PennyPress®

MW01571298

PUZZLER'S GIANT BOOK OF CROSSWORDS™ 29

Penny Press is the publisher of a fine family of puzzle magazines and books renowned for their editorial excellence.

This delightful collection has been carefully selected by the editors of Penny Press for your special enjoyment and entertainment.

PENNY PRESS, INC.
6 Prowitt Street, Norwalk, Connecticut 06855-1220

Printed in Canada

PENNY PRESS PUZZLE PUBLICATIONS

✦ PUZZLE MAGAZINES ✦

All-Star Word Seeks
Approved Easy & Fun Variety Puzzles
Approved Variety Puzzles
Classic Variety Puzzles Plus Crosswords
Easy Crossword Express
Family Variety & Crosswords
Family Variety Puzzles & Games
Favorite Easy Crosswords
Favorite Fast & Easy Crosswords
Favorite Fill-In
Favorite Number Fill-In
Favorite Quick & Easy Crosswords
Garfield's Word Seeks
Good Time Crosswords
Good Time Easy Crosswords
Good Time Variety Puzzles
Master's Tournament Variety Puzzles
Master's Variety Puzzles
Merit Variety Puzzles & Games
Original Logic Problems
Original Logic Problems: British Invasion!
Penny's Famous Fill-In Puzzles
Penny's Fill-In Puzzles
Penny's Finest Favorite Word Seeks
Penny's Finest Good Time Word Seeks
Penny's Finest Super Word Seeks
Spotlight Celebrity Word Seek
Spotlight Movie & TV Word Seek
Ultimate Favorite Variety Puzzles
Ultimate World's Finest Variety Puzzles
Variety Puzzles and Games
Variety Puzzles and Games Special Issue Plus
Word Seek Puzzles
Word Seek Puzzles: Large-Print

✦ SPECIAL COLLECTIONS ✦

Selected Anagram Magic Square
Selected Brick by Brick
Selected Codewords
Selected Crostics
Selected Crypto-Families
Selected Cryptograms
Selected Diagramless
Selected Double Trouble
Selected Flower Power
Selected Frameworks
Selected Letterboxes
Selected Match-Up
Selected Missing List Word Seeks
Selected Missing Vowels
Selected Patchwords
Selected Places, Please
Selected Quotefalls
Selected Syllacrostics
Selected The Shadow
Selected Wizard Words
Selected Word Games Puzzles
Selected Word Math
Selected Zigzag

✦ PUZZLER'S GIANT BOOKS ✦

Crosswords Sudoku Word Games Word Seeks

✦ ✦ ✦

Puzzler's Giant Book of Crosswords, January 2009, No. 29. Puzzler's Giant Books are published quarterly by Penny Press, Inc., 6 Prowitt Street, Norwalk, CT 06855-1220.On the web at pennydellpuzzles.com. Penny Press is a trademark registered in the U.S. Patent Office.

ISBN-13: 978-1-55956-941-5
ISBN-10: 1-55956-941-7

Printed in Canada

PUZZLE 1

ACROSS

1. Religious brother
4. Heels
8. Equal: prefix
12. Bun
14. Jewel weight
15. Augury
16. Largest continent
17. Marble
18. Go on and on
19. "—— Mallothi, . . ." (1 Chron. 25:26): 3 wds.
22. Conclusion
23. —— Angeles
24. —— Commandments
27. Aunts, in Madrid
30. Metal fastener
34. Before, to a bard
35. Remainder
36. Chop finely
37. "—— of Immer . . ." (Jer. 20:1): 4 wds.
42. This: Sp.
43. Constellation star
44. Stale
45. Trials
47. Poe, e.g.
48. Legal thing
49. Devour
51. Salt: Fr.
53. "—— to save me . . ." (Isa. 38:20): 4 wds.
62. Toss
63. Get up
64. Medicinal plant
65. Inter ——
66. Complains
67. Aromatic herb
68. Bits of land: Fr.
69. Woolly ones
70. —— Aviv

DOWN

1. College group, for short
2. —— Hashanah
3. "I cannot tell ——": 2 wds.
4. Zoo enclosure
5. Smell ——: 2 wds.
6. Appointment
7. Hard metal
8. Left part of a vessel
9. Asian nurse
10. Apartment fee
11. Division word
13. Country path
14. Bonbons
20. Within: prefix
21. And not
24. Belief
25. Worn away
26. Salamanders
28. Cigar residue
29. Confound
31. Cap part
32. School for Jeanne
33. Minds
38. Kneecaps
39. "Flying Down to ——"
40. Locks of hair
41. Hostile person
46. —— Paulo
50. Vestige
52. Direct
53. Siamese
54. Shell
55. Ohio Indian
56. Sketch
57. Telephone line
58. Vipers
59. Dismounted
60. Welfare
61. Holler

PUZZLE 2

ACROSS

1. Makes edging
5. Still snoozing
9. Go-devil
13. "Who's the ____?"
17. Met solo
18. Unclothed
19. Present
20. Aid in crime
21. Mementos
23. Throw a tantrum
24. Traditional knowledge
25. Attention
26. Function
27. Subsequently
29. Word on a coupon
31. Metric land measure
32. Kind of cut
33. Carry on
34. Slip of the memory
37. Mullins of the comics
38. Taped
42. Pretense
43. Extremely
44. Warms up
45. Brew
46. Pres. monogram
47. Steak order
48. Chars
49. Voyage
50. Hate
52. Mourning drops
53. October 31st choice
54. Slacken
55. Small nails
56. Material for Gepetto
57. Common or horse
59. Pleases
60. Makes a difference
63. Choir voice
64. Single thicknesses
65. Oversee
66. Compete
67. Opposite of NNW
68. Unwritten exams
69. "____ Little Acre"
70. Keep from sight
71. Silt deposit
73. Wild plum
74. Heaped
75. Baseball glove
76. Mountain summit
77. Columbia, in a song
78. Produce
81. Raised dogs
82. Neptune's domain
83. Track circuit
86. Lengthy
87. Actor Franco ____
89. Resolve
92. African lily
93. Sketch
94. Special nights
95. Dines
96. Sunday benches
97. Droops
98. Back of the neck
99. "True ____"

DOWN

1. Seize
2. Jurisdiction
3. Cake layer
4. Fool
5. Degrade
6. Cook cupcakes
7. Before, in poems
8. Demolish
9. Virago
10. Rely (on)
11. Marine eagle
12. Takes away
13. Having less hair
14. Woodwind
15. Dry
16. Stalk of bananas
22. Certain
28. Biddy
30. Selves
31. Onager
32. Essence
33. Has on
34. Cheryl or Diane
35. Assistant
36. Introduced
37. No more than
38. Nurtures
39. Knievel, e.g.
40. Essay writer
41. Division: abbr.
43. Place for a bouquet
44. Leaders
47. Soar
48. Cushions
49. Horse gait
51. El ____
52. Endeavors
53. Carryall
55. Constructed

PUZZLE 2

56. Armed conflicts
57. Talk back
58. Otherwise
59. Bias
60. Formed
61. Revere's journey
62. Bird food
64. Feigns
65. Restaurant VIP
68. Pass over
69. Cause a smile
70. That man
72. Reflections
73. Grasp
74. Bartlett, e.g.
76. Ships' fronts
77. Gaggle members
78. Bit of thunder
79. Actor's quest
80. Plenty, to a bard
81. Boast
82. Pace
83. Fibber
84. Person against
85. Nuisance
88. Historical period
90. Stowe heroine
91. A March sister

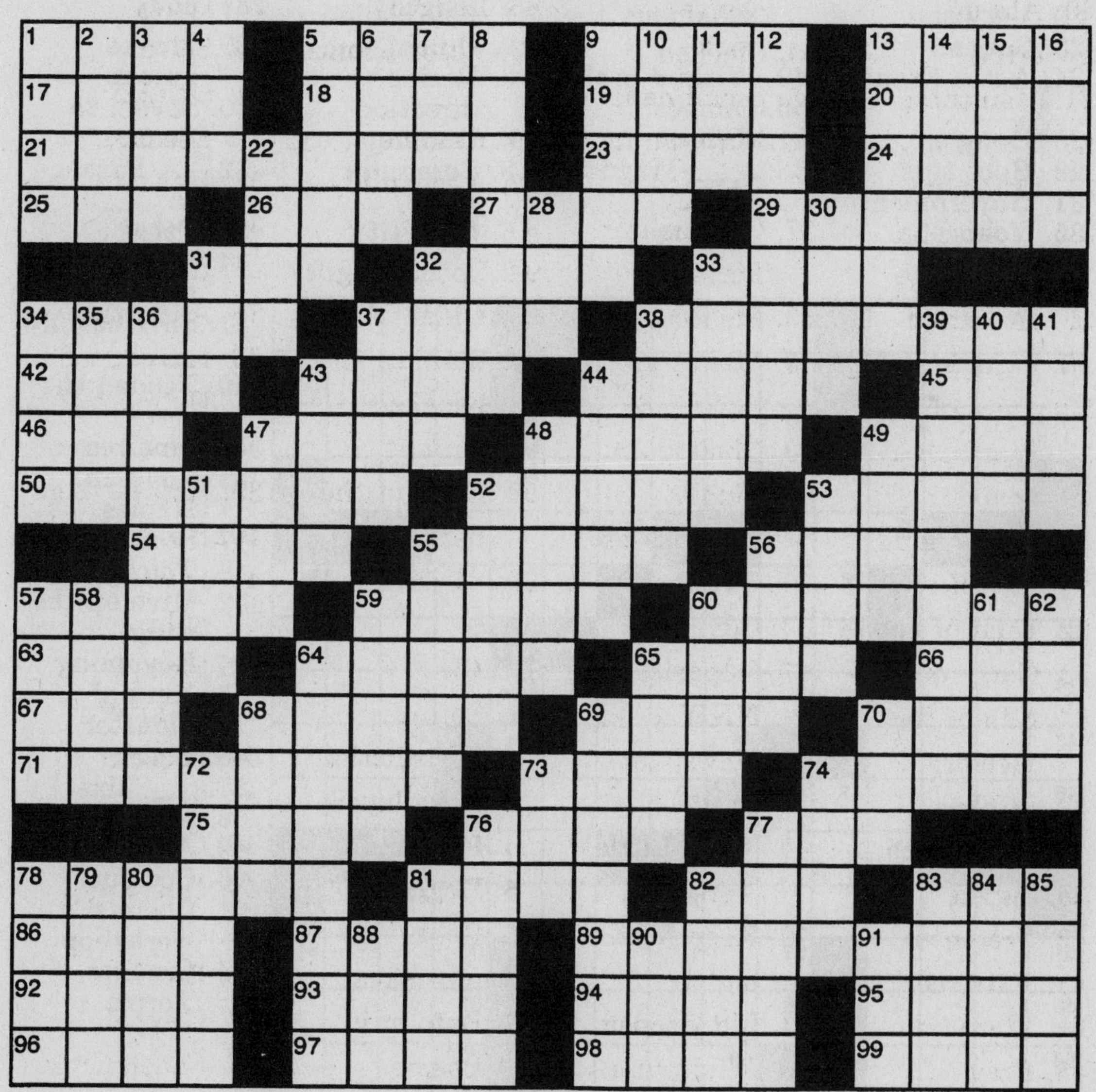

PUZZLE 3

ACROSS

1. Where nice guys finish
5. Asset
9. Mrs. Nick Charles
13. Johnson of “Laugh-In”
14. Moreno and Gam
16. Party to
17. Achieve
18. Adult insect
19. Sea swallow
20. Very tan
23. Squeal
24. Actor Franco ____
25. Douglas ____
28. Boot tips
31. Government
35. Yoko ____
36. Nobel surname
38. Arthurian lady
39. Nabbed in the act
43. Architectural pier
44. Stanley’s power source
45. Like two peas ____ pod
46. Gave a villainous look
49. Within: pref.
50. Onager
51. Rinses
53. ____ -Magnon
55. Highly jealous
61. Property attachment
62. ____ Hawkins Day
63. Appear
65. “I cannot tell ____”
66. Upright
67. First name in mystery
68. Marching musicians
69. Jumble
70. ____ drink of water

DOWN

1. Fall behind
2. Omani, e.g.
3. Recipe direction
4. Domingo, e.g.
5. Computer yield
6. Ohio city
7. Actress Hagen et al.
8. Astronomer Carl ____
9. Atmosphere element
10. Unique sort
11. Actor Calhoun
12. Actress Jillian
15. Like a judge
21. Wrist ticker
22. “ . . . ____ I saw Elba”
25. ____ point
26. Nonsensical
27. Path
29. Proves human
30. Seven, to Pedro
32. “A Passage to ____”
33. Faces
34. Norse anthologies
37. Sir Anthony ____
40. Tended the roses
41. Small axes
42. Love, in Naples
47. Storm center
48. Thick
52. Hive on the wing
54. Beginning
55. Kind of monster
56. Check
57. ____ fixe
58. Quirks
59. Actress Miles
60. Cry out
61. Chemist’s workshop
64. Crooner Torme

PUZZLE 4

ACROSS

1. Netting
5. Chalcedony
9. 007, e.g.
12. Choir member
13. Turning tool
14. Lily plant
15. Fish duck
16. Dominant
17. Unusual: Lat.
18. Host's question
20. Water pitcher
21. Danish money
22. Singer Williams
24. Grant Clarke's question
28. Eras
32. Truant from service
33. Venetian-blind strip
35. More confident
36. Farm tower
37. Miscalculate
38. Mailed
39. Rogue
41. Actor Pickens
43. Singer Cantrell
44. Concurs
46. "Won't ___ Sweetheart"
48. Dobbin's pace
50. ___ Rose du Lac
51. Cross one's ___
54. Bugs Bunny's question
60. English horn
61. Medieval guild
62. Old Celtic church site
63. Unsullied
64. Record of events
65. Playwright Coward
66. Porky's pad
67. Salty drop
68. Small weight

DOWN

1. Jam
2. Sailors' saint
3. Mulligan ___
4. E.B. Browning's question
5. Healthy, in Italy
6. Aleutian island
7. Valerie Harper role
8. Testify
9. Side dish
10. Skin opening
11. 52 weeks
13. Faithful followers
14. Question for Frere Jacques
19. Globe
23. Refugees: abbr.
24. Overwhelming
25. Grinding tooth
26. Rubber trees
27. Ahead of time
29. Rich milk
30. Youngman of comedy
31. Sp. miss
32. ___ silly question . . .
34. Chamber group
40. At all, to poets
42. Freshwater clam
45. Defiant question
47. Heat qty.
49. Clan chief
51. Bursts
52. Be next to
53. Whig's opponent
55. Actress Magnani
56. Russian emperor
57. Portal
58. SSS category
59. Serene

PUZZLE 5

ACROSS

1. Pakistani language
5. Abraham's wife
10. Glacial ice
15. "For ___ jolly . . ."
19. Bellow
20. Last
21. An archangel
22. "If ___ I Would Leave You"
23. Suburban design
25. Musical show
27. Indeed, matey!
28. M. Coty
29. Get home, in a way
31. Cozily warm
32. Goal
33. Indefinite pronoun
34. Injure
35. Mail boat
39. Barrel part
42. Most rigid
45. Muffed it
46. "___ Life Is It Anyway?"
47. Asian peninsula
48. Pronoun
50. Scheme
51. Gyrate to rap music
53. Agog
54. News director in "WKRP in Cincinnati"
55. Watchman
56. Flusher or poster
57. Petty swindler
58. ___ Wednesday
59. Kitty feeder
60. Packs
62. Herb of horn fame
63. Man of the ___
65. Three wood
66. Tissue layer
67. Victor's take
69. Sudden fright
70. Mediocre
71. Network initials
74. Junkets
75. Reno opening
76. Charlotte Corday's victim
77. Paleozoic, for example
78. Allure
79. Wags' specialties
82. Actor Muni
83. Penn. and B. & O.
84. Homer works
86. Author Joyce Carol ___
87. Hazard for Pauline
88. Route for the "QEII"
90. Quire component
91. Merriment
92. Network
93. Moms' and dads' org.
94. Scull
95. Attitude
98. Sigurd's steed
100. Perry's creator
101. Letter addendum
104. Floor covering
106. Ghost-town refuse
109. Per
110. Author of "The Cloister and the Hearth"
111. "Silas Marner" heroine
112. Gumbo ingredient
113. Scope
114. "The Highway-man" poet
115. "Play ___ for Me"
116. Half a fortnight

DOWN

1. Bear on high
2. Threadlike
3. Actor Robertson
4. Psychic Geller
5. English channel
6. Set right
7. Pierre's dream
8. Stone or Iron
9. Dutch painter Frans ___
10. Lying down
11. Wear away
12. Ready to eat
13. Early nuclear agcy.
14. Debate ender
15. Underworld goddess
16. Plumb and Brenner
17. Muralist Jose ___
18. Sporting cultural airs
24. Forced out on a limb
26. Field film, with 81 Down
30. "If I ___ You"
34. Employer
35. Garment flounces
36. City on the Rhone
37. Hurry-up lesson
38. Hockey's Dryden
39. Range of knowledge
40. Loathesome sort
41. Inquire
42. Concentrate
43. The Bard
44. Shark or moth
46. Outrage
47. Experienced
49. Trade center
51. Diamond ploys
52. In the works
53. Yawn
55. British lockups
57. Ogler
60. Torrent
61. Rocky Peak
62. A.k.a.
64. Como currency, once
65. Hillside affected by a glacier

PUZZLE 5

66. Central and Hyde
67. Top banana
68. Decants
69. Golfer's gaffe
70. Gem surface
72. Rumor
73. "When Harry Met ____"
75. Cast pearls before ____
76. Aussie chum
80. "Over There" composer
81. See 26 Down
82. Architect I.M. ____
84. Make an "in" of
85. Seamstress's aid
87. "Gay ____"
89. Soul-singer Franklin
90. Phases
91. Ship's kitchen
93. Stuffed shirt
94. Celestial path
95. Cruising
96. Cicatrix
97. Raceway gait
98. Gloomy
99. Agenda entry
100. Caesars: abbr.
101. Small dog, for short
102. "____ Goriot"
103. Neighbor of Minn.
105. Vintage car
107. Wire-service initials
108. Impress mightily

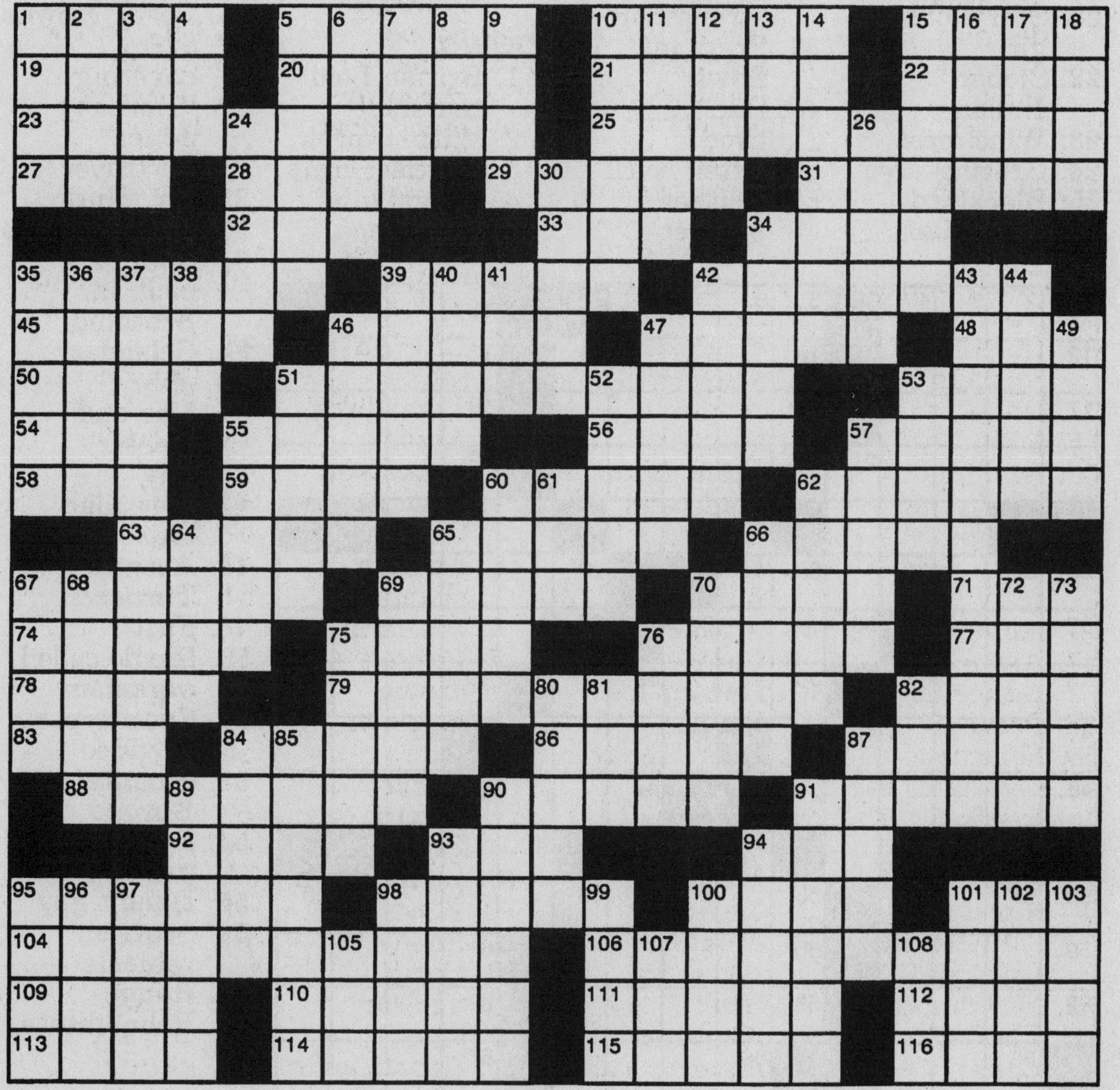

PUZZLE 6

ACROSS

1. Calls for attention
5. Castle trench
9. Scale units: abbr.
12. Once again
13. D sharp, on a piano
15. Apiece
17. Motionless
18. Like a gymnast
19. Caesar's 1052
20. Storybook girl
22. Siouan Indians
23. Wine: pref.
24. Grazing area
25. Blackbird
26. Paint the ____
29. Cossack chief
32. Science suffixes
33. "____ Holder"
35. Made over
36. Plant genus
38. Quick drink
40. Buffalo's lake
41. Scold
43. Bridal ____
45. Overhead railways
46. Biblical strongman
47. Fragrant flower
49. One ____ time
50. After Avril
52. Neither's partner
53. Taj Mahal site
55. The fourth estate
59. Burrow
60. "A Passage to ____"
61. Run with bounding steps
62. Walden, e.g.
63. New England state
64. ____ Bator
65. Them: Fr.
66. Poodle and Puli, e.g.
67. Hang fire

DOWN

1. British field marshall
2. Within: pref.
3. Beatles' craft
4. Bergman's birthplace
5. Diner's intake
6. "A host ____ daffodils"
7. Wonderland girl
8. ____ blue streak
9. Summer cooler
10. Maryland state bird
11. Shadow: pref.
14. Your: Fr.
16. Towel word
21. About
25. Had breakfast
26. Poetic crowns
27. Stem covering
28. "Barnaby Jones" portrayer
29. Mr. Shaw
30. Indigo plants
31. Sign of a cold, in Scotland
34. Calendar abbr.
37. Gas and plaster
39. Shy
42. Hawaiian tree
44. Actress Turner
48. Furl
50. Single-celled organism
51. Counterpart of video
53. Mountain of Europe
54. British prison
55. Dandy guy
56. Scottish refusals
57. Range
58. Rehabilitate

PUZZLE 7

ACROSS

1. Destruction
5. Imprint
10. Tears apart
14. Support, in wrongdoing
15. Court proceeding
16. Sandusky's lake
17. Activist
18. Riva ___
19. Toff
20. Devote
22. Site of Mount McKinley
24. Ballet bend
25. Consumer
26. Tilt
29. ___ money
33. In the past
34. Time periods
36. Spanish title
37. Plow the soil
39. Not as moist
41. Capitol feature
42. New York City isle
44. Puts money in the pot
46. Society-page word
47. Jittery
49. Mean
51. Muscle condition
52. Snarl
53. Wall or Fleet
56. Firs
60. General Bradley
61. Goodnight girl
63. ___ language
64. Behind schedule
65. Bind again
66. John-Boy's sister
67. Humdinger
68. Asian VIP
69. Fill

DOWN

1. "Shane" star
2. Reed instrument
3. Sesame, e.g.
4. Hash mark
5. Filtered
6. Hackneyed
7. ___ -de-camp
8. Periodical: abbr.
9. Amuse
10. Held dear
11. Exasperates
12. "Pretty in ___"
13. Bristle
21. Ball of yarn
23. Camera part
25. Topple
26. Supply refreshments
27. Spry
28. Sandwich breads
29. Peels
30. Hole ___
31. Title: Lat.
32. Avarice
35. Obliterate
38. Messy person
40. Donder or Blitzen
43. ___ gin fizz
45. Break suddenly
48. Complete
50. Clans
52. Supernatural spirit
53. Alone
54. Revenuer
55. Velocity
56. Network
57. Mrs. Nick Charles
58. Correct
59. Auld Lang ___
62. Radiation dosage

PUZZLE 8

ACROSS

1. River to the Baltic
5. Limber
10. Hooded vipers
14. Commedia dell'___
15. Base number
16. Blackthorn
17. Personal mail
19. Curly cabbage
20. Sale items
21. Martini garnishes
23. Moody and Ely
24. Small valley
25. "Mona ___"
26. Devastating
30. Swab
31. Jottings
32. Defendants, in law
33. Vacation mail
37. Santa ___
38. Later
39. From ___ Z
40. Ocelots
42. Pottery
44. Auto pioneer
45. Kismet
46. Exodus water
49. Glee club selection
53. Son of Aphrodite
54. Mail exec
56. Cleo's river
57. Ordeal
58. Lab heater
59. Antlered animal
60. Impertinent
61. Acts

DOWN

1. Louts
2. Faucet leak
3. To be: Fr.
4. Edict
5. Mysteries
6. Vexes
7. Lupino et al.
8. Fleur-de-___
9. Separates minerals
10. Inquiring
11. Eastern European
12. Flagstaff
13. Dioceses
18. Spanish relatives
22. Smallest
24. Croc's kin
25. Slow train
26. Know the ___
27. Provoked
28. Sleuth Wolfe
29. Sheep disease
30. Subcompact
31. Salamanders
33. Dog's foot
34. "___ Buck" (John Candy film)
35. Converts again
36. Petted
41. Pannier
42. Cordially
43. Tropical ant
45. ___ a pig
46. Cleave
47. Buffalo's lake
48. Allot
49. Greek letters
50. Sarge's dog
51. State bird of Hawaii
52. Mardi ___
55. Mouths: Lat.

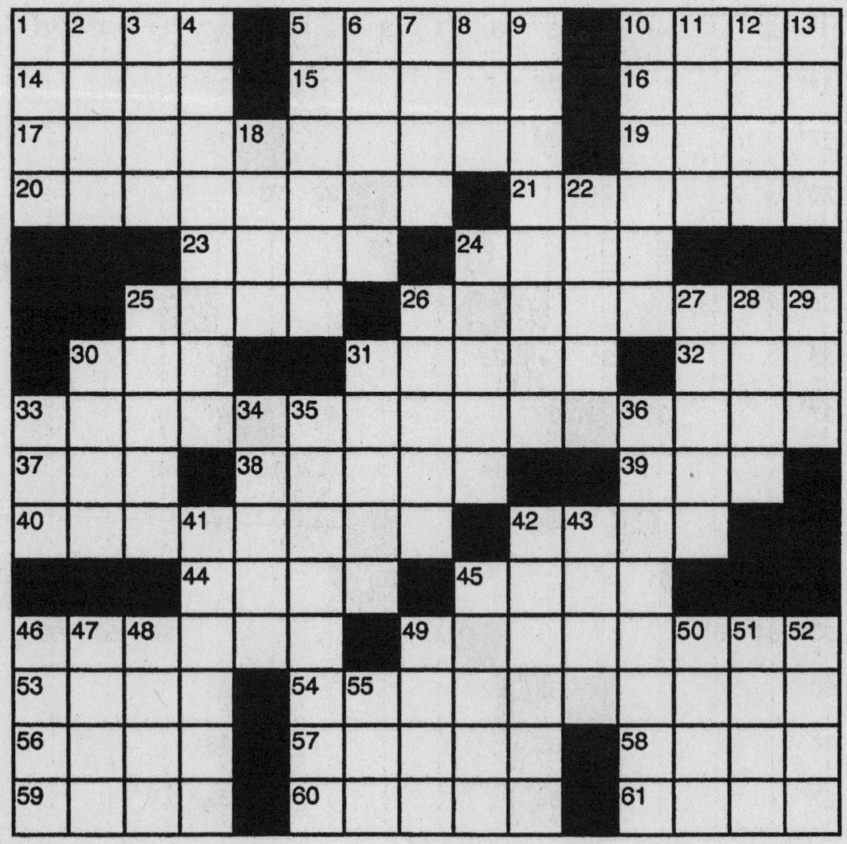

PUZZLE 9

ACROSS

1. Doris ——
4. Shine
8. "Veni, ——, vici"
12. Love god
14. Of flight
15. Snake poison
16. Rabbit's tail
17. Nasty
18. Plowed land: Sp.
19. Story author: 3 wds.
22. So-so grades
23. Writer Wiesel
24. At —— for words: 2 wds.
26. Bus tokens
28. Dove sound
31. Base person
32. Tra ——: 2 wds.
33. Wyatt ——
34. Kind
35. Son of Terah
36. Actor Paul
37. Dutch painter
38. Egyptian god
39. City in Georgia
40. Corrida cheer
41. "—— is a terrible thing to waste": 2 wds.
42. Keen
43. Actor Alda
44. Baseballer Speaker
45. Story character: 4 wds.
52. Souvenir
53. Gen. Bradley
54. Dog's end
55. Choleric
56. Noun suffix
57. Beige
58. "Auntie ——"
59. Location
60. Always, in poems

DOWN

1. Offspring: abbr.
2. Foot part
3. Story line, "Allow me to sell ——?": 3 wds.
4. Pastimes
5. Dregs
6. Spoken
7. Story site
8. Brink
9. Actress Claire et al.
10. Story creature
11. "—— Old Cowhand": 2 wds.
13. Accents
15. "Quo ——"
20. —— majesty
21. N.Y. city
24. Even if, for short
25. Faithful
26. Story's croquet mallets
27. VP Burr
28. Story activity: hyph.
29. Ready ——!: 2 wds.
30. Think
33. Make lean
35. Purim villain
39. Foal's mother
41. Story heroine
43. High as ——: 2 wds.
44. Trio
45. Haircut
46. Zeus's wife
47. Susiana
48. All: pref.
49. Datum
50. Exhaust
51. Disparagement

PUZZLE 10

MOVIES AND TELEVISION

ACROSS

1. Actor Vigoda et al.
5. Davis of "North Dallas Forty"
8. Polio vaccine discoverer
12. TV comedy show "Super ___"
13. "Gone With the Wind" family name
15. Actress Gray of "Six Pack"
16. Arkin of "Wait Until Dark"
17. "Fan-Fan the ___" (Philipe film)
18. Actor Auberjonois
19. Balin of "The Comancheros"
20. Actor Williams of "Prince of the City"
21. "___ What You Did" (John Ireland film)
22. "All This and Heaven ___"
24. Minor league letters
26. Actress Mary et al.
29. Russell or Gish
33. Songstress Dinah ___
34. James Mason's role in "A Star is Born"
36. Highway: abbr.
37. "___ We Meet Again" (Oberon film)
38. "___ Just Want to Have Fun"
39. Mothers
40. Wrath
41. Role on TV's "Laverne and Shirley"
42. "Thou ___ Not Kill" (Lee Grant film)
44. Peter Finch film
46. Songstress Della et al.
47. Yoko ___
48. TV sitcom "___ a Living"
49. "Charlie ___ on Broadway"
52. Famous
56. Actor Cassidy of "The Addams Family"
59. Thing of "The Addams Family," e.g.
60. ___ ear and out the other
61. Prop for the Frugal Gourmet
63. English composer
64. Madge the manicurist portrayer
65. Captain of the "Nautilus"
66. "The ___ Hunter" (De Niro film)
67. Inhabitant: suff.
68. Disney's "___ White and the Seven Dwarfs"

DOWN

1. Susan Hayward film
2. "___ Ha'i" ("South Pacific" tune)
3. Writer Hunter
4. "The ___ Was Indiscreet" (Powell film)
5. "The ___ Animal" (Fonda film)
6. Song in "Amadeus"
7. "___ Courageous" (Malden film)
8. "The Perils of Pauline," e.g.
9. Greek Mars
10. Director Wertmuller
11. "They ___ What They Wanted" (Lombard film)
13. Director Preminger et al.
14. "Ben-___"
23. Lode load
25. Tavern brew
26. "Freaky Friday" actor
27. "Old Boyfriends" actress
28. For rent
29. "Presenting ___ Mars" (Garland film)
30. Role for MacLaine and Wilson
31. "___ of Two Cities" (Sarandon film)
32. Birds' homes
34. "Make Mine ___" (Terry-Thomas film)
35. Scottish alder tree
38. Role for Chuck Connors

PUZZLE 10

41. Chaney of "The Cyclops"
42. "Desk ____" (Tracy-Hepburn film)
43. 14 Down actor et al.
45. Lynda Carter's TV adventure "____ Woman"
46. "Pale ____" (Eastwood film)
49. "____ Hanna" (Henry Fonda film)
50. Tortoise's racing opponent
51. Actress Bancroft of "Agnes of God"
53. Step ____!
54. Actor Franchot ____ of "Dark Waters"
55. Opposite of WSW
57. "Never Give a Sucker an ____ Break" (W.C. Fields film)
58. Dealer's car, for short
62. "____ Voyager" (Bette Davis film)

PUZZLE 11

ACROSS

1. Outsmart
5. "____ Is Born"
10. Fascinated
14. Olfactory stimulus
15. Responsibility
16. Mr. Lamb
17. Verdi opera
18. Actor Richard ____
19. Nation
20. In position
22. Banquets
24. Zip or Morse
25. Bog fuel
26. The long or short of a shirt
29. Mailmen
33. Green pegs
34. Inscribe
36. Appear suddenly
37. Leer
39. Ebb and neap
41. Palm
42. Jetties
44. Award
46. 100 yrs.
47. Flaunted
49. Rental agreements
51. Young salmon
52. Official stamp
53. Uneven in quality
56. Gatherings
60. Actress Anderson
61. Oregon city
63. Radiate
64. Toast spread
65. Triple
66. Recruit
67. Web-footed bird
68. American saint
69. Stone or stool starter

DOWN

1. Large snakes
2. Redact
3. Fountain order
4. Stupor
5. Mishap
6. Glittered
7. Chinese gang
8. Museum offering
9. Kind of jacket
10. Kin
11. "____! poor Yorick"
12. Half quart
13. Shavers
21. Noah's scout
23. Wild West Wyatt ____
25. Skinned
26. Desist
27. On the up and up
28. Certain fisherman
29. Gave up
30. Sagas
31. Indian coin
32. Reaches
35. Kitchen gadget
38. Outburst
40. Willy Loman and others
43. Photocopy, for short
45. Pastures
48. Shady meetings?
50. Burning
52. ____ evil
53. Opening
54. ____ vault
55. Unique thing
56. Skirt feature
57. Hodgepodge
58. Author Ephron
59. Scandinavian country: abbr.
62. "Chances ____"

PUZZLE 12

ACROSS

1. Used a cuspidor
5. Soap plant
10. "____! in the Name of Love"
14. Soda-machine choice
15. Dressed to the ____
16. Clock reading
17. Astronaut Shepard
18. Pick up the tab
19. Lively dance
20. Rudolph, e.g.
22. Always, in poetry
24. Morays
25. Actress Miles
26. Hi-fi
29. Keep in mind
33. Important period
34. Ask, in Dundee
36. Strange
37. ____ processor
39. Wipe out
41. Take the bus
42. Tools for duels
44. Nymph
46. Actor Beatty
47. Cardinals
49. Cowboys, sometimes
51. Toward the sheltered side
52. Poker term
53. Pull the plug
56. Lesions
60. Solar plexus
61. Slugger Hank ____
63. Stumble
64. Cogwheel
65. Colorful language
66. Grafted, in heraldry
67. Becomes a baseball statistic
68. Thinkers
69. Action

DOWN

1. Wound memento
2. North ____
3. Jai ____
4. Roscoe of tennis
5. ". . . where the deer and the ____ play"
6. Bogs down
7. Individual
8. Grassy area
9. Honor
10. Pennant
11. Stratum
12. Sign
13. Name in soccer
21. Ruby and Sandra
23. Banyan or baobab
25. Poem
26. Ed Norton's domain
27. Rhetorical device
28. Auriculate
29. Brings up
30. Salt water
31. River duck
32. Bulrushes
35. Eat away
38. Polemicists
40. Salary
43. Rural sight
45. ____ and dashes
48. Go by again
50. Stroked
52. "Home ____"
53. Impulse
54. ____-do-well
55. Celebrity
56. Talk big
57. Sea eagle
58. Formality
59. Went over 55
62. ____ mode

PUZZLE 13

ACROSS

1. Pale gray
4. Margin
8. Bloke
12. Phoenician deity
16. Chirp
18. Space
19. Function
20. Crooked
21. Indira's garment
22. Spin like ____
23. Water holder
24. Get closer
25. Mormon priests
27. Trifle
30. Once more
32. ____ de Janeiro
33. Hebrew prophet
34. Spanish town
37. Wild goat
39. Finds
43. Zhivago's love
44. Resorts
45. Observes Lent
46. Chemist's lair
48. Thickness
50. Posts
51. Bring action against
52. Ticked off
53. Donkey
54. Mount
56. Morning moisture
57. Pear-shaped instruments
58. Thai language
59. Pay
62. Blended
63. Tempera-ments
67. Not her
68. Fodder holders
69. Sewing need
70. "____ to Billie Joe"
71. Sir's opposite
72. Absent
73. Curly 'do
74. Heavenly
76. "Rebel Without a Cause" actor
77. 007, for one
78. Purpose
79. Cheat
80. Famed university
82. Whiskey cocktail
88. Bobs along
92. Bread purchase
93. Isinglass
94. Indian queen
96. Minor or Major
97. Spanish pronoun
98. Mars, to Plato
99. Road: Lat.
100. Dross
101. Did in, as the dragon
102. Plover's dwelling
103. Grant
104. Natural resource

DOWN

1. Recess in a church
2. Emblem
3. Flock of cattle
4. Wipe clean
5. Speck
6. Blunder
7. Dominions
8. Summary of beliefs
9. Ululate
10. Away from the wind
11. Improves
12. Desperado
13. Struck silent
14. Inland sea of Asia
15. Ancient Greek instrument
17. Dessert choice
26. Genetic inits.
28. Reformer Dorothea ____
29. Exclamation of regret
31. Sponged
34. "The Four Seasons" actor
35. Pompous
36. OPEC nation
38. Saloon
39. Dens
40. Norwegian seaport
41. Ms. Lanchester
42. Author Bellow
44. Simmer
45. Ate
47. Spelling contest
49. Looks at
50. Softens
53. Plump

PUZZLE 13

54. Jade
55. Brave
57. Fragrant shrub
58. Overdue
59. Reporter's question
60. Verdi opera
61. FBI agents
62. Skirt length
63. Nursemaid
64. Teeming
65. Hold down a job
66. Vegas machine
68. Hawker
69. Flightless bird
71. Plateau
72. Brand X
75. Laugh heartily
76. Wear
77. ____ of a sudden
79. Beach
81. Excited
82. Bullfighter's cheers
83. Relax
84. Roy's cowgirl
85. Engage
86. Sherbets
87. Escort
89. Singer Guthrie
90. Russian ruler
91. Kitchen herb
95. Actor Beatty

PUZZLE 14

ACROSS

1. Rose fruit
4. Fossil resin
9. At a distance
13. Cajun seasoning
17. Cry of woe
19. Stooge
20. Actor Andrews
21. Rectify
23. Gallop
24. Guffaw
26. Ebb
27. Allegorical stories
29. Choreographer de Mille
30. Ascended
31. Challenged
32. Breakfast choice
34. Threads
35. Baseball's Mel ____
36. Catches a fly
37. Staff
38. Repeat
41. Great house
43. Tossed
45. Make like a bunny
48. Lumberjack's commodity
49. Trojan
50. Wields
51. Wild hog
52. Miscalculate
53. Lawn game
56. Viennese treat
57. St. Bernards, sometimes
60. It gives you a pane
61. Boggy
62. Let out
63. Important official
64. Soupy food
65. Swayed
67. Annoy
68. Rain shoes
71. Dawdled
72. Shrewdness
74. "Butterflies ____ Free"
75. Close
76. Makes bread
77. Scribble
78. Liquid measure
79. Merry
80. Kohoutek, for one
81. Topics
84. Miners' quests
85. Hamilton bills
86. Two-spot
87. Moreover
89. Scale
92. ____ out (discover)
94. Start walking
97. Beach
98. Algonquians
99. Leaping
101. Choice
102. Oater
105. You are something ____!
106. More rational
107. Elevator name
108. Twist
109. Dumbfound
110. Herring and maple
111. Curds' companion
112. Vikings
113. Interview

DOWN

1. Orchestra member
2. Homer work
3. Spanish priest
4. Sportsman
5. Made like a Holstein
6. Forbids
7. Newspaper execs
8. Corned beef's partner
9. Maxims
10. Animal life
11. Seraph
12. Cheers
13. Suspecting
14. Drink
15. Car-buyer's option
16. Submit a contest solution
18. Lobster tails, e.g.
22. Bears' retreats
25. Jumbo
28. Speck
32. Scorches
33. Snack
34. Blowers
36. Leading ladies
37. Prompts
38. Jug
39. Geologic sample
40. Rough-and-tumble fun
42. Foil
43. Embroidery thread
44. Commits perjury
45. Upholstery material
46. Pledge
47. Target
50. Stages
51. Dull people
53. Listen
54. Exit
55. Work hard

PUZZLE 14

56. Polynesian tuber
58. Gambol
59. Previously owned
61. Slipper
63. Tete covering
64. Stickum
65. Nick
66. Brainstorm
67. Elbow
68. Fairy-tale creature
69. Aquatic bird
70. Thickens
72. Airwave buffs
73. Bail out
76. 007
78. French dogs
80. Some basketball players
81. Concise
82. Tint
83. Bin or battery
85. Analyzed
86. Elegant
88. Out of the ordinary
89. Becker boomers
90. Clean energy
91. Actor Michael ____
92. Cappuccino topping
93. Ghostly
94. Curdles
95. Hums
96. Follow
98. Black-tongued dog
99. Beneficiary
100. Trait carrier
103. Possess
104. In favor of

PUZZLE 15

ACROSS

1. Game preserve
5. Stimulus
9. Liability
13. Serpent tooth
17. American Indian
18. ____ in point
19. Higher up
20. Russian mountains
21. Infinitesimal
22. One-dollar bills
23. Soap opera, e.g.
25. Was situated
26. British beer
27. Bridge support
29. Flower patch
30. Not utilized
32. Frog's kin
33. Feature of luxury
35. Artificial waterway
37. ____ of plenty
38. Sundae toppings
43. Crafty
44. Band of turtles
45. Channel marker
46. Unwritten
47. Luau souvenir
48. Extend credit
49. Ringlets
50. Give someone the slip
51. Human race
53. Whittle
54. Sharpened
55. Bob the head
56. "Animal ____"
57. Enjoyment
58. Twirler's need
61. Barbecue
62. Snarled
66. Be an accomplice
67. Imitation gem
68. Dray
69. Gardner of films
70. Lath
71. Bronze and Stone, e.g.
72. Fragrant ointment
73. Entwine
74. Chose
76. Kennel sound
77. Move obliquely
78. Bespeckle
79. Unprepared
80. Sluggers' needs
81. Paleozoic, for example
84. A few
87. What Fido shakes with
88. Daunt
91. Permeate
93. Etching substance
95. Hirsch vehicle
96. Pop star
97. Prime-time time
98. Spilled the beans
99. Frank
100. Hit on the head
101. Ginger cookie
102. Orchard item
103. Remain unsettled

DOWN

1. Coddles
2. Met melody
3. Movie dog
4. Anthem poet
5. Piano exercise
6. Walk like a father-to-be
7. ____ one's noggin
8. Renew
9. Like the Capitol
10. Special nights
11. Bible, for one
12. They go "clang, clang, clang"
13. Mink, e.g.
14. Spirited horse
15. Identify
16. Light-hearted
24. Cherished
26. Whole
28. Operated
31. Sunup
32. Blabbed
34. Draw out
35. Tranquil
36. Scope
37. Applause
38. Pitcher's pitch
39. Burrow
40. Inflexible
41. Naturalness
42. Husky's load
44. Curve
45. Explode
48. Leo
49. Reason
52. Snarled

PUZZLE 15

53. Paint layers
54. Search (for)
56. Did garden work
57. MacDonald's place
58. Food fish
59. Fit
60. River duck
61. Conniption fit
62. Gab
63. Vista
64. Pernicious
65. Calendar notation
67. Sewing aids
68. Wag
72. Stability for a ship
73. Scout Carson
75. Face value
76. Feathery scarf
77. Maxim
79. Crawl
80. Sheriff's emblem
81. Legendary
82. Decorator's advice
83. Soon
85. "You're So ___"
86. Sicilian volcano
87. Cleanser fragrance
89. Cattle
90. Gust
92. Wapiti
94. Sedan
95. Crest

PUZZLE 16

ACROSS

1. Food fish
5. Rabble
9. Cut grass
12. Mrs. Dithers of "Blondie"
13. Always
14. Black cuckoo
15. Adjoin
16. Father
17. Acquire
18. Sparkler: 2 wds.
21. Those not in office
22. Spanish stewpot
25. Machine part
28. Golf mound
29. Kind of bear
30. Marbles
32. "Top ___"
33. Mexican gentleman
34. Lion's lair
35. Take prisoner
36. Stumble
37. Peruse
38. Fourth of July item
44. Paid athlete
46. Sour
47. Traditional knowledge
48. Petroleum
49. Constructed
50. Dash
51. Seed capsule
52. Raced
53. Rapid

DOWN

1. Wound mark
2. Vagabond
3. Cuckoopint
4. Facts
5. Saves
6. Fly
7. Flowerless plants
8. A Flintstone
9. Portuguese navigator
10. Single
11. Humor
19. Observer
20. Diving bird
23. Actress Turner
24. Desert dweller
25. Hurl
26. Dyer's device
27. Numerous and varied
29. Zoo celebrity
31. Pith helmet
32. Having whiskers
34. Settle
37. Summary
39. St. Louis footballers
40. Musical symbol
41. Kind of nut
42. Epochs
43. Lease
44. Soft drink
45. ___ Grande

PUZZLE 17

ACROSS

1. Waist wear
5. Overcharge on tickets
10. Rhode Island fowls
14. Bread spread
15. Mistake
16. Songstress Adams
17. Bank of seats
18. Racket
19. Citrus fruit
20. Male deer
21. —— rule: 2 wds.
22. Babbled
24. Chooses
26. Tense
27. Go on pension
30. Exercise weights
34. Got up
35. Big books
36. Break bread
37. —— on (fancy)
38. Hyde Park sights
39. Facts and figures
40. Cooling drink
41. Dagwood's dog
42. Skinflint
43. Prohibit
45. Sahara, for one
46. Rate
47. Penny
48. Write illegibly
51. Informer
52. Mimed
56. Dry
57. Chosen people
59. Memo
60. Sit for an artist
61. Passover feast
62. Scotsman's group
63. Drove too fast
64. Fortune-tellers
65. House wings

DOWN

1. The two of them
2. Writer Kazan
3. Villainous look
4. Hare's opponent
5. Upper House
6. Cranky
7. Diva's song
8. —— Angeles
9. Gets ready
10. Tell
11. Prepare copy
12. Ten cents
13. Kernel
23. Chafes
25. Before: affix
26. Actress Grimes
27. Electronic speed check
28. Eat away
29. Carries
30. Brag
31. Rent
32. Procrastinator's word
33. Begin
35. Treat's alternate
38. Not hurting
39. Mileage
41. Sketch
42. Fellows
44. Swapped
45. Discourages
47. Furnish food
48. Exhausts
49. Cultivated produce
50. Ascend
51. Midway attraction
53. Public opinion
54. And others: abbr.
55. Cozy rooms
58. Peggy or Pinky

PUZZLE 18

ACROSS

1. Resort for dieters
4. Martial art
8. Observe Lent
12. Actor Gossett, Jr.
13. English rock group
14. Territory
15. Word a suitor seeks
16. Penny
17. Moos
18. Trampled
20. Biker's headgear
22. Pulsate
24. Prepared
25. Demolish
26. Gray matter
29. Docs' org.
30. Stop
31. Bliss
34. Value
35. Grow dim
36. Sully
39. Tablecloth fabric
40. What bees spread
42. Cab
43. Correct
44. So be it!
46. Spigot
49. Overhang
50. Hoodlum
51. Corrida shout
52. Tinted
53. Swirl
54. Conducted

DOWN

1. Foxy
2. Mystery writer
3. Vienna's locale
4. Esau's twin
5. Manipulated
6. Clamor
7. Vow
8. Dishonored
9. Fragrance
10. Basted
11. Delicious
19. Opie's portrayer
21. Border lake
22. ____-la-la
23. Sing without words
26. Prohibit
27. Furrow
28. Cinder
30. Corn bread
31. School employee
32. Type of poem
33. Japanese currency
34. Drooped
35. Repair
36. Exceed the limit
37. Present time
38. "Staying ____"
39. Ungracefully tall and thin
41. Neck part
42. Look after
45. Sludge
47. ____ mode
48. Cage

PUZZLE 19

ACROSS

1. Bark
4. Crow
8. Applies gently
12. French coin
13. Unaccompanied
14. Robert ____
15. Meetings
17. Celt
18. Search
19. Customs list
21. Musical sound
23. Unadulterated
24. Great affection
25. Seethes
29. Writer Burrows
30. Shades of colors
31. ____ pro nobis
32. Parts
34. A ____ apple
35. Colleague
36. Topic
37. Turns aside
40. Did garden work
41. Sharp flavor
42. Delightful
46. Misfortune
47. Goals
48. Victory sign
49. Measure out
50. Mexican money
51. Lamprey

DOWN

1. You bet!
2. King topper
3. Sucker
4. Window shade
5. Basal part
6. Dancer Miller
7. Motions
8. Extent
9. Jai ____
10. Meat
11. Ego
16. Confident
20. Weapons
21. Applaud
22. Vagrant
23. Cent
25. Size of paper
26. Sudden drop
27. Decorate
28. Rational
30. Slant
33. Muddle
34. Throat-clearer
36. Trunk
37. Plant stalk
38. Own
39. Division
40. Stage hogs
43. Scurry
44. By birth
45. Solidify

PUZZLE 20

ACROSS

1. "A ____ Is Born"
5. TV units
9. Marsh
12. Cab
13. Eve's garden
14. Ostrichlike bird
15. Building wings
16. Twenty less one
18. Most timid
20. Merits
21. Wrath
22. Coffee server
23. Gold digger
26. Donkey
27. "____ Hat" (Astaire film)
30. Above
31. Be in debt
32. Taxi's fee
33. Brief farewell
34. "____ About Eve"
35. Striped cat
36. Had dinner
37. Lend an ____ (listen)
38. Separate
41. Fathers, e.g.
45. Some citrus coolers
47. Additional
48. Point-scoring serve
49. Adorable
50. Fencing sword
51. ____ Francisco
52. Gardening tools
53. Require

DOWN

1. Wineglass feature
2. "The Handmaid's ____"
3. Wheel shaft
4. Not as safe
5. Rationality
6. Correct text
7. Decade number
8. Scornful expressions
9. Lager
10. Sign
11. Revolvers
17. Cure, as leather
19. Make a mistake
22. Function
23. Unruly crowd
24. Climbing vine
25. Formerly named
26. Hole-making tool
27. Price label
28. Mine rock
29. For each
31. Mexican cheer
32. Blaze fighters
34. Affix
35. ____ and feather
36. "You ____ My Sunshine"
37. Loosens
38. Woe is me!
39. Type size
40. Prayer ending
41. Townshend of The Who
42. Slangy negative
43. Cedar or chestnut, e.g.
44. Bird food
46. Pair

PUZZLE 21

ACROSS
1. House
5. Viper
8. Donations
12. Concept
13. Fish eggs
14. Fleece
15. Playrooms
16. To the bitter ____
17. Helper
18. Stocking color
20. Mended
22. Picture taker
25. Fib
26. Warning
27. By means of
28. Convent occupant
31. Complain
32. "____ Alibi"
33. Frozen-yogurt holder
34. Favorite
35. Admirer
36. Kiwi or pear
37. ____-dried tomato
38. Mighty ones
39. Marzipan nut
42. Tiny tunneler
43. Take in the sights
44. Testing area
46. Wicked
50. Rubberneck
51. Building annex
52. Pilaf ingredient
53. Colleague
54. Date
55. Plant beginning

DOWN
1. Concealed
2. Keats poem
3. Some YMCA members
4. Oriental
5. Hippodrome
6. Male child
7. Hawker
8. Mindful
9. Cut of pork
10. Fashion
11. Huskie's burden
19. Handicraft
21. Tire input
22. Lejeune, e.g.
23. Shampoo ingredient
24. Animal flesh
27. ____ and ink drawing
28. Part of speech
29. Component
30. Circus safeguards
32. Treats
33. Depressions
35. Enjoyment
36. Fish part
37. More aching
38. "GWTW" actor
39. Upon
40. Theater box
41. Stubborn animal
45. Brewery product
47. Contest
48. Rink surface
49. Headed

PUZZLE 22

ACROSS
1. Domicile
5. Ship's stern
8. Pack down
12. Went by horse
13. Shad's output
14. Mock butter
15. Performs
17. Selects
18. Slovenly
19. Pigpen
21. Yo!
22. Moray
24. Divan
26. Spicy
29. Carpenter's tool
31. Honorable
34. Breezy
36. Herd of whales
38. Stench
39. Sparkle
41. Do wrong
43. Digit
44. Hymn ending
46. Certainly!
48. Onager
50. Vat
52. Antlered animals
56. Boxing match
58. Microscopic organisms
60. Tempt
61. Bikini part
62. Dairy product
63. Foil's relative
64. Desire
65. Shopper's event

DOWN
1. "____ Here to Eternity"
2. Gait
3. Fruit coolers
4. Succinct
5. Picasso's specialty
6. Opponents
7. Experiments
8. As well
9. Set of letters
10. Distribute
11. Bouquet
16. Favorable votes
20. Over there
23. Baby's seat?
25. Supporting
26. Crone
27. Frying need
28. Cherish
30. Grief
32. Astrological lion
33. Augment
35. Southern potato
37. Parched
40. NYC opera house
42. Take it easy
45. Lumpy
47. Flower parts
48. Fit
49. Consomme
51. Exposed
53. Domingo ditty
54. Bass feature
55. Purpose
57. Golfer's mound
59. Tin container

PUZZLE 23

ACROSS

1. Competent
5. Vehicle
8. Comparative word
12. Headliner
13. Untruth
14. Hawkeye State
15. Roof overhang
16. Enthusiastically
18. Wading birds
20. Firmament
21. Wheel part
23. Constrictor
26. Cigar residue
30. Far
32. Close
33. Actor Chaney
34. Choir voice
35. Boston ____ (dog)
37. Adage
38. Football position
39. Files
41. Vessel for preserves
42. Cheerful
47. Rookie
51. Soften
52. Type of horse
53. Hesitation sounds
54. Famous canal
55. Scruff
56. Ruby ____
57. Loud noise

DOWN

1. Actor Guinness
2. Smokey or Yogi
3. Etna output
4. Paradise
5. Necklace part
6. Ventilate
7. Washington athlete
8. Wee
9. Spicy
10. Leather-working tool
11. Negative vote
17. Makes do
19. Shapely curve
22. Smells
23. Indonesian island
24. Atop
25. Small particle
26. Stake
27. Discovered
28. Tough
29. Botch
31. Duty
33. Educated
36. Persia, now
37. Viper
40. Bag
41. Agree
43. Pollinators
44. Nobleman
45. China's site
46. Pour
47. Forbid
48. Epoch
49. Cavity
50. Before

PUZZLE 24

ACROSS

1. Fragment
5. Money: Ger.
9. Stinging insect
13. Poet's plaint
17. Wing-shaped
18. Regan's father
19. Theater award
20. ____ driver (wrestling move)
21. All roads lead here
22. Accord
24. Arabian gulf
25. Fix
27. Strong point
28. Atoll
30. "Star ____"
32. Family room
33. Etc.'s kin
34. Nairobi's republic
37. Playwright Coward
39. Jailbird
43. "You ____ So Beautiful"
44. Harsh
46. Gauze weaves
47. Generation
48. Riviera resort
50. Moscow Square
51. Caesar's language
52. "The Sultan of ____"
53. Foes
55. "A Delicate Balance" author
56. Rubber cement
57. Father
58. Parquet
59. Beatles song
60. Corridor
62. Woodland deity
63. Type of roof
66. "Dies ____"
67. Emulated James Bond
68. Freight weight
69. Armadillo
70. Ladies' gp.
71. Bart or Ringo
72. Bearcat
74. Topsy's playmate
75. To some extent
77. Bedouin dwelling
78. Baseball's Rod ____
80. Philosopher Descartes
81. Pro
82. "See no ____ . . ."
84. Overseas
87. Dressy fabric
89. Newscaster Murrow
93. Breakfast flake
94. Autumn festival
97. "Nessun dorma," e.g.
98. "Auld ____ Syne"
99. Ed or Leon
100. Obi container
101. Holler
102. Nog ingredients
103. Load cargo
104. Bacterium
105. Willy Loman's transaction

DOWN

1. Henry VIII's wife
2. Lily plant
3. Highway exit
4. Pact
5. Fierce look
6. Brain scan: abbr.
7. Pasternak heroine
8. German china
9. Femmes
10. Aid in wrongdoing
11. Misdeed
12. Request
13. NASA spacecraft
14. Succotash ingredient
15. Lyricist Lerner
16. Transmit
23. Donkey: Ger.
26. Cleopatra's maid
29. Rudeness
31. Leg joints
33. Bert's buddy
34. Actress Carol ____
35. Ireland, in verse
36. Required
38. Fort ____, California
39. Paul and Mary's co-singer
40. "USA Today," e.g.
41. Quod ____ demonstrandum
42. Pace
45. Banyan, e.g.
46. Toil

PUZZLE 24

49. French sociologist Durkheim
51. Actor Bridges
52. Lively dance
54. Wrath
55. Amend
56. Put down in writing
58. Laissez ____
59. Worker
60. Opera slave
61. Boxer Barkley
62. Fifth wheel
63. Gambling game
64. Great review
65. Sketch
67. French novelist
68. Beige
71. Flushing field
72. Fake hair
73. Etching fluid
76. Injustices
77. "Africa" singers
79. Constantly
81. Counterfeit
83. Poison
84. Palindrome start
85. Boast
86. Used the doorbell
87. Pung
88. Hawaii's state bird
90. Expanse
91. Moon valley
92. Senator Bumpers of Arkansas
95. Japanese pearl diver
96. Prove human

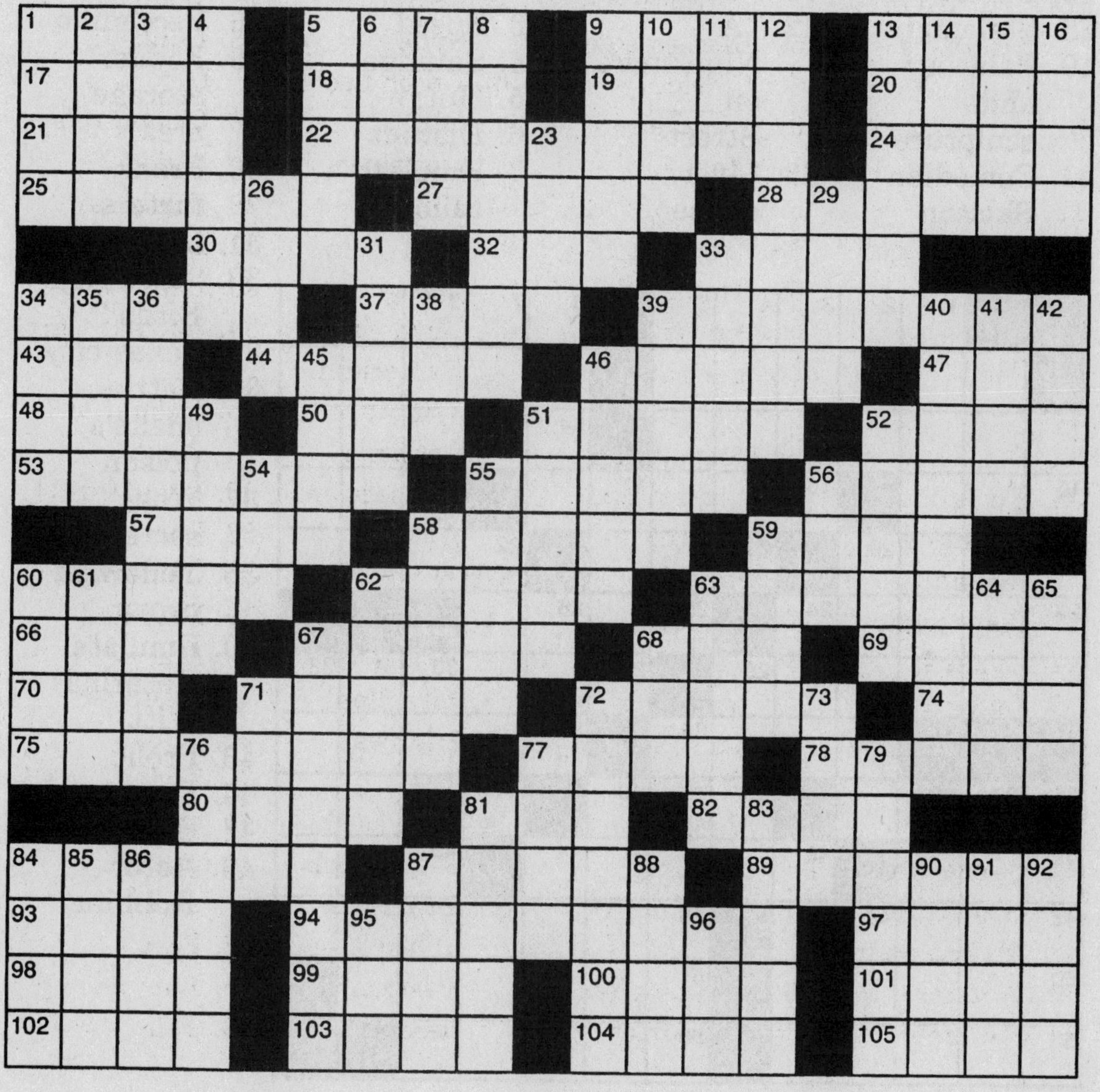

PUZZLE 25

ACROSS

1. Rough
6. Valuable possession
11. Famous canal
12. Not as many
13. Dribbles
14. Informed
15. Sprint
16. Diner
18. Stalemate
19. Painting and sculpture
21. Comedian Skelton
22. Manipulates
23. Retains
25. Cozy dwelling
27. Whirlpools
29. Foolish one
33. Deposited
35. Whinny
36. Scaloppine meat
39. ____ Vegas
41. Nevada city
42. "A Nightmare on ____ Street"
43. Lively dance
45. And not
46. Peace prize
48. Camper's light
50. "Carmen" or "Aida"
51. Garb
52. Cheerful
53. Appears to be

DOWN

1. Spooky
2. Dancer Miller
3. Speed
4. Smudge
5. Hurry
6. Distant
7. Emulate a tailor
8. Kills a fly
9. Weird
10. Oaks and maples
11. Served the wine
13. Slow down
17. Biblical garden
20. ____ the beans (blab)
22. Say
24. "The Old Man and the ____"
26. Peccadillo
28. Fodder storage area
30. Frankfurters
31. Disregard
32. "The ____ Birds"
34. Texas city
36. Rattlesnake's poison
37. Wed secretly
38. Yellowish brown
40. Emulate Katarina Witt
43. Frolic
44. Poker stake
47. Blunder
49. Actor Robbins

PUZZLE 26

ACROSS

1. At once
4. Dilemma
8. Melt
12. Actor Wallach
13. "____ Around"
14. Singer Coolidge
15. Steak order
17. "As ____ Dying"
18. Highway fees
19. Force
21. Director Preminger
23. Donkeys
26. "____ Sings the Blues"
29. Vexes
31. Not well
32. Deteriorated
34. Noggin
36. Fresh
37. Attorney General Janet ____
39. Peruse
40. Barbara or Cruz
42. Diminishes
44. Sample
46. Fragrant flowers
50. Sun god
52. Chide
54. Harvey's pal Elwood ____
55. Farming implement
56. Chowed
57. Reject
58. Stitched
59. Furious

DOWN

1. Salamander
2. Bread spread
3. Humorist Rogers
4. Among
5. Conceit
6. Elder
7. Stalk
8. Attempts
9. Landscape feature
10. ____ loss
11. Mode
16. Actress Emily ____
20. El ____, Texas
22. Oceanic movement
24. Mother Bloor
25. Rosebud, e.g.
26. Camera part
27. ____ code
28. Business section
30. Handle
33. Time periods
35. Director Welles
38. Tailor's implement
41. Actress Jessica ____
43. Cartoon kid Charlie ____
45. Bugle song
47. Thailand, formerly
48. This, to Juanita
49. Molt
50. Attach
51. Piggy
53. Cut the lawn

PUZZLE 27

ACROSS

1. ___ Hawk, North Carolina
6. Soup dish
10. Highlander
14. Worship
15. Solo from "Aida"
16. Relax
17. Summer TV fare
18. Poker players' need
20. Young miss
21. City in Ohio or Spain
22. Male child
23. Moisturizer
25. Mailed
27. Miss Piggy, e.g.
28. Made a public disturbance
32. Paid athlete
35. Recently
39. Arc
40. Bound
42. Tier
44. Bridle part
45. Up to the time that
47. Varnish ingredient
49. Some city trains
50. Rumors
52. Permit
54. Actor Baldwin
56. Gauges
59. Resort hotel
62. Overseas
64. Convent sisters
66. "Superman," e.g.
68. Leather band
69. Pre-owned
70. Be idle
71. Military color
72. Small plateau
73. ___ out (gets with difficulty)
74. Small land mass

DOWN

1. Basketball's Malone
2. Perfect
3. Trunk
4. Relies on
5. Japanese money
6. Breakfast meat
7. Taken by mouth
8. Cables
9. House painter's tool
10. Dead ___ Scrolls
11. Taxis
12. Norway's capital
13. High schooler
19. Remedy
21. Throw in the ___ (give up)
24. Charged atom
26. Guided trip
29. Sycamore, e.g.
30. Wicked
31. Studies
32. Cork
33. Gambling town
34. Cereal grains
36. "The ___ of the Roses"
37. Soap-making substance
38. Affirmative answer
41. Leaning Tower city
43. Angered
46. Fragrant, flowered shrub
48. Fisherman's snare
51. Small stone
53. Decimal units
55. Kermit's comment
56. Builds
57. Rustic
58. Slithery reptile
59. Film of algae
60. Sit, as for a portrait
61. Iowa State site
63. Seep
65. Turning barbecue skewer
67. Mont. neighbor
68. Hit the slopes

PUZZLE 28

ACROSS

1. Strong wind
5. Fat
10. Annoys
14. Genesis garden
15. Hilo hello
16. Breakfast, e.g.
17. Told an untruth
18. More rational
19. Wan
20. Caresses
22. Enraged
24. Relax
25. Knight's title
26. Halt
29. Solar-system center
32. Dressed to the ____
36. UFO pilots
38. Recent
40. Passionate affection
41. Public-transit vehicle
42. Cream of the crop
44. Arthur of "The Golden Girls"
45. Lazy
47. Humor
48. Sahara or Mojave
51. Must-haves
53. Part of MPH
55. Thaws
56. Hairpiece
58. Sinful
60. Crooner Frank ____
64. Irrigated
68. Smell
69. False name
71. Nat King ____
72. Unwanted plant
73. Shop
74. Bathroom-floor covering
75. Mineo and Maglie
76. Small lakes
77. Smack

DOWN

1. Hairstyling products
2. Mine entrance
3. Lewd look
4. Sign, as a check
5. Watering holes
6. Explosions
7. Very long time
8. Stadium of the Mets
9. Deserves
10. Endanger
11. Back end
12. Cabbagelike vegetable
13. Toboggan
21. Sharp
23. Martini ingredient
26. "Uncle Tom's ____"
27. Escape from
28. Bride's walkway
30. Join together
31. Volleyball-court barrier
33. Prestigious prize
34. Chris ____ (tennis star)
35. Chairs
37. Baste
39. Tie the knot
43. Facial feature
46. Film director Blake ____
49. Radiate
50. Chooses
52. Pose
54. Bonus
57. Clutch
59. Flower holders
60. Female pigs
61. Notion
62. Christmas
63. Female voice part
65. Stir up
66. Singer Fitzgerald
67. Profound
70. Charged atom

PUZZLE 29

ACROSS

1. Pigs' swill
5. Certain Vegas machine opening
9. ____ de Triomphe
12. Molten rock
13. Pathway
14. River: Sp.
15. Footwear for Hamill
17. Hotel's kin
18. Ball-point ____
19. "____ Got a Secret"
20. Swap
22. Sault ____ Marie
23. Undershirt
24. Sea mammals
27. Propels a canoe
31. Singer Guthrie
32. Elbow's locale
33. The Flintstones' pet
34. " . . . where'd you get those ____?"
36. Garden nuisances
37. First lady
38. Went quickly
39. Rent
42. ____ Alamos
43. School org.
46. Be mistaken
47. Those who live next door
50. Gift for dad
51. Mellow
52. Word with stick or happy
53. Body of water
54. Play the lead
55. Swiss mountains

DOWN

1. Petticoat
2. "Arsenic and Old ____"
3. Kiln
4. Mates for mas
5. Work hard
6. Better ____ than never
7. Singleton
8. Examined
9. Opera solo
10. Lemon skin
11. Frozen-yogurt holder
16. Baby beavers
21. Blush
22. Skiers' inclines
23. Highlander's hat
24. Tree fluid
25. Before, poetically
26. Pub brew
27. Couples: abbr.
28. Fib
29. Football position
30. Distress call
32. "You ____ There"
35. Happenings
36. Clean
38. Actor Moore
39. "____ Call the Whole Thing Off"
40. New York canal
41. Vicinity
42. Type of bean
43. Electoral survey
44. Snare
45. Vipers
48. Have a snack
49. Youth group: abbr.

PUZZLE 30

ACROSS
1. Chowder ingredient
5. Long-tailed parrot
10. Twilight hooters
14. Fashionable beach
15. Genus of oats
16. Pageant
17. Surrounded by
18. Promontory
19. Aspect
20. Monet painting
23. Item for Nancy Lopez
24. German ballad
25. New
27. Cabana needs
30. Uncultivated
32. Circumvent
33. Thousand: pref.
34. Research centers, for short
37. Trawl
38. Tolerate
41. Make a stab at
42. Canasta card
44. One kind of mule
45. ____ business!
47. Blissfully
49. Silent-star Renee ____
50. Long-tailed finch
52. Old Hebrew zither
53. Uris character
54. Relaxes in the pool
60. Hardens
62. Wedding-cake figure
63. Cast a ballot
64. Sonora sandwich
65. Waves of la mer
66. Sharing
67. Old English letters
68. A long time
69. Hindu fire god

DOWN
1. Hammer part
2. Variety of bean
3. Mine passage
4. Emulated Twiggy
5. Shade trees
6. Skirt around
7. Do a plastering job
8. Years: Lat.
9. Crushing defeat
10. WWII agcy.
11. Rapids
12. Deep green
13. Adeline's adjective
21. Irritates
22. Poivre's pal
26. S.Amer. country
27. Home on the trail
28. Finished
29. Dowser
30. Sheer
31. Colleague
33. Marx or Malden
35. Scottish hillside
36. Ago, to Macduff
39. Avery Robinson song
40. Black ____ spider
43. Derisive sound
46. Former Austrian province
48. Favorite
49. Estimate
50. Mouthful
51. Mountain nymph
52. Viper
55. Raptorial bird
56. Operatic heroine
57. Chinese society
58. Town on the Thames
59. Italian painter
61. Telegraphic Mayday

PUZZLE 31

ACROSS

1. Restaurant employees
6. Of the planet Mars: pref.
10. Fairy tale villain
14. Soup spoon
15. Actual
16. Defunct
17. New York city
18. ____ quam videri
19. Diminutive suffix
20. Home of the Nittany Lions
22. Star flower
23. Wedding announcement word
24. Like some excuses
26. Diamond feature
29. Australian bird
31. Foreboding atmosphere
34. Fittingly
36. Homer work
38. Tramp
39. Theater sign
40. ABA member
42. Metaphysical entity
43. Gums
44. Foil metal
45. Origins
47. Bakery offerings
49. City in northern Ohio
51. Black gold
53. Sponsorship
54. Call
56. Rowboat adjunct
58. Vice ____
60. New Hampshire college
65. Bitter drug
66. Oz dog
67. Put into circulation
68. Kind of machine
69. Spanish linen
70. French river
71. Disapproving noises
72. "Back in the ____"
73. Hits

DOWN

1. Hoof sound
2. Vigorous
3. Utopia
4. Nightgown material
5. Intelligence
6. Vicinity
7. Quiet
8. Canvas holder
9. Bullfight cheer
10. Ukraine seaport
11. Keystone State college
12. Pace
13. Westphalia river
21. Golf mound
22. Among
25. "____ Ordinary Man"
26. Moisten the turkey
27. Spring month
28. New York state university
30. Small arachnid
32. Many: pref.
33. Gather
35. ____ Abajo, Dom. Rep.
37. Italian commune
41. Furniture wood
46. Contributes
48. Hair spray, e.g.
50. Adjusts
52. Destiny
55. Fragrances
57. Faulty
58. Huge
59. House wings
61. Lion's comment
62. West Point letters
63. Small hill
64. Laughter sounds
66. Fort Worth col.

PUZZLE 32

ACROSS

1. Quotes
6. Bread unit
10. Squealer
13. Rugged ridge
14. Actress Raines
15. Venus de ____
16. Airline employee
17. Hebrew month
18. Allege
19. Compass pt.
20. Office items
23. Entreaty
25. Unmoving
26. Shrill
27. Templeton and Waugh
29. Kind of collar
30. Mexican state
32. Male swan
35. Copenhagen natives
37. Mil. officers
38. Range
40. Norwegian coin
41. Baby hooters
44. Leave out
45. Atmospheres
46. Brotherly love
48. Describe gram-matically
50. Humdinger
51. Office items
55. Label
58. Anger
59. "Kiss Me, ____"
60. Inhabitant of Stockholm
62. Timeworn
63. Verve
64. Bizarre
65. British rock group
66. To distribute
67. Quizzes

DOWN

1. Garment for Dracula
2. Eye part
3. Office item
4. DDE's command
5. Irish ____
6. Jump
7. Ye ____ Shoppe
8. " . . . ____ unto themselves"
9. Blacksmith
10. Danube, e.g.
11. Animated
12. Craggy peaks
15. Counterparts
21. Yelps
22. Peruvian Indians
24. Lois ____ of "Superman"
26. Headliner
27. Poker terms
28. Bewildered
29. Tokyo, formerly
31. Spanish cooking pot
32. Office items
33. Ron Howard role
34. Track transaction
36. March composer
39. Newcastle product
42. Destroyed
43. Mall event
45. Carrying a gun
47. Shirt insert
48. Satchel ____ of baseball
49. Wheel shafts
51. Battle
52. Nimbus
53. Eur. country
54. Hawaiian goose
56. Mine access
57. Honey makers
61. Very small

PUZZLE 33

ACROSS

1. Encounters
5. Exclude
9. Fire residue
14. Dr. Zhivago's love
15. Hindu queen
16. Cubic meter
17. Stratford-on-____
18. Potential steel
19. Coach
20. U.S. Military Academy site
22. Rent again
23. Scottish island
24. Garden implement
25. Uzbekistan sea
27. Piano novelty
30. Ballet step
33. Greek letters
35. Kind of code
36. Inlet
38. U.S. Air Force Academy site
42. ____ Baba
43. Actor Chaney
44. Sana native
45. Heathrow abbr.
47. Grows older
49. Mil. ranks
50. Dorm room feature
52. Of an epoch
54. Authentic
57. U.S. Naval Academy site
62. Pass over
63. Winter garment
64. Impolite
65. Name: Lat.
66. Noble Italian family
67. Governor Grasso
68. Cares for
69. Colored
70. Composition for two

DOWN

1. Cabbage dish
2. Gutter locale
3. Cupid
4. Capital of Chile
5. Celestial hunter
6. Singer Anderson
7. Privy to
8. Shade
9. Star: pref.
10. "Out of Africa" actress
11. Cure
12. Sandusky's lake
13. Dispatched
21. Bear or cap
24. Elated
25. Soap substitute
26. Illuminated again
28. Atmosphere layer
29. Fleur-de-____
31. Drapery fabric
32. Indications
33. Wood sorrel
34. Vegetarian's order
37. "____ was going to St. Ives"
39. Canine
40. Summarize
41. Begged
46. Stayed
48. Legislative body
51. Actress Barbara and family
53. Appraised
54. Opening
55. African succulent
56. Describe, of old
57. Passed with flying colors
58. Inquisitive
59. Outstanding person
60. Dormant
61. Subway rarity

PUZZLE 34

ACROSS

1. German organist
5. Food fish
8. ____-relief
11. Unearthly
12. Money, in Genoa, once
14. Saucy
15. Review
16. Trebeck of "Jeopardy!"
17. Inter ____
18. Elastic wood
19. Mohammad Ali, once
22. Natives of Rome: abbr.
24. Ontario and Huron
25. Argue
27. Riga inhabitants
29. Kind of exam
30. Scanty
32. Mahayana movement
35. Trickery
37. Dancer Miller
38. Grin
40. Author Buntline
41. Respect
44. Skip
45. Poker stakes
46. Scents
48. 1492 vessel
50. Mediterranean island
51. Roy Rogers, once
54. Greek p
57. Caesar's utterance
58. Faithful
59. Citrus fruit
61. Close tightly
62. Poet Teasdale
63. Obliterate
64. Bitter vetch
65. Actor Kingsley
66. Bear caves

DOWN

1. Social insects
2. Cary, once
3. Covert org.
4. Jazz lover
5. Category
6. Certain paintings
7. Three, in Berlin
8. Ball VIP
9. Costa Rican president
10. Remain
11. Period
13. Rejoices
14. Prepares for a trip
20. Frothy brews
21. Gluts
23. Story
25. Comforter filler
26. New York Indian
27. Road divisions
28. Irish river
31. Head
32. Dylan, once
33. Lamb
34. Catches
36. Actress Berger
39. Debatable
42. Activates
43. Contrary gardener
45. Negate
47. Staggered
48. Actor Ustinov
49. Jots
50. Launder
51. ____ majesty
52. Bland
53. Certain
55. Dan Blocker role
56. "A Chorus Line" tune
60. Bard's before

PUZZLE 35

ACROSS

1. Provoked
5. Hormone producer
10. Pack
14. Floor model
15. Juliet's love
16. Daddy
17. Of a lyric poem
18. Mellowing
19. Canned
20. Renaissance man
23. Formerly named
24. Wonder
25. Make a speech
28. High card
31. Composition
35. Spoil
36. Like some ions
39. Individuality
40. Swallowed
41. Quibble
42. Small boy
43. Female fowl
44. Withdraws
46. Shoshonean
47. Saying
49. Needle feature
50. Place for a boutonniere
52. Circle part
54. Small truck
55. Renaissance man
64. Neuron appendage
65. Icicle sites
66. Atmosphere
67. Magnitude
68. Certain cadet
69. English princess
70. Editor's term
71. Encamps
72. Dregs

DOWN

1. Golden calf, e.g.
2. Make over
3. Arab leader
4. College lecturer
5. Slight scratch
6. Company symbol
7. Surrounded by
8. Hawaiian state bird
9. Doctrine
10. Shovels
11. Hack
12. Oil-producing gp.
13. African valley
21. Want
22. Water pitcher
25. Nebraska Indian
26. Evaluated
27. Stadium
28. Quickly
29. Flock
30. Omit a vowel
32. Construct
33. Type of type
34. Swiss song
37. Rink surface
38. Stout
44. Evening: Ital.
45. Eastern European
48. Large seabird
51. One of the Muppets
53. Stole
54. Flower holders
55. Maiden
56. Egress
57. Slime
58. Broad valley
59. Kiln
60. Loan
61. Nothing
62. Frozen yogurt holder
63. Bad day for Caesar

PUZZLE 36

ACROSS

1. Filly
5. Capri or Man
9. Pour forth
13. Light beige
14. Kind of whale
16. First name in mystery
17. Public meeting place
20. That, in Barcelona
21. Podium
22. Thumbed (through)
23. Fast time
24. "La ____ Vita"
25. Nicene ____
27. '20s art style
28. Cleaning cloth
31. Luge
32. Eject
33. WWII sector
34. Twain territory
39. Mouths: Lat.
40. Land of the Kurds
41. Coll. sports group
42. ____ shelter
43. Thrice minus twice
44. Passover feast
46. "____ Cat"
48. Hand, in Seville
49. Shaw et al.
51. Dear: Ital.
52. "Exodus" character
55. Live it up
58. Crossword cry
59. South, in Germany
60. Actor Jannings
61. Transmit
62. Ice mass
63. British river

DOWN

1. Holiday
2. U.S. publisher
3. Province
4. Schisgal play
5. "Treasure ____"
6. Gymnastic maneuver
7. Grasslands
8. Energy unit
9. Glacial ice form
10. Druthers
11. Robt. ____
12. Travel
15. Tuneful
18. ____ fixe
19. Italian ice cream
23. Mother of Pollux
24. Hoover and Aswan
25. Nurse Barton
26. Rest and ____
27. Diplomat Silas ____
29. Essence
30. Prado painter
31. Burns, e.g.
35. Purple flower
36. Borgnine et al.
37. Risque
38. Defeat
44. Malaysian wear
45. Poet's plenty
47. Wrinkled
48. Alma ____
49. "Planet of the ____"
50. Carry on
51. Hand over
52. Host
53. Bridle part
54. Unemployed
56. Core
57. After expenses

PUZZLE 37

ACROSS

1. Attired
5. Medicinal root
10. Soda-fountain drink
14. Scalp growth
15. Speechify
16. Winglike
17. Spy
20. Body-rub expert
21. Hollow stone
22. Sober
23. Raised
25. On ship
28. Actor Bates
29. Taken
32. Ice mass
33. Musical sound
34. Harem room
35. Indisposed
39. Rorqual
40. Trinity denier
41. Domineer
42. French season
43. "On Golden ___"
44. Accused
46. Hawk
47. Charley horse
48. "The ___ Mutiny"
51. Slow as ___
55. Sotto voce
58. Rind
59. Prop for Roy Rogers
60. Malay boat
61. Hit, as a fly
62. Lost
63. Sharp taste

DOWN

1. Buddy
2. Actress Turner
3. Assists
4. Art of training a horse
5. Cheerful
6. Got up
7. Wash
8. Devoured
9. According to
10. Penned
11. Muffin topper
12. Country
13. Comedian Johnson
18. "___ Window"
19. Meeting plan
23. Inflated
24. Scarce
25. Mistreat
26. Stephen Vincent ___
27. Do ___
28. In the lead
29. Dull
30. Dancer Astaire
31. Risked
33. Backbone
36. Long sword
37. Quick pace
38. Church part
44. Panamanian coin
45. Phony
46. Genuflected
47. Sheriff's group
48. Hot-beverage holders
49. Over again
50. Impression
51. Disorder
52. FDR's mother
53. English school
54. Matted wool
56. Palm leaf
57. Slave Turner

PUZZLE 38

ACROSS

1. African land
5. Wyatt et al.
10. Takes steps
14. Submarine
15. Drink noisily
16. Liner
17. Writer Ambler
18. Lion trainer
19. Secrete
20. Was cheerful
23. Buddy
24. Metallic dirt
25. Breakwater
27. Lively
32. Winter flakes
33. Long time
34. Slant a rim
36. Tricks
39. Sandboxers
41. Psalm interjection
43. Borneo native
44. Garden pest
46. Wanderer
48. ___ Baba
49. Literary Lamb
51. Tells a tale
53. Greets
56. Dolores ___ Rio
57. Stadium yell
58. Dried meat
64. Guardhouse
66. Sky hunter
67. Unemployed
68. KGB forebear
69. Reagan's attorney general
70. Leer
71. Optimistic
72. Finished
73. Tidy

DOWN

1. Head cook
2. Neither ___ nor there
3. Seed covering
4. Physician
5. Beauty lovers
6. Jai ___
7. Cut of beef
8. Gets ready
9. Binges
10. Fire residue
11. Make slow progress on
12. ___ wave
13. Enchantment
21. Baby's bed
22. Talk wildly
26. Promise
27. Bristle
28. Exhaust
29. Rich
30. Tied up
31. Actor Alain ___
35. Tibetan monk
37. Colorless
38. Slaloms
40. Fodder tower
42. Inured
45. LP
47. ___ Scott case
50. Open house
52. Michigan city
53. Bower
54. Freight
55. Warning horn
59. "The ___ Piper"
60. Stance
61. Advantage
62. Actress Raines
63. Yard sections
65. Bloke

PUZZLE 39

ACROSS

1. TV's "___ Old House"
5. Vaccinations
10. Bounders
14. Word on Mexican mail
15. Biblical book
16. Opera melody
17. Anthem author
20. Weight
21. Region
22. Musical pause
23. Arctic birds
24. ___ pressure
26. Square-dance locales
29. Swiss city
30. Haul
33. Lessens
35. Blow one's top
36. Eggs
37. Machine parts
38. Self-confidence
40. Make yarn
41. Poem variety
42. See to
43. Salty
45. Composer Rorem
46. Speed
47. Cuts into cubes
48. Phony
49. Wee drop
51. Condemn
53. "___ Russia, With Love"
54. Crow
57. March composer
61. Miner's entrance
62. In existence
63. Check
64. Meadow sounds
65. Nero or Frampton
66. Sheep cry

DOWN

1. 27th president
2. Protagonist
3. Neighbor of Turkey
4. Hagman, to Martin
5. Avoid duty
6. Waters
7. Greek peak
8. Shamus, for short
9. ___ Paulo
10. Provide refreshments
11. Flatboats
12. Give up seconds
13. Authority
18. Reason
19. Council city
23. Hill dwellers
24. ___ and carrots
25. Sea eagles
26. Egg accompaniment
27. Home
28. Stormed
29. June notable
30. Subject
31. Sheeplike
32. Fades away
34. Give an address
39. Story starter
40. Thin
42. Vagrant
44. Photographer Ansel ___
48. Banks of type
49. Auto gear
50. Cowboy
51. Bygone bird
52. ___ Express ('60s band)
53. Move swiftly
54. Fight
55. Global region
56. Lack
57. Sticky situation
58. Luck
59. ___ de France
60. Form into a circle

PUZZLE 40

ACROSS

1. Belch
5. Score
10. Chase away
14. Spoken
15. Fasten again
16. Uncomplicated
17. Ocean's bottom
20. High priest
21. Unwrap
22. Cowboy's rope
23. Twist
24. Sea craft
26. Challenged
29. Balkan
30. Page of an atlas
33. Disney's "Peter and the Wolf" cat
34. Singer Crystal ____
35. Conceit subject
36. Handyman
40. Epic poem
41. Politician Richard ____
42. Turpin and Vereen
43. Actor Vaughn
44. Wee bit
45. Argue
47. Pollinators
48. Cleopatra's river
49. Pots
52. Porkpies
53. In one ____ and out . . .
56. Life of the party
60. Called
61. Actor Peter ____
62. Slippery trees
63. Rim
64. Light beam
65. Hemp

DOWN

1. Presage
2. Eurasian mountains
3. Sitar-player Shankar
4. Wield
5. Felt around
6. Start over
7. Egyptian sun god
8. God of the underworld
9. Elver
10. Review
11. Shade trees
12. Puts to work
13. Amateur
18. Say in fun
19. Orphan Twist
23. Go under
24. By underhanded means
25. Cease
26. Spicy mustard
27. Avoid
28. Confronted
29. Witch town
30. Jason's wife
31. 007, for one
32. Sheriff's men
34. Celebrations
37. Most strange
38. Passenger
39. French priest
45. State of confusion
46. Fashion-designer Schiaparelli
47. Pass
48. Mother-of-pearl
49. Tyrant
50. Fill
51. Lengthy
52. Word on a towel
53. Poet Wilcox
54. Goals
55. Lie down
57. Under the weather
58. Flightless bird
59. Dixie's Johnny ____

PUZZLE 41

ACROSS

1. Stereo
5. Fortas or Beame
8. In the distance
12. Biblical garden
13. Settle a debt
14. Easter or tiger
15. Green vegetables
16. Rage
17. Sweeten the pot
18. Come up
20. Cowboy's rope
22. One of the Seven Dwarfs
23. Irritate
24. Peaceful
27. Church official
31. Amazement
32. Be obligated to
33. Awards
37. Rebellion
40. Space
41. Life span
42. Shipload
44. Lisa ____ of "The Cosby Show"
47. Baseball's Ruth
48. Steal
50. Spring flower
52. ____ of Capri
53. Cycle or angle starter
54. ____ Cod
55. Accomplishment
56. Put down
57. Something different from

DOWN

1. With it
2. Hunch
3. Worry
4. "The ____ Story"
5. Each
6. Saloon
7. Facial feature
8. Anchorage's state
9. Sharks' characteristics
10. Kind of saxophone
11. Deli bread
19. "Sanford and ____"
21. Exist
24. Detective Spade
25. Lamb's mom
26. Primary color
28. Bird sound
29. Wise bird
30. New Jersey cager
34. Concurred
35. Linger
36. Soccer and swimming, e.g.
37. Hare's relative
38. Conceit
39. Canal city
42. Example
43. Competent
45. Of an epoch
46. Gratuities
47. Request
49. Miner's quest
51. Watch

PUZZLE 42

ACROSS

1. ____ Vegas
4. Deighton or Dawson
7. "____ and Prejudice"
9. Nat King ____
10. Citrus fruit
11. Chinese, e.g.
13. Catch one's breath
14. Water barrier
16. Goulash
18. Devoured
19. Drinks with a straw
21. Important time
22. Midler or Davis
25. Is contingent
27. Unusual
29. Collie, e.g.
30. Daisies and tulips
34. Molar, e.g.
38. Not high
39. Approach
41. Actress Remick
42. Jerk
44. Grow
45. Cain's father
46. Jeans material
48. Covers a road
50. Trust
51. Worship
52. Perceive
53. Craving

DOWN

1. Wilted
2. Fuss
3. Transmits
4. ____ Angeles
5. Yale students
6. Straighten up
7. Saucer
8. Establish again
9. Slept outside
12. Dweeb
13. Talk
15. Support
17. Existed
20. Locate
23. Haul
24. Paradise
26. Kind of trip
28. Fanciful
30. Travel by plane
31. Heavy burden
32. Proprietors
33. Droop
35. More ancient
36. Deride
37. ____ and haw
40. Reimburse
43. Leg joint
45. English river
47. ____ de France
49. Summer drink

PUZZLE 43

ACROSS

1. Speed trap
6. Rocker Dylan
9. Opposite of NNE
12. Idolize
13. Exist
14. Oriental drink
15. Silly birds
16. Book club members
18. Aroma
20. Sketch
21. Antler
24. Golfer Hogan
26. Further
27. Reverence
28. Refuses
30. Mixture
32. In a prying manner
36. Irregular
38. Sound of a pigeon
39. Knife handle
42. Small spot
43. Basted
44. Storybook meanies
46. Breed
48. Kind of bridge
50. Jingle writers
54. Permit
55. "____ the land . . ."
56. Easily deceived
57. Certainly!
58. No longer is
59. Signed-off

DOWN

1. Dust cloth
2. Thirst quencher
3. Female deer
4. Fire crime
5. Organ pipe
6. Unproductive
7. Lode load
8. Droplet
9. Rob
10. Servants
11. Debris
17. Put on clothes
19. Followed orders
21. Stage hog
22. Have bills
23. Scarlet
25. One hundred minus ten
28. Cozy room
29. Long time
31. Stringed instruments
33. Arctic abundance
34. Humble
35. Over there
37. Politicians' targets
39. Ardently
40. Have the same opinion
41. Worries
43. Limousine
45. Put away
47. Sheet of glass
49. Grassland
51. Halfway
52. Adam's wife
53. Actor Beatty

PUZZLE 44

ACROSS

1. Lounge
4. Plays the horses
8. Serling or Steiger
11. Actor Vigoda
12. Zone
13. Type of sandwich
14. Army brass
16. First gardener
17. Range animal
18. Mop part
20. Faucet problem
23. Singer Turner
24. Had brunch
27. Fib
28. Leases
31. ____ a hand
33. Fade
35. The ____ McCoy
36. Tied shoestrings
38. Third word of "America"
40. Wipe
41. "Now I ____ me down . . ."
42. Dislike intensely
44. Ladies' wraps
47. Choice
51. Come in last
52. Type of cheese
55. Unique person
56. Strong wind
57. Comic Philips
58. ____ and breakfast
59. Singer Guthrie
60. ____ Moines

DOWN

1. Sacks
2. Help in crime
3. Clair or Descartes
4. Wooden container
5. Age
6. ____ Aviv
7. Window part
8. Blushed
9. By mouth
10. Cupola
13. Yearn for
15. Moray, e.g.
19. Broadcast
21. Relief
22. Actor Brian ____
24. "____ the king's horses . . ."
25. London brew
26. Shut in
29. ____ and feather
30. Crafty
32. Casino employee
34. Actress Farrow
37. Color fabric
39. Music system
43. Inventor Whitney
44. Untidy one
45. Dial ____
46. Heroic tale
48. Frosted
49. Docile
50. Space chimp
53. Deface
54. House wing

PUZZLE 45

ACROSS

1. "____ But the Brave"
5. Not well
8. Take it easy
12. Wicked
13. Type of whiskey
14. Opera solo
15. Serve
16. Small barrel
17. Skate-boarder's apparatus
18. Cold symptom
20. Shoppers' quests
21. Mouse or rat
24. Telephone greeting
27. Tarzan's son
28. Mature
31. Absent
32. Knuckle under
33. Small bird
34. Evergreen tree
35. Chunk of eternity
36. Old-fashioned
37. Marshy areas
39. Cancel
43. Emcee's assistant
47. Hideaway
48. Gardening tool
50. Foil's kin
51. Duke or Cross
52. Dynasty
53. Not fully cooked
54. Hamsters and parakeets
55. Husbands
56. Winter coaster

DOWN

1. Fishing boat items
2. Cookie cooker
3. Number of lives for a cat
4. Up in years
5. Provoked
6. Caustic substance
7. Without a ____ to stand on
8. Zhivago's love
9. Spoken
10. Citrus tree
11. Drinks like a dog
19. Menagerie
20. Porky's pad
22. Black wood
23. At this time
24. Dried grass
25. Lamb's mom
26. ____ and order
28. Skill
29. Horse command
30. Finish
32. Large snake
33. Laundry machines
35. Recede
36. Twosome
38. The deep
39. Blunder
40. Be concerned
41. Civil disorder
42. Coffee pots
44. Valuable stone
45. Arid
46. ____ off (not happy)
48. Border
49. Mineral bearing rock

PUZZLE 46

ACROSS

1. Dracula, at times
4. Self
7. Baby's dinner wear
10. Pub order
11. Alumnus, for short
12. Tender
13. Denver's state
15. Algonquian tribe
16. "____, Dolly"
17. Least common
19. Drysdale and Knotts
22. That guy
23. Mineral spring
26. Brewer's vessel
27. Arthur of tennis
31. Where students gather
35. Not working
36. ____ "King" Cole
37. Sure!
38. Sound of disappointment
40. Selects
42. North American Plains Indian
46. Let up
50. Opposite of aweather
51. Tall, skinny person
54. Celestial body
55. River turn
56. Actor Duryea
57. Coal unit
58. ____ as a fox
59. Backyard tunneler

DOWN

1. Johann Sebastian ____
2. African lily
3. Relate
4. Pitcher's stat
5. Flit about socially
6. Fragrance
7. Drill
8. Angers
9. Red vegetable
11. Record feature
12. Horror movie sound
14. Over the hill
18. Sound of satisfaction
20. Carp
21. Office worker, for short
23. ____-fi
24. Whale herd
25. Everyone
28. Secret agent
29. ____ and cry
30. Double curve
32. Near ringer, in horseshoes
33. Hat's kin
34. Go to the theater
39. "____, the people of the . . ."
41. Dope
42. Gone by
43. Choir voice
44. Break from a habit
45. Recedes
47. Cola, for one
48. Verve
49. Fender casualty
52. Lamprey, e.g.
53. ____ which way

PUZZLE 47

ACROSS

1. Ceremony
5. Increase
8. Tiny particle
12. Poems
13. Regret
14. Yep's opposite
15. Thaw
16. Fox lair
17. Place for a patch
18. Queen's home
20. Ability
22. 2,000 pounds
23. Birthday number
24. Not here
27. Those in last place
31. ____ is me!
32. Sticky stuff
33. Attorney
37. Collided
40. Before, poetically
41. Lode load
42. Holy tables
45. Not as far
49. Layer
50. Tavern
52. Manufactured
53. Warning sign
54. Teamster's command
55. Gawks at
56. Authors' tools
57. Butterfly catcher
58. Dimple

DOWN

1. Prance
2. Opinion
3. Explain
4. Belongings
5. Anxious
6. Owed
7. ____ hygiene
8. Where some wear bracelets
9. Dial ____
10. Candid
11. Join
19. Prisoner
21. In the past
24. Boring tool
25. ____ constrictor
26. Embroider
28. Chick's beginning
29. Shad's output
30. Turf
34. Hungers for
35. Be mistaken
36. Give up
37. Baby's hat
38. "Where the Boys ____"
39. Drilled
42. Over
43. Rickey ingredient
44. Adolescent
46. Comedienne Martha ____
47. Utopia
48. Relax
51. Born

PUZZLE 48

ACROSS

1. ____ it up (overact)
4. Shade tree
7. Stinging insect
11. Time periods
13. Affirmative vote
14. Vocal range
15. Abuse
17. Went like mad
18. Sailor's greeting
19. Small cottage
21. Breather
24. Sixth ____
28. Blink
31. Assistant
33. On in years
34. Wrath
35. Actress West
36. Be bothersome
37. Pitch
38. Houseplant
39. Carry
40. Slumber noise
42. Opposite of nays
44. Wise bird
46. Refrain syllables
49. Heed
52. Roundabout
56. Roman wear
57. In favor of
58. Delhi dress
59. Hammer, e.g.
60. Give it a whirl
61. Energy

DOWN

1. Tailor's concern
2. Met highlight
3. Crush
4. Catch someone's ____
5. Meadow
6. Arithmetic
7. Squander
8. Heidi's mountain
9. ____ Jeanne d'Arc
10. Seed holder
12. New baby deliverer?
16. Grain
20. Put to good ____
22. Matching
23. Coronet
25. Forbidden thing
26. Blind part
27. Advantage
28. Live by one's ____
29. Persia today
30. Roman ruler
32. Reject
38. Not many
39. Ivan and Peter, e.g.
41. ____ flush
43. Actor Wallach
45. Raise
47. Lover's ____
48. Land measure
49. Baseballer Mel ____
50. Sound of disapproval
51. Freudian topic
53. Neither's companion
54. Cleaning or goods
55. Pencil end

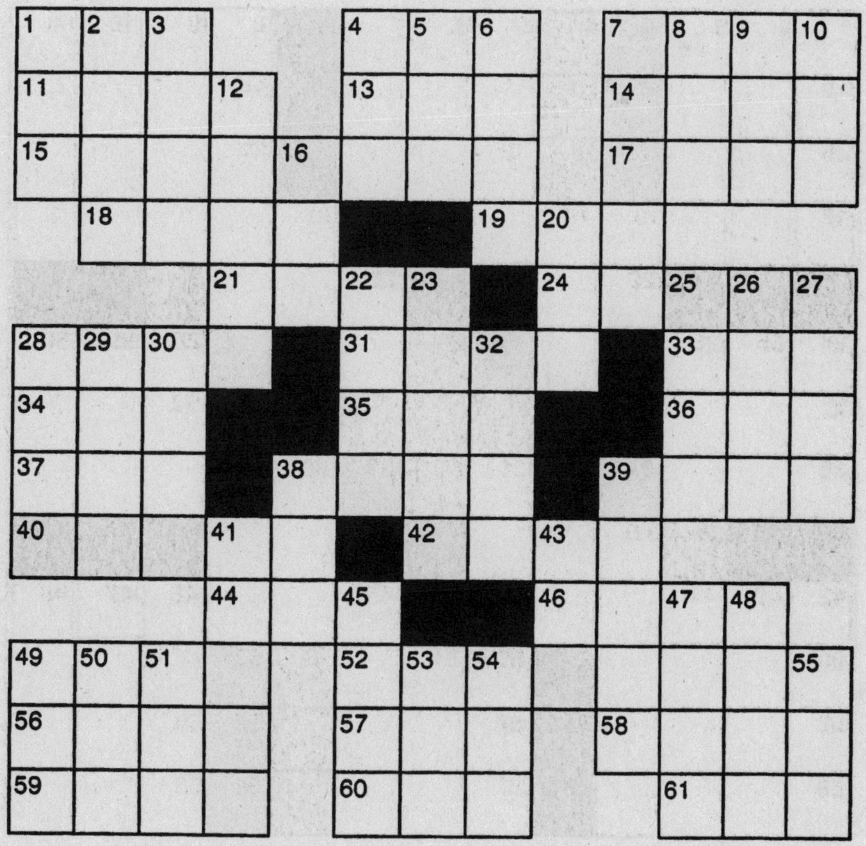

PUZZLE 49

ACROSS
1. Shack
4. Election campaign
8. Songstress Lane
12. Some
13. Eagerness
14. Stalemate
15. Pen point
16. Shrewd
17. Ponder
18. Belly
20. Actors' words
21. Exist
22. Airline entrance
23. Boil milk
26. Condensation
27. Duet number
30. Fit
31. Be under the weather
32. Leading performer
33. Australian bird
34. Extension
35. Attack
36. "Gorillas in the ____"
38. Took a chair
39. Makes ready to publish
41. Part of FBI
45. Cooked fully
46. Desert condition
47. Age
48. Moody
49. Left
50. Melody
51. Shade trees
52. Handwriting on the wall
53. The old man

DOWN
1. Sombreros
2. Single part
3. Spelling goof
4. Wanted-poster word
5. Wonderland girl
6. ____ and carry
7. Compass heading: abbr.
8. Allow to enter
9. Having dark hair
10. Diamond bag
11. Mas that baa
19. Fellow
20. Established rules
22. Congeal
23. That girl
24. Machine part
25. Light metal
26. Darken
28. Move the tail
29. Pay dirt
31. Talent
32. Location
34. Burro
35. Depress
37. Articles
38. Fishing net
39. Advantage
40. Barbie, for one
41. ____ bad to worse
42. Enjoy a novel
43. Opera part
44. Tub of ____
46. Past

PUZZLE 50

ACROSS
1. Hold tightly
5. Wander
9. Pop
12. Helper
13. Loosen
14. Freudian topic
15. Water racer
17. Yule ____
18. Store happening
19. Dole out
21. Terminates
24. Within the law
27. Daring
30. Beet color
32. Evans or Robertson
33. Gibbon
34. A Gardner
35. 2,000 pounds
36. Ditto
38. Precious stone
39. ____ off (started a golf game)
40. Vegas machines
42. In the neighbor-hood of
44. Takes a rest
46. Circus performer
49. Age
51. Hockey equipment
55. Turf
56. Hard to find
57. Dial ____
58. ____ the light
59. Sicilian volcano
60. Petty quarrel

DOWN
1. Home utility
2. Makes a hole in
3. Concept
4. Pared
5. Massage
6. Yoko ____
7. Actor West
8. Traveler's stop
9. Convention attendee
10. Past
11. Collie or poodle
16. Rec room
20. Danson of "Cheers"
22. Type of race
23. Number of Snow White's companions
25. Medicinal plant
26. Extend credit
27. Male singer
28. October stone
29. Citrus drink
31. "There Is Nothin' Like a ____"
37. Greek letter
39. Foots the bill
41. Steeple topper
43. Request
45. Word to a pesky cat
47. Over
48. Singer Horne
49. Double curve
50. Fish eggs
52. Coastal eagle
53. Caspian or Black
54. Word between ready and go

PUZZLE 51

ACROSS

1. List extender
4. Whitecap
8. Hock
12. ___ Hari
16. Attire
18. Egg on
19. Turkish regiment
20. Face shape
21. Song for Sills
22. Singer Bush
23. Standard
24. Pit
25. Toy
27. Likeness
30. Atoms
32. Vote against
33. Garland
34. Fastener
37. Corrode
39. Rooted
43. Weeded
44. Ring
45. Consecrate
46. Jack Lemmon film
48. Doctor's group: abbr.
49. Sharpen
50. Chlorophyll manu- facturer
51. Tokyo, of old
52. Idolize
54. Gets closer
55. Talking birds
57. Popeye's girl Olive ___
58. Novelist Jules ___
59. Gunk
60. Flutters
63. Inlet
64. Actor/comic John ___
68. Boat propeller
69. Shrewd
70. Sweet wine
71. ___ to lunch (unaware)
72. Spanish queen
73. Teases
74. Southern corn bread
75. Goad
76. Refers
78. Perjured oneself
79. Join
80. Tack on
81. Moccasin
82. Dog-team's vehicle
84. Comfort
89. Evaded
93. Lean against
94. OPEC nation
95. Bit
98. Parasites
99. Presage
100. Hawaiian goose
101. Greek letters
102. Ancient times
103. Caraway, e.g.
104. Wisecracks
105. Any
106. Caribbean liquor

DOWN

1. Mild oath
2. Scarlett's first love
3. Manger
4. Arouse
5. Sleeveless cloak
6. Dog's doc
7. Timeless
8. Violet
9. Lotion ingredient
10. Heat
11. Most agile
12. Kind of wool
13. Shake- speare's river
14. Soft mineral
15. Toward safety
17. Pampered
26. Moo
28. Pinna
29. Grant and Remick
31. Overwhelm- ing win
34. Bandleader Artie ___
35. How, in Honduras
36. Tail-end
38. Consume
39. Writer Booth Luce
40. Pullets
41. Genesis home
42. Art movement
44. Football's Simms
45. Tasteless
47. Two, in Tijuana
49. Motives
50. Designer Ellis
53. Drench
54. Bright signs
55. Shed
56. "___ Are My Sunshine"
58. Ivy and wisteria

PUZZLE 51

59. "Final Analysis" lead
60. Rival
61. Actress Turner
62. Inland sea
63. Artificial
64. Ties
65. Kind
66. Immense
67. Caesar's road
69. Indulging
70. "The Raven" author
73. Martial art
74. Summer outings
75. Excessively
77. Prevailed
78. Tai language
79. Slippery critter
81. Longs painfully
83. Rent
84. Taxis
85. Reed instrument
86. Stocking shade
87. Territory
88. Zip
90. Designer Christian ___
91. Tan
92. Judge
96. Exclamation
97. Actor Conway

PUZZLE 52

ACROSS

1. Canal feature
5. Trudge
10. Specks
14. Lotion ingredient
15. Bronco rider's show
16. Iniquity
17. Wee
18. Go-between
19. Bus charge
20. Torrid
21. Preholiday nights
22. Grated
23. Large diving duck
25. Biblical brother
27. Soft color
29. Concurred
32. Frequently
33. Veins of ore
35. Swear
37. Thailand, formerly
38. Lamb's mom
39. Yield
40. Sea eagle
41. Huge
43. Ravine
44. Principles
46. Got into the game
47. Help
48. Defect
49. Steeple
52. Clamp
53. Sing without words
56. Lumber
57. Particular viewpoint
59. Sage
60. Feed the kitty
61. Tanker
62. Unique person
63. "It Was a Very Good ___"
64. Requiring help
65. Monster

DOWN

1. Narrow strip
2. Mixture
3. Entrant
4. Door opener
5. Go on tour
6. Baseball's Clemens
7. Summer drinks
8. "Twelve Angry ___"
9. Kettle
10. State the meaning of
11. Racetrack shape
12. Grow weary
13. Winter vehicle
21. Actress Barbara ___
22. Evergreens
24. Short news article
25. West Point student
26. "The ___ of Innocence"
27. Sit for a portrait
28. Blazing
30. All
31. Evade
33. Smallest amount
34. Possess
36. Remove unwanted plants
39. Anthracite fuel
41. Jeer
42. Skater's surface
43. Paste
45. More difficult
46. Napoleon, e.g.
48. Penalized
49. Move back and forth
50. Corn bread
51. Smidgen
52. Mountain pass
54. Consumer
55. Simple
57. Offspring
58. Deception
59. Court

PUZZLE 53

ACROSS

1. Rushed
5. Reckless
9. Struck
14. Warsaw native
15. Medley
16. Wished
17. Kazakh sea
18. Grain elevator
19. "____ of Two Cities"
20. Peter Sellers film
23. Prong
24. Mousse alternative
25. With full force
28. Play the lead
31. Deserve
35. Fortune-tellers' aids
37. Kansas City to Savannah dir.
38. Female ruff
39. Aesop fable, with "The"
43. Printing measures
44. "____ Town"
45. Nicknamed
46. Prophet
48. Harvest
50. London apartments
51. Pub specialty
53. Italian wine center
55. Stockton short story, with "The"
62. Farewell, in Madrid
63. Nurture
64. Admit
66. French river
67. Wild buffalo
68. Actress Yothers
69. Media
70. Flat-topped hill
71. Verve

DOWN

1. Vichy, for one
2. Harbor
3. Biblical king
4. Removal
5. Violinist's substance
6. Straightens
7. Sheet material
8. Large ring
9. Classic western
10. Mark with spots
11. Colorful fish
12. Gram prefix
13. German river
21. One of Columbus's ships
22. Assented
25. Tamarisks
26. New England state
27. Came up
29. Four: pref.
30. Powdery residue
32. Caribbean island
33. Change an alarm
34. Inadequacies
36. Sleep disturber
40. Scheduled
41. Civilian clothes
42. Compel
47. Synthetic fabrics
49. Songs of joy
52. Forfeits
54. Narrow furrow
55. Light source
56. Jewish month
57. Dreadful
58. Streetcar
59. Present
60. Misfortune
61. Author Jaffe
65. Pale

PUZZLE 54

ACROSS

1. Hindu melody
5. Largest mammal
10. Mother of Hermes
14. Countess's spouse
15. Dubuque native
16. Gudrun's husband
17. Bedouin, for example
18. Pairs
19. Loam
20. Goddess of agriculture
22. Cadmus's sister
24. Actor Moody
25. Fair
26. Eastern Orthodox monastery
29. Take to the skies
30. Norse love goddess
34. "___ and the Swan"
35. Rest
36. Baroque and Georgian
37. Energy unit
38. Woodchucks' cousins
40. Singer Davis
41. Favor
43. Water, to Brigitte
44. Mother of Artemis and Apollo
45. Innsbruck province
46. Explosive letters
47. Most faulty
48. Raises
50. ___ Vicente
51. Mother of Dionysus
53. Mother of Hercules
57. Actor Ray
58. Some steaks
60. Novelist Turgenev
61. Litigates
62. Select group
63. Verne captain
64. Wife and sister of Zeus
65. Rekindled
66. Developed

DOWN

1. Scan
2. Rhine feeder
3. Small weight
4. Saskatchewan's neighbor
5. Broaden
6. Time of day
7. Respect
8. Recently
9. Result
10. Concrete work
11. On the summit of
12. Hipbones
13. Afflict
21. Water tester
23. Log boats
25. Twain
26. Caught a few z's
27. Tralee's county
28. Garden tool
29. Conifer
31. Playwright Rice
32. Irish poet
33. English racetrack
35. White-handed gibbon
36. Senator Symington
38. Skirmish
39. Cereal
42. Taiwan
44. Towering
46. High in pitch
47. Military woman
49. Modify
50. Frozen rain
51. Swing around
52. German river
53. Con
54. Someday
55. Call
56. Adequate
57. Coal residue
59. Color or paint

PUZZLE 55

ACROSS

1. Irascibility
7. Vacation spot
12. "____ of Paris"
13. Make beloved
15. Keeps quiet
18. Van Gogh's town
19. Goes out with
20. Mil. rank
21. Level
22. German river
23. Umpire's call
24. Hostelry
25. Meditated
26. Antitoxin
27. Moved up and down
29. Benign
30. Like many summer drinks
31. Floor coverings
32. Connected
35. Molly Ringwald et al.
39. Favorites
40. Aviator
41. Cluster of wool fibers
42. Attend a banquet
43. Tennis cup
44. Broker's letters
45. Heathrow abbr.
46. Prods
47. Females
48. Keep quiet
51. Ronald or Nancy
52. Accompanies
53. Pairs
54. Germ cells

DOWN

1. Rockette, e.g.
2. Greek
3. Sequence
4. Colleen
5. Self
6. Made
7. Outdid
8. Door sign
9. Foofaraws
10. Time per.
11. Drawn
12. Id est
14. Deplorable
16. Let up
17. Adversary
22. Floored
23. Perception
25. Steps
26. Spectacle
28. Move furtively
29. Glory
31. Enjoys
32. Increase
33. Newspaper employee
34. Provided
35. Metal fastener
36. Nowadays
37. Maroons
38. Consumes
40. Irreligious people
43. Trepidation
44. ____ never
46. Ulan Bator, formerly
47. Texas city
49. Howl
50. Clairvoyant's letters

PUZZLE 56

ACROSS

1. Instance
5. Buenos ____
10. Vintage
14. Highly spiced stew
15. Incline
16. Single
17. Actress Dawn Chong and others
18. Nigh
19. Rent
20. Country on the Aegean
22. Up on the deck
24. Commandeer
26. Cereal plant
27. Consummate
29. Actress Jackson
32. Tailed amphibian
35. Vertical part of a frame
37. Cruise
38. Bruin great
39. Ike's command: abbr.
40. Wildebeest
41. Grande and de la Plata
43. Confront
45. Reckon
46. Creme de ____
48. Defense pact: abbr.
50. Inventory
52. Cloth merchants
56. Twitched
59. Walk with stealth
60. Arabian nights number
61. Coffee or stew
63. Desire
64. Weapon of yore
65. Large artistic work
66. Work on a manuscript
67. Salts
68. Type of board
69. "Anything Goes" character

DOWN

1. Welsh dog
2. Frighten
3. Lie dormant
4. Prevail upon to go
5. Climbs
6. Negatively
7. Essence
8. Kind of salt
9. Drainage
10. Court sessions
11. Great time
12. Novelist Wiesel
13. Covers sporadically
21. Share
23. Part of RSVP
25. Hinder
28. Coolidge and Mae Brown
30. Sup
31. Silver-white metal: abbr.
32. Standard
33. Cleveland's water
34. Guilty party
36. Cherished
42. Cigars
43. Children's hour
44. Temporal
45. ____ shift
47. Long-handled implement
49. ____ chi
51. Milk whey
53. Piano piece
54. Pitcher's aid
55. Argument
56. Stallone film
57. Island off Scotland
58. Urgent
62. Patriotic organization: abbr.

PUZZLE 57

ACROSS

1. Confine
5. Caustic remark
9. Authority
13. Facility
14. Donkey, in Bremen
15. Diminish gradually
16. Cutting beam
17. Alaskan island
18. Uncertain
19. Transforms
21. Sculls
23. Smoke solids
24. Links gadget
25. Credit
28. Ms. Bombeck
30. Sora
31. Chinese animal
34. Protozoan
36. Test
37. Resume
39. Musical group
40. Vigilant
41. Grasp at ___
43. Track-and-field objects
44. Plato's porch
45. Hassles
48. Agreed
51. Former gov. agency
52. Paleozoic, e.g.
54. Festive
55. IOU giver
57. Speech defect
59. Lab burner
61. Seasonal visitor
62. Toward
63. Leases
64. Pulled the trigger
65. Timeworn
66. Neighbor of Neb.
67. Sarge's dog

DOWN

1. Varnish base
2. Snail's adage?
3. Certain plaintiff
4. Land
5. Arthur of "Maude"
6. Oregon port of entry
7. Sell
8. Book-jacket rave
9. Bath, e.g.
10. Penny pincher's adage?
11. Locality
12. Decade component
16. Delayed
20. Throat ailment, for short
22. "The Last ___"
26. Typewriter key
27. Wild horse of Asia
29. Punish arbitrarily
32. Warren denizen
33. Sternward
35. Jaunt
37. Bit
38. "The Greatest"
39. Stephen King book, with "The"
41. Dogwood City
42. ___ Canals
44. Like some pretzels
46. Cave
47. Fleetwood Mac tune
49. Oriental weights
50. Painting surface
52. Essayist
53. Boxer's milieu
56. Tical
58. Pea's place
60. Invite

PUZZLE 58

ACROSS

1. Soho pad
5. Wash anew
10. Vitamin C source
14. Ornate fabric
15. Evergreen shrub
16. Spanish waves
17. Surface measurement
18. Students' locales
20. Hearty breakfast fare
22. Exam-taker
23. Vietnamese coins
24. French resort
25. Of a mountain range
28. Culpabilities
32. Activist
33. Untidy one
35. Kind of dance
36. Sea or stew
38. Western Indian
39. Florida's Lake ____ Apopka
41. "____ the season . . ."
42. Garden enhancers
45. Steamer, e.g.
46. Term
48. Rear skull bulges
50. Depots: abbr.
51. Diana's sister-in-law
52. Buckle
55. Escalated
59. Report-card matter
61. Custody
62. Aldebaran, e.g.
63. Biblical witch's home
64. Certain collegians
65. Basins
66. Maternally related
67. Solicit

DOWN

1. Babble
2. "Dr. Zhivago" character
3. Mass response
4. School staff
5. Calculates
6. Kenton et al.
7. Sara and Slavenska
8. Military educational center: abbr.
9. Diversion
10. Less restrictive
11. Small key
12. Broadway role
13. Latin being
19. Up-to-date
21. Roadsters' club: abbr.
24. In no case
25. Pitmen's portals
26. British cormorant
27. Belief in god
28. Pamperer
29. Novelist Calvino
30. Colorless hydrocarbon
31. Joints
34. Pear-shaped instruments
37. Accelerate
40. Astronomy and physics
43. Strapholder
44. Bona fide
47. Chemical compounds
49. Compass pt.
51. Neckwear
52. Mooring chain
53. Alaskan island
54. Casual attempt
55. Pianist Geza ____
56. Auto-racer Earnhardt, Jr.
57. Sandusky's lake
58. Office item
60. Author Beattie

PUZZLE 59

ACROSS

1. Brake or camera
5. Speed-setter
10. Club or course
14. Jewish month
15. Worship
16. Hero
17. Mother, in Marseilles
18. Demon
19. First-class
20. Carouse
23. Caspian and Salton
24. Former GI
25. Crushes
28. Impudent child
30. Tourist's need
33. Acclaim
34. Fink
35. Before gram or log
36. Symbol of cowardice
41. Corded fabric
42. Sandra or Ruby
43. Nobel prize category
44. NY time
45. Attired
46. Strikes
47. Rival
48. Fragrant ointment
49. Rarely
57. Gush out
58. Wading bird
59. Adept
60. Hill builders
61. English Channel feeder
62. Money drawer
63. Shake
64. Caraway and poppy
65. Useful abbr.

DOWN

1. Dank
2. Notion
3. Hindu dress
4. Pinkish melon
5. Semolina and durum
6. Isaacs Menken and Esau's wife
7. Sheep's shelter
8. He was, to Pliny
9. Overhaul
10. Ogre
11. Stink
12. Ranger or wolf
13. Departed
21. Eye and wisdom
22. Sodden
25. Race-unit, in Bath
26. Throbs
27. Dozed
28. Produce
29. Brit. flyers
30. Historian Alfred Thayer ____
31. "____ God made . . ." (A.E. Houseman)
32. Reduces
37. Inactivity
38. Afternoon gathering
39. Pandowdy ingredient
40. Cohort
45. 102, in Pompeii
46. Fries
47. Stanza
48. Recipe instruction
49. Colorful gem
50. Words to Nanette
51. Gashes
52. Writer James ____
53. Camembert's kin
54. Newspaper sect.
55. Spanish jar
56. Actress/singer Carter

PUZZLE 60

ACROSS

1. Bible food
6. Chocolate units
10. Chowder ingredient
14. Use rollerblades
19. More freezing
20. Take ____ (accept the blame)
21. De ____ (elegant)
22. Sadat
23. Bristles
24. Church area
25. City on the Oka
26. Sub
27. Come to a sudden halt
31. Hither's companion
32. Galilee miracle town
33. Membership fee
34. County in Ohio
35. "____ Rebel" (Crystals tune)
36. Minus
37. Nero's garb
38. Composer Rorem
41. ". . . let him first cast ____ at her"
44. Peel
45. Delights greatly
46. "Bloom County" character
47. Diamond positions
49. Marooned Ben of "Treasure Island"
50. GI's picture
51. Reimburses
52. Fictional sleeper
53. Small fishing boat
54. Mix together
55. Theater sign
56. Beach toy
58. Dutch painter
59. Twinge
60. Goes whole hog
66. Dobbin's dinner
67. Paris airport
68. "____ the valley of death . . ."
69. Pied Piper follower
71. "Fats" ____
74. In apple-pie order
75. Neighbor of Tenn.
76. Throwing weapon
77. Separately
78. Spring flower
79. Did what the cop ordered
82. Take out, in printing
83. River islets
84. Loony
85. Famous cellist
86. Literary collection
87. ____ no good
88. Two-wheeled vehicle
89. Perukes
90. French painter
92. Singer Horne
93. Aria, e.g.
94. Western Indian
97. Regains control
101. Bandleader Shaw
102. Screen star Hayworth
103. Nobleman
104. Lariat
105. Wails
106. Doer: suff.
107. Reigns
108. Flynn of films
109. Basilicas' sections
110. Country road
111. Noblewoman
112. Inclines

DOWN

1. Actress Gold
2. Vinegary: pref.
3. Radon, formerly
4. Kind of tide
5. Isn't worth ____
6. Top ____
7. Cultivated land
8. Sitarist Shankar
9. Big ____ (lavish ones)
10. Duplicates
11. Entices
12. Chops
13. Nuclear accident
14. Very dry region
15. Rap
16. Revival
17. Labels
18. Suffix with trick or witch
28. Alleviates
29. English river
30. Scruffy dog's name
35. ____ d'oeuvre
36. Northern Scandinavian
37. Theater award
39. Hebrew month
40. Info
41. Deadly snakes
42. Acute
43. "I'm Leaving It All Up ____"
44. French soldier
45. Sausage
46. ____ Junction, Ohio
48. Small musical groups
49. Gee!
50. Mottled
53. Trifle
54. Schooner part
56. Sow
57. Regarding
58. Robust

PUZZLE 60

59. ____ code
61. French river
62. Slaves
63. Steep
64. Utah city
65. Massachusetts seaport
70. Ancient home of Irish kings
71. Modern art fad
72. Bid first
73. Alaskan sled dogs
74. Josep Broz
75. Mom's sister
76. Young men
78. Of the seashore
79. Counterpart
80. Staring at
81. Inferior poetry
83. Simians
84. Western author Grey
87. Aside from
88. A Borgia
89. Thickly treed
91. Dress shape
92. Reveal
93. Valuable violin
94. Scarlett ____
95. Grand ____ National Park
96. Some exams
97. Kind of school
98. Actress Talbot
99. ". . . my kingdom ____ horse!"
100. Spare or radial
101. Alias initials

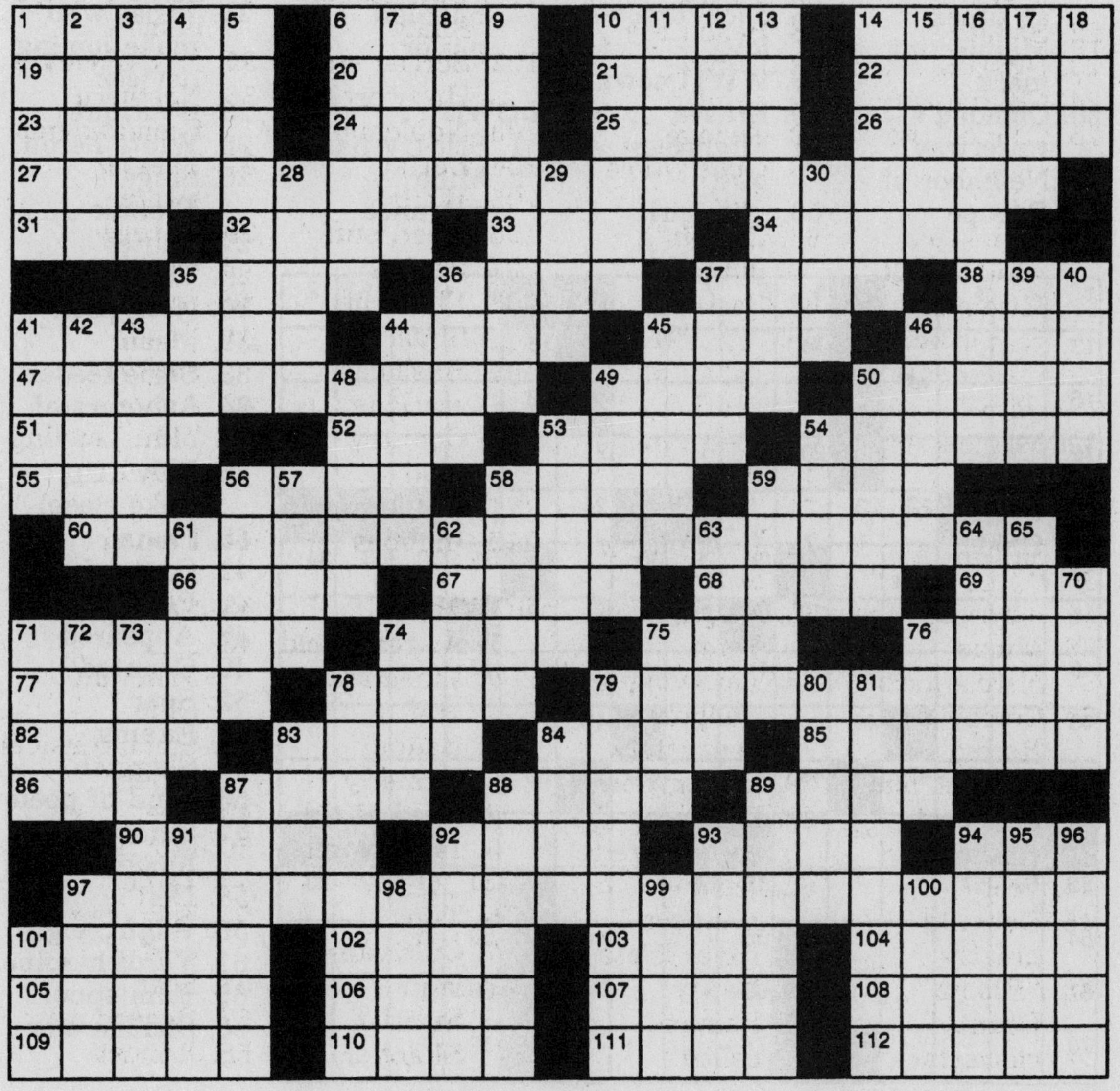

PUZZLE 61

ACROSS

1. Float
5. "The Incredible ___"
9. Cease
13. Garfield's pal
14. Fencing weapon
15. Armadillo
16. Drying oven
17. Amantium ___
18. Shoemaker, at times
19. Manuscript mark
20. Osmond's waterway?
22. Neighbor of Europe
24. Cereal grain
25. Choose
28. Standing
31. Zenith
35. Run rapidly
37. Necessity
39. Ethiopian prince
40. Irreversible waterway?
43. Opposite of WSW
44. Son of Isaac
45. Peaceful
46. Dick Tracy's love
48. WWII town
50. Erases
51. Flightless bird
53. ___ girl!
55. Queued up waterway?
60. Challenge
64. Weaving machines
65. Questions
66. Property right
67. Beginning
68. "___ a Song Go Out of My Heart"
69. First garden
70. Unwanted plant
71. Cincinnati team
72. Spanish parlor

DOWN

1. Stir-fry pans
2. Mine entrance
3. Manicurist's tool
4. Feeler
5. Spyri character
6. Din
7. Slim
8. Sharp
9. Rival of Athens
10. Mexican treat
11. Mountain: pref.
12. Place to play
15. Canadian prov.
21. Those who make joining devices
23. Boutique
25. White heron
26. Singer Frankie ___
27. Fairies
29. Void
30. New: pref.
32. Mean
33. Seine feeder
34. Laborers of old
36. Play ___ (fake sleep)
38. Feats
41. Overweight
42. Pedals
47. Appeared
49. Grunted
52. Spar
54. Exams
55. Sluggish
56. Kind of poem
57. Summer bloom
58. Den
59. Wight, e.g.
61. Verdi heroine
62. Film spool
63. Sicilian city

PUZZLE 62

ACROSS

1. Diamond necessities
6. Chorus member
10. Sleeveless robe
13. Money, in Madras
14. ____ vera
15. Burrower
17. Ring-shaped reef
18. Desire
19. Dauntless
20. Baby
21. Wise
24. Shoe fasteners
26. Combat area
27. Kind of bean
28. ____ & Peppa (musical duo)
31. Actress Diana and family
32. He takes for granted
37. Dull pain
38. Cowboy's rope
40. Not one
41. American Indian ceremony
43. Tolerated
44. Existed
45. Equine controls
46. Playing marble
50. Speakers' group
51. Coastal sights
55. Psychological entities
58. Weed
59. Taj Mahal site
60. Gaseous element
62. Unusual individual
63. Duck
64. Western lake resort
65. Links need
66. Steering device
67. ____ nous

DOWN

1. Spoiled one
2. Maserati, e.g.
3. Theatrical device
4. Slitherer
5. Picks
6. Cries
7. Jai ____
8. Vocal offering
9. Third son of Adam
10. Yellowish brown
11. Singer Debby ____
12. Director Irwin ____
16. Norse saga
22. Start of something new
23. Makes doilies
25. Heavenly one
27. One trillionth: pref.
28. Hall of Fame pitcher
29. Sisley's forte, e.g.
30. Pasture
31. Sharp blow
33. Release
34. Nocturnal illumination
35. Space traveling monkey
36. Magenta
38. Abbreviated highway
39. Sherbet
42. Be an accomplice
43. Feeling
45. ____ Dawn Chong
46. Tall, in Tegucigalpa
47. Colossal
48. Concur
49. "____ Goes My Heart"
50. Religious hymn
52. Olde verb
53. Molding
54. Asian river
56. Entrance
57. Ancient weapon
61. Kurosawa film

PUZZLE 63

ACROSS

1. ____ Vegas
4. Squabble
8. Forward end
10. Set of three
11. Obscured
13. Italy's capital
14. Young pig
15. Cover with asphalt
17. Rain heavily
18. Large tubs
20. Footed vase
21. Chop up
22. Cincinnati team
24. Turf
25. Farm worker
28. Cream of society
30. Enemy
31. Actor's part
32. Be interested in
33. Shed tears
35. Night crawlers
36. Green stone
39. Buccaneers
41. Grows older
42. At no time
43. Habit
44. Plaything

DOWN

1. Oaf
2. Likewise
3. Staircase part
4. Extend
5. In favor of
6. Intention
7. Foot digit
8. Flat fish
9. Bellow
11. Task
12. "____ Copperfield"
14. Goad
16. Moving truck
19. Sailor
21. One of the Stooges
23. Most sluggish
24. Precipitous
26. Standards
27. Below average grades
29. ____ de France
32. Dove's home
34. Ale measure
35. Uneven
36. Mandible
37. In the past
38. Lair
40. Classic car

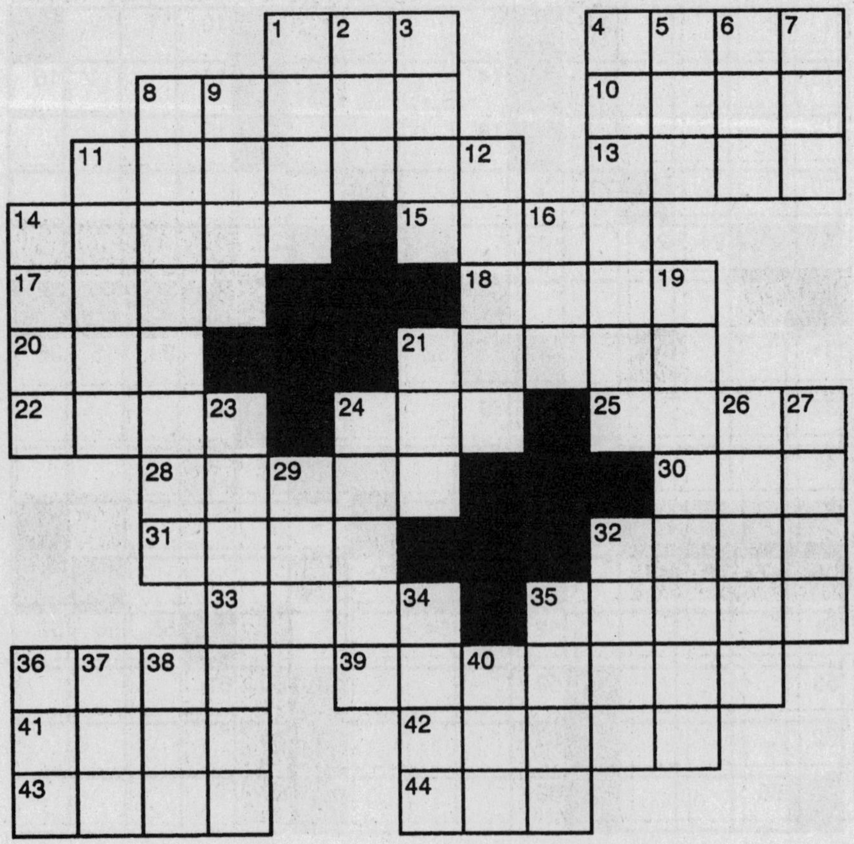

PUZZLE 64

ACROSS

1. Scarlet shades
5. Yale students
9. Actress Maureen ____
14. Opposite of aweather
15. Anklet
16. Bracer
17. Deer
18. Jingle bell journey
20. Date: abbr.
21. Urban railroad systems
22. Charters
23. Recommend
25. Direct
27. Hwy. choices
29. Soul: Fr.
30. Cushions
34. Devoured
36. Barbarian
38. Locale
39. Hepburn film
42. Spent time idly
43. Fountain treats
44. Pub offering
45. Mas that baa
46. Hamilton bill
47. Luminary
49. Flowered evergreen
51. Formed a rainbow
54. Component
58. Plumbing joint
60. Nebraska tribe
61. ____ Snowman
63. Legal agreement
64. Delight in
65. Small bird
66. Opposite of alkali
67. Paradises
68. Earth
69. Without: Fr.

DOWN

1. Gary Burghoff role
2. Wed in secret
3. Chill food quickly
4. Any stanza of six lines
5. Being: Lat.
6. Lounges
7. Rock Hudson film
8. Go schussing
9. One of two
10. Romanian dance
11. Tropical cuckoos
12. Take the bus
13. Experts
19. Music club
24. Bridge term
26. Rectify
28. Sign of a hit show
30. Corral
31. Ice-covered continent
32. Conflict with epees
33. Saharan
34. Salt tree
35. Melt
37. Famed auto racer
38. Scene
40. "____ Miserables"
41. Used to be
46. "The ____ of the Screw"
48. Whiffs
49. Kitchen wrappers
50. Actress Terry
52. Red dye
53. Accomplishments
54. Passenger
55. Slumbering
56. Inlet
57. Feds
59. Let someone use
62. Shoemaker's tool

PUZZLE 65

ACROSS

1. Cold or ginger follower
5. Deer
9. Clean up
13. Turkey portions
17. Molten rock
18. Potpourri
19. Operatic highlight
20. Friend, in Toulon
21. Heroic poem
22. House member
25. Patterns
27. Takes a siesta
28. Doles out
29. Entrance charge
30. Singing voice
31. Char
33. Business-letter request
36. Constructed
37. Congers
38. Little devil
41. Actor Guinness
42. Sports car
43. Shari or Jerry
44. Originally named
45. Child
46. Charity
47. Helen's abductor
48. Monster
49. Conundrum
51. Shiny fabric
52. Glossy
53. Safety slogan: 4 wds.
57. Step
59. Novelist's medium
60. Skirt gore
63. Baseball glove
64. Hirsute
65. Religious group
67. Caviar
68. Bard's before
69. Thick soup
70. Attache or brief follower
71. Promontory
72. Tied the knot
73. Virginia, for one
74. Drill
75. Apertures
76. Overtake
77. Time periods
78. Through
79. Plus value
82. Helper: abbr.
83. Became husband and wife
87. Stowe book: 3 wds.
91. Advantage
92. Well-groomed
93. Bright thought
94. Songwriter Porter
95. Tribe
96. Decades
97. Numerous
98. Lofty
99. Danson et al.

DOWN

1. Christmas toy
2. Back of neck
3. Rara ____
4. Largest ocean
5. "Stormy Weather" songstress
6. Pub orders
7. Let 'er ____!
8. Twister
9. Hornets
10. God of war
11. Go astray
12. Fedora
13. After a while
14. Send forth
15. Make a donation
16. Observes
23. Pave the way
24. Gather
26. Obtain
30. Belfry occupants
31. Needlework
32. Yale grads
33. Appraise
34. Dash
35. Treated with a prescription
36. Fall flower, for short
37. Weird
38. Usually: 2 wds.
39. Nothing more
40. Glance
42. Woeful word
43. Machine-shop need
46. Love, in Granada
47. Scapegoat
48. Bullfight cheers
50. "True ____"
51. Saw wood
52. Dispatched
54. Extras

PUZZLE 65

55. Bay window
56. Ruffle feathers
57. Diving bird
58. Wear down
61. Do ranch work
62. Golf mounds
64. Colors
65. Cable and trolley
66. Take advantage of
69. Babble
70. ___ lens
71. Suitable
74. Pear variety
75. Him's counterpart
76. Animal skins
77. Theme paper
78. Jury
79. Mother's sister
80. Snick's partner
81. Look over hastily
82. So be it!
83. Grain grinder
84. At a standstill
85. My word!
86. Rec rooms
88. "Christmas Carol" boy
89. Harem room
90. Scarf

PUZZLE 66

ACROSS

1. Altercation
5. Hack
9. Scorch
13. Beer ingredient
17. Sound of contentment
18. Strop
19. Theater box
20. Songstress Adams
21. Poetess Lazarus
22. Blue bloom
23. Mimicked
24. Thrusts
25. Stingers
27. Famous
29. Shellfish
31. Augment
33. Fish trap
34. Gulp
35. Flaming
39. Bank of seats
41. Attorney's subject
42. ____ of roses
45. Infrequent
46. Apply gently
48. Wanderer
50. Leaning Tower locale
51. Moll's diamonds
52. Actress Farrow
54. Dust cloth
55. "Call Me ____"
56. Substance
58. Flapjack
60. Surrender: 2 wds.
61. Actual
63. Pedro's river
64. Indoor messenger
65. Wasteland
68. Studies
70. Even score
74. Communion table
75. Ocean
76. Old salt
77. Opposite WSW
78. Lath
79. Spree
81. Porker
83. Copenhagen native
84. Witch
85. Household animal
86. Corn unit
88. Floating leaf: 2 wds.
90. Drink for O-lan
91. Droop
93. Convent dweller
94. Banishes
98. Mixes
100. Judge's hammer
104. Ireland, in poems
105. Merry caper
107. Uttered
109. Runner's distance
110. Queue
111. Needle case
112. Inoperative
113. Terrible tsar
114. Fewer
115. Forward
116. Sign gas
117. Jargon

DOWN

1. Erupt
2. Cougar
3. Weapons
4. Acrobat's swing
5. "The Sweetheart of Sigma ____"
6. Trumpet
7. Pungent bulb
8. Hassle
9. Dressed
10. Skip
11. "Rock of ____"
12. Carrot-top
13. Deserve
14. Ant of rock
15. Wilted
16. Miss D'Urberville
26. Glide on snow
28. English school
30. Uncooked
32. Finale
35. Hat edge
36. Openwork fabric
37. Location
38. ____ Abdel Nasser
40. Do aerobics: 2 wds.
41. Fall behind
42. Wait
43. Edom
44. Humid
47. Storage drawer
49. Daisy ____
50. Blacktopped
53. Quantity of land
55. Russian-built fighter jet
57. Pick up the check
58. Actor O'Brien
59. Atmosphere
60. Cooking fuel
62. Make a mistake

PUZZLE 66

64. Danger
65. Morse code symbol
66. Miss Raines
67. Male deer
68. Quill writer
69. Vital fluid
71. Gather a crop
72. "___ Karenina"
73. Garden pest
75. Take a load off your feet
79. The Fab Four
80. Toward the rising sun
82. ___ rummy
83. Energetic
85. ___ capita
87. Dried grape
89. Carry with effort
90. Musical sounds
92. Mark exams
94. Small valley
95. Cleveland's lake
96. On ___ and needles
97. Satisfy
98. Slip sideways
99. Fodder tower
101. ___ voce
102. Brilliance
103. Fasting period
106. Campaign
108. Library

PUZZLE 67

ACROSS

1. Laundry bar
5. Lion's den
9. Head cook
13. Mop
17. Apple of one's eye
18. Farm unit
19. Cowskin
20. Sharpen
21. Solitary
22. Cease
23. In the center of
24. Actress Magnani
25. Tire pattern
27. Scoff
29. Enticed
31. Male heir
33. Morose
34. Fish eggs
35. Welcomed
39. Baseballer Williams
41. Capture
42. Network
45. Highway
46. Soggy
48. Stairway post
50. Folder
51. Beast of burden
52. Seed container
54. Approve of
55. Wash out suds
56. Milwaukee product
58. Turned
60. Vegetable plot
61. Dismounted
63. Gym pad
64. Rational
65. Drowsed
68. Protects an invention
70. Brief attempt
74. In the lead
75. Satchel
76. Payable
77. Tint
78. Dock
79. Apple juice
81. Nickname
83. Gasp
84. Turf
85. Crone
86. Beknight
88. Pours carefully
90. Folding bed
91. Actor Mineo
93. Large cup
94. Lowered in rank
98. Artist's cap
100. Flogs
104. Small particle
105. Ready for plucking
107. Unusual
109. Toward shelter
110. Beauty spot
111. Smooth
112. Always
113. Not any
114. Termini
115. Dimple
116. Antlered animal
117. Mrs. Dick Tracy

DOWN

1. Sediment
2. Fragrance
3. First-class: hyph.
4. Gratified
5. ____ Vegas
6. Variety-show segments
7. Actor Jeremy
8. Say again
9. Scorch
10. That man
11. Work on copy
12. Part of FBI
13. Contour
14. Accustomed
15. English queen
16. Draw a ____ on
26. Polka ____
28. Paradise
30. Mass
32. Modern
35. Clutch
36. National flower
37. Comfort
38. Railroad station
40. Removed from print
41. Take-home pay
42. Breeze
43. Different
44. "Where Have You ____?"
47. Tyke
49. Bond
50. Discharges
53. Injured
55. Competed
57. Plane spotter
58. Disencumber
59. Make lace
60. Service-station item
62. Conducted

PUZZLE 67

64. Lieu
65. Dozes
66. Buckeye State
67. Achievement
68. Apartment
69. Bolt holder
71. "More ____ You Know"
72. Uncle's wife
73. Lays odds
75. Sizeable
79. Furnished food
80. Trick
82. Jewel
83. Christmas show
85. Sultry
87. Excluded
89. Young bear
90. Arrives
92. Sabbatical
94. Female knight
95. Certain collar
96. Matrix
97. Enter a pool
98. Warped
99. Genealogy diagram
101. African lily
102. Hamilton bills
103. Uses vision
106. Ink writer
108. Be human

PUZZLE 68

ACROSS

1. Young horse
5. Covers
9. Slightly wet
13. Medicine portion
17. Efficient
18. Look flirtatiously at
19. Pitcher
20. Eternally
21. Basis
22. Part of speech
23. Final outcome
24. Projecting prong
25. Convocations
27. Through
28. Hat fabrics
29. ____ long
30. Stripling
31. Hair coil
32. Remedy
36. Portion
37. Pulls apart
41. Fuss
42. Slum dwellings
45. Sandusky's waterfront
46. Famous fillets
49. Relief
50. Pair
51. Cubes
52. Handles
54. Golf score
56. Test to the limit
58. Comedian Sparks
59. Cereal grains
61. Pull the ____ out from under
63. Sets of tools
66. Scientist's workshop
69. Like Willie Winkie
71. Cut short
73. Documents
77. Very eager
79. ____ carte: 2 wds.
81. Nautical affirmative
83. Pertaining to the Holy See
84. Dole out
85. Intimidates
88. Self-esteem
89. Urges
91. Home: abbr.
92. Most somber
95. Herd of seals
96. Pasture
97. Expected
98. Swift
101. Poetic for 20 Across
102. Depressed
107. High cards
108. Half: prefix
110. Seed coat
111. Egyptian river
112. Biblical pronoun
113. Stratford-on- ____
114. Departed
115. Norwegian explorer
116. Sniggler's' catch
117. Band
118. Dollar bills
119. Drip slowly

DOWN

1. Till the soil
2. Woodwind
3. Bitter drug
4. Missive
5. Join together
6. Excited
7. Also
8. Japanese coin
9. Vanquished
10. Prize
11. Assembled
12. Before: Latin
13. Protected
14. Egg-shaped
15. Forwarded
16. Units of energy
26. Anger
27. Choice
28. Pleasure
31. Public conveyance
32. Throw
33. Stink
34. Portrayal
35. Oriental beverage
36. Fragrant wood
37. Long-legged bird
38. One of John Boy's sisters
39. Chinese grain
40. Sow
43. Pinch
44. Pistachio, e.g.
47. Attention
48. Eye sore
53. Baste
55. Abrade
57. Bark
60. Scorches
62. Capricorns
64. Faucet
65. Mineral spring
66. Source of illumination

67. Declare positively
68. Morsel
70. Inventor Whitney
72. Inciden-tal
74. Fencing weapon
75. Crusader Rabbit's sidekick
76. Narrow opening
78. Loathes
80. Concurring
82. Conclusion
85. Nourished
86. Listen
87. Outfits
90. Turf
93. Lament
94. Doghouse
96. Citrus fruit

PUZZLE 68

98. Charge
99. Soreness
100. Pare
102. Do a laundry job
103. Three times three
104. Homemade tree swing
105. Director Kazan
106. Pack of cards
108. Droop
109. Miss Gabor
110. In the past

PUZZLE 69

ACROSS

1. Brute
6. Covers up
11. 1963 Sophia Loren film
17. Less plump
18. Give last rites, of old
19. Southwestern poplars
20. Orphan Annie's guardian: 2 wds.
22. Actress Elaine
24. Bhutan neighbor
25. Ouse feeder
26. Walled portico
28. Own, in Oban
29. Singer Adams
30. Enrich
32. Typeface
34. Govt. agency
35. Sign of sunshine
36. Senate runner
37. Jogs
39. Personnel manager
41. Well-heeled backer: 2 wds.
45. Numero ____
46. Spumed
47. Jetty
48. ____-de boeuf
50. Actress Massey
51. Insult
54. Gaze
55. Type of saw
58. Courage
59. Nursery-rhyme author: 2 wds.
61. Royal inits.
62. Affected
63. Ride a log
64. Samovars
65. ____ da capo
66. Fan's sound
67. Australian nurse: 2 wds.
71. Nasty winter stuff
72. Promotes
74. Grinder
75. Toughens
76. More unique
77. Time division
78. Winged
79. Roof beam
81. Kooky
82. Miss Lonelyhearts et al.: 2 wds.
87. "Fur ____"
88. Ice pinnacle
90. Make a design on glass
91. Havana has one
92. It's in the ____
93. Ancient Greek post
95. Actress McDaniel
98. Door section
99. Ostrich's kin
100. Aleutian island
101. As to: 2 wds.
102. Duck down
103. On the button
106. 1955 Astaire-Caron film: 2 wds.
110. Term of affection
111. Tinker-Chance connection
112. Hindu poet
113. Holdings
114. Bowler's button
115. Auditions

DOWN

1. Sheets and cases
2. "____ Was a Lady"
3. Writer Seton
4. Embroider
5. Singer's syllable
6. Smoking, for one
7. Toughen
8. Fair-minded
9. Wapiti
10. Composer Roger
11. Perry and James
12. Russian range
13. Patriotic gp.
14. Francois's friend
15. Irish ballad: 2 wds.
16. Runaway
17. Actor Martin
20. Counts calories
21. Gave a 10 to
23. Learned
27. Dog who bit Miss Gulch
30. Disappeared gradually
31. Seaweed yield
33. Go for
36. Reporter's medium
38. Teacher's tool
40. Fleming and Carmichael
42. Mime's medium
43. Pipe ash
44. Sure!
46. Dentist's order
49. Annoy
50. Dramatic device
51. Chicago airport
52. Wild
53. Surrogate dads: 2 wds.
54. Classifies
55. Camp
56. Milton's "regent of the sun"
57. "____ Entertainment"
59. Skinflint
60. Charged up: 2 wds.

PUZZLE 69

63. Eager fish
65. Tocsin
67. Ranees' attire
68. Valerie Harper's role
69. Heyerdahl's "____ Tiki"
70. Pigs out
71. Cache
73. Cisterns
75. Golfer's problem
77. Pirate, at times
78. Italian wine area
79. Renaissance fiddle
80. Pie style: 3 wds.
81. Defrost
83. Climbing pepper
84. Sidestepping chaps
85. Goof at bridge
86. Wise ones
88. Sofa
89. Takes to task
94. Understood
96. Pianist Watts
97. Covert meeting
98. Ferryman
102. Prods
104. Hairpiece
105. Time frame
107. Hail!
108. Baseball Hall-of-Famer
109. Glasgow turndown

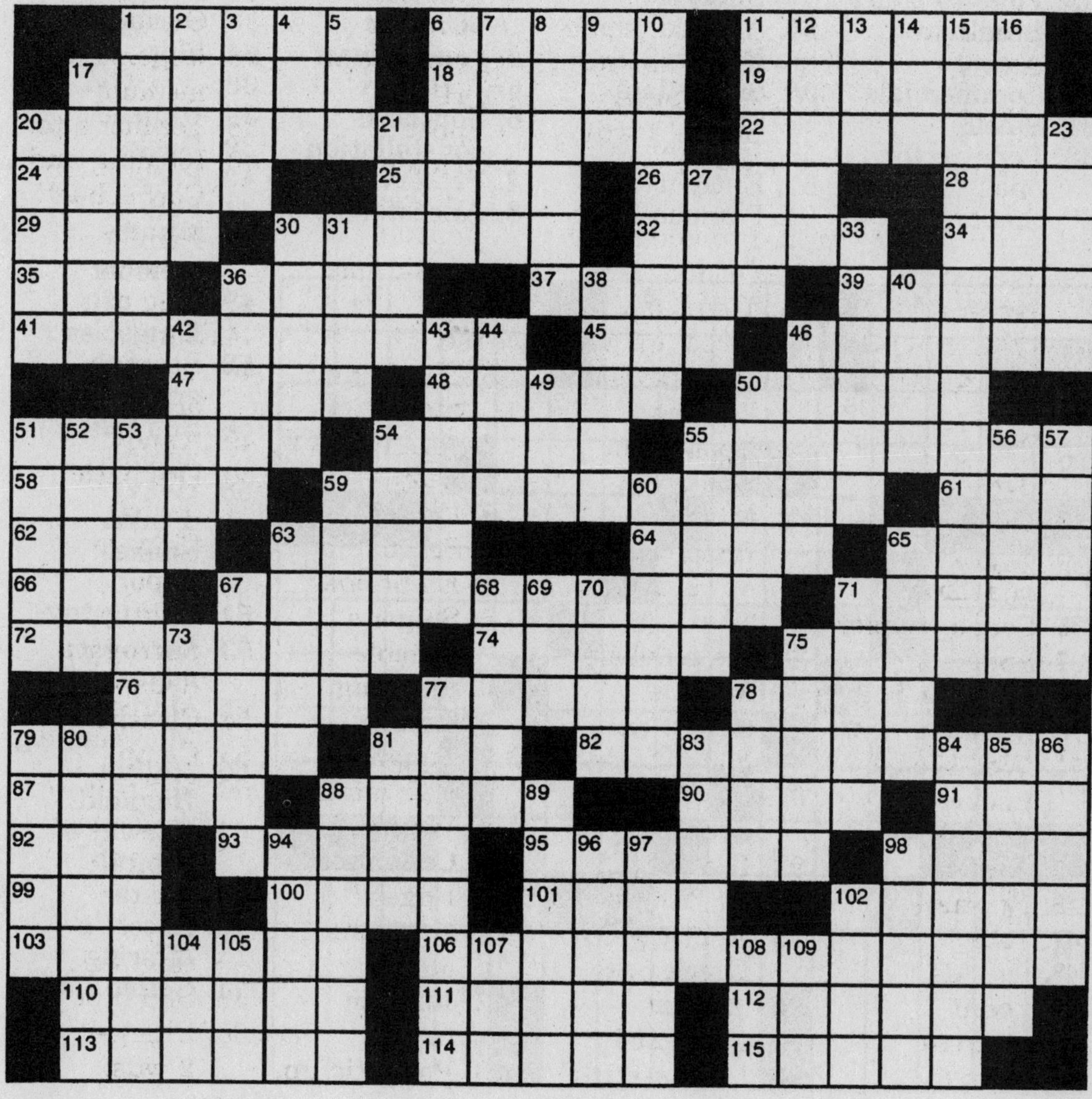

PUZZLE 70

ACROSS

1. Has a bawl
5. Spice
9. Restrain
14. Opposite of aweather
15. Of the mouth
16. Come into being
17. Sewing tools
20. Eastern nation
21. Fasten
22. Take to court
23. Break
26. Agitate
28. Commercials
31. Smell
33. Popeye, for one
37. Spoil
38. Viewpoint
40. Grin
41. Is in arrears
43. Tested
45. Indigo
46. Butchers' wares
48. Movie-rating indicators
50. Topsy's friend
51. Metes
53. Like a tortoise
54. Actor Reason
55. Small dam
57. Stain
59. Inquire
62. Entreaty
64. Famous lover
68. Sewing-box items
72. Porch
73. Well-ventilated
74. Actor Jannings
75. Violinist Isaac ____
76. Moniker
77. Make over

DOWN

1. Hit the river bed
2. Table spread
3. Oscar Madison's beverage
4. Jewish feast
5. A Stooge
6. Southern constellation
7. Preserves
8. Ancestor
9. Perennial flowers
10. Make a mistake
11. Binds
12. Jacob's twin
13. Counsel, of old
18. Hideaways
19. New Mexico city
24. Hat material
25. Severs
27. City in Peru
28. Scent
29. Peg
30. Swipe
32. Makes a sweater
34. Ship
35. ____ Oyl
36. Unbend
39. Ducks
42. Pack
44. Fall
47. Family member
49. ____ of Damocles
52. Storage space
56. Showed again
58. Heavy drinker
59. Snakes
60. Shoo!
61. Spring toy
63. Largest continent
65. Marcel Marceau, e.g.
66. Author Bagnold
67. Norway's capital
69. Mister
70. Escort's offering
71. Comic Louis ____

PUZZLE 71

ACROSS

1. Lunch dish
6. Small fly
10. ____ and sciences
14. Residence
15. Traveled
16. Metal thread
17. Sailing vessel
18. Once, of old
19. Once more
20. Biddy
21. Article
23. Armies
25. Highlander
26. Adam's mate
27. Country home
30. Folk myths
32. Scottish grain
35. Quarrels
36. Crow's call
37. "Home on the ____"
39. Bargain
40. Becker boomer
41. Tarts
42. Stood up
44. Conducted
45. Facade
46. Japanese coin
47. Upper limbs
49. Sharp tips
50. Notable age
51. Lass
52. Rides a bike
55. Curved lines
56. YMCA member
59. Chimps
60. Grotto
62. Swiftly
64. Evergreen
65. Neighborhood
66. Hindu fate
67. Play divisions
68. For fear that
69. Penetrate

DOWN

1. Cloth belt
2. Skillful
3. Diving bird
4. Commotion
5. Portrays
6. Welcome
7. Standard
8. TV spots
9. Horse restraint
10. Cognizant
11. Fruit skin
12. Woody plant
13. Mends clothes
22. Water tester
24. ____ and out
25. Gluts
27. School theme
28. Extra tire
29. Eagle's claw
30. Shoestrings
31. Was obligated
32. Pungent bulb
33. Representative
34. Experiments
36. Serene
38. Fourth month
43. English count
45. Abandon
48. Scamp
49. Snapshot
50. Soothes
51. Magnificent
52. Mama's mate
53. Majestic
54. Make a ____ in
55. Prayers
56. Supermarket
57. Peak
58. Close-by
61. "We ____ the World"
63. Piping god

PUZZLE 72

ACROSS

1. Actor who played Klinger
5. Smudge
10. ___ and pepper
14. Part of HOMES
15. Remain
16. The Kingston ___
17. Pinball-machine warning
18. Attorney Becker on "L.A. Law"
19. Symbol of fidelity
20. Pact
22. Snaps
24. Drummer Buddy ___
25. Genuine
26. Wit
29. Jeepers ___
33. Eve's garden
34. Walk
35. Actor Kilmer
36. Chinese political group
37. Race
38. Hemingway's nickname
39. Mine find
40. Scenes
41. Revise
42. ABC, NBC, and CBS
44. Goes over 55
46. Supports
47. Cancel
48. Tolerates
51. Parties
55. Terra firma
56. Bert's pal
58. Take on for work
59. Comic Johnson
60. Traffic sign
61. Greek peak
62. Sudsy drink
63. Fencing swords
64. Have on

DOWN

1. Greek cheese
2. Seed pod
3. Small brook
4. Quitting
5. Position
6. Hike
7. Water bird
8. Jackie's second husband
9. Deli choice
10. "Sophie's Choice" actress
11. Melody
12. Chain piece
13. Dresses
21. Make public
23. Lamented
25. Elm and oak
26. Attack
27. Love foolishly
28. Belief
29. Workmen
30. Shun
31. Very fast
32. Bed boards
34. Journeys
37. Seen from above
38. Raree
40. Idle
43. Gad about
44. Spirited horses
45. Soda
47. Gate
48. Thick piece
49. Plant of the Bible
50. Feed the kitty
51. Sword
52. River in France
53. Sky bear
54. Briny drop
57. Actor Torn

PUZZLE 73

ACROSS

1. ____-friendly
5. Earth: pref.
8. Scads
12. Reception room
14. Work cart
15. Particular space
16. Enjoy the ice
17. Dobbin's delight
18. Money, in Teheran
19. Some paints
21. Operatic leads, often
23. Sounds
24. Fix copy
25. Most submissive
28. Foul-up
30. Singer Yoko ____
31. Comfort
33. Peter and Ivan
37. Not gross
38. Curve
39. Orange drink
41. Caviar
42. Zorro's weapon
44. Assembled
46. "____ Got Sixpence"
47. Moved sideways
49. Dramatic devices
52. More secure
54. Paddled
56. Pace
57. Certain business transactions
60. Nuisance
61. Water jug
63. Weary
65. Otherwise
66. Learner
67. Long-billed game bird
68. Ruby and Sandra
69. Aves.
70. Procures

DOWN

1. Starship ____ "Enterprise"
2. Benefit
3. Spirit
4. Turn
5. Pastures
6. Dine
7. Shellfish
8. Gathers in
9. Constellation
10. Goatee
11. Mineo and Marciano
13. Verne's captain et al.
14. Ration
20. Submit a contest solution
22. Ham it up
25. Heavy weights
26. Again
27. Film detective Mr. ____
29. Peruse
32. Summit
34. Saharalike
35. Meander
36. Bishoprics
38. Totaled
40. Darlings
43. Makes purer
45. Worshipers
48. Hails
50. Chairs
51. Avoiding work
52. Outdated
53. Come about
55. Start of something "airy"
56. Hurried
58. Cleveland's water
59. Back-to-school mo.
62. Quick thinker
64. ____ Moines

PUZZLE 74

ACROSS

1. All-stops train
6. Breathe hard
10. Fido's feet
14. Perceive
17. Fragrance
18. Most populated continent
19. Nutmeg cover
20. Skillet
21. Bookkeeping word
22. Chime
23. Sun-worshiper
25. Ten years
27. Brother or sister, for short
28. Manufacturer
29. Traveler's guide
32. Storm
33. Understood
35. Bank (on)
36. Feels pain
38. Even chance
40. Be concerned
42. Creative person
44. College teacher, for short
46. Role for Stallone
50. Wholesaler
51. Used a sieve
53. Actor Ritchard
54. Rouse from sleep
56. Came up
58. Pub order
59. Attired
62. Half of a dance
63. Acquired
64. '70s group
65. Concealed
66. World carrier
68. Stickler for language or style
70. Garner
72. Musical studies
74. Public procession
78. Outlying
80. Vitality
81. Bank robber's escape
82. Barbie, for example
84. "Barney Miller" actor
86. "The Way We ___"
87. Lawn spoiler
90. Bus tokens
92. Fishing poles
94. ___ Moines
95. She's Reddy to sing!
97. Convent resident
98. Participates in an auction
100. Exhibiting sarcasm
102. Enthusiastic review
103. Lively dance
107. Taste, as wine
108. Dove shelter
109. St. Pierre and Miquelon
110. Sports palace
111. Pipe fitting
112. Water pitcher
113. Friendly nation
114. Gathered leaves

DOWN

1. Young man
2. Native metal
3. Male swan
4. Within
5. Afterwards
6. Model of excellence
7. Stage whispers
8. Number of lives for Garfield
9. Label
10. Overreact
11. ___ numeral
12. Jokester
13. Rundown area
14. Timber nail
15. Artist's tripod
16. Means of access
24. Once in a blue moon
26. Waterfall
27. Tropical fruit
29. Hotel employee
30. Staff officer
31. Entreaty
33. Sod
34. Small flap
37. Greens
39. Make yarn
41. Nation
43. Cat's cry
45. Legendary first king of Scotland
47. Spoiled child
48. Like some suntan lotion
49. Role for Michael J. Fox
51. Legislative body
52. Dutch, for one
55. Garden harvest
57. Salaries

PUZZLE 74

59. Blacken
60. Citrus fruit
61. West of "Batman"
64. Soda sipper
66. Concerning
67. Brooding
68. Keystone State founder
69. Took a chair
71. Soaking wet
73. Speaker's platform
75. Struck with wonder
76. Challenge
77. Sight for sore ____
79. Santa's helper
81. Earth mathematics
83. Woolly
85. Nonsensical talk
87. Card game
88. Ghostly
89. Flee, romantically
91. Measuring device
93. Sweetener
96. Pleasing
98. Formal dance
99. Brazilian rubber
101. Milk producer
102. Small inlet
104. Albanian currency
105. Dollar bill
106. Lily ____

PUZZLE 75

ACROSS

1. Turn left
4. Billed hat
7. Healthy place
10. Heroic poem
12. Mixed greens
14. Chimney dust
15. Flat-topped hill
16. Sports area
17. Aquatic bird
18. Formal argument
20. Pact
22. "You ____ My Sunshine"
23. Rich milk
24. Penny
26. For what reason
27. Equipment
30. Songstress Logan
31. Behold
32. Blush
34. Pasture sound
35. Stanley car
37. Bullring cheer
38. Furnish
40. Government levy
41. Actress Barrymore
42. Expunge
43. Tie fabric
44. Sugar root
45. Moray fisherman
47. "Peter ____"
48. Harvested
50. Small pebbles
53. ____ d'oeuvre
54. Hawk's nest
56. Wickedness
58. Ronny Howard role
59. Arctic explorer
60. Divorce city
61. Golf peg
62. Singer Torme
63. Confederate soldier

DOWN

1. Shirt edge
2. Emulated Rich Little
3. Intelligent
4. Be concerned
5. Strong beer
6. Kitchen closet
7. Classify
8. Small horse
9. Had a snack
11. Bathhouse
12. Satisfy fully
13. Challenge
14. Stitched
19. Actor Carney
21. Ready to go
23. Swindler
24. Cumulus
25. Marry in haste
26. Very small
28. Admire greatly
29. Sublease
30. Type measures
31. Messy home
32. Actor Harrison
33. Modern
35. Slumber
36. Atlas chart
39. Gratify
41. Colorado's capital
43. Get out of hock
44. Sheep sound
46. Jump
47. Victim
48. Cable
49. Great Lake
50. Young woman
51. At any time
52. Pitch
53. Torrid
55. Actress Charlotte
57. Tennis stroke

PUZZLE 76

ACROSS

1. Thin strip of wood
5. Settler in South Africa
9. Physicians: abbr.
12. Carried on furiously
14. Choice word
15. Hillside, in Scotland
16. Contemptuous look
17. Spin
18. Pro ____
19. Individual part
21. Not vegetable or mineral
23. Plumed bird
25. Giant
26. American inventor
28. Legal representative
30. Zero in
31. Captain ____
33. Inventor Howe
37. Rattling sound
40. Agrees
42. Strange
43. Mineral deposit
45. Small bed
46. Less intense in color
48. Fantasy
51. Temporary forgetfulness
53. Intertwine
55. Money, in Lahore
56. Conclusion
59. Bakery worker
60. Stumble
63. Certain collars
65. Round Table titles
66. Irish republic
67. Pony Express was one
68. Asner and McMahon
69. Actual
70. Daybreak

DOWN

1. Last year's juniors: abbr.
2. Alight
3. Pulitzer Prize-winning author
4. Wobble
5. Comic Milton ____
6. "Rah!" in Barcelona
7. End of many nationalities
8. Explain
9. One kind of play
10. Wickerwork material
11. Close securely
13. Pulls along
15. Crumbly
20. Actress Dunne
22. Baseball teams
24. Beret's cousin
26. 5,280 feet
27. General Bradley
29. Prod
30. Pilot's pilot
32. First name in mystery
34. Old Peruvian
35. Nuclear concern
36. Fast plane
38. Gratuity givers
39. Taunt
41. Car style
44. Sphere
47. Smaller
49. Equestrian
50. Redacted
51. Clear-headed
52. Copy cats
54. Drive back
55. Move upward
57. Lopez's theme song
58. Chew, as a bone
61. Falsehood
62. Author Levin
64. Together: pref.

PUZZLE 77

ACROSS

1. Meadow sounds
5. Macaw
10. ____ mater
14. Inter ____
15. Fraught
16. Turns right
17. First Tudor king
20. Cowboy show
21. "Ghost-busters" goo
22. Billy ____ Williams
23. Parry
25. Connections
27. Pitcher Maglie
29. Actor James ____
32. Fleet
36. Altar vow
37. Gallery item
39. Sashes
40. Duke of Windsor
44. Actor Will ____
45. Cultivated land, in the southwest
46. Native: suff.
47. Printing mistakes
50. ____ the air (undecided)
51. Darling of baseball
52. Birds' beaks
54. Grandstand unit
56. In the past
59. Let
62. Spheres
65. Bishop of Rome (1049-54)
68. Noted
69. Thread holder
70. Court proceedings
71. Old slave
72. Abounds
73. Sewing junction

DOWN

1. Cowardly Lion
2. Muffin spread
3. Anemone
4. Hindu attire
5. High, in music
6. Stadium sounds
7. Town near Des Moines
8. Convene again
9. Blood deficiency
10. Era
11. Impart
12. Apportion
13. Tennis great
18. Far away
19. Slue
24. Center or end starter
26. Environ-mental woe
27. Onslaught
28. Reptile
30. Film canine
31. Indian statesman
33. Hatred
34. Again
35. Ghostly
38. ____ year
41. Irish island group
42. Correct copy
43. Group of Greek islands
48. Greenish-blue
49. Best qualified
53. Incline
55. Silkworms
56. Part of a church
57. Leaves
58. Up-front
60. Indian
61. ". . . for ____ the bell tolls . . ."
63. Wheat flour
64. Hoax
66. Hydrocarbon suffix
67. City trains

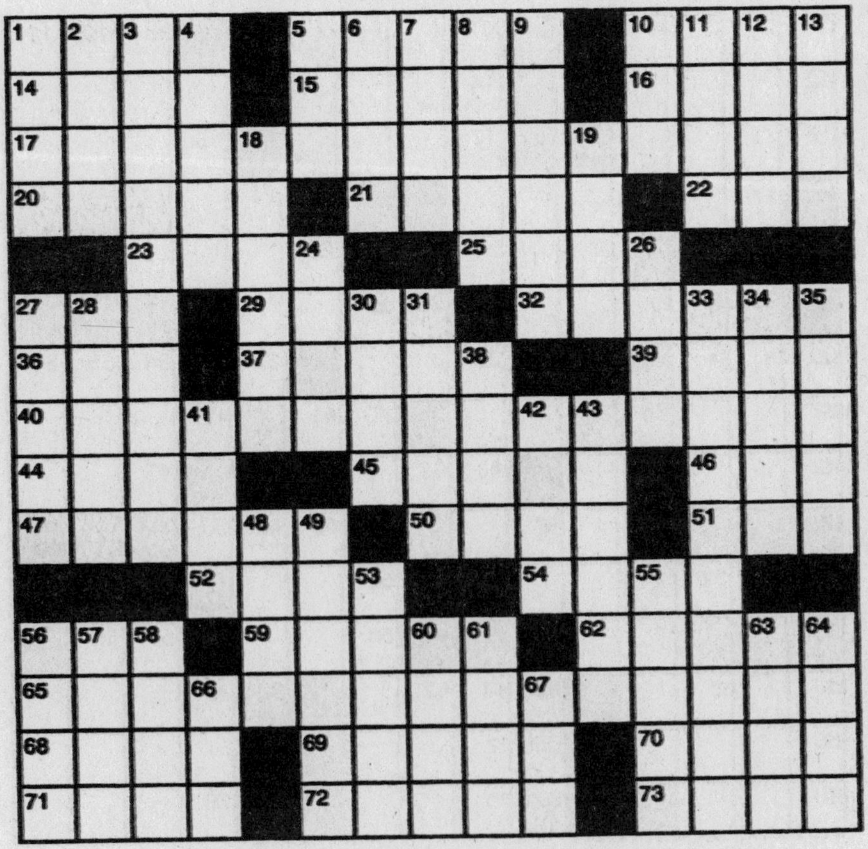

PUZZLE 78

ACROSS

1. Beach covering
5. Outlaws
9. Hindu writing
14. Playhouse locale
15. "Essays of ___"
16. Verses
17. Spool of film
18. Best man's concern
19. French cathedral city
20. Harrison Ford's role
23. Stipend
24. Abode, in Granada
25. Levy
29. Winter sound
30. Crossed paths
31. "___ Tin Tin"
32. Cathedral in France
37. Outlet
39. Samoan seaport
40. Cycles
42. Polish-German border river
43. Forwards
45. Notable college town
47. Metric measure
48. Bill and ___
50. Singer Charles
51. Bound
53. A la mode items
55. Mel's waitress
58. Racetrack locale
61. Lyric poem
64. Streetcar, in Soho
65. Incarnation of Vishnu
66. Enthusiastic reviewer
67. Trig function
68. Composer Satie
69. Smooth and slippery
70. North Sea feeder
71. Bristle

DOWN

1. Slat
2. Part of a Roman amphitheater
3. Indigent
4. Cold cuts counter
5. Baruch and Shaw
6. Aka
7. "Teenage Mutant ___ Turtles"
8. Starch source
9. Puts the cuffs on
10. Shot in the dark
11. Black cuckoo
12. Hebrew letter
13. Onager
21. Israeli seaport
22. Glasgow refusal
26. Abrade
27. Vamp
28. Mortimer ___
29. Nail
30. Waiter's offering
32. Of the nose
33. Gluck's forte
34. Prongs
35. Llasa ___
36. Chinese ruler, once
38. ___ Beau (Texas pop quintet)
41. Narrow flag
44. Stage set
46. Door clasp
49. "The ___ Couple"
52. Not the seeker
53. Plaster of ___
54. Foolish
55. Burst forth
56. Brink
57. Japanese metropolis
59. Bitsy's buddy
60. Crude metals
61. Energy unit
62. Amigo
63. An avis lays them

PUZZLE 79

REVELATION

When you have solved this crossword puzzle, the tinted letters, reading from left to right, will reveal a quotation.

ACROSS

1. Historic site
6. Knots
11. Dashed
16. Mandatory
17. Dormant
18. School, for Jacques
19. Battery pole
20. Trifling
21. Savage
22. D.C. figure
23. Purpose
24. Reasonable
26. Had a meal
27. Mucho
29. Top draw
31. Trill
33. Rose fruit
35. Dreyfus in "Pink Panther" films
37. Truly
38. Bow
41. "Maltese Falcon" lead
43. Merinos
46. Ribbed
48. French state
50. Cowardly Lion
52. Blade
53. Multitude
55. Open
57. Opinion
58. Connected riv.
60. Follows in the footsteps of
62. Spartan
64. Chair
66. Litter
68. Holders
69. Maximum limit
71. Hydrocarbon suffix
72. Likely
73. Hocks
76. Shoot!
78. Gaelic country
82. Halloween, e.g.
83. Auspices
85. Dabble
86. Hazy
87. Animate
89. "____ Life"
91. Cara or Worth
93. Sharp
94. Score well below par
95. Cancel
96. Stable dwellers
97. Pumps
98. Sniggler

DOWN

1. Nautical command
2. Interior
3. Do penance
4. Humor magazine
5. Gaucho's cry
6. Bound
7. Creatures
8. Number of yrs.
9. Son of Aphrodite
10. Stalk
11. Judge
12. Maven
13. Marine structure
14. Make happy
15. Cross out
23. Viper
25. Indeed
28. Transmit
30. Routine
32. Cry
34. Misfortunes
36. Baseball's Manny ____
38. Tie
39. Approaches
40. Unsettling
41. Handy
42. Leader in India
44. Paves
45. Ration
47. Guido's highest note
49. Greek cross
51. Dark breads

PUZZLE 79

54. Existed
56. Letters for an answer
59. Support
61. Polish
63. London gallery
65. Ancient monetary units
67. Mariners' home
70. Cribbage piece
72. A few
73. Saint Theresa of ___
74. ___ mind
75. Places
77. Peace and Tropicana
79. Paradigm
80. Immerse
81. Middle Eastern leader
82. Actor Jack ___
84. Persian ruler
88. Afore
90. "Long, Long ___"
91. Decorate
92. Caddoan Indian

PUZZLE 80

ACROSS

1. Still
5. Tease
9. Torch
13. Dog's wagger
14. Work on a manuscript
15. Courage
16. Cheese town
17. Mortgage
18. Arctic habitation
19. French anthem
22. Guitarist Montgomery
23. Holy oil
27. Expressed disapproval
30. Actress Anna ____
32. Average grade
33. Tropical pig
34. Pistons' guard
36. Pearl divers
37. Nabokov novel
38. "Exodus" writer
39. Opossum, for instance
42. Sticky
43. Broad-antlered deer
44. Brooks and Ferrer
45. Reckon
46. Second-hand purchase
48. Snakelike fish
49. Campfire goodies
56. French farewell
59. Two of a kind
60. Orchestra member
61. Charred
62. First name in mystery
63. Swiss capital
64. Mild oath
65. Act
66. Stared at

DOWN

1. Topic
2. Baby's first words?
3. Deceiver
4. Graceful trees
5. Depended
6. Baals
7. Tune in
8. Lab burner
9. Ale
10. Wholly
11. Pasture sound
12. In favor of
15. Hindu deity
20. Jug
21. Frosted
24. Mythical flying man
25. String
26. Unkempt
27. Hot Mexican dish
28. Flint flames
29. Smooch
30. Soft drinks
31. Blue-winged ____
33. Not as wild
34. Imprison
35. Share-cropper's stock
40. Pronunciation mark
41. One's equal
42. Sea scavenger
45. Harnessed
47. Change
48. Novelist Zola
50. Went like the devil
51. Leveret
52. Ear part
53. Follow
54. Became frayed
55. Mail
56. Humorist Burrows
57. Excavated
58. Tax-free pension: abbr.

PUZZLE 81

ACROSS

1. Become boring
5. West and namesakes
9. Only
13. Away from the weather
14. Mason, at times
15. High notes
16. Side dish-youth
19. Printing units
20. Praises
21. India VIP
22. Purposes
23. Dance: Fr.
24. Body of water-navigation
32. Weird
33. Dark haze
34. Time
35. Dry
36. Playground equipment
38. Former boxer Max ___
39. Two, in Toledo
40. Ore residue
41. French department
42. Laundry appliance-tyrannical
46. Race unit
47. Sad word
48. Astonish
51. Misplaces
53. ___ culpa
56. Pharos-servants
59. Actress Nazimova
60. Secondary map
61. Cut
62. Game's advances
63. Hart
64. Uses a fist

DOWN

1. Speed rate
2. Writer Paton
3. Remick and Majors
4. Them, in France
5. Misapplication
6. "When I was ___ . . ."
7. Long fish
8. Spanish Mrs.
9. Olympic prizes
10. Enthusiasm
11. Actress Martha ___
12. Being
14. Public vehicles
17. Similar
18. Swallowed
22. Tart
23. Reveal
24. Rosary units
25. European dormouse
26. Soar
27. Chihuahua chum
28. Mire
29. Center part
30. One of the Horae
31. Cut
36. Glide
37. Household god
38. Fish
40. Sting
41. Noxious swamp matter
43. Island calls
44. Former Egyptian president
45. Swift
48. Fatness
49. Easter flower
50. Flirt
51. Single
52. Cockney's 'ome
53. Skirt length
54. Correct
55. Snakes
57. Stashed
58. Tree

PUZZLE 82

ACROSS

1. Newsman Brokaw
4. Fraudulent scheme
8. Soft drinks
13. Shake ____! (get moving)
15. Native of Warsaw
16. White poplar
17. Typesetting machine, for short
18. Came to earth
19. Madrid mister
20. Song from "Follies"
23. Island off Scotland
24. Humorist George ____
25. German river
27. Engine track
30. Moist
34. Page the singer
35. Stretched tight
37. Female deer
38. Song from "West Side Story"
42. Hockey's Dryden
43. Midday
44. Chest sounds
45. God of love
47. Refusals
49. Russian port
50. Sock end
52. Actor Sean ____
54. Song from "Follies"
61. Toss
62. ____ avis
63. Not messy
64. Flambeau
65. "It ____ Me Babe"
66. Critic Siskel
67. Pleasant
68. Choice word
69. Attorney's field

DOWN

1. After-bath sprinkle
2. Medley
3. Bill of fare
4. Portugal's neighbor
5. Neckband
6. What Washington couldn't tell
7. "I ____ man with seven . . ."
8. Checked out
9. Complied
10. Comic Jay ____
11. Baseballer Matty ____
12. Sunday speech: abbr.
14. David's foe
21. "The Picture of ____ Gray"
22. Worth
25. Of sounder mind
26. "____ 'clock scholar"
28. Repent
29. Actor Keith
31. Allan- ____ (Robin Hood's friend)
32. Mushroom variety
33. Favorites
34. Jab
36. Crowd
39. Composition for nine
40. Cartoon dog Scooby- ____
41. Making
46. Posture
48. Turns down
51. Should
53. Gladden
54. Disappointment
55. Emerald Isle
56. "Dies ____"
57. Do not succeed
58. Film spool
59. Actress Turner
60. Fret
61. Aves.

PUZZLE 83

ACROSS
1. Read rapidly
5. Cache
10. Pigments
14. Toledo's lake
15. Martinque volcano
16. Garner
17. Gulf fish
19. Actress Lanchester
20. Main attractions
21. Conductor Kurt ____
22. Gidget in "Gidget"
23. Buzzwords
25. Postpones
29. Troublesome fungi
31. Lays off
32. Peanut butter's companion
33. Apple seed
35. Greek letters
36. Pairs
37. Byron work
38. Unclose, in verse
39. Fabric holders
40. Knots
41. Flowered archway
43. Reasons
44. Angry
45. Greek tycoon
46. Morocco's capital
48. Camera accessory
53. Encircles
54. Nursery
56. ____ gin fizz
57. Wish for
58. Dun-colored songbird
59. Eternities
60. Walter ____
61. Tempt

DOWN
1. Peasant
2. Ontario Indian
3. Opera role
4. Refuge
5. Extras
6. Lodge
7. Yodeler's home
8. Grasp
9. That woman
10. Clear, as a channel
11. Office supplies
12. Loosen
13. Boxers do it
18. Artists' models, sometimes
21. Actor Griffith
23. Hums
24. Maladies
25. Former Yugoslavian leader
26. Conform
27. Fair prize
28. Guitarist Paul
29. Encounters
30. No ____!
32. Actress Andrews
34. Permit
36. Blockhead
37. Singer Rawls
39. Utter loudly
40. Actor J. Carrol ____
42. Wipes out
43. Nook and ____
45. Perceptive
46. Rambler
47. Singer Guthrie
48. Deed
49. Bay
50. Spiritual advisor
51. ____ -friendly
52. Hawaii's state bird
54. Athletic facility
55. Defendants

PUZZLE 84

QUOTEWORD

A humorous quotation runs clockwise around the edges of this diagram. To find the quotation, work the puzzle as a regular crossword, filling in the remaining blank squares with the letters given below.

A E E H H N O O R S U Y

ACROSS

15. European wild ox
16. Seine feeder
17. Biblical book
18. Polynesian chief
19. Linseed et al.
20. Poverty
21. Mumbles
22. Group
23. Bumpkins
25. Speak wildly
27. California city
29. Basketballer Archibald
31. Lowest tide
33. Matt Houston's uncle
34. Air
38. Concurred
40. Fido's foot
42. Diamonds
43. Misbehave
45. Decline
46. Indian dress
47. '80s pop duo
49. Irish county
51. Pear-shaped instrument
54. Swiss song
56. Queenly
58. Concierge
59. Cribbage jack
61. Bodies
63. European beetle
64. Quack medicine
68. Slits
70. Parking timer
73. Flowering plant
75. Hits
77. Goddess of the moon
78. Coarse powder
79. Johnny ____
81. Bungling
83. Negative word
84. Partner for hither
85. Pierces
88. Show on the tube
90. Choice word
91. Computer fodder
93. Landing
94. Large antelopes
98. Mend
100. African muscoid fly
103. Chow
104. Thailand
106. Lantern
108. Beloved
109. Fiddling emperor
110. "Lohengrin" heroine
111. "Dies ____"
112. Cetacean genus

DOWN

1. Huey, Dewey, and Louie
2. Unwieldy ship
3. Palestinian ascetic
4. Like coated cookware
5. Untruth
6. North Sea feeder
7. Family car
8. Motley crowds
9. Aussie bird
10. Place of development
11. Guarantee
12. Spinster
13. Spanish jar
14. Massive meson
24. Volcanic flow
26. Teachers' gr.
28. Gat
30. Organic compound
32. Baby carriage
35. She loved Narcissus
36. Heavy metal
37. Large kangaroos
39. Mild oath
40. Victory
41. Formal song
44. Comedian Richard ____
46. Reddish-brown
48. Of the chin
50. Chinese Empire official's residence

PUZZLE 84

52. Assent
53. Condemn
55. Forsaken, in literature
57. Hawaiian veranda
60. Potential flower
62. Restrict
65. Butter replacer
66. Mr. Connery
67. Mate for pere
69. Snooze
71. Food fish
72. Son of Seth
74. Narrate
76. Divided legume
80. Hindu priest
82. Plumbing joints
85. White or Red
86. Controlled by a timer
87. ___ Anne de Beaupre
89. Attribute
90. Wealthy person
92. Hawaiian shrub
95. German number
96. Grain sorghum: var.
97. Sediment
99. Escapade
101. La ___
102. Levantine ketch
105. Japanese volcano
107. Singer Davis

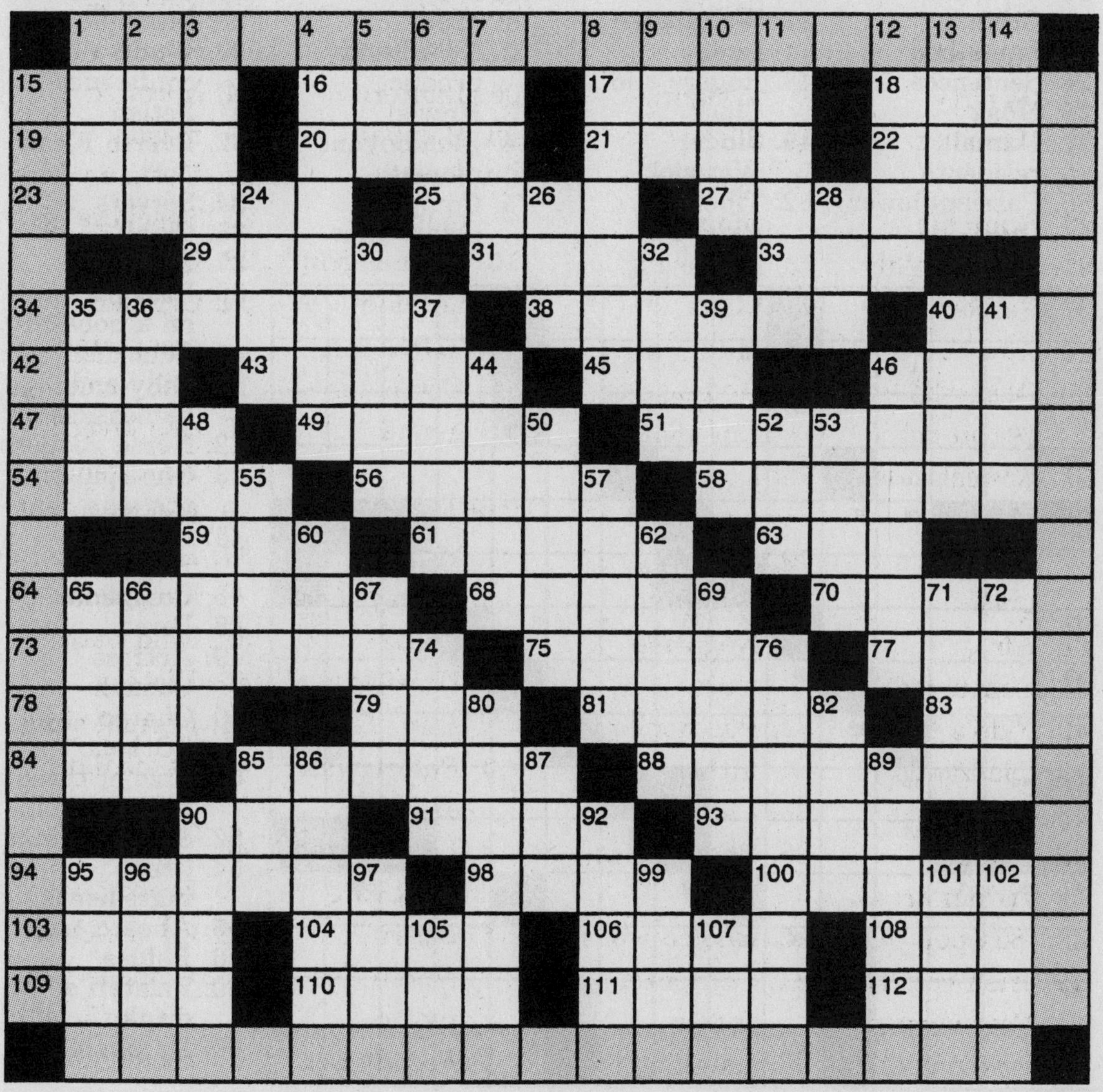

PUZZLE 85

ACROSS

1. ____ of contents
6. Wick for dynamite
10. Seurat trademarks
14. One more time
15. Egg-shaped
16. Singer Brickell
17. Chuck Berry hit
19. Theater
20. Celtic
21. Mountain in Crete
22. Smoothed
24. Sentences
26. Hoax
27. Uxmal residents
30. Passion-flower fruit
33. Precise
34. Dilutes
36. Feathery accessory
38. Trick
39. "The Young Lions" actress
40. One hundred yrs.
41. Piece of land
42. Upset
43. Ancient Greek lawgiver
44. Sea plea
46. Uproar
47. Web-footed birds
48. Rogers and Clark
49. Singer Warwick
52. Tibetan gazelle
53. Prince in disguise?
57. Jerk
58. BLT condiment
61. "A Death in the Family" author
62. Poor-box donations
63. Actress Barkin
64. Beak
65. Termitarium
66. Emerson's specialty

DOWN

1. Mild
2. Gelatinlike product
3. Howls
4. Flamboyant pianist
5. Compass point: abbr.
6. Creases
7. Part of the eye
8. Japanese title of respect
9. Tusker
10. Run away
11. Norse Zeus
12. Fork point
13. Pod's content
18. They're meant for kissing
23. Sets
25. Ergate
26. Wallop, Old Testament style
27. Complain
28. Principle
29. World War II conference
31. Fetish
32. Puerto Rican port
34. Servers
35. Clunk
37. Iota
39. Last person on a bobsled
40. Comedian Billy and namesakes
42. Norse goddess
43. One spin on the axis
45. New Englander
46. Complain
48. Perch
49. Actress Cannon
50. Character in "Othello"
51. Five of these for a Lincoln
52. Sch. buildings
54. Cruet ingredients
55. Aboard ship
56. Refuse
59. Falstaff's drink
60. By birth

PUZZLE 86

ACROSS

1. Andy's partner
5. "____ Princess" (TV movie)
10. Moist
14. The two
15. Separate
16. Toledo's lake
17. Singer Adams
18. Herring
19. Ice-cream holder
20. Olympic category
22. A, e.g.
23. On the house
24. "____ the Mood for Love"
26. Peer Gynt's mother
29. Vipers
31. Of stars
35. Sprinkle
37. Trip plan
39. Grandstand section
40. Microscopic
41. Czech river
42. Augmented
44. ____-glass window
45. Sharp reply
46. Judge's garment
48. Legal matter
49. Aim
51. Sumptuous
53. Court arguments
56. Same
61. Gain
62. "The Main ____"
63. Biblical weed
64. Mr. Sevareid
65. Serenity
66. Ontario Indian
67. Sheet of glass
68. Loafed
69. Get wind

DOWN

1. Sleeping
2. Fashion
3. Of the ear
4. Bundle of grain
5. Reduces to a pulp
6. Pastry items
7. Gambling game
8. Tehran native
9. Barrister: abbr.
10. Remove a price freeze from
11. Lined up
12. Excavation site
13. Skin
21. Salver
22. Gripping tool
25. Quite a few
26. Bustling about
27. Backbone
28. Straight up
30. Guide
32. Intruder detector
33. Mountain crest
34. Stringed instruments
36. Haughtiness
38. Laziness
40. Toodle-oo
43. Cupid
44. Nuisance
47. Hit a ball, in a way
50. Existed
52. Fasten
53. Nestling sound
54. "Dr. Zhivago" role
55. Ireland
57. Transaction
58. Concern
59. L x W
60. Sly look
62. Spire ornament

PUZZLE 87

ACROSS

1. Central points
5. Scoop
8. Cool ones
12. Bill
15. "The Thin Man" pooch
16. Stop —— dime: 2 wds.
17. On the sheltered side
18. "Ben ——"
19. Palmetto State: 2 wds.
22. Zeta's follower
23. Consume
24. Conversations
25. Urban pall
26. Chilly and damp
29. Cut the lawn
31. Golf item
32. French royalty
33. Barcelona cheers
35. Less usual
37. Walk unsteadily
40. Donkeys
42. And not
43. Columnist Buchwald
44. Morning moisture
45. Speckled
47. Stage device
49. —— - gin fizz
50. Some letters
52. Used-car deal
54. Trouble
56. —— Dame
58. Dozes
61. Fourth mo.
62. Cherry stone
63. Windup
65. Norman Vincent ——
66. Strays
68. Ovine animals
70. Nicholas or Alexander
71. Caravansary
72. Soup vegetable
73. Cover
75. Explosive: abbr.
76. Care for
78. Desist's partner
80. Poolroom item
82. Actor Wallach
83. Flickertails: 2 wds.
88. Wing
89. Pa. port
90. Threshold
91. Fairy-tale heavy
92. Operated
93. Actress Tuesday
94. Actor Beatty
95. Close at hand

DOWN

1. ——-been
2. GI's club
3. Heat meas.
4. Glut
5. Welby or Kildare
6. One —— million: 2 wds.
7. Role
8. Visitor
9. Similar
10. Decimal units
11. "By the Beautiful ——"
12. Persian Gulf area: 3 wds.
13. Detroit product
14. Boast
20. Stage hog
21. Horse operas
25. The Auld ——
26. Paved way
27. Furthermore
28. Mountain State native: 2 wds.
30. Pallid
32. Nonsense
34. Author Anya
36. Fete satirically
37. Curl
38. Summer sign
39. Ma that maas
41. Embroider
43. Fruit drink
46. Patron saint of France
48. Goodnight girl
49. Icy precipitation

PUZZLE 87

51. Fate
53. European peak
54. Cushion
55. Mil. addr.
57. Go over again
59. Lay out
60. Spanish painter
62. Confine
64. Neighbor of Md.
67. Midwest st.
68. Did usher's work
69. Chose
72. Hazard
74. Twosome
76. Lachrymal drop
77. Actress Raines
78. Pith
79. Biblical garden
81. Harrow rival
83. Novel
84. "—— Maria"
85. Mature
86. Blue Eagle letters
87. Sunday talk: abbr.

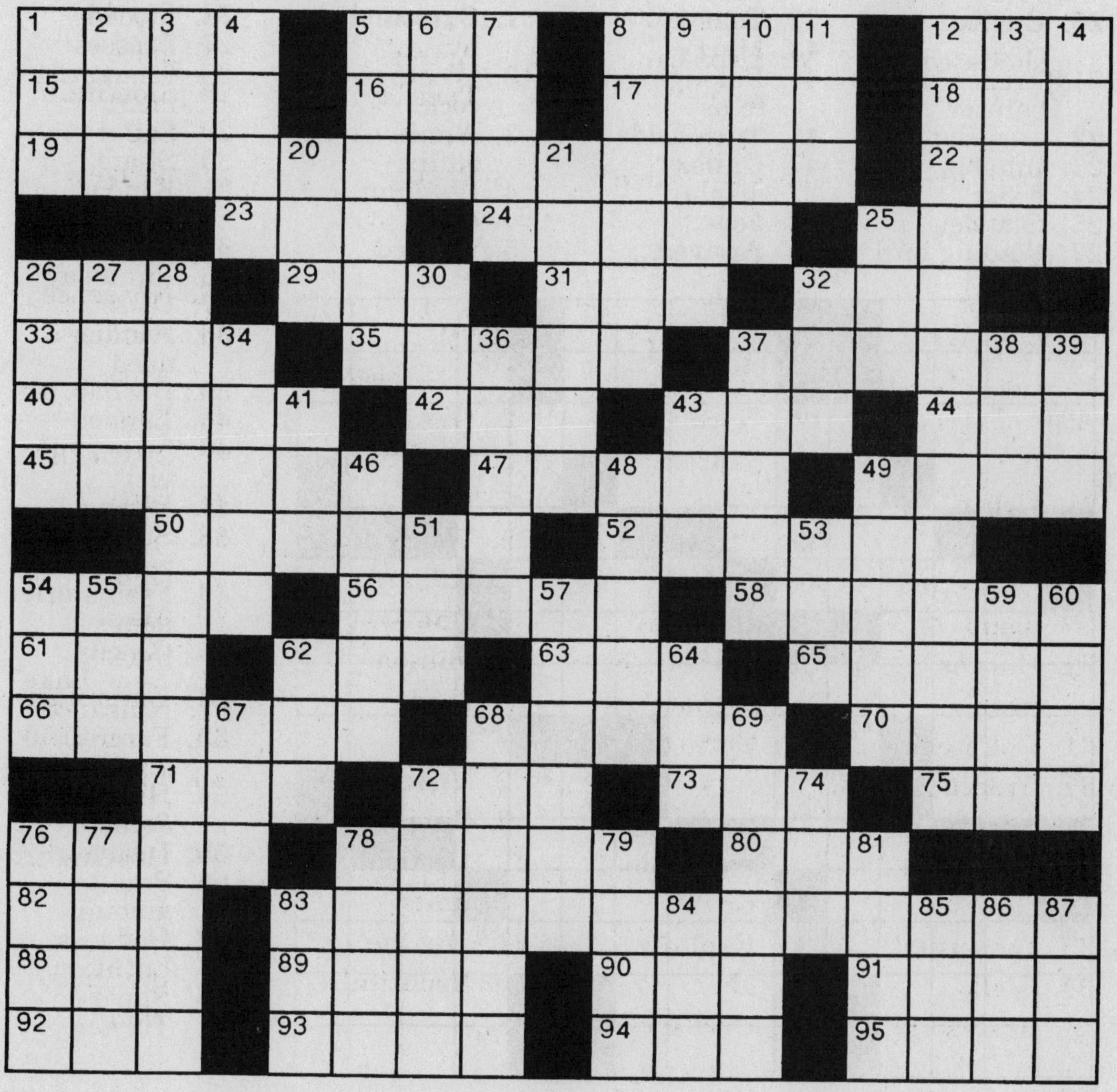

PUZZLE 88

ACROSS
1. State
5. Petty quarrel
9. Historic times
13. —— Hari
14. Noon, e.g.
15. Super: hyph.
16. "—— thy seed . . ." (Eccles. 11:6): 4 wds.
20. English river
21. French painter
22. —— Bator
23. Inhabit
24. Exist
25. Gladden
27. Wading bird
29. Switch position
32. The Bard of ——
33. Motor
34. Oolong or pekoe
35. "—— letter . . ." (1 Kings 10:2): 5 wds.
40. Supplement
41. Comparison word
42. Tear
43. Marry
44. Belonging to us
45. Turn aside
47. Gallery display
48. Joy
49. Arrived
51. Castilian country
53. Unhappy
56. "And —— castle . . ." (1 Chron. 11:7): 4 wds.
59. Rara ——
60. Facilitate
61. Thicke or King
62. Resting places
63. Small colonists
64. Figure mug

DOWN
1. Surrounded by
2. Weather-cock
3. Diminutive suffix
4. Stadium cheer
5. Glowed
6. Minute opening
7. Uncle's wife
8. Cycle starter
9. National bird
10. —— Bonheur
11. Shortly
12. Mend
17. Give out
18. Relocate
19. Hospital personnel
23. Ms. Turner
24. Verdi opera
25. Call forth
26. Mooed
27. Presses
28. Compart-ment
29. Different
30. Sham
31. Kind of track
32. Freshly
36. Put away
37. Close
38. Paddler's need
39. Baobab, e.g.
45. Landed
46. "——, vidi, vici"
47. Wrong
48. Strong winds
49. Prehistoric home
50. Greedy
51. "—— Lake"
52. Nuisance
53. Fr. city: 2 wds.
54. Husband of Jezebel
55. Disavow
56. Small amount
57. Goddess: Latin
58. Slave Turner

PUZZLE 89

ACROSS

1. Cut short
4. Prevaricated
8. Chores
13. Before
14. Architect Alvar
15. Foreign
16. Poorly
17. Struck, of old
18. Muppet Miss
19. King Midas?: 2 wds.
22. In succession: 2 wds.
23. Give
26. Superlative suffix
27. Mr. Waugh
29. Mikhail of chess
30. Former Milano masher?: 2 wds.
34. Elec. unit
35. "Deadly" seven
36. Infatuation goddess
37. Malay craft
38. Guided
39. Urge for sushi?: 2 wds.
43. Continental cont.
44. Hebrew month
45. And not
46. Kind of bath
48. Struggled
52. Play the silver-smith?: 2 wds.
55. Scent
57. Guido's love
58. Harem room
59. Van man
60. Party hearty
61. Oahu garland
62. Warrant officers, for short
63. Require
64. Fuss

DOWN

1. Ecru
2. Synthetic fabric
3. Chimes
4. Boxer Jake
5. "The Man ——": 2 wds.
6. Feminine suffix
7. Person of action
8. Pudding type
9. Put arow
10. Inker
11. Tavern unit
12. Curved plank
14. Umbria town
20. Affairs of honor
21. Town in Judah
24. Resort lake
25. Violinist Mischa
27. It's down the aisle
28. Property claim
30. Scilly ——
31. Snarl: hyph.
32. Soviet leader Yuri and kin
33. Vinous valley
37. Danger
39. S.Amer. cats
40. Yemen seaport
41. Recorded
42. Equine hue
47. Name
48. Range
49. Pansy, e.g.
50. Finished
51. Author Marsh
53. Mend, in a way
54. Capt. Hook's sidekick
55. Legate: abbr.
56. Outback beast, for short

PUZZLE 90

ACROSS

1. Actor Guinness
5. Poky
9. Bark
12. Heroic tale
13. "M*A*S*H" regular
14. Fuss
15. Fencing
17. Director Howard
18. Split ____ soup
19. Foolishly
21. Cast about
24. Tubs
25. Listens
26. Kitchen area
29. Dolt
30. Tiny
31. A Gershwin
32. Rock group ____, Lake, and Palmer
35. Chops
37. Mature
38. ____ business
39. Solomon's queen
41. Antique
42. Neutral color
43. Cultured
49. Curve
50. Periods
51. Pop
52. Quilting ____
53. Dispatched
54. Informed

DOWN

1. Donkey
2. ____ and order
3. Self
4. Nagged
5. Land of the Rising Sun
6. Entirely
7. Actress Lupino
8. Amateur
9. Ruler
10. Matinee ____
11. Small horse
16. Moistens, to a poet
20. Had breakfast
21. Pump
22. Matched pair
23. Source
24. Compete
26. Study
27. Sycamore, e.g.
28. Simple
30. Misfortune
33. Umbrella part
34. Blanks
35. Barbie, e.g.
36. Charge
38. Clammy
39. Attempt
40. Hound's quarry
44. Fury
45. Delivery truck
46. Bronx attraction
47. House wing
48. June honoree

PUZZLE 91

ACROSS
1. Bluish-green
5. Auction offers
9. Delicious
14. Young dogs
15. Vicinity
16. Eskimo's abode
17. Jeopardy
18. Wild pig
19. Available
20. Indignation
21. Author's alias
23. Court
24. "The Scarlet ____"
26. Artist's subject
28. Burst forth
31. Washington bill
35. Avoid
38. Excursion
40. Blaze
41. Cereal grain
42. Tourist's residence
44. Nothing
45. Current of air
48. Entreaty
49. Whirlpool
50. Stick
52. Nudge
54. Cordial
56. Pacific state
60. Leap
63. Old saying
66. ____ de la Paix
67. See 63 Across
69. Fruit skin
70. Golden ____ Bridge
71. Yellow gem
72. Largest continent
73. Secondhand
74. Rub out
75. Lord's wife
76. Full of life

DOWN
1. Showery month
2. Measure of paper
3. Capsize
4. Inquire
5. Famous slugger
6. Press
7. College official
8. Plastic wrap
9. Bored with
10. Bronze or Stone
11. Cabbage salad
12. Commotion
13. Toy with ups and downs?
21. Apiece
22. Wet dirt
25. "____ Little Indians"
27. Building wing
29. Actor's tool
30. Book-cover info
32. Touch down
33. Surrounded by
34. Depend (on)
35. Pop
36. Like a diamond
37. Western state
39. Do KP duty
43. September holiday
46. ____ and far between
47. Daring young man's swing
49. Female sheep
51. Be mistaken
53. Sphere
55. End of an Aesop fable
57. Understand
58. "The ____ Limits"
59. In want
60. Despise
61. Fragrance
62. Mama's mate
64. Passport endorsement
65. Author Bagnold
68. Cooking fuel
70. Astronaut Grissom

PUZZLE 92

ACROSS

1. Interval
6. Rich milk
11. Cigars
13. Earns before expenses
15. Recite
16. North Carolina city
17. Shop sign
18. Drizzly
20. Scottish negative
21. Mine entrance
22. Courage
23. Tiny insect
24. French nobleman
25. Revise, as a bill
26. Purport
27. Omen
29. Make tardy
30. Sword handle
31. Lawyer's job
32. Lacy trimming
34. Regulate
37. Cede
38. ____ de Leon
39. Cat or canary, e.g.
41. Put on freight
42. Talk foolishly
43. Lily plant
44. Cuckoo
45. Crimp a piecrust
46. Atomize
47. Type of wagon
49. Cloy
51. Position
52. Ran, in a way
53. Pennies
54. "En garde" weapons

DOWN

1. Type of comedian
2. Covered walk
3. Plumed bird
4. Fibber
5. Rent
6. Irritable one
7. ____ -poly
8. Opposite of WNW
9. Silly
10. One million tons
11. Sam of golf
12. Footless creature
13. Difficult task
14. Like some nylons
19. Mom's sister
22. Reek
23. Measuring device
25. Lopsided
26. Sample
28. White wine
29. Spear
31. Sporting match
32. Greatly excited
33. Send out beams
34. Jacket
35. Do a surgeon's job
36. Ambassadors
37. Tumbler
38. Dried fruit
40. Trifled
42. Schemes
43. Malice
45. Command
46. Prevent
48. Cask
50. "You ____ My Sunshine"

PUZZLE 93

ACROSS

1. Ammo for toy pistols
5. Scottish dance
9. Window ledge
13. Woodwind
14. Roof parts
16. Faithful
17. Burrowing animal
18. "____ and Prejudice"
19. The walls have ____
20. Seth's mom
21. "____ out the barrel . . ."
22. First word of Bob Hope's song
24. Examiners
26. Tiny particle
27. Abzug's trademark
28. Passage between buildings
32. Change
35. More cunning
36. Regret
37. Precipitation
38. Small branches
39. Ms. Moreno
40. Feel poorly
41. Gloss
42. Engine
43. Church members
45. Saucer's partner
46. Overwhelm
47. Short jackets
51. Skirt folds
54. Un-adulterated
55. Football's Donovan
56. "On the ____ Again"
57. Crocodile ____
59. Impulse
60. Monster
61. Hogs
62. Sewing juncture
63. Cages
64. Formerly, formerly
65. Sea eagles

DOWN

1. Halley's ____
2. Overhead
3. Fishing rods
4. Look at?
5. Bulletin
6. English nobles
7. Wicked
8. Guided
9. Like a sauna
10. Persia, today
11. Lie hidden
12. Minus
15. Sinks to the bottom
21. Back
23. Garden worker
25. Now and ____
26. Set in a row
28. Foreigner
29. Judge's order
30. Car
31. January through December
32. Desert dweller
33. Den
34. Ceramic square
35. Like Adeline
38. Lunges
39. Lasso
41. Fired
42. Army mascot
44. Swaps
45. Girdle
47. Comedian George ____
48. More remarkable
49. ____ grinder
50. Stalks
51. Brace
52. Theater box
53. Merit
54. Twosome
58. Farm female
59. Employ

PUZZLE 94

ACROSS

1. Actress Moore
5. Labyrinths
10. Pokes
14. Portent
15. Singer Cooper
16. Double curve
17. Says briefly
20. Making certain
21. Open shoe
22. "Tobacco ____"
23. Blurs
24. Lacquers
27. Quintet
28. Conducted
31. Suppose
32. ____-Coburg-Gotha
33. Stone wharf
34. Tchaikovsky opus
37. Commedia dell'____
38. Troubles
39. Basketball player
40. "For ____ a jolly . . ."
41. Baton
42. Finches
43. Accept
44. ____ Blanc
45. Field
48. Has faith
52. Poser
54. Authorizes
55. Harden
56. Noun suffix
57. Shrill sound
58. Doctored
59. Insightful

DOWN

1. Amino acid
2. Flightless birds
3. Shea nine
4. Liability coverage
5. Crazes
6. "____ flowing with milk . . ."
7. Vitality
8. Old French coin
9. Puts in charge of
10. Adela Rogers St. ____
11. Grown old
12. Actor Lugosi
13. Vend
18. Mangle
19. Wise
23. Mends
24. Minor Prophet
25. ". . . clean hands, and ____ heart"
26. Actress ZaSu ____
27. Simulated
28. Playwright Pirandello
29. Corroded
30. Colorers
32. Teacake
33. Drawn and ____
35. Aroused
36. Picturesque
41. Precinct
42. Flew alone
43. Pithy
44. English measure
45. Season
46. Sound of relief
47. Loathe
48. Heat measures: abbr.
49. Weather ____
50. ____ homo!
51. Straw beehive
53. Numero ____

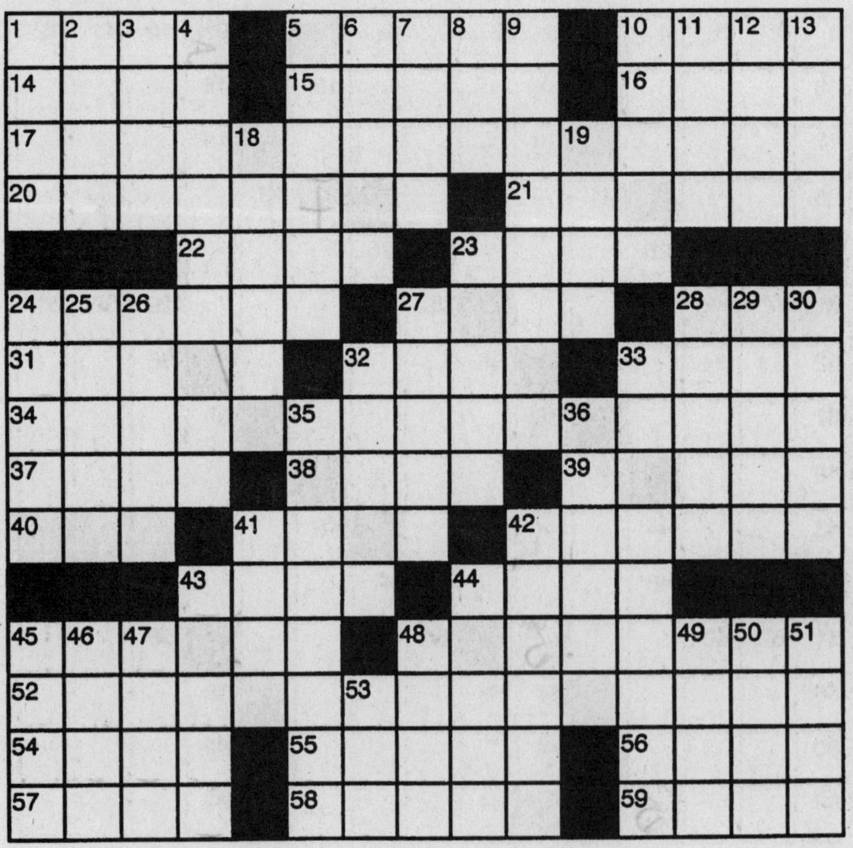

PUZZLE 95

ACROSS
1. Killer whale
5. Bivouacs
10. Skimmer
13. Pork cut
14. Aromatic herb
15. Policy
16. Wolverine's capital
19. Curved line
20. ____ model
21. Ledger entry
22. Silly
24. Smash review
26. Doctrines
28. Glued firmly
32. Broadway musical
33. ____ Berets
34. Employ
35. Mideast nation
36. Rosary ____
37. African fox
38. Fortune
39. Petticoat junctions?
40. Masher, in a way
41. Glides, as a snake
43. Family cars
44. Informers
45. Bethlehem product
46. Distant
49. Belgium river
50. Texas tea
53. Lake Superior port
57. Help
58. Paddled
59. Glacial ridges
60. Antique auto
61. Equals
62. Hairless

DOWN
1. Wide-mouthed jar
2. Bellow
3. City on the Ohio River
4. Reply: abbr.
5. Church laws
6. Fish
7. Marcel Marceau, for one
8. Fraternity letter
9. Part of a min.
10. Enfolds closely
11. Wings
12. Bivouac
15. Ascended
17. Seething
18. Safe spot
23. Bonn denial
24. Donna and Walter
25. Iowa city
26. Formal wear
27. Recruit
28. Stuffs
29. Alabama city
30. German city
31. Bambi's pals
33. Transmission parts
36. Red veggie
37. Assistant
39. Spear handle
40. Della ____
42. Game fish
43. Bleachers
45. More rational
46. Hebrew month
47. Garage job, for short
48. Butter alternative
49. Deep muck
51. Type style: abbr.
52. Fat
54. Short trip
55. Actress West
56. Kind of sister

PUZZLE 96

ACROSS

1. Lessen
6. Remove feathers
11. Witch's pet
14. Breakfast meat
15. Talk a lot
16. Falsify
17. Clarify for
19. Historic age
20. Total
21. Speech problem
22. Abyss
24. Resembling
25. North Carolina town
27. Mate
30. Suaver
33. Tithe
34. Clipped
35. Mouths: Lat.
36. Appraise
37. Pan-fry
38. Harmed
39. German exclamation
40. "Beau ___"
41. Assail
42. Unequaled
44. Selfish
45. Gray with age
46. Seed coat
47. Soup utensil
49. Mine entrance
50. Atlas chart
53. Indonesian islands
54. Effective
58. Auto fuel
59. Spooky
60. At no time
61. Needle hole
62. Iron setting
63. Used money

DOWN

1. ___ Eban
2. Poet
3. Tart
4. Coal weight
5. Our tongue
6. Ordinary writing
7. Clot
8. One: Fr.
9. Folding bed
10. ___ wood
11. Improve efficiency
12. Ventilates
13. Sports group
18. Nature walk
23. Strike
24. Old guitar
25. Overact
26. Folk knowledge
27. Shoulder band
28. Dove's goal
29. Free
30. Closes
31. Went astray
32. Tattered
34. Impudent
37. Oracle
38. Shoe lift
40. Peeks
41. Early Celts
43. Kanga's child
44. Sand
46. Take away, in law
47. Herb
48. Entreat
49. Orient
50. Chess play
51. Hymn ending
52. Cheeky
55. Permit
56. Crude metal
57. With it

PUZZLE 97

ACROSS

1. Safecracker
5. ____ Lady
9. Hebrew letter
13. Make eyes at
14. Actor Lugosi
15. Soccer great
16. Ohio city
19. Greek letters
20. Of bone: pref.
21. Nevada attraction
22. Hwys.
23. Alone: Lat.
25. Cosmetic queen
27. Barnyard home
30. More pleasant
32. She needs taming
35. Gardener, at times
37. Tie silk
38. Badger
39. Shield border
40. Stage whisper
42. Title
43. ____ Simpson
45. Roman 104
46. Colored
47. Pumps
48. River of Holland
50. Grads-to-be
51. Ralph ____ Emerson
53. End-of-school dance
55. Society girls, for short
57. Culture medium
59. Suspicious
63. He had an Irish Rose
64. Former European nation
66. Singer Vikki ____
67. Dream, in France
68. Clock sound
69. Finishes
70. Oak, e.g.
71. Affirmatives

DOWN

1. String toy
2. Self-images
3. Oversupply
4. Heredity factors
5. Literary monogram
6. Goes back over
7. Medicinal plant
8. One showing boredom
9. Collar
10. Past times
11. Nastase of tennis
12. Stack's TV role
17. Hoodlum
18. Numerals: abbr.
24. Italian coins, once
26. Mao ____-tung
27. Displays
28. Religious scroll
29. Hit song of 1961
31. Sagas
33. Mr. Fudd
34. Dandelions
36. Freedom givers
38. Denial
41. Refute
44. Manhattan, e.g.: abbr.
48. Dieter's lunch, perhaps
49. Lounge
52. 24 hours
54. Rich in thought matter
55. Cyprinoid fish
56. Israeli VIP
58. Ripener
60. Ancient shout
61. Costa ____
62. Beasts of burden
65. Understand

PUZZLE 98

ACROSS

1. Temptress
5. Vise
10. Shoo!
14. Agave
15. Designate
16. Luau dance
17. Small stream
18. "Phantom of the ___"
19. Vigoda and Lincoln
20. Site of Old Faithful
23. Vein site
24. Air holes
25. Paragon
28. Plait
31. First victim
32. Deft
34. Impudent talk
37. Beatles film
40. Affirmative vote
41. Snare loops
42. Bit
43. ___ corgi
44. "___ for You" (Dylan song)
45. Take to dinner
48. Fifty percent
50. Oz thoroughfare
57. Nuisance
58. Don't exist
59. "Rule Britannia" composer
60. Singer Adams
61. "Home on the ___"
62. Sham
63. Tinter
64. Finished
65. Flutter

DOWN

1. Differ
2. "I cannot tell ___"
3. Actor Richard of "Night Court"
4. Helter-skelter
5. Buffoon
6. Expire
7. Connive
8. Grouper
9. Make arrangements
10. Formed
11. Castro, e.g.
12. Vigilant
13. Chores
21. Black gold
22. A Peron
25. Yucatan Indian
26. Mind
27. Strike out
28. Run-in
29. Lounging garment
30. Ambitions
32. G.I. hooky
33. Milit. awards
34. Simba
35. "___ the wild blue . . ."
36. Fuel
38. ___ a customer
39. Rabble
43. Mr. Cronkite
44. Kind
45. Used a word processor
46. Thin
47. Ms. Dinsmore
48. Joint
49. Performed
51. Merchandise
52. Type of cereal
53. Rive
54. Aloud
55. "My Way" lyricist
56. Far down

PUZZLE 99

ACROSS

1. Pealed
5. Provide food
10. Stable food
14. Egg-shaped
15. Think
16. Entreaty
17. Rounded roof
18. Annoying ones
19. Twinge
20. Cardigan, e.g.
22. Gives an account
24. Angry
25. Gluts
26. Refuge
29. With it
30. Discontinue
34. Greedy
35. ___ and haw
36. Burrowing animal
37. Traffic color
38. Tijuana native
40. Atmosphere
41. Small earthquake
43. Fireplace fuel
44. Dig for ore
45. Rose
46. Ocean inlet
47. Diminished
48. Measuring device
50. Writer's need
51. Pittsburgh player
54. Envisioned
58. Cornet, e.g.
59. Courtyard
61. Donate
62. Prepare for publication
63. News articles
64. First garden
65. Vets
66. Thick
67. Transgressions

DOWN

1. Fishing poles
2. Declare
3. Title
4. Shone
5. Contended (with)
6. Copycat
7. Third word of "America"
8. Catch
9. Adjust
10. Against
11. Winged
12. Canvas shelter
13. Droops
21. Sunbather's goal
23. Pie variety
25. Matching
26. TV detectives
27. Turn aside
28. Part of VCR
29. Jinx
31. Once more
32. French river
33. Went astray
35. That woman
36. Sack
38. Mannequin
39. Coquettish
42. Instants
44. Gets along
46. Scold
47. Tiny
49. Lukewarm
50. Ordinary writing
51. Lean-to
52. Commotion
53. Novelist Ambler
54. Becomes indistinct
55. Skirt length
56. Level
57. Cozy rooms
60. X

PUZZLE 100

ACROSS

1. Chess piece
5. Sew loosely
10. Dish of chopped meat
14. Healing plant
15. Marriage
16. Author Ferber
17. Window section
18. Observed
19. Hideout
20. Also
21. "Auld Lang ____"
22. Entice
23. Singer Fitzgerald
25. "____ River"
27. Dark brownish-red
29. Patio
32. Permit
33. Put off
34. Coop denizen
36. Barnyard animal
37. Jury
38. Unadorned
39. Country hotel
40. Feeling
41. French capital
42. Teach
44. Gun cartridge
45. Seize
46. Suit to ____
47. Eating utensil
50. Short
52. Total
55. Cartoonist Al ____
56. Separated
58. Lab burner
59. Jai ____
60. Big
61. Disturb
62. Actor Lugosi
63. Go in
64. Feed the kitty

DOWN

1. Mama's mate
2. Actor Alda
3. "Alice in ____"
4. By birth
5. Legendary lumberjack Paul ____
6. Soon
7. Location
8. Digit
9. Conclusion
10. Capital of Montana
11. Eden denizen
12. Cut quickly
13. Lyricist Lorenz ____
21. Sluggish
22. Whig's opponent
24. Plunder
25. Confused fight
26. Spoken
27. Wise men
28. By oneself
29. Taut
30. Flapper's dance
31. Weird
33. "Inferno" author
35. Bird's home
37. Summit
38. Hay bundle
40. Scrutinize
41. Green stroke
43. Ideal place
44. Trade
47. Wound covering
48. Ashen
49. Milky gem
50. Wagon
51. Desire
53. Army division
54. Masculine
56. Tavern order
57. Bad review
58. Period of note

PUZZLE 101

ACROSS

1. Zoo enclosures
6. Semester
10. Gambling game
14. Energetic
15. Diva's solo
16. Arabian Sea gulf
17. Translator's forte
20. Elongated fish
21. Supplement
22. Rich cake
23. Quills
25. Applaud
26. Ganders
28. Fill again
31. Author Bombeck et al.
32. Views
34. Blind part
36. Sly look
37. Tit for ____
38. Domesticate
39. Ship part
40. Father
41. Fiend
42. Rehearsal
44. Important industrialist
45. Band
46. Uses needle and thread
47. "Beauty and the ____"
49. Summer: Fr.
50. School group: abbr.
53. Island off Cape Cod
57. "I cannot tell ____"
58. File or polish
59. Peep show
60. Monster's loch
61. Shoe bottom
62. Fencers' weapons

DOWN

1. Bistro
2. African lily plant
3. Lass
4. Adam's mate
5. Kind of whale
6. Armored vehicles
7. Mystery writer Gardner
8. River inlet
9. Sleeveless cloaks
10. Certain beds
11. Amo, amas, ____
12. Violent anger
13. Small bill
18. Dancer Kelly
19. Soccer score
23. Entrance to heaven
24. Double curve
25. Greek island
26. Selfishness
27. Arab chieftain
29. Texas mission
30. ____ and Pythias
31. Large deer
32. Robert Redford movie, with "The"
33. Hearing organ
35. Finger count
40. Baskers' desires
41. Crow's relative
43. Reckless
44. "I've ____ Working on the Railroad"
46. Fence steps
47. Cotton bundle
48. Greek goddess of discord
49. Bad
50. Peel
51. Maple or willow
52. Fruit beverages
53. Husband
54. ____ Paulo
55. Poet's before
56. Bark shrilly

PUZZLE 102

ACROSS

1. Umpire's call
5. Bates and Hale
10. Force down
14. Shipshape
15. Waltz or tango
16. Away from the weather
17. Wallet fillers
18. Cut
19. Cartoonist Thomas ____
20. Feel poorly
21. Presumption
23. Hay spreaders
25. Businessman Onassis
26. Clothing
27. Explode
32. Dawn
33. Crawl
34. Previously known as
35. Douse
36. Thwarts
37. Cliff
38. Friend
39. Foot parts
40. Cheers
41. Responded
43. Wine: pref.
44. Broke a fast
45. School penalty
48. Seamstresses, sometimes
53. Periodontists' group: abbr.
54. Smallest of the litter
55. Atlantic, e.g.
56. "Rock of ____"
57. Lotion ingredient
58. Fissile rock
59. Beef or pork
60. Mrs. Truman
61. Tries
62. The Emerald ____

DOWN

1. Ermine
2. Attorney Becker on "L.A. Law"
3. Certain football scores
4. Printing measures
5. Gather matter on a surface
6. Bert and Warren
7. Over again
8. University sports organization: abbr.
9. Makes notches
10. Astringent compound
11. Wings
12. Clutter
13. Caresses
21. Common house plant
22. Decrease
24. Gloomy
27. Helped with the dishes
28. Morays
29. Harbors, e.g.
30. Afternoon socials
31. Always, in poetry
32. Sound of suffering
33. Old King ____
35. Mineral spring
36. Leading
37. Sensible
39. Tennis match components
40. Edges
42. Squanders
43. Novelist Jules and family
45. Apportioned
46. Model
47. Flavor
48. Dull
49. Govern
50. Son of Seth
51. Dull pain
52. New Zealand parrots
56. French friend

PUZZLE 103

ACROSS

1. Poet
5. Firm
10. Door fastener
14. Declare
15. Circumvent
16. N.Y. canal
17. Godiva's title
18. Kingly
19. Thaw
20. Cigar residue
21. Marshland
22. Perfect models
24. Intervene
26. Praline ingredient
28. Uncommon
29. King of comedy
30. Draw from
33. Madame Curie
35. Growing out
36. Hasten
37. Seed covering
38. Roofing tile
39. Ancient Persian's kin
40. Trans- gression
41. "Star Trek" locale
42. Discourage
43. Droop
44. Evergreen
45. Gist
46. Bearlike animal
47. Reluctant
50. Crossword- column heading
53. Color
54. Greek letter
55. Trickle
56. African capital
59. The Seven ____
60. Axlike tool
61. Habituate
62. Heraldic border
63. Fortuneteller
64. Graded
65. Manipulated

DOWN

1. Rosy mineral
2. Stop, to Popeye
3. Misleading clue
4. Left high and ____
5. Tranquil
6. Prop for Julia Child
7. Hang back
8. Ms. Lupino
9. Fragile
10. Macho guys
11. Vicinity
12. Window ledge
13. Fondles
21. Conflagration
23. Great ____
25. Jack and Jill's bucket
26. Cure-all
27. Fill with joy
30. Funda- mentals of learning
31. ____ -memoire
32. Equal
33. Church service
34. Diva's forte
35. African antelope
38. She never tied the knot
39. Apportion
41. Health resorts
42. Leap headlong
45. Hesitated
46. ____ face
48. Like day-old bread
49. Comforted
50. Woe is me!
51. Yield
52. Demolish
53. Charter
57. Actress Merkel
58. Pistachio, e.g.
59. French coin

PUZZLE 104

ACROSS

1. "The ____ Who Loved Me"
4. Mustang, for short
9. Scatter
14. Cake or down
15. Musical show
16. ____ a point
17. Winglike part
18. Change, as a law
19. Slander
20. Land's end
22. Plain as day
24. Danger color
25. War hero
26. Leathernecks
30. Pattern
34. Musical composition
35. London elevators
37. Scholarly book
38. Ewe's mate
39. Menagerie
40. Delay
41. God of love
43. Lukewarm
45. Roman wrap
46. Kind of bass
48. Commissioned officer
50. Bounding main
51. Illuminated
52. Water tank
56. Abandons
60. Prior to
61. Overhead
63. Umpire's call
64. Breakfast bread
65. Trial site
66. Singleton
67. Stroked roughly
68. Give in
69. Make use of

DOWN

1. Iran's former ruler
2. Water sport
3. Fiscal or solar
4. Impudent
5. Alter, as a house
6. Kitchen appliance
7. Convent dweller
8. Grant
9. Interweave
10. Neptune's spear
11. Dressing gown
12. Uniform
13. Strengthening seam
21. Rainbow goddess
23. Large casks
26. Ethnic customs
27. Detached
28. Grapevine traveler
29. Graded, in a way
30. Impassive
31. Punctuation mark
32. Mirror view
33. Lawful
36. Beau Brummel
42. Vatican chapel
43. Go like sixty
44. Teary-eyed
45. Handy bag
47. Skinned
49. Enumerated
52. Apex
53. Ancient Peruvian
54. Pack away
55. "McHale's ____"
56. Finished
57. Source
58. Albacore
59. Gait
62. Hawaiian symbol of welcome

PUZZLE 105

ACROSS

1. Thirty days
6. Hindu princess
10. Callao's land
14. Dino's song subject
15. Cheese variety
16. Sponsorship
17. Alpine area
18. What some 4 Downs led
20. Eradicate
22. Hinnies
23. Sash
24. Snoozes
26. Concurrence
29. Band members
32. Blue-green hues
33. My fault!
34. ABA member
36. ____ of Cleves
37. March king
38. Color changer
39. Racket
40. Sharp
41. Utah town
42. Band clashers
44. Trimmed
45. Shade trees
46. Small wedge
47. Gamut
50. Dog-paddlers
54. Baton twirler
57. Hilltop house
58. Biblical bk.
59. Told a whopper
60. Overused
61. Disagreeable
62. Fortune's pal
63. Ruhr city

DOWN

1. Doilies
2. Neglect
3. Asta's mistress
4. One of 76 in a song
5. Assistants
6. Disprove
7. Mine passage
8. Carp
9. Mischief-maker
10. Study
11. Same, to Pierre
12. Torment
13. Expends
19. In abundance
21. Antique
24. Nanny
25. Indian city
26. School: abbr.
27. Pessimist
28. Skilled
29. Contests
30. Dress fabric
31. Eydie's hubby
33. Persons
35. Walked
37. Con game
38. Rhythm keepers
40. More competent
41. Man or ape
43. Marching tune, for one
44. ____ Beta Kappa
46. Ingmar or Greta
47. City problem
48. Cape: Sp.
49. Almost shut
50. Goblet part
51. Sister of Ares
52. Inauguration, e.g.
53. Espied
55. Pixie
56. Pedro's aunt

PUZZLE 106

ACROSS

1. Mountain range
6. Fiery gem
10. Time divisions: abbr.
14. Chili con ____
15. Clematis, for one
16. Horse's gait
17. Separated
18. Make ____ meet
19. Exceptional
20. Arguing
22. Toddler's delight
24. Comes by
25. Sneaky ones
26. Globe
29. Bakery treats
30. Asian export
31. Sting
33. Car style
37. Organs of sense
39. Race
41. Painful
42. Primp
44. Spooky
46. Order's companion
47. Approaches
49. Glorifies
51. Placards
54. ____ of Bethlehem
55. Part of HRE
56. Depict in words
60. Drizzle
61. Mr. Coward
63. Grows weary
64. Quaker pronoun
65. Biblical brother
66. Put out
67. ____ of Fame
68. Drinks slowly
69. Office furniture

DOWN

1. Private sch.
2. Neck part
3. Dull
4. Make furious
5. Long-haired bird dogs
6. Cake bakers
7. Engine sound
8. In addition to
9. "Children of a ____ God"
10. Accents
11. Remove
12. Reef material
13. Simmers
21. List units
23. Pleases the cook
25. Irrigate
26. ____ on it!
27. Bosc, e.g.
28. Jack rabbit
29. Loggers' targets
32. Mimes
34. Raggedy Ann, e.g.
35. I smell ____
36. Reporter's quest
38. Guard
40. Tries to lose weight
43. ____ -do-well
45. Demanded
48. Areas of conflict
50. Get there
51. Australian city
52. Nebraska city
53. Carnival pitch
54. Vends
56. Penetrating
57. Spring bloom
58. At one's ____ and call
59. Superlative suffixes
62. Sash

PUZZLE 107

ACROSS

1. ____ spumante
5. Freight-train units
9. Gemayel of Lebanon
13. British gun
14. Potpourri
15. Office worker
16. ____ hat
18. Asian tribesman
19. Vend again
20. Cantina selections
22. Lode load
23. "____ Girls"
25. Darkroom chemical
26. Barbecue locale
28. Fairy queen
31. ____ of Riley
34. Pablo's uncle
35. Void
37. Sulawesi oxen
39. Tough ____ to crack
41. Iroquoian Indians
42. Cave
44. Rocky hill
46. Fruit drinks
47. Tennis division
48. Hairless caterpillar
51. Oscar de la ____
53. Negative vote
54. Milit. decoration
57. Racetrack clientele
59. Page's workplace
61. "Beau ____"
62. Small
64. Sacrificial site
65. North Sea feeder
66. Granular snow
67. ____ transit
68. Elsa's sound
69. Confused

DOWN

1. Texas player
2. Range ranger
3. Uptight
4. Playwright William ____
5. Kind of call
6. Entirely
7. Laugh-a-minute
8. "Moonlight ____"
9. "____ of Two Cities"
10. Beatles' Rita, e.g.
11. Balin and Claire
12. And not
15. Hit patron, often
17. Actress Nazimova
21. "September ____"
24. Epidermis
26. Rhythm
27. Childhood
29. Suit to ____
30. Actress Armstrong
31. Falls behind
32. Concerning
33. Ottomans
36. Small weight
38. Penny pincher
40. ____ crier
43. Undeceived by
45. Large chicken
49. Fault finder
50. Bread and whiskey
52. Singer James et al.
54. Stuns
55. "My Three Sons" dad
56. Jason's wife
57. Actor Lugosi
58. Grain warehouse
60. Actress Foch
61. Actress Rita ____
63. Cagers' gp.

PUZZLE 108

ACROSS

1. Snow toy
5. Defect
9. Weight
13. Volcanic rock
14. Hideaway
15. O'Grady of song
16. Related
17. Greasy
18. Burning crime
19. Assail persistently
21. Use a caret
22. Remnants
25. Brawl
29. Dispatch boat
30. Hardship
31. Singer Laine
32. City on the Arno
36. Dutch cheese
37. Clipped
38. Always
39. Period
40. Blow a horn
41. Kind of cheese
42. Squirrel treat
44. Glides
45. Immediately obvious
49. Baby bed
50. Attack
55. Sum
56. Sweet wine
58. Malayan canoe
59. Equalizes
60. Add to the pot
61. Stravinsky
62. Civil-action case
63. Hart
64. Transmitted

DOWN

1. Concrete piece
2. Huron or Ontario
3. Wicked
4. Actor Andrews
5. Inundations
6. Scottish landowner
7. Be sick
8. Distorted
9. Western
10. German city
11. Norwegian inlet
12. Tepees
15. Shoe parts
20. Wild hog
21. Skull section
23. Taverns
24. Prevent
25. Worry
26. Tease
27. Seaweed product
28. Military officer
31. Set of musical tones
33. Currier's partner
34. Install in office
35. Weapons
37. Pebble
41. Folding beds
43. Telephones
44. Little Big Horn casualty
45. Eightsome
46. Utah city
47. Diner
48. Writer Bret ____
51. Sacred bull
52. Exhort
53. Crazy bird
54. Pastry
56. Writing tablet
57. ____ for the books

PUZZLE 109

ACROSS

1. Pedro's love
5. Storybook elephant
10. "____ La Douce"
14. Extremely distasteful
15. Make amends
16. Zoo attraction
17. Ages
18. "____ Entertainment"
19. Bell town
20. Echo
23. ____ Tin Tin
24. Elsa and Leo
25. Rectangular
27. Spins again
30. Aberdeen hillside
31. Yale students
32. Goes back in
36. Beverage
37. Donkeys, at times
40. Chart
41. Emulate a Labrador
43. Quote
44. Wheat flour
45. Fixed the floor
48. Bad egg
51. Absorb knowledge
52. ____ Marie Saint
53. Ponders anew
58. Jenny ____
60. WWII soldier: abbr.
61. Author Hunter
62. Stake
63. San ____
64. Puerto ____
65. Twelvemonth
66. Police-car feature
67. Did in

DOWN

1. Assert
2. Bog down
3. Norwegian king
4. Makes a used-car deal
5. Ball-park worker
6. Capital of Greece
7. Wild pigs
8. Thespian gp.
9. Antique improver
10. Biblical book: abbr.
11. Kind of rocket
12. California county
13. Ding-____
21. Estuary
22. Abba and family
26. "____ the Good Times Roll"
27. Back
28. French pronoun
29. Painter Mondrian
30. Quilter's party
32. Deli bread
33. Actor Jannings
34. Estimate
35. Hied
37. Angry dog, at times
38. Certain tires
39. Actress Gardner
42. Hair pad
43. Ashes
45. Pull a bridge no-no
46. Singer Sheena
47. Prefix with pod or sect
48. Transmit
49. Sheeplike
50. City in Egypt
51. Romeo
54. 902, Roman-style
55. Sinister
56. Grand Prix, e.g.
57. Winter white
59. German article

PUZZLE 110

ACROSS

1. Obligation
5. Morocco's capital
10. Decorate
14. Bitter herb
15. Love, Italian-style
16. Roof overhang
17. Idee ____
18. Items for tourists?
20. ____ Mahal
21. With skill
22. Toga wearers
23. Bandleader Shaw
25. Dreadful
26. Fragrant bag
28. Bigger than a ____
32. Help oneself to
33. Animal tracks
35. Yoko ____
36. Mountain nymph
38. Graceful tree
39. Band instruments
41. "You dirty ____!"
42. Simplified
45. Canyon mouth
46. Tuneful container?
48. Door
50. ____ ex machina
51. User
52. Poplars
55. Spoken
56. Pirate's drink
59. Loge
61. Skid-row dweller
62. Like many cagers
63. Poker term
64. Make over
65. Iowa town
66. Invite a police siren
67. North Sea feeder

DOWN

1. Silly
2. Writer Kazan
3. Overcoats
4. "Message" shirt
5. Magicians' stock
6. Soap plant
7. Square
8. Rainbow
9. More weepy
10. Abounded
11. ____ avis
12. Tennis's Lendl
13. Disorder
19. Quagmire
21. Eroded
24. Mother of Zeus
25. Running suffix
26. Hurricane
27. Swiss town
28. Bungle
29. Wintergreen fruit
30. Unique things
31. South African natives
34. Mexican bread?
37. Proper
40. Swiss river
43. Wrongdoers
44. Took it easy
47. Concepts
49. Actor Gerard
51. Ordinary language
52. Tropical ant
53. Rip-off
54. Soccer great
55. Off-Broadway award
57. Wavy, in heraldry
58. Fasten
60. Chew the fat
61. Distorted

PUZZLE 111

ACROSS
1. Atomize
5. Restaurants
10. Food store
14. Largest continent
15. Sky hunter
16. Medley
17. Bridge aim
18. River in France
19. Byway
20. Shirley Black, nee ____
22. Medals
24. Devour
25. Imposter
27. Creepy
30. Roasting vessel
31. Fall flower
35. Silent ____ Coolidge
36. Paymaster
38. Night before
39. Collection
40. Anger
41. Ironic
42. Quill
43. Neither's partner
44. Eye part
46. Dissolve
47. Beat
49. ____ and feather
50. Counts calories
52. Pester
54. Massachusetts cape
55. Rough
58. "____ 11" (Sinatra movie)
62. ____ mater
63. Terms of a bet
67. Seed covering
68. Bulrush
69. Pursue prey
70. Moon goddess
71. Corn bread
72. Screams
73. Merganser

DOWN
1. Pole
2. Capri or Man
3. Thailand, once
4. Meddle (with)
5. Heavenly streaker
6. Coach Parseghian
7. Evergreen
8. Age
9. Furtive one
10. Grinders
11. Winged
12. Skin
13. "... bells on her ____"
21. Put (down)
23. All in
25. Distant
26. Reply
27. Meager
28. River craft
29. Frighten
30. ____ Rico
32. Tent
33. Happening
34. Rips
36. Expert
37. Period
40. Images
45. Aye's opposite
48. Military review
50. "What's Up, ____?"
51. Role models
53. Full of gossip
54. Stoppers
55. Goldfish, for one
56. Muffin topper
57. Assuredly
59. Calla lily
60. Muses' number
61. Cabbage salad
64. Pleased the cook
65. Guy's date
66. Annex

PUZZLE 112

ACROSS

1. Massages
5. Scrap
10. Drop in water
14. Jacket type
15. Sheer linen
16. Storm
17. Actor Andrews
18. One of the Fords
19. Freshly
20. Christmas activity
22. A square has four
23. Printers' measures
24. Cuckoo
26. Heavenly visitors
30. Pass on
34. Dress style
35. Summer TV show
36. Mourn
37. Locate
38. Singer Reese
39. Evil eye
40. Adam and ____
41. Sample
42. Long time ____!
43. Snakes
45. Supplies food
46. Inquires
47. Beat-walker
48. Begin
51. Symphony section
56. Hawkeye State
57. Sky-blue
59. Ohio Indian
60. Related
61. Metric unit
62. "____ Christie"
63. Otherwise
64. Copycats
65. Ogle

DOWN

1. Cincinnati team
2. Beehive State
3. Cher's ex
4. Break suddenly
5. Beer mugs
6. Trumpets
7. Use a doorbell
8. Mr. Whitney
9. Billy ____ Williams
10. Laud
11. Come down
12. Curved molding
13. Sunday seats
21. Singer Seeger
22. Astound
24. Uncle Miltie
25. Greenish-blue
26. Bistros
27. Martini topper
28. Digger
29. Cease
30. Hits hard
31. Come up
32. Piano worker
33. Bewitches
35. Takes five
38. Unpleasantly moist
39. Iota
41. Exam
42. Back of the neck
44. "Easter ____"
45. Lids
47. Kitchen gadget
48. Location
49. Thingamajig
50. Piercing instruments
51. Silent
52. Chow
53. Sea eagle
54. Playing card
55. Rip
57. Pie ____ mode
58. Kind of code

PUZZLE 113

ACROSS

1. Fifty-two, to Brutus
4. Bouquet
9. Legume abode
12. Actress Best
14. Architectural style
15. China or dry
16. Have no hope
19. Bank
20. Most: suffix
21. Old-timer
22. Half ems
24. Women's or ad
25. Resist
34. Auricles
35. "La ____ Vita"
36. Bewildered
37. King's superior
38. Salt
39. Punch
40. Fork segment
42. "____ de Milo"
44. Molding
45. Party leaders
48. ____ back at
49. Bonn single
50. Chilling
53. Enervate
56. Female knights
60. Accolade
63. Add
64. Pique
65. Fish-eating bird
66. End for ethyl
67. Actor Dolph ____
68. Wind dir.

DOWN

1. Fisheye, e.g.
2. Hero
3. "Come ____ my parlor . . ."
4. One ____ time
5. Cryptic mark
6. Probability
7. Deep trench
8. Curved path
9. Lagoon
10. Previously
11. Stag
13. Some poplars
15. Pacific Ocean's discoverer
17. Serve
18. Successor
23. Instant grass
24. Dress size: abbr.
25. Has room for
26. Understood
27. Battlefield
28. Annotator
29. Antelope
30. Cancel, NASA-style
31. Practice
32. Fresher
33. Small valleys
41. "The Little ____ That Could"
42. Vintner's need
43. Find out
44. Flamboyant
46. Owner's proof
47. Verdi heroine
50. This, in Madrid
51. Collar type
52. Deserve
53. Crystalline downfall
54. Fever and shakes
55. Masquerade
57. Swamp
58. Endless ages
59. Dagger
61. Treasury Dept. div.
62. Ex-GI

PUZZLE 114

ACROSS

1. Midwest airport
6. Actress Negri
10. Harrow's rival
14. Talked and talked
15. Aviators
16. Steak order
17. Lose one's cool
20. Neighbor of Ga.
21. Son of Hera and Zeus
22. ____ the joint (examined)
23. Battle wound
24. Presently
26. Island off New Jersey
29. New Guinea waterway
33. Clocked, as a race
34. Stranger
35. Conquistador's quest
36. In line
37. ____ one's throat
38. Bridge triumph
39. Pro
40. Tree trunks
41. Terra ____
42. Insect trapper
44. Small plum
45. Bone: pref.
46. Spelunker's milieu
47. Old French coins
50. Singer Guthrie
51. Maiden-name word
54. Airborne rodents
58. Yard sections
59. Entre ____
60. Seer's card
61. Positive
62. Colorado's neighbor
63. Fruit pit

DOWN

1. "Carmina Burana" composer
2. Corridor
3. Novelist Seton
4. Kanga's child
5. Wrote on a document, e.g.
6. Father: Lat.
7. American publisher
8. Golfer Trevino
9. ____ Wednesday
10. Lesser-known Verdi opera
11. Little boys
12. Heraldic border
13. Deficiency
18. Kukla's friend
19. 54 Across's morsel
23. Mulligan, e.g.
24. Aka
25. Moscow denial
26. Advisory group
27. Alpine region
28. Author Cleveland ____
29. Handbill
30. Electrical units
31. Poetry Muse
32. Eternal City native
34. Tree-lined walk: Fr.
37. Dandies
38. Indefinite amount
40. Washbowl
41. Frolics
43. Mannerly
44. Spanish surrealist painter
46. Infatuation
47. Switch positions
48. Kind of cheese
49. Criminal trial
50. Turquoise
51. Pianist Peter ____
52. North Carolina college
53. Punta del ____
55. African antelope
56. Over-drinker
57. Hair pad

PUZZLE 115

ACROSS
1. Mixture of greens
6. Incite to attack
9. Hot tub
12. Mediterranean fruit
13. Bustle
14. Register
15. Belief
16. Share
18. Withered
19. Garbed
20. Noah's craft
22. Singer Charles
23. "____ of the South"
26. Brad
28. Jump
31. On the sheltered side
32. Tanker's cargo
33. Assistant
34. Evergreen shrub
35. Land measure
36. Goulash
37. Large deer
38. Even so
40. Politician Abzug
43. Tie
46. Gathered
49. Unimportant
51. Quarry
52. Crucial
53. Notched, as a leaf
54. Sounds of hesitation
55. "You ____ Sixteen"
56. Marry again

DOWN
1. Tippler
2. Pub drinks
3. Profession
4. Ordinary
5. Discourage
6. Maple syrup source
7. Actress Lupino
8. Horse enclosure
9. Thick slice
10. Jab
11. Ripened
17. Plaything
21. Rap
22. "The Life of ____"
23. Assert
24. Cheer for a toreador
25. Fresh
27. Ventilate
28. Success
29. "____ to Billie Joe"
30. Church bench
33. "Top Hat" star
35. 49th state
37. Chicago trains
39. "____ Gantry"
40. Wished
41. Arab ruler
42. Dawdles
44. Skier's delight
45. Watering device
47. Always, in poems
48. Color
50. Blushing

PUZZLE 116

ACROSS

1. "My ____ Foot"
5. Blemish
8. Vagabond
12. Gumbo ingredient
13. Wing
14. Rocker Ant
15. Driver's ____ mirror
17. Judge's garb
18. Amended
19. Desolate
21. Careless
22. Nonflying bird
23. Prayer ending
25. Famous
29. ____ Vegas
30. Linoleum pieces
31. The Gay Nineties was one
32. Valiant
34. Change
35. Minerals
36. Pad
37. News feature
40. Montana's capital
43. Purposes
44. Cosmetic item
46. Escape
47. Red or Black
48. Appear
49. Industrialist Henry ____
50. Melancholy
51. Singer Arnold

DOWN

1. Knowledge
2. Scraped
3. Most delicate
4. Kilt pattern
5. Damsel
6. Pub order
7. Rangy
8. Farmer's clod-breaker
9. Fragrance
10. Paul Bunyon's blue ox
11. Sign
16. Enrage
20. Stirs
22. Sandwich shops
23. ____ Pasha
24. Gent
25. Maturity
26. Tidied up
27. Go astray
28. Actor Daniel ____-Lewis
30. Period
33. Woke up
34. Satchel
36. Singer Torme
37. On the ____ (gratis)
38. Norwegian capital
39. Lascivious glance
40. Chief
41. Lack
42. Infantry
45. Pro vote

PUZZLE 117

ACROSS

1. Go by car
5. Sensed
9. In what manner
12. "____ Bede"
13. Clinton's canal
14. Before, in verse
15. Impertinent
16. Moistened
18. Tithe
20. Comfort
21. ____ the knot
24. Dancing spot
28. Japanese sash
30. Author Carnegie
32. Warm up
33. Observe
34. Period
36. Ripen
37. Swift stroke
39. Indian garment
40. ____ herring
41. Aquatic mammal
43. Dutch bulb
45. Have a meal
47. Lock
50. Football field
55. "____ Karenina"
56. Paddle
57. Soft drink
58. Tropical hardwood
59. "____ from the Heart"
60. Whirlpool
61. "The ____ of Night"

DOWN

1. Vehicle for rapids
2. Goof off
3. Finest
4. Drain
5. Nourished
6. Stat for Seaver
7. Butter bean
8. Warm
9. Barnyard fowl
10. Native metal
11. Married
17. Revise
19. Conceal
22. Dozes
23. Exult
25. Whetted
26. Parakeet's enclosure
27. Was under obligation to
28. Norway's capital
29. Triumphed over
31. Beige
35. Sword handle
38. Pay attention to
42. Grow
44. Angered
46. Walked
48. Obstacle
49. Benefit
50. Sticky stuff
51. Loped
52. Wrath
53. Unusual
54. Negative vote

PUZZLE 118

ACROSS

1. Ali, once
5. Make a goal
10. Burn
14. "The ____ Tattoo"
15. Refuge
16. Game on horseback
17. District
18. Lessen
19. In a line
20. Sneak
22. Italian coin, once
24. That girl
25. Narrative
27. Class brain
29. Enormous
32. Tosspots
34. Not me
35. In the past
36. "____ Frome"
38. Costume
42. "Cheers" patron
44. Cleave
46. Shopper's delight
47. Terrific
49. Strides
51. ____ nutshell
52. Glass edge
54. Kentucky Derby, for one
55. ____ Vegas
56. Nuclear device
60. Ships' records
62. Vase
63. Golf club
65. Awakens
69. Prime
71. Prize
73. Blunt
74. Norway's capital
75. French composer
76. Opera melody
77. Oliver or Rex
78. Hair net
79. Shipshape

DOWN

1. Bird's crop
2. Folk knowledge
3. Bewildered
4. Leavening agent
5. Onionlike plants
6. Taxi
7. Elliptical
8. Make another bow
9. Pep
10. Numbers man: abbr.
11. Trigger, e.g.
12. Hawaiian greeting
13. Used paddles
21. Comfort
23. Enraptured
26. Singer Merman
28. Colors
29. 4th of July noise
30. Inventor Sikorsky
31. Writer Vidal
33. Taste
37. High country
39. Rear end
40. Forearm bone
41. Legumes
43. Artist Chagall
45. Made a tape
48. Small monkey
50. Western lily
53. Swamp
56. Gossipy report
57. Eradicate
58. Old-womanish
59. ____ and Martin
61. African country
64. Defense gp.
66. Certain
67. Director Kazan
68. Bed support
70. Be drowsy
72. River, to Jose

PUZZLE 119

ACROSS

1. Vital
4. Do ____ others . . .
8. Conceal
12. Dander
13. Yuletide song
14. On top of
15. Noticed
17. Misplace
18. Porter, e.g.
19. Authorize
20. Malice
23. Cowboy's rope
25. Eternities
26. Island east of Java
27. Blob
30. Picnic pest
31. Florida city
32. Savings plan: abbr.
33. Flower wreath
34. Recedes
35. Bill
36. Jazz's Davis
38. Church walkway
39. Jewel from the sea
41. Request
42. Saxophone range
43. In a high voice
48. Secluded valley
49. High point
50. Jar
51. Simple
52. Refuge
53. Quick farewell

DOWN

1. Nanny's offspring
2. Before
3. Still
4. Mother's brother
5. Reminder
6. Golfer's peg
7. "The ____ Curiosity Shop"
8. Ponders
9. Regrets
10. Middling
11. Realized
16. Nibbles
19. Largest continent
20. Emblem
21. Corn bread
22. Cronies
23. Gentle animals
24. European range
26. "I Got You ____"
28. Verbal
29. Cook
31. Describe
35. Cycle
37. Sarcasm
38. Piece of property
39. Leaf
40. Singer Fitzgerald
41. Donations
43. Enthusiast
44. Topnotch
45. Large container
46. Attempt
47. Unit

PUZZLE 120

ACROSS

1. Prohibit
4. Took a dip
8. Singe
12. Bauxite, e.g.
13. Rabbit
14. Time past
15. Part of a play
16. Pulled out
18. "____ Amigos!"
20. Shout
21. Notice
23. Concise
27. Reach
29. Resound
32. Snaky fish
33. Carry
34. I see!
35. Qualified
36. ____-de-France
37. Londoner, for short
38. Singer Nat "King" ____
39. Cowboy show
41. Beige
43. Obstacle
46. Therefore
49. Deep dish
53. Pop
54. ____ vera
55. Solo for Domingo
56. Actress Arden
57. Soldiers in gray, for short
58. Sugar-producing vegetable
59. Cozy room

DOWN

1. Sloop, e.g.
2. St. Louis sight
3. Went back
4. Woolly animals
5. Paraffin
6. Pretentious
7. Only
8. Circular process
9. ____ potato
10. "Just the Way You ____"
11. Vermilion
17. Female voice
19. Feudal serf
22. "Same Time, Next ____"
24. Caromed
25. Vend
26. General Robert ____
27. Commotion
28. Game played on horseback
30. City in Ill.
31. Detest
35. "God's Little ____"
37. Clavicle, e.g.
40. Double curves
42. Swindle
44. Saudi, for one
45. Tipper or Al
47. Grotto
48. Paradise
49. Train component
50. Dark brew
51. Weep
52. Fib

PUZZLE 121

ACROSS
1. Task
4. Rushed
8. Herringlike fish
12. Reverence
13. Enclosure
14. Spouse
15. Power again
17. Actor Ladd
18. Staff member
19. Storage room
21. Jockey's colors
23. Solidifies
24. Pinnacle
25. Melody
26. Tear
29. Turn right
30. Yells
31. Significant period
32. Remark further
33. Gripped
34. Singer Campbell
35. Warmth
36. Lift
37. Themes
40. Rests
41. Retired for the night
42. Rain attire
46. Suffer defeat
47. Three squared
48. Make a mistake
49. Permits
50. Establishes
51. Behold

DOWN
1. Startle
2. Be indebted to
3. Deprived of a wind for sailing
4. Loads
5. Trim
6. Goad
7. Made more profound
8. Long-necked birds
9. Handle
10. A long way off
11. Declare untrue
16. Wilderness walk
20. Strong brews
21. Epic
22. Frosted
23. Remorse
25. Violations of allegiance
26. Pickle condiments
27. Infuriates
28. Huff and puff
30. Head cook
34. "Anything ____"
35. Stashes
36. Employs
37. Shopping area
38. Wind instrument
39. Trial run
40. Advanced
43. Contend
44. Mine output
45. Before, to a poet

PUZZLE 122

ACROSS
1. Ruse
5. Craze
8. Gentle
12. Lead performer
13. Brewed drink
14. Away from the wind
15. Uproots
17. Shopping center
18. Bind
19. Basks in the sun
20. Detecting device
23. Feel unwell
24. Cake decorator
25. Division
29. Born as
30. Manufactures
31. Help
33. Fancied
35. Take a bus
36. Lament
37. Brawl
38. Actual
40. Egg producer
41. Towel label
42. Complimentary words
47. Actress Bancroft
48. Type of paint
49. Director Kazan
50. Enterprising person
51. Attain
52. Moist

DOWN
1. "____ Wore a Yellow Ribbon"
2. Jinx
3. Actor Carney
4. Cement
5. Side
6. Dist. above sea level
7. ____ Moines
8. Mexican dish
9. Actor Bates
10. Brooks and Allen
11. Conger
16. Broadcast
19. Robbins and McCarver
20. ____ Tin Tin
21. Received a high grade on
22. Forest animal
23. Matured
25. Alike
26. ____ out a living
27. Metal fastener
28. Ocean movement
30. Paw
32. Actor Billy ____ Williams
34. Pencil end
35. Leased
37. Encountered
38. Nevada city
39. Sea eagle
40. Stop!
41. Owned
42. Mist
43. Falsehood
44. High note
45. Wheel edge
46. Bark sharply

PUZZLE 123

ACROSS

1. Jacket
5. Moist
9. Hullabaloo
12. Poker stake
13. Notion
14. "____ Are So Beautiful"
15. Pause
16. Memorial
18. Subject
20. Regulation
21. Valleys
23. Hurt
27. Barrel
30. Vapor
31. "Captain ____"
32. Tacked
34. Aphorism
35. Composition
36. Josh
37. Confederate general
38. Soaks
39. Fills
41. Denomination
43. Pilfer
47. Modernize
51. Impulse
52. Wrath
53. She, in Madrid
54. Demeanor
55. Small rug
56. Clairvoyant
57. Bother

DOWN

1. Play's group
2. Upon
3. Surmounting
4. Lukewarm
5. Murky
6. Worships
7. Bills of fare
8. Actor Reiser
9. Change the color of
10. Charged particle
11. Pecan, e.g.
17. Powdery
19. Shrewd
22. Boy
24. Mattress support
25. Sharpen
26. Border
27. Understood
28. Simplicity
29. Heart of the matter
31. Infants
33. Lariat
34. Pose
36. Unnerve
39. Climb
40. Confound
42. December 24 and 31
44. New York canal
45. Periods
46. Period before Easter
47. Brink
48. Baseball stat
49. Seine
50. Lend an ____

PUZZLE 124

ACROSS

1. Chasm
4. Male deer
8. Revise
12. Goof
13. "A ____ of Two Cities"
14. Greater amount
15. Affiliation
16. Took out
18. Adventurous journey
20. A Stooge
21. Sea eagle
22. Happen again
26. Bonus
28. Lure
31. Metal-bearing rock
32. Station sign abbr.
33. Steam bath
34. Contend
35. Pub drink
36. Annoys
37. Newspaper department
38. Made over
40. "____ All We Know"
41. Omaha's location: abbr.
43. Forest watcher
46. Intersection
50. Lyricist Gershwin
51. Staffer
52. Otherwise
53. Tear
54. Frost or Pound
55. Unwanted plant
56. Tennis call

DOWN

1. Acquires
2. Opera tune
3. Favored
4. Strict
5. Cab
6. Height: abbr.
7. Microbe
8. Host
9. Spot
10. Anger
11. Actor Danson
17. Major artery
19. Biblical boat
23. Model
24. Author Leon ____
25. Smell
26. TV host Jack ____
27. Author ____ Stanley Gardner
28. Saloon
29. Northern diving bird
30. ____ and outs
33. "Both ____ Now"
37. Baseball's Drysdale
39. Fabric panel
40. Dimmed
42. Potion
43. Tear down
44. Great Lake
45. Absorbed
46. Top
47. "____ Bravo"
48. Song of praise
49. Bullring cry

PUZZLE 125

ACROSS
1. Baden-Baden, e.g.
4. Overwhelm with humor
8. Droning sound
12. Set of tools
13. Colorless
14. Teased
15. Puts into a list
17. Harbinger
18. Frozen
19. Press and fold
20. Passage
23. Ladder parts
25. Kidney or lima
26. Lucy's partner
27. Small child
30. Rent
31. Himalayan land
32. ____ out a living
33. Before, in verse
34. Top pilots
35. Type of merchandise
36. Mean
38. Passenger vehicle
39. Wilderness guide
41. Colorless
42. Munitions
43. Immature
48. Eliot or Auden
49. Air
50. ____ Grande
51. Agile
52. Cattail
53. Lumberjack's tool

DOWN
1. Schuss down a slope
2. Hole in the ground
3. Dined
4. Hot
5. Slothful
6. Porter or stout
7. Positive response
8. Amiss
9. Settler's residence
10. Thought
11. Split
16. Bearing
19. Weave together
20. Proficient
21. Evil look
22. Tardy one
23. Revolt
24. Utilizes
26. Game cubes
28. Gumbo vegetable
29. High-school student
31. Stretched tight
35. Make (one's way)
37. Out of practice
38. Greens mixture
39. Dupes
40. Harvest
41. Telegram
43. Train component
44. Shade
45. Novelist Levin
46. Half-dozen
47. Garden tool

PUZZLE 126

ACROSS

1. Chowder ingredient
5. Haw's partner
8. Pop
12. First-class
13. Self-image
14. Take notice of
15. Hines/ Crystal film
18. Precious
19. Pitch
20. Super-market need
23. Choir voice
27. West of Hollywood
29. Weaponry
31. Climbing plant
32. Rower's need
33. Pekoe or Oolong
34. Confederate general
35. Dined
36. Sewing joint
37. Cozy place
38. Dine regally
40. Adhesive
42. Help
44. Tolled
47. Act as expected
53. Words of understanding
54. Norm
55. Project
56. Accomplishment
57. Time period
58. Meshes

DOWN

1. Automobile
2. Noisy
3. Diarist Frank
4. Threat
5. Egg layer
6. Quiche ingredient
7. More than half
8. Stock market unit
9. Poet's beyond
10. Actress Sandra ____
11. Attach
16. Author Wolfert
17. Felines
21. Tempo
22. Pay the bill
24. African river
25. Baker's need
26. Ham on ____
27. Chess triumph
28. Region
30. "I Remember ____"
32. Dolt
36. Mix
37. Stun with noise
39. Satisfied
41. Expert
43. Patsy
45. Alaskan city
46. "True ____"
47. Disencumber
48. Manipulate
49. Wedding announcement word
50. Corn serving
51. ____ la la
52. Alps: abbr.

PUZZLE 127

ACROSS

1. Kind
5. Wealthy man
10. Selves
14. Black bird
15. Montana's neighbor
16. Musical symbol
17. Oppositionist
18. Escalate
19. Charge
20. Loafer
22. Autumn or spring
24. Lucy's ex
25. Slug
26. Polo stick
29. Interrogate
33. Martian
34. Direct
35. "____ Na Na"
36. Shape
37. Says no to seconds
38. Bridge trick
39. Cry of discovery
40. Milling cutters
41. Metric unit
42. Church room
44. Oklahoma and Maine
45. Vow
46. Tense
47. St. Francis of ____
50. California port
54. Composed
55. Wed secretly
57. Arabian sultanate
58. Roofing piece
59. Engineer Georges ____
60. Longest river
61. Skidded
62. Stooge
63. Night sight

DOWN

1. Tropical fish
2. French department
3. Roman tribunal
4. ____ one's thumbs (did nothing)
5. Most pleasant
6. Statesman Stevenson
7. Chum
8. Unit of resistance
9. Winter olympic vehicles
10. In a trance
11. Tibetan gazelles
12. Historical German king
13. Caught sight of
21. Has- ____
23. Facility
25. Clubs and hearts
26. "____ Family"
27. Hilo hello
28. Purple shade
29. Doubt
30. Ait
31. Famous airport
32. Dubs
34. Size
37. Most dry
38. Grand Central and Penn
40. Slant
41. Poker game
43. Stirred up
44. In a rational manner
46. Recorded
47. "Hamlet" has five
48. Stain
49. Arias
50. Marsh rail
51. Give off
52. Showy
53. Unique occurrence
56. Old card game

PUZZLE 128

ACROSS

1. Big monkeys
5. Blob
9. Pub drink
12. Fluff
13. Landed
14. Not high
15. Poker stake
16. Eden
18. Throw about
20. Time period
21. Smell
24. Hobo
28. Knock
30. To ____ his own
32. General Robert ____
33. Little devil
34. Soda sipper
36. Allow
37. Bambi, e.g.
39. Big sandwich
40. Dwight's nickname
41. Bequeath
43. Parsley branch
45. Jeer
47. Wipe out
50. Aloof
55. Slanted
56. Yes vote
57. Like
58. Carry
59. Fresh
60. Otherwise
61. Gaelic

DOWN

1. Woe is me!
2. Half a quart
3. Snared
4. Maverick
5. Chart
6. Pie ____ mode
7. Father
8. Begin
9. Actress MacGraw
10. ____ Angeles
11. Female sheep
17. Challenge
19. Troubles
22. School subj.
23. Farm measures
25. Swamp dweller
26. Humble
27. Rose of baseball
28. Take the bus
29. Prayer ending
31. Complain
35. Had on
38. Toga
42. Less skillful
44. Teed-off
46. Egg-shaped
48. Poses
49. Fencing sword
50. Operated
51. Seeing organ
52. Use a needle
53. Printer's measures
54. Passing grade

PUZZLE 129

ACROSS

1. Unclothed
5. Luau garland
8. Excite
12. African lily
13. Tavern
14. Air
15. South Dakota's rock formations
17. Prune
18. Snake shape
19. Affirmatives
21. Command to a mule
22. Paddock
23. Grotto
25. Badger
28. Spins
31. On top of
32. Chair
33. Field
36. Parklike
38. Reasonable
39. "___ Town"
40. Hollow
42. English counts
44. Honest ___
47. Tart
49. Melted
51. Western resort
52. "All About ___"
53. Marsh grass
54. Trim
55. Directed
56. Crooked

DOWN

1. Baseball's Ruth
2. Cry of dismay
3. Poles
4. Conger, e.g.
5. Sheets
6. Boundaries
7. Bug
8. Used to be
9. Yearned
10. Buffalo's lake
11. Record
16. Not nays
20. Observed
22. Bamboo eater
24. Eyeshade
25. Bustle
26. Gorilla
27. Cooking slowly
29. ___ Vegas
30. Pigpen
34. Third person singular
35. This animal goes pop
36. Gobbled
37. Depose
40. Peel
41. Frosted
43. Wander
44. Again
45. Tavern fare
46. Swirl
48. Bambi's mother
50. Age

PUZZLE 130

ACROSS

1. Agenda
5. Festive occasion
9. Massage
12. Opera solo
13. Dollar bills
14. Sooner than, to a poet
15. Tradesmen
17. Become old
18. Tool set
19. Succession
21. Grownups
24. To and ____
25. Win by a ____
26. Decanters
30. Foot part
31. "____ Town"
32. Reverence
33. Chores
36. Kiln
37. Rocker Stewart
38. Chicken
40. Money stores
43. Chased
44. Tall tale
45. Attracts
51. Citrus drink
52. Peggy and Ruta
53. Genuine
54. Crib
55. Desires
56. Alluring

DOWN

1. Take it on the ____
2. Hard feelings
3. Galahad's title
4. Fishing gear
5. Billies and nannies
6. ____ -Margret
7. Rent
8. Separate
9. Enjoy a book
10. Motivate
11. Milwaukee product
16. Strike
20. Decay
21. Poker term
22. Portal
23. Consumer
24. In support of
26. City vehicle
27. Molten rock
28. Pitcher
29. Transmit
31. Weird
34. Noah's boat
35. Curiously
36. Proprietors
38. Salad green
39. Boat paddle
40. Tattle
41. Camp helper
42. Obligation
46. Formerly named
47. Bowling frames
48. Lay eyes on
49. Sales or income
50. Clever

PUZZLE 131

ACROSS

1. Smashes
5. Bounder
8. Donkey's cry
12. Neighborhood
13. Ripen
14. Play part
15. Fix
16. Actor Reiner
17. March date
18. Small boy
20. Basin
22. Whips
25. Allude
29. Assist
30. Alarm
34. Division of history
35. Hot or cold beverage
36. Neither here ____ there
37. Journal
38. Hen product
39. Dormant
41. "____ to Billie Joe"
42. Looks for
44. Had
46. Little devil
48. Cow bellow
49. Skip over
52. Pasture
54. Not shut
58. Speed contest
59. Consume
60. Salesman's model
61. Peepers
62. Part of to be
63. Comfortable

DOWN

1. Sandwich meat
2. Wrath
3. Half a score
4. Joylessly
5. Business ____
6. Before now
7. Loan
8. Payola
9. Fishing pole
10. Strong beer
11. You bet!
19. Burro
21. Vase
22. Kismets
23. Faithful
24. Saying
26. Convict
27. Chafe
28. Blew up
31. Lodge
32. Red deer female
33. Go astray
39. Doctrine
40. ____ close for comfort
43. Wind toys
45. Balsa and ply
47. Reason
48. One of a pair
49. Crude mineral
50. Can
51. Freezer cube
53. Bend an ____
55. Ink writer
56. Australian bird
57. New Year's drink

PUZZLE 132

ACROSS

1. Jewel
4. Gusted
8. Boutique
12. Amaze
13. Unusual
14. Treatment
15. Guardsman
17. Vigor
18. Peculiar
19. Erie and Suez
21. Foundation
23. Arrive
24. Pouches
25. Female knight
26. Likely
29. "We ___ the World"
30. Made on a loom
31. Pool stick
32. Scarlet
33. Did farm work
34. Simple
35. Titles of respect
36. Comfort
37. Alert
40. Lend an ___
41. Shoot up
42. Chair parts
47. Folk knowledge
48. Work hard
49. Cool
50. Barely gains
51. Establishes
52. Affirmative vote

DOWN

1. Auto fuel
2. Female sheep
3. Grown boys
4. Wedding-cake topper
5. Go ashore
6. Before, poetically
7. Greeted
8. View
9. Luau dance
10. By mouth
11. Corrals
16. Mix, as a salad
20. Hymn ending
21. Naked
22. Matured
23. Lairs
24. Block
25. Entrance rugs
26. High cards
27. Undiluted
28. Popular shirt
30. Fluttering sound
34. Mother horse
35. Tender spots
36. British noblemen
37. Key
38. Recess
39. Muddle through
40. Throw off
43. Fish eggs
44. Bashful
45. Fasten
46. Health facility

PUZZLE 133

ACROSS

1. Hint
5. Crow's sound
8. Infrequent
12. Countess's spouse
13. Japanese sash
14. Made do
15. Absorbed
17. Shaft
18. Build
19. Syria's neighbor
21. Spigot
23. Neither's opposite
24. Scottish port
28. Authorizes
32. Jabber
33. Actor Johnson
35. Singer Brenda ____
36. Legends
39. Friendliest
42. Sprite
44. Golf peg
45. Tropical fruits
49. Hard candies
53. Perched
54. Sled
56. Snout
57. Generation
58. Songstress Fitzgerald
59. Split
60. Library
61. Bottomless

DOWN

1. Grant
2. Lodge
3. Encourage
4. Chooses
5. Camp bed
6. Cain's brother
7. Enlarge
8. Comment
9. Like
10. Gambling city
11. Eve's garden
16. Doe's mate
20. Opposite of cheer
22. Shell
24. Fitness center
25. Place
26. Appropriate
27. Knock one's socks off
29. Tavern order
30. Affirmative
31. Collection
34. ____ "King" Cole
37. Stove
38. Like a fox
40. Decorate again
41. Joined
43. Destined
45. Gasp
46. Healing plant
47. Leaning Tower site
48. Painful
50. Eye
51. Colorless
52. Ginger cookie
55. Prohibit

PUZZLE 134

CODEWORD

Codeword is a special crossword puzzle in which conventional clues are omitted. Instead, answer words in the diagram are represented by numbers. Each number represents a different letter of the alphabet, and all the letters of the alphabet are used. When you are sure of a letter, put it in the code key chart and cross it off in the Alphabet Box. A group of letters has been inserted to start you off.

1	2	3	4	5	6	7	8	9	10	11 U	12	13
14 E	15	16	17	18	19	20	21 S	22	23	24	25	26

21	15	5	18	■	■	9	24	25	2	14	■	8	25	24
6	25	7	14	24	■	6	25	9	14	24	■	25	17	14
5	17	4	1	14	■	5	12	5	10	14	■	19	4	10
22	4	15	■	19	25	24	14	■	■	8	23	14	21	15
■	■	■	16	11	24	26	■	1	5	15	14	■	■	■
1	14	7	5	15	14	■	2	24	5	■	18	25	24	1
14	13	5	20	14	■	3	11	4	12	■	■	22	5	25
6	25	15	14	■	8	11	24	13	14	■	25	22	11 U	15
25	1	14	■	■	23	5	21	14	■	2	24	5	21 S	14
26	14	6	6	■	25	15	14	■	6	5	4	15	14 E	24
■	■	■	25	11	24	25	■	3	11	4	1	■	■	■
22	6	5	18	21	■	■	23	11	9	21	■	16	4	22
24	25	2	■	25	14	24	4	14	■	14	6	11	1	14
14	20	14	■	9	24	25	13	14	■	21	25	15	14	21
1	14	10	■	14	25	9	14	24	■	■	7	14	25	15

ALPHABET BOX

A B C D ~~E~~ F G H I J K L M N O P Q R ~~S~~ T ~~U~~ V W X Y Z

PUZZLE 135

ACROSS

1. Computer fodder
5. Upperclassmen: abbr.
8. Plant part
12. One who mimics
13. Bird call
15. Rose of baseball
16. Distance unit
17. Sights on the Mississippi
19. Kingly homes
21. Conditional releases
22. ____ Vegas
23. Summer cooler
24. Earn
27. Quick-witted
29. Ancient
32. Antitoxin
33. King: Fr.
34. Ice mass
35. Luxury-ship trip
39. Arabian gulf
40. Black cuckoo
41. Change
42. Spread hay
43. Small songbird
44. Roofer, perhaps
45. Recall subject
46. Derek-Moore film
47. Provided food
51. Spring holidays
56. Atlantic sight
58. Face shape
59. Rages
60. Shuts hard
61. Dole out
62. Wild Hawaiian goose
63. "____ Miserables"
64. Raised, as guppies

DOWN

1. Slightly wet
2. Samoan seaport
3. Squeal
4. Zone
5. ____ army knife
6. Gun, as an engine
7. Ooze
8. Soup utensil
9. Fresh-water duck
10. Diminutive suffix
11. GI's hall
13. Actor Williams
14. Kind of jam
18. Dennis the Menace, for one
20. Use a ladder
24. Gettysburg general
25. Went astray
26. Destroy
27. Sap
28. Geologic time period
29. Gentry
30. Also-ran
31. Forest creature
32. Beat it, kitty!
34. Filled to the brim
36. Wooden containers
37. Compass point: abbr.
38. Really comes down
43. Give notice of danger
44. Mourning drops
45. Desist
46. Abounds
47. Nickel or dime
48. Unit of land
49. Six follower
50. Pickle type
52. Pyramid
53. "____ in My Heart" (Stanwyck film)
54. Estimate
55. Coasting toy
57. Scottish negative

PUZZLE 136

ACROSS

1. Son of Noah
4. Symbol of power
8. Polite bloke
12. Author Ambler
14. Sew quickly: 2 wds.
15. German river
16. Guy, gal and another: 2 wds.
19. Tolerance
20. In a drastic way
21. Great amount
22. "The Way We ——"
23. "I'll —— You . . .": 2 wds.
26. Traffic tie-ups
27. Musical notes
30. Unanimously: 2 wds.
31. Arias
32. Miami's county
33. Do the impossible: 3 wds.
36. Kill Van ——
37. Oodles
38. Vexed
39. But, to Ovid
40. Guns a motor
41. Sweethearts
42. Shredded
43. Pass the peak
44. Tavern
47. Laterally
51. Tomb of Cheops, e.g.: 2 wds.
53. Wine casks
54. Makes an attempt
55. Ivy League school
56. Suggestive
57. Kennel sounds
58. Junior

DOWN

1. Lowlife
2. Comedian Johnson
3. Bearing
4. Fertilizer
5. Cash for cards
6. Mutt
7. Widespread outbreak
8. Category
9. Periphery
10. Entertainer Carter
11. Yarborough card
13. Felon
14. Cattleman's spread
17. Grammatical term
18. Makes public
22. Swansea's land
23. Sunbathes
24. Adjective ending
25. "If Ever I —— Leave You"
26. —— Hopkins
27. Twin crystal
28. Lazybones
29. Bird food
31. Kitchen feature
32. Garage adjunct
34. Forever
35. Mangle operator
40. Cheer
41. —— -slipper
42. Eva's playmate
43. Swabs
44. Groups
45. Malarial fever
46. Bobcat's kin
47. Rude one
48. "—— corny as Kansas . . .": 2 wds.
49. Rural structure
50. Utopian place
52. Onassis, familiarly

PUZZLE 137

ACROSS

1. Took court action
5. Put off
10. Scheme
14. Poker stake
15. Rust
16. Italian capital
17. Gets the prize
18. Huge
19. Notion
20. Metal fastener
22. Apartment house
24. Tiny amount
26. Good review
27. Small groups
31. Fragrant woods
35. Ceremonies
36. Defeats
38. Decay
39. Surrounded by
40. Church leaders
41. Wolf
42. Measurement
43. Danger
44. Singer Paul ___
45. Simmered
47. Turn away from
49. Terminates
51. Hosiery mishap
52. Pancake pans
56. Small earthquake
60. Nobleman
61. Type of poem
63. Storm
64. Musical instrument
65. Deadly gas
66. Concerning
67. Twist
68. Tip
69. Ogled

DOWN

1. Cutting tools
2. One measure
3. Volcanic peak
4. Hated
5. Strike out
6. Historical period
7. Knox or Lauderdale
8. Lawn tool
9. Performs again
10. Prepared
11. Vein of ore
12. Prayer ending
13. Tidy
21. Building sites
23. Nights before holidays
25. Place for plants
27. Packs tightly
28. Boundary
29. Useful
30. Shade of brown
32. Smell
33. Mechanical man
34. Stepping ___
37. Vends
40. Street sellers
41. Lacy underwear
43. Await
44. Burn slightly
46. Married
48. Meaning
50. Flower leaf
52. Drop of liquid
53. Lounging attire
54. Strong metal
55. Root beer, for one
57. Numerous
58. Grimm meanie
59. Marsh plant
62. Put on

PUZZLE 138

ACROSS

1. Downy mass
6. Persian
10. Multi-masted sailing vessel
14. Hindu princess
15. Algerian port
16. Fever
17. With sympathy
20. Hot diamonds
21. Racket
22. Concerns
23. Semester
25. "____ Maria"
26. Mythical British king
27. Other: Sp.
29. Lilt
30. Germany's Bad ____
33. Objecting
37. Race-track shape
38. Roamed
39. Follower: suffix
40. Fight site
41. Second son
42. Newspaper feature: 2 wds.
44. Sea, in Soissons
45. Shaw's "Arms and the ____"
46. Obi
47. Pierce
49. 2000 pounds
50. Early Irish alphabet
54. Management division
56. Denominations
58. ____ Baba
59. Beyond criticism
62. Thought
63. Fictional plantation
64. Synthetic fiber
65. Gratuities
66. Kind of exam
67. Borscht ingredients

DOWN

1. Kind of salad
2. Pike
3. "____ Milk Wood"
4. Tuition
5. Lobby greenery
6. Drive
7. Expunge
8. Marmaduke, the comic Great ____
9. To what ____?
10. Mundane
11. Offender
12. Govern
13. Islets
18. Flies high
19. Bakery worker
24. Highway inn
26. Ferber's "So ____"
28. Baseball's Williams
29. Hermitlike
31. "The ____ Love": 2 wds.
32. Cuff
33. Baby carriage
34. Gown
35. Ignore the alarm
36. Doctrine
37. Right: prefix
40. Ninny
42. Hansom
43. Poetic division
45. Gender: abbr.
48. Where everything is biggest
49. Prefix for four
51. Window type
52. Distribute
53. Bearings
54. Diamonds, e.g.
55. "The Egg ____": 2 wds.
56. Gaff
57. Bluenose
60. Ike's command: abbr.
61. "Happy Days ____ Here Again"

PUZZLE 139

ACROSS

1. Holy terror
5. Harden
8. Large primates
12. Facilitate
13. Limousine
14. Stuck on
15. Province
16. Part of to be
17. Witch's concoction
18. Explanation
20. UFO travelers
22. Finale
23. Heavy weight
24. Canasta boo-boo
28. Salute
32. Mineral bearing rock
33. Rim
35. ____ the line
36. Unwanted plants
39. Crisp fabric
42. Shad's output
44. ____ jacket
45. Stick up for
48. Sign up
52. Extremely dry
53. Elongated fish
55. Transport
56. Circle
57. Peeper
58. Wool producers
59. Leg joint
60. Rouge color
61. Preoccupied

DOWN

1. Grizzly, e.g.
2. Not fully cooked
3. On the water
4. Tormented
5. Discredit
6. Musical sense
7. Trick or ____
8. Pale-skinned mammal
9. Small opening
10. Smooth and level
11. Mends
19. ____ for the books
21. Land parcel
24. Do a lawn chore
25. Hard feelings
26. Witness
27. Ignited
29. Consumed
30. Lush
31. Hot beverage
34. Dressed up a room
37. Coat with flour
38. ____ of a gun
40. Quagmire
41. Fumble
43. Garden tool
45. Like some chocolate
46. ____ go bragh
47. Penalty
49. Minnesota's neighbor
50. Way of walking
51. Trial run
54. Sailor's yes

PUZZLE 140

ACROSS

1. "Planet of the ____"
5. ____ voyage
8. Stalk
12. Barbie, e.g.
13. Actress Remick
14. Employ
15. Wilmington's locale
17. Solo in an opera
18. Conditions
19. Guide
21. Dine
22. Whitney and Wallach
23. Decanters
26. Removes moisture from a window
29. Always, to a bard
30. Farrow of films
31. Cosmetics
35. Yield
38. Paul ____ of song
39. Adam's mate
40. Run
42. Realizes
46. You are something ____!
47. Superior
49. Close by
50. Cereal grain
51. Italian town
52. Hardy heroine
53. Opposite of SSW
54. Relax

DOWN

1. Inserts
2. T.S. Eliot, for one
3. Fitzgerald or Grasso
4. Blackboards
5. Explodes
6. "____ the ramparts . . ."
7. Essential
8. Actor Omar ____
9. Monotonous
10. ____ the Red
11. Beef
16. Feeble
20. ____ de France
23. Counterpart of masc.
24. Grassland
25. Little Rock's locale
27. Sloe ____ fizz
28. Had a chair
32. Sets foot in
33. Tiny Tim's instrument, for short
34. Clergyman
35. Connect
36. Not odd
37. "____ of the Pack"
40. Penny
41. Sheltered direction
43. ____-colored glasses
44. Crazy
45. Printer's direction
48. Light brown

PUZZLE 141

ACROSS

1. Recall subject
4. Not as much
8. Sunday seat
11. Muffin spread
13. Arthur ____ of tennis
14. Lobster eggs
15. ____ Ernie Ford
17. Off the deep ____
18. Use a swizzle stick
19. Lemon and orange drinks
21. Without repetition
24. Winter toys
27. Mend, as a sock
30. TV alien
32. Break suddenly
33. "____ Loser"
34. Guy's date
35. Refrain syllable
36. In the center of
38. Heathrow abbr.
39. Inquires
40. Hermit
42. Old oath
44. Thicken
46. At a ____ for words
49. Dairy-farm sound
51. Hawaiian export
55. Pitcher's stat
56. A Great Lake
57. Implement
58. Obtain
59. Valley
60. ____ Aviv

DOWN

1. Folding bed
2. Pub drinks
3. Lease
4. ____ Vegas
5. It precedes tee
6. New York stadium
7. Apple starters
8. Christmas packages
9. Long time period
10. Join together
12. French ____ soup
16. Marine bird
20. Overhead trains
22. Zoo enclosure
23. Gladden
25. Pitch-black
26. Health spots
27. Radio feature
28. Soldier's need, for short
29. Foul weather wear
31. Jolly Roger, for one
37. Dover's state: abbr.
39. Take as one's own
41. Lassoed
43. Pie ____ mode
45. Fizzle out
47. Primer pooch
48. ____ gin fizz
49. Ryan or Tilly
50. Lode load
52. Nothing
53. Lamprey
54. House extension

PUZZLE 142

• FILM FESTIVAL •

ACROSS

1. Toledo's location
5. Float
9. "Tosca," e.g.
10. Poet T.S. ____
12. Drama with Minnelli
14. Thriller with Stewart
17. Director B. De Mille
18. Pig's nose
20. Nape hair
21. Hot tub
24. Washington bills
26. Museum display
27. Paving material
28. Co. bigwig
29. Concluded
31. Musical biography with Hulce
35. New York team
36. Historic period
37. Author Fleming
38. Curve
39. Cinder
40. Bizarre
43. Sarcasm
46. Outdo
47. Song of praise
48. Snake's poison
50. Fizzy drinks
52. Boxing great
54. Poppycock!
56. Unit of work
57. Off. in baseball
60. Actor West
61. Comedy with Hoffman
63. Famed boat builder
65. Steal
66. City plan
67. ____ de Janeiro
68. Set loose
70. Farm enclosure
71. Small landmass
72. Solemn poem
75. Ties together
77. Satire with Allen
81. Southern story with Davis
84. Homer's TV wife
85. Solitary
86. "Up on the ____"
87. Uproar

DOWN

1. Iridescent stone
2. "I Was Made to Love ____"
3. Dander
4. Cereal grain
5. Gun an engine
6. Pub brew
7. Pine tree
8. Kids
9. Kimono sash
11. Can material
12. Midpoint
13. Perfect serve
15. Sentimentality
16. Small weight units
17. Slice up
19. Incisors, e.g.
20. ____ Tse-tung
21. Baseball's Musial
22. Writing tablet
23. Zone
25. Distress call
30. Uncooked
31. Disaster film with Hayes
32. Angry
33. Mr. Geller
34. Holiday classic with Finney
35. Spring month
41. Summer, in Paris
42. Charged particle

PUZZLE 142

44. Peculiar
45. Teachers' org.
48. Vitality
49. Bovine call
50. ____ Lanka
51. Nearest star
52. Worship
53. Tags
55. Male cats
56. Catch a glimpse of
58. Tidbit
59. Buckets
60. Woof!
62. Tit for ____
64. Gardening tool
69. Lamprey
71. Rink surface
73. Onyx, e.g.
74. Earth's term of revolution
75. Allowed the use of
76. Actor Vigoda
78. In favor of
79. Self-esteem
80. Basketball official, for short
81. Startle
82. Inventor Whitney
83. Menagerie

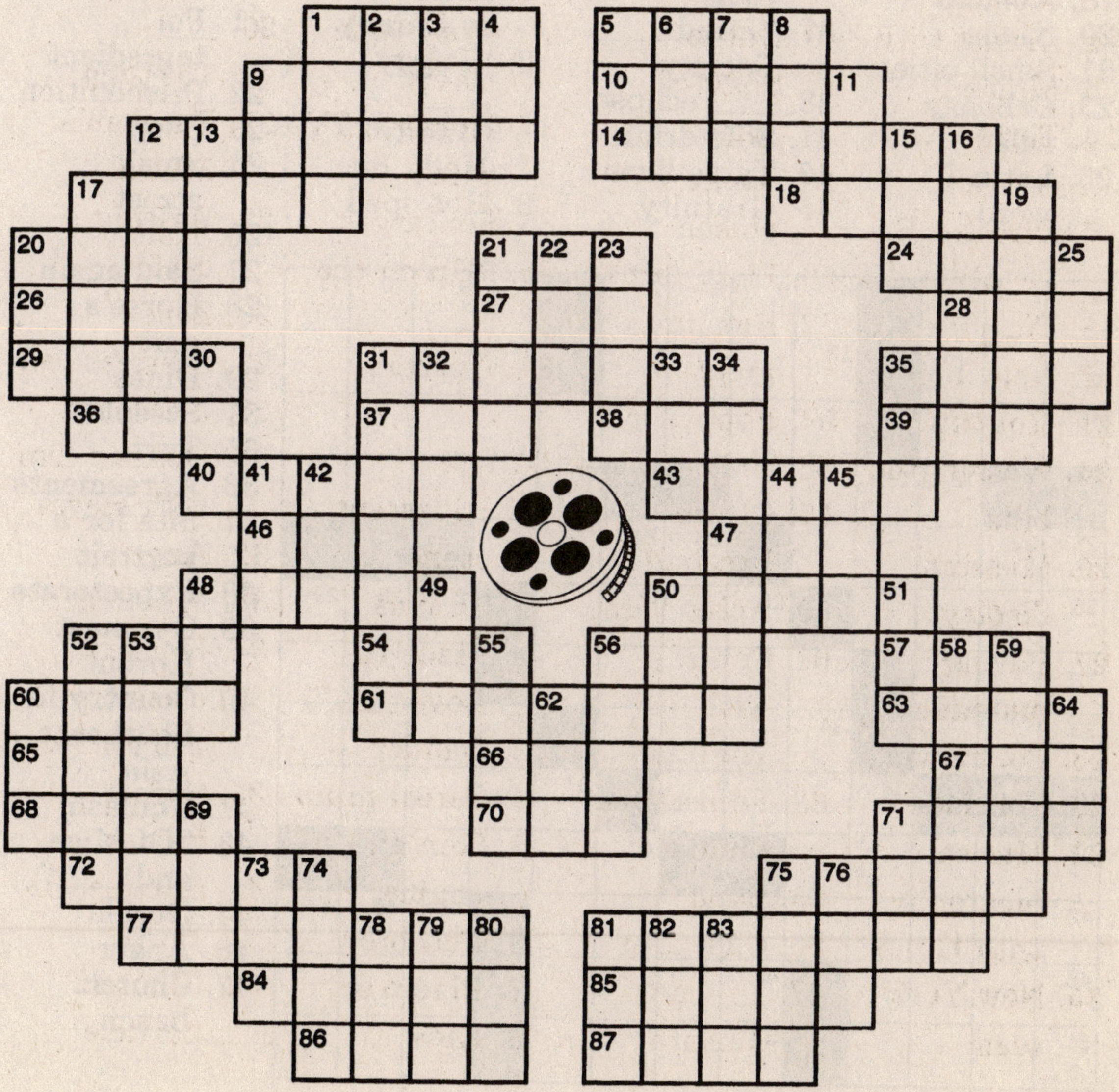

PUZZLE 143

ACROSS

1. Fire residue
4. Actress Moreno
8. First man
12. Regret
13. Small particle
14. Housecoat
15. Afternoon social
16. Daring
18. Abound
20. Kinds
21. Small cities
23. Cabbage salad
25. Latin I word
26. Male deer
27. Highway: abbr.
30. Gun the engine
31. Rock
32. Historic time
33. Single
34. Opening
35. Stain
36. Smoking tool
37. "Dead ____ Society"
38. ____ eclipse
41. Soft drink
42. Table linen
45. Gratuity
48. "____ Rhythm"
49. Fencing weapon
50. Before, to Keats
51. Soviet journalism organization: abbr.
52. Information
53. Morning moisture

DOWN

1. Linkletter or Carney
2. "Peggy ____" (Buddy Holly hit)
3. Hot spell
4. Good reviews
5. Article
6. Heavy weight
7. Quantity: abbr.
8. Bow's partner
9. "The Girl Next ____"
10. Border on
11. Confusion
17. Custom
19. Printer's measures
21. Poi ingredient
22. Premonition
23. Shop
24. Small street
26. Halt
27. Said again
28. Horse's gait
29. Dines
31. Steeple
35. Turf
36. Agreements
37. Sits for a portrait
38. Expectorate
39. Gymnast Korbut
40. Country in Southeast Asia
41. Goulash
43. "Of Mice and ____"
44. Gorilla
46. Anger
47. Church bench

PUZZLE 144

ACROSS

1. Ginger drinks
5. Twinkler
9. Tic-____-toe
12. Waiting room call
13. Faintly colored
14. Actor Vigoda
15. Dorothy's dog
16. Anticipated
18. Writer Bagnold
20. Blackboard
21. Dead duck
23. Egyptian queen, for short
25. Ancient
26. Diva's song
28. Highway vehicle
32. Ruta and Gypsy Rose
34. Strange
35. Way out
36. Extinct bird
37. "____ and the Swan"
39. ____ in the hole
40. Consumer
42. Monikers
44. Untied
47. Against
48. Made larger
51. Fairy tale opener
54. Victory sign
55. Information
56. ____-do-well
57. Tavern
58. Dog-paddled
59. First home

DOWN

1. Army insect
2. MGM lion
3. Made longer
4. Sly and the Family ____
5. Drove too fast
6. Levy
7. High mountain
8. Singer Della ____
9. Cheerio!
10. Aid in crime
11. Yield
17. Shut
19. A Gershwin
21. 24-karat ____
22. Bread spread
23. Fall drink
24. Actress Cheryl
27. Function
29. Looked over
30. Cats' quarries
31. Natives: suff.
33. The March King
38. ____ Arbor, Michigan
41. Mails
43. Make amends for
44. Famous pant manufacturer
45. Yoked animals
46. ____ for business
47. Actor West
49. Small crow
50. Greek letter
52. Bee follower
53. Sea eagle

PUZZLE 145

ACROSS

1. Dad's mate
4. Assist
8. Dry
12. Monkey
13. Spoken
14. Compete in a marathon
15. Hopping animal
17. Forewarning
18. Senior
19. Did the breast-stroke
21. Total
23. Rears
27. Burn
30. Competent
33. Fabricate
34. Bungalows
35. Coffee alternative
36. Fence opening
37. Gone by
38. Has lunch
39. Due
40. Wigwam's relative
42. Ocean
44. Singer Campbell
47. "Home ___"
51. "For Your Eyes ___"
54. Kind of rug
56. Jump
57. Snack
58. In addition to
59. Financial obligation
60. Toboggan
61. Of course!

DOWN

1. Construct
2. Iridescent gemstone
3. Repair
4. Collect greedily
5. Misjudge
6. Cambodia's neighbor
7. Cultivate
8. Scent
9. Male sheep
10. Frozen water
11. Lion's residence
16. Prepares, with up
20. Vigoda of "Barney Miller"
22. Information
24. Talon
25. Go fly a ___
26. Plant beginning
27. Gab
28. Enormous
29. On the summit
31. Wager
32. Scottish girl
36. Aims
38. Slippery fish
41. Cairo's nation
43. Type of seal
45. Recedes, as the tide
46. Astronaut Armstrong
48. All right
49. Number on a baseball team
50. Completes
51. Ancient
52. Wedding-announcement word
53. Science room, for short
55. Consumed food

PUZZLE 146

ACROSS

1. Desert nomad
5. Very small
8. Incline
12. Extinct bird
13. Notable period
14. Charles Lamb
15. Film with Darth Vader
17. Stumbled
18. Piece of corn
19. Showy flowers
21. Like the Milky Way
24. Very long time
25. Slippery fish
26. Agrees
30. Singer Torme
31. Boring
33. Please the cook
34. Guaranteed
36. Mr. Onassis
37. Drench
38. Share top billing
41. Spud
44. Crude metal
45. Like a bump on ____
46. Captain Kirk's TV series
51. Descartes
52. Hesitation sounds
53. Conk out
54. Digits
55. Occupied a chair
56. Ajar

DOWN

1. Paid notices
2. Spoil
3. Ohio college town
4. Driller
5. Exhausted
6. Make a mistake
7. Least difficult
8. Improve
9. Pub drinks
10. 5,280 feet
11. Chums
16. "____ of the Planets"
20. National flower
21. Trucker's rig
22. Adolescent
23. "____ Well That Ends Well"
26. Subsidize
27. Tidy
28. "GWTW" plantation
29. Move about
31. Horse's pace
32. Rests
35. Habits
38. Shoreline
39. Hockey great
40. Argument
41. Hair line
42. Toast topper
43. Actor Franchot ____
47. ____ la la
48. Split
49. Before, in verse
50. Barbie's boyfriend

PUZZLE 147

ACROSS

1. Masculine pronoun
4. Hairdo
8. Went by plane
12. Amazement
13. Increase
14. Helper
15. Canadian city
17. Zoo enclosure
18. Pay attention
19. Laid off
20. Edition
23. "____ for Two"
24. Borders
25. Never meeting
30. Fuss
31. Purchaser
32. Citrus drink
33. Nightgown
35. Mass reply
36. "Baby ____ Cold Outside"
37. Stadium
38. Boasts
41. Soda type
43. Vow
44. Without a saddle
48. Civic disturbance
49. "The Greatest Story ____ Told"
50. Caviar
51. "Desire Under the ____"
52. Wren's home
53. Mist

DOWN

1. "Green Eggs and ____"
2. ____ Jima
3. Males
4. Consent
5. Liberate
6. Street
7. Night bird
8. Beautifying treatment
9. Fibber
10. "The ____ of Night"
11. Do a garden chore
16. Therefore
19. Dread
20. Teheran's country
21. Facet
22. Air pollution
23. Oak or chestnut
25. Certain dogs
26. Sailor's affirmative
27. Shiny fabric
28. Paradise
29. Horne or Olin
31. Pieces
34. Lamps
35. Certain Mid-easterner
37. Warn
38. Dull person
39. Fence part
40. Little particle
41. Shelter in a rock
42. Minerals
44. Statesman Franklin
45. Dog's sound
46. Dove's noise
47. Beer container

PUZZLE 148

ACROSS
1. Trade
5. Vigor
8. Singe
12. Nobleman
13. Boat paddle
14. Ebb
15. Riches
17. Funnyman Johnson
18. Pecan, e.g.
19. Rotated
21. Concur
24. Microbe
25. Chimney dirt
26. Crooner Crosby
27. Away
30. Shade tree
31. Knife
32. Compete
33. Fruit drink
34. Contact ____
35. Cotton bundle
36. Clean house
37. Wind-storms
38. Gazes
41. Small rug
42. Simple
43. Dublin citizens
48. Great Lake
49. Butterfly catcher
50. Roof edge
51. Night light
52. Obtained
53. Actress Barrymore

DOWN
1. Place
2. Combat
3. Exist
4. Mars or Saturn
5. Sulk
6. Lend an ____
7. Makes believe
8. Flock
9. Make a buck
10. Feed the kitty
11. Woodwind
16. "A Boy Named ____"
20. Goad
21. On the ocean
22. Precious metal
23. Eternal City
24. Monster
26. Miracle
27. Face shape
28. Manicurist's item
29. Charges
31. Sky color
35. Took a shower
36. Laundry appliance
37. Auto fuel
38. Understands
39. Sour
40. India's continent
41. Catcher's glove
44. Old car
45. Month before Apr.
46. Night before a holiday
47. Recent

PUZZLE 149

ACROSS

1. Clear
4. Silky
8. Snow runners
12. Wrath
13. Request
14. Lofty
15. Think about
17. "For Your Eyes ___"
18. Complete
19. Puppy
20. Man's title
21. Deli meat
24. Brag
27. ___ Francisco
28. Wine or pepper color
29. Battalion
30. Tail action
31. Highway charge
32. Grab
33. Wages
34. Composed
35. Cut, as bread
37. Observe
38. Kind of dance
39. Dishes
43. Scoop
45. "The ___ Heart"
47. Military crime: abbr.
48. Great Lake
49. Practice
50. Comfortable rooms
51. Abilities
52. Knight of "Too Close for Comfort"

DOWN

1. Cereal grain
2. Pump ___ (lift weights)
3. Dimple
4. Ghost
5. Less adolescent
6. Price of entry
7. Paving material
8. Armless seat
9. Jumping animal
10. Under the weather
11. Stallone's nickname
16. Cowardly
19. Quayle or Rather
21. Droop
22. Turn to liquid
23. Still
24. Forbids
25. Verbal
26. Appetite for success
27. Declare
30. Lump
31. Indulge
33. Energy
34. Actor/director Orson ___
36. Names
37. Divide
40. Tight
41. You are something ___
42. Origin
43. Rotten
44. Wonder
45. Iced drink
46. Foul up

PUZZLE 150

ACROSS

1. Harden
4. Die down
9. Weep
12. Rowing blade
13. Soft drinks
14. Color
15. Hulk Hogan and Roddy Piper
17. First in a series
18. Mocked
19. Put up
21. Lightened
23. Rewards
25. Forehead
26. Shore up
27. Gunn from "Treasure Island"
28. Dish
29. Frenzied
32. Quick-tempered
33. Brave warrior
34. Heartaches
37. Travesty
38. Adobe materials
39. Next in line
40. Outfit
41. Wall covering
46. Actress Plumb
47. Tennis player Chris ____
48. Side sheltered from the wind
49. Unite in marriage
50. Values
51. Up to now

DOWN

1. Put in seeds
2. Hearing organ
3. Treachery
4. Performed
5. Unafraid
6. Beerlike beverage
7. Sailor
8. Substance
9. Sneakers
10. Unit of weight
11. Red veggies
16. Gush out
20. Regret
21. Ease off
22. "Car 54, Where ____ You?"
23. ____ tacks
24. Hot breakfast cereal
26. ____ up (explode)
28. Thrive
29. Gaily
30. Curve
31. Female rabbit
32. Have a bawl
33. Welcome
34. Have a ____ loose
35. Kind of oil
36. Boiled over
37. Hat materials
39. At this place
42. Frank's ex
43. Profit
44. Formerly named
45. Acquire

PUZZLE 151

Diagramless crosswords are solved by using the clues and their numbers to fill in the answer words and the arrangement of black squares. Insert the number of each clue with the first letter of its answer, across and down. Fill in a black square at the end of each word. Every black square must have a corresponding black square on the opposite side of the diagram to form a symmetrical pattern. Puzzles have been started for you.

ACROSS
1. Espy
5. Petty quarrel
9. Cubbyhole

11. Permission
12. Change
13. Boo-boo
14. Command to Dobbin
15. Likely
17. Sloth for one
18. Squirrel away
20. Nourished
21. Renter's contract
23. Baseball's Maglie
25. Common ____
28. TV's Brokaw
29. Canopy or bunk
30. Faucet
32. Silly
34. Degrade
36. Paris's ____ Quarter
37. Saltpeter
38. Journey
39. Waist wear

DOWN
1. Hang-up
2. Heaps
3. Eightsome
4. Common word
5. Sunday talk: abbr.
6. Analyze grammatically
7. Shun
8. Sea eagle
10. Clean the slate
11. Tennis call
16. Stage
19. Completely
20. Swamp
22. Auto type
23. Depth-finding device
24. Fine violin
26. Aver
27. Artist's stand
28. Slant
29. Dancer Vereen
31. Saucy
33. Pinch
35. ____ and tucker

PUZZLE 152

ACROSS
1. Grasp
5. Singer Davis
8. Mental flash

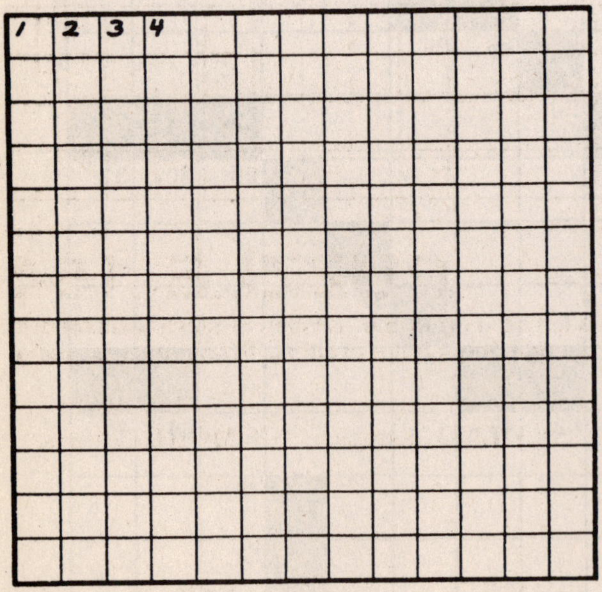

9. Upon
11. Missing
12. Put aside
14. Joyce Kilmer poem
16. Mr. Rogers
17. Add
19. London gallery
20. Tear
22. Those holding office
23. "____ All Odds"
25. Drink cooler
26. "____ the season . . ."
27. Breathe heavily
29. Groan producer
31. Louvre offering
32. Monet's support
36. Tether
39. Peruvian native
40. Land measure
41. Hog fat
42. Pull
43. Tater

DOWN
1. To the ____ (fully)
2. Aroma
3. ____ majesty
4. Palm fruits
5. "Welcome" site
6. One ____ time: 2 wds.
7. Snakes
10. Scheme
13. Regard
15. Sudden increase in flow
18. Actress Farrow
19. Explosive letters
21. Abyss
22. Publish
23. Behave
24. ____ in the bud
25. Whole
27. "____ Joey"
28. Neighborhood
30. Hits solidly
33. Ginger cookie
34. Light tan
35. Actress Cheryl
37. Angel's favorite initials
38. Chop

PUZZLE 153

ACROSS
1. Lowest female voice
5. Imp
8. Father
11. Sparrow
12. Melee
14. Completed
15. Supplemented
16. Solo for Sills
17. Paradise
18. "____ Little Indians"
19. Sleeveless Arab cloak
22. House addition
23. Solemn promise
24. Transfer design
26. Fencing sword
29. Withered
30. Nocturnal bird
31. Partiality
34. Male sheep
37. Mr. Durocher
38. Total
39. Three: Sp.
41. Unparented one
45. Ocean
46. Sick
47. Bullfight shout
48. Specimen
52. Unable to hear
54. Health resort
55. Help
56. Self-esteem
57. Nuisance
58. Remnant
59. Ruler's creation
62. Three, in cards
64. Sluggish
66. Gained the victory
68. Uris character
71. "____ Fine Day"
72. Liable
75. Undisguised
76. Bars
78. Healing plant
79. Seaweed's gelatinlike product
80. Roy's love
81. Tibia, e.g.
82. Set
83. Condensed moisture
84. Concludes

DOWN
1. Assist in wrongdoing
2. Prefer
3. Current style
4. Unusual
5. Time period
6. Monetary units of Italy, once
7. Prevent the success of
8. Clumsy, extinct bird
9. Once more
10. Lair
13. Story
14. Cause to grow
19. Highest card
20. Tavern
21. Keen
25. Double curve
27. Game played on horseback
28. Pitcher
31. Lowest male voice
32. Concept
33. First man
35. Very dry
36. Turmoil
40. Lava resembling cinders
42. Stockings
43. High mountains
44. Orderly
49. Spouse
50. Fibber
51. Brink
53. Number of each page
57. For each
60. Roadside hotel
61. Wedding-announcement word
63. Front lawn
65. Claw
66. Salary
67. Using speech
69. Street
70. Lazy
73. Small lake
74. Golf pegs
75. Purse
77. Join with stitches
78. Mr. Beame

Starting box on page 562

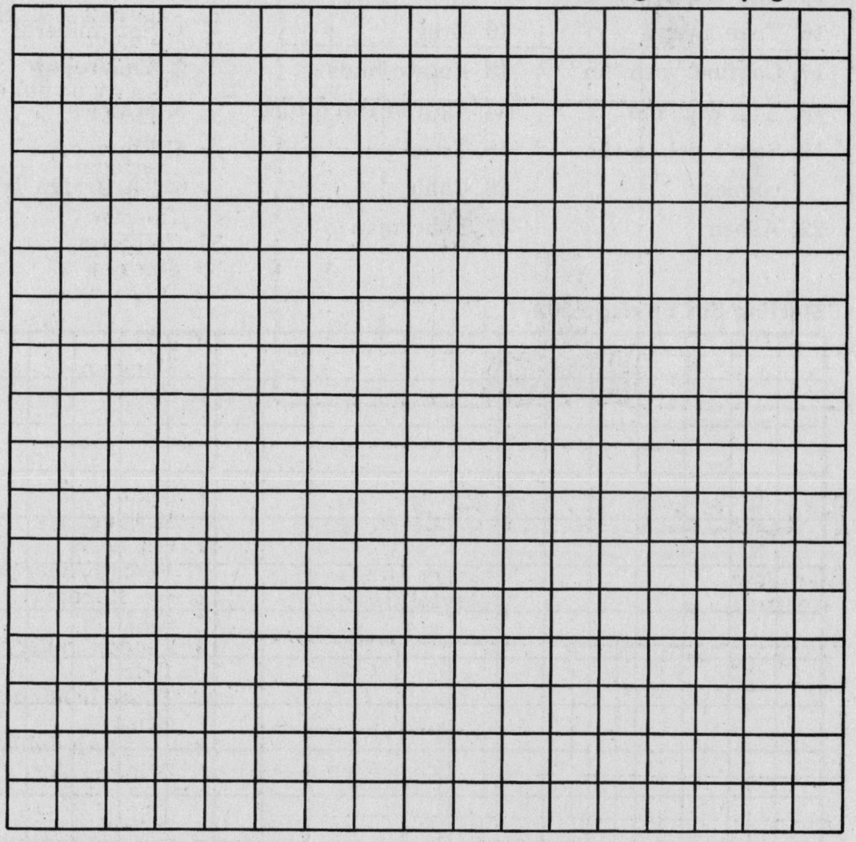

CHANGAWORD

PUZZLE 154

Can you change the top word into the bottom word in each column in the number of steps indicated in parentheses? Do not change the order of the letters, and change only 1 letter at a time. Proper names, slang, and obsolete words are not allowed.

1. HARD (4 steps)

ROCK

2. SAND (5 steps)

HILL

3. MEND (5 steps)

SOCK

4. MORE (5 steps)

RENT

PUZZLE 155

ACROSS

1. Pull behind
4. Director Burrows
5. Blockhead
6. Obese
9. Sketches through thin paper
11. Made amends
15. Cup handle
16. Take away
17. Confine, with "in"
18. ____ England
19. Sam's pal, in the comics
22. Ashen
25. Aroma
26. Walk restlessly
27. Least desirable
29. Sidewalk trash
31. Actress Wallace
32. Over there
33. Sick
36. Youngest Keaton on "Family Ties"
40. Brag
43. Potato buds
44. Sign of the future
45. Tread
46. Chair
47. Policeman
49. That girl
51. Federated
55. Stamping tool
56. Call it quits
57. Investment income
60. Piping god
61. Mangle
62. Pewter ingredient
63. Expert aviator

DOWN

1. Soft mineral
2. Woodwind
3. Marries
5. Limo, e.g.
6. "A Bridge Too ____"
7. Devoured
8. Paciorek of baseball
9. Ball holder
10. Male sheep
12. Not any
13. Night before a holiday
14. Morning moisture
17. Steed
19. Female hog
20. Marriage response
21. Nobleman
22. Unconvincing
23. Drama division
24. Grant's opponent
26. Brooch
28. Oriental beverage
29. Moo
30. Curved bone
32. Word of permission
34. At large
35. Gold fabric
37. Clear profit
38. Color
39. Corded fabric
41. Great expanse
42. Explosive: abbr.
45. Skewer
47. Mutt
48. Singleton
49. "Little ____ Echo"
50. Biddy
52. Pointed end
53. Period in history
54. Room for relaxation
55. Press for payment
57. Actress Moreno
58. ____ the Red
59. Quality of sound

Starting box on page 562

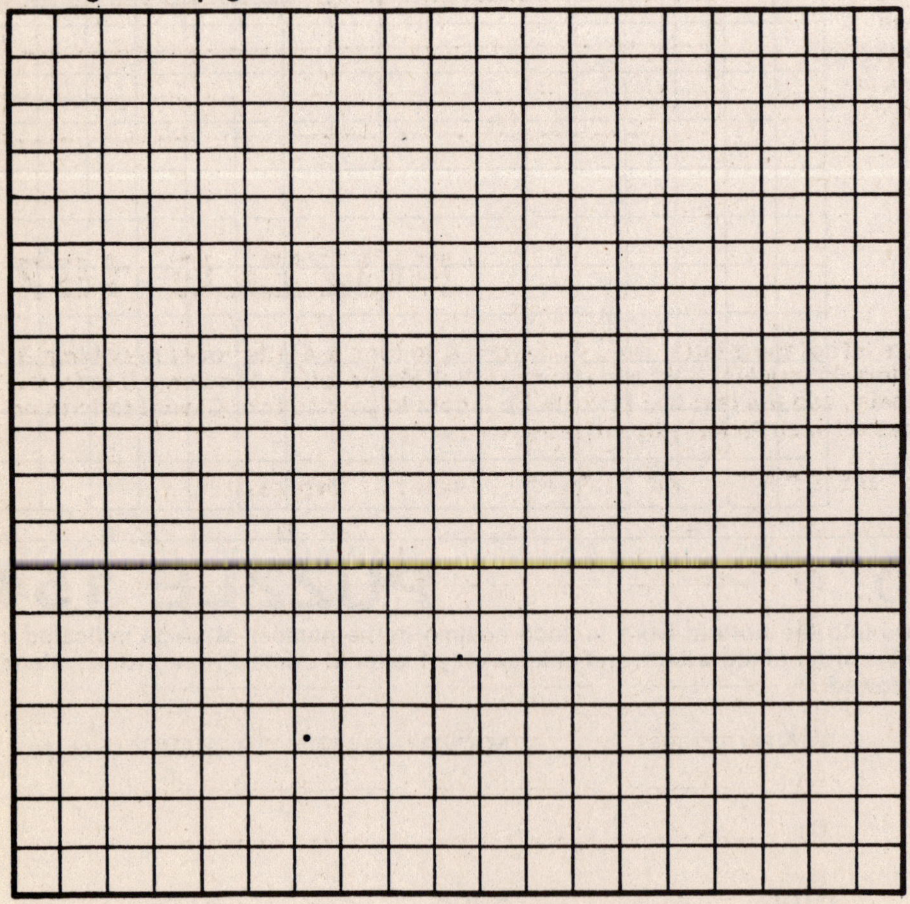

PUZZLE 156

ACROSS

1. Theme
6. Company of desert travelers
8. Twin-hulled vessel
10. Wall painting
11. Wanderer
13. Driller
14. Parking device
16. Doctrine
17. Pleasant-tasting
19. Desertlike
20. Great affection
21. Dab
22. Posed
23. Above
25. Flooring square
26. Asian antelope
28. Not now
29. Send payment
31. Two-footed animal
32. English breed of cattle
34. Rescued
35. Parts
37. Barbarous people
38. Greek letters

DOWN

1. Turkic language
2. Spoken
3. Knave of clubs
4. Terrible tsar
5. Billiards shot
6. Mark of omission
7. Identifies
8. Healed
9. Of birth
10. Supervised an exam
12. Opened a bank account
13. Scolder
15. Emulated
16. Mulberry cloths
18. Discourage
24. Pears and apples
25. Records a TV show
27. Old ____ tale
28. Resides
30. November birthstone
31. Actor Alan ____
33. Church part
34. Long narrative
36. "Brother ____"

Starting box on page 562

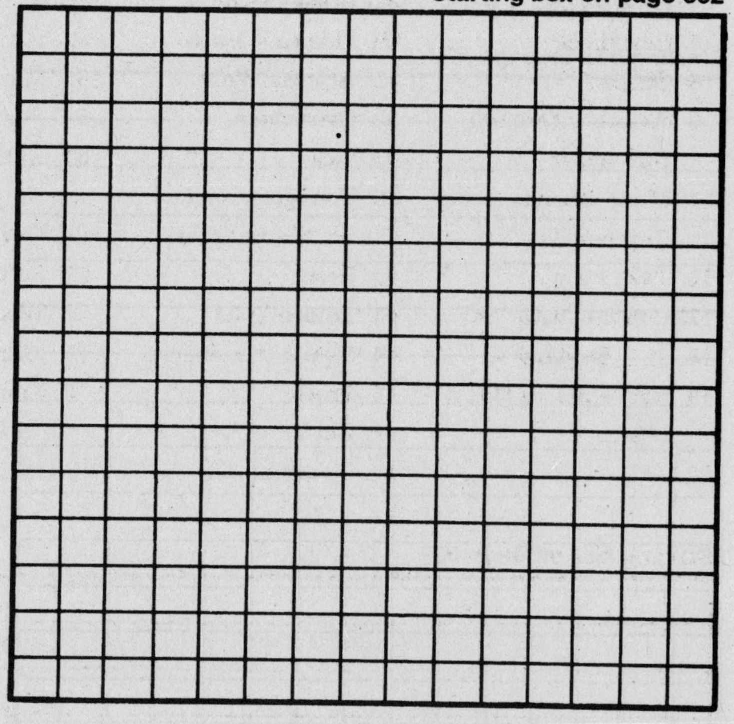

PICK-ME-UPS — PUZZLE 157

Add any two Pick-Me-Up letters left of the 2-letter word in column A to form a 4-letter word in column B, rearranging the order of the letters if you wish. Next add two more Pick-Me-Up letters to column B to form a 6-letter word for column C. Finally, add the last two Pick-Me-Up letters to your column C word to form an 8-letter word for column D. Cross off each Pick-Me-Up letter as you use it.

PICK-ME-UPS	A.	B.	C.	D.
EXAMPLE: D E E P R T	Ad	Read	Depart	Departed
1. E L N O P R	As	______	______	______
2. F F F I R U	El	______	______	______
3. E L M P R T	Da	______	______	______
4. E I N R S S	It	______	______	______
5. E F R T T Y	La	______	______	______
6. E N P S S T	Re	______	______	______
7. C C D N O T	Us	______	______	______

PUZZLE 158

ACROSS
1. Tilted
5. Son of Noah
9. Hebrew spy
11. Gawk
12. Copy changer
14. House flights
15. Three or four
17. Elgin ____
18. Mexican shawl
19. Grinned
20. Collection
21. Welcome or place
23. ____ diem
24. Bus station
26. ____ Moines
27. Open
29. Rodent
31. Palm
34. Faced
35. Distinctive time
36. Pesky pismire
38. Mountains, in Madrid
40. Candles
43. Uses leftovers
44. Recluse
46. Musical movement
47. Cower
48. Safe spot
49. Scissors quickly
50. Snow vehicle
51. Comfort

Starting box on page 562

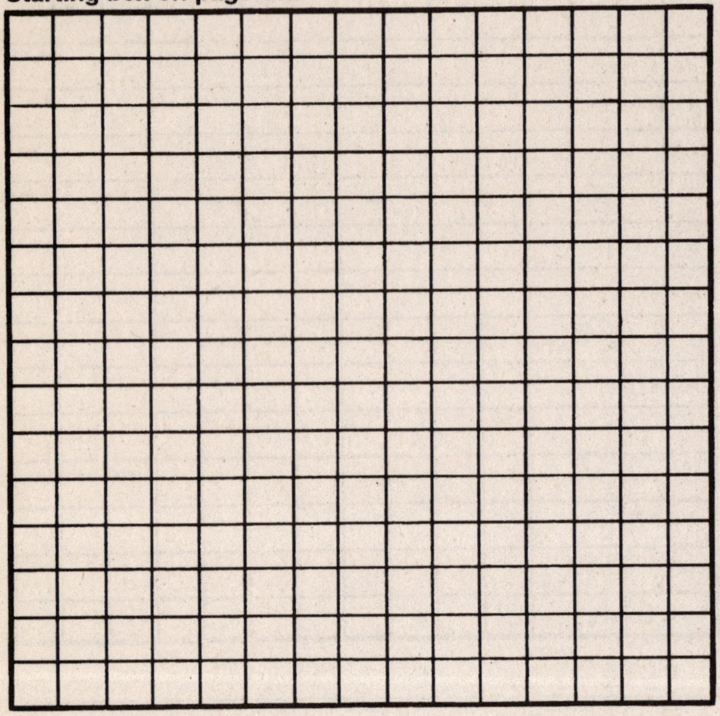

DOWN
1. Tennis serves
2. Stows cargo
3. Martini garnishes
4. ____ out (diminished)
5. Homes for Swale and Alysheba
6. Greeter
7. Did wrong
8. Military meal
10. Chemical salt
11. Chevron unit
13. Talk informally
14. "My Sister ____"
16. Dud
17. Time zone: abbr.
22. Essence
25. Place
26. River in Scotland
28. Furious
29. Weaseled out
30. Reach
32. Pickled garnishes
33. Spring flower
34. N.Amer. Indian
35. Curve
37. Popular table game
38. ____ of Honor
39. WWII area
41. S.Amer. country
42. "The Thirty-nine ____"
43. Cheers
45. Otherwise

PUZZLE 159

DAISY

Form six 7-letter words using the letters in each daisy petal PLUS the letter G. Next, form a bonus 7-letter word using the first letters of these words and beginning with the center letter G.

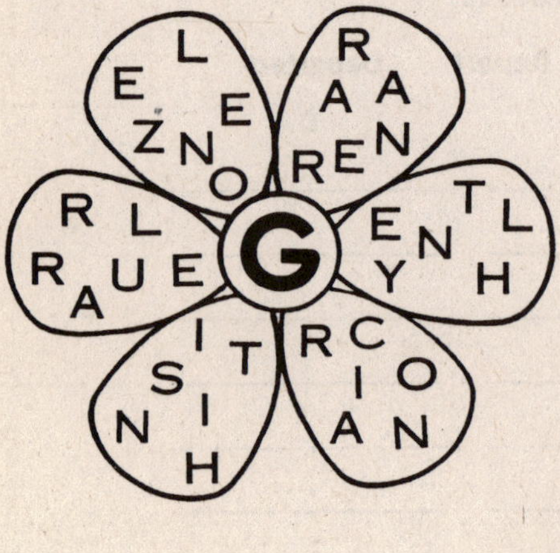

PUZZLE 160

ACROSS
1. Dog's foot
4. Sensible
5. Ship's record
8. Eighth interval
11. Declare positively
13. Border upon
15. Mediterranean ____
16. Diminish
17. Track circuit
18. Precious
19. "____ Miserables"
20. ____ Diego
21. Building wing
22. Foreign film captions
26. Baseballer Gehrig
27. Publicize
28. Expiation
31. "____ the fields we go . . . "
33. Us: Sp.
34. Go astray
36. Winglike parts
37. Ink writer
38. Uttered
40. Equipment
41. Boys
42. Ocean movement
43. Dog's neckband
45. Novelist Wallace
46. Republic of Ireland
47. Health resort

DOWN
1. Covenant
2. Picnic pest
3. "Pop Goes the ____"
4. Dinner course
5. Statute
6. Egg-shaped
7. Chromosome units
9. Calf meat
10. Cup handle
12. Consequence
13. Jai ____
14. Small chickens
18. ____ Moines
20. Astonished
23. Scare word
24. Fib
25. Novelist Hemingway
28. Exist
29. Long periods of time
30. Follow behind
31. Medley
32. Birds of prey
35. Go by car
36. Circle segment
37. Remove rind
39. Morning moisture
41. Zhivago's love
44. Cup rim

Starting box on page 562

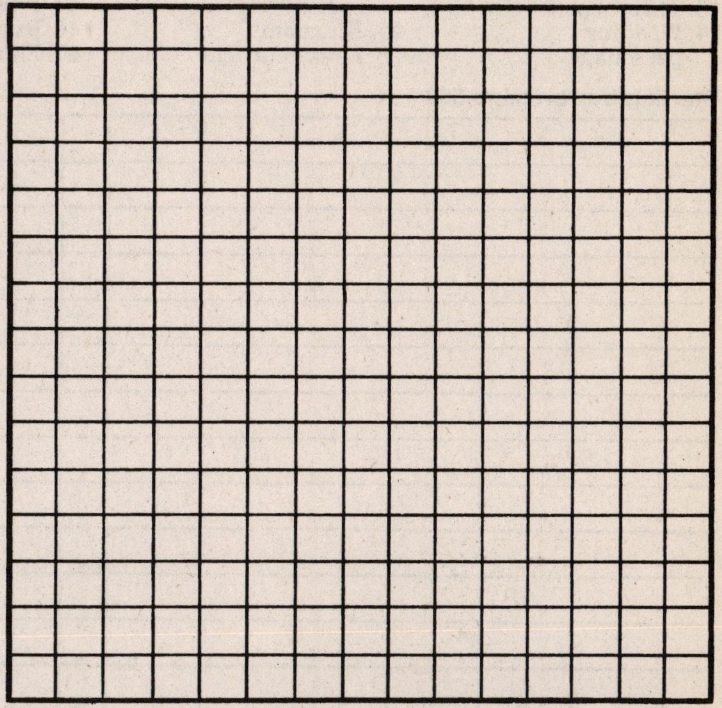

WORD MATH

PUZZLE 161

In these long-division problems, letters are substituted for numbers. Determine the value of each letter. Then arrange the letters in order from 0 to 9, and they will spell a word or phrase.

1

0	1	2	3	4	5	6	7	8	9

```
          A L E
HEAL | D A W D L E
       H E A L
       A T G H L
       A A L L T
         K D L O E
         K K E D L
           K E A T
```

2

0	1	2	3	4	5	6	7	8	9

```
          H O D
TRIO | E D I T O R
       Z I D T
       U T Z A O
       U A T R I
         T O O E R
         T H A Z I
           U O A D
```

3

0	1	2	3	4	5	6	7	8	9

```
          L E D
DALE | T O L L E D
       D A L E
       C K T D E
       C L B O E
         C U T B D
         C O A T B
           L D L D
```

PUZZLE 162

ACROSS
1. Indonesian boat
5. Of the pelvis
6. Fidel's land
10. Compact
11. Neighborhood
12. Dynamite
13. Throw open
14. Wedding personage
15. Accrual
16. Far Eastern
18. Genetic unit
19. Commitment
21. Chorus member
22. Dental concern
25. Ancient Palestine region
27. Kingdom
28. Letter curlicue
29. Grassland
32. Troops
33. Perspective
34. Caustic remark
35. Floor utensil
36. Middle age
37. Indian term of respect
38. Fracas
39. Actor Gordon ____
40. Toward shelter
41. Generator
44. Physique
46. Bucket type
47. Flaxen
49. Style
51. Pound subdivision
52. Exchange words
53. Genesis brother
54. Circumvent
55. Dry
56. Boring tool
57. Tall grass

DOWN
1. Implore
2. Washer cycle
3. Tobacco oven
4. Expert
5. Dawdling
6. Poem division
7. Of the city
8. Snout
9. Swiss river
12. Small nail
13. Disengage
14. Coffin stand
15. Whit
16. To a T
17. Bridge coup
18. Musical sign
20. Thrown out
21. Mine entrance
22. Mine car
23. Flying prefix
24. Inclined walkway
26. Nobel chemist
28. Place for valuables
29. Comedian Bert
30. Silkworm
31. French cleric
33. Portfolio
34. Breakfast meat
36. Serve a meal
37. Identical
38. Miss, in Marseilles
39. Construct
40. Assistant
42. Over there
43. Not a one
44. Mistake
45. Remus or Sam
47. Scarves
48. Car job
49. Estimate
50. Concluded
52. Despondent
54. Attention

Starting box on page 562

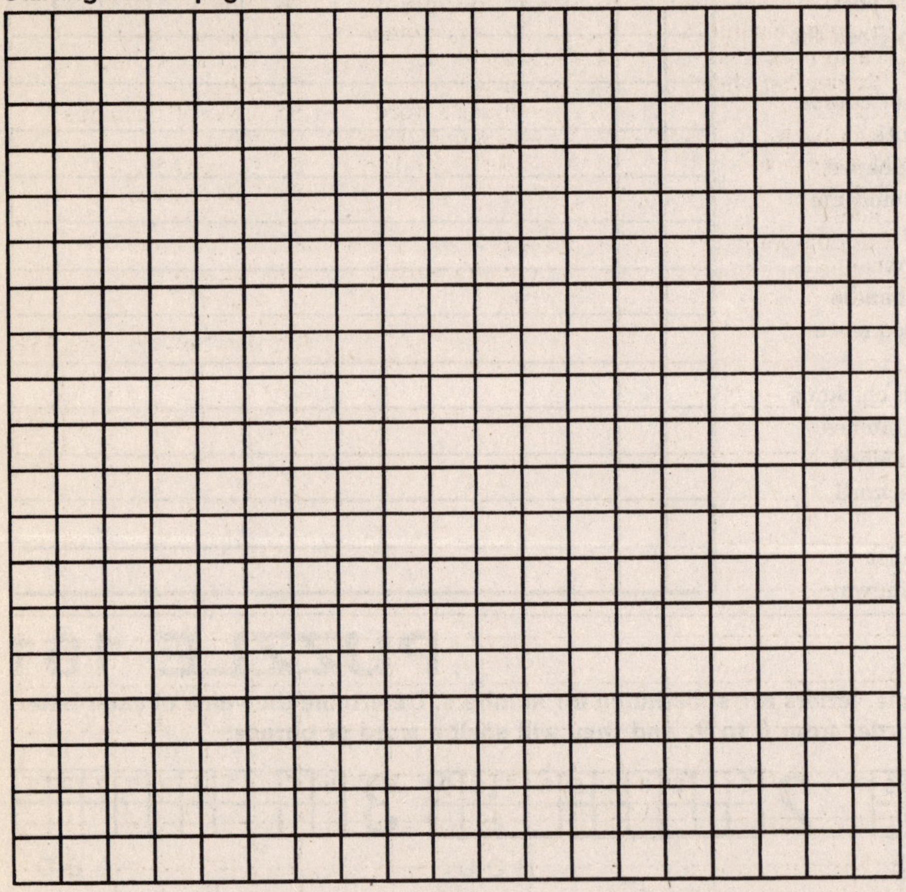

PUZZLE 163 Deduction Problem

GREEN THUMB

George arranged four flower beds in a square around a central birdbath. The spring bulbs he planted, one kind to each bed, were daffodils, hyacinths, crocuses, and tulips. George put only one color in each bed. The daffodils were yellow; the other flowers, in no particular order, were pink, white, and purple. If the hyacinths were diagonally across from the crocuses, the white flowers were next to the purple ones (in a clockwise direction), the tulips were not purple, and the crocuses were not pink, how did George lay out his garden?

PUZZLE 164

• U.S.A. TRIO •

ACROSS

1. ____ Alonzo Stagg
5. Sprite
8. Christie's title
9. Fateful phrase: 2 wds.
12. Duffer's quest
15. Tool's mate
16. Norwegian king
17. Corrode
18. Pub drink
19. Anger
20. Washington, D.C.: 3 wds.
26. Yemen's capital
27. Graf ____
28. Brando film, with "The"
29. Large tub
32. Refrain syllable
33. ____ as the hills
34. "I ____ Camera": 2 wds.
35. Spanish cheer
37. French composer
39. Tax agcy.
41. "A Lesson from ____"
46. Mr. Ritter
47. Olden times
48. ". . . the ____ of time"
49. Washington: 4 wds.
56. Kingly
57. New Mexico resort
58. Sugarloaf site, for short
59. Scents
60. Pose
61. Droops
63. War vessel: abbr.
65. ____-tse
66. Rodent
69. Owned
71. Compass pt.
72. Football's Haji-Sheikh
73. Poet Khayyam
75. Roman and Victorian
79. George Washington: 3 wds.
85. Gold to Cortez
86. Spot's doc
87. "____ a creature . . . "
88. ____ for thought
90. Go swiftly
91. Kind of turn
92. WWII agcy.
93. Ms. St. Vincent Millay
94. Linguistic suffix
95. Clarinet part

DOWN

1. "Much ____ About Nothing"
2. Fountain drinks
3. Nebraska city
4. Lucky number
5. Prepare copy
6. Italian coin, once
7. Sense
9. Author Levin
10. Period
11. Inventor Elisha
12. Warm boot-liner
13. "Remember the ____!"
14. Push back
21. Of a service branch
22. Choose
23. Fiddling emperor
24. Marine mammal: 2 wds.
25. Terre Haute's st.
30. Stradivari's teacher
31. Ancient weights
36. Baseball miscues
38. Type of soup
40. Ongoing movie fare
41. Baseball bat wood
42. Order's partner
43. ____ to a customer
44. Sullivan et al.
45. Concorde
47. Sycophant's word
49. Letters angels love
50. Spread hay to dry
51. Past
52. Asphalt
53. Subways' kin
54. Flashy show-off: 2 wds.
55. Roman wear
62. Planted
64. Press down
66. Battle of Britain monogram
67. Look ____!
68. Rolling stock
70. Patriotic gp.
74. Nevada city
76. Allude
77. Battery part
78. Author Irving
79. Seep
80. Leon of "Exodus" fame
81. Cowpunch
82. Kin of aves.
83. Distress call
84. ____ a boy!
89. Palindromic parent

Starting box on page 562

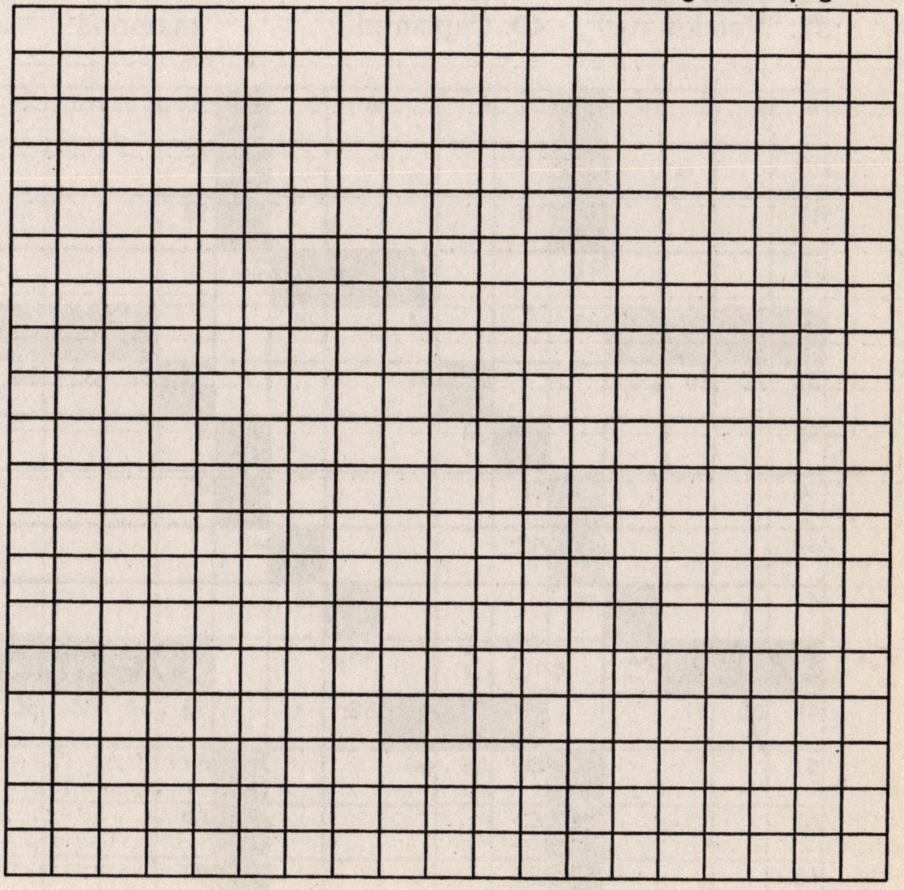

PUZZLE 165

ACROSS

1. Fret
5. Engine
10. Thick slice
14. Mama's mate
15. Expiate
16. "A Whiter Shade of ____"
17. Way out
18. Spirited horse
19. Kind of code
20. Decree
22. Restaurant request
23. Sweat
27. Count
31. Road
32. Wooden nail
35. Yearns
36. "The ____ Crystal"
37. Rotary-phone feature
38. Remedy
39. Canine treats
40. "Do ____ others . . ."
41. Type of bomb
42. ____ and ends
43. Gorges
44. Spider's creation
45. Actor Nicholas ____
46. Hues
47. Kind of instinct
49. Captured
52. Further
57. Sleeping
58. Raft wood
61. Went on horseback
62. Prayer
63. Model
64. Kitchen feature
65. Vend
66. Implements
67. Bucky ____ of baseball

DOWN

1. Hurried
2. Hack
3. Heroic
4. Electricity unit
5. Boss
6. Water mammal
7. Shoe tip
8. ____ for the books
9. Herring color
10. Bowling term
11. Animal fat
12. Out of the weather
13. Endure
21. Gibbons, e.g.
22. Swedish coin
24. Malign
25. Whittles
26. Writing fluids
27. Large parrot
28. Sharp
29. Vibrate
30. Abound
32. Kind of bean
33. Consumer
34. Luster
36. Sidestep
37. Twofold
39. Miss the ____
43. Unaccompanied
45. Soup container
46. Artificial waterways
47. Decoration
48. Of the nose
49. Touches
50. Fit
51. On an even ____
53. Trampled
54. Threw
55. Utopia
56. Monthly payment
58. Morsel
59. Activity
60. Zodiac lion

PUZZLE 166

ACROSS
1. Created
5. Paddles
9. Scientific workshop
12. ____ the Terrible
13. Dispute
14. Reasonable
15. McHenry or Knox
16. A new ____ on life
17. Shoot forth
18. Wild
20. Modernizes
22. Drab
24. Baseball statistic: abbr.
25. Poker payment
26. Evening meal
30. Entranced
33. Collar or jacket
36. American Indian
37. Actress Lupino
38. Version
40. Large weight
41. Was solicitous
43. Pace
44. Summer bloom
45. Corrects
47. Surrender
49. Hint
50. Expunges
53. Withdraws
58. Venerates
60. Part of HOMES
61. Perch
63. Knowledge
64. Baseball number
65. Overact
66. Border
67. Single
68. Groups
69. Buck or stag

DOWN
1. Offend
2. Evade
3. Risk taker
4. Plead
5. Miner's find
6. Food thickener
7. Ploy
8. Appeared
9. Shiny cloth
10. Indigo
11. Chances
13. Cautioned
14. Enclosed cars
19. Half of a French dance
21. Celestial hunter
23. Abominable Snowmen
27. Defense group: abbr.
28. Self-images
29. Philosopher Descartes
30. Wedding confetti
31. First name
32. Skin
34. Baseball great
35. Brother's daughter
38. Comedian Murphy
39. Do a surgeon's job
42. Menu item
44. Fixed a shoe
46. Some tires
48. Pop
51. Wear down
52. Worsted fabric
53. Gambling city
54. Actress Moran
55. Prong
56. Heavy reading
57. Chimney output
59. Palmist
62. Holy people: abbr.

PUZZLE 167

ACROSS

1. Unite
4. Spurt
7. ____ diem
10. Very large: pref.
11. Shoshonean Indian
12. Attest
14. Thus
15. "____ Done Him Wrong"
16. Essential
18. Against: pref.
19. Hog's home
20. Escape
21. Disorder
22. Aviator
25. Formerly named
26. Grand
28. Demon
31. Last letter: Brit.
34. Wallet item
35. Mexican liquor
38. Help
40. Speak
41. Printed cambric
44. Ocean
46. Edible tuber
47. Spooky
48. Kill time
50. Young boy
52. Square
54. Straight
58. Improve
61. Water barrier
62. Kinds
63. Film
64. Tavern
65. Playing marble
66. Furnace
67. Building addition
68. ____ Gemayel
69. Allow
70. Ingested
71. Sprinted

DOWN

1. Desires
2. Kind of tax
3. Expire
4. Fairness
5. Chemical compound
6. Popular shirt
7. Tar
8. Corrupt
9. Stoutness
10. Bill of fare
13. Play in water
14. Noah's son
17. Gypsy Rose ____
19. Twirl
23. Frequently, in literature
24. Cravat
27. Kind of bear
29. Peer
30. Pecan or cashew
31. Destroy
32. Abel's mom
33. Risk taker
36. English river
37. Appendage
39. Chill
42. Rim
43. Snaky fish
44. Large
45. Dutch town
49. Riddle
50. Flee
51. Berserk
53. Grown-up
55. Illinois city
56. Associated
57. Half of an African fly
59. Egyptian river
60. Depression
64. Legume
65. Swiss river

PUZZLE 168

ACROSS
1. Poplar
6. Peruvian Indian
10. Wooden pins
14. Cite
15. Birth covering
16. Writer Waugh
17. Ger. craft: hyph.
18. Do as a bear does
20. Cinder
21. Implement
23. Ohio town
24. Arctic
26. Weaver of myth
28. Eats away
30. Anoint, of old
31. Murmured
32. Big Dipper: 2 wds.
36. College cheer
37. Writer Horatio
38. Numero ——
39. Little Dipper: 2 wds.
42. Maryland town
44. Film barbarian
45. Scant
46. Scriptures
49. Woodland deity
50. Pronged
51. Artist Chagall
52. Cyprinid fish
55. Stuffed toy: 2 wds.
58. Hardship
60. Feminine suffix
61. Tangelo
62. Source of Solomon's gold
63. Rivers: Sp.
64. Tipplers
65. Electric units

DOWN
1. Turquoise
2. Stand-ins
3. Dismisses lightly: hyph.
4. Greek H
5. Vexed
6. Ethereal fluid
7. Brad
8. Young scout
9. Pub potable
10. Cure-all
11. Israeli port
12. Fare: 2 wds.
13. Vista
19. Empire
22. Hemisphere group: abbr.
25. Lyric poem
26. Goose genus
27. Raise
28. Neutral hue
29. Lion's cry
30. Lamp gas
32. Arm bones
33. Perfect, for Goldilocks: 2 wds.
34. Unique person
35. New York cinema name
37. Eldest: Fr.
40. Assents
41. Musty
42. Be humiliated: 2 wds.
43. Crafty
45. Golf norm
46. Water animal
47. Italian composer
48. "To Have —— Hold": 2 wds.
49. Indian gowns
51. Beer grain
53. "Let's ——": 2 wds.
54. Goofs
56. School vehicle
57. Self
59. Argentine Indian

PUZZLE 169

ACROSS

1. Male swans
5. Implicit
10. Cut
14. Cookie cooker
15. Speechify
16. Atmosphere
17. Information
18. Less good
19. Fall
20. Goes by
22. Fight site
23. Status
27. Shows sudden anger
31. Woody stem
32. Make clothes
35. Speedy
36. Tree skin
37. Scorch
38. Assist
39. Tough
40. Fury
41. Carnivore's fare
42. War partner
43. Cries
44. Mooselike deer
45. Alternately
46. Writing pad
47. Symbol system
49. Kitchen garment
52. "Mean Mr. ___"
57. Sudden growth
58. Snares
61. Zone
62. Soda
63. Art prop
64. Enumerate
65. Winter toy
66. Heel's neighbor
67. Overdue

DOWN

1. Set of signals
2. Egg-shaped
3. Second Greek letter
4. Fasten with a click
5. Rises
6. Came into being
7. Gas guzzler
8. "___ My Turn"
9. Fit to a ___
10. Military core
11. Attract
12. Unyielding
13. Hemingway's nickname
21. Raced
22. Improve, as wine
24. Bright red
25. Not on time
26. Black
27. Bowling division
28. Title
29. Vertical
30. Glove
32. Poncho
33. Coin worth a sawbuck
34. Extort
36. Light wood
37. King or hermit
39. Stop
43. Prohibits
45. Long time
46. Muss
47. Wanderer
48. Push forward
49. Simplest principles
50. Betting or swimming
51. Actor's part
53. High
54. Gluck solo
55. Take a breather
56. Palm fruit
58. Earl Grey, for one
59. Jogged
60. Request

PUZZLE 170

ACROSS

1. Primates
5. Bowler's term
10. Hazard
14. Genie's home
15. Light beer
16. Buffalo's lake
17. Robert ____
18. Mountain ridge
19. Blaze
20. Imitated
22. Selected
24. Stringed instrument
25. "____ Wars"
26. Pure
29. Island off Georgia
33. Fooled
34. Harangue
36. Musical
37. Medical school subject: abbr.
39. Decade units
41. Attempt
42. Juliet's love
44. Terror
46. Impatient sound
47. Differ in opinion
49. Brawls
51. Golf gadgets
52. Gaucho's weapon
53. Frightens
56. Coating
60. Big instrument
61. Papal crown
63. Go-getter
64. Mind
65. Mr. Fudd
66. Lab burner
67. Caresses
68. Land documents
69. Norma and Charlotte

DOWN

1. Out of the wind
2. Tropical tree
3. Aussie bird
4. Charms
5. Excessive praise
6. Street show
7. Senior
8. New York athlete
9. Constructs
10. Amended
11. Rainbow
12. Father
13. Acute
21. Car
23. Mane
25. Cubic meter
26. Beet variety
27. Vietnam's capital
28. John Quincy ____
29. Ogle
30. Egg-shaped
31. Hospital employee
32. Looks for
35. Mosquito genus
38. Pekoe servers
40. Urns
43. Curved molding
45. Take out
48. Took five
50. Pantry
52. Jaded
53. Anagram of tops
54. Dice shape
55. Help a felon
56. Approached
57. Mite
58. Hawaiian goose
59. Fat: Fr.
62. ____ de France

PUZZLE 171

ACROSS

1. Manner of running
5. Infiltrate
9. Basics
13. State or mural starter
14. Biblical weed
15. Developer's map
16. Squelched: 2 wds.
17. Malevolent
18. Indian prince
19. Popular tea: 2 wds.
22. —— amore
23. N.Y. college
24. Piled
26. Innocent one
29. Definite article
31. Indonesian islands
32. Hooters
33. Snigglers' catch
35. Tether
38. "—— Grant"
39. Declamation
41. —— Grande
42. N.Y. city
44. Extinct bird
45. Fr. city: 2 wds.
46. Record
48. Apprehend
49. Meat cut
50. "Our —— night to bear": 2 wds.
53. Taunt
55. Malleable metal
56. "Alice in Wonderland" character: 3 wds.
61. Hebrew month
63. Khayyam or Bradley
64. Author Sinclair
65. River into the North Sea
66. Wrinkle
67. Without aid
68. Colored, as hair
69. —— bien
70. Telescope part

DOWN

1. Growl
2. —— boy!
3. Incongruities
4. Ballroom dance
5. One up on the competition: 2 wds.
6. Roof overhang
7. Estrada and Satie
8. Jai alai
9. Cal. abbr.
10. Chernozem: 2 wds.
11. Kayak's cousin
12. Easel
13. One: prefix
20. Join the race
21. In advance
25. Runner Sebastian
26. Philippine knife
27. Mil. truant
28. Popular waltz: 2 wds.
30. Singer John
34. Fountain workers: 2 wds.
36. Storage place
37. Circle
39. Beginning
40. Clad like a judge
43. Broadcast
45. Qualm
47. Companion
50. Charger
51. Steep
52. Thighbone
54. Peer
57. Kind of track
58. Town on the Thames
59. Divisions of time
60. Vane letters
62. Was first

CRISS-CROSSWORD

PUZZLE 172

The answer words for Criss-Crossword are entered diagonally, reading downward, from upper left to lower right or from upper right to lower left. We have entered FIRS and WIT as examples.

TO THE RIGHT

1. Evergreens
2. Used to be
3. Felt concern
4. Statute
5. Competition
6. Come together
7. Iced or hot
9. As well
11. Peas
12. Hang in folds
15. Knight's title
17. Mate
18. Final
20. Family vehicle
21. Kind of dance
23. Eighth planet
25. Circular
28. Intelligence
29. Dull routine
32. Not as much
34. Green land
35. Printing fluid
37. Had a sandwich

TO THE LEFT

2. Humor
3. Comedienne Burnett
4. Lariats
5. Indy 500 entry
6. Cut the grass
7. Sawbuck
8. Saucy
10. Grow older
13. Fantasize
14. Regards highly
16. Card game
17. More pristine
19. Wheel shaft
20. Health spot
22. Young boy
24. Raises
26. Hawaiian dish
27. Moved furtively
30. Care for
31. Food fish
33. Facility
36. Football player
38. Draw

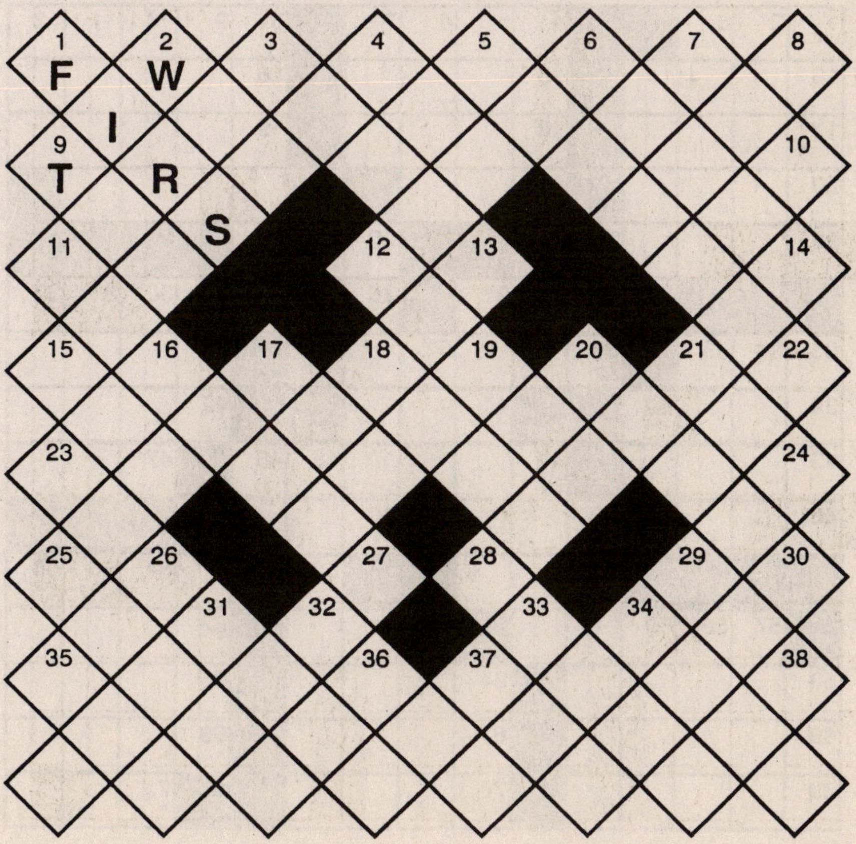

PUZZLE 173

ACROSS

1. At the stern
4. Slammer
8. Live coal
13. Blunder
15. Free
16. Innocent
17. Meat paste
18. Seaweed
19. Quoted
20. Capri, e.g.
21. Cote denizen
22. Lost cause
23. Angel
25. Woeful
26. Break off
28. List
33. Current unit: abbr.
36. Breathe out
38. Smell
39. Gather
41. Winter hazard
42. Puts on
43. Solo for Sills
44. Redress
47. Permit
48. Shouts
50. Spruce
52. Spring month
53. Harmony
57. Flock of partridges
60. Summer cooler
62. ____ regia
63. Reef or snake
64. Corn covering
65. Holy women
66. Stroll
67. Sandusky's lake
68. Poise
69. Harass
70. Scheme
71. Ottoman governor

DOWN

1. Meat jelly
2. Glint
3. Deed
4. Coin-operated phonograph
5. Afresh
6. Still
7. Hang limply
8. Do a cryptographer's job
9. Principal
10. Dracula's action
11. At all
12. Scarlet
14. Equals
22. Fence opening
24. Shoshonean
25. Mute
27. Fancy
29. British teen
30. Icon
31. Area
32. Formerly, formerly
33. Bedouin
34. Gigi's mom
35. Bucket
37. Hole in one
40. "____ Joey"
44. Absent
45. Tipsy
46. Wrong
49. Egg dish
51. Goliath
54. Nestling pigeon
55. Part of a pound
56. Mean
57. Advance
58. Globes
59. Latin farewell
60. Roll up
61. India's continent
63. Horse-drawn vehicle
64. Cool

PUZZLE 174

ACROSS

1. Actor's aid
5. Cry of sorrow
9. Mannerisms
14. Lariat
15. Some are fuzzy
16. Abundant
17. Brainstorm
18. Alter direction
19. Renter's concern
20. "____ in White"
21. Sight or smell
22. Gave to the pot
23. Placards
25. New Jersey team
27. No longer is
28. Curse
29. Received
32. Retreat
35. Gambler's concern
36. Hail!
37. Modify
38. Female rabbit
39. Depart swiftly
40. Annex
41. Verse
43. On a ship
45. Pigment
46. Night birds
47. British beverage
48. Independent
49. Wonderful
53. Brilliant
56. Units of heredity
58. Have being
59. Work
60. Hymnal word
61. Snooty one
62. Scene of action
63. Connected
64. Peak
65. Unimportant
66. Goofs
67. Bell sound

DOWN

1. Preen
2. Cowboy show
3. Unfolds
4. Green vegetable
5. Unlucky
6. Mortgages
7. Masters
8. Lover's song
9. Aesthetic tastes
10. Presages
11. Tiff
12. In addition
13. Plant starter
21. Char
24. Taunt
26. Terminate
28. Thunders
29. Celebration
30. Finished
31. ____ off (angry)
32. Interpret
33. Mary Baker ____
34. Current
38. Representative
39. Young horse
41. Depict
42. Have unpaid bills
43. Escorts
44. Quilting parties
48. "Storm ____"
49. Derisive smile
50. Spear
51. Fragrance
52. Revolt
53. Smack
54. ____ nostrum
55. Encourage
57. Arab prince
61. Tree fluid

PUZZLE 175

ACROSS

1. Phrygian king
6. Squash
10. Small bites
14. Grownup
15. Small ox
16. Woodwind instrument
17. South Carolina's state flower: 2 wds.
20. "My Gal ____"
21. Ship's bow
22. Intense beam
23. Mimic
24. Slithered
26. Elysium
29. Slender
30. Tree fluid
33. Mistake
34. Stage
35. Miscellany
36. Night-sky sight
37. Warn
38. Took to court
39. Donkey
40. Actor Gable
41. Submarine detector
42. Formerly named
43. Country road
44. Dance or root
45. Ultimate
46. King of Israel
47. Infuriate
50. Exhaust
51. Sleeping place
54. North Dakota's state flower: 3 wds.
58. French girl friend
59. Adept
60. Of an area
61. Lima or pinto
62. High-school student
63. Assume

DOWN

1. Willie ____
2. Inkling
3. Boring
4. Everything
5. Cork
6. Important
7. Again
8. Call for help
9. Owns
10. Vagabond
11. Wading bird
12. Corn bread
13. Sign spotter
18. Singing bird
19. Straighten
23. The Bard's river
24. "Jaws" star
25. Roster
26. Milktoast's opposite: hyph.
27. Irregularly notched
28. Occurred
29. "Over ____"
30. Steam bath
31. Lend ____: 2 wds.
32. Military chaplain
34. Sow seeds
37. Woe is me!
38. Spirit
40. Vise
41. Hug
44. Hindu robe
45. Loaded down
46. Rock singer
47. Use a mop
48. It flies when you're having fun
49. Lamb's pen name
50. Ceramic piece
51. Blofeld's foe
52. Jacob's dupe
53. Take out
55. Tattle
56. Politician Ribicoff
57. Director Howard

PUZZLE 176

ACROSS

1. Bulk
5. Humanities
9. Squeeze
14. Pa's sister
15. Uncommon
16. Follies
17. Main actor
18. Kitchen heater
19. Musical play
20. Expectant desire
21. Sports contest
22. Individuals
23. Duration
25. Corn unit
27. Mistake
30. Strew
34. Notable period
35. Letter charge
38. Yule or ship's
40. Junk mail
41. Genetic copy
42. Entirely
43. In no manner
44. Chemists' jars
46. Golf peg
47. Send out rays
49. Fat
51. Hotel
52. Wait
54. Quahog
57. Grain product
59. Store special
63. Grates
65. Relieve
66. Frosted
67. Foot joint
68. Stair
69. Residue
70. Assail
71. Exam
72. Ghostly

DOWN

1. Alda show
2. Car
3. Take a picture of
4. Pressure
5. Scent
6. Poe's bird
7. Maple or willow
8. Transmitted
9. Paid expert
10. Recount
11. Divisible by 2
12. Certain
13. Seven ____
24. Energy
25. Anxious
26. Ingested
27. Thin
28. Zeal
29. Italian entree
30. Tend a furnace
31. Walking stick
32. Make ecstatic
33. Movie parts
36. Pacific or Atlantic
37. Strip of wood
39. Mirth
44. Food container
45. Turf
48. Cheek hollow
50. Nigh
52. Military installations
53. Clumsy
54. Grouch
55. Road strip
56. Inquires
57. Most desirable
58. Grade
60. Realty unit
61. Lascivious look
62. Irritable
64. Play place

PUZZLE 177

ACROSS
1. Called
6. Flop
10. Lhasa ____
14. Nod
15. Eros
16. Pro ____
17. Sing
18. Change the decor
19. Small insect
20. Summer color
21. "Albert's Son" artist
24. Strives
26. French rooms
27. Ivanhoe's love
29. Spectacle
31. English school
32. Warhol's forte
34. ____ Cuarto
37. Set upright
39. Witticism
40. Used
42. Mass of ivy
43. Kind of show
46. Mine: Fr.
47. Hum
48. Red dyes
50. Belfast's county
53. Roasting bird
54. "The Bath" artist
57. Opening
60. Eye part
61. Sullen
62. Yucca fiber
64. Go first
65. Pliny's road
66. Picked
67. Superlative suffixes
68. French statesman
69. Spanish title

DOWN
1. Treaty
2. Turkish general
3. "American Gothic" artist
4. Poetic contraction
5. Hold up
6. Poets
7. Hebrew measure
8. Way
9. Shopper, sometimes
10. Sock pattern
11. Triptych part
12. Washington
13. Vows
22. Kind of tide
23. Needs
25. Splitsville
27. Musical pause
28. ____ von Bismarck
29. Froth
30. Miracle site
33. Available
34. "Downing the Nigh Leader" artist
35. Party to
36. Elevator name
38. Classical order
41. El ____
44. Like the Bedouins
45. Undiluted
47. Woodland nymphs
49. Science of light
50. Stubborn as ____
51. Church areas
52. Pick up the tab
53. Convey
55. Hernando De ____
56. Tallow source
58. In addition
59. Nobleman
63. "Thar ____ blows!"

PUZZLE 178

ACROSS

1. Market wagon
5. Quote
9. Reserved
12. Garden worker
13. Fighting ring
15. Greek porch
16. Singer Gibb
17. Tears at
18. Lanky
19. Fresh
20. Apartment payment
21. Party
23. ____ of cards
25. Rains heavily
26. ____ and dines
27. Section
28. Loudspeaker, for short
31. Detests
32. Lingers
33. Modernist: pref.
34. Affirm
35. Raggedy ____
36. Utopia
37. Meadow
38. Plebe
40. Dated
41. Aquatic bird
42. Singing brothers
43. Speed
44. Challenged
46. Kitchen gadget
47. Kind of check or stamp
49. Eternal City
50. Rhoda's mom
53. Mystery writer Gardner
54. Hanker for
56. Bridge piece
57. Chills and fever
58. Consumer
59. Nuisance
60. Billy ____ Williams
61. Towel word
62. Tennis great

DOWN

1. Chinese detective
2. Topnotch: hyph.
3. Old Glory: 4 wds.
4. Attempt
5. Pet
6. "Good Night" girl
7. Wigwam
8. Cease
9. Old Glory: 3 wds.
10. Golf goal
11. Ivy League school
14. Classify
15. Fidget
20. Grieves about
22. There are three per inning
24. Humdinger
25. Sketch
26. Teeter
27. Window squares
29. Edwin ____
30. Corn cake
31. Regretful American patriot
32. Walked through water
36. At ____!
38. Have feelings
39. Punish
40. Flay
43. Simpson patriarch et al.
45. Busy as ____: 2 wds.
46. Lid
47. Study
48. Egg on
49. Fee
51. Sprint
52. Pot-filler
55. Cheer
56. Fitness resort

PUZZLE 179

ACROSS

1. Jaunt
5. Pioneer Daniel ____
10. Nimble
14. Take on cargo
15. Musical group
16. Shades
17. Some paintings
18. Canadian town
20. Railroad bridges
22. Soother
23. "____ the land . . ."
24. Alpine abode
26. Commission
30. Smears
31. Fossil fuel
32. Endowment
33. ____ Moines
36. Georgia mountain
40. "____ to Joy"
41. Chews
42. Sitarist Shankar
43. Ditch
44. Beldams
46. Continuous
48. Spring month, in Bonn
49. Israeli port
50. End
55. Sioux leader
58. Yugoslavian president
59. ____-beche
60. Unescorted
61. Musical symbol
62. Washington bills
63. Gauge
64. Command

DOWN

1. Vacancy
2. Darby and Joan
3. Inert
4. Famous loch
5. Played tenpins
6. Artist's pigment
7. Cornelia ____ Skinner
8. Ensnare
9. Dijon's summer
10. Throngs
11. Handbag
12. Adjust
13. French river
19. Fireplace
21. High fashion
24. North Pole denizen
25. Like some juries
26. Reverberate
27. Crucifix
28. Exceptional
29. Hirt and Capp
30. Ukrainian city
32. Interrogate
33. Faculty head
34. Gutter locale
35. Hits the slopes
37. Parity
38. Russian city
39. For
43. Scrapes
44. Calling
45. Edge
46. Warning sound
47. Delight
48. Intervening, in law
49. Outer: pref.
50. Gait
51. Yen
52. Cleo's river
53. American Indians
54. Yielding
56. Ark passenger
57. Bullring cheer

PUZZLE 180

ACROSS

1. Stakes
5. Publicizes
9. Barrier
13. Kind of law
14. Billy or nanny
15. Like the Gobi
16. Salisbury Plain sight
18. Chinese secret society
19. Mr. Van Winkle
20. Not yet final, in law
21. Submerge
23. Shish-kebab need
25. Frolics
27. Words of under-standing
29. D.C. VIP
32. Stitched
35. Blouse's kin
37. Unwrap, poetically
38. Anesthetic
40. Jot
41. Confess
43. Before, to Shelley
44. Sharp ridge
46. Dame Myra ___
47. Person who no longer works
49. Madras wear
52. Cooks over water
54. Punch or Judy
58. Slow down
60. Mint
62. Pub quaff
63. Chemist's compound
64. "___ do not a prison make . . ."
67. Skirt length
68. French vase
69. Red as ___
70. Impression
71. Dock
72. Knitter's need

DOWN

1. Hand-dyed fabric
2. Run off to wed
3. ___ Pan Alley
4. Act parts
5. "Rock of ___"
6. Type style
7. Kind of doll
8. Lippizaner, e.g.
9. Jimson weed
10. Hard white china
11. Chess piece
12. Brink
13. Uzbek and Tajik, once
17. For ___
22. Slowly, in music
24. Cellar or press
26. Dramatic whispers
28. Honor
30. Literary work
31. Corded fabrics
32. Psychic
33. To be, in Paris
34. Knife sharpener
36. Headwear
39. More unique
42. Beat
45. Studies, with "on"
48. Roma's country
50. Cap-___
51. Takeoff site
53. Scottish village
55. Less colorful
56. Designer Tracy
57. Experiment
58. Oar: pref.
59. Arthurian lady
61. Unusual person
65. Angular prefix
66. Arab garment

PUZZLE 181

ACROSS

1. Ottoman title
4. Comice or Anjou
8. Charity
12. White House pet
14. French hall
15. Tease
16. Alack's partner
17. Valuable
18. Singer Moffo
19. Shed light
22. Province
23. Female ruff
24. Coaches
27. Candor
31. Golf score
32. Slant
33. Above, poetically
35. Epic
36. Butter's mate
37. Aggravate
38. Title for Olivier
39. Warble
40. Chimes
41. Cheese producers
43. Of greatest age
44. Lassie or Benji
45. Algonquian language
46. Spill the beans
54. Cruising
55. "Don't ____ on me"
56. Unconnected
57. Blind part
58. Gladden
59. Cola
60. Soccer great
61. Catches
62. ____ Darya

DOWN

1. To a distance
2. Festive
3. Kirghiz range
4. Turkish official
5. What ____ is new?
6. Actor Guinness
7. Came back
8. Lets up
9. Actress Turner
10. Skirt type
11. Jazzman Kenton
13. Attacks
14. Surfeits
20. Aquatic flier
21. Bobbin
24. English river
25. Swift
26. Greek marketplace
27. Shoe parts
28. Race-track shape
29. Transparent linen
30. Hollers
32. Soft cheese
34. Repose
36. Illuminate
37. Distributes again
39. Horse's gait
40. Wafted
42. Think
43. Eat out
45. Makes small talk
46. Pant
47. Man or Wight
48. Kind of cutlet
49. Mr. Gardner
50. Chair
51. Courts
52. Artist Warhol
53. 1990

PUZZLE 182

ACROSS

1. Prepare for a trip
5. Turkish titles
9. Highway
13. Oop of comics
15. Play
16. Firth of Lorn port
17. Fence steps
18. Tower
19. Actress Miles
20. Daddy's little girl
23. Author Deighton
24. Doze
25. Willie Tyler's dummy
29. Munro's pen name
31. Distress signal
34. Get ___ of
35. Upsettable item
37. Sulk
38. Comply
39. Conceal
40. Famous planter
42. Quarry worker
43. Spanish king
44. Church recess
45. Middle
46. Schedule abbr.
47. Sighs of relief
48. Teacher pleaser
55. Trumpeter-swan genus
56. Flatten
57. Creepy
59. Aria
60. Weeping willow
61. A votre ___
62. Ajar
63. Unlikely tale
64. Hammer part

DOWN

1. Faux ___
2. Banff's prov.
3. Snip
4. Seaweed ash
5. Firebug's crime
6. Blunder
7. Asian nurse
8. Light rain
9. Meandered
10. Follow orders
11. Berne's river
12. Genetic inits.
14. Whooped
21. Always, to Byron
22. French silk
25. U.S. politician
26. Run off to Gretna Green
27. Drenched
28. Liang
29. Buying frenzy
30. Played copycat
31. Patrick or Elmo
32. Directive
33. Cordwood measure
35. Gets older
36. Take it on the ___
38. ___ as a picture
41. Nobleman
42. Binds
45. Greek letter
46. Protective garment
47. Glow or horn prefix
48. Unbalanced
49. Native of Gdansk
50. Brazilian estuary
51. Part of an ephah
52. Mass
53. Irish river
54. Liturgy
55. Barcelona bear
58. Still, in poems

PUZZLE 183

ACROSS

1. Icelandic work
5. Wooden shoe
10. Scrutinize
14. Stew
15. Bell town
16. Part of TLC
17. Georgia or Virginia
18. Vocalize
19. Unicorn fish
20. Trail opened by Daniel Boone
23. "Jane ___"
24. Curl
25. Winged
28. Regretful
31. Rani's garment
32. Thoroughfare
34. Stop ___ dime
37. 1923 movie
40. Altar constellation
41. Stop working
42. Run into
43. Actress Leslie ___
44. White poplar
45. Pilfer
48. European river
50. Great National Pike
56. Indigo plant
57. Greased
58. Bridge coup
60. Volcano goddess
61. Swiss tune
62. Particle
63. God of war
64. Capture
65. Solar disk

DOWN

1. Newt
2. Sketched
3. Numerical prefix
4. Some scholarships
5. Rescuer
6. Cherish
7. Actor Conrad ___
8. Formerly
9. "On Your ___"
10. Skedaddle
11. Indian boat
12. 1987 Nobelist
13. Inadequacies
21. Coloring agent
22. Disperse
25. Film pooch
26. "Wizard of Oz" actor
27. Sphere
28. Canary's kin
29. Pip
30. Discourteous
32. Allege
33. Presidential action
34. Curved arch
35. Seasonal song
36. Poker term
38. Religious vestment
39. Food of the gods
43. Telegrams
44. Rhine feeder
45. ___ Flow, Scotland
46. Piano-store employee
47. Author Zola
48. Scoff
49. Confuse
51. Cowboy Rogers et al.
52. Pride member
53. "Same Time, Next Year" star
54. Oodles
55. Social engagement
59. Dog's best friend?

PUZZLE 184

ACROSS
1. Feigns
5. ____-a-brac
9. Invented
13. Castle ditch
14. Texas mission
15. Concerning
16. Belem
17. Bulges
18. Biblical preposition
19. Celestial combats?
21. Savage person
23. Clenched hand
24. Horse
25. Blemish
28. Amazing
33. Preacher
35. Laughter: Fr.
36. Pierre's refusal
37. Linear measure
38. Express a thought
40. Portico
41. Big: abbr.
42. Oak or hickory
43. Loathe
45. Guiding lights
48. Chances
49. Actor Bert ____
50. Maple genus
52. Coniferous trees
55. Heavenly journey?
59. In ____
60. Dutch flower
62. Shamrock land
63. Dig for ore
64. In regard to
65. European capital
66. ____ of the realm
67. Baseball team
68. Comic Freberg

DOWN
1. Current units: abbr.
2. Outer garment
3. Movie plantation
4. Sea animal
5. Blabs
6. Sheep
7. Brat
8. Shared top billing
9. Emblem of victory
10. Does not exist
11. Kett of comics
12. Portal
14. Word of woe
20. Toper
22. Comic Johnson
24. Chief
25. Overflow
26. Dance
27. Formed a luminous bridge
29. Judge
30. ____ alia
31. Loop
32. Pesky insects
34. Polaris
39. Fruit
40. Race officials
42. Autocrat
44. German river
46. Beetle
47. Glossy fabrics
51. Mil. rank
52. Set up tents
53. Lake or canal
54. Sand hill
55. Winter toy
56. Uproar
57. Author Bombeck
58. Avid
61. One: Fr.

PUZZLE 185

ACROSS

1. Break
5. Range
10. Greek hero
14. On the Atlantic
15. Kind of phobia
16. Decant
17. Comedian
19. Home of Irish kings
20. "Puts all Heaven in ____"
21. Lip
23. Any anagram
24. Countess's man
27. Chopper
29. Flattery
33. Cowboy's rope
36. Frank's ex
37. Whole
39. Instigator
40. Landlord's due
42. Gave the axe
44. Dried up
45. Cartoonist Peter et al.
47. White salt
49. Inlet
50. Barn loft
52. Taunton's county
54. Beneath
56. Lopez theme song
57. Scratch
59. London district
61. Foolish
65. Step ____!
67. Comedian
70. Fairy-tale opener
71. Organic compound
72. Missing
73. Shortcoming
74. Hangman's loop
75. Feminine suffix

DOWN

1. ____ California
2. Consumer
3. Antitoxins
4. Quarry
5. Guy's date
6. Ripen
7. Does a summer chore
8. Bathsheba's husband
9. Mortarboard ornament
10. Fitting
11. Comedienne
12. Mood
13. Medical picture
18. Bread ingredient
22. Emulated Janet Evans
25. TV antenna locale
26. Pliny's language
28. Love god
29. Actress Bernhardt
30. ____ barrel
31. Comedienne
32. French city
34. Eagle's abode
35. Halloween handout
38. Pretend
41. Large book
43. Sample, for short
46. Peruvian coins
48. Memento
51. Stiff
53. Fester
55. Pronoun
57. Satellite
58. Actress Bancroft
60. Aware of
62. "____ of Livin' To Do"
63. Cardinal's home
64. Italian family
66. Mr. Koppel
68. Legal matter
69. Choler

PUZZLE 186

ACROSS

1. Door clasps
6. Fire
9. Pepper's companion
13. Contribution of ideas
14. Sound
15. Composer Novello
16. Metric measure
17. Samovars
18. Terrible
19. Secondary business
21. Smudges
23. Camera parts
25. Slave of old
26. Associate
29. Eden inhabitant
31. Edgar Allan ____
32. Place
33. Aerial
37. Blackboard cleaner
39. Duplicator
40. Yens
42. River to the Rhine
43. Actress Dawber
44. Maids, sometimes
46. Vipers
47. King toppers
49. Devourers
51. Less speedy
53. Certain cocktails
57. Carbonated beverage
58. Wading bird
60. Casaba
61. Blue dye
62. Yard components
63. Loosen
64. Bottle part
65. Seaman
66. Took

DOWN

1. Snake sound
2. Opposer
3. Rushed
4. Only
5. Inscribed pillar
6. Profession
7. Ms. Landers
8. Loch ____
9. Evade
10. Relating to birds
11. Actor in "The Maltese Falcon"
12. Very: Fr.
14. "____ Boulevard"
20. Warrants
22. Teacher
24. Resort hotel
26. Copied
27. Wisdom
28. Grassy areas
30. Enclosed
32. Study
34. Pinches
35. Certain tide
36. Weapons
38. Pedestrian's path
41. Fr. holy woman
42. Painter
45. Less difficult
46. Climb
47. Solitary
48. Horse's complaint
50. Romulus's twin
51. Skim
52. Break
54. Singing voice
55. Stir up
56. Dirk
59. Actress Arthur

PUZZLE 187

ACROSS

1. Place for a swing
6. Nail
10. Gee!
14. Actress Bow
15. Time past
16. Singer Paul ____
17. Catches
18. Tense
19. Bridle attachment
20. Union ploy
23. Baby's plaything
24. Israeli port
25. First or third
28. Start of a children's song
31. Tree trimmer
35. Alaskan mountain
36. Shakespearean sprite
38. Genoa grandma
39. Some inn comforts
42. Texas landmark
43. Diver's complaint
44. ____ anemone
45. Hit the hay
47. Sun
48. "Cheers" quaff
49. Bistro
51. "Long ____ Tomorrow"
53. Treat for Mom
60. Ewe's child
61. Will-____-wisp
62. Follow
64. Wickedness
65. Antique cars
66. "I ____ Be Loved by You"
67. Cable
68. Crib
69. Condition

DOWN

1. Math abbr.
2. Norwegian king
3. Roue
4. Make
5. Must
6. Computer unit
7. Surf sound
8. West Indies island
9. Notice
10. Bosch's "The ____ Delights"
11. "The ____ Love Belongs to Someone Else"
12. Husk
13. Suspend
21. Got word
22. Imbibes
25. Fictional pachyderm
26. Fred's sister
27. Egyptian leader
29. Lettuce type
30. Goddess of agriculture
32. Bag
33. Develop
34. Subsequent
36. Parka
37. Comic Jay ____
40. Friendly
41. Politician Stevenson
46. Endeavor
48. Bay lynx
50. Peter, for one
52. Nibbles
53. Gusted
54. Mr. Shankar
55. Arab chieftain
56. Scram
57. Final
58. Sicilian hot spot
59. "____ Look Back"
63. Scottish negative

PUZZLE 188

ACROSS

1. Infix
6. Loafers
10. Chatter
14. Fry lightly
15. On the briny
16. Singer McEntire
17. Gangster's lingo
18. Big-top supporters
20. Nautical initials
21. Legal do-over
23. Italic lang.
24. Oyster find
26. Subject for Gray
28. "The ____ Worker"
30. Mineral suffix
31. Confounded
32. Light holders
36. Low island
37. French artist
38. To such an extent
43. Tirana's republic
47. Forearm bone: pref.
48. Fall and spring
49. In proportion
52. Dried orchid tubers
53. Feel poorly
54. Busybodies
56. Lizard
59. Park areas
61. "L.A. Law" role
63. Hot times, in Paris
64. Shipshape
65. Former attorney general
66. Baglike structures
67. Direction suffixes
68. Kinds

DOWN

1. Biblical twin
2. War god
3. Bite preventers
4. Ike's command
5. Divert
6. Fought
7. Patron
8. Domestics
9. Devilish
10. ____-Magnon
11. Greeting
12. Builder's item
13. Cruel
19. Greek philosopher
22. A Gardner
25. Corrode
27. Toe count
28. 1601
29. Teheran's country
33. Kitchen gadget
34. Ireland
35. Resorts
39. Belonging to us
40. Pennants
41. French architect
42. Chicken, sometimes
43. Basketball statistics
44. Bound
45. Oleoresins
46. Chemical suffix
49. Makes like an expectant father
50. Lariat
51. Ancient Meso-american
55. Playwright O'Casey
57. Boxer's weapon
58. Palmer's gadgets
60. Letter addenda: abbr.
62. ____ Speedwagon

PUZZLE 189

MOVIES AND TELEVISION

ACROSS

1. Kaplan and Pressman
6. "Change of ____"
11. "____ Miner's Daughter"
15. "Home ____"
16. Obliterate
17. Attorney Becker
19. Spencer Tracy film
22. "sex, ____, and videotape"
23. Goddess of discord
24. Singer Smith
25. Rank for Charles Parker: abbr.
26. "A ____ With Judy"
27. "Bonanza" role
29. Diminutive suffixes
30. Papa Hansen on "Mama"
31. Pastime for Dagwood
32. "Charlie ____ on Broadway"
34. "Artists and ____"
37. Sounds of satisfaction
40. "The ____ Petticoat"
41. "____ Ballou"
42. King, at Versailles
43. She played Maude
44. Glenn Close TV film
49. ____ B. Davis
50. Inlet
51. Trig ratio
52. Suit to ____
53. "____ Geordie"
54. "Hill ____ Blues"
56. "Harper Valley P.T.A." lead
57. "The Lemon Drop ____"
58. Title for C.E.O.
60. Treasure seeker's aid
63. Actress Anna ____
65. Martin of "Second Chance"
66. Ranch animal
69. Ms. Dahl
71. Prepared to drive
72. Other things, to Caesar
73. "San Francisco" actress
77. Ouzo flavoring
78. Castle or Papas
79. "Hotel de ____"
80. Actor Roscoe ____
81. Shetland features
82. "____ in My Crown"

DOWN

1. "Red Dust" actor
2. Filmmaker Robbe-Grillet
3. Portends
4. "To the ____ of the Earth"
5. "____ of Love"
6. "____ and Minds"
7. Bandleader Shaw
8. Batgirl Gordon
9. Maui or Greenland: abbr.
10. "____ and Sympathy"
11. Birthday treats
12. Hockey's Bobby and family
13. Go into ____ dive
14. Legal
18. Increases, of old
20. "The ____ of Living Dangerously"
21. TV network
26. "Night Court" character
27. "It ____ To Be You"
28. Verdi creations
30. A Turner
31. Espied
32. Bob ____ of "Hogan's Heroes"
33. "Stormy Weather" singer
34. Meadow sound
35. Champagne Lady Alice ____
36. Puppeteer Krofft
37. Lessen
38. Actress Hayes
39. "____ of the Century"
40. "____ What You Did"

PUZZLE 189

41. Director Shirley ____
45. "Another 48 ____"
46. "The Money ____"
47. "____ As a Stranger"
48. Playwright Mosel et al.
55. Bonn article
56. Electric fish
58. "Five Easy ____"
59. Funnyman Foxx
60. "The Naked ____"
61. Gig Young film
62. Hairdo for Heidi
63. Large knives
64. Asian holiday
65. Cartoonist Bil ____
66. "Nutcracker" girl
67. Edmonton athlete
68. Walks in water
70. Otherwise: Scot.
71. Dennis O'Keefe film
72. Subj. for Doogie Howser
74. Comic Conway
75. Box score letters
76. Goddess of plenty

PUZZLE 190

ACROSS

1. Look goggle-eyed
6. Full speed ____!
11. Took affect
16. Particular union
17. Food
19. Mount ____ (highest Adirondack peak)
20. Sign of approval: 5 wds.
22. French soup
23. Butterfly catcher
24. Church council
25. Can be rented
27. Damage allowance
29. Varnish ingredient
30. Flight of steps
32. Espies
33. Epic poetry
35. Most severe
37. Rabbit fur
39. Put to flight
40. Metal fastener
44. ____ of Troy
45. Beam of light
46. Thai or Chinese
47. Make eyes at
48. Neck warmer
49. Algerian city
52. Neighbor of Ore.
53. Summer shirt
54. Mental condition: 3 wds.
56. Before cycle or pod
57. Educating: abbr.
58. Burning glass
59. Palm off
60. Kismet
61. Swelling
63. Blackboard
64. Soars
65. Give a hand
67. Moves with difficulty
68. Hammers and saws, e.g.
69. Braggarts: hyph.
71. Timber wolf
72. Entranceway
75. "The Divine Comedy" author
76. Tourist aid
77. Vale
81. Thurmond and Kennedy. e.g.
83. Trumpeter Armstrong
85. Shad's output
86. Slither
87. Select carefully: 3 wds.
91. Anglo-Saxon laborers
92. Record envelopes
93. More senior
94. Adolescent years
95. French legislature
96. Noble ones

DOWN

1. Bias
2. Slender candle
3. Ease off
4. Nonsense!
5. God of love
6. Kind of committee: 2 wds.
7. Scurried
8. ____ tide
9. According to: 2 wds.
10. Make known
11. ____ Alonzo Stagg
12. Melds, in a certain card game
13. Family
14. School, in Rouen
15. Metric units of force
17. Lab burners
18. Flock of geese in flight
21. Hose material
26. War god
28. Indian home
30. Bread: 3 wds.
31. Feel out
34. Wrestling move
35. Piece of the action
36. Rise up
37. Photo captions
38. Asserts without proof
39. Chin wags
41. Kind of duck
42. Ophelia's brother
43. Begrudges

PUZZLE 190

44. Afternoon refresher: 2 wds.
45. Scrutinize
48. Fr. holy woman: abbr.
49. Deletes
50. ____ and shine!
51. Aardvark's snack
54. Cut, as prices
55. Young horses
60. Surge
62. Misguided
63. Kind of touch?
64. Watch pocket
66. Fuss: hyph.
67. Throat tissues
68. Subject
70. Distorts
71. Praises highly
72. Something of value
73. Jam-packed
74. Foolish
76. "The Water Lilies" painter
78. Deteriorate
79. Also-ran
80. Suggestive looks
82. Hardy girl
83. Volcanic flow
84. Boutique
88. After bee
89. Actor Murray
90. Torero's hurrah

PUZZLE 191

ACROSS

1. Actress Turner et al.
6. Shellfish
10. Stained-glass window component
14. Represent-ative
15. "____ We Go Again"
16. Gift
18. Bible divisions
20. Position
21. Temporal zone: abbr.
22. Actor Donny ____
23. Pekoe and oolong
25. Heavy weight
26. Droop
27. General Bradley
28. Component
29. Gorge
32. Box
33. Flagstaffs
34. Scene of action
35. Sharp
36. Tiny ____
37. Heart
38. Endure
39. Zoo employees
43. Curved letter
44. Receptacle
46. Illuminated
47. Teeter-totters
49. Foot digits
50. Hawaiian dance
51. "____ the King's Men"
52. Type of bag
53. Broader
54. Tempest
57. Actress Miles
58. Gorgonzola, e.g.
59. Arizona tribe
60. Some reviews
61. Placed
62. Gravestone letters
63. Pool
64. Rifles
65. ____ Zeppelin
68. Marries secretly
70. Step beyond
73. Dry place
74. Cat-o'-____-tails
75. Forward thrust
76. Fender scar
77. Espies
78. Go in

DOWN

1. Overdue
2. Matures
3. Aerie
4. Social insect
5. Fortitude
6. Treasure holder
7. Lease
8. Columnist Buchwald
9. Groom's attendant
10. Garfield and Morris
11. Chicken ____ king
12. Of the mind
13. Repeat performance
16. Tyrant
17. Campground sights
19. Beauty spot
24. Pitcher's handle
26. Chablis, e.g.
27. Phone-company employees
28. Splendor
29. Marathons
30. Got out of bed
31. Rhyme
32. Bench
33. Wharf
35. Barbie's boyfriend et al.

36. Golf gadgets
38. Sugar holder
39. Leg joint
40. Baffle
41. Aggravates
42. Gawk
44. Serene
45. Bit
48. Rani's garment
50. Hastened
52. Muscle cords
53. Tea-kettle sound
54. Fragment
55. Labored
56. Contest
57. Moving aid
58. Soup containers
60. Mail
61. Fishing needs
63. Sassy
64. Dancer Kelly
65. Dryer fuzz
66. Brink
67. Doe or buck
69. Write
71. Contend
72. Stocking mishap

PUZZLE 191

PUZZLE 192

ACROSS

1. Fragments
5. Ignited
8. "____ of La Mancha"
11. Halt
15. Prepare copy
16. "A Chorus Line" song
17. Past
18. Volume
19. Shoe bottom
20. Began
22. Actress Moran
23. Winter precipitation
25. Issue
26. Competitions
27. Needy
29. Fixed
32. Skirt edge
35. Forty winks
36. Genuine
37. Weep
40. Verbal
42. Canter
45. Punster
46. Pool shark's need
47. Soothe
48. Cut in two
50. Upper House
52. Duped
54. Slender candle
56. Top an i
57. Camera stand
60. Luxury ship
62. On the summit
65. Attila the ____
66. Meadow
68. Medicine portion
69. Submarine
70. Omelet ingredient
71. Eye part
73. Cat's foot
75. Scarlet
76. Divided
78. Ajar
80. Lance
83. Maize
85. Exams
89. Caution
90. Coverlets
93. Telephone line
94. Came down
95. Choler
96. English brew
97. Director Kazan
98. Golf mounds
99. Tyke
100. Actor Byrnes
101. Weaver's need

DOWN

1. Porgy's love
2. False god
3. Game piece
4. Drench
5. ____ Angeles
6. Translate
7. Sports group
8. Substance
9. Ripen
10. Land of ____
11. Mount
12. Raced
13. Elide
14. Pig homes
21. Margin
24. 2,000 pounds
26. Defrosted
28. Horse food
30. Fresh
31. Podium
32. Weeding tool
33. Baseball letters
34. Crushing
37. Strew
38. "____ of the Blue"
39. Buzzing insect
41. Jump
43. Race-track shape
44. Lukewarm
49. Divorce city
51. Ark builder

PUZZLE 192

53. Monetary unit
55. Answered
57. Article
58. Carpet
59. Stag or fawn
61. Harvest
63. Norwegian coin
64. Home for peas
67. Picnic pest
72. Covert
74. Soggy
76. Trousers
77. John or Jane
79. Stairway post
80. Kill flies
81. Faint
82. Sandusky's lake
84. Pace
86. Fodder tower
87. Threesome
88. Baseball feature
90. Use a chair
91. In favor of
92. Sorry

PUZZLE 193

ACROSS

1. —— cum laude
6. Homily
11. Mollify
18. Cloth
19. Confederate soldier
20. Worshipful
22. Wayward
23. Hurtful
24. Fade away
25. Hot spots
26. Pronoun
27. Lend a hand
29. Coal weight
30. Lily or moth
31. Embankment
33. Mongrel
34. Simple
35. Actress Balin
36. Untainted
37. Repulsive
39. Plebe
40. Animal doc
41. Cohort
42. Condition
43. —— of the land
44. Without beginning or ending
46. Long cut
47. Stoker
51. Imaret
52. "—— Spirit"
53. Run-of-the-mill
54. Russian fur
57. Pair
58. Carried on
60. Company: abbr., Fr.
61. African plant
62. Desire
63. Criminal
64. Rumpelstiltskin's product
65. Scare word
66. Reproach
67. Absolve
68. Milk's partner
69. Get on board
71. Waste pipes
73. "The —— Game"
74. Reticence
75. Harold of music et al.
76. Curl
80. American poet
81. Scrooge, e.g.
82. Expense
83. Asian peak
84. Ford lemon
87. "Saturday Night ——"
88. Contest
89. Egyptian king, for short
90. Conceal
91. Prong
92. Intermediary
94. Favored ones
96. Snacked
97. Shade of yellow
99. Be a stool pigeon
100. More than one
101. Tyrannical
103. Having wings
105. Provide with oxygen
106. Reckon
107. Ore deposits
108. Part of UAW
109. Reduced gradually
110. Make an effort
111. Took on cargo

DOWN

1. Strict disciplinarian
2. Repeal
3. Serious
4. Forty- ——
5. Curtain raisers
6. Robin Hood's forte
7. Get from a source
8. Maltreat
9. Golly!
10. Miss Cinders
11. Suppose
12. Flippancy
13. Sea dog's word
14. Red ——
15. "We —— the World"
16. Checked for flaws
17. Cry at the Met
18. Joyous
21. Article of faith
28. Bits
31. Quiet
32. San Simeon, e.g.
34. Part of MGM
36. Formulation
38. —— La Rue
39. Was solicitous
41. —— of Cleves
42. Golf stroke
43. Animate
45. Vex
46. Hard taskmaster: 2 wds.
47. Small party gift
48. Georgia city
49. Sprightly
50. Disadvantaged
52. Kind of nail
54. Kind of saw
55. Unaided
56. You bet your ——
57. Pickle liquid

PUZZLE 193

59. Word of regret
62. Onion family member
63. Handbill
64. Oriental bell
66. Joyce —— Oates
67. Tourist's trademark
68. Intimation
70. Disgust
72. National flower
73. Pith
76. Utter defeat
77. Well-read
78. Schooled
79. Told Mom
81. Threatened
82. Dispute
84. Dodge
85. Abhor
86. Respite
87. Like some verbs
88. Egg mixer
91. Turkic language
93. Slope
94. Miss Verdugo
95. Sensational
97. Arrive
98. New Haven school
100. McCartney of music
102. —— -squeak
104. Smoked salmon

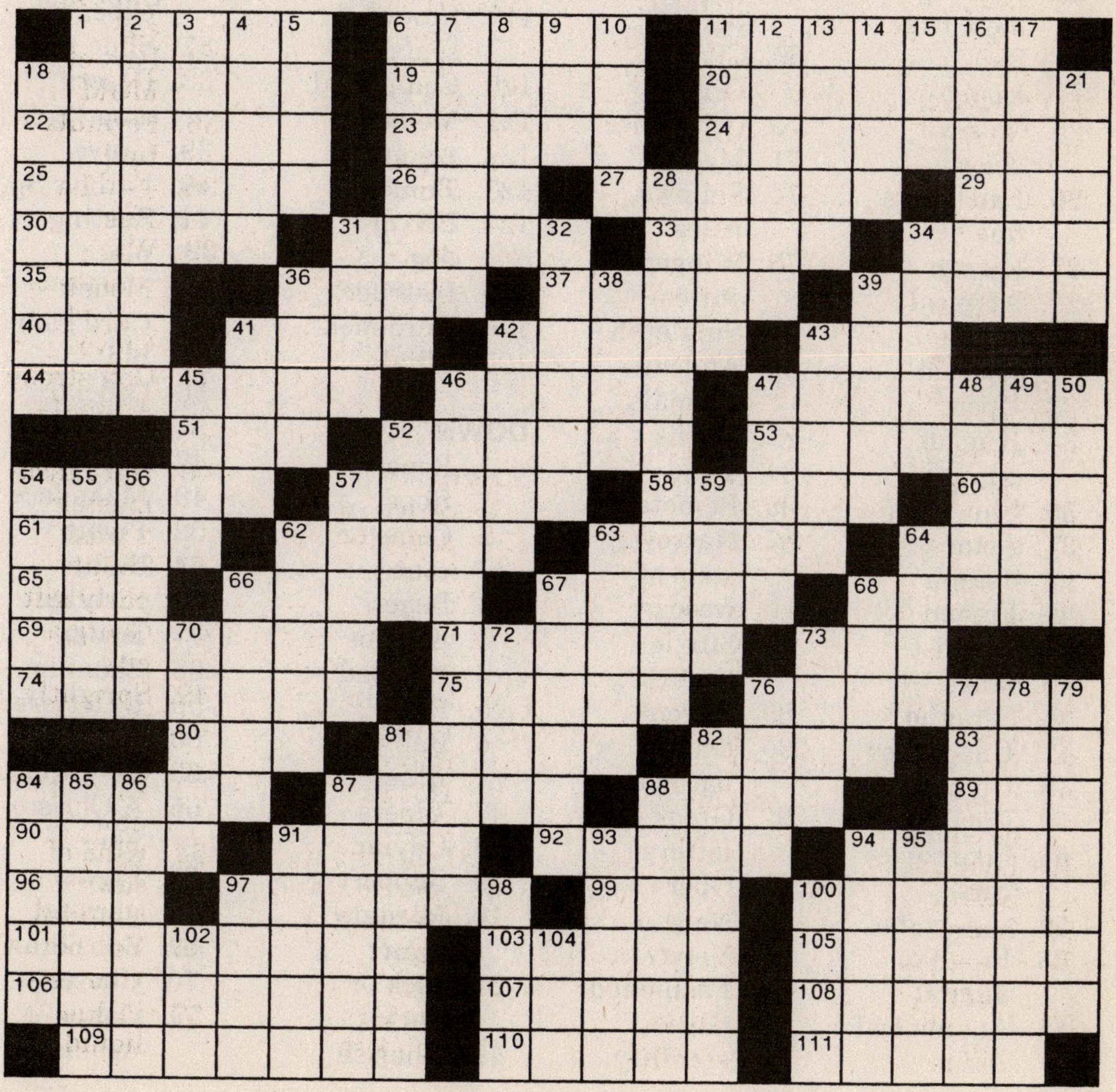

PUZZLE 194

ACROSS

1. Stockings
5. Intimidate
10. Makes attractive
15. Seasoning
19. Nefarious
20. Burning crime
21. Oak nut
22. Constant
23. Nothing more than
24. Ran easily
25. Musical show
26. Landlord's due
27. Former
29. Atypical
31. Undernourish
33. Upon
34. Kind of runner
36. Slip
37. Actor Joseph
40. French chemist
42. Mugs
46. Seraglio
47. Unadorned
48. Uproar
50. Provide
51. Like some cars
52. —— water
53. Froglike animal
55. Anatomical tissue
56. Attachment
57. Rapiers
59. Be alert
61. Entirely
62. Garnet variety
64. In progress
66. String instruments
68. Impose a tax
69. City in Ohio
70. Otherwise
71. Mess
74. Follows rules
75. Winged states
79. Singleton
80. Andean animals
82. Moths
84. Yield
85. Remote
87. Narrow strip of wood
88. Single time
89. Urgent
90. Lost patience
92. Greek letters
94. Opera song
95. Verify
96. Fashioned
98. Gives stability
100. Slanted
101. Donkey: Ger.
103. Pulverize
104. Duration
105. Canadian capital
109. Supped
110. Coolness
114. Mine passage
115. Stop!, at sea
117. Trot and gallop
119. Row of seats
120. Completed
121. Memento
122. Anoint
123. Troubles
124. Bob or dog
125. Instruct
126. Burdened
127. Whale

DOWN

1. Rope fiber
2. Come or coat
3. Beget
4. Kind of railroad
5. Bar
6. Baby illness
7. Vipers
8. Caviar
9. Support
10. Mystery man
11. Pick or pack
12. Cherish
13. Percussion instruments
14. Skulks
15. Harsh
16. Tract
17. An Alfred
18. Head: Fr.
28. Particular
30. Speck
32. Mention for bravery
34. Electrical unit
35. College expense
37. Slide
38. Desert stop
39. Grove
40. Father: Sp.
41. Resting place
43. Model
44. Card game bid
45. Official stamps
47. Spoils
49. Make lace
52. Pivots
54. State
57. Fishline leader
58. Benefits
59. Unfettered
60. Retreats
63. —— World
65. A Christopher
67. Flower garland
69. Subsiding
70. Chosen
71. Castle defenses

72. Not qualified
73. Darling
74. City in Nebraska
75. Ms. Moorehead
76. Leek's kin
77. Temerity
78. Stallion
81. High mountain
83. Calabash
86. Yielded
89. Histrionic
91. Mr. Arnaz
93. Withdraw from competition
94. County in Ireland
95. Jaunty
97. Deviate
99. B'way success

PUZZLE 194

100. Decrease
102. Riverbank
104. Legal paper
105. Rolls of money
106. Hero
107. Cloud number
108. Festivity
110. Expired
111. Egyptian waterway
112. Stone ax
113. Irish Gaelic
116. Thus
118. Actress Alicia

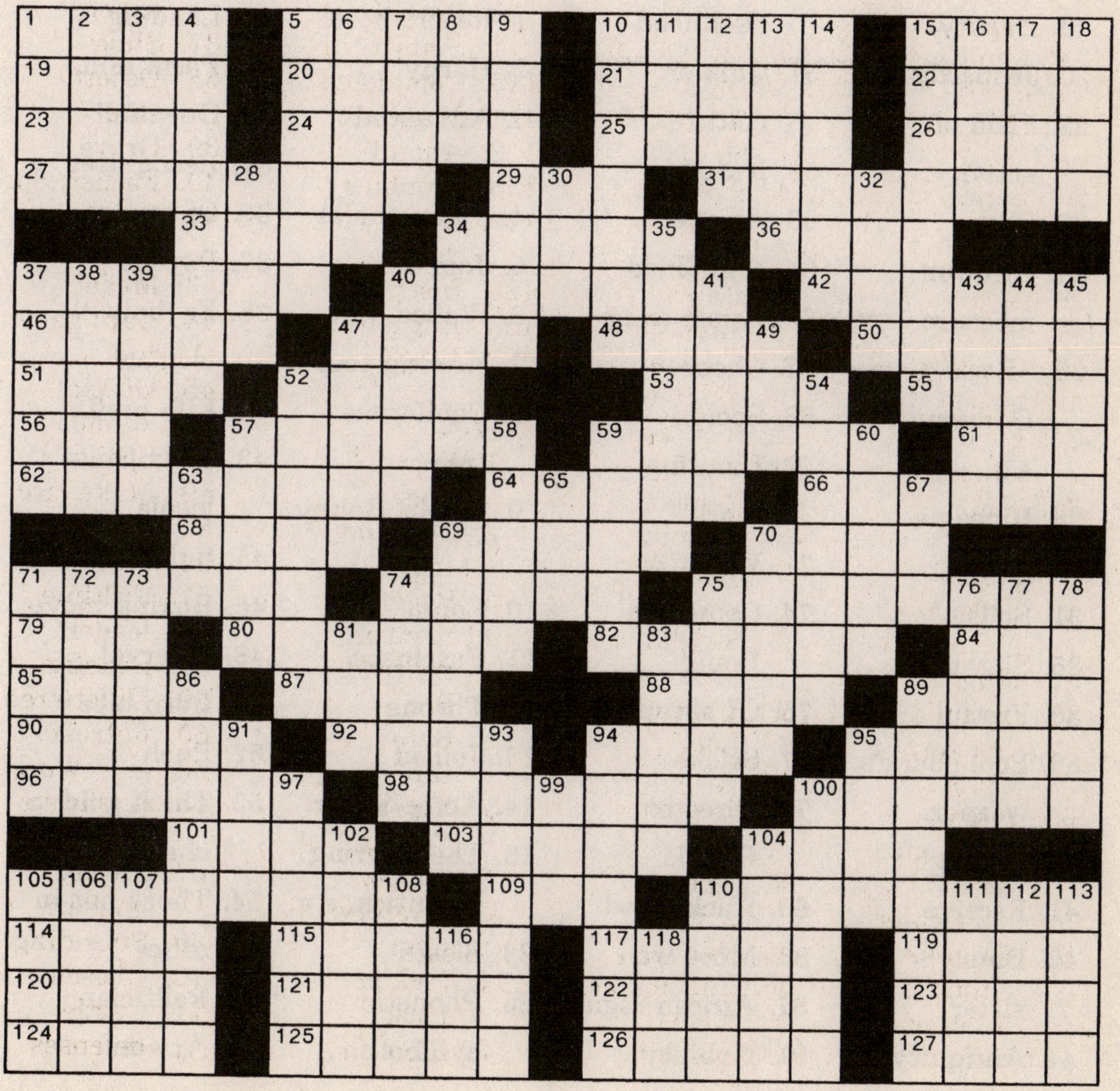

PUZZLE 195

REVELATION

When you have solved this crossword puzzle, the tinted letters, reading from left to right, will reveal a quotation.

ACROSS

1. Apportion
6. Thin cookie
11. Task
16. Hedonistic
17. Cast out
18. Respect
19. Deputy
20. Jeopardy
21. Field of activity
22. Chap
24. Gridiron measure
26. "Boris Godunov," e.g.
28. Bigwig's letters
31. Soils
35. Slight
36. Fretful
39. Pool shark's weapon
40. Through
41. Receive
42. Donny's sister
44. Antiquity
46. Fall down on the ____
47. Diets
49. Stole
51. Humorist George ____
52. In all likelihood
57. Quiz or culture
59. Nature
63. Awaken
64. Lightened
66. Apple treat
67. Choose
68. Scolds
70. Limiting mark
71. Want
74. Comedian Louis ____
75. Of sheep
77. Sticks
79. Director Pakula
80. Hackneyed
83. More wan
87. African region
91. Nobility
92. Dull green
93. Bizarre
94. Fables
95. Currents
96. Method

DOWN

1. Resort hotel
2. Harpy
3. Advanced years
4. Park official
5. Join
6. Wailed
7. Hewing tool
8. Coniferous tree
9. Singer Bobby ____
10. Count
11. Fascinate
12. Throng
13. Joined
14. Actor Silver
15. The Roaring Twenties, e.g.
23. Siesta
25. Phonetic symbol
26. Butterine
27. Sound of contentment
28. Sentence part
29. "____ Got Sixpence"
30. Landing
32. Farm unit
33. Downfall
34. Recognizes
35. Operative
37. Psyche
38. Fr. holy woman
42. Life prefix
43. Iowa State's locale
45. Subsides
46. Boxing move
48. Interval
50. Barn bite
52. Push
53. Thick gold chain
54. Those not in office
55. Politician Atwater

PUZZLE 195

56. Afghan material
57. Dog in "Our Gang"
58. Horatian work
60. Unwrap
61. Liturgy
62. Pipe joint
65. Relate
68. Lake bottom
69. Sun god
70. Stately dance
72. Incensed
73. Functions
76. Bud holders
78. Freckle
79. Son of Hera
80. Bookie's deal
81. Side petal
82. Zilch
84. Mohammed ____ Pasha
85. Top
86. First lady
88. Dehydrated
89. Feel poorly
90. Wedding announcement word

PUZZLE 196

ACROSS

1. Pistol case
8. Larceny
13. "One Day ——": 3 wds.
14. Tremble
15. Missouri city
16. Exalted
17. —— canto
18. Palaces
19. —— Palmas
22. Himalayan cedar
25. Move slowly
27. Trousers
29. Nourished
32. Ireland
33. Mr. Gazzara
34. Royal fur
36. Favorite haunts: 2 wds.
39. Persuading
40. —— Alamos
41. Hint
42. Dance step
43. Blacksmith
45. Mister, in Bonn
46. Experience
49. Even now
50. Meeting place
55. Flying mammal
57. Do away with
58. Brisk
62. Entertain
63. Line up
64. Trudges
65. Show-biz glory

DOWN

1. Possesses
2. Native: suffix
3. Youth
4. Random try
5. Like some floors
6. Writer Zola
7. Turmeric
8. Vats
9. Sentry's word
10. Wicked
11. Woman, in law
12. Very: Fr.
14. Place to live
16. Glance at quickly
19. Stays in bed: 2 wds.
20. "Peer Gynt" dancer
21. Scrawny ones
23. Unwrap
24. Swung loosely
26. Half: prefix
28. Theater sign
29. —— Peter Dunne
30. Last
31. Abandon
33. Slammer: 2 wds.
35. Great deal
37. Bankers' IOUs: abbr.
38. Skirt panel
44. Correct in doctrine: abbr.
47. Cut short
48. Singer Branigan
50. Angel's instrument
51. Cain's victim
52. Not ready: hyph.
53. Pleased
54. Certain paintings
56. Powerful leader
58. Ethiopian prince
59. Hoosier State: abbr.
60. —— Dinh Diem
61. Jewel

CLUES IN TWOS

PUZZLE 197

ACROSS

1. Become older
4. Blackthorn
8. Anglo-Saxon serf

12. 13.] Rent

14. Attention-getting sound
15. Repeats
17. Pacific island
18. In addition
19. Excessive
20. Arrange in order
22. Mine product

23. 24.] Left

29. Question
30. Sinks in mud
31. Reverence

32. 34.] Acts

35. Mexican hurrah
36. Kiss
37. Flat, as paint
40. Showy flower
42. Land measure
43. Electronic connectors
47. Son of Noah

48. 49.] Note

50. Golf pegs
51. Settled a debt
52. Plant

DOWN

1. Clay, today
2. Obtain
3. Summer: Fr.
4. Plant stem
5. Parking areas
6. Popular cookie
7. Printers' measures
8. "Hotel California" band

9. 10.] Close

11. Madame Bovary
16. Speak wildly
19. "Exodus" author
20. Pause
21. Singer Paul ____
22. First digits
23. Existed
24. Locale
25. Anger
26. New Mexico artist colony
27. Sheep
28. Matter, in law
30. Slipper
33. Clan emblems
34. Do a household chore
36. Two-legged support
37. Spar

38. 39.] Pine

40. Mental flash
41. Nerve branches
43. Electric-current unit
44. Nineteenth letter
45. Early automobile
46. Stitch

PUZZLE 198

ACROSS

1. Circus pinniped
5. Circus feline
10. Aerialist's insurance
13. Medley
14. Ridge
15. Venetian resort
16. Circus names: 3 wds.
19. Wind dir.
20. Network of nerves
21. Hammers
22. Fee
23. Male issue
24. Plots
27. Singer/actor Eddy
30. Irish island
31. Pare
32. Asian holiday
34. Circus family member: 2 wds.
39. Small one
40. Brainstorm
41. Counsel
42. Seasoned
44. Route
46. High card
47. Swiss river
48. Feel
51. English composer
52. Mother Gynt
55. Anthony Newley song: 4 wds.
59. Chip in
60. Erin
61. Check
62. Kanga's baby
63. Swiss/French lake
64. German river

DOWN

1. Blubbers
2. Greek resistance gp.
3. Early Irish nobleman
4. Chaney of films
5. Lion handlers
6. Fuming
7. Actor Wilder
8. JFK letters
9. Johnny ____
10. Cairo's river
11. Early garden
12. Trifles
15. Legal claims
17. Asian river
18. Sun god
22. Tiger tooth
23. Oracle
24. Dray
25. Soli
26. New Guinea sea
27. Beak
28. Else
29. Requisites
31. Links org.
33. Corner
35. Chinese nut
36. ____ fixe
37. Composer Rorem
38. Loyal
43. ____ Grand-Lieu, France: 2 wds.
44. French dance
45. Russian city
47. Circus site
48. Russian ruler
49. Wine: prefix
50. " . . . and ____ dust thou shalt return."
51. Attention getter
52. Inspires reverence
53. Tizzy
54. Serf
56. None
57. Three: Ital.
58. Cortez's quest

PUZZLE 199

ACROSS

1. Vassal
5. Launder
9. Excitement
13. Elliptic
14. Chili bean
15. Egg yellow
16. Note
18. Soared
19. Following
20. Not on time
22. Caviar
23. Rest
24. Unspoken
27. Young Kodiak
30. Clues
34. Biblical prophet
35. "Moonlight ___"
37. Gout site
38. "Jurassic Park" author
41. It's easily bruised
42. Like certain bases
43. The walls have ___
44. Bake
46. Moscow square
47. Stanza
48. Attention-getter
50. Massachusetts cape
51. Tourists' appendages
55. Contaminate
59. Opera song
60. Named, as a ship
62. Liturgical season
63. Lift
64. Fawn's father
65. Archimedes's forte
66. Nero's garb
67. Dover or lemon

DOWN

1. Not all
2. Tied
3. Stuffs
4. Thrive
5. ___ it (improvise)
6. Share ___ share alike
7. Ticket-holder's receipt
8. Dwellings
9. Whirl around
10. Plunder
11. Something other
12. Scraped by
14. Window square
17. Stampede
21. Pale purple
24. Gentler
25. Pedro's pal
26. Hot chocolate
27. Pigment
28. Fester, to Pugsley
29. Revealed
31. Petal extract
32. Jim Morrison's group, with "The"
33. Get the impression
35. Placed
36. Metallic element
39. Fall bloomer
40. Distracted
45. Slinky dress
47. Electrical unit
49. America's Cup contender
50. Expense
51. Reassure
52. Zone
53. After-dinner candy
54. Scat!
55. Leaning Tower site
56. "Do ___ others . . ."
57. Greenish blue
58. Trim
61. Furnish

PUZZLE 200

ACROSS

1. Everyone
5. Chew out
10. Proficient
14. Pump
15. "Uptown New York" star
16. Writer Stoker
17. TV host Jack ___
18. Wading bird
19. Norse symbol
20. Daisylike flower
23. Where nice guys finish
24. Plant parasite
25. Awhirl
28. "___ We All"
31. Handlers
32. Agree
34. Quiet sound
37. Fragrant-flowered plant
40. Greek letter
41. Lavishly
42. Marshal Wyatt ___
43. Pauses
44. Young stars
45. Prize marble
48. Pace
50. Wild carrot
56. Metric land measures
57. Mortgages
58. Highway
60. Arrest
61. Actress Van Doren
62. Opera star
63. On a ship
64. Cake or music
65. Luge's cousin

DOWN

1. Mind-reading ability, for short
2. Mighty whaler
3. Fossil fuel
4. Coats of arms
5. Footgear
6. Printer's mark
7. Approve
8. Don Juan's patter
9. Legal document
10. Sudden
11. Graze
12. Kauai porch
13. Correct
21. Low-lying island
22. Holiday visitor
25. Swig
26. Mother of Horus
27. Sandwich shop
28. Bonfire residue
29. Movie spool
30. Begrudge
32. Curly 'do
33. Big first for baby
34. Balkan
35. Greek Juno
36. Media excess
38. Frequently
39. Dancer's gear
43. Veracruz snooze
44. None
45. Sinai gulf
46. Hindu teachers
47. Migratory flocks
48. Jinn
49. Investment
51. Poor-box donations
52. Lexicographer Webster
53. Cognomen
54. Spring
55. Roof part
59. TV's "Major ___"

SCRAMBLE CROSS

PUZZLE 201

Unscramble each group of letters in the diagram on the top to form a word and put it into the corresponding group of squares in the diagram on the bottom. Do this for ACROSS WORDS ONLY. The completed diagram on the bottom will be a crossword puzzle with words reading across and down. For groups of letters that can make more than one word across, solve across and down together.

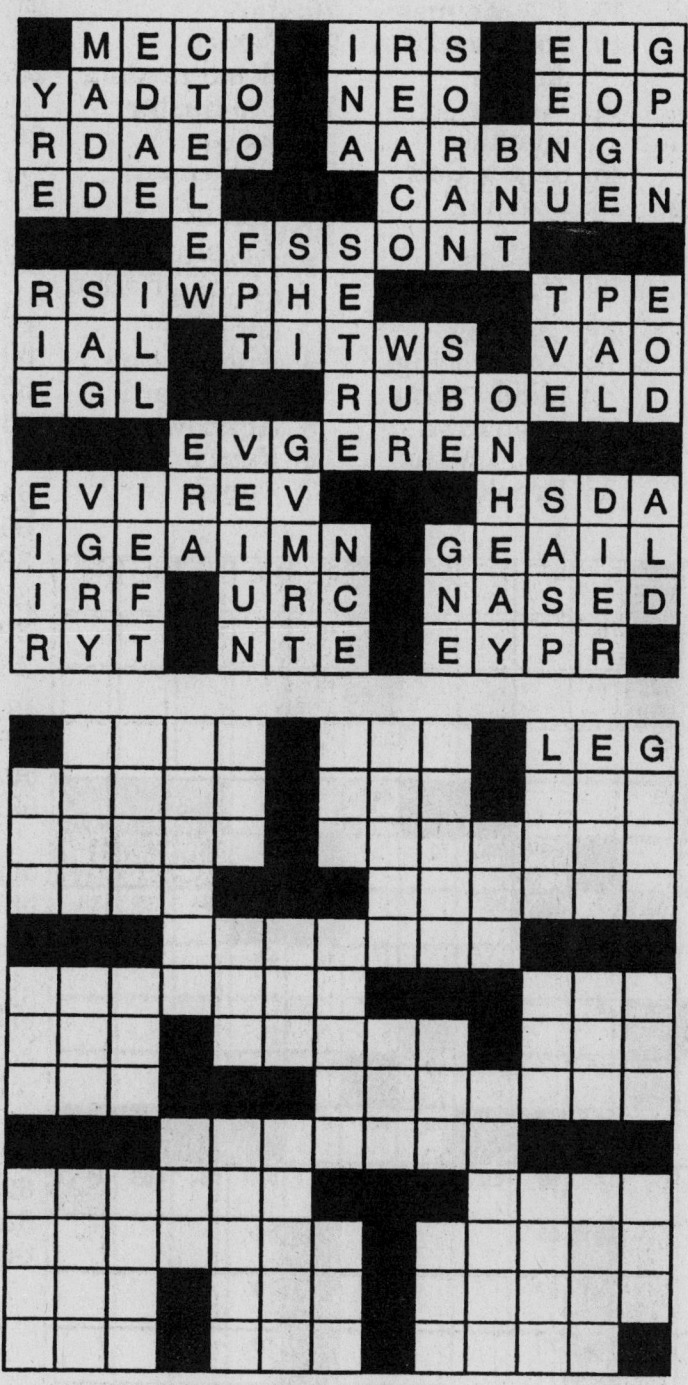

■	M	E	C	I	■	I	R	S	■	E	L	G
Y	A	D	T	O	■	N	E	O	■	E	O	P
R	D	A	E	O	■	A	A	R	B	N	G	I
E	D	E	L	■	■	■	C	A	N	U	E	N
■	■	■	E	F	S	S	O	N	T	■	■	■
R	S	I	W	P	H	E	■	■	■	T	P	E
I	A	L	■	T	I	T	W	S	■	V	A	O
E	G	L	■	■	■	R	U	B	O	E	L	D
■	■	■	E	V	G	E	R	E	N	■	■	■
E	V	I	R	E	V	■	■	■	H	S	D	A
I	G	E	A	I	M	N	■	G	E	A	I	L
I	R	F	■	U	R	C	■	N	A	S	E	D
R	Y	T	■	N	T	E	■	E	Y	P	R	■

■					■				■	L	E	G
					■				■			
					■							
				■	■	■						
■	■	■								■	■	■
							■	■	■			
			■						■			
			■	■	■							
■	■	■								■	■	■
						■	■	■				
							■					
			■				■					
			■				■					■

PUZZLE 202

ACROSS

1. Gives silent approval
5. Meander
9. Strike
14. Aloud
15. Bombeck the columnist
16. Gay ____
17. Choir member
18. Wild ox
19. Stage whisper
20. Composer of 40 Across and 56 Across
23. Baseball notable
24. Billy ____ Williams
25. Farewell
29. Small case
32. Step over the line
36. Actor Oscar ____
38. Spanish gold
39. ____ de mer
40. Song by 20 Across
44. Make a mistake
45. Singer Cole
46. Evening party
47. Spanish kings
49. Opening
51. Auto racing family name
52. Cay: abbr.
54. "____ Miss Brooks"
56. Song by 20 Across
65. Valletta's country
66. Batons
67. Conceited
68. Revoke, in law
69. To shelter
70. Jai ____
71. Comes close
72. Pre-Easter season
73. Nobleman

DOWN

1. First skipper
2. Column support
3. Information
4. Work hard
5. Acknowledge
6. Fancy
7. Cupid
8. Title of address
9. Astronaut's milieu
10. Crushed
11. Diva's number
12. Relinquish
13. Ship's timber
21. Youthful
22. Expressions
25. Author Horatio ____
26. Farm implement pioneer
27. Tusk material
28. Auricle
30. Blows a horn
31. Footed vase
33. Turkish titles
34. Hindu queen
35. Senior
37. Prickle
41. Motorist's org.
42. "____ My Best Friend" (Queen tune)
43. Sixty seconds: abbr.
48. Rock group Twisted ____
50. Tomboy
53. Shuts with force
55. Tip over
56. Federal agent
57. Walk through water
58. Olive genus
59. Of an epoch
60. Warsaw native
61. Stadium shape
62. Stick: Sp.
63. Fabler
64. Camelot lady

PUZZLE 203

ACROSS

1. Roman statesman
5. Barley's beard
8. Enjoying a yacht
12. Astringent
13. Defender of the Aesir
15. Become embedded
17. Tiny insect
18. Learn's partner
19. English composer
20. "The Clockmaker" artist
23. G.I. mail drop
24. Period
25. ____ the light
26. Unrefined materials
27. Fades
30. Baton
32. Reagan, to friends
33. Stainless ____
37. Lacks
40. Academy person
42. Bossie's comment
43. Specialized jargon
44. Cramp one's ____
45. Remove from a sack
47. Exist
48. Walk in water
50. Optical devices
52. Extended family
54. Kind of trip
57. Average
58. "____ the ramparts . . ."
59. "Water Lilies" artist
64. Additional
66. Hardy's pal Laurel
67. Alaskan seaport
68. Heat furnisher
69. Await determination
70. American lake
71. Cabbage dish
72. ____ judicata
73. Repair, as an argyle

DOWN

1. Bivouac
2. Inter ____
3. Costume for Marie Camargo
4. Breakfast choice
5. Minimally
6. Buzz (by)
7. Star blasts
8. On the protected side
9. Impresario Hurok
10. "Prima Ballerina" artist
11. Struck speechless
14. Actor Enriquez of "Hill Street Blues"
16. Son of Aphrodite
21. Peaked
22. Fresh
26. Unique item
27. Bows
28. Missed the ____
29. "Campbell's Soup" painter
31. Letter rearrangement
34. Ostrich's kin
35. Two or more eras
36. Tennis shot
38. Campus building
39. Canonized Fr. women
41. Eagerness
46. Affixes
49. Sushi fish
51. Got the wrinkles out
52. Cote sounds
53. Lithuanians
55. Noisy breath
56. Exterior
59. Complement
60. Hamlet, for one
61. Author Ephron
62. UAE member
63. Young person
65. Zsa Zsa's sister

PUZZLE 204

REVELATION

When you have solved this crossword puzzle, the tinted letters, reading from left to right, will reveal a quotation.

ACROSS

1. Support
5. Strain
9. Water or lick
13. Enameled metalware
14. Zodiac sign
16. Solo for Sutherland
17. Diving bird
18. Mortal
19. Indication
20. Venomous snake
21. Strokes
22. Sidesteps
24. Unproductive
26. Antelope's playmate?
27. Some
28. Told
32. Like some beer
35. Sot
36. Bauxite, e.g.
37. Split
38. Confusion
39. Poet's inspiration
40. Grain
41. Impose
42. Despised
43. Ward
45. Smallest part
46. Oven accessory
47. Part of FDIC
51. Brainy
54. Affected manners
55. Epoch
56. Pierce
57. Acclaims
59. Henhouse products
60. One
61. Convolution
62. Tense
63. Conceits
64. Guitarist Duane ____
65. Tavern quaffs

DOWN

1. Mainstay
2. Plug
3. Go to Gretna Green
4. Playing card
5. Securely
6. Incensed
7. Conforms
8. Afternoon party
9. African desert
10. Unimaginative
11. Come-on
12. Uses a shuttle
15. Shirt features
21. Liquid measure
23. Swerve
25. Great quantity
26. Train stop
28. Main course, at times
29. Oaf
30. Gaelic
31. Act
32. Decline

PUZZLE 204

33. Raise
34. Kitty food
35. Dim-witted
38. Recital
39. Chum
41. Order
42. Brick holders
44. Salad-dressing bottles
45. Athlete's shirt
47. Evil spirit
48. Splendid
49. Bicker
50. Prevails
51. Fever
52. Ditty
53. Tom, Dick, and Harry, e.g.
54. Fain
58. Cow
59. Greek letter

PUZZLE 205

ACROSS
1. Fluffy or Fido
4. Walk the ____
9. Male wool producer
12. Spanish cheer
13. Gymnast's aid
14. Easily bruised item
15. Hawaiian fruit
17. Actor Gibson
18. Pigment
19. Stop!, at sea
21. Quotes
24. European viper
26. French ____
27. Boot accessory
30. Ma that baas
31. Velocity
32. A Gershwin
33. Common
35. Beneficiary
36. Flaxen-haired
37. Burdened
38. Egg yellows
40. Train unit
41. Japanese sash
42. Newlyweds' vacation
48. Succeeded
49. Dodge
50. Actress Lupino
51. Not a ____ to stand on
52. Sword
53. Allow

DOWN
1. Soda
2. Inventor Whitney
3. Sawbuck
4. Says the rosary
5. Run easily
6. Serpent
7. None
8. Mixed dough
9. Tied the knot again
10. "Rock of ____"
11. Shed feathers
16. Adam and Eve's place
20. Horse doc
21. Restaurant VIP
22. Hawkeye State
23. Shaking
24. In the lead
25. Shaker and mover
27. Rotate
28. Buffalo's lake
29. Be entitled to
31. Splashes around
34. Sort
35. Injure
37. Tier
38. Squawk
39. Woodwind
40. Grant
43. Eggs: Latin
44. Catch
45. Olive or vegetable
46. "____ to Billie Joe"
47. ____ "King" Cole

PUZZLE 206

ACROSS

1. Miner's quest
4. Arab prince
8. Breaking story
12. Paraffin
13. Completed
14. Egg shape
15. Grassland
16. Vases
17. Quarry
18. Ceremonial staff
20. Resounded
22. Nimble
24. Street
25. Native of Copenhagen
26. Air hole
27. Wager
30. Bullfight shouts
31. Donkey
32. Change over
33. Melancholy
34. Great Lake
35. Margarine
36. Nickel or dime
37. Holy person
38. Monkey's treat
41. Positive
42. Matured
43. Back of the neck
45. By way of
48. Pear-shaped instrument
49. Walked on
50. Marine eagle
51. For fear that
52. Location
53. Ocean

DOWN

1. It gives a hoot
2. "Norma ___"
3. Inspected
4. Draw out
5. Additional
6. Roadside hotel
7. Reply
8. Wanderer
9. Bad
10. Slacken
11. Sleigh
19. Malt drinks
21. Consume food
22. Difficulties
23. Festive
24. Lac
26. Alternatives
27. Thinks
28. Paradise
29. Blow, as a horn
32. Lion's sound
34. Vast time span
36. Military student
37. Shoe leather
38. Keep the ___ rolling
39. Malaria fever
40. Profits
41. Stain
44. Onassis's nickname
46. Anger
47. Collection of sayings

PUZZLE 207

ACROSS

1. Styptic
5. Native's weapon
10. Beyond
14. Be overly fond
15. Winged
16. Frazzle
17. Inland sea
18. Drives a dragster
19. Anemia antidote
20. Delaware's popular beach resort
22. Flung
24. ____ to a turn
25. Celestial body
26. Cutting wood
29. Torments
32. Sigourney Weaver movie
33. Beer type
34. Greek letter
35. Misfortunes
36. Duplicates
37. Meat spread
38. Rara avis
39. Bounds
40. Trucked
41. Energetic
43. At ease
44. Actor Williamson
45. Pitcher's no-no
46. Approver
48. Delaware's military installation
52. Singer Smith
53. Pointless
55. Thought
56. Stravinsky
57. Ed Norton's domain
58. Void's companion
59. Lots
60. Inclines
61. Place to get a sandwich

DOWN

1. Jewish June
2. Learning
3. Salt Lake City's state
4. Euphonies
5. South Pacific skirt
6. Anodize
7. Per
8. Supped
9. Makes new
10. Comes into existence
11. Delaware's nickname
12. ____ vera
13. Split
21. European capital
23. General Bradley
25. Parakeets' homes
26. Asian antelope
27. Funt of "Candid Camera"
28. Delaware's major port
29. Couldn't stand
30. Fared
31. Napped leather
33. Jacket part
36. Driver
37. Pigskin
39. Tatting
40. London TV
42. Diggers
43. Hoarders
45. ____ up (studied)
46. Sketch
47. "Othello" villain
48. Birth
49. Musically together
50. Cut down
51. Indonesian island
54. Previously named

FOUR-MOST

PUZZLE 208

All of the four-letter words in this crossword puzzle are listed separately and are in alphabetical order. Use the numbered clues as solving aids to help determine where each four-letter word goes in the diagram.

4 LETTERS
ACRE
AMOS
ANIL
ANON
ARID
AXLE
EGAD
ERAL
ERIE
ETES
EXIT
GENE
GLEE
GNAT
IRAN
IRED
MELD
MESA
MILD
NOSE
PACE
PALE
PARE
PEAR
PINE
PISA
PITA
PLAN
PLAY
POLL
PURR
RANG
RAVE
SETS
SITE
SOLE
STAR
USED
VIES
VISA

ACROSS
1. Make a lap
12. Bedlam
15. Buddy
20. Egg dish
27. Cleo's killer
31. Derby, e.g.
33. Picnic drink
38. Rue
46. Astonish
51. Not against
54. Finger count

DOWN
1. Plant juice
2. Cider girl
3. Allow
6. Used a match
7. Uninhabited
8. Poe's bird
21. Spring month
24. Win, ____, or show
26. Ghost
27. Helicopter or plane, e.g.
34. Apple or Boston cream
36. Get the wrinkles out
45. A Stooge
47. ____ is me!
48. Sea bird

PUZZLE 209

ACROSS

1. Barber or repair
5. Eva or Zsa Zsa
10. Command to Rover
14. Nobleman
15. Mountain crest
16. Tabu
17. Wings
18. Delicate
19. Aleutian island
20. Role on "Who's the Boss?"
21. Without a care in the world
23. Weaver's reed
25. Charity
26. French port
29. Feathered friends
32. Rectify
33. Donegal Bay feeder
34. Ameche or Ho
37. Isaac Asimov tale
41. Ike's WWII command
42. Sicilian volcano
43. French river
44. Bristles
46. Splashed
47. Prayer word
49. Bouncy
50. Lively Spanish dances
54. Idol
58. ____ girl!
59. Hubbub
60. Be afraid of
61. Hatching site
62. By no means
63. Coax
64. Indian
65. On one's toes
66. Caustic substances

DOWN

1. Petticoat junction?
2. Ring of light
3. Algerian port
4. Nice
5. Social blunders
6. Adorn
7. Pole climber
8. Of the ear
9. Depend (on)
10. Growls
11. Tribal symbol
12. Feeds the kitty
13. Second person
22. Whim
24. "____ Rose" ("The Music Man" song)
26. Eatery
27. He loves: Lat.
28. Jay ____ of late-night TV
29. Salt water
30. Indian of Peru
31. Gun, as an engine
33. Kett of the comics
34. Podium
35. Fairy-tale heavy
36. Necessity
38. Place
39. Swan genus
40. Fresh
44. Lawmaking body
45. Terminal
46. Gobi or Sahara
47. Subsequent
48. Billiards stroke
49. Puzzle
51. She went to Siam
52. Playwright Coward
53. ____ the benefit of the doubt
55. Strange
56. Wrath
57. Mine finds
58. Business abbr.

PUZZLE 210

ACROSS

1. Toss
4. Summer cooler
7. Remove by cutting
13. Desert
15. Thief
16. Texas national park
17. Window trim
18. "____ Karenina"
19. Years, in Madrid
20. Sofa or flower
23. Poet Marvell
25. Fitness resort
28. Strong brews
30. Understand
31. Diamonds, e.g.
32. One who makes improvements
35. Serviceable
37. Zambezi River sight
39. Slanted
40. Dozing off
42. Western Indians
43. Beseech
44. Singer Ed ____
45. NASCAR driver Jarrett
46. Part of the ankle
49. Memorable time
50. Bald eagle's kin
51. Tropical ant
54. Divide proportionately
57. Manama's location
61. RSVP'd
62. Communication
63. Prolong
64. Tolkien creature
65. "Runaround ____"

DOWN

1. Chemist's milieu
2. Sash
3. Sack
4. Mideast gulf
5. Reed or Mills
6. Threaten
7. Make up for
8. Under
9. Boys
10. Former ring champ
11. Dudley Moore film
12. Unit for work
14. Basketball gp.
15. Intelligent
20. Pub
21. Raise
22. Explained
24. Ridicules
25. Heavenly
26. Kind of beer
27. Dined
29. Footwear
31. Hot sauce
33. Road map abbr.
34. Squad of the '70s
35. Sky phenomenon
36. Builder's tool
38. Debatable
39. Hamburger holder
41. Youth gp.
43. Sire
46. Prepare
47. Fed the kitty
48. Discolor
50. Mystery writer Gardner
52. "____ Old Black Magic"
53. Onassis
54. Before fix or sent
55. Harrison of Hollywood
56. Lean toward
58. Dolt
59. Promissory note: abbr.
60. Opposite of SSW

PUZZLE 211

ACROSS

1. Clinton's vice president
5. Equal to the task
9. Wide open
14. False god
15. Metallic element
16. Type of lily
17. Ballot
18. Obligations imposed by law
20. Built
22. Crazy
23. Make edging
24. Actor Knight
25. Corpsman
27. Ascend
30. Denver's st.
31. Eateries
35. Tom, Dick, or Harry
36. Barbie and Ken, e.g.
38. Marshal Dillon of "Gunsmoke"
39. Dutch export
41. Type of ink
42. Mountain's melody
43. Number of Muses
44. Cake topping
45. Slithery fish
46. Says no to desserts
48. Chang's twin
49. Framework
51. Ogling
53. Damage
54. Total up
57. Negative word
58. Beleaguer
62. Stockpiles of arms
65. Space org.
66. Auriculate
67. Brainstorm
68. Friendly nation
69. Sediment
70. TV's "Top ____"
71. Witnesses

DOWN

1. Donate
2. Smell
3. Mechanical performance
4. Chooses
5. Felt poorly
6. Raised rottweilers
7. Ship's history book
8. Painting
9. Sharp, biting taste
10. Gangster's gun
11. Dismounted
12. Alibi
13. Right of north
19. Young boy
21. Fairway gadget
25. Door trim
26. Arrived
27. Update
28. Spokes
29. Wacky
30. Having a common center
32. Went up against
33. Anesthetic
34. Burglarized
36. Caesar's 502
37. Slump
40. Hand out
47. Ecclesiastical councils
49. Heel
50. Amphitheaters
52. Charged particle
53. Flat-topped hills
54. Frightened
55. Beloved
56. Challenge
58. Roadrunner's sound
59. Singer Jerry ____
60. Small island
61. Puts down
63. Small dowel
64. Altar words

PUZZLE 212

ACROSS
1. Hair rake
5. Range
10. Kind of school
14. Enclosed space
15. Newsprint
16. Actress Anderson
17. Scrutinize
18. Teheran native
19. "____ for All Seasons"
20. On the other ____
21. Gingham dog's adversary
23. Tavern offerings
25. Hawaiian goose
26. Tacked
29. Hair styles
32. Stadium
33. French town
34. Average grade
37. Honor Blackman film, with "The"
41. Barcelona bravo
42. Church cross
43. Author Jules ____
44. Broths
46. Grimy
47. Mighty whale hunter
49. Circle
50. Maid Marian's love
54. Sound of laughter
58. Pigeon
59. Of the ear
60. Nail
61. Hebrew measure
62. Logic
63. Earthen jug
64. Auricles
65. Waste allowances
66. Chamber

DOWN
1. Country singer Johnny ____
2. Whale of a movie
3. Spiteful
4. Colorful handkerchief
5. Seasoned
6. "____ Bulba"
7. Iridescent gem
8. I came: Lat.
9. Norse explorer
10. Puts
11. Caesar or Cicero, e.g.
12. Maternally related
13. Fastener
22. Lennon's lady
24. Bend
26. Mexican morsel
27. Asian range
28. Nerve network
29. A Musketeer
30. Vamoosed
31. Mythical bird
33. Cease
34. Mr. Reiner
35. Irish river
36. Gazed at
38. Actress Joanne ____
39. Bard's stream
40. Family next door
44. Cavalry weapons
45. "Mikado" costume item
46. Moves furtively
47. Redolence
48. Make like a helicopter
49. Cut of meat
51. Political cartoonist
52. Alarm shouter
53. French department
55. A Guthrie
56. Heavenly headgear
57. Eden dweller
58. Bambi's mom

PUZZLE 213

ACROSS

1. Dispose of
6. Snip
10. Hyde Park buggy
14. Wall Street's Boesky et al.
15. Emanation
16. Rank
17. Hyperopic
19. Favorite
20. Horizontal
21. Dawn goddess
22. Serve the port
24. Rhine feeder
26. Adores
27. Mob
30. Forty-niners
31. Spry
32. Psalms
33. Musician Calloway
36. Sound
37. Strolled
39. Barrett the gossiper
40. Paid athlete
41. Actor Paul ____
42. Terminal
43. Dam on the Columbia
45. Spreads
46. Gust
48. Quayle and Rather
49. Depends on
50. Author Bracken
51. Vats
55. Caucasian language
56. Sight for a Winchester
59. Actress Austin
60. Learn
61. "____ Gay"
62. Meeting: abbr.
63. Sea eagle
64. Dogma

DOWN

1. Pique
2. Egg-shaped
3. Before graph or chute
4. Dangerous
5. Twenty-third Greek letter
6. City on the Truckee
7. Gullies
8. Great anger
9. Raised the dander
10. Grocer's gun?
11. NORAD's lookout
12. Repent
13. Defrosts
18. Actor Richard ____
23. Arden and Plumb
25. Ginger ____
26. Amusement-park offering
27. File style
28. Japanese gelatin
29. Birdwatcher's need
30. Flick
34. Later
35. Ash clubs
37. ____ roost
38. Pip
39. Alabama arsenal
41. Voiceless
42. Clamor
44. Egyptian deity
45. Moves the tail
46. Spoiled tykes
47. Riverbank
48. Tractor man
50. Layout
52. At the brink
53. Choler
54. Ella's forte
57. Eternally, in verse
58. Whale: pref.

DOUBLE CROSSER

PUZZLE 214

Fill in the missing letters in the crossword diagram, making sure that no word is repeated. Then transfer those letters to the correspondingly numbered dashes below the diagram to reveal a quotation.

■	34	A	S	P	■	12	A	S	T	■	■	22	A	N
P	A	36	K	A	■	I	D	I	23	T	■	O	W	3
A	S	S	18	T	■	7	O	28	E	R	■	14	A	W
S	T	O	P	■	A	I	R	S	■	I	20	E	R	T
T	E	10	T	1	C	L	4	■	16	B	U	S	E	S
■	■	■	I	D	E	A	■	■	W	E	N	T	■	■
B	24	A	C	E	■	5	A	M	E	33	■	A	S	P
O	A	26	S	■	25	C	R	I	D	■	B	30	U	R
31	P	T	■	K	N	E	E	L	■	29	L	L	E	Y
■	■	E	D	I	15	■	■	L	21	G	O	■	■	■
S	T	9	E	S	S	■	D	27	R	E	C	2	O	R
L	A	W	N	19	■	L	O	N	E	■	17	I	T	E
6	L	A	■	E	R	A	S	8	■	B	A	T	H	11
T	O	R	■	D	I	V	13	R	■	I	D	L	E	D
E	32	D	■	■	M	A	S	S	■	B	E	35	R	■

__   __ __ __ __ __ __ __ __   __ __ __ __ __
1   2 3 4 5 6 7 8 9   10 11 12 13 14

__ __ __ __ __   __ __   __ __ __   __   __ __ __ __ __
15 16 17 18 19   20 21   22 23 24   25   26 27 28 29 30

__ __ __ __ __ __.
31 32 33 34 35 36

PUZZLE 215

ACROSS

1. Heart of the wheat
5. Drawing room
10. Napoleon's place of exile
14. Range
15. Excited
16. Shape
17. Ho Chi ____
18. Stories
19. Dog's bane
20. Tot's vehicle
22. Sneakiness
24. Ford fuel
25. Pouch
26. Moroccan seaport
29. Country cabin
32. Stocking lines
36. Sir Anthony ____
37. Turn
39. Stadium sound
40. 007 thriller
43. Energy unit
44. Squinted
45. Hawk
46. Change the clock
48. Neither here ____ there
49. Empty
50. Meadow
52. Suit ____ tee
53. Shiver
57. Errand runners
61. Huron or Ontario
62. Scandalous city
64. Spicy stew
65. Singing brothers
66. Air a view
67. Aggravate
68. Experiment
69. Rose and Fountain
70. Out on the ocean

DOWN

1. Schools of whales
2. Suspense writer Ambler
3. Gambling town
4. Dark wood
5. Overfeeds
6. At a distance
7. "____ Abner"
8. Minerals
9. Fledglings' abodes
10. Wipe out
11. Lounge
12. TV's Maverick
13. Asian nurse
21. Make a doily
23. Soothes
26. Consult
27. Venerate
28. Floes
29. Hollywood's Sophia ____
30. Colorado county
31. Merrier
33. Golfer Palmer, to friends
34. Valletta's country
35. Less bold
37. Feel remorse
38. Newscaster Koppel
41. Chose
42. New Mexico's neighbor
47. First-born
49. Gendarme
51. Fable writer
52. Large books
53. Strip of wood
54. Part of a horse's collar
55. Polynesian instruments
56. Cowpoke's gear
57. Departed
58. Olympic site
59. Teeming
60. Couch
63. Morse code signal

PUZZLE 216

ACROSS

1. Pokes
5. Traffic-light color
8. Globe
11. Burn plant
12. Face shape
14. "Norma ____"
15. Excitement
16. Devote
18. More pungent
20. Servant
21. Bronx attraction
22. Vitality
23. Foreign
26. Sure!
27. Swimsuit top
30. Precious
31. Small barrel
32. Gibe
33. Moral offense
34. "____ Little Indians"
35. Stir
36. Straw
37. Brewed beverage
38. Cleansing agent
41. More savage
45. Foil wrap
47. Uncommon
48. Headed
49. Few
50. Omelet ingredients
51. Female deer
52. Marry
53. For fear that

DOWN

1. "All That ____"
2. Toward the sheltered side
3. Fluffy scarves
4. Carbonated water
5. Cowboy contest
6. At all
7. Father
8. Not written
9. Merit
10. Borscht ingredient
13. Dwells
17. Bottle top
19. Charged atom
22. Cribbage pin
23. Radio spots
24. Flower necklace
25. Actor Hunter
26. Desire
27. Partly opened flower
28. Outfit
29. Imitate
31. ____ lime pie
32. Brawl
34. Cabs
35. Hive dweller
36. Smoked pork
37. Used a stopwatch
38. Lacking hair
39. Butter substitute
40. Impolite
41. Seethe
42. Coop
43. Units of work
44. Relaxation
46. Presently

PUZZLE 217

ACROSS
1. Swiss mountain
4. Fitness center
7. Coin aperture
11. Hispaniola country
14. Word on a light bulb
16. California fruit valley
17. Mimes
18. Salt tree
19. Muscat's country
20. Elizabeth Taylor film
23. Roman poet
24. Sault ___ Marie
25. Gershwin musical
33. Wonderment
34. Coastal flier
35. Lure
36. Latvia's capital
38. Mr. Onassis
40. ___ Stanley Gardner
41. Battery terminal
43. Lower leg
46. Crew's control
47. Circus command?
51. Old-time car
52. Delineate
53. Koehler-Arlen song
59. Make a to-do over
60. Irritate
61. Moth
65. Water and skate
66. Search
67. Grow
68. Broadcasted
69. Make a lap
70. Composer Rorem

DOWN
1. Exclamation
2. One time around the track
3. Slapstick item
4. Barter
5. ___ of least resistance
6. Finally
7. Winter powder
8. Tibetan monk
9. Iridescent gem
10. Army vehicle
12. Roman fountain
13. "O, my luve ___ a . . ."
15. After ninth
21. German river
22. ___ off (irate)
23. It borders California
25. Teasdale and Gilbert
26. Cord
27. Actress Merkel
28. Freshwater fish
29. Spelling or quilting
30. "Uneasy lies the head that wears ___"
31. Actor Lloyd ___
32. Colorers
37. Append
39. Dublin's land: abbr.
42. Emerald Isle
44. Western campus: abbr.
45. Fast pitch
48. Advances
49. Themes
50. Greek letter
53. "Stanley & ___"
54. Shoestring
55. The Frugal Gourmet's prop
56. It has no sleeves
57. Asian range
58. First-of-the-month payment
62. Bathtub ___
63. Compass pt.
64. Moscow Square

PUZZLE 218

ACROSS

1. Cookie accompaniment
5. Stinging insect
9. Gospel author
13. Brainstorm
14. Musician Shaw
16. Understanding comment
17. Murder
18. Pythias's boat?
20. Senator Kennedy
21. Grizzly
22. Take umbrage
23. Each
25. Actress Tyne ____
26. Stepped on
27. First Christmas visitors
28. School org.
31. Tomato or wallpaper
32. Flag holders
33. Goof
34. Twinge
35. Gleans
36. Temper tantrum
37. Luau dish
38. After the bell
39. FDR's coins
40. Cleo's way out
41. Grand Ole ____
42. Time periods
43. Formicary inhabitants
44. Primp
46. ____ chango!
49. Lumberyard product
50. Enjoy Stowe
53. John Updike's boat?
55. Moby Dick's pursuer
56. Former French President Coty
57. Glimmered
58. Toe the ____
59. 6th Jewish month
60. Enjoys pretzels
61. Pinnacle

DOWN

1. Spray
2. Inactive
3. George W. Bush's boat?
4. Actress Francis
5. Cracker
6. Arrangement
7. Jail
8. Dessert choice
9. Actress Gold
10. Tennis great
11. Harness part
12. Retained
15. Infuriates
19. Places to get a sandwich
21. "Adam ____"
24. Participate in an election
25. Waste time
26. Mexican sandwiches
27. Like week-old bread
28. Calligrapher's boat?
29. Assays
30. ____ and crafts
31. One of the Three Bears
32. Expresses pleasure
35. Jailers
36. Father
38. Lone Ranger's sidekick
39. Homeowner's paper
43. Son of Jacob
44. West ____
45. Learning the ____
46. Rubber: pref.
47. Was penitent
48. Lab lamp
49. Stop, horse!
51. "Citizen ____"
52. European wild goat
54. Woman's pronoun
55. W. of Georgia

PUZZLE 219

MOVIES AND TELEVISION

ACROSS

1. 1978 Michael Douglas film
5. George ____ of "Mr. Ace" (1946 film)
9. "____ Joey"
12. "Once ____ a Honeymoon" (1942 film)
13. Sal ____
14. "____ Street" (1948 film)
15. Peter ____ Hayes
16. 1985 Scorsese film: 2 wds.
18. "Teacher's ____" (1958 film)
19. "____ for the Lamps of China" (1935 film)
20. "Ready, Willing and ____" (1937 film)
21. Clark ____
23. "El ____" (1949 film)
25. "The Big ____" (1983 film)
27. 1940 Davis film, with "The"
30. "____ and the Bachelor" (1957 film)
31. "The Wreck of the Mary ____" (1959 film)
33. Bested by DDE in 1952 and 1956
35. Actor Vigoda
36. "A ____ from Mrs. Cimino" (1982 film)
37. Mrs., to Montalban
38. Neither's partner
39. Howard Duff TV show
40. Ravi Shankar's instrument
42. ____ Power
44. ____ Massey
45. "____ the Top" (1987 film)
46. "____ La Mancha" (1972 film): 2 wds.
48. 1940s film actor ____ Clark
50. Hesitation sounds
51. King of Siam's expression: abbr.
54. "____ to Broadway" (1953 film): 2 wds.
58. 1966 Jennifer Jones film, with "The"
59. "This Is the ____" (1943 film)
60. Eller and Em
61. Honduran seaport
62. "____, Giorgio" (1982 film)
63. "Twin ____" (1942 film)
64. "The ____ Griffith Show"

DOWN

1. Robert ____ of "I Spy"
2. Character in 64 Across
3. Robert or Elizabeth
4. "____ Now Tomorrow" (1944 film)
5. "Springfield ____" (1952 film)
6. Rocker Adam
7. Performing charge
8. "High ____"
9. Hogan or Newman
10. "God's Little ____" (1958 film)
11. "____ Miserables" (1935 film)
13. "Jackass ____" (1942 film)
14. "____ Monster" (1953 film)
17. "Make ____ to Live" (1954 film)
19. ____ the law
22. "The Wrong ____ of the Law" (1962 film)
23. Prop in "Airport" movies
24. Of flying: prefix
25. Actor Laurel
26. Bruce ____, Fay Wray's savior
28. 1955 Dean film: 3 wds.
29. Showed a movie again
31. 1982 Kevin Bacon film
32. "You Are What You ____" (1968 film)

PUZZLE 219

34. Brenda Vaccaro TV series
36. Glass unit
39. Not hawks
40. "The ____ of Rachel Cade" (1961 film)
41. Dock workers' group: abbr.
43. Young Mr. Howard
46. "Frankenstein ____ the Wolf Man" (1943 film)
47. Linkletter and Carney
48. "They ____ Not Love" (1941 film)
49. Goals
52. "The Greatest Story Ever ____" (1965 film)
53. "____ Pigeon" (1971 film)
54. Comedian Elaine
55. Actor Hunter
56. Actress McClanahan
57. "The ____ of the Affair" (1955 film)
58. "Call ____ Day" (1937 film): 2 wds.

PUZZLE 220

ACROSS

1. Sports record, for short
5. Zhivago's love
9. Easy task
13. 1492 ship
14. Turn inside out
16. —— Linda, Calif.
17. Virgil's "Love conquers all": 3 wds.
20. Well-beings
21. Sets apart
22. Choose
24. Plus
25. Chaplains
28. Twaddle
33. Mr. Baba
34. French photographer
36. Chamber
37. Cicero's "I am a Roman citizen": 3 wds.
41. "—— Diary"
42. Communist hero
43. That: Sp.
44. Decayed again
47. Charters
49. "High ——"
50. Clairvoyance: abbr.
51. Ships' anchors
56. Campus girls
60. Alcuin's "The voice of the people is the voice of God": 4 wds.
62. To shelter
63. Shorthand, for short
64. Unique person
65. Monocle
66. Noticed
67. Scruff

DOWN

1. TV static
2. Watch data
3. Actress Case
4. Suit maker
5. "My Name Is Asher ——"
6. Eager
7. Director Clair
8. Rainbows
9. Maligns
10. Alaskan city
11. Minor Prophet
12. Stated value
15. Saturn moon
18. Poplars
19. Cans
23. Russian ruler
25. Harness track horse
26. Animated
27. Frogman
28. Nominated
29. Algerian city
30. Snouts
31. Drunkard
32. Mme. Bovary et al.
35. Allot
38. Chemical element forms
39. African river
40. International gp.
45. Bull: Sp.
46. Stumbles
48. "—— the girl" (Woolf): 3 wds.
51. Beauty spot
52. Draft animals
53. Soup to ——
54. Mirth
55. Without: Latin
57. —— May Oliver
58. Way down
59. King's title
60. French lace
61. Otto —— Bismarck

PUZZLE 221

ACROSS
1. Stir
4. Bonnet
7. Fourposter
10. Camera part
12. Rubbed
14. Painful
15. Once more
16. "Goodnight" girl
17. Musical sound
18. Bizarre
20. Aerobic shoe
22. Pull
23. Night bird
24. Overpass
28. Church spire
32. Olive or sunflower
33. Colonist
35. Pine or pepper
36. Eggs
37. Gardener's aid
38. "____ Got a Secret"
39. Permit
40. Hi-fis
44. Retreat
45. Clam
47. Spoils
49. Race
50. Wooden peg
51. Reel
55. Bonuses
59. "Little ____" (comic strip)
60. Come to a point
62. Rapper L.L. ____ J.
63. Woodwind
64. Begets
65. Sharpen
66. Tiny
67. Drowse
68. Gave lunch to

DOWN
1. Woe is me!
2. Imprint
3. Pip
4. "Monsieur ____"
5. Imitate
6. Sawbucks
7. Novel
8. Marine flier
9. Whitetail
11. Whacks
12. Writhe
13. Indicate
14. Banal
19. Barbra Streisand film
21. Water jug
24. Carpenter's need
25. Metal pin
26. Gladden
27. Flammable liquid
28. "To ____ With Anger"
29. Self-esteem
30. Crowbar
31. Blissful abodes
34. Cliff
40. Boastful
41. Beliefs
42. Westerns
43. Eurasian duck
46. Dispute
48. Georgia fruit
51. Subside
52. Boob ____
53. African lily
54. Type of forest
55. Oliver or Lou
56. Housetop
57. Complete
58. Pung or troika
61. Master

PUZZLE 222

ACROSS

1. Unseat
7. Waist tie
11. Value
17. Some football players
18. Verboten
19. Outstanding
21. New member
22. Lifeless
23. ___ non grata
24. Always, to a bard
25. And not
26. Life of the party
28. Geraint's wife
29. Gullet
31. Aloof
33. Seed coat
34. Cheerful: Fr.
35. Wished
37. Top-drawer
38. Aver
39. South American rodent
40. Slowly, in music
42. Printing direction
43. Beelzebub
44. Romantic poet
47. Mother ___
49. Defrost again
50. Australian marsupial
51. Swiss lake
52. Audience
53. ___ tower
54. Boat hoist
55. ___ Mead
60. Parcel out
61. National Guard job
63. Actor Jack ___
65. Wayne film
67. "Le ___ d'Arthur"
68. Quench
69. "___ Got to Be Me"
70. Sawfish snout
71. ___ Island
72. Avoid
76. Irritable
78. Forebode
79. NCO's nickname
80. Hire
81. Spokes
82. Baobab, e.g.
83. Toiler
85. Landing
87. Assume as a fact
91. South American people
92. Seep
93. When this happened
95. Knob
96. Say nay
98. Value too highly
100. Hot ___
102. Infinitesimal
103. Energize
105. European plant
106. Salad dressing
108. Young hare
109. Mountain crest
110. "___ -Six Trombones"
111. Shipworm
112. Smooth
113. Come into view

DOWN

1. Mexican money
2. Lure
3. For each
4. Arabian gulf
5. Mister, in Madrid
6. Plea
7. Medieval cloth
8. Upstairs
9. Aching
10. Predicament
11. ___ de corps
12. Addison's partner
13. Thrice: pref.
14. Different
15. Lengthen
16. Demented
17. Bloodsucker
18. Claw
20. Beaming
27. Overwrought
30. Refined
32. Low
36. Procrastinate
38. Amaze
39. Shriver of tennis
41. ___ worth
42. Pronouncement
43. Evening, in Palermo
44. Sink's opposite
45. Fly overhead
46. Ham it up
47. At no time
48. Within
49. Latest fad
51. Feeble
52. Celtic language

PUZZLE 222

54. Noah's scout
55. Gleeful
56. Theater gp.
57. Kinsman
58. Please
59. Captured
61. Busy spot
62. Tuning ____
64. Recover
66. Ready enough
68. Divest
70. Sound
71. Turf
72. Of summer
73. Silk for linings
74. Original
75. Birthday-cake number
76. Vogue
77. About-face
78. "____ Lost"
81. Female ruff
83. Dirtied
84. "I ____ Sing"
85. Small
86. Actress Papas
88. Planting seed
89. Think up
90. Minute
93. Refuge
94. ____ pole
97. Hebrew dry measure
99. Not common
101. Donated
104. Exist
107. Sea god

PUZZLE 223

ACROSS

1. Throw about
6. Wires
12. Comic strip ghost
18. Sports field
19. Ring of color
20. Downhill skiing event
21. Newspaper feature
23. Office greenery
24. Opposite of WSW
25. Banquet
26. Vicinity
28. Before, poetically
29. Slices wood
31. Caviar
32. Spud
34. Let it stand
35. Greek letters
37. Appointed
38. Weight allowances
39. Offends
42. Shoe parts
43. Auto wheel
44. Harden
45. Patton's army
46. Wild cries
49. Hit hard
50. Comic Soupy ___
51. Toledo's location
52. Witness
53. ___ board
54. Talkative person
56. Mulligan ___
57. A Gabor
58. Report card report
59. Coaxed
60. Use a VCR
61. Group of attendants
63. Actor Keith
64. Hose down
65. Danube feeder
66. Relic
67. Los Angeles team
68. Young salmon
70. Cleaving tools
71. General's assistant
72. Johnnycake
73. Pal
74. Fast jet
75. Tale
79. Long ___ of the law
80. Biblical word
81. Mirages
83. French pronoun
84. "The Rose of ___"
86. Busybody
90. Employers
91. Valley flowers?
92. Follow
93. Narrow sandy ridges
94. Conger catchers
95. Sobs

DOWN

1. Cooking herbs
2. Yellowish mineral
3. Baste again
4. Actual being
5. Homeless child
6. Chocolate sources
7. Met the day
8. Bible or corn
9. Actor Gossett, Jr.
10. Graceful shade provider
11. Councils
12. Escapade
13. ___ breve
14. Health haven
15. Maine's nickname
16. Main course
17. Turns back the odometer
22. Beautiful young girls
27. Danger color
30. Laurel
32. Is frank
33. Actor Leon ___
34. Hindu garment
36. "___ Haw"
37. Composition for nine
38. Beginner
39. Vex

PUZZLE 223

40. Smitten
41. Excerpt punctuation
42. Caesar, e.g.
43. Diamond feature
45. Nevada resort
46. Luster
47. Zoo employee
48. Drains
50. Rub
51. Church instrument
55. Lake Indians
56. Antes
58. Pest
62. ____ of Man
63. Blessing
64. Roll of money
66. Hardship
67. Metric unit
68. Bract
69. Famous finicky feline
70. To and ____
71. Tax
73. Fischer's game
74. Saw type
76. Delight
77. Clothes
78. Cigar residue
80. Region: abbr.
81. TV award
82. Pintail duck
85. Pasture
87. Incline
88. Whole
89. Wallet filler

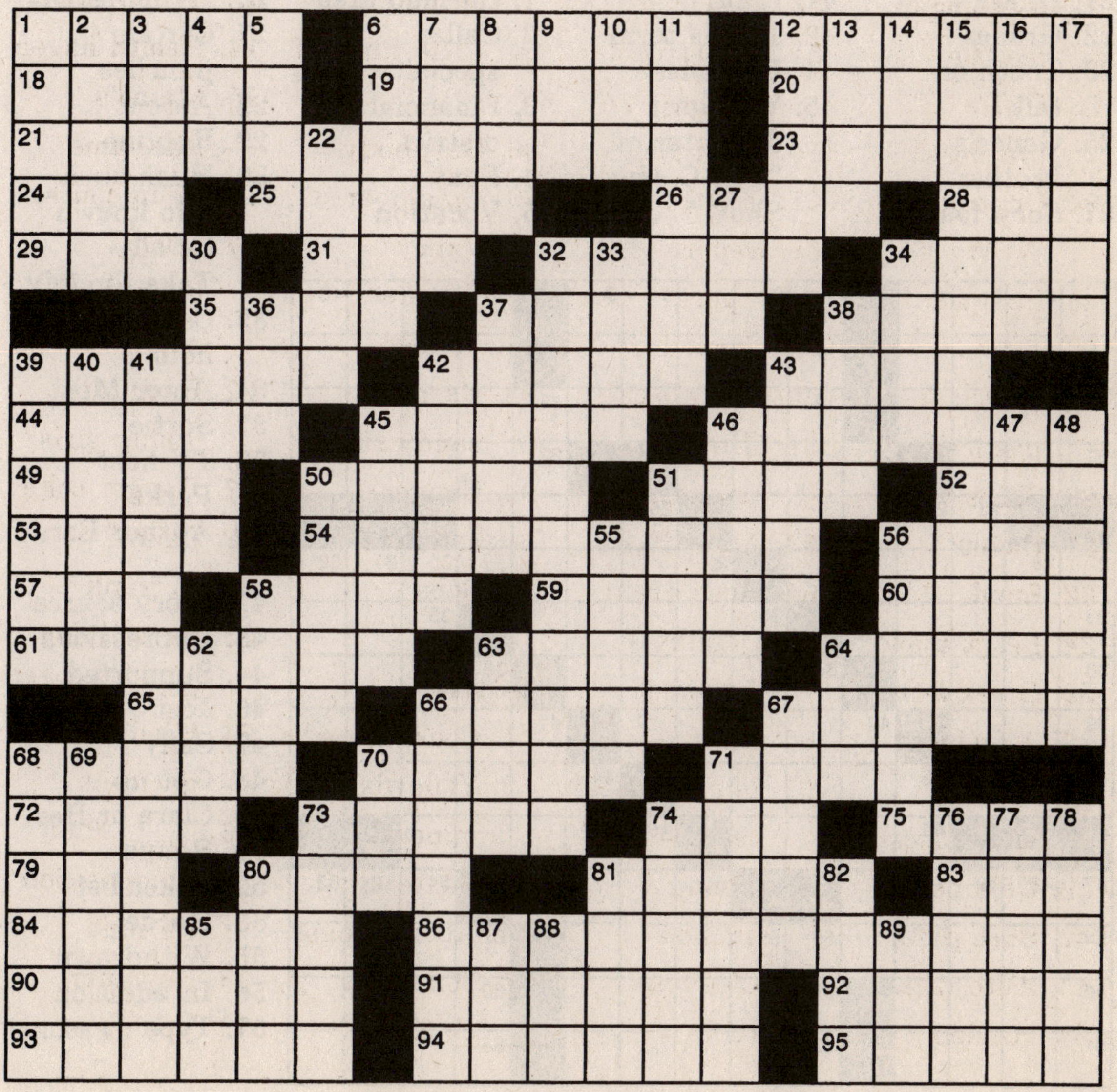

PUZZLE 224

ACROSS

1. Statutes
5. Confined
10. Norway's capital
14. Type of surgeon
15. Deft
16. Provisions
17. Greasy
18. Likeness
20. Chum
21. Knack
22. Grades
23. Tooth or talk
25. Genesis brother
27. Soap foam
29. Resident's city
33. White plume
34. "____ at Sea"
35. Paid athlete
36. Liberate
37. Batman's buddy
38. Auxiliary verb
39. Golf peg
40. Hysteria
41. Rigid
42. Tennis term
44. Explodes
45. Youngest daughter of "The Cosby Show"
46. Sample
47. Practice
50. Buss
51. Tabby
54. Beef cut
57. Coastal bird
58. Common contraction
59. Filly
60. Ration
61. Caresses
62. Joined
63. Pipe part

DOWN

1. Chicago area
2. Callas specialty
3. Financial district
4. Foxy
5. Vocation
6. Emissary
7. Present
8. Building shape
9. Scottish river
10. Eighth part
11. Climb
12. Appearance
13. Admits
19. Calls out
21. Root vegetable
24. Cry of delight
25. Henny Youngman, e.g.
26. Hymn ending
27. Certain punches
28. Assent
29. Routine
30. Hush-hush info known by all
31. Take forcibly
32. Canonical hour
34. Actor Most
37. Sortie
38. TV host Parks
40. Author Ezra ____
41. Ivory source
43. Impressions
44. Supported
46. Jest
47. Sally
48. Got up
49. Clara or Bee
50. Bonus
52. Poker bet
53. Horde
55. Withdrawn
56. In addition
57. Type measures

PUZZLE 225

ACROSS

1. Mauls
5. Perform
8. Woods
14. Sulawesi ox
15. Spoil
16. Devonshire city
17. Maestro
19. Adjust
20. German city
21. City on the Arkansas
23. "____ a Wonderful Life"
24. Does a tailor's work
26. Terrace
28. Last
29. Subjugates
33. Debilitate
34. "El Capitan" composer
36. Burlap fiber
37. Tow truck
39. Thrash
42. Soil: pref.
43. Lend ____
45. Type of shirt
46. Missile part
49. Actress Wilson
51. Ledger entry
52. Ven.'s locale
53. Playwright Shepard
56. Rodeo item
58. Egg-shaped
61. Recognition
63. Thankless ones
65. Lazy
66. Wind dir.
67. Type of cheese
68. Wallet item
69. Rummy
70. Ms. Bombeck

DOWN

1. Macadamize
2. Cuckoos
3. Congregation
4. Lustrous fabric
5. I love: Lat.
6. Hurl
7. Bands of performers
8. Regales
9. Kind of soup
10. Soak flax
11. Small case
12. Forwarded
13. Very, in Vichy
18. Expose
22. Woolly
25. Wild plum
27. Kauai's neighbor
28. Wells ____
30. Fresh-air contrivance
31. Host
32. Ger. admiral
33. Cygnet
35. One of the Muses
38. Certain student
40. Twigs
41. Cicero, e.g.
44. Meshwork
47. Red
48. ____ dictum
50. Demolish
53. Dundee denizen
54. Commedia dell'____
55. Chow ____
57. Years: Lat.
59. Lakers, e.g.
60. This, to Carmela
62. Put on
64. Milit. VIP

PUZZLE 226

ACROSS

1. Silent screen actress Theda ____
5. Leaves the singles scene
9. Zola
14. Pre-college exam: abbr.
18. ____ Bator
19. Song at the Met
20. To do with form
21. Light unit
23. Entrancing
25. Manipulators
26. Iowa colony
27. Ammonium carbonate
29. Ancient Greek coin
30. Coal unit
31. Novelist Seton
32. Utah's capital
35. Currier's partner
36. Compassion
37. Panache
38. Homes
41. Morse or dress
42. Keeps in reserve
47. ____ and onions
48. Sped
49. Doctor who delivered the Dionne quintuplets
50. Stretch of lowland
51. Lyric poems
52. Football's Starr
53. Defeat
54. Stick for Bernstein
55. Each
56. Computer fodder
57. Superboy's girlfriend Lang
58. Cuts into small pieces
59. Society's best
64. Proportion
66. Soaks
67. ____ Marian
68. Lard
71. Virile
72. Crude
74. Glacier's snowy part
75. Rickey ingredient
76. Chilled
77. Avoids
78. Goes bad
79. Rank of Snoopy's archenemy
80. Purifying sea water
82. Electrical units
83. Fishermen's boots
84. Wine prefix
85. Be introduced to
86. Venture
87. With ____ (skeptically)
92. Gainer or jackknife, e.g.
93. ____ culpa
96. Theater district
97. Fully deserving
100. Nimble
101. Take care of
103. Opera beginnings
104. Misfit
105. Powdered volcanic rock
106. Dry
107. Pilaf ingredient
108. Gets some sun
109. Consent
110. Stepped
111. ____ Morgana

DOWN

1. Explode
2. Texas shrine
3. Lustrous black
4. Dark blue dye
5. Polynesian women
6. The Furies
7. ____-ling (fool)
8. Bends in the middle
9. Try to equal
10. Chiefly
11. That is: Lat.
12. Household god
13. Urban railways
14. Typewriter parts
15. Poison ivy's cousin
16. Valuable violin
17. Principle
22. Never
24. Drool
28. Next to
29. Use the rink
33. Turns pages carelessly
34. Apportion
35. Fateful March date
36. ____ of entry
38. Off balance
39. Wait
40. Implications
41. Reef material
42. Actress Bernhardt
43. ____-garde
44. Night signal
45. Medicinal plant
46. Itches
48. Londoner's good-bye
49. Dos and ____
52. Rope fiber
53. Floats on air
54. Cockatoo, e.g.
56. Negate
57. Good soil
58. Water pipe
60. German goddess of marriage
61. Nasal tone

PUZZLE 226

62. Sends forth
63. Pitcher parts
64. In the center of
65. Ground spice
69. Cupid
70. Sawbucks
72. Uniform material
73. ____ the mill (ordinary)
74. Furniture part
75. Do a stevedore's job
77. Office worker
78. Butler in "GWTW"
79. Most meager
81. Lingers aimlessly
82. ____ Park, Illinois
83. Fluctuated
85. ____-tung
86. Money, slangily
87. Inland Asian sea
88. Leg of lamb
89. Mrs. Gorbachev
90. Ethan or Fred
91. Take oath
92. Delaware's capital
93. "West Side Story" heroine
94. Put into office
95. Confused
98. Greeter
99. Ride the waves
101. Depot: abbr.
102. Energy unit

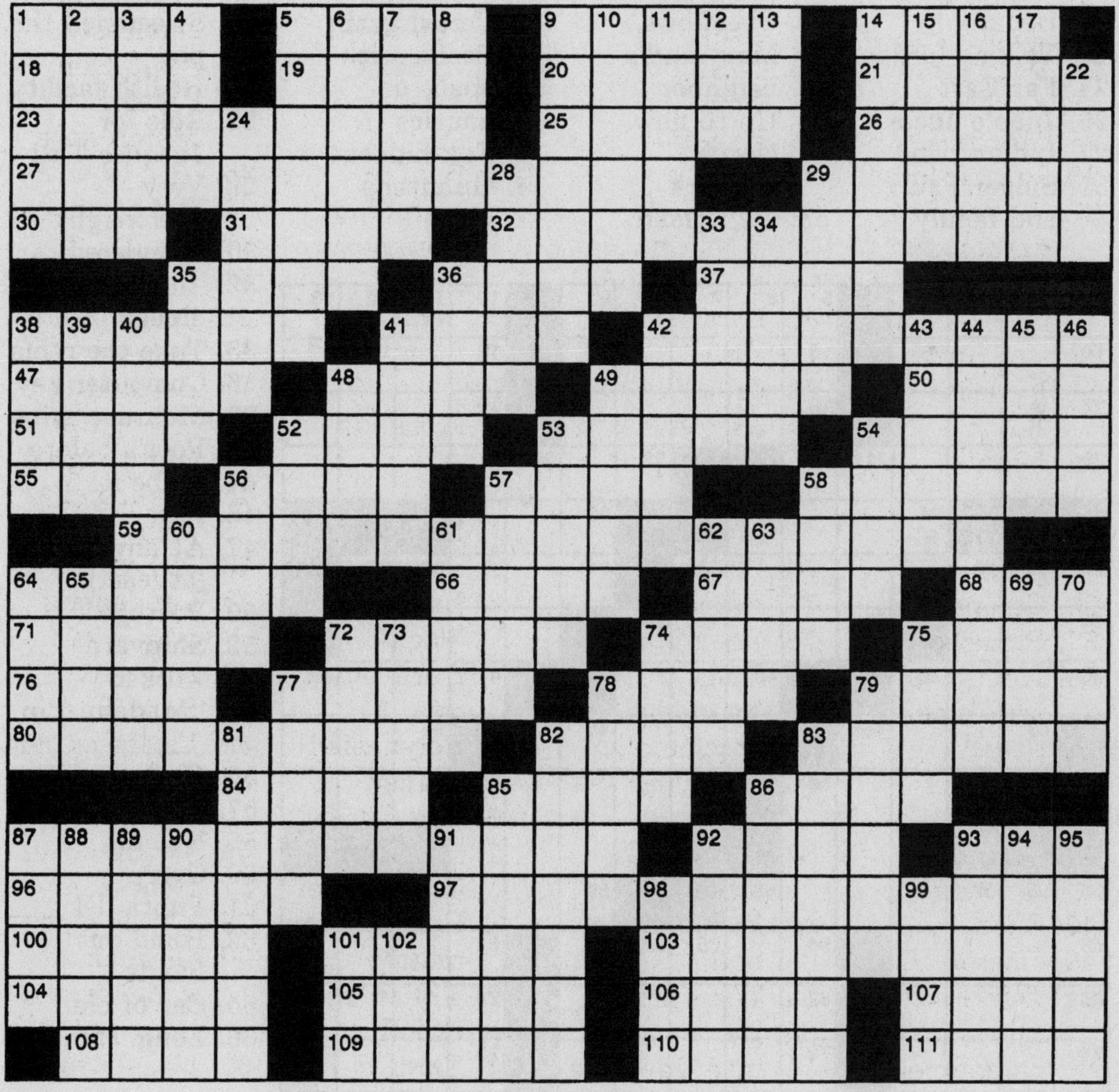

PUZZLE 227

ACROSS

1. Golf, base, or foot follower
5. Idaho's capital
10. Cut up
14. Believable
15. Before peace or tube
16. Where the heart is?
17. Song for Sutherland
18. Misfit
19. Exude
20. Usual
22. Talking birds
24. Far East
26. Juan's uncle
27. Indian tribe
31. Singer Paul and family
34. British bar
35. ____ vous
37. Money
38. Actor McCowen
40. Sea swooper
41. "En garde" weapon
43. Government job protection agcy.
45. Discourage
48. Feminine pronoun
49. Overflows
51. Maryland's neighbor
53. Up to now
54. Nerve network
55. ____ gland
59. How Frosty died
63. Campus VIP
64. Highway entrance sign
67. Medicinal amount
68. Infamous Idi
69. Song of joy
70. Singer James
71. Where coal comes from
72. Loud exhalation
73. Spool of film

DOWN

1. Cereal grain
2. Prefix with space or nautics
3. Fox hideout
4. Guanacos' kin
5. A thousand million
6. Lennon's Plastic ____ Band
7. ____ and outs
8. Leak
9. Printing errors
10. Rose of Georgia
11. ____ sapiens
12. Pass up
13. Dogs, cats, etc.
21. Arthur of the courts
23. Finger wear
25. Sweetened the pot
27. Health facility
28. Role for Jacques Tati
29. Very overweight
30. Blundered
32. ____ and omega
33. Take the reins
36. Computer key
39. Montana tribe
42. Poet's before
44. So be it!
46. Part
47. At any ____ (at least)
50. Postage
52. Shipyard worker
55. "Madam, I'm ____"
56. Half: pref.
57. Picnic spoiler
58. Not fat
60. Carry
61. Punta del ____
62. Hand out hands
65. Car of old
66. Long, thin fish

PUZZLE 228

ACROSS
1. Orient
5. Barn site
9. Missing Jimmy
14. Prance
15. Baseballer Matty ____
16. NYC isle
17. 45s' non-hit cuts
19. Freshen a stamp pad
20. Ol' Blue Eyes
21. D.C. group
23. Legume
24. "Norma ____"
25. Bloke
27. Postponement
31. Improvise
33. British howdy
34. Spray
36. ____ breve
38. Japanese sash
39. Box type
42. Yosemite ____
43. Clean
45. Not worth ____
46. Once ____ time
48. Old car
50. Disloyal
52. Optimally
54. Succeeded
55. Network inits.
57. Car protector
58. Firemen's cradle
62. Singer Pat ____
64. Rubber sandals
66. Simpleton
67. Republic of Ireland
68. Ancient Greek city
69. Guys
70. Interpret
71. Activist

DOWN
1. Barks
2. Arias
3. "____ the Mood . . ."
4. Garments
5. Less ruddy
6. Robert or Alan
7. Fish eggs
8. Louvre, e.g.
9. Messenger
10. Violinist Bull
11. TV comic
12. Delicate
13. ____ silly question . . .
18. ____ Bethlehem
22. Greek VIP
25. Go wild
26. Palm leaf
27. Arab boat
28. Musician Blake
29. Chooses by chance
30. Kingsley ____
32. French mont
35. Dumfound
37. Nursemaid, in India
40. Looser
41. Delay
44. Id ____
47. Like some dens
49. ____ Field
51. Filched
53. Less risky
55. " . . . carry ____ stick"
56. Foretoken
58. Milan money, formerly
59. ____ contendere
60. Dueling sword
61. Tyrant
63. Negative word
65. ____ down on the job

PUZZLE 229

ACROSS

1. The Georgia Peach
5. Calyx part
10. Sleep
14. Malarial fever
15. Repent
16. Writer Gardner
17. Anatomical network
18. Plane
20. Animal amigo
21. Rainbow
22. Refuges
23. Joyce Carol ____
25. Restaurateur Toots
27. Mined for gold
29. Backup: hyph.
32. Berry-bearing tree
33. Reporter's question
34. ____ and downs
36. Wild revelry
37. Skinned
38. Being: Fr.
39. Playing marble
40. Old World falcon
41. More shrewd
42. Showed contempt
44. Singer Julius ____: 2 wds.
45. Taboo item for Mrs. Sprat
46. Buffalo
47. Grab the tab
50. See you later
51. Topper
54. Detain
57. Nat King ____
58. Bitter drug
59. Raring to go
60. Frosty
61. Distress
62. Mild oaths
63. Related

DOWN

1. Find fault
2. Double curve
3. ____ collar: hyph.
4. Honey maker
5. Stuck with a sword
6. Carrying cases
7. ____ and pans
8. Aardvark fare
9. Astral cat
10. Bounty
11. Cupid
12. Wild plum
13. Spreads out for drying
19. Not a soul: 2 wds.
21. Roman road
24. Dill herb
25. Bum ____
26. Difficult
27. Saucy
28. Pen name
29. Tatter
30. Football play
31. Belgian commune
33. Rouse
35. Plant fluids
37. Amazon arm
38. Large 'roo
40. Take care of: 2 wds.
41. House: Sp.
43. Lifted up
44. Metric units
46. Bundled cotton
47. Ski lift: hyph.
48. As a ____
49. Short jacket
50. White robe
52. Asian range
53. Trio
55. Wedding announcement word
56. Ugly old Crone
57. Rolled tea

PUZZLE 230

ACROSS

1. With the addition of
5. Stage person
10. Labels
14. Smidgen
15. Camel's cousin
16. Soil: pref.
17. Aim
18. Fair
19. Sandbox toy
20. Long U.S. waterway: 2 wds.
23. Cash
24. Dogma
25. Old Testament book
28. Youthfully chic
29. Creek
31. Thanks ____!: 2 wds.
33. Line dance
38. Satellite's sight: 2 wds.
42. Dingo's prey
43. Squirrel's cache
44. Keystone ____
45. Perfect: hyph.
48. Pointless talk
49. Bulgarian capital
53. Bitter
55. Powell's conquest: 3 wds.
60. Fencing piece
61. "Waiting for ____"
62. King of the jungle
64. Jason's ship
65. Love, to Dino
66. Too
67. TV cop
68. Imparts
69. Nijinsky's no

DOWN

1. Suzanne Sugarbaker's pet
2. Spoils
3. Bountiful's site
4. Boston suburb
5. One lacking natural coloring
6. Shut
7. Strong-smelling weed
8. All: pref.
9. Beams
10. Rhino's relative
11. Wide open
12. Complain
13. Unhollowed
21. Elyse Keaton, to Alex
22. Barely enough
25. Hoisting tool
26. Spanish stew pot
27. Benefit
29. Cane product
30. One ____ million: 2 wds.
32. Pull
33. Fam. member
34. Yang's counterpart
35. 60 minutes
36. Aware of
37. Hey, you!
39. Capital of Senegal
40. To's partner
41. Alley ____
45. Mutual agreement
46. Talks from a soapbox
47. Relatives
49. Fine fiddle
50. "Pal Joey" author
51. Fabricate
52. Inuit abode
53. Extension: hyph.
54. "Like a Rolling Stone" singer
56. "I've Got ____ in Kalamazoo": 2 wds.
57. Alaska city
58. Slick
59. Meddling bit of anatomy
63. "____ As a Stranger"

PUZZLE 231

ACROSS
1. Arabian garment
4. Excel
8. TV host of old
12. Autumn pear
14. Less well
15. Verdi opera
16. ____ boy!
17. Doesn't mention
18. Oxford sport
19. Go beyond reason in argument: 3 wds.
22. African antelope
23. Scientist Rubik
24. Quill point
27. "L.A. Law" actress
28. Curvy letter
31. Kind of step or egg
33. Cohan song: 2 wds.
37. Mets' home
40. Bride's path
41. Gaze
42. Move: 3 wds.
45. Wabbit hunter Fudd
46. ____ King Cole
47. Stolen
50. Existed
51. Specks
55. Like Chauncy Gardner
57. Marie Dressler role: 2 wds.
60. Bakery employee
63. A Beatle
64. Garden site
65. Bonanza
66. Church official
67. Ties the knot
68. See!
69. Slope slider
70. Singer Orbison

DOWN
1. Lowered
2. "Time in a ____"
3. Wandering
4. "Brave New World" drug
5. Garbage
6. "Maltese Falcon" actress
7. Varnish ingredient
8. Treaty
9. Make public
10. Cool drink
11. Harsh
13. "A Bridge Too Far" actor
14. Triumphed
20. Noodle product
21. Impossible: 2 wds.
24. Point
25. ____ of Man
26. Tap liquid
29. Fingers' sound
30. Slaloms
32. Clumsy one's cry
33. Connecticut college
34. It is: Lat.
35. Spirit
36. Ten: pref.
37. Emit
38. Luau dance
39. Graceful trees
43. Indic language
44. Lab lamp
47. Deter
48. Province in Spain
49. Itty-bitty
52. Man-eaters
53. Government bond: hyph.
54. Weather balloon
56. Fresh
57. Journey
58. Old
59. Craggy hill
60. Suffering
61. Dove sound
62. Old Tokyo

PUZZLE 232

ACROSS

1. Pack
5. More evil
10. Mix
14. Middle
15. Run off to wed
16. Medley
17. Unique: 4 wds.
20. 4 o'clock drink
21. 0%
22. Showroom models
23. Monkshood
24. Violin
26. Actress Kidder
29. Actor West
30. Project-cut initials
33. About
34. Actor Harrison
35. German river
36. Superficial job: hyph.
39. Feels sorry about
40. Comic Johnson
41. Female ruff
42. Naughty one
43. Hindu god
44. Vagabond
45. Score
47. Fill-ins, for short
48. Crown
50. Lab need
51. Hanks film
54. ____ shy: 3 wds.
58. Brain tissue
59. "Lorna ____"
60. Agenda part
61. Dates
62. ____ Wences
63. Knight namesakes

DOWN

1. North European
2. Sound
3. Whale
4. Picayune
5. Marathoner Joan ____
6. Paton and Shepard
7. Flatfish
8. Finial
9. Game judge, for short
10. Sacred song
11. Got rid of
12. Long car, for short
13. Accomplishes
18. Wholly: 2 wds.
19. Dutch cheese
23. "____ of God"
24. Fred's sister
25. African nation
26. South Seas native
27. Per ____
28. Holder
29. Main artery
31. Balm
32. Chicken type
34. Rash
35. Casts off
37. Colorado town
38. Clutch for: 2 wds.
43. Thick piece
44. Marksman
46. Places
47. Office help, briefly
48. Children
49. Arrow poison
50. School
51. Sting
52. Cooled
53. Stones
55. Parts of psyches
56. Shoe tip
57. Mental agility

PUZZLE 233

ACROSS

1. European saltwater fish
5. Rice ____
10. Under covers
14. Cuzco's country
15. Seething
16. Punjab river
17. Like Pindar's poetry
18. Shylock's business
19. Counterpart of Mars
20. Hardwood
21. Favorite one
22. Ohio feeder
24. Hammer part
26. "____ Live"
27. Sturgeon product
30. Stout's lighter cousin
31. Yalie
34. Intermediary
35. Actor Sal ____
36. Operated
37. Little piggies
38. Doughnut-shaped roll
39. Taste
40. Make a gaffe
41. Make drunk
42. Nibbler
43. Manta
44. Oven
45. Eastern temple
46. Nucleus
47. Area or dress
48. Industrialist Hammer
51. Electrical unit
52. Hull members
56. Smear
57. Ancient port of Rome
59. Pale tan
60. Sicilian mount
61. Bizarre
62. Planetary revolution
63. Fastener
64. Mother-of-pearl
65. Norse poetry

DOWN

1. Espy
2. Allow
3. Sills offering
4. Lane game
5. Penniless one
6. Norwegian dramatist
7. Oaf
8. Broadcast
9. Engine part
10. Irving Berlin song
11. Actress Theda ____
12. Nights
13. Plate
23. Flight: pref.
25. Erode
26. Doctrine
27. Provide food for
28. Greek marketplace
29. Thrush
30. Prejudiced person
31. Greek Muse
32. Added alcohol to
33. ____ vitam
35. En ____
38. Try hard: 2 wds.
39. Yellow-brown stone
41. Blessing
42. Jackson album
45. Hair dressing
46. Secret group
47. Grasshopper sound
48. Arabian gulf
49. Pro ____
50. Bond type: abbr.
51. Of the ear
53. Bumped off
54. "Rocky Horror Picture Show" role
55. Koran chapter
58. Red or Dead

PUZZLE 234

ACROSS

1. Locality
5. Reef rock
10. Helmond show
14. Hand part
15. Rapidly
16. Buddy
17. To be: Lat.
18. Earn back
19. Repast
20. Hone
22. Settle
24. Fury
25. Sniggler's quarry
26. Disagreement
30. Went in
34. Brainwave
35. Former Egyptian president
37. Knight's wife
38. Anger's flipped item
39. Chasing game
40. Clamor
41. Mezzanine
43. Make valid again
45. Fedora and derby
46. Like a snifter
48. Anguish of repentence
50. Charged particle
51. Weaken
52. Star circlers
56. Try
60. Ore vein
61. Active
63. Phobia
64. Cooker
65. Tier
66. Annul
67. Trial
68. Unyielding
69. Intense desire

DOWN

1. Copies
2. Reckless
3. Actress Lanchester
4. Land of the free
5. Vocations
6. Doing business
7. Crude
8. Sour
9. Merciful
10. Tasted
11. Table spread
12. Alack
13. Gomer ____
21. Expert
23. Tennis-match component
26. Pickles
27. Moron
28. Marsh grass
29. Out of style
30. Avid
31. "M*A*S*H" role
32. Gives off
33. Thick
36. Rowan or Rather
42. Renowned
43. Vacation cars
44. Horse opera
45. Promising
47. Shemp's pal
49. Welcome sign
52. Scheme
53. Ardor
54. Summer drinks
55. Venetian-blind part
56. State
57. Bill of fare
58. Cushions
59. Horse's gait
62. Bump off

PUZZLE 235

ACROSS

1. Bluster
5. Sutures
10. Dough
14. Baseballer Matty ____
15. Danger
16. "____ from Muskogee"
17. Mister, in Munich
18. Stadium
19. Ship's work force
20. Ottawa breakfast entree?: 2 wds.
23. Gen. Robert ____: 2 wds.
24. Starling
25. Guardianships
28. Cross: Fr.
31. Dismounted
32. ____ last: 2 wds.
34. Play part
37. Bogota breakfast beverage?: 2 wds.
40. Witness
41. Blunt
42. One of Charlie's Angels
43. Plait
44. Buenos ____
45. ____ Minor
47. Stalk
49. London breakfast biscuit?: 2 wds.
55. Scottish hillside
56. Discolor
57. Great Northern diver
59. Whirring sound
60. Cloth of sheer linen
61. Suits to ____: 2 wds.
62. Honey makers
63. Rowed
64. Masculine

DOWN

1. Bowl yell
2. Actor Baldwin
3. Nick Charles's wife
4. Asked for help: 2 wds.
5. Shovel
6. Odd
7. Region
8. Gopher State: abbr.
9. Thick slice
10. Spinal column's lowest bone
11. Ohio city
12. Tuscan city
13. Cut
21. Capp and Pacino
22. Friend: Sp.
25. WWII female soldiers
26. Medicinal herb
27. Annoy
28. Santa ____
29. Howard and Reagan
30. Formerly
32. Monk
33. Small birds, for short
34. Distant
35. Forfeit
36. Kennedy and Knight
38. Ethical
39. Deception
43. Jungle cats
44. WWI group
45. Lofty nest
46. Trap
47. Grin
48. Adjusted for tone
50. Ratio phrase: 2 wds.
51. Portico
52. "Aquarius" musical
53. Particle
54. Carol
55. Consumer advocacy group: abbr.
58. Born

PUZZLE 236

ACROSS

1. Had a siesta
6. Song for Sutherland
10. Moslem official
14. Observer
15. Protracted
16. Spur
17. Beyond tasteful limits
18. Places
19. She: Sp.
20. Military officer: 2 wds
22. Bicycle built for two
24. Provo's state
25. Procures
26. Actress in "The Fan"
29. Wickerware material
30. Lyric poem
31. Retinal area
32. Joplin's specialty
35. Ready
36. Intimidated
37. Fidel's land
38. Interstice
39. Pugilist
40. Hebrew robot
41. Paint
43. Avaricious
44. Like a directional marker
46. Wild pig
47. View
48. Airtight
52. Obey
53. Theta's follower
55. Goddess of the hunt
56. Ellipse
57. ____ plaisir
58. Engine
59. Counsel, to some Britons
60. Renown
61. Concerning

DOWN

1. Smug one
2. Scowl
3. Singer James
4. Urge
5. Bridge frame
6. Moslem god
7. Cheer
8. Bus. abbr.
9. Annoyed
10. Schedule
11. Worthy precept: 2 wds.
12. Healthier
13. ____ apple
21. "2001" role
23. Pilaster
25. Road worker
26. Ship hazard, for short
27. Samoan port
28. Snake
29. Spur wheel
31. Deceived
33. Sleeping
34. Like venison
36. Berle or Skelton
37. Forced compliance
39. Cry
40. ____ Moses
42. Pasta piece
43. Glop
44. Revile
45. "Superman" star
46. Carpenter's tool
48. Object
49. Tardy
50. Soon
51. Game projectile
54. Caviar

PUZZLE 237

ACROSS

1. Court proceedings
5. "____ de Lune"
10. Position
14. Needy
15. Merchants' guild
16. Muse of history
17. Treacherous person
20. Close
21. Winning serves
22. Martha's family
23. Sounds of disapproval
24. Electrical unit, for short
25. Belongings
28. Cigar residue
31. Lone
34. Lighten
35. Couple
36. White or Red
37. Pliny's lucky number?
38. Lodgers
41. ____ semper tyrannis
42. Make bigger: abbr.
43. Prefix for cycle or corn
44. Unite by sewing
46. Old cars
48. Asian holiday
49. Shiny coating
50. Map abbreviation
52. Anglo-Saxon worker
53. Boundary
55. Helm position
56. Iranian language
59. Pour
63. Heavy beam
64. Cuts of meat
65. Field
66. Chances
67. Muslim decree
68. Hairdresser, sometimes

DOWN

1. Church part
2. Nutmeg State: abbr.
3. Object of disgust
4. Noah's creation
5. Get cold feet
6. Alleys
7. Pismires
8. Like: suff.
9. Ruff's mate
10. Gets out
11. Fake sleep
12. Belgian river
13. Throw
18. Spring holiday
19. Dear: Brit.
23. Hebrew letter
25. Young eel
26. Net
27. Avian stitcher
28. Allow
29. Take to court
30. Practical judgment
32. French river
33. Do well
39. "A Chorus Line" tune
40. Basked
45. To: Scot.
47. Duties
51. And so forth: abbr.
52. Large antelope
53. Jason's boat
54. ____ of honor
55. Burma's locale
56. Whig's foe
57. Author James ____
58. Russian ruler
60. Boxing great
61. Rocky crag
62. "Major ____"

PUZZLE 238

ACROSS

1. Adhesive
5. Exhaust
8. Campus area, for short
12. Proverb
13. Anagram of eta
14. Seize illegally
16. Deport
17. Drop the ball
18. Eagle's nest
19. Smarter
20. Card game
22. Capable
23. Car food
25. ____ and crafts
27. Group of wives
30. Mexican Indian
33. Highway section
34. Newspaper notice, for short
38. Ellipsoidal
40. "Stanley & ____"
41. Sacred text of Islam
43. Overdue
44. 100 centavos
45. Large, hairy beast
46. Fancy
47. Woolen fabric
50. Apple drink
52. Nero's garb
54. Bog
55. Many times
58. Ravine
60. Gem
65. Toss
67. Uncooked
68. Deteriorate
69. Last
70. Corrida cheer
71. Catlike mammal
72. Sort
73. Conflict
74. High-schooler

DOWN

1. Vehicle for Tony Danza
2. Spindle
3. Mound
4. Appear
5. Stairs
6. Prefix for gram or dynamics
7. Winter jacket
8. Crystal
9. Purpose
10. Emanation
11. Leak
12. Sea gull
15. Kitten, e.g.
21. Period of note
24. Frenzied
26. Impassive
27. Long-eared mammals
28. Flavoring seed
29. Spa
31. Elude
32. Provide food
33. Impudent talk
35. Tarzan's son
36. Wrath
37. Knot thread
39. Grazing land
42. Pleasant
48. Stare
49. Freudian term
51. Introduce
53. Bull's-eye hitter
54. Less
55. Down
56. Dart
57. Wee
59. Festival
61. Border lake
62. Interlaced
63. Heaven on earth
64. "____ It Be"
66. Doze

PUZZLE 239

ACROSS

1. Aptitude
6. Saharan
10. Audacious
14. Sheer fabric
15. Medicinal measure
16. Caesar's road
17. French city
18. Airport abbreviations
19. Kuwaiti coin
20. Japanese political leader
21. Bret Harte locale
23. Bread, in Bonn
25. James Whitcomb ____
26. Oust
29. Pilasters
31. Leontyne's solo
32. Oppose
34. Belgian resort town
37. Rains lightly
39. Normal: abbr.
40. Scottish river
42. Spanish queen
43. Value
46. Singing syllables
47. More exact
48. Noah's landing place
50. Rot
52. Aid's partner
53. Bonneville ____
56. In the distance
59. City map
60. Wedding vows
61. French painter
63. Old man: Ger.
64. Margin
65. Robes of office
66. Kind of admiral
67. Back talk
68. Rock

DOWN

1. Dollar parts: abbr.
2. Sorrows
3. Actor Alan ____
4. Scow
5. Some singers
6. Skillful
7. Newspaper section, for short
8. Author Dinesen
9. Abandons
10. Turn hastily
11. Usable
12. Dawdle
13. Once, once
22. Lasso
24. "____ the ramparts . . ."
26. Female knight
27. Character on "The Waltons"
28. Tower locale
29. Fall bloom
30. Pheasant brood
33. Noble Italian family
34. Luminary
35. Actress Negri
36. Gray's subject: abbr.
38. Letter stroke
41. Cop
44. Tarnishes
45. Fairy queen
47. Stagger
49. Answers
50. Maison room
51. Rio de la ____
52. Onagers
53. Bandy words
54. Italian river
55. Clothing
57. Mythical ship
58. Horse color
62. Pipe joint

PUZZLE 240

ACROSS

1. Competent
5. Biblical spy
10. Prayer ending
14. Shakespearean king
15. Texas shrine
16. French composer
17. "M*A*S*H" star
18. Mongrel
19. Muslim leader
20. Negative votes
21. Little bit
22. Stolid
24. Hannah Van ____
26. Melville novel
27. More just
29. Diamond feature
30. Persona
33. Strayed
34. Georgia city
35. Babylonian war god
36. Swards
37. Chalice
38. Mother of Horus
39. ____ Mahal
40. Kind of aid
41. Perfume
42. Box-office sign
43. '80s rock group
44. Exhausts
45. Stops
47. Fuzzy fruit
48. Ice-cream treat
50. Mouths
51. Character on"thirty-something"
54. Celestial bear
55. Fit for a king
57. Mas that baa
58. Biblical kingdom
59. Actor Nick ____
60. Cliques
61. Dull colors
62. Grimace
63. Woody plant

DOWN

1. Ladd or King
2. Composer Bartok
3. Wife of LBJ
4. Deletions
5. Furniture wheel
6. Northern highway
7. Cooking fat
8. Large bird
9. Adolescent
10. Dynamic
11. Wife of DDE
12. Pep
13. Alaska seaport
23. Honest
25. Mr. Skelton
26. Silent
27. Celebrations
28. Loud
29. Buoyant wood
31. Tedium
32. Kilns
34. Baseball's Roger ____
37. Water collectors
38. Picnic equipment
40. FDR's pet
41. Hot springs
44. Painting preparation
46. Presidential family name
47. Chatter
48. Brought to court
49. Pakistani language
50. Leer
52. Sampras of tennis
53. To be: Lat.
56. Millennium

PUZZLE 241

ACROSS

1. Hurried
5. Everything
8. Surmounting
12. Greasy
13. By way of
14. Agitate
15. Toward shelter
16. Authorizes
18. Vigor
19. Upright
20. Small child
21. TV host Mary ____
23. Egg producer
25. Hackneyed
27. Keepsake
31. Gasp
32. Downhearted
33. Stick around
34. Effort
36. Attack
37. Fish eggs
38. Wagon
39. Eastern title
42. More faded
44. Mischievous one
47. Learned thoroughly
49. Ascertain
50. Entreaty
51. Night before
52. ____ of Wight
53. Coal bed
54. Accomplished
55. Stride

DOWN

1. Detergent
2. Stack
3. Pachyderm
4. Tint
5. Prevent
6. Boundary
7. Fastened
8. Singer Garfunkel
9. Lean
10. Table spread
11. Nuisance
17. Article
19. Before, to Keats
22. Modify
24. More recent
25. Baden-Baden, e.g.
26. Make lace
27. Small rug
28. Meanest
29. Connect
30. Baseball's Mel ____
32. Harpooned
35. Pout
36. Watering hole
38. Yielded
39. Electrical units
40. Strong wind
41. Confused
43. Son of Jacob
45. Man
46. Type of school
48. Scottish hat
49. Towel monogram

PUZZLE 242

ACROSS

1. Actor Carney
4. Sharp knock
7. Miscalculate
10. Minuscule
11. Vegetable dish
13. Born as
14. Actress Gardner
15. Chicago airport
16. ____ Moines
17. Moves upward
19. Sign up
21. At any time
22. Strange
24. Nights of anticipation
25. Chalk remover
27. Binds
28. Wear away
30. Divide
33. Surface covering
37. Shoe bottom
38. Stitch
39. On the briny
41. Promise
43. Speak
44. Keep one's ____ to the ground
45. Kitchen appliances
48. House addition
49. Hill dweller
50. Commence
51. Wide shoe size
52. Thoroughfares: abbr.
53. Steal
54. Physicians: abbr.

DOWN

1. Mindful
2. Rejuvenate
3. Kidder
4. Cheer
5. In the manner of
6. Trimmed the outer coating of
7. Young chicory plant
8. Singer Della and others
9. Takes a break
11. Distress signal
12. Cozy room
18. Epoch
20. Pacific wreath
22. Poet's above
23. Induced
26. Group
27. "____ Little Indians"
29. Morning condensation
30. Cracow's location
31. Warns
32. Scarlet or ruby
34. Ingest
35. Value highly
36. Spun
37. Stab
38. Cut off
40. City on the Rhone
42. Lump
43. American military branch: abbr.
46. Self-image
47. Tip

PUZZLE 243

ACROSS

1. Old salt
4. Eager
8. Tantrum
11. Poems of praise
13. Painful
14. Fruit cooler
15. Religious leader
16. "The Black ____"
18. Miss ____ of "Dallas"
20. Rings
21. Weighing devices
23. Turn brown
24. Friend
25. Director Preminger
27. Valise
31. Ripens
33. Suffer
34. Very dry
35. Make over
36. Urgency
38. Female hog
39. Gamble
41. Williams and Leach
43. Cut
46. Spouses
47. Goodman's instrument
49. Smallest part of an element
52. Inquire
53. Grow weary
54. Nevada city
55. ____ the line
56. Rushed
57. Condensed moisture

DOWN

1. Pinnacle
2. "Much ____ About Nothing"
3. Cancelled
4. Helper
5. Cast a ballot
6. Lyricist Gershwin
7. Actress Burke
8. Fizzle
9. False god
10. Sawbucks
12. Vend
17. Yearns
19. Lion constellation
21. Box
22. Enclosure
23. Put up with
26. Bind
28. Withstood
29. Shackle
30. Sunday seats
32. Rational
37. Speck
40. Redacts
42. Kodiak or polar
43. Scram!
44. In addition
45. Arouse
46. Lake
48. Bite
50. "____ Day at a Time"
51. Trim

PUZZLE 244

ACROSS

1. Singer Davis
4. High card
7. Currency
11. Alone
12. "Man of a Thousand Faces"
13. Zone
14. "Down by the ____"
17. Type of glass
18. Musical pauses
19. Tin
20. Always, in poetry
21. Director Kazan
24. Actress Lupino
25. Take a turn at the plate
28. "Paper Doll" singers
32. Western Indian
33. Hasten
34. Little: suff.
35. Actor Kingsley
36. Goof
38. Yet
41. Made wavy
45. "The Ten Commandments" director
47. Pub orders
48. Type of room, for short
49. Lacquered metal
50. Knight and Lange
51. Frequently, to a bard
52. Baden-Baden, e.g.

DOWN

1. Shed feathers
2. "Betsy's Wedding" star
3. Funny
4. Comedian Steve ____
5. Frigid
6. Printers' measures
7. One who is concerned
8. God of war
9. Chair
10. Amateur radio operators
11. Mayday letters
15. ____ lather (agitated)
16. Cure
20. Tokyo, formerly
21. Flightless bird
22. Ignited
23. ____-de-France
24. Anger
25. Wager
26. Columnist Buchwald
27. Mao ____-tung
29. Hard coating
30. Storage place
31. Recluses
35. Rapture
36. Build
37. Edge
38. Go away!
39. Over a distance: pref.
40. Decorated
41. Followers of AB
42. Set down heavily
43. She, in Madrid
44. Actress Ruby ____
46. Sis's sib

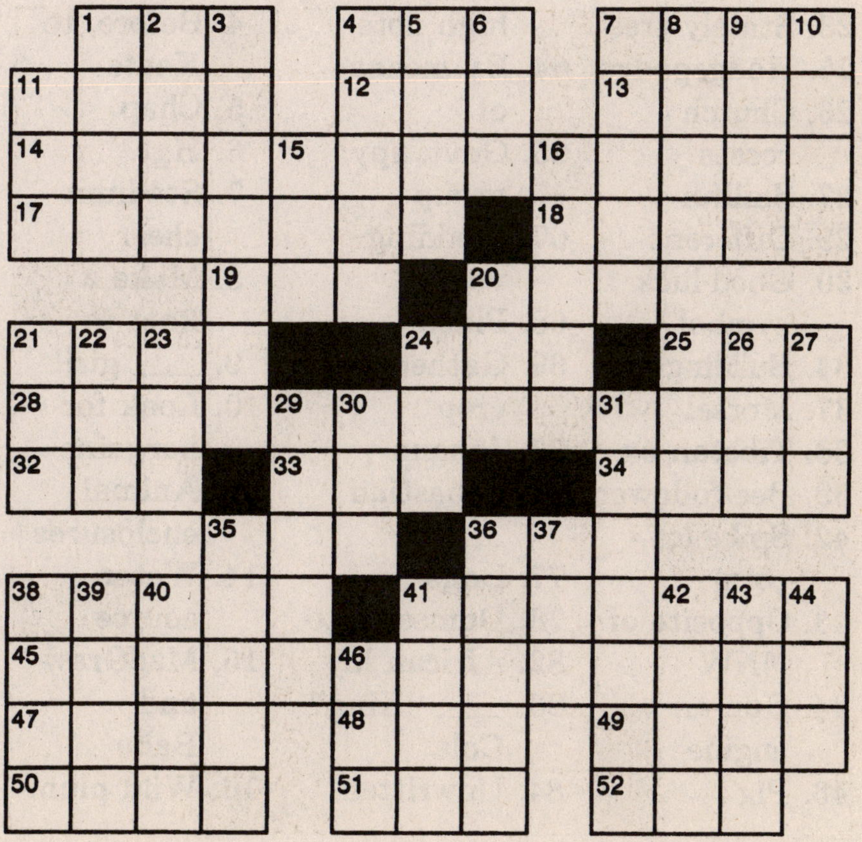

PUZZLE 245

• OLD MACDONALD'S REALM •

ACROSS

1. Unit of land
5. Shopping center
9. Egyptian snake
12. Lion's den
13. Jai ___
14. No longer is
17. Game song, with 20 Across
20. See 17 Across
22. Shade
23. Stately tree
25. Hodgepodge
26. Church recess
27. Skillful
29. Different
30. Good-luck symbol
34. Building site
37. Morsel
38. Tibetan ox
39. Bee follower
42. Spike (of corn)
43. Opposite of NNW
44. Gun an engine
46. Pig
47. Animal shelter
49. ___ wood (snoring)
51. Dove sound
52. Varnish ingredient
53. Spud
56. Domestic fowl
59. Confusion
60. Total
62. Have being
63. Guido's high note
64. By means of
65. Govt. spy group
67. Wedding vow
68. Pinch
69. Gathered a crop
73. Johann Sebastian ___
77. Bogs
78. Domesticate
82. African lily
83. ___ "King" Cole
84. Unwritten
85. Hoedown
90. " . . .crying over ___"
95. Conclude
96. Small intestine: pref.
97. Margarine
98. ___ Moines
99. Turn the soil
100. Story outline

DOWN

1. In the manner of
2. Limousine
3. Brink
4. Before, to Keats
5. Chap
6. Hgt.
7. Stadium cheer
8. Make a knot in
9. ___ girl!
10. Look for bargains
11. Animal enclosures
14. Water source
15. MacGraw and Baba
16. Wild plum
18. Professional charge
19. Ruby and cerise
20. Sprites
21. Female antelope
24. "Malcolm X" director
27. Columnist Buchwald
28. Biblical pronoun
30. Stockings
31. Native metal
32. Rowing blade
33. Supplements
34. "___ Miserables"
35. Kind of meal
36. Farm vehicle
39. Leghorn, e.g.
40. Eternity
41. Nest deposit
43. Coin openings
45. Worth
48. Feather scarf
50. "___ and Peace"
53. Baby food

PUZZLE 245

54. Pindaric poem
55. Cry of pain
56. Trampled
57. Inventor Whitney
58. Shrill bark
61. Actress Sara
62. Summer beverage
66. Branch
67. ____ a girl!
70. Grape plant
71. Historical period
72. Congeals
73. Baseballer Ruth
74. Comedian King
75. Heavy string
76. Coop dweller
78. Journalist Brokaw
79. Dry, as a desert
80. Masculine
81. BPOE members
86. Scoop of ice cream
87. Everything
88. Modern: pref.
89. Female bovine
91. Dad
92. Sick
93. Author Buscaglia
94. Tyke

PUZZLE 246

ACROSS

1. Bingo, e.g.
5. Section: abbr.
9. Grouping
12. Portent
13. Theory
14. Malt beverage
15. Shipshape
16. Richmond's locale
18. Ask earnestly
20. Move aimlessly
21. Footed vase
22. Tithes
25. Appaloosa, e.g.
28. Offer
29. Author Bradbury
30. Give off
31. Chasm
32. "Fire and ____"
33. Toupee
34. Rested
35. Syrup source
36. Walking poles
38. Angora or Manx
39. Mold
40. Small chickens
44. Energetic
47. African lily
48. Folding bed
49. Companion
50. African river
51. Endeavor
52. Tiff
53. Stalk

DOWN

1. Left
2. Final word
3. Substance
4. Make responsible for
5. Couch
6. Work on copy
7. Each
8. Labeled
9. Golf hazard
10. Inventor Whitney
11. Social gathering
17. Singer Janis ____
19. Sooner than, in poems
22. Hint
23. "____ Columbia"
24. "Auld Lang ____"
25. Chops down
26. Overlook
27. Inflexibility
28. Take one's turn at the plate
31. Step on the ____
32. Wicker materials
34. Boils
35. "A ____ for All Seasons"
37. Restriction: abbr.
38. Military trainee
40. Phi ____ Kappa
41. Descended from a vehicle
42. Burrowing animal
43. Appear
44. Behave
45. And also not
46. Draw off

PUZZLE 247

ACROSS
1. Cat's foot
4. Conflict
7. Mineral spring
10. Dismounted
12. Pub order
13. "The ____ Earth"
14. Dorothy's dog
15. Sick
16. Actor's part
17. Specter
19. Furious
21. Actor Majors
22. Long time period
23. Felt
26. Roundabout way
30. Actress Gardner
31. Dined
32. Wood-turning devices
36. Squanders
39. "____ for My Baby"
40. Bullring cheer
41. Chinese mammal
43. More pleasant
46. Sea eagle
47. Sorrowful
49. Horse's gait
51. Magician's prop
52. Lyric poem
53. Farm structure
54. Hurricane's center
55. Neither's partner
56. New Haven tree

DOWN
1. Butter unit
2. Sleep like ____
3. Accompanied by
4. Stood in line
5. "____ Shook Up"
6. Depended
7. Chimney problem
8. Warsaw native
9. Cool drink
11. Awl and hammer
13. Donation
18. Observe
20. Fish eggs
23. Actor Mineo
24. Actress Marie Saint
25. Singer Cole
27. Cereal grain
28. Colorado Indian
29. Inhabitant: abbr.
33. Sharpened
34. Conclude
35. Fall, e.g.
36. "My Cherie Amour" singer
37. Boxing great
38. Religious groups
41. Offer petition
42. "____ of Green Gables"
44. New York canal
45. Biscuit
46. Lamb's mom
48. Hubbub
50. Poston or Bosley

PUZZLE 248

ACROSS

1. Cotton applicator
5. Prison unit
9. Label
12. Needlework
13. Opposed to aweather
14. Prior to, to a Bard
15. Concept
16. Steer
18. Unkempt
20. Mexican dollar
21. Torment
23. State of inactivity
27. Reverent fear
30. Copy
31. Accept
32. Explosive noise
34. Dims
35. Surfaces
36. Shad's output
37. Positioned
38. Busy insects
39. Bicycle parts
41. Deserve
43. Makes docile
47. Racing sleds
51. Pierce
52. Summer fruit drink
53. Flow out slowly
54. Solo
55. Clear profit
56. Gumbo vegetable
57. Transmitted

DOWN

1. Thin
2. Walk in water
3. Expert pilots
4. "Beauty and the ____"
5. Ont. locale
6. Glide by
7. Embankment to prevent flooding
8. Flowery necklaces
9. Oriental drink
10. Handicraft
11. Turn to the right
17. Ravine
19. "The Wonder ____"
22. Inclined
24. Periods in history
25. Dried up
26. Trial run
27. Type of horse
28. "The Way We ____"
29. Sword
31. Sharp
33. Desert watering holes
34. Fluffy scarf
36. Melt down fat
39. Athens native
40. Epics
42. In addition
44. Supplemental
45. The Emerald Isle
46. Couch or sofa
47. Prohibit
48. Lyric poem
49. Gamble
50. Resort of sorts

PUZZLE 249

ACROSS

1. Wise guy
4. Bay
8. Green gem
12. Actress MacGraw
13. Berate
14. Nautical hello
15. Sprinted
17. Coop
18. Singer Buddy ____
19. Pack of cards
21. Crowd
23. Boom boxes
27. Vermilion
30. Apprehend
32. Winter jacket
33. Chilled
35. Children's game
37. Caution
38. Dairy product
40. Cloth
42. Pester
43. Cheer
45. Chemist's lair
47. Playwright Simon
49. Actor Hayes
53. Mongolian desert
56. Australian marsupial
58. Pizzeria appliance
59. Malicious
60. Botch
61. Biting flavor
62. Valley
63. Tiny

DOWN

1. Cleanse
2. Tall, in Tijuana
3. It's a ____!
4. Wax pencil
5. Hardwood
6. Contended
7. Church official
8. Small crow
9. Cry of triumph
10. Lassie, e.g.
11. Look at
16. Freddy's street
20. Head covering
22. Flying mammal
24. OPEC nation
25. Podded vegetable
26. Warbled
27. Wealthy
28. Light brown
29. Doe
31. Saloon
34. Mending with stitches
36. Guy's date
39. Daisy ____
41. Flock
44. Walked
46. Bleat
48. Molten rock
50. Beer or ale
51. Drill
52. Time past
53. Acquired
54. Roe
55. Big ____ (London landmark)
57. Nothing

PUZZLE 250

ACROSS

1. Love god
5. That girl
8. Discuss
12. Donated
13. Marble
14. Actress Moran
15. Doing business
16. Cancel
18. Bizarre
20. Omit
21. Remain
22. Countdown ending
23. Hail
25. ____ Albert
26. Slant
29. Potato feature
30. "____ of the Roses"
31. Grotto
32. Always, to a bard
33. Long-jawed fish
34. Relic
35. Chinese sauce
36. Evergreen
37. Ravioli, e.g.
40. Mend
43. Neglect
45. Corrupt
46. Columbus's ship
47. Bustle
48. Hardens
49. Whirlpool
50. Peg
51. Family ____

DOWN

1. Selves
2. Ecstatic
3. Boss
4. Councils
5. Cigar
6. Own
7. Flock female
8. ____ Haute, Indiana
9. Diva's forte
10. Covers
11. Leg joint
17. Crevice
19. Slave leader Turner
22. Bireme's need
23. Observe
24. Caustic
25. Distant
26. Conquer
27. "____ Got A Secret"
28. Writing tool
30. Road
31. Tournament
33. Aim
34. "My country ____ of thee . . ."
35. Drift
36. Tea
37. Southern bread
38. Passionate
39. Dispatch
40. Took the bus
41. Ceremony
42. Different
44. Cereal grain

CRISS-CROSSWORD

PUZZLE 251

The answer words for Criss-Crossword are entered diagonally, reading downward, from upper left to lower right or from upper right to lower left. We have entered the words BOB and TOWN as examples.

TO THE RIGHT

1. "Our ____"
2. Feathered stole
3. Generous
4. Pelt
5. Mail carrier
6. Fundamental
7. "Top ____"
9. Flatter
11. Carmine
12. Yield
16. Choose
18. Forehead
19. Epoch
21. Ecstasy
23. Research room
25. Bar bill
28. Stunned
29. Tumult
30. Van Gogh's need
32. Ivory ____, Africa
34. Pilfer
36. Show agreement
38. Pismire

TO THE LEFT

2. Rocker Dylan
3. Demote
4. Woman engaged to be married
5. British tavern
6. Ennui
7. Mask or meter
8. Metal corrosion
10. Deft
13. Force back
14. Convertible, e.g.
15. Redolence
17. Rearward
20. Denial word
22. Siesta
24. Hairpiece
26. Authorization
27. Behavior
28. Swarm
31. Chef's need
33. Stage
35. James Woods film, with "The"
37. Creative work
39. Flying mammal

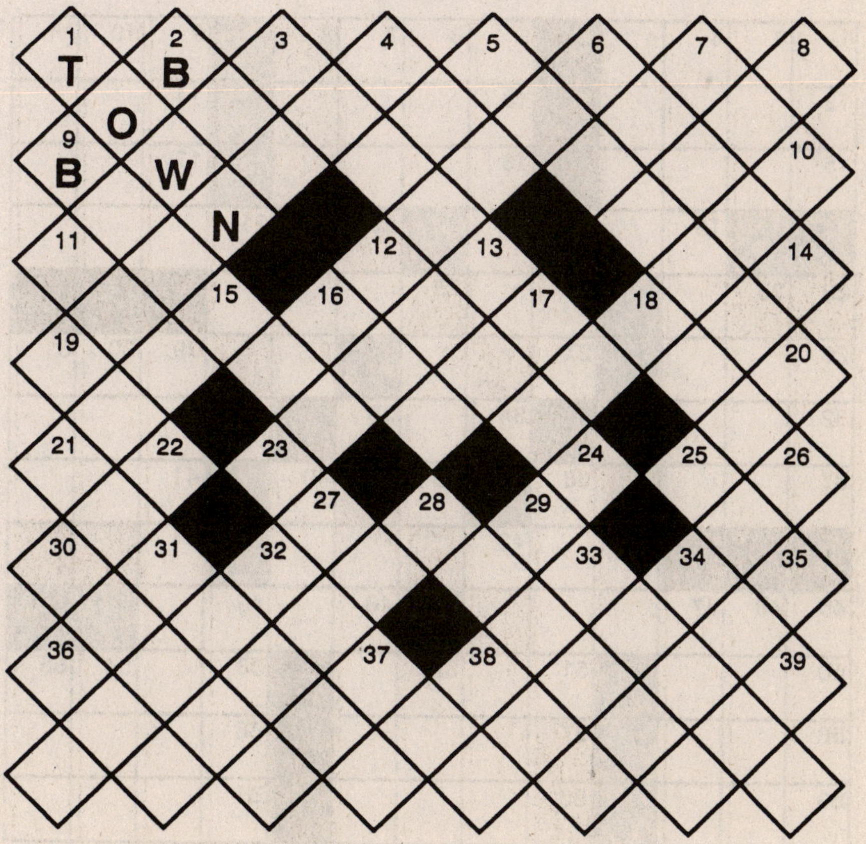

PUZZLE 252

ACROSS
1. Dutch cheese
5. Football toss
9. Rotten
12. Went on horseback
13. Landed
14. Mimic
15. Throb
16. Row
17. Direction abbr.
18. French state
20. Eccentric man
22. Auto
24. Subscribes again
26. Strong brew
27. Sooner than, poetically
28. Smirk
32. Gasp
34. ____ "King" Cole
36. Other
37. Chemical compound
39. Spoil
41. Kind of curve
42. Playground feature
44. Favored pupil
45. Issue
48. Was a frosh last year
50. Galena or bauxite
51. Speedy
53. Noshes
56. Football's Dawson
57. Noted Italian family
58. Years, in Barcelona
59. Superlative suffix
60. Actor Oliver ____
61. Let it be

DOWN
1. Aeon
2. Medic
3. Follower
4. Encounter
5. Design
6. Boxing great
7. Attack
8. Scatters
9. Folk singer Joan ____
10. Church part
11. Whitetail
19. "We ____ Not Alone"
21. Serf
22. "____ Fear"
23. Word of despair
25. Gets close
29. Babar, e.g.
30. Fin follower
31. Take ten
33. Try out
35. Browned the bread
38. Kind of coat
40. Pair
43. Rub out
45. Burrowing rodent
46. Greek god of war
47. Camping need
49. Legumes
52. French female saint
54. Piggy
55. Concorde

PUZZLE 253

ACROSS

1. Testing place
4. Imitated
8. Sewing joint
12. Frozen cube
13. Platter
14. English queen
15. Exist
16. Ripped
17. Cast a ballot
18. Withholds
20. Poorest
21. Intense anger
22. Till the soil
23. Digging tool
26. Evergreen
27. "____ Town"
30. Walk the floor
31. Bonnet
32. Blend
33. Painting or sculpture
34. Shack
35. Sat for a photographer
36. Detail
38. ____ diem
39. Casanova, e.g.
41. Imperfection
45. Tennis's Lendl
46. Float aloft
47. Female deer
48. Profits
49. Poker bet
50. Bullfight shout
51. Sycamore or cypress
52. Accomplishment
53. Guided

DOWN

1. Fibber
2. "God's Little ____"
3. Sugar source
4. Garb
5. Inclined
6. Listening organs
7. Color
8. Enjoy thoroughly
9. Huge
10. Aardvark's food
11. Sports competition
19. Assistant
20. Armed conflict
22. Tantrum
23. Mineral spring
24. Golfing norm
25. Arouse
26. Portly
28. Employ
29. Blushing
31. Buzz
32. Shape
34. "____ Alibi"
35. Gazed
37. Nervous
38. Dish
39. Fuzz
40. Above
41. Rover's treat
42. Object of devotion
43. Shoe part
44. Pay attention
46. Gloomy

PUZZLE 254

ACROSS

1. Fishing rod
5. Domestic animal
8. Punch
11. Fans' hero
12. Fish eggs
13. Villain's foe
14. Tiny skin opening
15. First digit
16. Singing voice
17. Construct
19. Young actress
21. "____ and Sympathy"
23. Towel marking
24. Nearest
28. ____ Island (New England state)
32. Be unwell
33. Buddy
35. Affirmative
36. Foot lever
39. Prods
42. Rascal
44. Image of oneself
45. Gymnast
49. Glimmer
53. Dolt
54. Immediately
56. Frilly trim
57. Borrowed money
58. Stage prompt
59. Voyaging
60. New Haven tree
61. Poet's before
62. Take a break

DOWN

1. Peace ____
2. Smell
3. Legends
4. Chooses
5. In favor of
6. Geologic time periods
7. Dentist's concern
8. Congeal
9. Comedian Johnson
10. Footwear
13. Severe
18. Golfer's gadget
20. Broadcast
22. Egyptian cobra
24. Beanie or beret
25. Speak falsely
26. Aged
27. Light brown
29. Olive ____ (Popeye's gal)
30. Actress Ruby ____
31. Road curve
34. TV's Kathie ____ Gifford
37. Oak seed
38. Scientist's milieu
40. Omelet ingredient
41. Small bill
43. Emulate Baryshnikov
45. Competent
46. ____ as a cucumber
47. Wander
48. Journey
50. Comfort
51. Serves for a point
52. Beef or pork
55. Minuscule

PUZZLE 255

ACROSS

1. Flag down
5. Extremely dry
9. Water source
12. Wind instrument
13. Ore vein
14. Help
15. Camper's cover
16. Noticed
18. Melody
20. One's equals
21. Incite
24. Showed the way
25. Because
26. Moral wrong
27. Ink holder
30. Pillar
31. Bolt's mate
32. Cavity
33. Pig's home
34. Male offspring
35. Sheriff's group
36. Tablet
37. Bashed in
38. Fundamental
41. Type of package
42. Situated within
44. Loafer or pump
48. Had breakfast
49. One of the Great Lakes
50. Labor
51. Do needlework
52. Rather and Quayle
53. Scream

DOWN

1. Fiery
2. Presidential nickname
3. Charged particle
4. Salad ingredient
5. "Home ___"
6. Pajamas topper
7. Freud's concerns
8. Intensify
9. Rescue
10. Wharf
11. Appends
17. Blushing color
19. Purpose
21. Venomous serpents
22. Melee
23. Solely
24. Fired up
26. Bask
27. Assignment
28. Additional
29. Want
31. Show agreement
32. Integrity
34. Consecrated
35. According to
36. Easy as ___
37. Challenges
38. Inclination
39. Poker stake
40. Fume
41. Nickel, e.g.
43. ___ Gershwin
45. Gardening tool
46. Olive or canola
47. Building extension

PUZZLE 256

ACROSS

1. Traffic barrier
5. Thumbs-up
8. Dance move
12. Zenith
13. Fib
14. Book leaf
15. Roman general Antony
16. Otis product
18. Church official
20. Golfer's aim
21. Walkway
24. Taunt
28. Bothered
32. Fodder tower
33. "You ____ My Sunshine"
34. ____ Baba
35. Press for payment
36. Fuzz
38. Large serving dishes
41. Purple Heart, e.g.
43. Bread spread
44. Chart
46. Correct
50. Clam dish
55. Succulent plant
56. Of the mouth
57. Cut off
58. Use a camcorder
59. Show all
60. Afternoon affair
61. Unique chap

DOWN

1. Arrived
2. October's stone
3. Blockhead
4. Excluding
5. Tavern treat
6. Lubricate
7. Retain
8. Extras
9. Make lace
10. Freudian topic
11. According to
17. Large tub
19. Actress Dawn Chong
22. Snare
23. Aloha
25. General's helper
26. Disparaging remark
27. Eternities
28. Tropical tree
29. Great Lake
30. Dispatch
31. Use the phone
37. Mexican dish
39. Ess follower
40. Love apple
42. On the ____ (escaping)
45. Hide
47. Gusto
48. Yep's opposite
49. Forest denizen
50. Weep
51. ____-la-la
52. Corn unit
53. Fish delicacy
54. Place to rejuvenate

PUZZLE 257

ACROSS

1. Inoculation
5. With it
8. Market
12. Sign on
13. "People ____ Funny"
14. Window glass
15. Utopia
16. Born, in Paris
17. Preacher's word
18. Blue
20. Small boy
22. Munch
24. Revolt
28. Time span
29. Wading bird
33. Orangutan
34. Yup!
35. Ventilate
36. Family room
37. Sup
38. Borders
40. Procure
41. Sniff
43. Mellows
45. Current measure, for short
47. Wildebeest
48. Drove
51. Not well
53. Prunes
57. Egg-shaped
58. Grassland
59. Cost
60. ____ de foie gras
61. Showed the way
62. Put away

DOWN

1. Pronoun
2. Stashed
3. Mineral
4. Anxious
5. "Cool ____ Luke"
6. Rage
7. Pare
8. Deck suit member
9. Prosciutto
10. "It Happened ____ Night"
11. Cage
19. Amaze
21. Pollock's forte
22. ____ of the crop
23. Speed
25. Sheriff's star
26. Dueling swords
27. Advanced
28. Gawks at
30. Roam aimlessly
31. Large truck
32. Before, poetically
38. Tall tree
39. Puerto Rico's ____ Juan
42. Bail
44. Chasms
46. Tablet of medicine
47. Cheerful
48. Dance
49. Actress Marie Saint
50. Informer
52. "Malcolm X" director
54. Type of meal
55. For
56. Fasten with thread

PUZZLE 258

ACROSS

1. Barks sharply
5. Tarry
9. Pierre's friend
12. Prepare for publication
13. Off-white
14. Jar cover
15. Legend
16. Weaken
18. Take the bus
20. Bird homes
21. Guides
24. Honey producer
25. Raccoon's cousin
26. Food fish
30. Clay, today
31. Lively dance
32. Talk amorously
33. Lost weight
36. Composed
38. Turf
39. Hums
40. Ski resort
43. Howls
44. Benevolence
46. Lofty
50. Crude mineral
51. Therapeutic plant
52. Fencer's equipment
53. Precious stone
54. Evergreens
55. Take five

DOWN

1. Positive response
2. Mont.'s neighbor
3. Swine
4. Gazed
5. Unwanted plants
6. Skin problem
7. Anger
8. Lana or Tina
9. Woeful word
10. Catcher's glove
11. March 15
17. Swerve
19. Author Levin
21. Box
22. Story
23. Oklahoma city
24. Plead
26. Covered up
27. Symbol
28. Memo
29. "Mr. Deeds ____ to Town"
31. Pa Clampett
34. Applied
35. Singer Twitty
36. Twisted
37. List
39. Valleys
40. Fascinated
41. Achy
42. Browning work
43. Hard hit
45. ____ du Diable
47. Mimic
48. Bandleader Brown
49. Allow

PUZZLE 259

ACROSS

1. Spinning toy
4. Behaves
8. Personnel
12. Brew
13. Metal fastener
14. Bee's home
15. Household animal
16. Sycamore, e.g.
17. Blue-pencil
18. Eye part
20. Impressionists' stands
22. Loft
24. Sputtered
25. Placed
26. Dog-paddle
27. Flap
30. In favor of
31. Fencing weapons
32. Perfect serve
33. Male offspring
34. Ruminant mammal
35. Revolve
36. Fender bender mark
37. Molts
38. Marzipan flavor
41. Low islands
42. Honk
43. Plan
45. Gymnast's goal
48. Byway
49. Playwright Coward
50. Deli bread
51. Singer Nelson ____
52. Hardens
53. Nonetheless

DOWN

1. Emulate Gregory Hines
2. Bullring shout
3. Appeal
4. Tomfoolery
5. Sedans
6. Cravat
7. More tired
8. Bureau
9. Sally ____
10. Bad
11. Saturates
19. Clear (of)
21. Directs
22. European mountains
23. Tropical plant
24. ____-talk (flatter)
26. Depleting funds
27. Ruglike wall hanging
28. Biting
29. Hogan and Vereen
31. Shangri-la
35. Bashful
36. One of the seven dwarfs
37. Stickers
38. Accomplished
39. Starring role
40. Recuperate
41. ____ over (faint)
44. Fawn's mom
46. Stare at
47. Mesh

PUZZLE 260

REVELATION

Solve this puzzle as you would a regular crossword. Then read the circled letters from left to right, and they will reveal a quotation.

ACROSS

1. Bask
4. Little ones
8. Mound
12. Before, in verse
13. Connecticut town
14. Border lake
15. Loathed person
17. Harangue
18. God of thunder
19. Hags
21. Broadway's orphan
23. Pelt
24. Competes
25. Podium
26. Football holder
29. ____ and outs
30. Pigs
31. Actor Linden
32. ____ Moines
33. Part of a bird
34. Strokes lightly
35. Gasp
36. Parsonage
37. Run aground
40. Stroll
41. Destitute
42. Searches
46. Dismounted
47. Irish river
48. Actress Hagen
49. Depend
50. Polka followers
51. Deep in pitch

DOWN

1. Dead or Red
2. Footed vase
3. Cleanliness
4. Resort lake
5. Finished
6. Twain's Sawyer
7. Dieter's no-no
8. Egret
9. Mideast land
10. Spiel
11. Allows
16. "____ is Your Life"
20. Shine's partner
21. Ardent
22. Number of Muses
23. Holy person
25. Wasted away
26. Appreciative
27. Victuals
28. Or ____!
30. Cygnet
34. Playmates
35. Political group
36. Manufactures
37. Shadowbox
38. Lacquered metalware
39. Bother
40. Accustomed
43. Spanish gold
44. Nebraska Indian
45. Unrefined

CIRCULAR CROSSWORD

PUZZLE 261

To complete this Circular puzzle fill in the answers to the Around clues in a clockwise direction. For the Radial clues move from the outside to the inside.

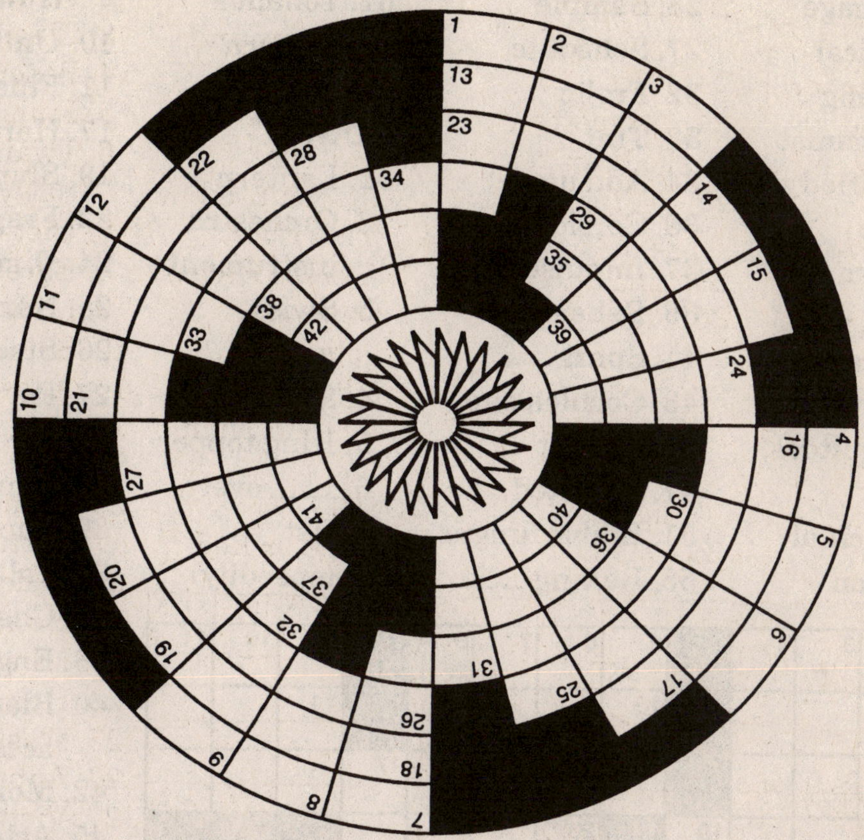

AROUND (Clockwise)

1. Luxury hotel
4. Venomous snake
7. "The ____ Squad"
10. Classifieds
13. Australian city
16. Lend
18. Upper crust
21. Speed
23. Functional
26. Promotion
29. Verdi opera
30. Pub
32. Car
33. Most sensible
35. Tread
36. Bill of fare
37. Raced
38. Have to
39. Double curve
40. Actor Alda
41. Before, in poetry
42. Locale

RADIAL (Out to in)

1. Dot
2. Energy
3. Zones
4. Muhammad ____
5. Chimney dirt
6. Canal or hat
7. Cruel
8. Ancient
9. Prima donnas
10. "You ____ There"
11. Water barriers
12. Emits vapor
14. Commonplace
15. Greek underworld
17. Type of orange
19. Brownish gray
20. Go in
22. Boredom
24. Faucets
25. Actress Olin
27. Morse or ZIP
28. Quiz
31. Dash
34. Sault ____ Marie

PUZZLE 262

ACROSS

1. Mortgage
5. Nautical greeting
9. Antagonist
12. Qualified
13. Crate
14. Tavern
15. Floor cleaners
16. Expanded
18. Mosquitoes, e.g.
20. Medicinal portion
21. Mr. Tolstoy
23. Sample
27. Schedule
32. Frolic
33. Tint
34. Add up
36. Corrida cry
37. Impulse
39. Rehearsed
41. Spars
43. Cochlea site
44. Abrupt
47. Sprinted
51. Edible fungus
55. Baking ____
56. Rearward
57. If not
58. Continuously
59. Plaything
60. Remains
61. Tenant's concern

DOWN

1. Lantern
2. Orchestra instrument
3. Swiss peaks
4. Snuggle
5. King topper
6. ____ over fist (speedily)
7. Norway's capital
8. Leavening agent
9. Pear-shaped fruit
10. United
11. Finale
17. Harvest
19. Shipped
22. Fragrance
24. Dim-witted
25. Narrative
26. Stared at
27. Pal
28. Air
29. Limbs
30. Supped
31. Talk wildly
35. Charlatan
38. Engrave
40. Blackboard accessory
42. More certain
45. Actor's part
46. Throw
48. Bay
49. Blissful abode
50. Pub missile
51. Small rug
52. Alien spacecraft
53. Hog's home
54. "When Harry ____ Sally . . ."

PUZZLE 263

ACROSS

1. Sheer force
5. Staff
8. Musical group
12. Stench
13. Common verb
14. Butter substitute
15. Gambling city
16. Emerald or garnet
17. Horse color
18. Stoneworker
20. Commands
22. Saga
24. Formerly named
25. Adult male
27. Expert
29. Theatrical fare
33. In addition
35. Bark
37. Destroy
38. Swarms
40. Uncooked
42. Citrus drink
43. Charged particle
45. Den
47. Armed conflict
50. Cavorts
53. Assist
54. Morrison of song
57. Shower-wall piece
58. Merriment
59. Id's counterpart
60. Confused
61. Convey
62. Paddle
63. Asterisk

DOWN

1. College housing
2. Concept
3. Balderdash
4. TV's "F ____"
5. Dustcloth
6. Mine yield
7. Fiend
8. Perimeters
9. Burn soother
10. Not far
11. Puts on
19. Bite
21. Blushing color
23. Weep
25. Welcome item
26. Brewery product
28. Boat equipment
30. One easily frightened
31. Incensed
32. Sailor's affirmative
34. Left out
36. Buddy
39. Sun god
41. Conflict
44. Not once
46. Very small quantities
47. Purses
48. Qualified
49. Juvenile
51. Request
52. Char
55. Way back when
56. At this time

PUZZLE 264

ACROSS

1. Soft drink
5. Swiss mountain
8. Lamb's pen name
12. Mine yields
13. Contend
14. Small stream
15. Thrives
17. Inactive
18. Variable
20. Tropical bird
23. Dodged
27. Disembarked
28. Strive
29. Have being
30. Tears
31. Possesses
32. Grouch
33. Frost
34. Sweet potato
35. Remainder
36. Feels
38. Shovels
40. Landed properties
42. Spirits
45. Circus animal
49. TV's Hawkeye
50. Neither's partner
51. Actress Sedgwick
52. High schooler
53. Member of Congress: abbr.
54. Valley

DOWN

1. Officer
2. Hockey star Bobby ___
3. Author Tolstoy
4. Declares
5. Ward off
6. Italian money, once
7. Bothers
8. Author Jong
9. Cover
10. Sick
11. Pub drink
16. Con's foe
19. Building vine
20. City on the Seine
21. "Wonderland" girl
22. Mature
24. Challenged
25. Rub out
26. Financial obligations
28. Scottish cap
31. Accelerates
32. Collided
34. No's counterpart
37. Family car
38. Harsh
39. Vigor
41. Lotion ingredient
42. Wrestling pad
43. Bullring cry
44. Lyric poem
46. City in Oklahoma
47. Nothing
48. Golfer's peg

PUZZLE 265

ACROSS

1. New York City vehicle
4. Make cookies
8. Envelop
12. Tint
13. Arab chieftain
14. Overhang
15. Generation
16. Chromosome
17. Sector
18. Alarm
20. Salesman
21. As well
22. Perched
23. Dress
26. Shy
30. Self
31. Fragment
33. Mineral
34. Conference
36. Darn
37. Egg layer
38. Dove call
40. Tooth
43. Trash
47. Spirit
48. Ground
49. Offer
50. Connect
51. Medicinal plant
52. Night before
53. Little piggies
54. Bar drink
55. Finger count

DOWN

1. ____ the fat
2. Atmosphere
3. Grizzly, for one
4. Start
5. Revise
6. Royal ruler
7. Previously, in poetry
8. Riches
9. Uncommon
10. Profess
11. Summit
19. Seize
20. Valise
22. Pouch
23. Jewel
24. Eternity
25. Caviar
26. Plead
27. Enemy
28. Footed vase
29. Conducted
31. Wharf
32. "Holiday ____"
35. Gratitude
36. Throng
38. Dugout
39. Command
40. Defrost
41. Medley
42. Alley
43. Wind gust
44. Help
45. Donate
46. Adam's garden
48. Research room

PUZZLE 266

MOVIES AND TELEVISION

ACROSS

1. "That Certain ____" (1938 film)
4. "Happy Days" actress
9. Locale of "Golden Girls": abbr.
12. Actress Witherspoon
14. "____ in the Head" (1959 film): 2 wds.
15. "True ____" (1969 film)
16. Actress Markey (original Jane)
17. Michael or George
18. Reporter Lois ____
19. "The ____ Was Indiscreet" (1947 film)
21. "The ____ of Iwo Jima" (1949 film)
22. Actress Munson of "GWTW"
23. "The Night ____ Eyes" (1942 film)
24. Actress Marjorie of "Stella Dallas"
27. 1979 David Soul film: 2 wds.
33. Comedian Dean ____
35. Actress Thompson et al.
36. "____ Got a Secret"
37. Alan or Robert
38. More unusual
40. Actor Burl
41. TV's 66, e.g.: abbr.
42. Backwater
43. Arthur Godfrey's "____ Scouts"
45. 1953 film with Actor Cameron: 2 wds.
48. Singer Diana
49. Larry's friend
50. Actress Joanne of "Wagon Master"
52. "The Enemy ____" (1957 film)
55. 1927 Buster Keaton film, with "The"
60. "____ in my Heart" (1933 film)
61. Ruth or Susan
64. ____ Jill Miller of "Gimme a Break"
65. "What's My ____?"
66. On to
67. Comedian Kamen
68. Jolson and namesakes
69. Actress Sharon of "Cagney & Lacy"
70. "Meet John ____" (1941 film)

DOWN

1. "Four ____," 1950s singing group
2. "____ Are the Days" (1963 film)
3. Actress Gray
4. "____ Fire" (1957 film): 2 wds.
5. Maureen and Catherine
6. ____ Serling's "The Twilight Zone"
7. Tavern brew
8. King Saul's grandfather
9. Ollie's pal
10. Peter ____ Hayes
11. Actor Roscoe
13. 1961 Hayward film
15. "The ____ Menagerie" (1950 film)
20. Singer Tennille
21. Waterston and Elliott
23. "Dear ____" (1964 film)
24. "The ____ Story" (1953 film)
25. Eve or Mary
26. Carol ____ White
28. Terri ____ (Priscilla Barnes TV role)
29. Grant or Majors
30. "Private ____" (1931 film)
31. Props for Julia Child
32. "____ Pilot" (1938 film)
33. "Presenting Lily ____" (1943 film)

34. Actor Nick of "48 Hours"
39. "The Dynamic ___" (Batman and Robin)
40. Labor initials
42. "The ___ Queen" (1959 film)
44. "___ for Your Money" (1949 film): 2 wds.
46. "That's ___" (Martin song from "The Caddy")
47. Buchanan and Barrier
51. Auberjonois and Clair
52. Lugosi or Bartok
53. "The ___ Mind" (1934 film)
54. Camera part
56. "A Nightmare on ___ Street" (1984 film)
57. "___ on Rommel" (1971 film)
58. A Guthrie
59. "The ___ George Apley" (1947 film)
61. Dusting cloth for "Hazel"
62. "The ___ and the Pussycat" (1970 film)
63. Actress West

PUZZLE 266

PUZZLE 267

ACROSS

1. Inner hand
5. Shock
10. Thrust
14. Balm
15. Unite
16. Bern's river
17. Bass tuba
19. Future sign
20. Lazy ____
21. Defeat
23. Vampire
24. Game fish
27. Region for Eisenhower: abbr.
29. Instruments for Benny Goodman et al.
33. Wine jug
36. Houston University
37. Inhabitant: suff.
38. Tibetan
39. Rise
41. Watches
42. Shortstops' equipment
43. Park it
45. Cleves lady
46. More dried out
47. Flamenco instruments
49. Medal initials
50. Gas consumers
51. Greek letter
53. Progeny
55. Bid
60. Ship call
62. Keyboard instrument
65. Not a soul
66. Rile
67. Old cars
68. Trial
69. Yorkshire city
70. Depression

DOWN

1. ____ judgment on
2. Baseball family
3. Costello and Rawls
4. High land
5. Stereo component
6. Exclamation of disgust
7. Will procedure
8. Actor James ____
9. Sodium hydroxides
10. ____ Paulo
11. Gypsy's instrument
12. Place
13. Committed
18. Opposed
22. Cal and Georgia, e.g.
25. Singles
26. Minnow catcher
28. Boring tool
29. Rugged rocks
30. Cloth type
31. Instruments for Judy Tenuta et al.
32. Actor Keanu ____
34. Worn out
35. Lets up
38. Fracas
40. Franco and Peter
43. Meat link
44. Suffix with novel or social
47. Dog
48. Until
51. Gasp
52. If the ____ fits . . .
54. October stone
56. Harrison or Henry
57. Liberate
58. Harrow's rival
59. Remainder
61. Thus far
63. Composer Rorem
64. Correlatives

PUZZLE 268

ACROSS

1. Moon exploration vehicle
4. Squeal
7. Go out with
11. Met offering
13. Ms. Maxwell
15. Challenges
16. Spot's breed, perhaps?
18. Brilliance
19. Part of U.S.A.: abbr.
20. Healthcare facility
22. Spanish galleon's loot
23. Marvin and Trevino
24. Football scores, for short
27. ____ de France
29. Outlines sharply
32. Does more business
35. Dummy
36. Cheeky
37. Tree
39. Vincent Lopez's theme song
41. Orchestra members
44. Fixed a cushion
47. Music maker
49. Drench
50. Compass heading: abbr.
51. Teheran money
52. Singer Zadora
54. Accrued
58. Discover
60. More of the same
61. Racing breed
65. Wakes up
66. Gratify
67. Wipe out
68. Pass
69. Roll of money
70. Summer on the Seine

DOWN

1. Young man
2. Memorable time
3. Uris's "____ 18"
4. Fish again
5. Actress MacGraw
6. Russian ruler
7. Short-legged dog
8. Woody's boy
9. Sports group
10. Noted Italian family
12. Bullets
14. Anoint
15. Discover
17. Eagle's nest
21. Parts of a tennis match
24. Spinning toy
25. Singing twosomes
26. Prance
28. Fairy
30. Poem
31. Tennis champ Monica ____
33. Brandy carrier
34. Knight's title
38. Second notes of the scale
40. Summer drink
42. Gazelles
43. Scorch
45. Having bulging peepers
46. Silly
48. Designer Cassini and namesakes
53. Punctuation mark: abbr.
54. Stream
55. Dog in "The Thin Man"
56. Mar
57. Tie
59. Christmas season
62. Airport initials
63. Slave-leader Turner
64. Change color

PUZZLE 269

ACROSS

1. Eva or Zsa Zsa
6. ____ on the vine
10. Artist Chagall
14. Crockett's last stand
15. Sulk
16. African shrub
17. Deceives
18. Kimono features
19. Noisy
20. Breakfast drink
22. Roman garment
23. Van Gogh's loss
24. Short jacket
26. Uphold
30. Destined
32. Guinness and others
33. "Quoth the Raven, ____"
37. On this spot
38. Went with
39. Inventor Sikorsky
40. Jacksnipe
42. Dimness
43. Nat and Natalie
44. Cookie cookers
45. Sea creatures
48. "____ the ramparts . . ."
49. Medieval sharecropper
50. Soft drink
57. Treble or bass
58. Demonic
59. Major artery
60. Away from the weather
61. Hawaiian bird
62. Twinkle
63. Took a cab
64. Peter or Nicholas, e.g.
65. Millay and Ferber

DOWN

1. Fisherman's hook
2. Winglike
3. Azerbaijan capital
4. Buddhists' sacred mountain
5. Registers
6. Love affair
7. Mongolian desert
8. Spectacular
9. Abandoned
10. Soda-fountain treat
11. Distant
12. Red, in Paris
13. Aromatic wood
21. Wedge
25. Byron's eternity
26. Delightful sounds
27. Fido's bane
28. Houseplant
29. Java drink
30. Celebrations
31. Allege as fact
33. Neck part
34. Double curve
35. Laugh loudly
36. Goes astray
38. Thorough
41. Burst
42. Heavy fire
44. Social insect
45. Hollywood prize
46. Violin's kin
47. Cornered
48. Girl watcher
51. Currier and ____
52. Columbus's ship
53. Aggressive
54. Literary Ireland
55. Volcano in Sicily
56. Charlie Brown's exclamation

PUZZLE 270

ACROSS

1. Word of regret
5. Foreman
9. Harness part
13. Stillness
14. A la ____
15. West of Afghanistan
16. Anderson fairy tale
19. Common verb
20. French kings
21. Bulrushes
22. Cut
23. Right and left, e.g.
24. Punishment method of yore
28. New York city
29. Electrical particles
30. Auto trip need
33. Carry on
34. Movie film units
36. Ditto
37. "High Hopes" insect
38. Breathing: abbr.
39. Southeast of Cleveland
40. Easy targets
43. Auspices
44. Author Bombeck
45. Playful act
46. Wild plum
47. Literary collection
50. Had ____ (was prepared)
53. Habit
54. Apply
55. Liturgy
56. Inside: pref.
57. Genesis home
58. Dressed

DOWN

1. Proceedings
2. Cowardly Lion
3. Aweather's antithesis
4. Dallas sch.
5. Howling
6. Commands: abbr.
7. Original Beatle Sutcliffe
8. Parts
9. Famous Jewish scholar
10. Northern constellation
11. Supplies the crew
12. A Siamese twin
14. Emmet Kelly, e.g.
17. Rye or wheat
18. Praise
22. Old card game
23. Converti-plane: abbr.
24. Dumb girl
25. ____ Bator
26. Wallet coin
27. Basso Cesare ____
30. Artist Chagall
31. Frenzied
32. Writes
34. Small purse
35. Assessments: abbr.
36. Seagull's relative
38. Unbending
39. Madison Avenue denizens
40. Begins
41. Actor Craig T. ____
42. Architectural joint
43. Concerning
45. Soon
46. Terrier type
47. Seed covering
48. Part of N.B.
49. Thunderstruck
50. Have bills
51. Heel
52. Circle part

PUZZLE 271

ACROSS

1. Parking attendant
6. Poplar trees
12. Components
17. Likeness
18. Germinates
20. Bay window
21. Rocky Mountain tree
22. Pennsylvania: 2 wds.
24. Remnant
25. Quaker pronoun
27. Meager
28. ____ the mark
29. Crucifix
31. Totaled
34. Tease
35. Tirade
36. Type assortment
38. Festive nights
40. Timber wolf
42. Wild plum
43. Coarse files
45. Harvester
49. Stopwatches
52. Plugs
54. Mohawk, e.g.
55. Cooking utensil
56. "____ of Wine and Roses"
58. Iraqi's neighbor
60. Baseballer Slaughter
61. Killer whales
63. Purpose
65. Fender-bender mark
66. Pack away
67. "____ Rae"
68. Writer Ephron
70. "____ the season to . . ."
71. Fitzgerald and Logan
73. Twosomes
75. Sahara or Mohave
77. Contradicts
79. Lindens
81. Perennial plant
82. Actress Patricia
84. Complete defeat
85. Sugar plant
86. Automobiles
89. Brooks of "Blazing Saddles"
91. Approaches
93. Jacob's twin
96. Fuss
97. French painter
99. Scan
101. Sandboxer
102. West Virginia: 2 wds.
106. Divided
108. Unit of work
109. ____ glass
110. Ms. Midler
111. English city
112. Artemis's nymphs
113. Lance

DOWN

1. Fanged one
2. ____ acid
3. Illinois: 3 wds.
4. Conceit
5. Scout's shelter
6. Catechized
7. Radar trap's quarry
8. Use leverage
9. Greek's Aurora
10. From soup to ____
11. Business share
12. Station
13. Ovid's "____ of Love"
14. Lariat
15. Wyoming mountain
16. Winter precipitation
19. Sluggard
23. The witch of ____
26. Fedora or beret
30. Tragic fate
32. Gabor and LeGallienne
33. Goal
35. Bellowed
37. If ____ be
39. Athletic activity
41. "You ____ Your Life"
42. Shock
44. Basque country
46. Maine: 3 wds.
47. Vulcanite
48. Slumbers
50. April shower
51. Church council

PUZZLE 271

53. Hairnet
55. Modeled
57. Swagger
59. Concerning: 2 wds.
62. Beaus
64. Arabian ruler
69. Movie dog
72. Bishop's jurisdiction
74. Swing around
76. Ocean eagle
78. Formerly Navigators Islands
80. Embarked on
83. Unaspirated consonant sound
85. Civil War govt.
86. Dromedary
87. Dote on
88. Cosmetic
90. Slow, in music
92. Oboes
94. Way to the heart
95. Speak
97. Rockies: abbr.
98. Russian ruler
100. Pats softly
103. Land of sleep
104. Cravat
105. Literary collection
107. Energy

PUZZLE 272

ACROSS

1. Cicatrix
5. Hunters' settlement
9. ____ au rhum
13. Podium
17. Meat paste
18. Ellipsoidal
19. Cain's victim
20. In addition
21. Excited
22. Back of the neck
23. Bedouin shelter
24. Wheat grinder
25. Meal
27. Flavor
29. Contended
31. Smirk
33. Curling marks
35. Area or scatter
36. Degraded
40. Nancy of fiction
42. Obtuse
46. Welcome!
47. Spread widely
49. Time period
51. ____ to the world
52. Money-maker?
54. New Orleans Bowl
56. Stage item
58. Ice or Iron
59. Senior
61. Part of USNA
63. Dampen
65. Wail
67. Cut in two
69. Fellows
70. Desert hazard
74. Stately
76. Ballplayer Maris
80. "Mr. ____" (George Raft film)
81. Vault
83. Not now
85. Expansive
86. British streetcar
88. Place for money
90. Even
92. Perjure oneself
93. Horse or truth
95. Lounge
97. Chose
99. Russian fighter jet
101. Stumble
103. Truckee city
104. Falls down
108. Cogwheel
110. Expiated
114. Unwritten
115. Snout
117. Talks
119. Mound
120. Gawk
121. Emulates Bojangles
122. Genealogy diagram
123. Actress Martinelli
124. "____ Fall in Love"
125. Tiff
126. Darns
127. Spool

DOWN

1. Bandy words
2. Confine
3. At the acme
4. Entertain
5. Appeases
6. At all: Scot.
7. Charts
8. Skirt fold
9. Flashlight need
10. Humorist Burrows
11. South ____, Ind.
12. Change
13. Broken
14. Dismounted
15. Key
16. Vended
26. Caspian and Andaman
28. Showed the way
30. Potential flower
32. Second showing
34. Ooze
36. Female knight
37. Corrupt
38. Get better
39. French painter
41. Enthusiastic
43. Straight
44. Wise
45. Actress Barbara ____
48. Vacillate
50. Chamber
53. Final
55. Perplex
57. Dock
60. Bakery purchase
62. Lawful

PUZZLE 272

64. TV static
66. Red vegetable
68. Ranks
70. Squeals
71. Farm unit
72. Kind of duct
73. Sora
75. Crowbar
77. Young female swine
78. Plimpton book
79. Clarinet, e.g.
82. Conspire
84. Press ____
87. Mutters
89. Most capacious
91. Fasting time
94. Wire measurement
96. Piffle!
98. Barrelmaker
100. Refined guys
102. Hair lines
104. Useful item
105. Coax
106. Beer ingredient
107. Detergent
109. Scarce
111. Cleo's river
112. Where's preceder
113. Business transaction
116. Belgian resort
118. Church seat

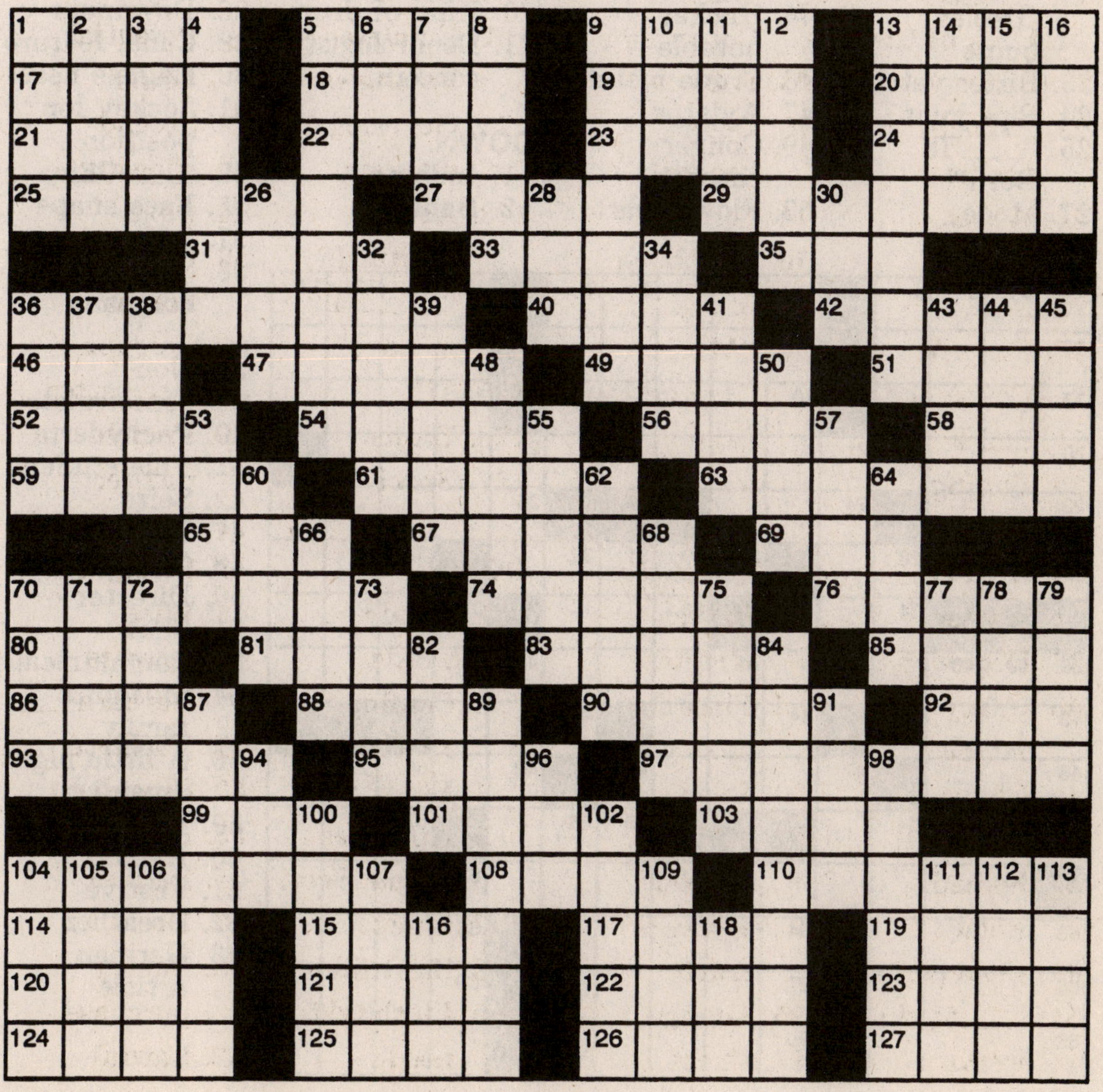

PUZZLE 273

ACROSS

1. Bookies' quotes
5. Trances
10. Quarrel
14. Antitoxins
15. Weaken
16. European river
17. Footless
18. Actress Berger
19. Weird
20. Horace Greeley quote
23. Bitter vetch
24. Pipe joint
25. "___ Is Born"
27. Mode
29. Letterman
33. Actress Claire
34. Lennon's lady
36. German article
37. "The King ___"
38. Conestoga
43. Bandleader Lawrence ___
44. "The Greatest"
45. Hockey notable
46. Crude metal
47. Aviator
49. Conger catcher
53. Flower part
55. CIA predecessor
57. Actress Arden
58. Famous pioneer route
63. Pair
64. Muse of poetry
65. ___ St. Vincent Millay
66. Complexion woe
67. Tanker
68. Clan
69. Concordes
70. Kind of drum
71. Dendrologist's concern

DOWN

1. Indians
2. Banish
3. Sleepy
4. Marquis de ___
5. Rank
6. Carried out
7. Spanish hand
8. Aleutian island
9. Penn of films
10. Abounds
11. Thinking
12. Explorer De Soto
13. Saute
21. Office worker
22. Flit about
26. Downpour
28. Canal feature
30. Eagle's nest
31. Jockey for position
32. ___-China
35. Face shape
37. Swiss river
38. "___ company . . ."
39. Non-conformists
40. Pachyderm
41. Yale student
42. Seize
47. Ziegfeld
48. Cheering fan
50. Director
51. Show
52. Communicate
54. Mosquito family
56. A little night music?
59. Vintage cars
60. Ireland
61. Festive
62. Breather
63. German article

PUZZLE 274

ACROSS

1. Dough
5. Originate
9. Fictional elephant
14. Nora's dog
15. Comic Johnson
16. Informed
17. Legume
18. Japanese seasoning
19. Pianist Peter et al.
20. Wayne-Agar film
23. Type type: abbr.
24. Former king of Albania
25. More secure
28. Jane Austen novel
31. Stag
35. Alarm
37. Ventilates
39. Beetle
40. Southern constellation
41. Wayne-O'Hara film
43. Grow older
44. Edge
45. Yodeling feedback
46. Monument
48. ____ off (irritated)
50. Trumpeter Al ____
52. Suit material
53. Fish eggs
55. Willow
57. Wayne-Janssen film
64. Self-confidence
65. Seaweed
66. Seep
67. Telegraph inventor
68. Layer
69. Logan or Fitzgerald
70. Weaver's reeds
71. Impudence
72. Bambi, e.g.

DOWN

1. Taxis
2. On the briny
3. Comedian Laurel
4. More convenient
5. South Pacific islands
6. Treat lightly
7. Although: Lat.
8. The cat's ____
9. " . . . with a ____ on my knee"
10. "Anchors ____"
11. Brewer's yeast
12. Venezuela city
13. Legal matter
21. Photographic device
22. Missouri mountains
25. Begin
26. Lofty shelter
27. Casing
29. "____ Dad"
30. Actress Farrow
32. "____ With Judy"
33. Scoundrel
34. Cornered
36. Wealthier
38. Seat for two
42. Alphabet trio
47. Gave a medal to
49. Showy
51. Colors lightly
54. Moldings
56. Ski-lift components
57. Pickax, e.g.
58. Rent
59. Cafe sign
60. Lamb's pseudonym
61. First name in mystery
62. Mosaic piece
63. Boxers do it
64. Afternoons: abbr.

PUZZLE 275

ACROSS

1. Dogpatch cartoonist
5. Official deeds
9. Skillful
13. Eastern nobleman
14. Unsharpened
16. "Dies ____"
17. Aquarelle
19. Actress Thompson
20. Pointed instruments
21. Seacoast
23. Street: abbr.
25. Mexican coins
26. ____ tell: 2 wds.
30. Spare
34. Bandleader Brown
35. Globes
38. Sierra ____
39. Oscar winner for Kazan: 3 wds.
43. Descendant
44. Talking Francis of films
45. East Indian hemp
46. Gave audience
47. "____, pick up sticks": 2 wds.
50. ____ pole
54. Fort ____
55. Strong drink
59. Day's march
63. Wrought ____
64. Having serious problems: 3 wds.
66. Untruths
67. Door part
68. Songstress Carter
69. Villa d'____
70. Rice wine
71. Pierre's head

DOWN

1. Certain bird calls
2. Amo, Amas, ____
3. Feel for
4. D.A.'s undergrad program
5. Three of twenty-six
6. Congeal
7. Spring flower
8. Battery part
9. Popular film genre
10. Part of QED
11. Diminish
12. Salty drop
15. Very French
18. ____ Ridge
22. Mrs. Dalloway's creator
24. "... were Paradise ____!"
26. Go through a puddle
27. Ergo
28. Ancient Roman port
29. Sixty grains
31. Circlets
32. Boredom
33. Demand further tribute
36. Energy abbr.
37. Ego
40. Maid in "Bleak House"
41. Provide with income
42. Actor Wallace
48. Panorama
49. Surviving
51. Shadow
52. Lab burners
53. Conductor Zubin
55. Drum's partner
56. Rainbow goddess
57. ____ E. Lee: abbr.
58. Before bottom or candy
60. Suit to ____: 2 wds.
61. Fur
62. Perry's creator
65. Article

PUZZLE 276

ACROSS

1. Fashionable
5. Unwritten
9. Austere
14. Reckless
15. Soccer notable
16. Golfer Palmer
17. Vehicle
18. Idi ____
19. Consumer-advocate Ralph ____
20. Is inconsistent
23. Threw
24. Carbohydrate: suff.
25. Actress Arlene ____
27. Tallinn native: abbr.
30. Lost in
34. Fortune-teller's card
35. Pigeon sound
36. China's former ruler
37. Boast
42. Capone et al.
43. Monk's title
44. Uncanny
45. Bread grains
47. Use a stopwatch
49. God of war
50. Before, to poets
52. Get by
54. Venting one's anger
62. Animate
63. Amo, amas, ____
64. Unemployed
65. Hebrew measures
66. Speed contest
67. Quote
68. Keyed up
69. ____ Fox
70. RBI, e.g.

DOWN

1. Grouch
2. Lug
3. Ratio phrase
4. Dog breed
5. Colorful fish
6. Far off
7. Dismounted
8. "Stormy Weather" singer
9. Smoothes
10. Investigator
11. Within: pref.
12. Cambodian money
13. Dull person
21. Like some pretzels
22. Not in any way
25. Dawdle
26. Originated
28. Beat it!
29. Furthermore
31. Love, Italian style
32. Capital of France
33. Quality
34. Aspen conveyance
38. Frequently
39. Swiss lake
40. Approaches
41. Dissenters
46. Quilters
48. Expunge
51. Laundry cycle
53. Subsequent
54. Smudge
55. Key ____ pie
56. Baking chamber
57. Costume
58. Actor Sharif
59. Reword
60. Canadian prov.
61. Convene

PUZZLE 277

ACROSS

1. Tourist's need
4. Angler's catch
7. Have an ____ on
11. Grinder shop
12. Broad st.
13. ____ the way
14. Kind of exam
15. Look like
17. Male singer
19. Equipment
20. Hamilton bill
21. Heavy weight
23. Sticky stuff
25. Dove call
28. City
30. Autumn
34. Bee, to Opie
36. Through
37. Canine pest
38. Steep, as tea
39. Involved with
41. Tabby's foot
42. Decide
44. Time period
46. Health resort
49. Feel unwell
51. Spree
55. Gripe
58. Burn
59. Opposite of aweather
60. As well
61. Den
62. Lease
63. Finish
64. Coastal flier

DOWN

1. Simple
2. King of comedy
3. Jet jockey
4. Auto
5. Done
6. Specify
7. Shade provider
8. Liability
9. Wind gust
10. Adam's place
11. Polka ____
16. Conceit
18. Decompose
22. Beginner
24. Switch position
25. Taxi
26. "____ Miss Brooks"
27. Billfold note
29. Come in first
31. Swiss peak
32. Actress Thompson
33. Rule
35. Duo
40. Sphere
43. Chum
45. Walkway
46. Old wound
47. Post
48. So be it!
50. King of beasts
52. ____ at hand
53. Profit
54. Blunder
56. Family pooch
57. Bow

PUZZLE 278

ACROSS

1. Kills flies
6. Blemish
9. Health club
12. Aviator
13. Frozen water
14. Paraffin
15. Texas attraction
16. Breathe
18. Caesar's X
19. Mine find
21. Egged on
22. Ripen
23. Foxy
24. Appliance
28. Suggestion
31. Booty
32. Street: abbr.
33. Top-notch
34. Clip
35. Therapy
37. Biblical boat
38. Answer
39. Sew
42. Change the color
43. Type of sandwich
46. Cost
48. Coil
50. Pub drink
51. Pool stick
52. Uncanny
53. Novel
54. Feminine pronoun
55. Naps

DOWN

1. Quarrel
2. Trickery
3. Poet Seeger
4. Author Clancy
5. Larry, Curly or Moe
6. Bog
7. High card
8. Outcome
9. Gulp
10. Use a kitchen gadget
11. Chopped
17. Snoop
20. Say
22. Model Carol ____
23. Conniving
24. Sickly
25. Cow's cry
26. Dad
27. Holiday lead-in
28. Pedal digit
29. Lodge
30. Favored one
33. Gospel singer Grant
35. Ditch
36. Reel
37. Took food
39. Pinto or lima
40. Wheel shaft
41. Jet
42. Antlered animal
43. Gentlemen
44. One
45. Wasps
47. Take to court
49. Tiny

PUZZLE 279

ACROSS

1. Cap, in Scotland
4. Diva's song
8. Type
12. Famous boxer
13. "Star ____"
14. Entreaty
15. Makes into a different form
17. Enjoy a novel
18. Sailors
19. Expressions
21. Dish
23. Wide-eyed with curiosity
24. Lawn tool
25. Tennis court official
29. Single unit
30. Diamond bags
31. Actor Vigoda
32. Capable of being fixed
34. Say no to seconds
35. Woodwind
36. Furs
37. Bank employee
40. Location
41. Asian sea
42. Burden
46. Isinglass
47. Oliver or Donna
48. Set down
49. Equal
50. Dry
51. Bard's before

DOWN

1. Pitch
2. Tavern order
3. In error
4. Informed
5. Knocks
6. Rage
7. Trust recipient
8. Parsley units
9. Muffin topper
10. Paper measure
11. Little fellows
16. Despise
20. Female rabbits
21. School dance
22. Path
23. Corridor
25. Workmen
26. Approved by the post office
27. Aid
28. Gains
30. Baseballer Ruth
33. Buck
34. Consider
36. Overly modest person
37. Force down
38. Great Lake
39. Chantilly, e.g.
40. Maple genus
43. Formerly named
44. Corn unit
45. Bread choice

PUZZLE 280

ACROSS

1. Actor Alan ____
5. Fedoras
9. That girl
12. Jai ____
13. Overlook
14. Skirt fold
15. Offers
16. Fork prong
17. Clockmaker Terry
18. Piled
20. Conform
22. OPEC concern
23. Actress MacGraw
24. Show an old show
27. Assignment
31. "____ the Rainbow"
32. Armed conflict
33. Frozen-yogurt holder
34. Argued
36. ____ up (studied hard)
37. Chat
38. Clergy mem.
39. Antic
42. Food supplier
46. Frost a cake
47. Moral
49. Took the bus
50. X
51. Mother Bloor
52. Level
53. Curvy letter
54. Shred
55. Hollow

DOWN

1. Test sites
2. Came down
3. Early 20th-century art form
4. Deter
5. Inn
6. Between
7. Badge metal
8. Thieves
9. Mets' stadium
10. Assist
11. Expel
19. Aunts and uncles
21. Found
23. Broadcast
24. Staff
25. Actress Brenner
26. Confederate soldier
27. Teed off
28. Charged particle
29. Dollar bill
30. Comedian Sparks
32. Spider's creation
35. Bull's-eye
36. Chance
38. Detecting device
39. Quote
40. High cards
41. Writing tools
42. Soft drink
43. Meander
44. Utopia
45. Lease
48. Bullring cry

PUZZLE 281

ACROSS
1. Pistol ____ Maravich
5. Club's golf expert
8. Iraqi, e.g.
12. Section
13. "Swing ____, Sweet Chariot"
14. ____ Ranger
15. Laces, as shoes
16. Vigoda of "Fish"
17. Spouse
18. Guard
20. Baseball competitions
21. With no difficulty
24. Rigid
27. Cover
28. Kitten's foot
31. Advance
32. Falsehood
33. Zoo building
34. Neverthe-less
35. "The Streets of ____ Francisco"
36. Lubricated
37. Trimming
39. Kind of diving
43. Church official
47. Misplace
48. Witness
50. Bicycled
51. What's the big ____
52. Split ____ soup
53. Ceases
54. Student's table
55. "____ the king's horses . . ."
56. Tryout

DOWN
1. Touches lightly
2. Great Lake
3. High-school senior
4. Not western
5. Broadway offerings
6. Steal
7. Be indebted to
8. ____ mater
9. Meander
10. Poker stake
11. Buzzing insects
19. Fled
20. Swindle
22. Cake topping
23. Kind of dog, for short
24. Crafty
25. ____ the line
26. Have a snack
28. Chum
29. Time period
30. Marry
32. Craze
33. Smoke
35. "____ of Love" (Pacino film)
36. Small bill
38. Standard
39. Glided
40. Secret message
41. Takes ad-vantage of
42. Bird's nose
44. Pine or ice-cream
45. Betting probability
46. House of sticks
48. Health club
49. Long fish

PUZZLE 282

ACROSS

1. Gigantic
5. Amino ____
9. Top pilot
12. Kind of exam
13. Army's kin
14. Promise
15. Gape
16. Elm, e.g.
17. Certain poem
18. Nectarines' relatives
20. Speed contests
22. Brown in the sun
23. Mountain resort
24. Crone
27. Fastener
30. Knife blade
33. Self
34. Skins, as fruit
36. Rowing need
37. Spider's creations
39. Browse
40. Columbus to Savannah direction: abbr.
41. Stake
43. Wail
45. Certain tooth
47. Unruly
51. Lincoln's nickname
52. Prayer ending
54. African succulent
55. Neither hide ____ hair
56. Castle's protection
57. Beer ingredient
58. Affirmative answer
59. "My Three ____"
60. Results

DOWN

1. Basketball player's target
2. Encourage
3. Celebration
4. Choose by vote
5. Aerials
6. Automobiles
7. "____ Got a Secret"
8. Tinters
9. Guacamole ingredients
10. Area or zip
11. Rams' mates
19. Yarn spindle
21. Gorilla
24. Cut
25. Period in history
26. Turkeys
28. Circle part
29. Laborers
31. Fuel
32. Poetic before
35. Winter precipitation
38. Baltic or Yellow, e.g.
42. Cable vehicles
44. Hold responsible for
45. Various
46. Reed instrument
47. Not fatty
48. Excitement
49. Convinced
50. Places
53. Cow sound

PUZZLE 283

ACROSS

1. Police officer
4. Grand story
8. Accomplishment
12. Have being
13. Pianist Peter ____
14. Pay to play
15. Marine
17. Notion
18. Northern Indian
19. Directed
21. Vereen or Gazzara
22. Capture
26. Inn
29. Summer beverage
30. Date
31. Done
32. Frozen water
33. Tiers
34. Males
35. Social insect
36. Postpone
37. Goes in
39. Paddock
40. Slide downhill on snow
41. Unobstructed
45. Too bad!
48. Maryland's neighbor
50. Festive occasion
51. At any time
52. Container
53. Heed
54. Take it easy
55. Place

DOWN

1. Lawsuit
2. Metal sources
3. Pike's ____
4. Lacquer
5. Argentine leader
6. Wrath
7. Rot
8. Vague
9. Termination
10. Devoured
11. Oolong or Earl Grey
16. Thread
20. Lincoln, familiarly
23. Military infraction
24. Midwestern state
25. Inquisitive
26. Dwelling
27. Kiln
28. Canvas hut
29. Carry out
32. One in the know
33. Subscribe again
35. Noah's vessel
36. Leave
38. Composition
39. Posts
42. Grabs
43. One of the Great Lakes
44. Scar on a car?
45. Before
46. Research place
47. Lager's kin
49. First woman

PUZZLE 284

ACROSS
1. Performs
5. Big boats
9. Warsaw's locale: abbr.
12. Sigh of relief
13. Runs with the pres.
14. One-spot
15. Small quantity
16. Light opera
18. Visually pleasing
20. Small spike
21. Married women in Madrid: abbr.
23. Faux pas
27. Cultivating tool
30. First garden
32. Effortless
33. Competent
35. Have bills
36. Mosaic piece
37. Whine
38. Place in office
40. Show agreement
41. Transports
43. Fall
45. Female wool producer
47. Requisite
51. Annoyance
55. Pressing
56. Limb
57. Rainbow
58. Blood-related
59. Break
60. Crackpots
61. Eyepiece

DOWN
1. Sacred bull of Egypt
2. Milk shake flavor: abbr.
3. Head, to Chantal
4. "The Wild ____ at Coole" (Yeats)
5. Pear-shaped fruits
6. Corded fabric
7. Protect
8. Celebration
9. Author Conroy
10. Tenth month: abbr.
11. Pasture
17. Long-plumed heron
19. Rage
22. Hemmed a skirt
24. Shower
25. Capital of Norway
26. Hollow stalk
27. Amateur actors
28. Woodwind
29. Enthusiasm
31. Closeness
34. Wrapped up
39. Shoe tip
42. Gentleman friend
44. Bicycle part
46. Off-white
48. Water barrier
49. Paddy's land
50. Hiding places
51. Crone
52. Period in history
53. Unit of current: abbr.
54. Punch

PUZZLE 285

ACROSS

1. Observes
5. Canary, e.g.
8. War memento
12. ____ moss
13. Time period
14. Saga
15. Singing voice
16. Signed a check
18. Tennis score
20. Ceremonies
21. Tranquil
24. Knock
25. Wipe out
26. Set free
30. Goal
31. Mortar tray
32. Olive center
33. Answered
36. Belief
38. High card
39. Made of oak
40. Elf
43. Wedding band
44. Went back
46. Rim
50. Neighbor of Turkey
51. "____ to Billie Joe"
52. Genuine
53. Blockhead
54. Refusal abroad
55. Vend

DOWN

1. Health resort
2. Moray
3. Have a burger
4. Fur pieces
5. Make angry
6. Marine bird
7. Boy
8. Bar
9. Hurl
10. Sea call
11. Cubs' rival
17. Spoken
19. Unit
21. Dry up
22. Pennsylvania port
23. Incline
24. Senator Kennedy
26. Staff
27. Copied
28. Flank
29. Jacket type
31. "____ Haw"
34. Rue
35. Bakery employee
36. Prisoner
37. Cowboy Roy ____
39. Broaden
40. Metal grating
41. Roman emperor
42. Arena shape
43. Make over
45. Heir
47. Passing grade
48. "My ____ Sal"
49. House wing

PUZZLE 286

ACROSS

1. Venerable
4. Draw a ____ on
8. Genre
12. Cow sound
13. At rest
14. Next in line
15. Tavern
16. Fine sand
17. Wide-mouthed jug
18. Hot water vessel
20. New Haven tree
22. Two thousand pounds
23. Technology
27. Parched
29. Appointment
30. Biblical craft
31. Bill and ____
32. Lucky number
33. Foot part
34. Managed
35. Emulated
36. Gratuities
37. Made certain
39. Disapproving sound
40. Brooch
41. Fair-haired
44. Lucid
47. Valley
49. Assist
50. Harbinger
51. Self-images
52. Relay part
53. Hurried
54. Obligation
55. Animal enclosure

DOWN

1. Pass over
2. Singular
3. Contributions
4. North American buffalo
5. Blue-pencil
6. "____ by Myself"
7. Discovered
8. Motif
9. Evergreen tree
10. Tart
11. Do wrong
19. Seedcase
21. Hold on property
23. Put aside
24. Citizens
25. Prune
26. Supplements
27. "God's Little ____"
28. Horse color
29. Relied
32. Eastern draped garment
36. Additionally
38. Affect drastically
39. Consecrated
41. Lump
42. Regimen
43. Tense
44. Call of alarm
45. Stereo component, for short
46. Born
48. Iron or Bronze

PUZZLE 287

ACROSS

1. Baseball cap, for one
4. Play players
8. Pea holders
12. ____ Marie Saint
13. Before: pref.
14. Wicked
15. Newspaper employee
17. Tennis star Lacoste
18. Genuine
19. Lasted
21. Surf sound
23. "____ the World Turns"
24. Swiss mountain
27. ____ -fi
28. Wooden duck
32. Garment edge
34. Terminate
36. Challenge
37. Syngman Rhee's land
39. "I ____ Rhythm"
41. Little Indians number
42. Hirt or Capone
43. "The Way We ____"
45. Equip
49. "____ Three Lives"
52. Toledo's lake
53. Kiddie game
56. Souffle ingredient
57. Of flying
58. Actress Gardner
59. Exam
60. Begged
61. Tennis unit

DOWN

1. That girl
2. State as truth
3. Gift-wrapping need
4. Musician Santana
5. Social insect
6. Car horn's locale
7. Sea bird
8. Read
9. Atop
10. Eat
11. Toboggan
16. Dory stick
20. June honoree
22. ____ up one's sleeve
24. Inquire
25. Durocher of baseball
26. Golfer's delight
29. Mouser
30. Bauxite, for one
31. Desire
33. Most ornery
35. Female deer
38. Actress MacGraw
40. Camera stand
44. Sprite
45. Place for shoes
46. Goad
47. Trucks
48. Hit in the face
50. Ages
51. Noah's bird
54. "You ____ So Beautiful"
55. Gangster's weapon

PUZZLE 288

ACROSS

1. Like a jalapeno
4. Besides
8. Cried
12. Commotion
13. Broadway light
14. Moroccan native
15. Property
16. Timetables
18. Just picked
20. Lay eyes on
21. Voting place
24. Slip-up
28. Tweety Pie and others
32. Miffed
33. Expert pilot
34. Circus performers
36. Foundation
37. Cause to ravel
39. Pure
41. Weird
43. Influence
44. Wing of a building
46. Posteriors
50. Most slender
55. Persian or calico
56. Lacking rain
57. Supper, for one
58. Arctic abundance
59. Health clubs
60. She, in Paris
61. Mountain ____

DOWN

1. Fifty percent
2. Skunk feature
3. Transport
4. "____ Aweigh"
5. Meadow
6. The sun
7. Dollar bills
8. Waterproof boots
9. Distinctive period
10. ____ for the course
11. Kitchen measurements: abbr.
17. Born
19. Mineral spring
22. Stretches out
23. By ____ and bounds
25. Evening wear
26. Metals
27. Ruby and carmine
28. Bistro
29. Land parcel
30. Close at hand
31. Sluggish
35. Sneak up on
38. Surrenders
40. Caustic liquid
42. Wapiti
45. Lollipop flavor
47. Sour
48. Speed contest
49. Meat and vegetable dish
50. Droop
51. Make an effort
52. Point
53. Elongated fish
54. Actor Mineo

PUZZLE 289

ACROSS

1. Maple genus
5. Greek mountain
10. Lab burner
14. Traversed
15. Wedding-party member
17. Keen
18. Like Austria
19. Pledge
20. Nullify
21. Swindle
22. Deterioration
24. More inexperienced
25. Flood
26. Shape, in Britain
27. Porcupine protector
28. Madness
29. ____ de guerre
32. Asian river
33. Mob
34. Lucy's love
35. Slippery fellow
36. Pluto's realm
37. Attics
38. Liliaceous plant
39. Split
40. Foreign traveler's need
43. Different
44. Average
45. Minute
46. Freezer product
47. Devotee
49. Former Dutch coin
50. Acrobatic action
51. Greek drink
52. Beginning
53. Cardinal number
54. Fortune-teller's words?

DOWN

1. Ballet pose
2. Shelter
3. Newspaper department
4. Basketball's Auerbach
5. Flowering
6. Retinue
7. Hart's mate
8. Weird
9. Autonomy
10. Hosted a show
11. Occupied
12. Female relative
13. Math student, at times
16. Only
20. Glass container
23. Peddle
24. Olympic medals
26. Edible mushroom
28. Dutch violinist
29. Wicked
30. Shun
31. Holiday hanger
33. "There's no ____ between us"
34. Fool
36. Balloon filler
37. Tax
38. Used cloves
39. Indicate
40. Stockpile
41. "Robinson Crusoe" author
42. Stop on ____
43. Move furtively
45. Bull: pref.
48. Nope
49. "____ Love You?"

PUZZLE 290

ACROSS
1. Panache
5. Fundamental
10. Racing boat
14. Until: 2 wds.
15. Actress Verdugo
16. Roue
17. 19th-century luggage
19. Spring blossom
20. Inspectors' tools
21. Feminine suffix
23. Favorite
24. Brenda or Bart
25. Christmas meanie
28. Mixture
30. Prima ____
33. Almond cookie
37. Packing box
38. Levin and Gershwin
39. Author Loos
41. Actress Rowlands
42. Kit ____
44. New Jersey town
46. "____ Gantry"
47. Commedia dell'____
48. School for Pablo
51. Slipknot
56. Coolidge's nickname
58. Hill builder
59. Figure shaper
60. Mr. Gemayel
62. Thanksgiving kit: 2 wds.
65. Repetition
66. Bis
67. Assistant
68. Supplemented
69. Pound portions
70. Mysterious loch

DOWN
1. Conduits
2. Asunder
3. Groove
4. Aspiring one
5. Wagers
6. Church vestment
7. Black or Red, e.g.
8. Bitterness
9. Roper's rope
10. ____ Lanka
11. Cabinetmaker
12. "____ from Muskogee"
13. Mr. Greeley's direction
18. Faux pas
22. Fountain drink
25. Hebrew nation: var.
26. Like a dunce hat
27. Canyon
29. Bank transaction
31. Not a soul
32. Med. school subj.
33. Mickey and Minnie, e.g.
34. Asian sea
35. White friar
36. Mule sires
37. Two-wheeled wagon
40. "GWTW" plantation
43. Killer whale
45. Mortise's partner
49. Remove the top
50. French floor
52. Church instrument
53. Actor Davis
54. Plants
55. Diminutive endings
56. Give a rap
57. Out of control
59. Movie: Spanish
61. Sparks or Beatty
63. Operated
64. Singer Damone

PUZZLE 291

ACROSS

1. Channel
5. Cotton bundler
10. Engrossed
14. Tennis great
15. Winged
16. Drunken cry
17. Athletes' domain
20. Seeing organ
21. Light black
22. Social cream
23. Quarry
24. False fronts
26. Take on gas
29. Unite
30. Wife of Osiris
31. Misrepresent
32. Humor
35. TV soap
39. "____ Girls"
40. Thresholds
41. Poetess Teasdale
42. Rocky debris
43. More profound
45. Marble works
48. Female deer
49. Auriculate
50. Best
51. Science room
54. "All ____"
58. Table d'____
59. Downy duck
60. Portent
61. Progeny
62. Flat hills
63. Ancient Persian's kin

DOWN

1. Meat spread
2. Deadly pale
3. "Of ____ I Sing"
4. Chop down
5. Keg
6. Pacify
7. Godiva, e.g.
8. Ike's command: abbr.
9. Hockey official
10. TV sports fixture
11. Shun
12. ____-cochere
13. Heads: Fr.
18. Monster
19. Undercover
23. Shove
24. Drops
25. Desertlike
26. Iranian coin
27. Being: Lat.
28. Shapes
29. Blackbird
31. Tree trunks
32. Evening coat
33. Concerning
34. Russian ruler
36. Portuguese coin, once
37. Metal thread
38. Secondhand
42. Simmered
43. Algerian coins
44. Chemical suffixes
45. Clockmaker Thomas et al.
46. Resort lake
47. Mountain ridge
48. Minor prophet
50. Does sums
51. Gold fabric
52. Old
53. Part of N.B.
55. Radiation unit
56. ____ down on the job
57. Male cat

PUZZLE 292

ACROSS

1. Statesman Eban
5. Salvages
10. Swindle
14. Actress Patricia
15. Knowing
16. Poorly
17. Countrywide: abbr.
18. Biblical food
19. Castle ditch
20. Reliable source
23. Highway
24. Peruvian peaks
25. Sausage herb
27. Allan-____
30. ____ me tangere
31. Upper House
33. "The Gold Bug" author
36. Great, to oldsters
39. Ad-____ committee
40. Igneous rock
41. "____ It Romantic?"
42. Speculation
43. Knowing about
44. Moral system
47. Forest member
49. Timid
55. Chain segment
56. Rows
57. "____ corny . . ."
59. Poker kitty
60. Tie holder
61. Quote
62. Exam
63. Start of a toast
64. Worry

DOWN

1. Miss Sothern
2. Rhythm
3. English spa
4. Hyper-sensitive
5. Pacific islands
6. Grant
7. Moving trucks
8. Sea bird
9. Vast expanses
10. Actress ____ Signoret
11. On ____ nine
12. Having wings
13. Legends
21. Weeding tool
22. Men
25. London area
26. Actor Guinness
27. Mr. Sadat
28. Arlene of filmdom
29. Keep ____ (persevere)
30. Highest degree
31. Doe's mate
32. To be: Lat.
33. Scourge
34. Yes ____?
35. Superlative suffix
37. Taken ____ (surprised)
38. Science of motive forces
42. Croquet hoop
43. "____ the ramparts . . ."
44. Brilliance
45. "To ____ own self be true"
46. Suggestions
47. Concise
48. Grates harshly
50. Engrave
51. Egyptian river
52. Get wind of
53. Give off
54. Palm fruit
58. Embroider

PUZZLE 293

ACROSS

1. Metallic fabric
5. ____ facto
9. Wound covering
13. Organic compound
14. Debonair
16. ____ breve
17. ____ parmigiana
19. Kiss
20. Diner
21. Gumbo ingredient
22. Reed instrument
23. Vetch
24. Sprite
26. Smudges
28. Ragout
30. Reception
33. Repair shoes
36. Lock openers
38. Eight: Sp.
39. ____ leaf
40. Informer
41. Hurdle top
44. Fence posts
46. Big ____
47. Entree
49. Clan chief
51. Writer Rand
52. Sault ____ Marie
55. Songstress Irene ____
57. Israeli statesman
59. Western movie
61. News item, for short
62. Entree
64. Toga
65. Threaded nail
66. Wigwam
67. Disarrange
68. Composer Jerome
69. Russian city

DOWN

1. Reception
2. Lend ____
3. Castle ditches
4. French pronoun
5. Ames campus: abbr.
6. Delay
7. Polio-prevention pioneer
8. Wear out a welcome
9. Wooden shoe
10. Aka Delmonico
11. As well
12. Foundation
15. Troop camps
18. Fishing basket
25. Golfer Trevino
27. Sounds of pain
28. Sounds of disapproval
29. Flash
31. Rochester's love
32. Invites
33. Aerial bombs
34. Beige
35. Entree
37. Hilltop
39. Saddleless
42. Health oasis
43. Goofs
44. Timid
45. Like a ____ bricks
48. Mouth sore
50. Detests
52. One of a flight
53. Arizona city
54. Iraqi town
55. Crocus bulb
56. "____ Ben Adhem"
58. Land measure
60. Palo ____
63. Have title to

PUZZLE 294

ACROSS
1. Scads
6. Shopper's paradise
10. Tax gp.
13. Wrath
14. Extent
15. Dill
16. Be of use
19. Leave in print
20. Wanes
21. Other: pref.
22. Mama sheep
23. Depots: abbr.
24. Scorn
25. L.A. team
27. Meadow
28. Roman bronze
29. Zodiac lion
30. Moccasin
31. Norm: abbr.
32. Entertainment
35. Heir
36. ____ League
37. Goddess: Lat.
38. His: Fr.
39. Epoch
40. Recliners
44. Blab
46. Gasp
47. Bolt holder
48. Across the keel
49. ____ the Red
50. Handle
51. Work
54. Fasting time
55. Locale
56. Roman official
57. Double curve
58. Plodded
59. Slackened

DOWN
1. Expired
2. Boxing punch
3. Consented
4. Skillful
5. Theater sign: abbr.
6. African snakes
7. Swift horses
8. Not so much
9. New Guinea port
10. Induct
11. Tapered off
12. Cubic meters
15. Affirm
17. Ignite, at stage-separation time
18. Ostrich's kin
23. Astrologer
24. Corruption
26. Valley
27. Take it on the ____
30. Snoop
31. Beat it!
32. Back doors
33. Eggs
34. Bird's home
35. Naval builders
38. Paper holder
39. Sailor's saint
40. Poured
41. Boredoms
42. Steal cattle
43. Lingered
45. 27th president
46. Foremost: pref.
49. Eastern VIP
50. Egyptian skink
52. Q-U fillers
53. Bishopric

PUZZLE 295

ACROSS

1. "L.A. ____"
4. Shoo!
8. Shade of green
11. Constrictor
14. Came down
16. Soap plant
17. Alabama city
19. Unlucky person
20. Actress Powers
21. Aka William Bonney
23. Robt. ____
24. Wallet
26. Skid-row dweller
27. October gem
29. "The Man ____"
30. Coal holder
31. Hindu princess
32. Navy engineer
34. FBI agents
36. Eileen or Walter
39. Sailor's saint
40. Demeanor
41. Certain deer
42. Bushed
44. Occupied
45. Mingo's friend
47. Fearful filly
49. Felix Unger's daughter
50. Flurry
51. "Golden Boy" star
54. D.C. figure: abbr.
55. Store fodder
57. Charged particles
58. Worthy
60. Woody's son
61. Armor
63. Passable
64. Lion constellation
65. Grin
66. Ant attracters
69. High trains
72. Perennial pinks
77. "____ a Living"
79. Stadium sounds
81. Beer mug
82. Score constituents
83. Show approval
84. Uprisings
86. Toward the stern
87. Actor Glass
88. High, in Roma
89. Breakfast offerings
91. Cozy rooms
92. Stocky tropical bird
94. Kodiak, e.g.
95. Jitney
96. Illinois city
97. Collection suffix
98. Rhine feeder
100. Cara or Anson
103. Thwart
105. NFL member
109. Part of QED
110. Actress Sheedy
111. Sting
112. Wadi
113. June 6, 1944
114. Petrol
115. ____ rata
116. Sunken fence
117. Sault ____ Marie

DOWN

1. Mary's pet
2. Russian range
3. Fred of "Julia"
4. Funt's admonition
5. Freezing
6. 100%
7. Author Josephine
8. Hammer head
9. Nevada town
10. Bon ____
11. Pool
12. Individual
13. Halberd
15. Chest-on-chest
16. Superior in rank
17. Tibia's locale
18. Love rapturously
19. Barbara Eden's TV role
22. Carbon copy
25. Enemy
28. Gasp
30. Ohio town
32. Biblical country
33. Dodge
34. British pokey
35. Short skirt
36. Seethes
37. Rattan
38. Hawaiian goose
41. River in France
43. Dapper gent
45. Waves
46. Bread spread
47. Pot or hot
48. Betterments
51. Cables
52. Crockett and Tubbs's city
53. Impulse

56. ____ volatile
59. Mr. Brokaw
61. Kind of point
62. Sheer fabric
63. Cicatrix
65. Complains
67. Road signs
68. Say
69. Stray
70. Non-professional
71. African birds
73. Kin of etc.
74. Old harps
75. Boxer Spinks
76. Fleming and McShane
78. Primer pooch
80. Irregular
83. Lugged
85. Actor Penn
90. Mecca men
91. Fence

PUZZLE 295

92. Galas
93. Suffer
95. Devilish child
96. Eyelashes
98. Remote
99. Hair style
100. Desire
101. Justice deity
102. Eye problem
103. Valise
104. Wing
106. Ref's kin
107. Admiring sound
108. Flock cry

PUZZLE 296

ACROSS

1. Booby ____
5. Stride
9. Slightly open
13. Assistant
14. Western lake
15. Assumed part
16. Nightstand light
17. Expiate
18. Ostrichlike bird
19. Yale nickname
20. Remove the cream from
21. Smoothed
23. "Ivanhoe" heroine
25. Horned viper
26. Festive affairs
27. Counterfeit
30. That chap
33. Actor Arbus
34. Sixth month
35. Skating surface
36. Fishing hook
37. Navy
39. Berg
40. Epoch
41. Feudal estate
42. Corrupt
43. "____ Rosen-kavalier"
44. Table extension
45. Complains
46. Be contrite for
48. Delights
50. Aspects
53. Frog genus
54. Dope
57. Theater box
58. Stickum
60. Blend
61. River to the Okhotsk
62. Hawaiian greeting
63. Court great
64. Court dividers
65. Prong
66. Week units

DOWN

1. Narrative
2. Iranian coin
3. Hero of Mobile Bay
4. Spunk
5. Glossy fabric
6. Third president
7. Very long time
8. Chirp
9. Rich tapestry
10. The March King
11. Downwind
12. Interpret
14. Captures
20. "____ Lake"
22. Limping
24. King of Norway
26. Stare angrily
28. Shade
29. Hill insect
31. Sacred pictures
32. Come together
33. Ripened
37. For shame!
38. Pasture
39. Taxi passenger
41. Hightail it
42. Farewell
45. Capital of Crete, once
47. Utility customers
49. Turning machine
50. Diagram
51. Residence
52. Lovers' quarrel
55. Pallid
56. Charges
59. Mohammad ____
60. Vogue

PUZZLE 297

ACROSS
1. Dawdle
4. Walks in water
9. Violence
13. Dollar bill
14. Actor Andy ____
15. Tied
16. "____ Little Indians"
17. Florida fruit
18. Peddle wares
19. Turn aside abruptly
21. Sports officials
23. Road, in Paris
24. Throbs
26. Tadpole's mom or dad
28. Cream-filled pastry
29. Tears apart
33. ____ Angeles
34. Singer Perry
35. Inform positively
36. Kimono sash
37. Wing
38. Batman and Robin, e.g.
39. Water tester
40. Idaho or Irish
42. Scorch
43. Rocker Stewart
44. Format
45. Actress Turner
46. Lulus
47. Instructs
49. Away
50. Bears witness
53. "The ____ Strikes Back"
56. High-priced
57. Capital of Canada
60. Rowing blade
61. Valley
62. Closer
63. Footed vase
64. Hill coaster
65. Go in
66. Understand

DOWN
1. Scads
2. Afresh
3. Unselfishness
4. "The Way We ____"
5. Actress Gardner
6. Commotion
7. Overwhelm
8. Appears
9. Makes a new version of
10. Declare positively
11. Kelly or Hackman
12. Remnants
14. Bird of peace
20. Braided or hooked
22. Human being
24. Cougar
25. Mystery craft?
26. Complete failures
27. R2D2, e.g.
28. Horseback game
30. Good for you
31. Slouch
32. Plants
34. Provides food
35. Atmosphere
38. Demands payment from
41. Made different
42. Prohibit
45. Lend an ear
46. ____ tent (two-man tent)
48. Make amends
49. Actor Sharif
50. Says further
51. Small river duck
52. Yarn
53. Vase-shaped jug
54. Uncommon
55. Sea eagle
58. Make lace
59. Land measure

PUZZLE 298

ACROSS

1. D.E.A. agent
5. Canter
9. Applications
13. Actor Sharif
14. Unique person
15. Coral island
16. Canfield, e.g.
18. March king
19. Look over
20. Bridge strategy
22. French cheese
23. Roman three
24. Black suit member
26. Chemin de fer
31. Cheap cigar
32. Went down
33. Speed
34. Nudge
35. Apertures
36. Ibsen woman
37. Scottish uncle
38. Labyrinth
39. Chair worker
40. 4 Down, e.g.: 2 wds.
43. Like Batman
44. Eternally, in verse
45. Board competition
46. Two-deck rummy
50. Adore
54. Verbal exams
55. Bridge holding
57. Engraved stone
58. Canadian Indian
59. Choreographer White
60. Upper: Ger.
61. Mister: Ger.
62. Negatives

DOWN

1. Face part
2. Chinese seaport
3. Murmur
4. Competition involving pegs
5. Hockey defender
6. Old-womanish
7. Comparative suffix
8. Elm, e.g.
9. More's opus
10. Type of food
11. Literary lion
12. Murder
15. Brit. sonar
17. Late
21. Notches
24. Leaf pore
25. Five-card stud, e.g.
26. Billiard-table material
27. Pay the kitty
28. French river
29. Ventilated
30. Rend
31. On ____ (on approval): abbr.
32. Bridge coup
35. ____ aleck
36. Pastime involving chips
39. Yule song
41. Distributor
42. Plaster
43. Sponger
45. More choice
46. Tropical palm
47. Semite
48. "____ That Tune"
49. Author Sholem
51. Pay ____ mind: 2 wds.
52. Region
53. Spanish queen et al.
56. Anger

PUZZLE 299

ACROSS

1. Cries of surprise
5. Diplomacy
9. Mother of Horus
13. Cowsheds
15. "____ the Merry-O"
16. Forever ____ day
17. ____ Detoo
18. At another time
19. Ponder
20. Flighty person
23. Private eye, for short
24. Nineteenth letter
25. Wheel tracks
26. Peculiarity
28. Swiss painter
29. Emblem: abbr.
32. Swallow
33. Italian river
35. British pal
37. Creeks
38. Sand bars
40. Persia, today
41. Starts a pot
43. Suffragist
44. Tableland
45. Manipulate
46. Sleeping
48. Caucasian
50. Not care ____
51. ____ Dolorosa
52. Spanish aunt
54. Sondheim song
59. Request
60. Cake layer
61. Ohio Indians
62. "I met ____ with seven wives"
63. Writer Hunter
64. Billiards stroke
65. Dog in Oz
66. Counsel, in England
67. So that not

DOWN

1. To the rear of
2. Buffoons
3. Fluent
4. Social climber
5. Asian wild goats
6. "____ We Got Fun"
7. Church gallery
8. Language
9. Metrical feet
10. Social affront
11. At rest
12. Great ____ Lake
14. Not drunk
21. Glacial ridge
22. Thing
27. ____ dixit
28. Work dough
29. Resourceful
30. Exuberance
31. Talking bird
32. Writer Shirley Ann ____
34. Open to ideas
36. Intentions
39. Impassive
42. Indian dress
47. Raillery
49. Witch town
50. "A Bell for ____"
51. Writer Jules ____
53. Property
54. Petty dispute
55. Pollster Roper
56. Spiffy
57. ____ over heels
58. Verbal

PUZZLE 300

ACROSS

1. Chinese noodles
5. Clans
11. Brink
14. Director Preminger
15. "Lifeboat" actor
16. Cry of triumph
17. Unit in a brazier
20. Daughter of Loki
21. Fabric trademark
22. Provo's state
23. Up in the air
25. Those complying with RSVPs
28. Sculls
31. Red Sea gulf
32. Melville novel
35. High credit rating
37. Catnappers
41. '40s radio show
44. Jewelry-box item
45. Totally
46. Chef
47. Greek love god
49. "Star Wars" princess
51. Sea gods' scepters
55. Batter's dry spell
59. King of Thailand
60. In a muddle
63. Modern prefix
64. Printed
68. Apple dessert
69. Counted calories
70. Fraternity letters
71. Stop
72. Bandleader Tommy
73. Depend

DOWN

1. Coffee-chocolate flavor
2. Singer Merman
3. Novelist Calvino
4. Neither's companion
5. Thunder god
6. Stable hue
7. Lazybones
8. Gideons' texts
9. Sound receiver
10. Snow glider
11. "____ 66"
12. "Do ____ a Waltz"
13. Garment varmints
18. Down: pref.
19. Puzzled
24. Piano feature
26. Cloudburst remnant
27. Trotsky
29. "Don't ____ My Parade"
30. ____ Clemente
32. Fall mo.
33. Printemps month
34. Unlock, poetically
36. Medical org.
38. The self
39. 17th Greek letter
40. Wall St. commodity
42. Leeds's river
43. Under the weather
48. One who bets
50. "____ Mommy Kissing . . ."
51. Inferior stuff
52. Took to jail
53. Fix securely
54. Sports-page figures
56. Combine
57. "Full ____ Jacket"
58. Metrical composition
61. Partner of snick
62. Ocean motion
65. Do sums
66. AFL's partner
67. Ship pronoun

PUZZLE 301

ACROSS
1. Mart
5. Crude
10. Be an accomplice
14. Cassette
15. Soldier's weapon
16. Baseballer Winfield
17. Historic periods
18. Fed the kitty
19. Location
20. Thawing
22. Big and Little
24. Lucy's mate
26. Asian holiday
27. Harbinger
31. Chief support
36. Reflection
37. Kitchen garment
38. Self-esteem
39. Art ____
40. Overwhelmed
41. Oklahoma city
42. Before, poetically
43. Stone pillar
44. Serving spoon
45. City in central New York
47. Tidbit
48. Flop
49. Dull
51. Deciphered
55. Windflower
60. Concluded
61. Mane sites
63. Withered
64. Bona ____
65. Tent
66. Cod or Ann
67. Escaped
68. Masts
69. Dash

DOWN
1. Goblet part
2. Famous race loser
3. Milky gem
4. Nuisance
5. Stretched to see
6. Tolls
7. Sternward
8. Santa's vehicle
9. Treason
10. Accommodates
11. Unclad
12. Eternally
13. Social gatherings
21. Not in use
23. Quaker William ____
25. Pierced
27. Animal skins
28. Abrasive substance
29. Indy 500 entrant
30. Earlier
32. Opera highlight
33. Sees to
34. Sprightly
35. Alpine music
37. Types of brew
40. Schoolgoers
41. Auricle
43. Driving shower
44. Leaf part
46. Revered
47. Clerical homes
50. Yard worker
51. Take off, as a hat
52. Wicked
53. Give up
54. Profound
56. Medieval weapon
57. Spoken
58. Type of palm
59. First garden
62. Nos. man

SUSPENDED SENTENCE PUZZLE 302

The words in each vertical column go into the spaces directly below them, but not necessarily in the order they appear. When you have placed all the words in their correct spaces, you will be able to read a quotation across the diagram from left to right.

EXPRESS ALONE LANGUAGE TO	AND THE HAS EXPRESS	GLORY CREATED THE THE	WORD OF PAIN THE	SOLITUDE WORD BEING OF	TO BEING ALONE LONELINESS

PUZZLE 303

ACROSS

1. Power network
5. Golfer's memento
10. Role on "The Cosby Show"
14. Wedding, e.g.
15. Unnaturally
16. Animal's cry
17. Verily
18. Thirst-quencher
19. Soft cheese
20. Deplore
22. Kind of convertible
24. "Sound of Music" family
27. "___ Folks" (Schulz cartoon)
28. Navigator's guide
31. Jots down
35. Misjudges
36. Itinerant
38. Zip
39. Grazed
40. Diva Rise ___
42. Southeastern electrical initials
43. Wild sheep of southern Asia
44. Marking post
45. Hands
46. Drum
48. Cutters
51. Puppy's complaint
52. Scout's rider
53. New Zealand racehorse
57. Dictator
61. Saint's headgear
62. Swedish inventor
65. Dr. Frankenstein's assistant
66. Author Turgenev
67. Join
68. Verne captain
69. ___ majeste
70. Kind of maid
71. "East of ___"

DOWN

1. Seize abruptly
2. Frost
3. Columnist's tidbit
4. Indicates
5. ___ the heels
6. Mrs. Cantor
7. Computer screen and keyboard: abbr.
8. Corrida cheers
9. Certain style of dress
10. Romeo's victim
11. Thyme or savory
12. French art historian Faure
13. Newspaper page
21. ___ gratia artis
23. Breakthroughs
25. Discussion group
26. University official
28. Last but not ___
29. Adjacent on a benzene ring
30. Sleeper's adventure
32. ___ nous
33. Indus, e.g.
34. Picnic side dishes
37. ___ Park, New Jersey
40. Pamper
41. Middle ear
45. Rockette
47. Mr. Power
49. Stag feature
50. Squalid place
53. Comedian Silvers
54. Beget
55. Wellaway!
56. Cornmeal creation
58. Long in the tooth
59. Alaskan seaport
60. Sci-fi flick
63. Type of part
64. Hiver's opposite

PUZZLE 304

SUNRAYS

Form 4-letter words using only the nine letters in the center of the diagram. Do not repeat a letter within a word. Place your words into the rays of the diagram so that no two words which are next to each other share a letter.

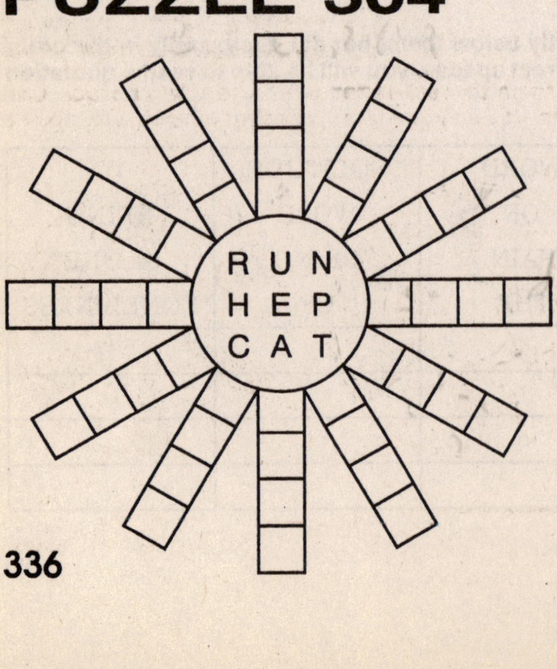

PUZZLE 305

ACROSS

1. Tropical plants
6. Glut
10. Facts
14. Warn
15. Sci-fi flick
16. Mideast priest
17. Ongoing
19. Space or drome preceder
20. Asian New Year holiday
21. Tear
22. Mr. Dangerfield
24. Waste allowance
25. Packaging material
26. Exercised leniency toward
29. Changed
33. Was human
34. Boutonniere spot
35. Baseball stat
36. London gallery
37. Type of charge
38. Glaswegian
39. Colorado brave
40. Madras princess
41. "____ porridge hot"
42. Annoyed
44. Smoothed, as wood
45. Unique person
46. Outerwear
47. Monterey's neighbor
50. Greek love god
51. Floral garland
54. Song for Sills
55. Pays the bill
58. Thaw
59. Locale
60. Actor Flynn
61. ____ Alto
62. Tater
63. Singer Della ____

DOWN

1. Finesse
2. Bitter herb
3. Hire
4. Table scrap
5. Mixed
6. Inhibit the growth of
7. Dry
8. Cargo weight
9. Wedding-invitation maker
10. Crown
11. Sherman Hemsley sitcom
12. Biblical vetch
13. Formosa Strait island
18. Require
23. Milky gem
24. Arboretum growth
25. Wigwam's cousin
26. Arrangement
27. Chatter
28. Comedian Johnson and namesakes
29. Was enthusiastic
30. Pie nut
31. Jagged
32. Passé
34. Hermit
37. Negligent
38. Bench
40. Tennis star Lacoste
41. Ceiling material
43. Salad ingredient
44. Destitute
46. Belief
47. David or Pendleton
48. Length times width
49. Small stream
50. "____, Brute!"
51. Italian money, once
52. Seth's son
53. Small land mass
56. Swallow
57. "Roses ____ red . . ."

HUBCAPS

PUZZLE 306

Insert two letters into the center of each circle below to form three 6-letter words reading across and diagonally (top to bottom). When you are finished, the letters you have entered, reading across, will spell a word.

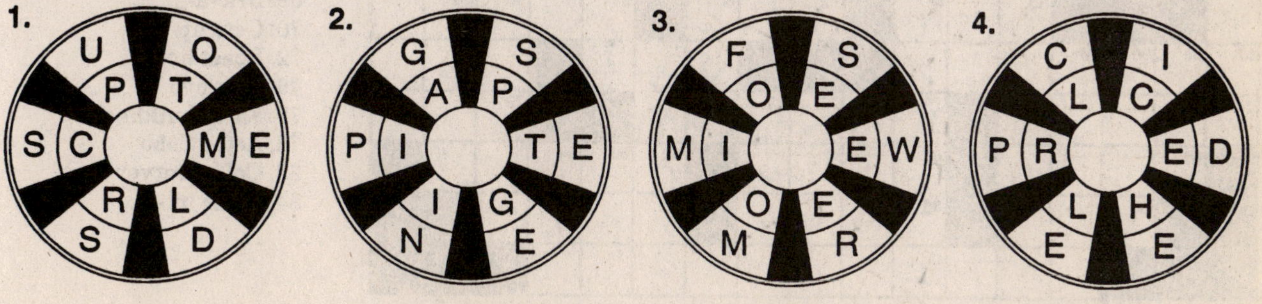

BONUS WORD: ____________

PUZZLE 307

QUOTEWORD

A humorous quotation runs clockwise around the edge of this diagram. To find the quotation work the puzzle as a regular crossword, filling in the remaining blank squares with the given letters.

A D H N N R R Y

ACROSS

10. Actress Donna ___
11. Toward shelter
12. Horned viper
14. Consumers
15. Meaning: Fr.
16. Dance move
18. Food scrap
19. Votes in
21. Bad links score
22. Greek letter
23. Boxer Muhammad ___
24. Kind of swimming stroke
26. Santa's little helpers
28. Male cat
31. Formerly called
32. Schuss
34. Saloon
36. Naval standard
40. "How now! ___?"
43. Decaying
46. Jai ___
47. Baseball team
48. Shoulder adornment
50. Birds' beaks
51. Ye ___ Shoppe
52. Vehement speech
53. Concept: pref.
54. Toady
57. Volleyball court divider
58. ___ King Cole
60. Soup vegetable
62. Singer Clark
64. Bike
67. Involve in conflict
71. Nevertheless
73. Evergreen tree
74. Nostril
75. Adherent of Islam
79. Utmost
80. Orient
81. Steinbeck character
82. Knickknack
85. Animator's sheet
86. Store event
87. ___ the Red

DOWN

1. Summer shirt
2. "___ Alibi"
3. A Ford
4. Comfort
5. Actor Baldwin
6. Pre-Easter period
7. School assignment
8. Washed-up star
9. Capitalist John Jacob ___
10. Q-W connection
13. Remora
14. ___ Mountains (Eurasian range)
17. For each
20. Ignited
23. Question
25. Certain neckline
27. Value highly
29. Acquire
30. Came of age
33. Wrath
35. Narrate
37. Mental health
38. "___ Three Lives"
39. Actor Kaplan
41. Aggravate
42. Ifs, ___, or buts
44. Make a choice
45. Author Buntline
49. X
55. Peter or Paul
56. Egyptian flute
59. Deed
61. Nearly
63. Organ of sight
65. Pessimist
66. Apollo's mother
68. Ms. Busch
69. Bric-a-___
70. Gets up
72. Roast host
76. Approve
77. Farm building
78. Actor Cobb
83. Coffee server
84. River inlet

PUZZLE 308

ACROSS
1. Soaks up
5. ____ detector
10. Female knight
14. Cave
15. Ship of the desert
16. At any time
17. Capital of Norway
18. Modify
19. Hayworth or Moreno
20. Apple or blueberry
21. Emerald Isle
22. Martini garnishes
24. Crux
26. Moistureless
27. Adam's rib
28. Police surveillance
32. Young female horse
35. English china
36. Philippine native
37. Blue bloom
38. ____ acid
39. Phooey's kin
40. French refusal
41. Miss by ____
42. Turkish title
43. Spellbind
45. Grown boy
46. Realty unit
47. Absence of noise
51. St. Francis of ____
54. "West ____ Story"
55. Lubricate
56. Billiards game
57. Jacket part
59. Measure of wood
60. First name in mystery
61. Feudal lord
62. Single time
63. Achievement
64. Requisition
65. Letter opener

DOWN
1. Skier's inclination
2. Desert Eden
3. Heaps
4. Theater sign
5. In short supply
6. Dwight's first lady
7. Sign
8. Understanding
9. Very wealthy place
10. Mock
11. Tel ____
12. Allot
13. Periods in history
21. Jealousy
23. Similar
25. Lampreys
26. Do penance
28. Cause to fall out
29. Sculls
30. Mormon State
31. Bye-bye, in London
32. Of superior quality, as wine
33. Rust element
34. Dark suit's scourge
35. Grin
38. City in Texas
39. Native of Copenhagen
41. Curved lines
42. Ashen
44. Called out to
45. Singer Bette ____
47. Attack
48. Nary a soul
49. About
50. Church official
51. Emulated Rich Little
52. Miffed
53. Dover or lemon
54. Hurried
58. Aura
59. New England cape

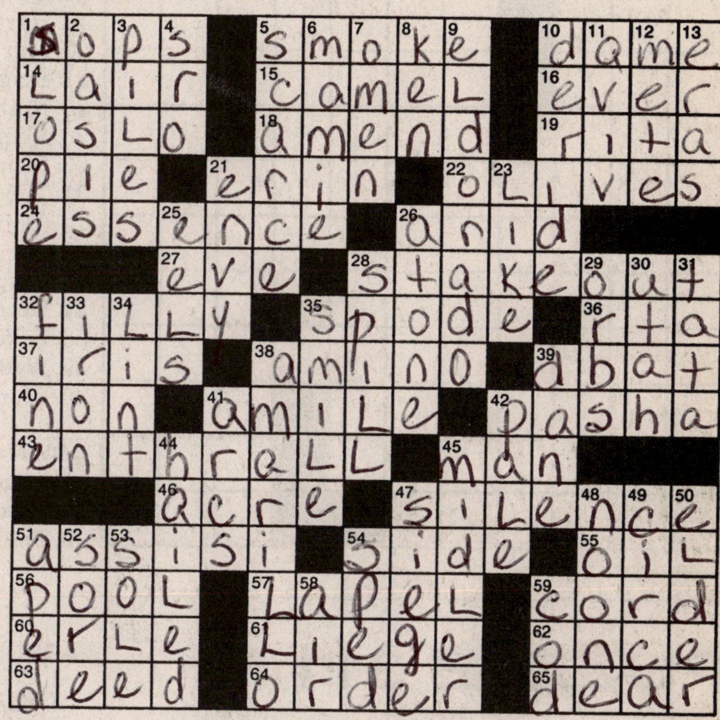

A TO Z MAZE

PUZZLE 309

Find your way through the alphabet three times in succession by starting at the circled A and moving in consecutive order from A to Z to A, etc. Move in one continuous line to reach the circled Z. Do not skip over any letters.

J M E (A) F I N O
I E S B W Z B N P L
M F A D C P K A D V W U
X Q G N Y Q R S E U B E X I
L S H E X P L C H T K Z D N Y Z
M I K Y O B D J Z A P E M C B A
J X W I N A K U I B F C G X F H
V K O M Q R L O H G M K C D E A
H Z L S L E M N J Z A B E S G F
U V R A P O X Y I C L K V H
S B Q A W C O N M W J I
T O V G P Q U V Y X
U S T R S T H (Z)

PUZZLE 310

Diagramless crosswords are solved by using the clues and their numbers to fill in the answer words and the arrangement of black squares. Insert the number of each clue with the first letter of the answer, across and down. Fill in a black square at the end of each word. Every black square must have a corresponding black square on the opposite side of the diagram to form a diagonally symmetrical pattern.

ACROSS
1. Peter ____
4. Flirt
8. Grand ____ Opry

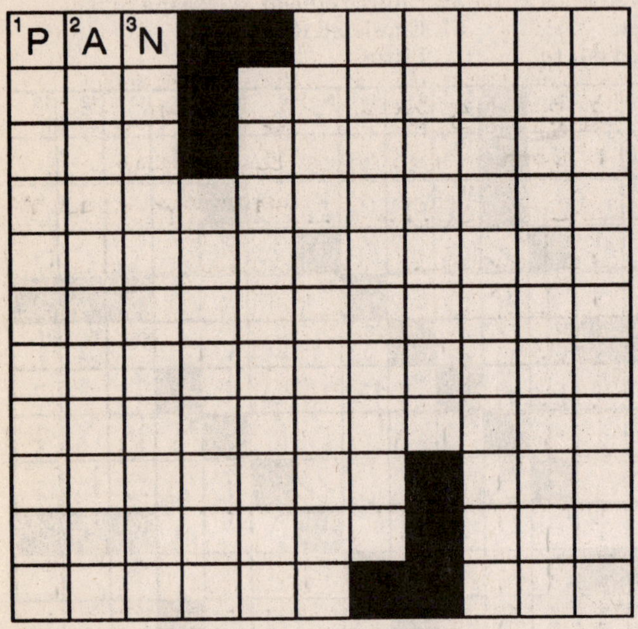

9. Comment
11. Knight's title
12. Heroic action
14. Chaos
16. Stringed instrument
17. Harsh
20. Lair
21. Stage whisper
23. Nothing
26. Elan
29. Biting
31. The Red ____ (Snoopy's adversary)
33. Army rank
36. Respect
37. Deceive
38. Pekoe or oolong
39. Walter or Donna
40. Blunder

DOWN
1. Ritzy
2. Pseudonym
3. Boldness
4. Irk
5. Electrical unit, for short
6. Shoppers' mecca
7. Haughty
9. School break
10. Franklin's flyer
13. Countdown starter
15. Eggs
18. Rend
19. Appetizing
22. Epoch
23. Pester
24. Frosted
25. Steamship
27. Angry
28. ____ of Babel
30. Erase
32. Close
34. Regret
35. Total

PUZZLE 311

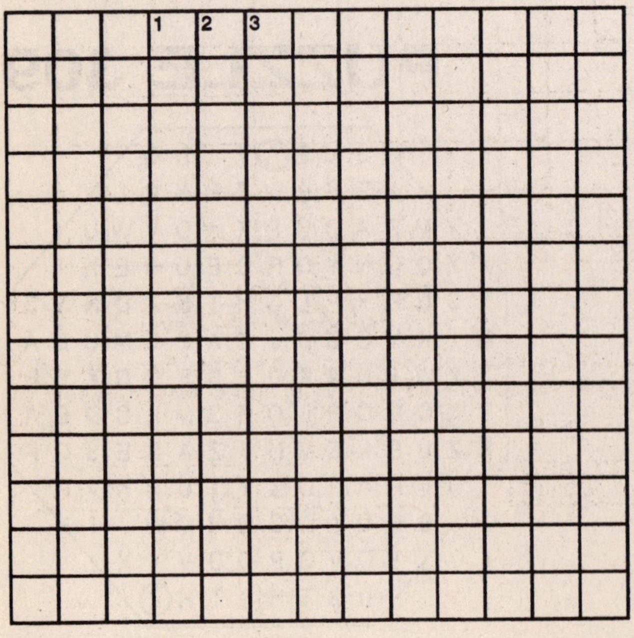

ACROSS
1. Cover
4. Mist
7. Flightless bird
8. Actress Lupino
9. Sleeveless coat
10. Peels
12. Gratuity
13. Summer color
14. "____ and Peace"
15. Writing fluid
16. Circle segment
17. Baby's toy
20. Sweet's counterpart
22. Sick
23. Way out
26. Taste
28. For
29. Foot digit
30. Years and years
31. Make a mistake
32. Footed vase
33. Shovel
36. Price
38. Head covering
39. Reverence
40. Before, poetically
41. Resting place

DOWN
1. Jump
2. Mischievous child
3. Payable
4. Evergreen
5. Lyric poem
6. Natural fuel
9. Three-ring attraction
10. Gasp
11. Leg joint
12. Poi source
13. Name
14. Existed
17. Mellower
18. Everything
19. Ace
21. Graded
24. Press
25. Heavy weight
27. Oliver's word
32. Employed
33. That woman
34. ____ for the course
35. Had a meal
36. Taxi
37. Part of IOU

PUZZLE 312

ACROSS

1. Cracked open
5. Joan of Arc, e.g.
8. ____ avis
9. Peel
10. Printers' measures
13. Motorcycle support
15. Small rug
16. Make happy
17. Epoch
18. Fireplace adjuncts
19. Actress Moran
20. Roofing liquid
22. Word of consent
23. Summoned
24. Winged insects
26. Canary's home
27. Bridge bid
31. Musical key
32. Church halls
33. Throb
34. Sweet treat
35. Hole-maker
36. Body of moral values
37. Pub drinks
38. Dixie dish
39. Supply food
40. Outdo
41. ____ and shine
42. Mom or dad
43. Stage comment
45. "The Winds of ____"
46. Legal matter
47. Baseball team
48. Touch lovingly
50. Cozy room
51. Preach
52. Night before a holiday
53. Park feature
57. Blushing
58. To ____ (exactly)
59. Biblical pronoun
60. Acted
61. Feed bag filler

DOWN

1. Noah's craft
2. ____ alai
3. Rainbow
4. Garden worker
5. Uses an ice rink
6. Prongs
7. Cease
9. Ohio and Utah
10. Comes out
11. Singer Osmond
12. Those who oppose change
14. Very funny person
18. Showboater
19. Avid
20. Mexican treat
21. Straightens
23. Does road work
25. Plaything
26. ____ blanche
28. One-seeded fruit
29. Blouses
30. Dry, as wine
32. Static
34. Taxi
35. Newlywed
36. Something to lend?
38. Smiled broadly
39. Insert marks
42. Event for floats
44. Filter
45. Alerted
48. Raccoon's cousin
49. Brawl
53. Evil
54. Exclamation of discovery
55. Seine
56. ____ Moines

Starting box on page 562

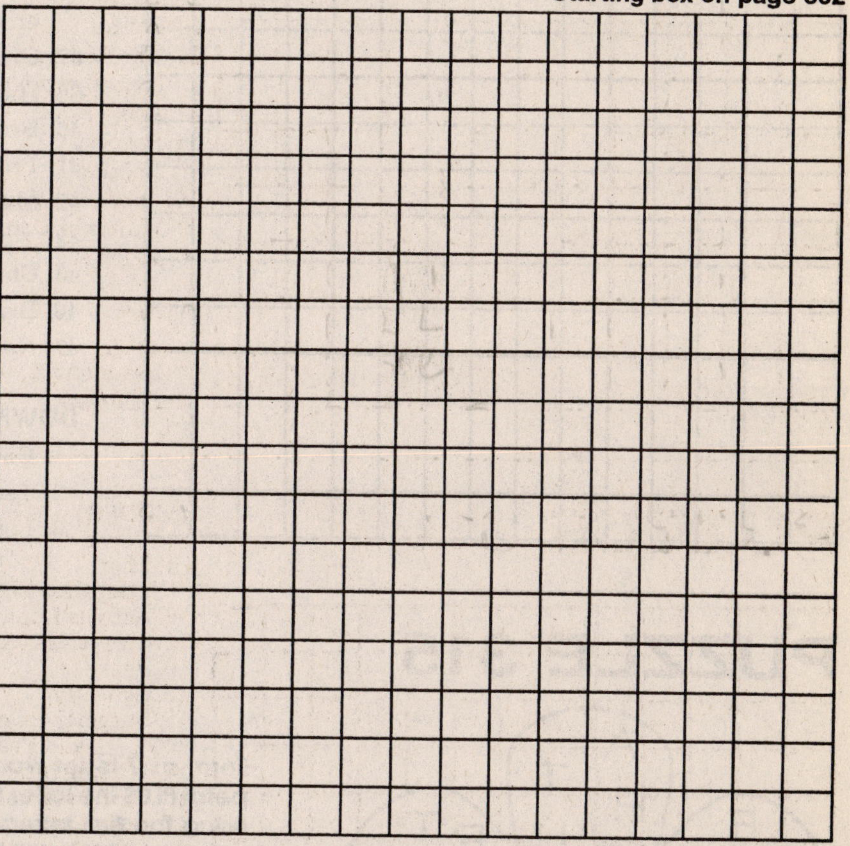

IN THE MIDDLE

PUZZLE 313

Fill in the squares to form a word which is the missing link to connect the two given words. For example, if the two given words were CRAB and SAUCE, the missing link would be APPLE (Crab apple, Applesauce).

1.

2.

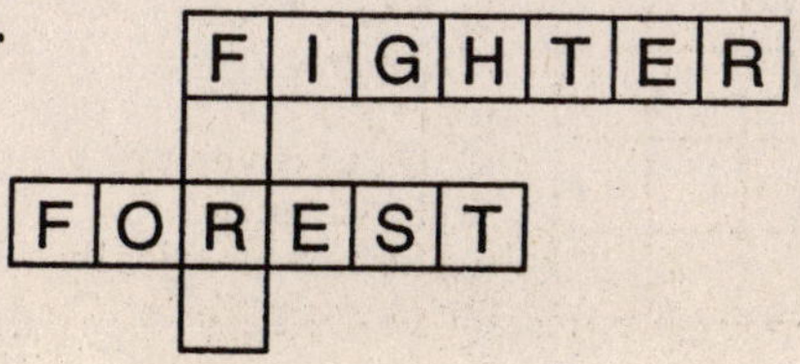

3.

PUZZLE 314

ACROSS
1. Practice
4. Ice mass
5. Tavern
8. Bonus for a car buyer, e.g.
11. Newspaper notice, for short
13. Region
15. Mr. Reiner
16. And
17. Permit
18. High-hat
19. Moray
20. Legume
21. Doer: suffix
22. Quelled
26. Tool and ___
27. Paddle
28. Agreed
31. Bering or Baltic
33. Commercials
34. Weep
36. Daffodil's origin
37. Grow old
38. Hard wood
40. Branch
41. Property right
42. Mall event
43. ___ counter
45. Chess pieces
46. Bright
47. Noshed

Starting box on page 562

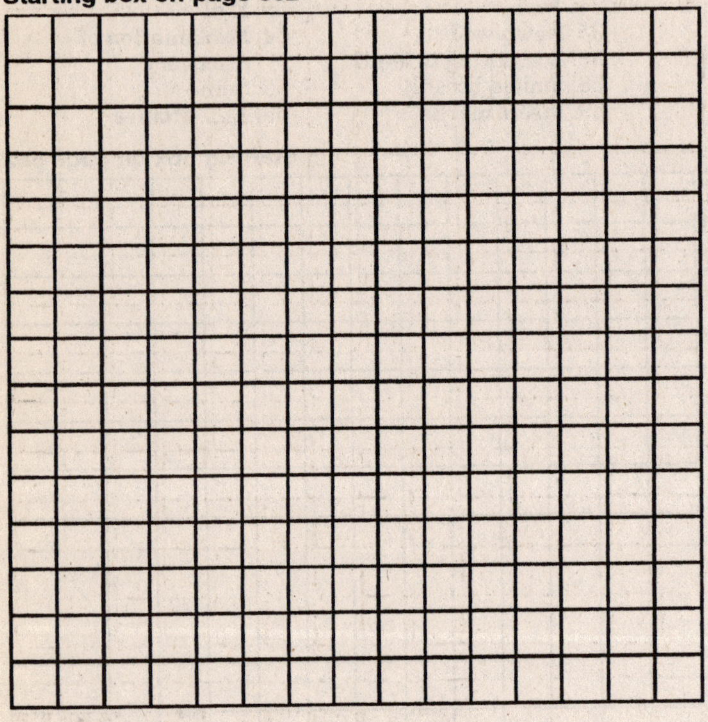

DOWN
1. Entreaty
2. Tennis shot
3. Longs
4. Stew
5. Large snake
6. Competent
7. Stair part
9. Give a tip
10. Wane
12. City in Spain
13. Toward shelter
14. Motives
18. Comic Caesar
20. Omen
23. Wrestling hold
24. Perched
25. Builds
28. Taxi
29. First garden
30. Reverie
31. Certain
32. N.Y. city
35. Conn. university
36. Purse
37. Well-ventilated
39. Rosewall of tennis
41. ___ majesty
44. Received

PUZZLE 315

DAISY

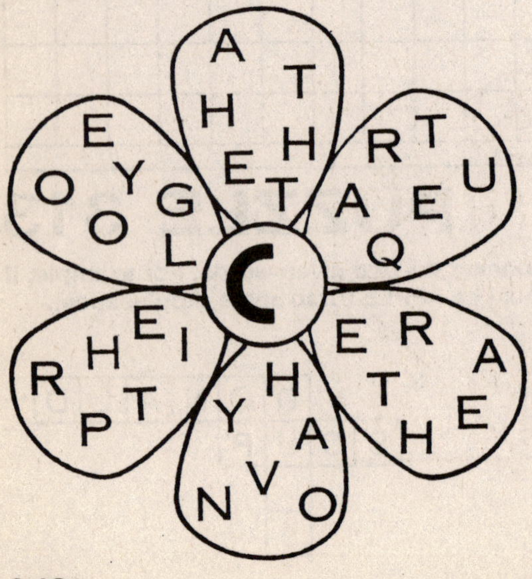

Form six 7-letter words using the letters in each daisy petal PLUS the letter C. Next, form a bonus 7-letter word using the first letters of these six words as well as the letter C, which will be the first letter of the word.

ACROSS
1. High card
4. Individual
7. Unload
9. Territory
10. Warehouse
12. Apple drink
13. Blue flag
15. Secret language
16. Financial reputation
18. Exaggerate
21. Strong beer
22. Conceit
23. Flower plot
24. Sports palace
26. Timid
27. Tooth doctor
30. Drama division
33. Pace
34. Cooking fuel
37. Sticky stuff
38. Affirmative answer
39. Attack by surprise
41. Each of two
43. Large pond
44. Actress Patricia ____
45. Night twinklers
47. Road units
50. Benevolent
51. Great affection
52. Writing fluid
53. Very small

DOWN
1. Say further
2. Billiards stick
3. Domain
4. Command
5. Born
6. Spike of corn
8. Study
9. Helped
11. Ocean movements
12. Inlet
14. Sound of relief
15. Corn center
16. Assert as true
17. Trifle
19. Father
20. Metallic rock
21. Contributes a share
25. Go in
28. Health resort
29. Male cat
30. Vital statistic
31. Metal money
32. Indian ____ pole
34. Sentry
35. Inquires
36. That woman
38. Cowardly
40. Unfilled
42. Frozen rain
45. Snow runner
46. Roofing metal
48. First woman
49. Espy

PUZZLE 316

Starting box on page 562

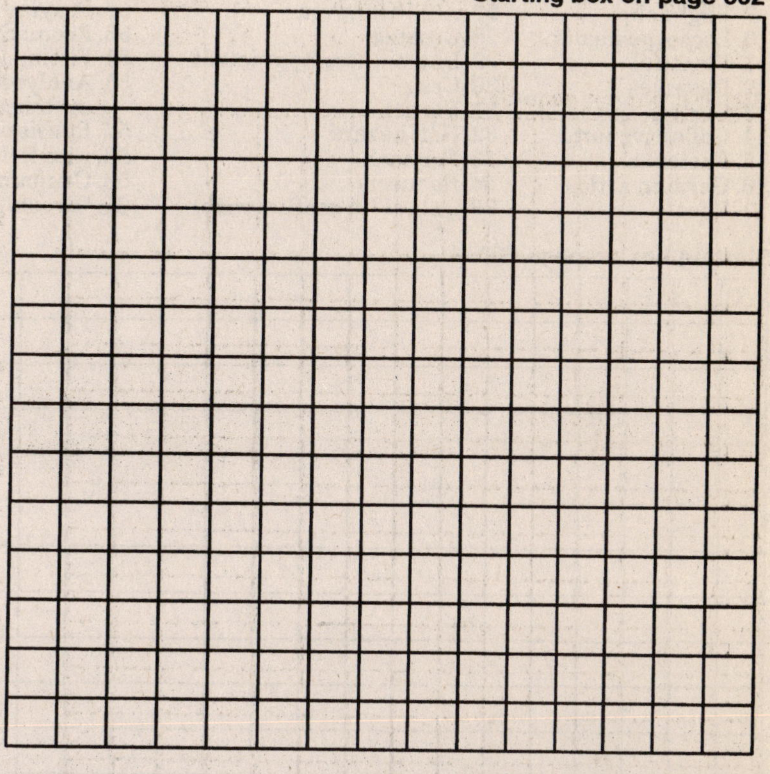

SUM TRIANGLES

PUZZLE 317

Each triangle, lettered A through I, has its own number value from 1 to 9. No two triangles have the same value. Each number shown in the diagram is the sum of the triangles that meet at that corner. For example, 11 is the sum of the triangles A and B. Can you determine the value of each triangle?

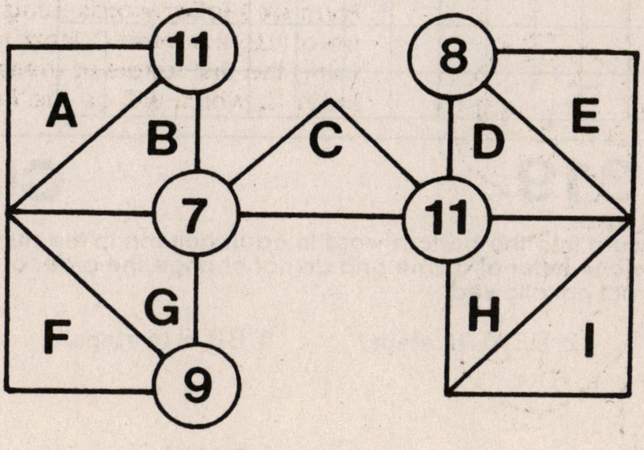

PUZZLE 318

ACROSS
1. Leave port
5. Football's Rozelle
9. Slight slip
10. Loose garments
11. Plentiful
12. Deserves
13. Certain spies
14. Collective farm
15. Fastener
16. German article
17. Pass
23. Albacore and bonito
24. Indigo
26. Sky hunter
27. ____ Khayyam
28. Created
29. Entree accompaniment
30. Crag
31. Border
32. Golf hazard
33. For each
34. Requests
36. ____ of (in conflict with)
38. Colony of bees
43. Sweltering
45. ____ du jour
47. Olive genus
48. Apply lightly
49. Wish-granting spirit
50. Arab land
51. Theater box
52. Praying figure
53. Room: Sp.
54. Fitting loosely
55. Analyzed a sentence
57. Russian plane
58. Rice field
59. Confound
61. "Broom ____"
62. Katerina Witt, e.g.
63. Kirstie ____ of "Cheers"
64. Tops of heads
65. Suggestive looks
66. Sandarac
67. Certain military ships

DOWN
1. Tea maker
2. Delicious and Cortland
3. Ait
4. Peggy and Pinky
5. Pear tree dweller
6. Ohio Indian
7. Appellation
8. Letter
9. Arranged in scales
10. Romantic entertainment
12. Titles of respect
15. Unconfirmed stories
18. "Paradise ____"
19. Mountain in Turkey
20. Rice dish
21. TV serial
22. Finale
23. Lug
25. Onion's kin
33. White ____ (city in New York)
35. "Scooby-Doo" character
37. Of an arm bone
39. Courts
40. The school you left
41. Understands
42. Foreman
44. What every child should do
46. Head, in Monaco
48. Period of stagnation
49. Republican initials
51. Firemen's equipment
54. "Coppelia," e.g.
56. Seaport in Senegal
58. Heaps
60. Spy Hari
61. Corridor
62. Health conscious resort

Starting box on page 562

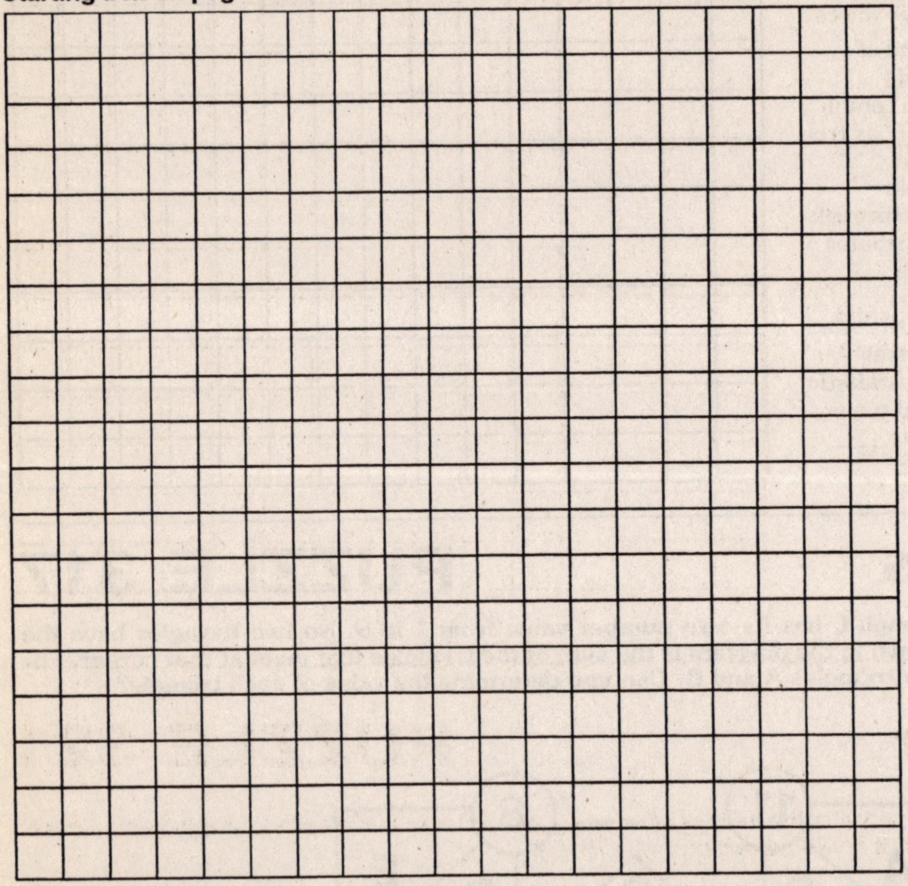

PUZZLE 319 Changaword

Can you change the top word into the bottom word in each column in the number of steps indicated in parentheses? Change only one letter at a time and do not change the order of the letters. Proper names, slang, and obsolete words are not allowed.

1. HAND (3 steps)	2. DEAL (4 steps)	3. BIDS (4 steps)	4. CARD (6 steps)
LEAD	PILE	RANK	DECK

PUZZLE 320

ACROSS
1. Savory jelly
6. Lanky
7. Season
11. Works of fiction
13. Bread spread
14. Supplement
15. Big
19. "___ Dark, My Sweet"
20. Primary color
21. Antlered animal
22. Mall unit
23. Extols
25. Skirt bottom
26. Retreat
27. Zilch
28. Fido's doc
29. Bottle top
30. Earl Grey, e.g.
31. Murmur
33. Rob
35. In addition
37. Burro
40. Iron
41. Beg
43. Transportation term
44. Military assistant
45. Modern
47. Fling
48. Pianist Victor ___
49. Carried

DOWN
1. TV's Lou Grant
2. Uttered
3. Covered with asphalt
4. Fury
5. Prison pad
7. Become more lenient
8. Choir voices
9. Ogle
10. Raced
12. Blue
16. Drive back
17. Seed
18. Noteworthy age
19. Object of value
24. Brainchild
25. Place for a Hula-Hoop
27. Talons
28. Song part
29. Pursues
30. Recite
31. Nick Nolte film
32. Infant's food
33. Minor quarrel
34. Kingston ___
36. Paddle
37. Ward off
38. Scorch
39. Glutted
42. Obligation
46. Dove's call

Starting box on page 562

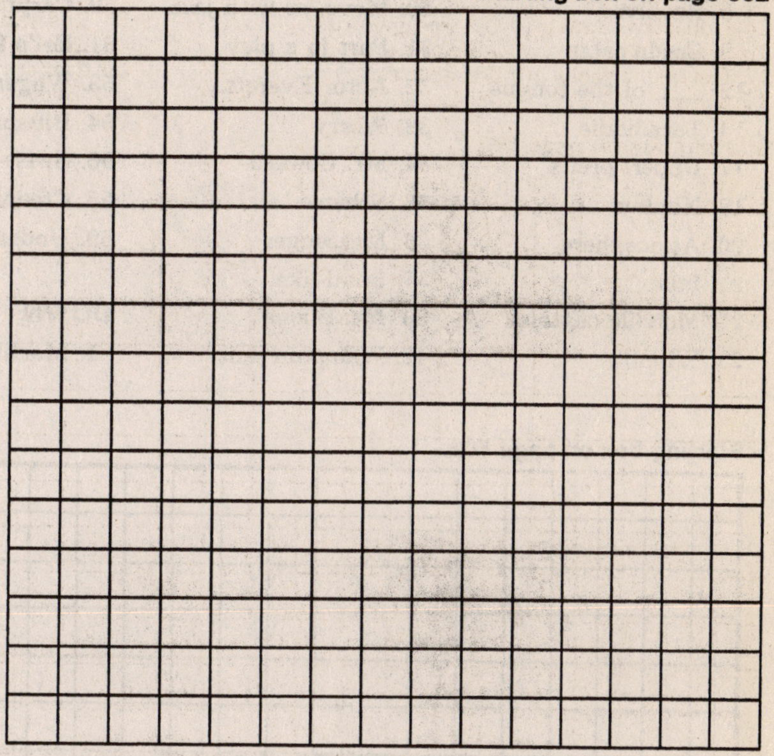

Rapid Reader

PUZZLE 321

Ten 5-letter words appear backward in these lines of letters. Can you find them all in four minutes or less? Underline each word as you find it as we have done with THEME.

O	P	A	D	E	M	E	H	T	A	T	U	O	B	A	R	F	F	O	G
T	R	E	D	I	O	L	X	N	E	L	B	O	N	G	A	W	A	S	T
T	E	M	L	A	S	P	A	K	S	A	L	F	T	C	E	N	I	V	O
P	O	H	G	R	A	L	R	A	N	G	P	S	A	L	C	O	R	A	P
H	S	R	A	M	L	R	U	H	T	E	S	P	U	X	I	W	U	R	C

PUZZLE 322

ACROSS

1. Festive occasion
5. Moslem leader
6. Marshy inlet
8. Revolve
9. Crude cabin
12. ____ of the tongue
14. Taradiddle
17. Upper: prefix
18. Nimbus
20. Atmosphere
21. Palo ____
22. Melville captain
23. Winnow
25. Farm structure
26. "Welcome" site
27. Balustrade
28. White water
30. Move, as with jazz
31. Part in a play
32. Actor Everett
33. Worry
34. Mr. Coward
35. Scheme
36. Messenger
38. Snail-like
39. Mr. Boone
42. Wampum unit
43. "The ____ Rose of Texas"
45. Spy Mata
46. Musical sign
47. Grass-to-be
48. Highest point
49. "____ Town" (Wilder)
50. Carplike fish
51. Eri's fabric
53. Wager
54. Blueprint
56. Swiss song
58. Creeping palm
59. Understands

DOWN

1. Machine fastener
2. Famous violinmaker
3. Basketball shot: hyph.
4. Love god
7. Spread out, as a flag
9. Corridors
10. Toward
11. Also
12. Lath
13. Tennis shot
15. Choler
16. Boxer Max
18. Emoter
19. Cry of triumph
20. Sour
21. Military assistant
23. Hourglass grains
24. Restricted
25. Sediment
27. In truth
29. Bard
30. Mets' stadium
32. Firewood measure
33. Stream
34. Keen
35. Trudge
36. "____ and Soul"
37. Mr. Arnaz
38. One of Snow White's pals
39. Crowd together
40. Branch
41. Four-in-hand
42. Melancholy
44. Directed
45. Actor Linden
46. Watch chain
51. ____ Hawkins Day
52. Bumbling
55. Wish earnestly
57. ____ Vegas

Starting box on page 562

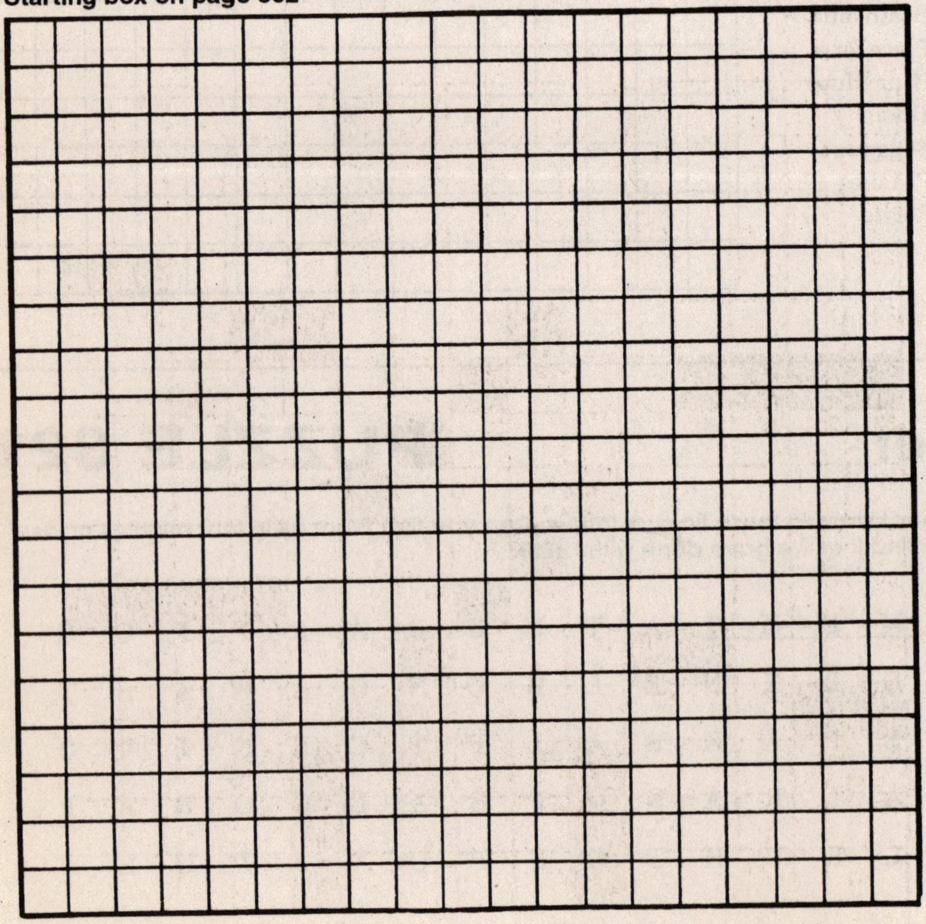

PUZZLE 323

ACROSS

1. Cartoonist Peter ____
5. Sage or thyme
9. Dull
14. Fare
15. Zone
16. "Home ____"
17. Actor John ____
18. Hampers
19. Saturn moon
20. Monroe-Lemmon movie
23. Harpsichord
24. Wine: pref.
25. Put two and two together
28. Vessel
30. More slender
33. Jocks
38. Awkwardness
39. Sand bar
40. Two, in Toledo
42. Negotiations
43. Soaked
45. Fearfulness
47. Electrical measurements
49. Statute: abbr.
50. Recent: pref.
51. Printers' measures
53. Pince-nez
58. Vegas cry
62. Panache
64. Godiva's title
65. Reduce
66. Joyce Carol ____
67. Bald eagle's kin
68. Leak
69. Lyric poem
70. Bolt or end
71. Itchings

DOWN

1. Lay up
2. Swab again
3. Judd the singer
4. Comedian Ole ____
5. Milieu
6. Actor Rhodes
7. Tennis-player Richards
8. Inlets
9. "Lord ____ taken away ..."
10. Stew
11. Mexican entree
12. Actress Merkel
13. Guys
21. Smoother
22. Perfume resin
26. Work stations
27. Kind of code
29. Jane Fonda's husband
31. Number
32. Signify
33. Nile dam
34. Motif
35. Risky situation
36. Off schedule
37. Greensward
41. English senor
44. Act
46. Passed on
48. Beamed
52. Intimidate
54. Indigent
55. Divvy up
56. Silk dye
57. Dancers' concerns
59. Scooted
60. Celtic language
61. Author Ferber
62. Contender
63. Once around the track

PUZZLE 324

ACROSS

1. Actor Mineo
4. Hindu title
9. Rest against
13. Civil-rights pioneer Parks
14. Rink
15. Oom-pah instrument
16. "Iliad," e.g.
17. Nonets
18. Journey
19. Grant-Hepburn thriller
21. Refugee
23. Girasol
24. Fourth person
25. Swiss city
27. Lancelot comrade
31. Flubs a grounder
32. Bathroom item
34. Highest note, to Guido
35. Joe South tune
39. Gardner of Hollywood
40. Shade
41. Charged particles
42. Go down
44. Dollar makers
46. ____ to riches
47. Han ____ of "Star Wars"
48. Set up a bivouac
51. Night noisemaker
55. String
56. Frequently
59. Conceal
60. Certain exam
61. Not a soul
62. Advance
63. Vital statistic
64. Actress Garson
65. ____ Marie Saint

DOWN

1. Senior to a frosh
2. Tibet's locale
3. American Indian sport
4. Summer footwear
5. "The Tempest" sprite
6. Layer
7. Made of: suff.
8. Gooden's sport
9. Noted Hun
10. Hamlet
11. Over, in Bonn
12. Snatch
13. Family room
20. Tarzan's neighbor
22. Brawl
24. Wide open
25. Valiant
26. Former Red Sox Tony ____
28. Spartan slave
29. Arkin and Alda
30. Doris and Dennis
31. Mild expletive
32. Ships
33. Gear part
36. Engine or bath
37. Paddle sport
38. Card game
43. Baby's bed
44. Jack Horner's place
45. "Ace ____ and Rodger of the Skies" (Spielberg story)
47. Play part
48. Business subj.
49. Nick's wife
50. Crowd
52. Russian port
53. Author Ferber
54. Senator Kennedy
57. In favor of
58. Tip of Italy

CAMOUFLAGE

PUZZLE 325

The answers to the clues can be found in the diagram, but they have been camouflaged. Their letters are in the correct order, but sometimes they are separated by extra letters which have been inserted throughout the diagram. You must black out all the extra camouflage letters. The remaining letters will be used in words reading across and down. Solve Across and Down together to determine the correct letters where there is a choice. The number of answer words in a row or column is indicated by the number of clues.

	1	2	3	4	5	6	7	8	9	10	11	12	13
1	K	E	E	R	N	E	L	A	B	A	R	K	D
2	E	N	T	E	N	R	A	L	I	T	O	R	E
3	P	L	A	T	E	E	R	A	B	O	V	I	E
4	Y	A	L	L	E	M	I	V	A	P	S	O	R
5	W	R	E	U	I	C	K	N	P	O	E	M	D
6	I	G	N	U	A	E	N	A	P	I	E	E	R
7	T	E	N	S	T	O	A	T	O	L	I	N	E
8	B	E	T	R	G	Y	S	A	L	O	L	N	E
9	T	O	A	N	A	L	B	L	E	R	R	O	D
10	A	P	H	I	T	D	B	E	P	D	A	T	E
11	G	W	O	E	N	E	E	D	D	E	N	A	N
12	S	A	N	C	A	W	T	S	A	R	T	E	D
13	S	L	E	E	T	W	A	M	D	E	E	N	D

ACROSS

1. Seed • Poet
2. Join • Landed • Miner's find
3. More tardy • Overhead
4. Elihu ____ • Steam
5. Demolish • Verse
6. Large lizard • Wharf
7. Dress type • Grain • Fib
8. Attempt • Solo
9. Heavy weight • More fit • Reel's partner
10. Plant insect • Cot • Consumed
11. Left • Paradise
12. Behaves • Comic Johnson
13. Icy rain • Walked in water

DOWN

1. Lock opener • Humor • Stubs
2. Expand • Milky gem
3. Knack • Garden tool
4. Come back • Frozen water
5. Tidy • Pismire
6. Bard's before • Shy • Moisture
7. Spree • Catch • Greek letter
8. Hot rock • Stories
9. Baby apron • McIntosh, e.g. • Mom's man
10. On • Lubricant • Command
11. Wander • Angry
12. Italian city • Memo
13. Doe • Stem • Stop

PUZZLE 326

ACROSS

1. Traffic problem
4. Forearm bone
8. Fencing weapon
13. Continent
15. Tag or football
16. Pseudonym
17. Malt beverage
18. Horsehair
19. Dagger handles
20. Don Quixote's sidekick
23. Golf-ball location
24. Parasite's home
25. Catherine of ____
27. Throw out
29. African antelope
31. Wading bird
32. Faux pas
33. Cain's nephew
36. Anglo-Saxon letter
37. Alike
40. Forty winks
41. Fairy's rod
43. Of the earth
44. Irish writer Thomas ____
46. Commanded
48. Anthony and Barbara
49. Slow, musically
51. Arab chieftain
52. Wrestler's surface
53. Secret Squirrel's sidekick
59. Short-lived David Soul TV series
61. Woodwind
62. Skating jump
63. Lime or brim
64. Soccer great
65. Football's Anderson
66. Male voice
67. "The ____ of Laura Mars"
68. New Deal org.

DOWN

1. Short punches
2. Cruising
3. Appearance
4. Extreme
5. Jumped
6. Darling dog
7. Sherman Helmsley TV series
8. Desert
9. Actress McGraw
10. Joe Friday's sidekick
11. 7:1
12. German city
14. Actress Anne ____
21. Pawns
22. Mothers of Invention leader
26. Tankard contents
27. Kett, e.g.
28. Sherlock Holmes's sidekick
29. Homer epic
30. Factory
31. Baste
32. "Peter Pan" villain
34. Crew members
35. Mole
38. Snow house
39. Marconi's medium
42. Excavate
45. "Call Me Madam" star
47. Supple
48. Game-show hosts
49. "____ to Avoid" (Herman's Hermits)
50. "Divine Comedy" author
51. French school
54. Alfred Hitchcock film
55. Heed
56. Yoke animals
57. Limerick writer Edward
58. Fitzgerald of jazz
60. Numero ____

PUZZLE 327

ACROSS
1. Nick and Nora's pet
5. Beaver creations
9. Mil. ranks
13. Highway
14. Inventor Howe
16. Seed coat
17. Part of BPOE
18. Biblical mount
19. Stuff
20. Summer drink
21. Midnight rider
22. Ski slope covering
23. Mall components
25. Skirt opening
27. Most secure
29. Church tower
32. Jogs
33. Has a different opinion
35. Always, in verse
36. Food scrap
37. Hosp. workers
38. Absorbs
42. Ike's wife
44. Former prisoner
45. Small houses
46. Prayer ending
47. Shows consideration for
49. Miracle site
51. Conceive
53. Gal of song
56. Italian city
57. Harangue
58. Water conduit
59. Mortgage
60. Scorer
61. Gypsy ___ Lee
62. Load cargo
63. Rocky crags
64. Extraordinary thing

DOWN
1. Locality
2. Realtor's sign
3. Assumes
4. Newspaper notices, for short
5. Wasteland
6. Active
7. Excavations
8. German territory
9. More impudent
10. Allow
11. Josip Broz
12. Large amount
15. Afternoon nap
21. Singer Diana ___
24. Asian holiday
26. Lower limb
27. Exorbitant
28. Amphitheater
29. Fast jets
30. Soviet premier
31. Dangerous curves
33. Doctor's amount
34. Dander
39. Kind of lettuce
40. Corrida cry
41. Certain college student
42. Colt's mom
43. Judge Fortas
45. Provides food
47. Defense gp.
48. Father: Lat.
49. Phone
50. China's continent
52. Darn!
54. Church recess
55. Sideways glance
58. Opposite of con

PUZZLE 328

ACROSS

1. Forage plant
7. Alma ____
12. Level
16. Gorge
17. Martini garnish
18. Lazy
19. Corrects
20. ____ America
21. Chick sound
22. Neck hair
23. Nigerian town
25. Elderly
26. Preserve
27. Tackle
29. Hamilton bill
30. Night club
34. Aligned
36. Father or mother
39. La Scala offering
40. Caustic
41. Japanese sash
42. Harbor
43. Turn right
45. Sudden drop
50. Purpose
51. Wail
52. Shrewdness
53. "Three ____ in a tub"
54. Lab glass
57. Fixed
58. Desire
59. Jug handle
60. Baby's seat
62. Culture medium
63. Esteem
66. Apartments
69. Depend
70. ____ Marie Saint
71. Malay boat
72. Politician's concern
74. Orange seed
77. Actor Howard
78. Merganser
82. Educator Young
83. Profit
85. Blue river
87. Stratford-on-____
88. Polka, e.g.
89. Arthurian paradise
90. Give freely
91. Scoff
92. "The ____ of Sleepy Hollow"

DOWN

1. Stuff
2. Tibetan priest
3. Kiln
4. Climbing plant
5. Terminate
6. Withstand
7. Part of an element
8. ____ carte
9. Yugoslavian leader
10. Wrong
11. Split
12. Hints
13. Think
14. Football team
15. Regret
24. Distant
28. Lock opener
30. Headlike expansion
31. Ascended
32. Flames
33. Corrode
35. Cozy room
36. Affirm
37. Assist in crime
38. Disencumber
43. Pepo
44. Decline
46. Have debts
47. Mirror sight

PUZZLE 328

48. Open to bribery
49. Doorway
51. Luminary
55. Boston ____ Party
56. Santa's helper
57. Diamond
58. Conflict
61. High mountain
63. Cancel
64. Develop
65. Four quarts
67. ____ the line
68. Summer footwear
73. Come to earth
74. Cushions
75. Scientist Pavlov
76. Window glass
78. Glitch
79. Stubborn animal
80. Black
81. Proceed
84. Skater's milieu
86. Hail!

PUZZLE 329

ACROSS

1. Walked in water
6. Tennis shot
11. Makes watertight
16. Solo
17. Macaroni
18. Custom
19. Donates
20. Bride-groom's attendant
21. Make amends
22. First woman
23. "—— Miniver"
24. Actress Mae ——
26. Old-timer, for short
27. Relax
29. And others: abbr.
31. Female parent
33. Away from home
35. Cooking fuel
37. Hive dweller
38. Extra money at Christmas
41. Lukewarm
43. Fixed charge
46. Run
48. Pack away
50. Lily pool
52. Current
53. Air circulators
55. Took to court
57. —— was saying: 2 wds.
58. Sketched
60. Plant bottom
62. Stands the strain: 2 wds.
64. Woe is me!
66. Rule the ——
68. Carryalls
69. Still
71. In addition
72. Morning moisture
73. Used glue
76. Place for an earring
78. Bed board
82. Tie the knot
83. Rip
85. Capture
86. —— Maria
87. Angry
89. Tangle
91. Senior
93. Striped feline
94. Eradicate
95. Prophets
96. Toboggans
97. Fender mishaps
98. Sample food

DOWN

1. Bet
2. —— and kicking
3. Birds of peace
4. Compass dir.
5. —— Plaines
6. Gush forth suddenly
7. Rubdown
8. Cigar residue
9. Cook slowly
10. Seraglio
11. Fragment
12. Sup
13. Over
14. Luxury ship
15. Let it stand!
23. Convened
25. Weep
28. Guided trip
30. Drinks like a dog
32. Pile
34. Military branch: abbr.
36. Takes a chair
38. 007, James ——
39. Music drama
40. Stairway post
41. Choir member
42. Be unsure
44. Browned bread
45. Follow after
47. Roofing liquid
49. Willie Winkie's size
51. Scoops of ice cream
54. Coal dust
56. Escort
59. Methods
61. Implement

PUZZLE 329

63. Quarrels
65. Irish dogs
67. Earliest
70. Suits to a ___
72. Society girl
73. Danger
74. Old saying
75. Challenged
77. Cotton bundles
79. Spoons out
80. Avoid
81. Concise
82. Punsters
84. Infrequent
88. Emcee Mack
90. Moving truck
91. Superlative ending
92. Grazing ground

PUZZLE 330

ACROSS

1. Loser's place
5. Gossip
9. "____ Out of Control"
13. Requisite
17. Tennis great Arthur ____
18. ____ avis
19. Young horse
20. Writer Stanley Gardner
21. Have in mind
22. Unwritten
23. Korea's continent
24. Workbench item
25. Tatum O'Neal film, with "The"
28. More timid
30. Motel
31. Stir ____
32. Son of Venus
33. Violet
36. Astringent
38. Climb down
42. Southern constellation, the Altar
43. Heavenly messenger
45. Twosome
47. Comedienne Martha ____
48. More or ____
50. Columnist Buchwald
51. Florence's river
52. North Sea feeder
53. Gospel singer Jackson
55. Gather
56. Mas that baa
57. Actor Kilmer
58. Sports field
59. Andy Capp's wife
60. Ball of yarn
62. Sip
63. Greenbacks
67. Teasdale, e.g.
68. Oliver or Rex
69. Corp. chairman
70. Defect
71. Chinese nurse
72. Permit
73. Thin rock
75. "Three ____ Match"
76. Bouquet
78. Tennis tournament
79. Flight of fancy
81. Hardy's heroine
82. Lancelot's title
83. Coconut cream, e.g.
84. Illinois city
87. 1986 animated film
93. Enthusiastic
94. Atop
96. Mrs. James Joyce
97. Theater award
98. Nobel Peace Prize winner Cassin
99. Called up
100. ____ and bear it
101. Columnist Barrett
102. Prophet
103. Sommer of Hollywood
104. To a degree
105. Eye drop

DOWN

1. Mary's follower
2. At a loss
3. Food fish
4. Ken Rosewall's racket
5. Mahogany
6. Papa Hansen on "Mama"
7. Steed breed
8. Hurtful
9. Hair-raising
10. Little Joe's brother
11. Part of REO
12. Speech defect
13. Farley Mowat filmization
14. Actor Estrada
15. Or ____ (ultimatum)
16. White-tailed animal
26. Singer of "Orinoco Flow"
27. Prepare for battle
29. Goddess of the dawn
32. Tijuana ta ta
33. Grease one's ____
34. Precinct
35. Humorous poet
36. Indian city
37. Give the go-ahead
39. Alleviate
40. Bill and Louis
41. "____ Rosenkavalier"
44. Catch in the act
45. Practical joke
46. Vase handle
49. Jack Lemmon film
51. Modify
54. Statute
55. The Ram
56. Building wing
58. Hera's son

PUZZLE 330

59. Stooge
60. Crooner Perry ____
61. Grazing grounds
62. Carts
63. Jagger or Jones
64. Burn reliever
65. Frog genus
66. Emulated Spitz
67. Find fault
69. Latin American revolutionist Guevara
72. Put out to ____
73. Mattress components
74. Actress Sedgwick
77. Teamster's command
78. Mineral or olive
80. Write-up
82. "Riders to the Sea" author
83. Woodworking tool
84. Startles
85. Double curve
86. Solitary
87. Friar
88. Pamplona bull
89. Svelte
90. Hautboy
91. 1492 ship
92. Vintage
95. Comrade

PUZZLE 331

• BEST FRIENDS •

ACROSS

1. "____ Can I Turn To"
4. ____ Angeles
7. Angels and Padres
9. Assistance
10. Fireman's friend
14. Large dog breed
19. Chicago trains
20. Mountain group
21. Attempts
22. Fresh
23. Mimic
25. Sheepshank, e.g.
26. Borscht or chowder
27. Clamp
28. Walking stick
30. Longfellow, for example
31. Nick's wife
32. "The ____ and the Pussycat"
33. Body
34. Come up
38. Marsh
39. "The ____ from Laramie"
42. Solo
43. Schuss
44. Mahogany-colored dog
48. Heat meas.
51. Santa ____
52. Miner's goal
53. Guitarist Paul
54. Main subject
55. Singer Pat ____
57. Green vegetable
59. Atop
60. Fly high
61. Wall support
62. Lure
63. Snare
67. Distinctive region
70. "Pyg-malion" playwright
73. Columnist Landers
74. Singer McEntire
75. Oratorio solos
77. Be in debt
78. Furry fetcher
81. Racing dog
83. Roof overhang
84. Cloudless
85. Seeded bread
86. Actor Beatty

DOWN

1. Cardiff canine
2. Overact
3. ____ Sharif
4. Tennis call
5. Former
6. Springer or cocker
7. Powder
8. Money at risk
9. Door clasp
10. Below-average grade
11. Tavern
12. In the past
13. Clear profit
14. Auto's need
15. ____ Grande
16. Flightless bird
17. Comfy home
18. Ram's mate
24. Rowboat propellers
27. Solemn promise
29. Model Campbell
30. "The Raven" author
31. Cranny
33. Cable network: abbr.
34. Porter or stout
35. Hogwash
36. Division word
37. Soothsayer
40. Foot part
41. African river
42. Pack animal
45. Newsman Donaldson
46. Shade

PUZZLE 331

47. Argue against
48. Doggy detective
49. Nashville's state: abbr.
50. Utilize
54. ____ with the same brush
56. Comic penguin
57. Hunter's helper
58. Consume
60. Rational
61. Remains
62. Forbid
63. Oak or cherry
64. Gun a motor
65. Actor Vigoda
66. Average
67. Satchel
68. Make a mistake
69. Untruth
71. Bristly
72. Unite
76. Avoid
79. Author Bradbury
80. "____ Got a Secret"
82. Washington bill

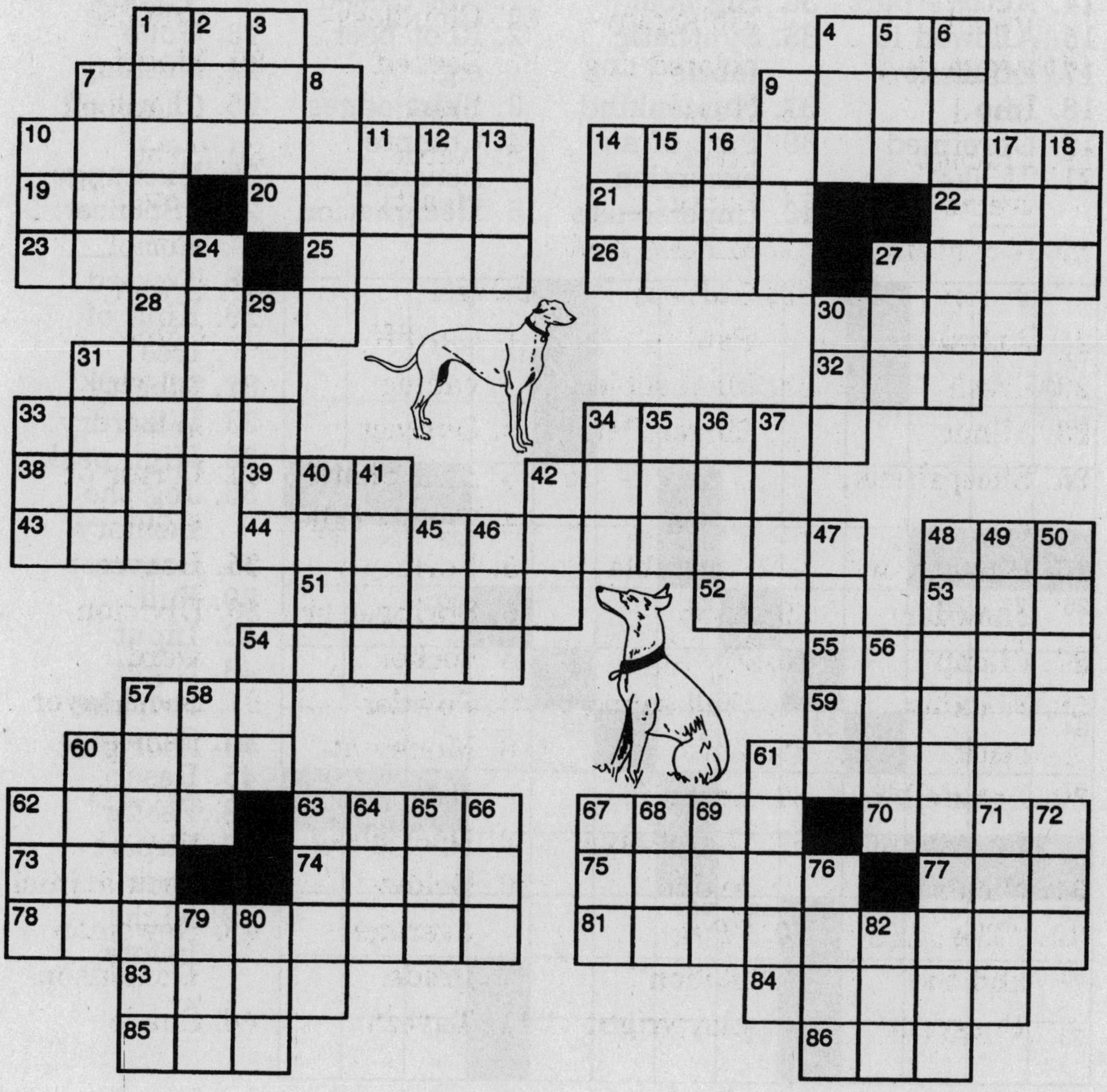

PUZZLE 332

ACROSS

1. Cigarette leftover
4. Salt Lake City's state
8. Gloat
12. DiMaggio or Garagiola
13. Feel compassion for
14. Actor's part
15. Allowed in
17. Efficient
18. Imp
19. Unrefined
21. "I like ___"
22. Flaming
26. Glow
29. Individual
30. Get hitched
31. Bird appendage
32. Lard
33. Certain horse
34. Sculpture or pottery, e.g.
35. Big boat
36. Synthetic fabric
37. Humankind
39. Part of an excursion
40. Impersonate
41. Among
45. Obstacle
48. Devote
50. Cadence
51. Baking place
52. Road-surfacing material
53. Eons
54. Correct
55. Twist my ___

DOWN

1. Not closed
2. Root beer, e.g.
3. Skirt edges
4. Comprehension
5. Designation
6. Consumed
7. Firefighter's spigot
8. Fight
9. Character on "The Dick van Dyke Show"
10. "___ the President's Men"
11. Golly
16. Frosting
20. Actor Vigoda
23. Gone
24. Nothing
25. "East of ___"
26. Exchange
27. "Spenser: For ___"
28. Toward
29. Kind of tree
32. Liberty
33. Wizardry
35. High peak
36. Jog the memory
38. Leaves
39. Full
42. Input
43. Night twinkler
44. Semester
45. Resort
46. Pester
47. Expert flyer
49. Night before

PUZZLE 333

ACROSS

1. High card
4. Deface
7. Howl at the moon
10. Parcel of land
11. Comedian Carvey
12. Colt's mom
13. Honda riders
16. Shorthand, for short
17. Lets up
18. Atop
21. Society girl
22. Roofing stuff
25. Ages
27. Frenzy
30. Singer-actor Burl ____
32. Wire measure
33. Cabbage dish
34. Opposite of fem.
35. Freshly
37. Soap ingredient
38. ____ la la
40. Did the backstroke
42. Bea Arthur role
44. Rule the ____
48. Boat pusher
51. "Cheers" orders
52. Dead and Black
53. Water tester
54. Blushing color
55. "____ Little Indians"
56. Song from "A Chorus Line"

DOWN

1. Charity
2. Crotchety person
3. Suffix with luncheon or major
4. Singer Davis
5. Unspecified amount
6. Track event
7. Game for Strawberry
8. ____ and crafts
9. Okey-dokey
11. Herd
12. Stingy ones
14. Yoko ____
15. Lassie's pal
19. Author Bombeck
20. Sprinkles
22. Comedian Conway
23. A Gardner
24. Said again
26. Killed
28. "Enola ____"
29. Flock member
31. Cleanses
36. Heats up
39. Fuss
41. Cow call
42. Stubborn animal
43. "____ of Eden"
45. Director Preminger
46. In the near future
47. Playhouse locale
48. Dory stick
49. Ruff's mate
50. Quayle or Rather

PUZZLE 334

ACROSS

1. Public vehicle
4. Pack down
8. Word before house or robe
12. Viper
13. Affirm
14. Dull pain
15. Media story part
17. Equipment
18. Ancient
19. ____ chango
21. Sarcasm
24. Drive a spike
25. Today's paper
26. Maidenhair
27. In the dumps
30. High note
31. ____ down (became quiet)
32. Sash
33. Say further
34. Cry of woe
35. Glen
36. Satisfied
37. French cap
38. Sigh
41. Golfer's peg
42. Small amount
43. Storage shack
48. Strong wind
49. Wicked
50. Paddle
51. Ogled
52. Author Carnegie
53. Snoop

DOWN

1. Exclamation of contempt
2. Put to work
3. Mineral spring
4. Add up
5. Zealous
6. Crew
7. Sets up
8. Roll with a hole
9. Fighter pilots
10. "____ Girl"
11. The good guy
16. Spanish noblemen
20. Cheese skin
21. Ancient Peruvian
22. Singer Lou ____
23. Was in debt
24. Site of the Himalayas
26. Deboned
27. Glide aloft
28. Proficient
29. Count calories
31. Painter Gauguin
35. Goose formations
36. Celebrated
37. ____ of the ball
38. Border
39. Medical photo
40. Patriot Nathan ____
41. Labor
44. Roe
45. Jump
46. Corn unit
47. Parched

PUZZLE 335

ACROSS

1. Amusement
4. Sibling, for short
7. Edge of a cup
10. Climbing plant
11. Drag
12. Comfort
13. Flower
14. Sorrow
15. Suffers
16. Strength
18. Points of view
20. Singer Peggy ____
21. Caviar
22. Warnings
26. Pick up the check
30. Tint
31. Algonquian
33. Abel's mother
34. Bestow
37. Propelled
40. Assistance
42. ____ Alamos
43. Reliable
46. "The Scarlet ____"
50. Rabbit's kin
51. Colonist Yale
53. Ambience
54. "Green ____ and Ham"
55. Relieved
56. Skinny
57. Formerly called
58. Notice
59. Envelope abbr.

DOWN

1. Blaze
2. Compartment
3. Snuggle
4. "The ____ of San Francisco"
5. Debt letters
6. Curse
7. Wading bird
8. ____ of Man
9. Hodgepodge
10. Energy
12. Avid
17. Meadow
19. Forget-me-____
22. Article
23. Attila, e.g.
24. Crimson
25. Drain
27. Always, to a poet
28. Road: abbr.
29. Kennedy or Danson
32. Run together
35. Desert havens
36. Humor
38. Grief
39. Landed property
41. Colorists
43. "That Was ____, This is Now"
44. Indignation
45. Prod
47. Revolve
48. Journalist Sevareid
49. Ewe's mate
52. Fabricate

PUZZLE 336

ACROSS

1. Alan or Robert
5. Golly!
8. Iowa city
12. Dirt
13. Raced
14. "Miami ___"
15. Trespassers
17. Tennis great Arthur ___
18. Ripen
19. Souvenir
21. Cover
22. Play on words
23. Richard ___ of "Pretty Woman"
25. Take for granted
28. In the vicinity
31. ___ d'etat (overthrow)
32. Bambi, e.g.
33. Subjects
36. Card suit
38. Napoleon's island
39. ___ capita
40. Damage
42. Grin
44. Ecology group: abbr.
47. Bullets
49. William Shatner series
51. Not nice
52. Baseball's Mel ___
53. All: pref.
54. "___ of Green Gables"
55. Negatives
56. Horace or Thomas

DOWN

1. Largest continent
2. Endless
3. Plunge
4. Chicken ___ king
5. Lorne of "Bonanza"
6. British nobleman
7. Certain navy officer
8. Gardner of films
9. TV's talking horse
10. Reverberate
11. Leak
16. Snare or kettle
20. Average grade
22. Student
24. Walter O'Reilly on "M*A*S*H"
25. Perform
26. Jack ___ of "Barney Miller"
27. Christopher Reeve role
29. Spelling contest
30. Calendar units: abbr.
34. Certain network: abbr.
35. Delilah's mate
36. Smacks
37. Equal
40. Mother
41. Prayer ending
43. Tell ___ the marines
44. Columnist Bombeck
45. William or Sean
46. Related
48. Dollar bill
50. Jerry's cartoon nemesis

PUZZLE 337

ACROSS

1. Tidbit for Flicka
4. Expensive
9. NBC rival
12. Evergreen
13. Dance for two
14. Squeal
15. Pink birds
17. ____ was saying
18. Standard
19. Preference
21. Western Indians
23. ____-and-cream complexion
25. Adam's son
26. Canal vessel
27. Can top
28. Pickle juice
29. Cribbage counter
32. Across: pref.
33. Salve plant
34. Says again
37. Author Stephen ____
38. Indebted to
39. Tennis call
40. D.C. VIP
41. Alumni
47. Dander
48. Spooky
49. Zsa Zsa's sis
50. Kind of curve
51. Legal documents
52. Blushing color

DOWN

1. On one's way
2. Be under the weather
3. Caught in a snare
4. Blends
5. Summer hue
6. Part of G.B.: abbr.
7. ____ trip
8. Meter or stamp
9. Attend uninvited
10. Stitch loosely
11. Pigs' havens
16. Letter-carrier's burden
20. King's better
21. Actor Holbrook
22. Kimono sash
23. Aches
24. Sea eagles
26. Spoiled tot
28. Boasted
29. Dish
30. Vast time frame
31. ____ whiz!
32. Sawbuck
33. Neighborhood
34. ____ the Riveter
35. Water pitchers
36. Maine's trees
37. Indications
42. Ruff's mate
43. "____ You Lonesome Tonight?"
44. Performed
45. New Year's ____
46. Downcast

PUZZLE 338

ACROSS

1. Bridge
5. Tippler
8. Angered
12. Outer edges
16. Cassette, e.g.
17. Cut back
19. Flower jar
20. Cleveland's lake
21. Soothe
22. To the sheltered side
23. Waiting servant
25. Decide in advance
28. Aim a finger
29. "____ Got Sixpence"
30. Suffocating snake
31. Screen star Lugosi
32. "____ How She Runs"
33. Ready for business
35. Played a king-rook move, in chess
38. "Planet of the ____"
40. Fragrance
41. Diminutive suffix
42. Decay
44. Placed in the middle
46. Queen ____ furniture
48. In the ____ (healthy)
49. Terminate
50. Roofing substance
51. African fly
53. Aware of
54. Wager
55. Fishing cords
56. Shoe tip
58. Johnson of "Laugh-In"
61. Worn away
63. ____ Na Na
64. Everyman John ____
67. Lunch time
68. Unique person
69. Breaks into pieces
71. Mountain peak
72. To be, to Caesar
74. Anytime now
75. Medicinal plant
76. Instructor
78. Type of football kick
79. Building addition
80. Fish eggs
81. Former Mideast country: abbr.
82. Exist
83. Moonshiner's device
85. One who trades places
91. Unending
93. Withered
94. "A ____ of Two Cities"
95. Peel
96. Perry's creator Gardner
97. Swarm
98. Songstress Fitzgerald
99. Hymn closing
100. Venison source
101. "____ Miser-ables"
102. Hold as an opinion

DOWN

1. Pace
2. Carson's predeces-sor
3. Cathedral end
4. Most wanting
5. Declare
6. Heraldic border
7. Row
8. Donald Trump's ex
9. Grade
10. Superlative suffix
11. Going down farthest
12. Try the number again
13. Persia, today
14. Money factory
15. Tennis match unit
18. Part of a group
24. Actor Nick ____
26. Adam's wife
27. Charged particle
31. Actress Kathy ____
32. Dispatch
33. Baltic feeder
34. Pea envelope
35. Pennies
36. Ireland, to poets
37. "____ Tread on Me"
38. Hole in one
39. Enclosure
40. Speak pompously
43. Boxing de-cision: abbr.
45. French summer
46. Actor Ed ____
47. Lack
48. Author of "The Raven"
51. Spring, neap, or flood
52. American patriot Allen
54. TV's Matlock

PUZZLE 338

55. Lover of solitude
57. Cereal grain
58. Picnic pest
59. Tree's anchor
60. Ripped
62. Fragrant red flowers
63. Struck by a bullet
64. "The Farmer in the ____"
65. Spanish gold
66. Opposite of WNW
69. Boy baby
70. Naturally skillful
72. School, in Paris
73. Removed the husk from
74. Most certain
77. Gotten up
78. TV host Sajak
79. Historic age
81. Racecar driver Bobby ____
82. Attention getters
83. Joint
84. Weight allowance
85. ____ of Wight
86. Spool
87. Algonquin tribe
88. High wind
89. French fashion magazine
90. Measure of paper
91. Auditor: abbr.
92. Before

PUZZLE 339

ACROSS
1. Sport fish
5. Rips
10. Bridge
14. Bouncing sound
15. Large black bird
16. Gap
17. Parched
18. Out of the way
19. Total defeat
20. Asked for insistently
22. Bells, whistles, etc.
24. Snaky fish
25. Dermal layer
26. Expand
30. Glossiest
34. Wide-awake
35. Pledged
36. Blemish
37. Rural road
38. Small stores
39. Skeletal material
40. Carpenter or army
41. Expositions
42. Palm fruits
43. Left alone
45. Apple beverages
46. Family quarrel
47. Female deer
48. Would rather have
51. Spaghetti's partner
56. Advertising emblem
57. Songs for two
59. Europe's neighbor
60. Aroma
61. Thing of value
62. Film critic Rex ____
63. Trial
64. Many ____ ago . . .
65. Alleviate

DOWN
1. Necklace component
2. Farm measure
3. Thin wedge
4. Bicarbonate of ____
5. Swapped
6. Painter's stand
7. Eager
8. Comedian Buttons
9. Athletic footwear
10. Reduced
11. Destitute
12. Grad
13. Receives after taxes
21. Orderly
23. Legal claim
25. Spills
26. Dish of fresh greens
27. Aircraft
28. Leases
29. Sooner than, poetically
30. Saber, e.g.
31. Show feeling
32. Mentally healthier
33. Long lock of hair
35. Flinched
38. Seventh day of the week
39. Not good
41. Without charge
42. Eat less
44. Exertion
45. Slides
47. Prevent
48. Story line
49. Went by horse
50. Selves
51. Plateau
52. Uncover
53. On the ocean
54. Falsehoods
55. Put a burden on
58. Utilize

PUZZLE 340

ACROSS

1. Frolic
5. Incline
10. Shut hard
14. State with confidence
15. Swiss call
16. Role model
17. Fence opening
18. Frown
19. Garage entrance
20. Lift
22. Wash
23. Frozen treat
24. Chowder ingredient
26. Buy back
29. Wrestled
33. Promises
34. Original source
35. Chopping tool
36. Small child
37. Weary from overwork
38. Health resort
39. ____ out a living
40. Fortune-telling card
41. Guide
43. Confine
45. Unsatisfactorily
46. Ace in the ____
47. Close to the ground
48. Noted
51. Adolescent
56. Butter substitute
57. "La Boheme," e.g.
59. Move quickly
60. Back
61. Dreads
62. Extreme
63. Refute
64. Inaccurate
65. Wall support

DOWN

1. Fury
2. Egg-shaped
3. Allot
4. Advance showing
5. Method
6. Crazy
7. Smell
8. Church seat
9. Building addition
10. Prawn
11. Slender
12. Weapons
13. Sulk
21. Experts
22. Fascinated
24. Glass bottle
25. Touch down
26. Estimator
27. Call forth
28. Loves to excess
29. "Waiting for ____"
30. Focused beam
31. Oust
32. Darling
34. Mockery
37. Hoosegow
40. Walked
41. Before long
42. In the direction of
44. Supposition
45. Gratify
48. Tennessee Ernie ____
49. To shelter
50. Intend
51. Greenish blue
52. Sins
53. Horse's stride
54. Light brown
55. Marsh grass
57. ____ and running
58. Green vegetable

PUZZLE 341

ACROSS

1. Dominate
5. Alert
10. Scarlets
14. Spanish jar
15. Private teacher
16. Lamb's pen name
17. Garden pest
18. Boredom
19. Competes
20. Foster strife
23. Take it on the ____
24. Destroy
25. Ignobility
30. Invalidate
34. Sheep mother
35. Expanse of land
37. Evil spirit
38. Actor Alan
40. Golf norm
41. Papal court
42. Peculiarity
44. Sniff
47. ____ King Cole
48. Felt
50. Ern
52. But: Sp.
54. Battle
55. Commit youthful follies
63. Pub brews
64. In reserve
65. Eye tunic
66. Egyptian river
67. Mr. Standish
68. Male children
69. Precious metal
70. Appears
71. Terminates

DOWN

1. Curtsies
2. Bread spread
3. Killed
4. Seat on a horse
5. Soft-shell clam
6. Suspended
7. ____ time
8. Circular
9. Pokey
10. Retaliator
11. Writer Wiesel
12. Eating plan
13. Cummerbund
21. Carry on
22. Knotted
25. Waistbands
26. Cognizant
27. Family car
28. Weakens
29. Con games
31. Surrounded by
32. Sum up
33. Maternally related
36. Coatrack
39. Inclined
43. Adolescent
45. Unruly
46. Show the way
49. Reveries
51. Excite
53. Actor Davis
55. Crooned
56. Hodgepodge
57. Healthy
58. Stratagem
59. Same: Lat.
60. Bard's river
61. Baby-sit
62. Nerve

PUZZLE 342

ACROSS

1. Equal
5. "The ____ Luck Club"
8. Astringent
12. Press
13. Sooner, poetically
14. Get up
15. Hire
16. Stockpiles
18. Looks for
20. Achievers
21. Misguided
23. Sunday bench
24. Applaud
25. Ashen
26. Typewriter key
29. Cattle group
30. Diaper fastener
31. Speed contest
32. McMahon and Sullivan
33. Like father, like ____
34. Hooded snake
35. Baseball stick
36. Wine glass
37. Guardian ____
40. Perhaps
41. Rewards
43. Kind of collar
46. Direct
47. Head cover
48. Actor's part
49. Shade providers
50. Chicago Loop trains
51. Gush out

DOWN

1. Baronet's title
2. Part of to be
3. Creatures
4. Signed up
5. Beef ____
6. Unrefined metals
7. Okay
8. Bow's missile
9. Not taped
10. Consumer
11. Confusion
17. Adam's garden
19. Hearing organ
21. In need of a massage
22. Cast off
23. Skillet
25. Triumph
26. Family's eating surface
27. Farmhold
28. Throb
30. Spaghetti cooker
31. Thieves
33. Seasoning
34. Modest
35. Zigzags
36. Puffs
37. Qualified
38. Yuletide
39. Pacific island
40. Repast
42. Winter driving hazard
44. "Grand ____ Opry"
45. Just bought

PUZZLE 343

• A FINE KETTLE FULL •

ACROSS

1. Singer Garfunkel
4. Female military flyers: abbr.
7. Australian marsupial
10. Courtroom excuse
12. More frosty
13. Comes in last
14. Imbibe excessively
20. Belonging to that girl
24. Actor Steiger
25. Beer's cousin
26. Persia, today
27. Willing's partner
29. Delaware or Kansas
31. "And Then There Were ___"
32. Orange covering
33. Thing of value
34. Brink
35. Norse saga
36. Agent 007, e.g.
38. Cleopatra's snake
41. Prophet
42. Basketball's Archibald
44. Vexed
46. Formerly named
47. Lubricate
48. Following
50. "___ and the Swan"
52. Dress of India
54. Pounds, shillings, and pence
56. Do sums
57. Foal's mother
61. Whitney and Wallach
62. Covered with water
66. Design
67. Table setting item
68. Brubeck and Winfield
69. Kind
70. High cards
71. Styling goo
72. "___ the ramparts . . ."
73. Sparrow's home
74. Better things to do
82. Speak what you think
84. Equip with weapons again
85. Leases
86. Follow
87. Tibetan ox
88. Mad as a wet ___

DOWN

1. Related
2. Actor Hudson
3. Horse's fly chaser
4. Hope
5. Honest ___ Lincoln
6. Questionable quality
8. Hawaiian garland
9. Noah's boat
10. Boxing great Muhammad ___
11. ___ Angeles
14. Heavy curtain
15. Dressed
16. Ran in neutral
17. Has dinner
18. Word of woe
19. Gala celebration
21. Wears away
22. Scope
23. Scornful smile
28. Verve
29. Utter
30. Airport abbr.
36. Refined iron product
37. Equals
39. Reprimand
40. Snooped
43. Tiny hill builder

PUZZLE 343

45. Elderly
48. Gets up
49. Tall tale
51. Electrical units
52. Type of car
53. "____ in Wonderland"
55. Mom's spouse
56. Exclamations
58. Distantly cool
59. More unusual
60. Way in
63. Salary
64. Assert
65. Ego
74. Pig's comment
75. Explosive initials
76. "For ____ a jolly good fellow"
77. Fury
78. Member of Congress: abbr.
79. Leftover serving
80. Not false
81. Sign of the future
83. Split ____ soup

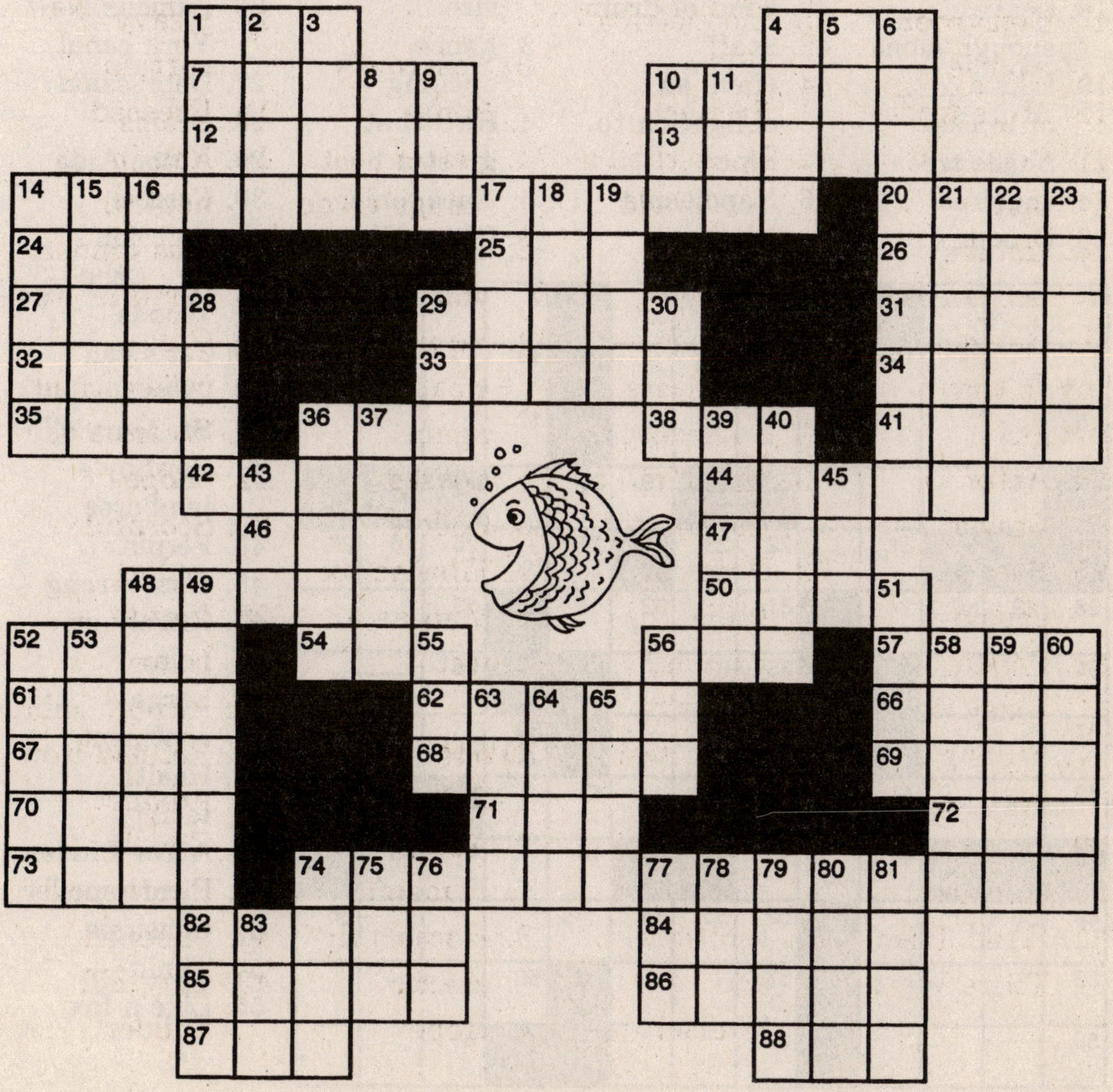

PUZZLE 344

ACROSS

1. Souffle ingredient
4. Light-switch position
7. Time spans
11. Steed breed
13. Court
14. Distasteful
15. Storekeeper
17. Radiate
18. Leave ___ enough alone
19. Like a ___ of bricks
21. Shade trees
24. Inquired
28. Droops
31. Landed
33. Wrath
34. Pie ___ mode
35. Cozy room
36. Can metal
37. Chum
38. Make both ends ___
39. Borsch ingredient
40. Kind of drum
42. Staff
44. Have an obligation to repay
46. Napoleon's isle
49. Roe fish
52. "The Young and the ___"
56. Window unit
57. Good cheer
58. Jib, for one
59. Singing range
60. Porky's pad
61. Beam

DOWN

1. Spike of corn
2. Increased in size
3. Fence opening
4. Bird that gives a hoot
5. Antagonist
6. Dix or Knox
7. Ties, as the score
8. Edge
9. Mr. Baba
10. Gel
12. Cotton bundles
16. Under the weather
20. Feed-bag morsel
22. Fabricated
23. Hit the hay
25. Go fly a ___
26. Famous New York canal
27. Depression
28. Drains
29. Actor Alda
30. Festive occasion
32. "___ the Woods"
38. Cat's call
39. "The ___ of St. Mary's"
41. Cowboy's jamboree
43. Permit
45. Goes wrong
47. Grizzly or polar
48. Large continent
49. Health facility
50. Actor Linden
51. Picnic spoiler
53. Consume
54. Timid
55. Like a fox

PUZZLE 345

ACROSS

1. Actress Merrill
5. Agent, for short
8. Pound in
12. Eve's son
13. Grow old
14. Great Lake
15. Authentic
16. Oath
17. "____ Misbehavin' "
18. Unmask
20. Swap
21. Cold season
24. Actor Woody ____
27. Beam of light
28. Health facility
31. Nourish
32. Drill part
33. Bring up
34. Child's game
35. Canary or cat, e.g.
36. Core
37. Teetered
39. Tale
43. Flee
47. Busy place
48. Epoch
50. Alda of "M*A*S*H"
51. Prayer ending
52. Part of L.A.
53. "On Golden ____"
54. Fender bender
55. Brenda or Ruta
56. Observes

DOWN

1. Defy
2. Wild mountain goat
3. ____ tide
4. Permitted
5. Black bird
6. Self
7. Sunday seat
8. Salty drop
9. Elaborate solo
10. ____ over matter
11. Guitarist Townshend
19. Transgress
20. Attempt
22. Dull
23. Have a hotdog
24. Toward the back, matey
25. Meadow
26. Support
28. Ocean
29. Average
30. Mr. Carney
32. Spelling contest
33. Porters
35. Snoop
36. "For ____ a jolly good . . ."
38. New ____ on life
39. Food fish
40. Once upon a ____
41. Baking need
42. Landlord's due
44. Bitter herb
45. Window ache?
46. Ceases
48. House addition
49. Fish eggs

PUZZLE 346

ACROSS

1. ____ of the party
5. Recedes
9. "____ to Billy Joe"
12. Scent
13. Song refrain
14. Feather stole
15. Bull, to Juan
16. Boundary
18. Toboggans
20. "The World ____ Me a Living"
21. Criminals
23. Hair style
27. Blunder
29. Painful sounds
30. Swashbuckler Flynn
31. Unfasten
33. Do a cobbler's job
34. Baseball ploys
35. "____ Alibi"
36. Modern: pref.
37. Suffix with kitchen or major
38. Withstand
40. Lamb's pen name
42. Sea duck
45. Displeases
49. Short letter
50. Automobile
51. Curved molding
52. Get one's ____
53. Venture
54. Shredded
55. ____ Stanley Gardner

DOWN

1. Oodles
2. False god
3. Position of importance
4. Wear away
5. Fairy
6. British titles
7. ". . . when the wind ____ the cradle . . ."
8. Rational
9. Japanese sash
10. Forest creature
11. Hearing organ
17. Russian rulers
19. Wild plums
22. Of one's ____ free will
24. Entranceway
25. Actor's part
26. Bread spread
27. German river
28. Defeat badly
30. Scary
32. Guide
33. Legal matter
35. Furnace
38. Drummer Starr
39. Char
41. Plunder
43. And others: abbr.
44. Nerve network
45. Perform
46. Distant
47. Saute
48. Japanese coin

PUZZLE 347

ACROSS

1. Highlander
5. Less ornate
10. Composer Franz ____
11. Like a tank
13. Merge
14. Film length
15. Charles Dutton's TV role
16. Sailor's stories
18. ____ Angelo, Texas
19. Ages of note
21. Extra bed
22. Animal hide
23. Wisest
25. Lamprey
27. Single
28. Gain
31. Swab
33. Ballet cheers
35. Spanish painter
38. Wire serv.
40. Like most cagers
41. Pig ____ poke
42. Singer Sinatra
44. Inlet
45. Nuttier
47. Decree
49. Wrecked completely
50. Reduces to tiny bits
51. Appoints
52. Requirement

DOWN

1. Spanish women
2. The Windy City
3. Stable morsel
4. Playing card
5. Novelist Charlotte ____
6. Famous cookie man
7. Decay
8. Wipe out
9. Kingly
10. Anglers' needs
11. Hairdo
12. Fender mark
17. Behave
20. City in Alabama
22. Fold
24. ____ Canals
26. Go astray
29. Greed
30. Patrolled
32. Blender products
33. Container
34. Bed boards
35. Main point
36. Tear provoker
37. WWII conference city
39. Cowboy's comrade
42. Manicurist's tool
43. Composer Jerome ____
46. On the ____ (fleeing)
48. Gaming cube

PUZZLE 348

ACROSS

1. Singer Davis
4. Cathedral section
8. Orient
12. Metallic rock
13. Chair
14. Wedding band
15. "____ the ramparts . . ."
16. "The Scarlet Letter" author
18. Armadas
20. Goal
21. Actress Jillian
22. Nevada lake resort
26. Standing
28. Legendary
31. Generation
32. Louvre exhibit
33. "Lifestyles of the Rich and Famous" host
34. Spoil
35. Compete
36. Friendly nation
37. Invoice
38. Abated
40. Clamor
41. Singer Sayer
43. Bachelor's status
46. "Of Mice and Men" author
50. Crumple
51. Harbor
52. Siouan
53. Gardner of "The Night of the Iguana"
54. Yesteryear
55. Breaks bread
56. Thanksgiving vegetable

DOWN

1. Once in a blue ____
2. Province
3. "Don Quixote" author
4. Sickly
5. Garden vines
6. Witnessed
7. Jazz songstress James
8. Fragrance
9. Masculine title
10. Hotel kin
11. Season
17. Tether, as a horse
19. Writing fluid
23. "A Farewell to Arms" author
24. Of the mouth
25. British blueblood
26. Praise
27. Song for Sills
28. Lamprey
29. Amigo
30. Frigid
33. Loaded
37. Hamper
39. Select group
40. River embankments
42. Double reed instrument
43. Glasgow native
44. Etna flow
45. Dutch cheese
46. Saboteur
47. Also
48. Misjudge
49. Greek vowel

PUZZLE 349

ACROSS

1. Baste
5. Prone
8. Munch
12. ____ of thumb
13. Beach
15. Turkey's neighbor
16. Quickest
17. Chessmen
19. ____ and bones
20. Pitcher handle
22. Grates
26. Billiards parlor
31. Actor Wallach
32. Ordinance
33. Jerk
35. Fellow
36. Piece (out)
37. Shoving
39. Prospector's test
42. Health facility
43. Soup dish
46. Edge up to
50. Brave
54. Greenish blue
55. ____ hour (last minute)
56. Graceful trees
57. Current
58. Summer shirt
59. Ready for picking

DOWN

1. Stumble
2. Air
3. Lobster gripper
4. Doghouse
5. Cigar residue
6. ____ and carrots
7. Chore
8. Porcelain
9. Work in a garden
10. Sounds of hesitation
11. Soaked
14. Move
18. Hindu garment
21. Went by horseback
23. 18-wheeler
24. Blueprint
25. Harmonize
26. Entreaty
27. They begin as acorns
28. Has unpaid bills
29. Frying need
30. Gangs
34. Exceeds
38. Cafe worker
40. Superior
41. Days of ____
44. Custom
45. Stringed instrument
47. Cold cuts shop
48. Torch
49. Otherwise
50. Fido's doc
51. Mohammed ____
52. Took by the hand
53. Haggard novel

PUZZLE 350

ACROSS

1. British beer
4. Mineral spring
7. Let the cat out of the ____
10. Depression
12. Narrow road
14. GI's hangout: abbr.
15. Muttonchops
17. ____ Tin Tin
18. Pester
19. Uptight
21. Fire remains
24. Hardens
25. Sulk
26. Marches
29. Hockey star
30. Snakelike fish
31. Lode load
32. Capitol Hill VIP
35. Dither
36. Golfer's item
37. Strands
39. Washbowl
41. Exist
42. Cigarette residue
43. Kookie of "77 Sunset Strip"
49. Course: abbr.
50. Earth
51. Royal title
52. Smidgen
53. Horse command
54. TV's "L.A. ____"

DOWN

1. Paid notices
2. Oahu garland
3. To the bitter ____
4. Punches
5. Golfer's aim
6. Massachusetts cape
7. Puts a match to
8. Sales term
9. Disappeared
11. Doctrine
13. Chemical compound
16. Prohibit
20. Guido's high note
21. Heroic poetry
22. Additional
23. Polished
24. "My ____ Sal"
26. Through
27. City in Pennsylvania
28. Places
30. One billion years
33. Mr. Onassis
34. Sounds
35. Layers
37. ____ of contents
38. Twisted
39. "The Simpsons" son
40. Movie pooch
44. German Shepherd, e.g.
45. Never say ____
46. Nothing
47. Pitcher's concern: abbr.
48. Stitch

PUZZLE 351

ACROSS

1. Olympic medal color
5. Key
9. Highlander's cap
12. Hidden place
13. Ornery
14. Bullfighter's cheer
15. Lab burner
16. Stringed instrument
18. Native Alaskan
20. Rounded roof
21. Apprehends
23. Sale items
26. More reliable
30. Anger
31. Snack
32. Church official
34. Coal weight
35. Stalk
37. Most gung-ho
39. Voice above bass
41. Shade of green
42. Glide
44. Me
48. Correspond
51. Russian emperor
52. Night bird
53. Utopia
54. Soothe
55. Yup
56. Apartment fee
57. Tidy up

DOWN

1. Mirth
2. Dobbin's dinner
3. Chain part
4. Empties
5. Not moving
6. Body of water
7. Make shore
8. Donate
9. Permit
10. ____ Baba
11. Blokes
17. Persian poet Khayyam
19. Aussie's buddy
22. Family car
24. Easily bruised items
25. Mailed
26. Evaluate
27. Price
28. Kitchen tools
29. Army
33. Depend
36. Satellite
38. Took it easy
40. Ten-speed bike
43. Tease
45. Isaac's son
46. Young girl
47. Stew
48. Reserved
49. Have money problems
50. Study

PUZZLE 352

ACROSS

1. Winter outerwear
5. ___ Van Winkle
8. Poker word
12. Cry of pain
13. Actress Lupino
14. "___ Homeward, Angel"
15. Elm or maple
16. Mythology
18. Bowling ___
20. Baseball teams
21. Courteous
24. Hog
25. Old saying
26. Escape
30. Hair accessory
31. It's in the ___
32. Floor square
33. Handled
35. Pitcher's powder
36. Pug, e.g.
37. Proofreaders' marks
38. Ragouts
41. Royal splendor
42. Huge
44. James ___ Jones
48. Cain's brother
49. Behave
50. Met song
51. Coral deposit
52. Positive word
53. Mr. Foxx

DOWN

1. Small bed
2. "___ Town"
3. ___ in the hole
4. "The Three Little Pigs" enemy
5. Firearm
6. Matinee ___
7. School mate
8. Avocado
9. Lunch time for some
10. Ripped
11. ___ out (supplements)
17. Make a sweater
19. Broke bread
21. Agreement
22. Skunk feature
23. Metallic fabric
24. Wooden nail
26. Move about
27. Street smart
28. Touched down
29. Longings
31. Plead
34. Turn's partner
35. Male sheep
37. Young horses
38. Battle reminder
39. "I Want ___ Happy"
40. General Robert ___
41. Walk to and fro
43. Utter
45. "You ___ My Sunshine"
46. Disencumber
47. Young gentleman

PUZZLE 353

ACROSS

1. Clutter
5. Female swine
8. That girl
11. So be it
12. Stalemate
13. Pack away
14. Out of ____
15. Strong beer
16. Leisure
17. Respect
19. Jeopardy
21. Kill
22. Bro's sibling
23. Enraged
27. Pick up
31. Female rabbit
32. Excavate
34. Quilting session
35. Sugary
38. Come before
41. Up-to-date
43. Hole-making tool
44. Haircutter
47. More orderly
51. Lily's relative
52. Inclined
54. Flutter
55. ____ at hand
56. Fixed charge
57. Fencing weapon
58. Jewel
59. Small amount
60. Writing table

DOWN

1. Partner
2. Australian birds
3. Forwarded
4. Ahchoo
5. Put an emblem on
6. Lubricant
7. Dandelions
8. Without a date
9. Stocking
10. Pitcher
13. Meaning
18. Hearing organ
20. Be under the weather
23. Newspaper notices
24. At this time
25. Command to a horse
26. Sag
28. Humorist Burrows
29. "The Hunt for ____ October"
30. Society-page word
33. Awarded
36. Smoldering coal
37. Boot tip
39. Ram's mate
40. Scratched
42. Rough sketch
44. Whack
45. Away from the wind
46. Meander
48. Adhesive strip
49. Plumb and Arden
50. Strong smell
53. Black-eyed ____

PUZZLE 354

ACROSS

1. Move the tail
4. Astound
7. Pop
11. Pity!
13. Singer Torme
14. Fragrance
15. Explain
17. Given temporarily
18. Free
19. Large deer
21. Consider
23. "Leave ____ to Heaven"
24. Epic
25. Of currency
30. Molecule part
31. Likely
32. One of the Great Lakes
33. Answering-machine calls
35. Dryer residue
36. Cover
37. Dressed
38. Frenzy
41. "A Boy Named ____"
42. Ahead of the ____
43. Depositor's concern
48. American author
49. Expert aviator
50. Shopper's quest
51. Turn
52. Forget-me-____
53. Bread choice

DOWN

1. Roll of money
2. Beer's relative
3. Step on the ____
4. Within
5. Spider's trap
6. Basics
7. Individual effort
8. Some poems
9. Over and ____ with
10. Special skill
12. Shrieks
16. Edge
20. Mine yield
21. Social event
22. I's
23. Wished
24. America's uncle
25. Houdini, for one
26. Bank employees
27. Diva's highlight
28. Skin
29. As of now
34. "The Greatest"
37. Actor's signal
38. Use the beeper
39. So be it!
40. Require
41. Printer's notation
42. Gossip
44. Sgt., e.g.
45. Head feature
46. Shady
47. Short-sleeve shirt

PUZZLE 355

ACROSS

1. Astonish
5. Does sums
9. Enemy
12. Employ
13. Challenge
14. Uncooked
15. Rim
16. Dawdler
18. Legal documents
20. Always
21. Illuminated
23. Able to be eaten
27. Fully developed
31. Frame of mind
32. "We ____ the World"
33. Merrily
36. "A Chorus Line" number
37. Waterproofed canvas cover
39. Postal carriers
41. Goes in
44. Mineral spring
45. Hourglass contents
47. Fragment
51. Burgers and fries, e.g.
55. Site of Des Moines
56. Self-image
57. Canned fish
58. Building wings
59. Unite in marriage
60. Plant stalk
61. Sleep

DOWN

1. Storage building
2. Ocean movement
3. Coax
4. Pointy sewing tool
5. Commercials
6. Valley
7. Operated, as a car
8. Made a seam
9. To's partner
10. Acorn bearer
11. Lamb's mother
17. Prissy
19. Make music with the voice
22. Afternoon social event
24. Prosperous time
25. Solitary
26. Original garden
27. Grade, as a movie
28. Site of Tehran
29. Sassy
30. Not very bright
34. ____ Vegas
35. Small barks
38. Nuisance
40. Frillier
42. Flat boats
43. Muzzle
46. Finished
48. Theatrical part
49. Hole-punching tools
50. History
51. "A ____ Good Men"
52. Birthday number
53. Turf
54. Water barrier

PUZZLE 356

ACROSS

1. Drag
5. Choose
8. Vagabond
12. As well
13. By way of
14. Was in debt
15. Thought
16. Signed up
18. Climbing structure
20. Buddy
21. Has dinner
23. Compel
27. Morning moisture units
31. Lumber
32. Significant period
33. Ode writers
35. Sty dweller
36. ____-de-camp
38. Lantern fuel
40. Ogles
42. Broad valley
43. Chest bone
45. Greatly desires
49. Tubular pasta
53. Hammer or saw
54. Once ____ a time . . .
55. Sprinted
56. What ____ is new?
57. Repair
58. Omelet ingredient
59. Feat

DOWN

1. Flag down
2. Alan ____ of "M*A*S*H"
3. Secondhand
4. Piled on
5. Caught up with
6. Needle's cousin
7. Canvas cover
8. Empty inside
9. Night bird
10. Hive insect
11. Not even
17. Bumpkin
19. Marshal Wyatt ____
22. Drive too fast
24. Heavy cord
25. Dime or nickel
26. Border
27. Pass out, as cards
28. New York canal
29. Walk through water
30. Wandering off
34. Shoe bottom
37. Chore
39. In a chair
41. Knight's title
44. Tiresome person
46. Actor's part
47. Proboscis
48. Winter slider
49. Silent
50. Orangutan, e.g.
51. Pro's counterpart
52. Old horse

PUZZLE 357

ACROSS

1. Stroke, as of lightning
5. Lamb's father
8. Grow weary
12. Not at home
13. "We ____ the World"
14. Adam's abode
15. Cornhusker State
17. Starring role
18. Volcano's dust
19. Lettuce-based dishes
21. Unlocks
24. Wick
25. Following
26. Photograph-developer's need
30. Historic time
31. Locales
32. Health club
33. Called for
35. Bed support
36. Impresses
37. Entire
38. Painter or sculptor, e.g.
41. Deception
42. Shipment
43. High-schooler
48. Cowgirl Evans
49. Santa's helper
50. Babble
51. Hymn ending
52. Take a chair
53. Hurried

DOWN

1. Prohibit
2. Be in debt
3. Place for experiments
4. Cruel dictator
5. Hotheaded
6. Noah's ship
7. Determined the size of
8. Bank clerk
9. Concept
10. Interpret
11. Odds and ____
16. Donkey
20. Inquires
21. Small bills
22. South American country
23. Quiz
24. Destinies
26. Kitchen alcoves
27. Norway's capital
28. Whitish gem
29. Partner
31. Female pigs
34. Lass
35. Clips, as sheep
37. Triumph
38. Hawkeye Pierce portrayer
39. Wander
40. Anecdote
41. Opposite of right
44. Inventor Whitney
45. Opening
46. Other resident of 14 Across
47. Scarlet

PUZZLE 358

ACROSS

1. Mouth bone
4. Disorder
8. Rub dry
12. Actress Lupino
13. Spoken
14. Baking chamber
15. Biting insect
17. Repair
18. Function
19. Itty-bitty
21. Film
24. Benefactor
28. Touched down
29. Thug
30. Chimpanzee, e.g.
31. Nothing
32. Recreation areas
33. Table support
34. Adam's mate
35. Toward shelter
36. Scarlett's plantation
37. Member of Congress
39. Bike's foot lever
40. Donkey
41. Chum
42. Fly high
45. Family antique
50. "____ the Woods"
51. Sea eagle
52. Lemon cooler
53. Hammerhead feature
54. Plant's beginning
55. Knockout number

DOWN

1. Olympian Thorpe
2. Ruckus
3. Existed
4. Mickey or Minnie
5. Pennsylvania port
6. Made a lap
7. Dawdler
8. Grown girls
9. "____ Got a Secret"
10. Writing tool
11. Finale
16. Throw in the towel
20. Long time periods
21. Lions' ruffs
22. Martini garnish
23. Female fox
24. More painful
25. Dieter's dish
26. Musical drama
27. Majestic
29. Overshoes
32. Butter servings
36. Relate
38. Baseball great Hank ____
39. Peeled
41. Evergreen tree
42. Drink slowly
43. Small bill
44. Had dinner
46. Prior to, in poems
47. Feedbag grain
48. Poem of praise
49. "3 ____ and a Baby"

PUZZLE 359

ACROSS

1. Fruit preserve
4. Rotated
8. Grain-storage tower
12. Boxer Muhammad ____
13. Notorious Roman emperor
14. Dry
15. Cowboy movies
17. Bee's home
18. Bed, as of coal
19. Foundations
20. Frog's sound
22. Rower's need
23. Sixty minutes
24. Steam-heating device
29. Play it by ____ (improvise)
30. Christmas song
31. First woman
32. Having more ruffles
34. Sense
35. Liquid for frying
36. Child's nursemaid
37. Gathering
40. Site of Des Moines
41. ____ a hand (help)
42. Mightier
46. Contribute to the kitty
47. Green legumes
48. Prior to, in poetry
49. Room opening
50. "____ of Green Gables"
51. Mom's partner

DOWN

1. Chat
2. Pub beverage
3. Site of St. Louis
4. Go stealthily
5. Hair wave, for short
6. Vase
7. Negative answers
8. African desert
9. Colored part of the eye
10. Exist
11. Certain poems
16. Rip
19. Remove water
20. Skilled cook
21. Lion's sound
22. Smell
24. Banister
25. "Just the Way You ____"
26. Adolescent
27. Appliance for baking
28. Depend
30. Trim
33. At a higher volume
34. Young deer
36. Lasso
37. Pleased
38. Nevada gambling city
39. Aware of
40. Tehran's country
42. Mineral spring
43. ____-gallon hat
44. Notable time
45. Caught ____-handed

PUZZLE 360

ACROSS

1. Hawaiian dance
5. Writing tablet
8. Determination
12. October's gem
13. Citrus drink
14. Territory
15. Disk-shaped bell
16. Solemn promise
17. Immense
18. Ahchoo!
20. Sight or smell
21. Diocese head
24. Acute, as pain
27. Chicken ____ king
28. Mom's fellow
31. Salad fish
32. Assistance
33. Soda flavor
34. Longing
35. "Wise" bird
36. Devoured
37. The Sahara ____
39. Plunged headfirst
43. Made coffee
47. Thought
48. Chest bone
50. Great review
51. Army beds
52. Mine yield
53. Paradise
54. What ____ is new?
55. Marry
56. Lease

DOWN

1. Gluttons
2. Once ____ a time . . .
3. Bowling alley
4. Branch of math
5. Surfaces, as a road
6. Hubbub
7. Morning condensation
8. Ocean breaker
9. Teheran's nation
10. Not as much
11. Tardy
19. Postal code
20. Health resort
22. Greets
23. Antique
24. Pigpen
25. Tint
26. Columnist Landers
28. Polka ____
29. Beer's kin
30. Former VP Quayle
32. Fearful reverence
33. Food provider
35. Peculiar
36. Be mistaken
38. Subsided
39. Gaming cubes
40. Worshipped object
41. Ex-soldiers, for short
42. Alleviate
44. Walk in water
45. Tied, as a score
46. Dimple
48. Use oars
49. Rage

PUZZLE 361

ACROSS

1. Plunge into water
5. Boston ____ Party
8. Wooden pins
12. Poems of praise
13. Possesses
14. Way out
15. Sweets
17. Farm measure
18. Cereal grain
19. Thorny-stemmed flowers
21. Shade tree
22. Overalls feature
23. Asian staple food
25. Dining surfaces
28. Plod
31. Not working
32. Pare
33. Pitchers' places
36. Stays
38. Garden of Adam and Eve
39. Craze
40. Wheel center
42. Fret
44. Actress West
47. India's continent
49. Cooking in the oven
51. Period
52. Inventor Whitney
53. Atop
54. Whirlpool
55. "Little ____ Riding Hood"
56. Golf-ball stands

DOWN

1. Extinct flightless bird
2. Notion
3. Sleeveless garment
4. Curvy letter
5. Pulsates
6. Ingests
7. Declare
8. Pod vegetable
9. Outdid
10. Lass
11. Plant support
16. Cleveland's lake
20. Knight's title
22. Mix
24. Valentine's Day figure
25. Comic actor Conway
26. "Much ____ About Nothing"
27. Symbol of happiness
29. Gosh!
30. Some city trains
34. Morning condensation
35. Noisy sleeper
36. Fearful
37. Inlets
40. Detest
41. Secondhand
43. Actor's part
44. Coal source
45. Poker starter
46. Vanities
48. Actress Irving
50. Small child

PUZZLE 362

ACROSS

1. Real-estate unit
5. Small flap
8. Sentence part
12. Rich soil
13. "____ to Joy"
14. At any time
15. Completed
16. Small barrel
17. Highway division
18. Off course
20. Let
21. Reprimands
24. Plane flier
27. Annoy
28. Domino spot
31. Garden of Paradise
32. Frosty
33. Rabbit's kin
34. Old horse
35. Noah's boat
36. Strength
37. Type of nut
39. Figure out
43. Sung dramas
47. Reed instrument
48. Cozy room
50. Flower urn
51. Take a break
52. Years of life
53. New York canal
54. Organs of sight
55. Head motion
56. ____ between the lines

DOWN

1. Alan ____ of "M*A*S*H"
2. Dove's cries
3. Speak wildly
4. Ralph Waldo ____
5. Japan's capital
6. Summer drink
7. Beseech
8. Watering hole
9. Racetrack shape
10. Nevada city
11. Sketched
19. Play a role
20. Inquire
22. Beats soundly
23. Remove moisture
24. Fountain or ballpoint
25. Ms. Lupino
26. Table support
28. Cat's foot
29. Wrath
30. Part of MPH
32. Nest egg plan
33. Nevertheless
35. High card
36. Vivacity
38. Sharpened
39. Achy
40. Follow orders
41. Misplace
42. Animal docs
44. Seldom seen
45. Largest continent
46. Bird food
48. Newsman Rather
49. Self-image

PUZZLE 363

ACROSS

1. Gardening tool
4. Sheep's comment
7. Butter servings
11. Small hotel
12. Swiss mountains
14. Too
15. Devote
17. By the ___ of your pants
18. Opposite of pro
19. Changes
21. Little brown songbird
23. China's continent
24. Serving both men and women
25. Medicinal plant
26. ___ up to (admit)
29. "Roses ___ red . . ."
30. Fad
31. Gaming cube
32. Sleeping place
33. Blunders
34. Air duct
35. Distance measures
36. Judge's concern
37. Blossoms
40. Sun-bronzed
41. Chief Justice Warren
42. Designated as a goal
47. Scored on a tennis serve
48. Swing around
49. Amazement
50. Disarray
51. Guided
52. Church bench

DOWN

1. Concealed
2. Half of a pair
3. Goal
4. Breakfast meat
5. Astronaut Shepard
6. Likely
7. Linguine, e.g.
8. On the sheltered side
9. Russian ruler
10. Tipplers
13. Adds spices to
16. Frosted
20. Told untruths
21. Had on
22. Film critic Rex ___
23. Wide-awake
24. Taxi
25. Takes into custody
26. Lyric poems
27. Chablis or Chardonnay, e.g.
28. Butterfly catcher
30. Swarm
34. Wind direction indicator
35. Creases
36. Penned up
37. Grin broadly
38. Openwork fabric
39. Metallic deposits
40. False's opposite
43. Entirely
44. Faucet
45. Ram's mate
46. Morning moisture

PUZZLE 364

ACROSS

1. Plant's underground part
5. Fitness club
8. Grand celebration
12. Building curve
13. Beer barrel
14. Press, as clothes
15. Odd
17. Curved
18. Fruit drink
19. Pekoe portions
21. Common people
24. Self-esteem
25. Boxing great
26. Tattered cloth
28. Bestow
32. False god
34. Edgar Allan ____
36. Certain
37. Copenhagen residents
39. Dolt
41. Damage
42. Chatter
44. Wander
46. Infuriated
50. Bar bill
51. Chilly
52. Umpires
56. Ship's bottom
57. Inventor Whitney
58. Merriment
59. Solely
60. Can metal
61. Singer Fitzgerald

DOWN

1. Music of Will Smith and Ice Cube
2. Mine yield
3. Event
4. Sounds of heavy impacts
5. Hit the slopes
6. Bog fuel
7. Consent
8. Small, slender apes
9. Telephone ____ code
10. ____ Island Sound
11. Picnic pests
16. Ogle
20. Mature
21. Female servant
22. Actor Alan ____
23. Tree fluid
27. Sticky glop
29. Small hand-held weight
30. Verbal
31. Existed
33. Lawfully
35. Lend an ____ (listen)
38. Droop
40. Destiny
43. Frenchman's cap
45. Mother on "The Simpsons"
46. Resounding sound
47. Name of a person, place, or thing
48. Turn over and over
49. Cold-cut shop
53. Shark part
54. Slippery as an ____
55. Ocean

PUZZLE 365

ACROSS

1. Locale
5. Tropical tree
9. Honest ____ (Lincoln)
12. Immediately following
13. New York canal
14. Night's opposite
15. Tidy
16. Apronlike garment
18. Confess
20. Peddle
21. Dice
23. Nights before holidays
27. Small bus
30. Outlaw
31. Distributed, as cards
32. Ran off to marry
34. Wine container
35. Graven images
36. Beam
37. Tree fluid
38. Large pond
39. Unsightly
41. Poisonous vipers
44. Dirt
48. Friendly feeling
52. Existed
53. Age
54. Largest continent
55. Hammer's target
56. Chat
57. Barnyard animal
58. Spill, as liquid

DOWN

1. "____ and the King of Siam"
2. Cattail, e.g.
3. Test
4. Garret
5. Liveliness
6. Gotten up
7. Stripe
8. Dinner, e.g.
9. Hubbub
10. Saloon
11. Organ of sight
17. Group of ships
19. Hoses
22. Naughty
24. Tanks
25. "____ Cinders" (Plumb cartoon)
26. Footfall
27. Bride's headgear
28. "The Four Seasons" star
29. Cozy corner
31. Author Arthur Conan ____
33. Beg
34. Sack
36. Moscow's country
40. Signs of drowsiness
42. Catch
43. Mexico's monetary unit
45. Genuine
46. Group of three
47. Assist
48. Barrel
49. Lyricist Gershwin
50. Seize
51. Used a chair

PUZZLE 366

ACROSS

1. Cupola
5. Uncooked
8. Pleasant
12. Malevolent
13. High card
14. Worshipped object
15. Feudal peasant
16. Fur hunters
18. Savings plan: abbr.
19. Snail's home
20. Fruit cooler
21. Hint
23. Boston ____ Party
25. More sacred
27. Get a ____ on (understand)
31. Rams' mates
32. ____ ground (progress)
33. Snuggle
36. Followed orders
38. Turf
39. Temperate
40. Hired car
43. Pointed, as a gun
45. Fish eggs
48. Of the East
50. Broadcast
51. Darling
52. Needle's hole
53. Stride up and down
54. Soothe
55. Polka ____
56. Prayer's last word

DOWN

1. Bandleader Arnaz
2. ____ and above
3. Divine occurrences
4. Santa's helper
5. Anchorman Dan ____
6. Real-estate measure
7. Affluence
8. Small bite
9. Notion
10. Strong twine
11. You are something ____!
17. Appeal
19. Bring to court
22. Inventories
24. Halo-wearer
25. Mother chicken
26. Have unpaid bills
28. Conscious reverie
29. Fib
30. Finish
34. Give temporarily
35. Revised copy
36. Egg dish
37. Auction offer
40. Zip numbers
41. Zone
42. Prejudice
44. Rochester's ____ Clinic
46. Single time
47. Biblical garden
49. Poet's before
50. Health resort

PUZZLE 367

ACROSS

1. Roll of money
4. Garden tool
9. Pop
10. Fishermen's boots
12. Clinches
13. Thrift
15. Switch position
16. Pelts
18. Expected
19. Furlough
21. Bright color
22. Offers
23. One of a pair
25. Joint
26. Duplicates
29. River boats
30. Separate
31. Party giver
32. Fetches
33. Prospect for gold
34. Sentry's command
38. Bungle
39. Cares
41. Retainer
42. Wisconsin farms
44. Wedding gift, perhaps
46. Hard to find
47. Not theirs
48. Bow down
49. Summer shirt

DOWN

1. ____ down (devours)
2. Sum up
3. Bolt
4. Norway's neighbor
5. Walked back and forth
6. Hubbubs
7. Family room
8. Washing away
9. Settee
11. Dirty spot
12. Make like a bunny
14. Affirmatives
17. Blue bloom
20. Wakes up
22. Beginning
24. Waterlogged
25. Possesses
26. Cooped up
27. "Carmen" and "Aida"
28. March 17th saint
29. Adhere
31. Gretel's brother
33. Slice
35. Excited
36. Camera's eye
37. Londoner's beverage
39. Mud
40. Highlander
43. Operated
45. Color

PUZZLE 368

ACROSS
1. Daddy
5. Office cabinet
9. Catch
12. Highly excited
13. Verbal
14. Doctors' group: abbr.
15. Suggestive stare
16. Newshound
18. Before, in poems
20. Soup utensils
21. Yell
24. Snakelike fish
25. Do a garden chore
26. Opening
28. Sticker
32. Egg-shaped
34. Pester
36. Low-price offer
37. Foot lever
39. Bar bill
41. Ocean
42. Small rug
44. Took a break
46. Erase
49. "A Few Good ____"
50. Courtroom proof
52. Sleeping
56. Author Tolstoy
57. In the near future
58. Pocket bread
59. Lodging house
60. Horse's gait
61. Remain

DOWN
1. Buddy
2. "The ____ of Innocence"
3. Edgar Allan ____
4. Concur
5. Factory boss
6. Anger
7. Backslide
8. Wed on the run
9. Western alliance: abbr.
10. So be it!
11. Saloons
17. What actors play
19. Cloth scrap
21. Boutique
22. Inlet
23. Interpret
27. Mrs. Nixon
29. Playbill listing
30. Toward shelter
31. Guide
33. Made defective
35. Item of clothing
38. Newest
40. Busy buzzer
43. High male voice
45. Fasteners
46. Sub store
47. Equal
48. Tawny big cat
51. Dove's call
53. Nipped
54. Timetable term: abbr.
55. Singer Doris ____

PUZZLE 369

ACROSS

1. Heavens
4. Baby's bed
8. Hairless
12. Filled pastry
13. Atmosphere
14. Lotion ingredient
15. Lawyer
17. Back of the neck
18. Jokes
19. Ebbed
20. Maps
23. Sun-browned
24. Metallic cloth
25. Processions
29. "Just the Way You ____"
30. Bunch of bees
32. Citrus drink
33. Antarctic bird
35. Indication
36. Social insect
37. Rubbed out
39. Eyelid flutter
42. Family group
43. Tear apart
44. Wrist ornament
48. Poker stake
49. Evaluate
50. Mine product
51. Entryway
52. Overwhelmed
53. Roll of money

DOWN

1. Fitness facility
2. Set of tools
3. Thus far
4. Diamond-weight unit
5. Ladder steps
6. Enrages
7. Inlet
8. Slippery-peeled fruit
9. Actor Arkin
10. Bounding gait
11. Legal document
16. Monster
19. Heat up
20. Applaud
21. Jack rabbit
22. Prayer ending
23. Sticky pitch
25. Frying vessel
26. Speaker's platform
27. Border
28. Dispatch
30. Went down, as a ship
31. Humor
34. Male goose
35. Rational
37. Fill with joy
38. Ran
39. Small nail
40. TV host Jay ____
41. Division word
42. Bird's crop
44. Bikini top
45. Moo
46. Notable period
47. Baseball's Williams

PUZZLE 370

ACROSS

1. Hen's product
4. Evergreen
7. Bubble-blowing chew
10. Ring
12. Ruckus
13. Too
14. Close securely
15. Large rodent
16. Membership fees
17. Respect
19. Gentlest
21. Blvd.
22. Actor Wallach
23. Swung at a baseball
26. Blockhead
30. Spanish cheer
31. Time period
32. Juneau's state
36. Scatter trash
39. Spider's snare
40. Expert pilot
41. Cottages
44. Depended
48. Lubricates
49. Woolly mother
51. Ore vein
52. Poems of praise
53. Indicate yes
54. Simmer
55. Church bench
56. 1 + 1
57. Some

DOWN

1. What ____ is new?
2. Leaves
3. Nanny or billy
4. Worked the land
5. Actress Lupino
6. Decayed
7. Paste
8. Purposes
9. Majority
11. Kilt feature
13. Own up to
18. Cain's mother
20. Boxer Muhammad ____
23. Feather scarf
24. 100%
25. Herbal drink
27. Drenched
28. Outrage
29. Roofing material
33. Cheese with holes
34. Tenn.'s neighbor
35. Not in class
36. '60s TV western
37. Skating surface
38. Relates
41. Chicken pen
42. Staffer
43. Gusted
45. Tiny bit
46. Adam's garden
47. Moist
50. Amazing!

PUZZLE 371

ACROSS

1. Mongrel dog
4. Up to the job
8. Mimicked
12. Purpose
13. Close at hand
14. Baseball's Winfield
15. Label
16. Domesticate
17. Unlock
18. Magazine edition
20. Speak wildly
21. Suit, in court
23. Pitfall
26. External
28. Neckwear
29. Likely
32. Amphitheaters
34. Unruly mob
36. ____ and feather
37. Corpulent
39. Contributor
40. Space under a roof
42. Soft feathers
43. "____ of the Flies"
46. Tardier
48. Throat-clearing sound
49. As well
50. Swab
53. Short skirt
54. Obtains
55. Fruit drink
56. Hiking shoe
57. Raw metals
58. Allow

DOWN

1. Slice
2. "Born in the ____"
3. Record book
4. Picnic pests
5. Women's sweethearts
6. Bemoan
7. Before, to a poet
8. Dote on
9. Mama's man
10. Balanced
11. Ding
19. Witnessed
21. Layer of paint
22. Atmosphere
24. Ventilate
25. Peruse
27. Floating platform
29. Not typical
30. Turn the soil
31. Gull's relative
33. Day after Fri.
35. Foreshadow
38. Rudder handle
40. Confess
41. Social class
43. Baby sheep
44. Cleveland's state
45. Nevada city
47. Throw
49. "Long, Long ____"
51. "____ to Joy"
52. Cherished animal

PUZZLE 372

ACROSS

1. Pitcher's stat
4. Boast
8. Female horse
12. Cover
13. Hawkeye State
14. Chilled
15. Dolphins' sport
17. Cast off
18. Shade tree
19. Recently
21. Sparkled
24. Songwriter Porter
25. Endure
26. Better
30. Grease
31. Drills
32. Pair
33. Made
35. Fast aircraft
36. Sour
37. Renter's agreement
38. Largest state
41. Title for Gielgud
42. Shove
43. Covers completely
48. Clinton's canal
49. Huron, e.g.
50. Sticky stuff
51. Precious
52. Bliss
53. Possess

DOWN

1. Mischievous creature
2. ____ Grande
3. Fuss
4. Holy book
5. Wander
6. Leather worker's tool
7. Rushed
8. Man's title
9. Soreness
10. Spool
11. Whirlpool
16. Canvas shelter
20. Porter and stout
21. Pig's meal
22. Bristle
23. Scandinavian capital
24. Healed
26. Friendly
27. Thought
28. Pitchers' goals
29. Went up
31. Dollar
34. One of Santa's team
35. Tug
37. Woven fabric
38. Copied
39. Bait
40. Japan's location
41. Rice wine
44. Boy
45. Self-esteem
46. Pull
47. Male offspring

PUZZLE 373

ACROSS

1. Baby dog
4. Plead
7. Flunk
11. Age
12. Fossil fuel
13. Nautical hello
14. Wherever
16. Lois ____ of "Superman"
17. Struts
19. Prejudice
21. Encounters
24. Milky stones
25. Harden
26. Regret
28. Raise crops
29. Father
30. Follow closely
31. Pear-shaped fruit
32. Flop
33. Fronts of the legs
34. More recent
36. Wounded by a bee
37. Looked forward to
39. Louts
42. Looking through
46. Cover, as a gift
47. Facial features
48. Expected
49. Camera part
50. Curvy letter
51. Lunched

DOWN

1. "The Princess and the ____"
2. Decorative vase
3. Remit money to
4. Brag
5. Every
6. Shone
7. Untrue
8. Cry of discovery
9. Charged atom
10. Soap-making substance
12. Family groups
15. Biblical poem
18. As of now
19. Madrid's site
20. Big
22. Wedding-gown trailer
23. Prosecuting
24. ____ the beaten path
25. Unhappy
27. Subways' kin
29. Long-lasting
30. Sounds of a fall
32. Moisten, poetically
33. Hearty soups
35. Stinging insects
36. Ceases
38. Colored eye part
39. Hooting bird
40. Exist
41. Admirer
43. Ore.'s neighbor
44. Cashew, e.g.
45. Command to a horse

PUZZLE 374

ACROSS

1. Pea container
4. Colored part of the eye
8. South American weapon
12. Tavern drink
13. Gaming cubes
14. Regrets
15. Tiny
16. Aid in crime
17. Upon
18. ____ Pole (Santa's home)
20. Bashful
22. Des Moines site
25. Donkeys
29. Yellow kerneled vegetable
32. Neutral color
34. "____ to a Nightingale"
35. "We ____ the World"
36. Wild, as an animal
37. Era
38. Small boy
39. Summer drinks
40. ____ out (barely earned)
41. Bread ingredient
43. Display
45. "Little ____ Riding Hood"
47. Sleeveless garments
51. Tulip starter
54. Fairy-tale monster
57. Lubricate
58. Cambodia's continent
59. Midday
60. Bullring shout
61. Adolescent
62. Female pigs
63. Senator Kennedy

DOWN

1. Smallest chess piece
2. Margarine
3. Bambi's mother, for one
4. Boise's state
5. Chest bone
6. Hockey-rink surface
7. Solidifies
8. Sounds made by 25 Across
9. Not at home
10. Lion of the zodiac
11. Poisonous viper
19. ____ Pan Alley
21. Tow
23. Unwanted plant
24. Land measures
26. Drench
27. On the cutting ____
28. Bird food
29. Baby cow
30. Of the mouth
31. Decorate again
33. Recklessly hasty
36. Bus money
40. Female sheep
42. Of the city
44. Baking appliances
46. Puts on, as clothing
48. Chimney clogger
49. Bathroom-floor material
50. Child's snow slider
51. "Casey at the ____"
52. Purpose
53. Falsehood
55. Sticky stuff
56. Paddle

CRISS-CROSSWORD

PUZZLE 375

The answer words for Criss-Crossword are entered diagonally, reading downward, from upper left to lower right or from upper right to lower left. We have entered the words SODA and FOG as examples.

TO THE RIGHT

1. Fizzy drink
2. Distant
3. Mint ____
4. Tabby
5. Processions
6. Flutter
7. Occupation
9. ____ up and go
11. Gathers
12. Blows up
15. Take to court
17. Noise
18. Small lizard
20. More exquisite
21. Galahad's title
23. Joy
25. Tilt
28. Shiny fabric
29. Food fish
32. Jungle creatures
34. Wild goat
35. Illuminated
37. Adult males

TO THE LEFT

2. London's haze
3. Tired
4. Church officials
5. Good buddy
6. Pond filler
7. Glass container
8. ____ Scotia
10. Fourposter
13. Fear
14. Withstands
16. Now payable
17. Sword fights
19. Actor Hackman
20. Not many
22. Moral wrong
24. Repeats from memory
26. Everyone
27. Holy person
30. Batman's partner
31. Shadow
33. Hymn ending
36. Cooking vessel
38. Lair

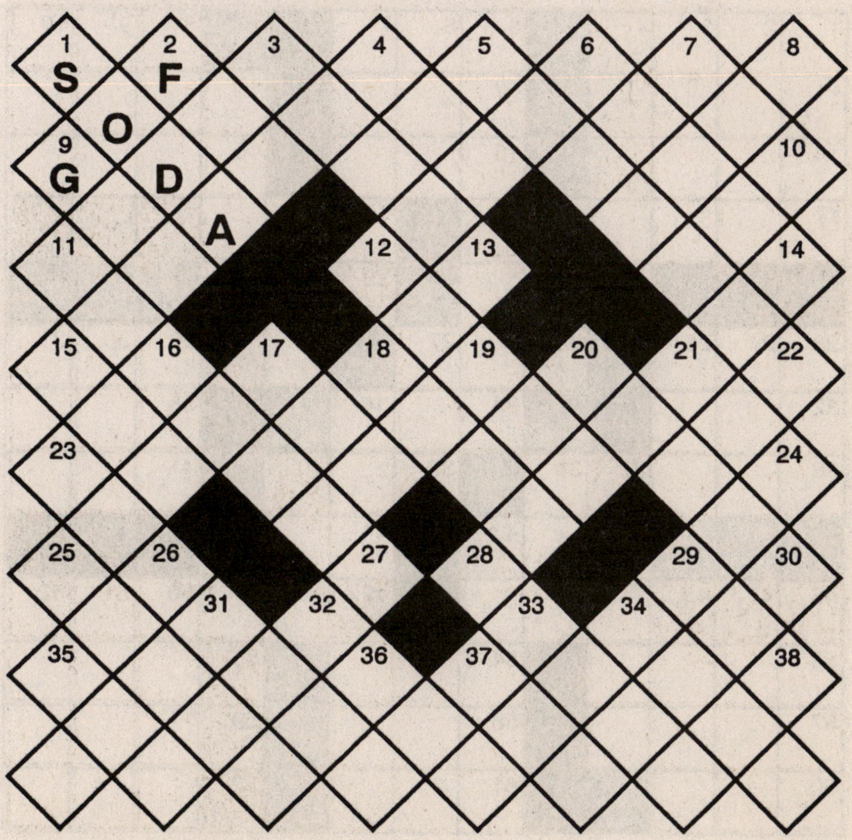

PUZZLE 376

ACROSS

1. Misplace
5. Vampire ____
8. Peculiar
11. Declare openly
12. Falsehood
13. Fencing sword
14. Female horse
15. Fury
16. Feeble, as an excuse
17. Warns
19. Suit maker
21. Used a chair
22. Punch
23. In what manner
26. Ruby-colored
28. Cantaloupe, e.g.
32. Have unpaid bills
33. Fishing pole
35. Hubbub
36. Beg
39. Joyous
41. Unite in matrimony
42. Arrow's partner
44. Crazed
46. Reduce in rank
49. Changes for the better
53. Hot and dry
54. Hen fruit
56. Tidy
57. Burgundy or Chablis
58. Bambi's mother
59. Carry
60. Actor Beatty
61. Turf
62. Crack

DOWN

1. Buddhist monk
2. Racetrack shape
3. Achy
4. Water pitchers
5. Scorch
6. Ventilate
7. Molars, e.g.
8. Milky gem
9. Showroom model
10. Stag or fawn
13. Select group
18. Roofing material
20. Goal
23. Bunny's jump
24. Nocturnal bird
25. Tiny
27. Canine beast
29. Statute
30. Lyric poem
31. Head gesture
34. Broken
37. Dwelling
38. Speck
40. Sweet potato
43. Unwanted plants
45. Dimples
46. Sunrise
47. New York canal
48. Brain
50. Sign gas
51. Computer input
52. Dance move
55. Sticky stuff

PUZZLE 377

ACROSS

1. Sinewy
5. Short snooze
8. Big smile
12. Zone
13. Actress Lupino
14. Vein of ore
15. Hockey net
16. Easily moved
18. Concluded
20. Smooched
21. Standards of perfection
24. Frequently, to a poet
27. Crazed
28. Phillies and Mets
32. Close by
34. Baby's apron
36. Smack
37. Trimmed, as a hem
39. Bar bill
41. Some
42. "____ the Snowman"
44. Sewing cord
47. Enthusiastic
52. Graduate's volume
55. Broad
56. Manuscript leaf
57. Feel remorse
58. Level
59. Otherwise
60. Hog's dwelling
61. Fender bender mark

DOWN

1. Salary
2. Steel ingredient
3. Peruse, as a letter
4. Ivy League school
5. Small bite
6. "Much ____ About Nothing"
7. Hooded winter coat
8. Bifocals, e.g.
9. Steals
10. Unoccupied
11. Require
17. Slant
19. Poorly lit
22. Little bit
23. Revises a manuscript
24. Single thing
25. Nourished
26. Label
29. Pie ____ mode
30. Grown boy
31. Secret agent
33. Umpire's cousin
35. Vampire ____
38. Dull and colorless
40. Brief farewell
43. Aromas
44. Ilk
45. Cure
46. Cloth shreds
48. Inspired with fear
49. Donate
50. Biblical garden
51. Landlord's fee
53. Not at home
54. Lock opener

PUZZLE 378

ACROSS

1. Male offspring
4. Lead actor
8. Hub of activity
12. Paid athlete
13. Havana's locale
14. Verbal
15. Soaked up
17. Light browns
18. Direct route
20. Catcalls?
22. Punctuation mark
25. Items of merchandise
26. Cushion
27. Atmosphere
29. Chicken ___ king
30. Snakelike fish
31. Mediterranean, e.g.
32. Positive answer
33. Cereal grain
34. Highly seasoned
36. Kernels
38. Pursue
39. Former soldier
41. Land measure
44. Volcano outburst
48. Tart
49. Get up
50. Pair
51. Small horse
52. Fish catchers
53. Comic actor Carney

DOWN

1. Hot tub
2. Sphere
3. Refusals
4. Wood fasteners
5. Toothpaste containers
6. Cain's brother
7. Extreme
8. Lodge
9. Pensioner's fund: abbr.
10. Small bus
11. Overhead trains
16. Reed instrument
19. Doze
20. Ram and rooster, e.g.
21. Wipe out
23. Caravan stopover
24. Sister's daughter
25. Method
26. Household animal
28. Boxer Sugar ___ Leonard
30. Oriental
33. Lyric poem
34. Geometric forms
35. Huff and puff
37. Each one
38. Pie shell
40. New York canal
41. Venomous snake
42. Dove's comment
43. Sprint
45. Actress Lupino
46. Belonging to us
47. Forget-me-___

PUZZLE 379

ACROSS

1. Near the ground
4. Casual shirt
7. Fall flower, for short
10. Volcano's dust
11. Vase
12. Half of a pair
13. Crafty
14. Ran, as colors
15. Do the backstroke
16. Throws
18. Lone Ranger's sidekick
19. Toddler's enclosure
22. Custom
25. Historic time
26. Baseball stick
29. Revise text
30. Singer/pianist Charles
31. Nevada city
32. Burglarize
33. Melody
34. Cent
35. Cues
37. Firm
40. Chief male servant
44. Someone who fibs
45. Chest bones
47. Inventor Whitney
48. Large deer
49. "____ to the West Wind"
50. Venomous viper
51. Change the color of
52. 24 hours
53. Payment

DOWN

1. Final
2. Capital of Norway
3. The ____ and wherefores
4. Northeastern Oklahoma city
5. Before, to a poet
6. Conclusion
7. Cut, as a lawn
8. Segment
9. Reminding note
14. Pants securer
15. Male child
17. Turning barbecue skewer
18. British beverage
20. Crave
21. Move with leverage
22. That woman
23. Stir
24. Baby's mealtime garment
26. Actor Kingsley
27. Actress ____-Margret
28. Plaything
30. Big truck
31. Relax
33. Assist
34. Addition word
35. Knight's title
36. "____ Road" (Beatles album)
37. Toboggan
38. Greasy
39. Large pond
41. Turn over a new ____
42. Otherwise
43. Mature
45. Curtain or lightning
46. Neighbor of Mont.

PUZZLE 380

ACROSS

1. Attorney's expertise
4. Towel or sheet
8. Fitness facility
11. Part of the eye
13. Size
14. Faucet
15. Sheet of stamps
16. Control knob
17. Lemon drink
18. Bauble
20. Church tables
22. Swab
24. Stitch
25. Out of control
29. Respond
33. Birthday number
34. Liquid gold
36. Favorable vote
37. Cowboy contest
40. Mexican menu items
43. "Violets ____ blue . . ."
45. Dull
46. Brass and iron
49. Meek one
52. Bounder
53. Foot digits
55. Eagerness
57. "____ to Joy"
58. Milky gem
59. Diminish
60. Stockade
61. Trust
62. Pipe joint

DOWN

1. ____ service
2. Swift horse
3. Grape juice
4. Harmful
5. Song for Sills
6. Wild ducks
7. Bridle
8. Asterisk
9. Writing tablets
10. Impersonate
12. Clothing joints
19. Female rabbit
21. Respectful fear
23. Not an amateur
25. Exclude
26. Self-esteem
27. Lipstick color
28. Scout Carson
30. Chum
31. Caustic substance
32. Okay
35. Small boy
38. Consume
39. Speaker
41. Unit of length
42. Surprise
44. Flee, romantically
46. Produced
47. Garden spot
48. Emblem
50. Veal or beef
51. Bottom
52. Police officer
54. Cunning
56. Lawyer F. ____ Bailey

PUZZLE 381

ACROSS

1. Tablet
4. Faucet
7. Health resort
10. Manipulate
11. Melodies
13. Necklace unit
14. Curved chest bone
15. Pat dry
16. ____ upon a time
17. Baby's noisemaker
19. Intense
21. Cherry-colored
22. Flying mammal
23. Refuse
26. Every bit
27. Conducted
30. In the past
31. Carved pole
33. Respectful fear
34. "The ____ Squad"
35. Expert
36. Not shut
37. Ginger drink
38. Fire residue
40. Country house
42. Mortar
46. Animal parks
47. Short letter
49. Cow's sound
50. Low female voice
51. Toboggan
52. Bed-and-breakfast
53. Pod vegetable
54. Begley, Jr. and McMahon
55. Pullover shirt

DOWN

1. Contented cat's sound
2. Largest continent
3. Unpaid bill
4. Dining-room item
5. Was sick
6. In favor of
7. Transmitted
8. Tempo
9. Fruit drink
12. Secure
13. Boxing match
18. Attempt
20. Tranquil
23. Beaver's structure
24. Self-image
25. Indicate yes
26. Gobbled up
27. Baby's seat
28. Ram's mate
29. Study
31. High
32. Pacific and Indian
36. Unit of resistance
37. In addition
38. Behaved
39. Kernels
40. Mouselike animal
41. Smidgen
43. Radiate
44. Zip
45. Sound quality
46. Jolt suddenly
48. Bravo!

PUZZLE 382

ACROSS

1. Speck
5. Ernie's friend
9. Pump
13. Stay
17. Arab ruler
18. Turmoils
19. Mama's mate
20. Small guitars
21. Crooned
22. Everest's range
24. Ooze
25. Fire crime
27. Hindu garment
28. Mardi Gras follower
30. "Once ___ a midnight dreary . . ."
32. Swig
35. Fragrant shrubs
39. Embarrassment
43. Rose
45. ___ of the ball
46. Decline
47. Perfumed
49. Hurried
50. Bandleader Shaw
51. Chili ingredient
52. Ewe said it!
54. Witch
55. Troubles
56. Young horses
57. Flow
58. "Butterflies ___ Free"
59. Edited
61. Meerschaum's country kin
63. Overhead trains
65. Sombreros
66. Fold
67. Running mate
70. Cheer
71. Actor Brynner
72. Arboreal mammal
73. Davis or Middler
74. Culture medium
76. Wins over
78. Greek garb
79. Lucky number
81. Circumference
82. Russian soup
83. Puts up
85. Seine
86. Ringing sound
87. Grounded bird
89. Neutral color
91. Sword
96. Honolulu's island
99. Stress
103. Tender
104. Asian range
105. Slide
106. Old Peruvian
107. Potter's oven
108. Pause
109. Bows
110. Nobleman
111. Winter vehicle

DOWN

1. Plateau
2. Actor Sharif
3. Cans
4. Therefore
5. Exclamation of contempt
6. Light bulb inventor
7. Numeral type
8. Ruler of yore
9. Healthy spot
10. Hit the ___
11. Role on "All My Children"
12. Artist's stand
13. Victorian fashions
14. Harry's successor
15. Irish Sea feeder
16. Psi power
23. Heeds
26. TLC provider
29. Pen point
31. Lemon meringue, e.g.
33. Charged particles
34. Lobster trap
36. In letter order
37. Prove innocent
38. Marsh plant
39. Gizzard
40. Hoagy
41. Men's cologne
42. Costume
43. Weight-watcher's tool
44. TV personality Norville
47. Judgment and hot
48. Intimidate
51. Moonshine
53. Circle part
56. Con game
57. Browning and Keats

PUZZLE 382

60. Detective's question
61. Silk or linene
62. Baking chambers
63. Rub off
64. Beer
66. Serving dish
68. Engrave
69. Plague
72. Waterless
73. Villages
75. New member
77. Shark part
78. Large weight
80. Ultimate
82. Rebound
84. Children's author Dr. ____
86. Sea water
88. Singer Paul ____
90. Trim
92. Inquires
93. Simmer
94. Gardner of whodunits
95. Split
96. Boathouse implement
97. London libation
98. Possesses
100. Burrow
101. Ames and Sullivan
102. Corn unit

PUZZLE 383

ACROSS

1. Grouchy one
5. Dill herb
9. Info
13. Come to a halt
17. Western weed
18. Hawaiian goose
19. Ripped
20. Jason's ship
21. Passe: hyph.
23. Portent
24. Cooking fat
25. "Beau ——"
26. Shunned ones
28. Bees
30. Easter meat
32. Paper quantity
33. Inclines
34. Small restaurants
38. Soil
39. Chop off
42. Cereal grain
43. Look-alike
44. Kleptomaniac
46. Record for TV
47. Profess
49. Behind time
51. Adds explanations
53. Lukewarm
55. This evening, in ads
57. East
58. Family member
60. Period
61. Pack away
62. Fastener
65. Alaskan seaport
67. Circus worker
71. Stamp gatherer
73. Hall runners
75. Calif. valley
76. Eye amorously
77. Scout activities
79. Add
81. Stone
82. Court
83. Weathercock
84. Favors
87. Like April
89. Planet
90. Flock mother
91. Dwarfed plant
93. Corsair
95. Israeli seaport
99. In a line
100. Cajole
102. "Bonanza" man: 2 wds.
104. "Peter Pan" pooch
105. Qualified
106. Sicilian resort
107. Be concerned
108. Small valley
109. Told tales
110. Stool
111. Walked

DOWN

1. Shoe
2. Debauchee
3. Bible book
4. Bazaar stalls
5. Also
6. Actress Patricia
7. Join: 2 wds.
8. Indian home
9. Tempest
10. Male cats
11. Common verb
12. Boy scout rank
13. Beauty parlor
14. Interpret
15. Monster
16. Peas' homes
22. Banquet
27. Bridge chair
29. Deserter
31. Whimper
33. Legal claim
34. Gravy dish
35. Enthusiastic review
36. On
37. Lariat
38. Eat
40. Unlock
41. Nuisance
45. "Mad" man
46. Formosa
48. Nun's headcloth
50. Withstand
52. Equine gait
54. Miss Evans
56. Charged atom
59. Routine
61. Sweetener
62. Garbage boat

PUZZLE 383

63. Takeout order: 2 wds.
64. Ultimatum: 3 wds.
65. Gag
66. Canterbury VIP
68. Creche trio
69. Sword
70. Football team
72. Like Tim
74. Buildable lot
78. Battle memento
80. Staircase post
83. By way of
85. Papal vestments
86. Elite
88. Dam town
89. Metaphor or doubles starter
91. Noise
92. Spoken
93. Ashen
94. Lab burner
96. Slightly open
97. Corrida animal
98. Listen carefully
101. Kimono sash
103. Make lace

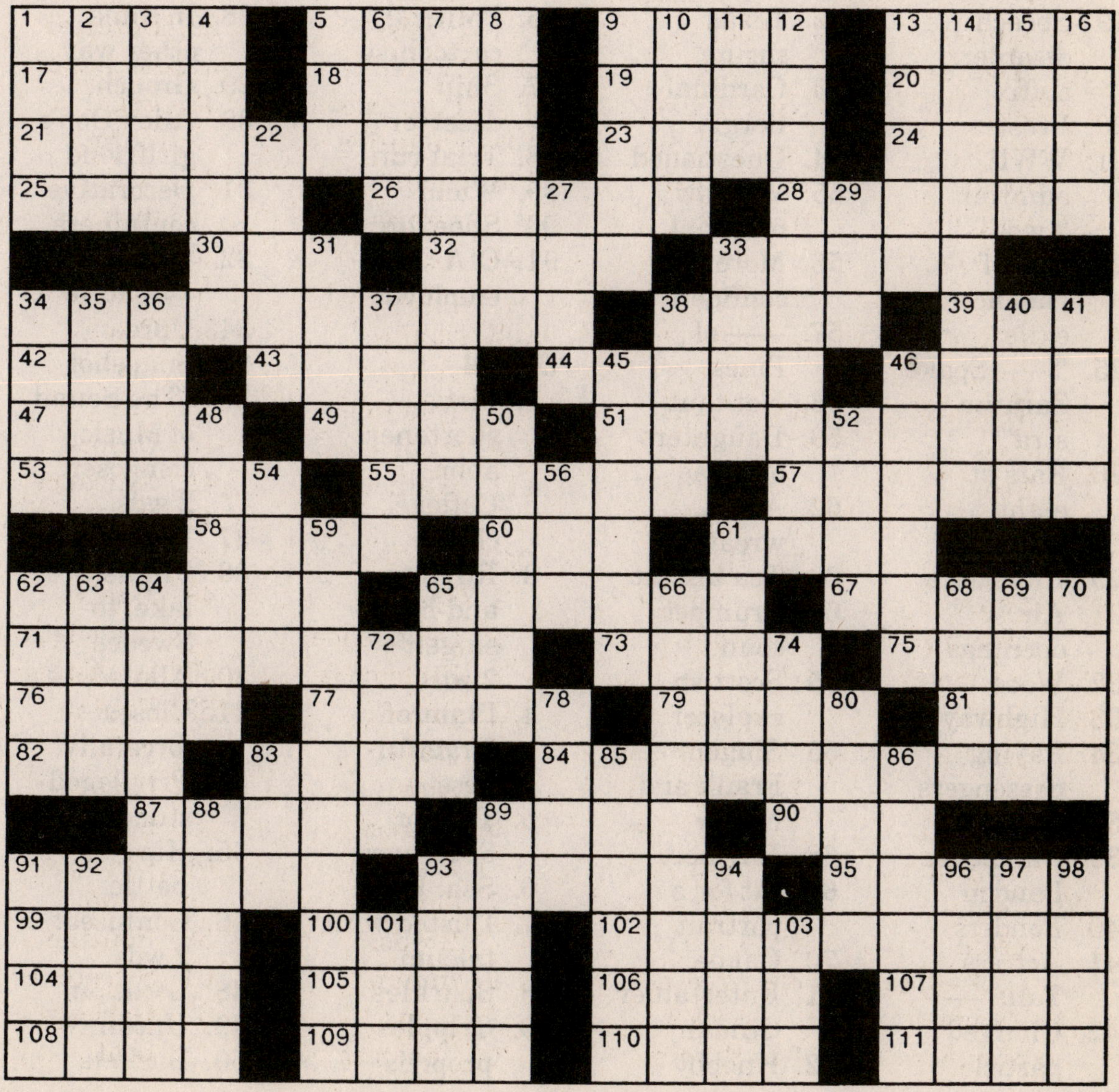

PUZZLE 384

ACROSS

1. Memorable period
4. Lantern
8. Lymph node
13. Small weight
17. —— and feather
18. Polyunsaturated spread
19. Speech disorder: suffix
20. Frost
21. WWII admiral: 3 wds.
24. Site of Napoleon's exile
25. "—— Spake Zarathustra"
26. Eats at eight
27. Fanatic
29. Blue jacks
31. Air openings
32. Woes
33. Highway
34. Paying passengers
35. Can fruit
39. Candidate Landon
40. Ponders
41. Actress Talia ——
42. Charged particle
43. Exchanged in trade
45. Dental thread
46. Official records
47. Limousines
48. Writer Sylvia ——
49. Anesthetic
50. Playwright Harold ——
52. Texas shrine
53. Cardinal Borgia
54. Questioned
55. Window material
56. More confident
57. —— of Pines
58. Not taut
59. Daughters of Atlas
62. Aloha wreath
63. Tea biscuit
64. Trumpet sound
65. Scottish explorer
66. Singers Frank and Nancy
68. Rhymers
69. Sit for a portrait
70. Canoe
71. Entertainer Guinan
72. Knobby
73. Madhouse
76. Candy stripers
77. Tennis star Bjorn ——
78. Pennsylvania city
79. TV interviewer: 2 wds.
84. "Desire Under the ——"
85. Tablecloth material
86. Political cartoonist
87. Ship deserter
88. Trial run
89. Wield
90. Shoe form
91. CIA employee

DOWN

1. List shortener: abbr.
2. College cheer
3. Rhythm-and-blues singer: 2 wds.
4. Plant of forgetfulness
5. Tavern beverages
6. Sea: Fr.
7. Dusted with talcum
8. Sparkles
9. Cripples propriis
10. MacGraw, et al.
11. Young insect
12. Beauties
13. Lubrication
14. Small stream
15. Early church desk
16. —— and potatoes
22. Wearing shoes
23. Baseball teams
28. In some other way
29. Grouch
30. Alley Oop's girlfriend
31. Decorative containers
32. "My Wild —— Rose"
34. Uproar
35. Snapshot
36. "The Sound of Music" composer: 2 wds.
37. Elector
38. Finnish lake, to Swedes
40. Alloted
41. Closes forcefully
44. Privileged student
45. Hip bottle
46. Confused: 2 wds.
48. Location
49. Uncanny
50. Buckets

PUZZLE 384

51. Japanese-American
52. Arkin and Mowbray
53. Prompters
55. Be smug in success
56. Bed boards
58. Mix up
59. Agreeable
60. Life of Riley
61. Germ
63. Portico
64. Pugilist
67. Most talented
68. Hairsplitter
69. Fortified wine
71. River through Rome
72. Actor Nick
73. Sugar vegetable
74. First name in mysteries
75. Loses brightness
76. "Rule Britannia" composer
77. Foundation
80. French city
81. Armed conflict
82. Knock sharply
83. Barnyard area

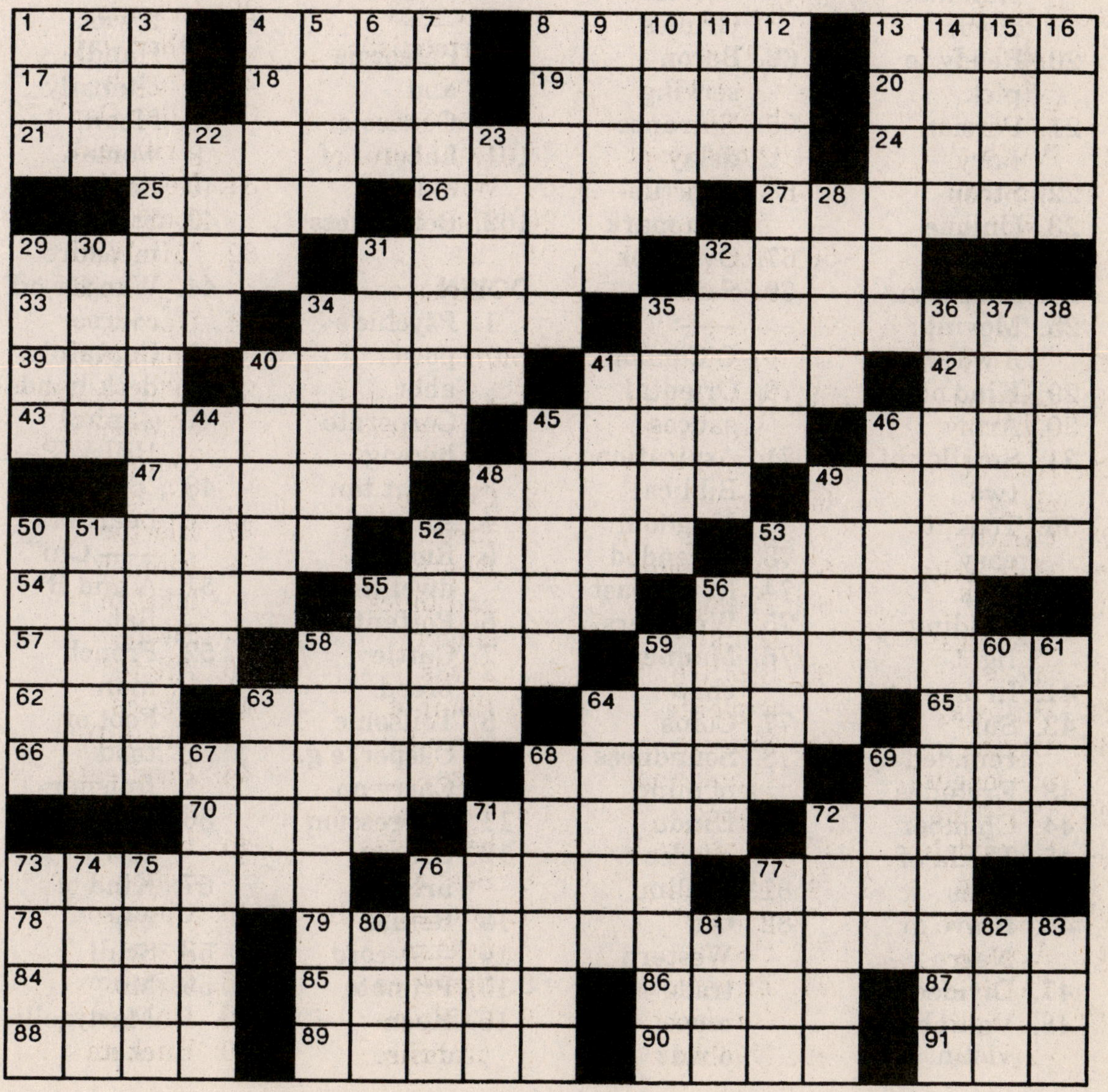

PUZZLE 385

ACROSS

1. Holiday nights
5. Soft drink
9. Hold firmly
13. Strong cart
17. Denomination
18. Roman love god
19. "If I —— Hammer": 2 wds.
20. Ready to pick
21. Persian fairy
22. Stoop
23. Unique chap
24. Shop sign
25. Moving: 3 wds.
29. Kind of ear
30. Army
31. Smaller of two
35. Took it easy
38. Sulk
39. Guiding light
41. In favor
42. Surrounded by
43. Excludes
44. Clamber
45. Theda of films
46. Bravo or Negro
47. Divided
48. Valuable violin
49. —— about: 2 wds.
50. Snoopy's home
52. Personnel worker
53. Dear ones
54. Pioneer transport: 2 wds.
59. Coup d'——
61. Actress Grimes
62. Bacon serving
65. Entrance delay
66. Punctuation mark
67. Overcook
69. Sandra —— O'Connor
70. Oriental sauces
71. Aspiration
72. Biblical kingdom
73. Ascended
74. In the past
75. Wrigglers
76. Mannerly chap
77. Coins
78. Soundness of mind
80. Hindu goddess
81. Decline
82. Old Western trade route: 4 wds.
88. Secular
91. Forbidden thing: hyph.
92. Famous fiddler
93. Crazy bird
95. Roguish
96. Cartoonist of yore
97. Enjoy the joke
98. Sicilian town
99. Bird of ——
100. Paleozoic and Cenozoic
101. Laborer of old
102. Bottomless

DOWN

1. Psychic's power: abbr.
2. Corporate bigwig
3. Light tan
4. Affected
5. Rustic dwelling
6. Portent
7. Cattle breed
8. Toilsome
9. Casper, e.g.
10. Carry on
11. Impression
12. Grassy area
13. Refuse
14. —— cord
15. Primate
16. Keen desire
26. Topper
27. Calif. zone
28. Always, in verse
32. Early ranchero: 2 wds.
33. Goof
34. Pride sounds
35. Caper
36. Yvette's chum
37. Utah attraction: 2 wds.
38. Handle clumsily
39. Mean woman
40. Coronet
43. Straw measure
44. Wander off course
45. Captain's deck hands
47. Capitol Hill VIP
48. "Sweetheart of —— Chi"
51. A and B flat
52. French man
55. Foot or toad finisher
56. Packs down
57. Kind of bag
58. Scull
59. Ms. Martinelli et al.

PUZZLE 385

60. N.Y. county
63. Vane direction
64. Some breads
66. Missouri feeder
67. Pine and fir, e.g.
68. Sunbonnet
72. Mixture
73. Delighted
75. Crossed d
76. Heavy's heater
77. Cable ——
79. Eager for action
80. Tie-ups
81. Rock or boulder
83. Go to great heights
84. Vase handle
85. Ireland, to poets
86. Pompeii girl
87. "Carry Me Back to the —— Prairie"
88. Circuit
89. Schedule abbr.
90. Winter hazard
94. Fabric pile

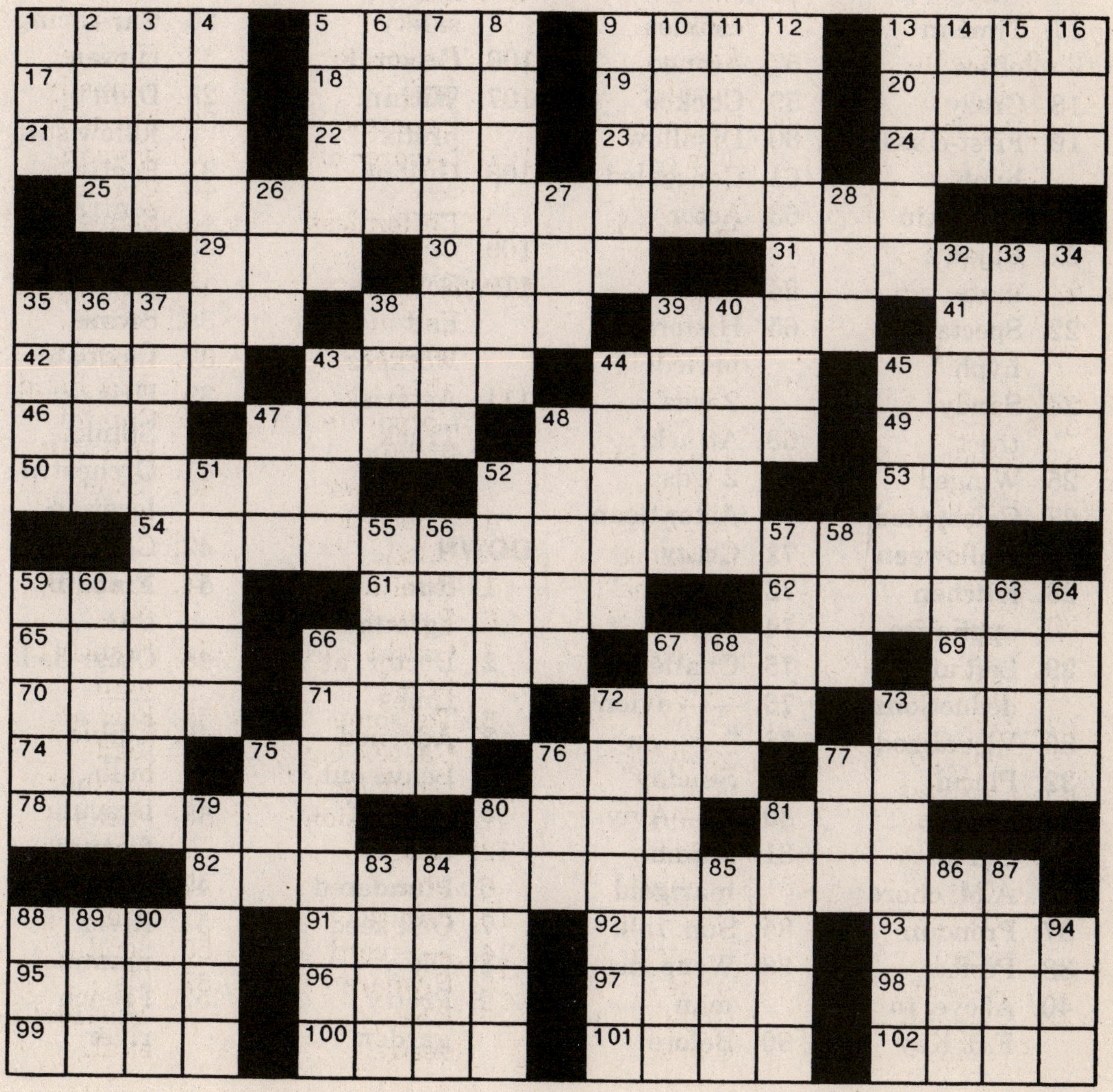

PUZZLE 386

ACROSS

1. Begone!
5. "When I was —— . . .": 2 wds.
9. Stage piece
13. "—— well that ends well"
17. Time in office
18. Crazy
19. First-class: hyph.
20. Bumpkin
21. Rajah's mate
22. Spectators: hyph.
24. Sandy tract
25. Winged
27. Celebrated Halloween
28. Kitchen appliance
29. Left after deductions
30. Visualized
32. Placid
34. Harden
35. Did an A.M. chore
37. Pronoun
38. Perfect
40. Above, to F.S. Key
41. Priest
43. Winged insect
44. Ships' fronts
47. Qualified
48. Feast
50. Loose beast
54. Optical glass
55. Unit of cookies
57. Atoned
59. Cuckoo
60. Disallow
61. Concealed
63. Actor Beatty
64. Bind
65. Historical period: 2 wds.
68. Attack: 2 wds.
70. Actor Sean
71. Crazy
72. Turf
74. Pro
75. Challenges
76. —— avion
78. "—— on Sunday"
80. —— Aviv
81. Marsh marigold
85. Sun. talk
86. Weapons man
90. Before
91. Sullen
93. Exchange premium
94. Compass pt.
95. Lively songs
97. Surplus
99. Tree houses
101. Vein
102. Exhaust
104. Extreme
105. To safety
106. Green: Fr.
107. Within: prefix
108. Gulf of ——
109. Colors
110. Soldiers and workers
111. Asterisk
112. Track event

DOWN

1. Run aground
2. Doctor, at times
3. Adorned
4. Leave out
5. "—— of Me"
6. Plundered
7. Oak seed
8. Okey- ——
9. Pretty garden
10. Not a winner
11. Positive poles
12. Urge
13. Actor Robert or Alan
14. Loaf
15. Surges forward
16. Strengthens
23. Comforted
26. Car-racing curves
28. Didn't follow suit
31. Poetic contraction
33. Point of a pen
36. Swine
37. Incubate
39. Uris or Spinks
41. Orchestra location
42. Corn unit
44. Proto or ecto
45. Oscar de la ——
46. Edible bulb
47. Dracula features
49. Voice
51. River mammal
52. French river

53. Nice places
55. Bleat
56. Towel word
58. Quill
60. Soothes
62. Put off
66. Bites
67. Many moons
69. High hill
70. —— Alto
73. Meal finales
75. Evil spirit
77. Brazilian resort
79. Swerves
80. Three: prefix
81. Basement
82. Baltimore ——
83. United

PUZZLE 386

84. Established
86. Program
87. Dwell
88. Menu item
89. Take umbrage
92. Apparent
93. FBI man
96. Golf pegs
98. Imitates
100. Yellow cheese
102. Reproductive units
103. "Le Coq ——"

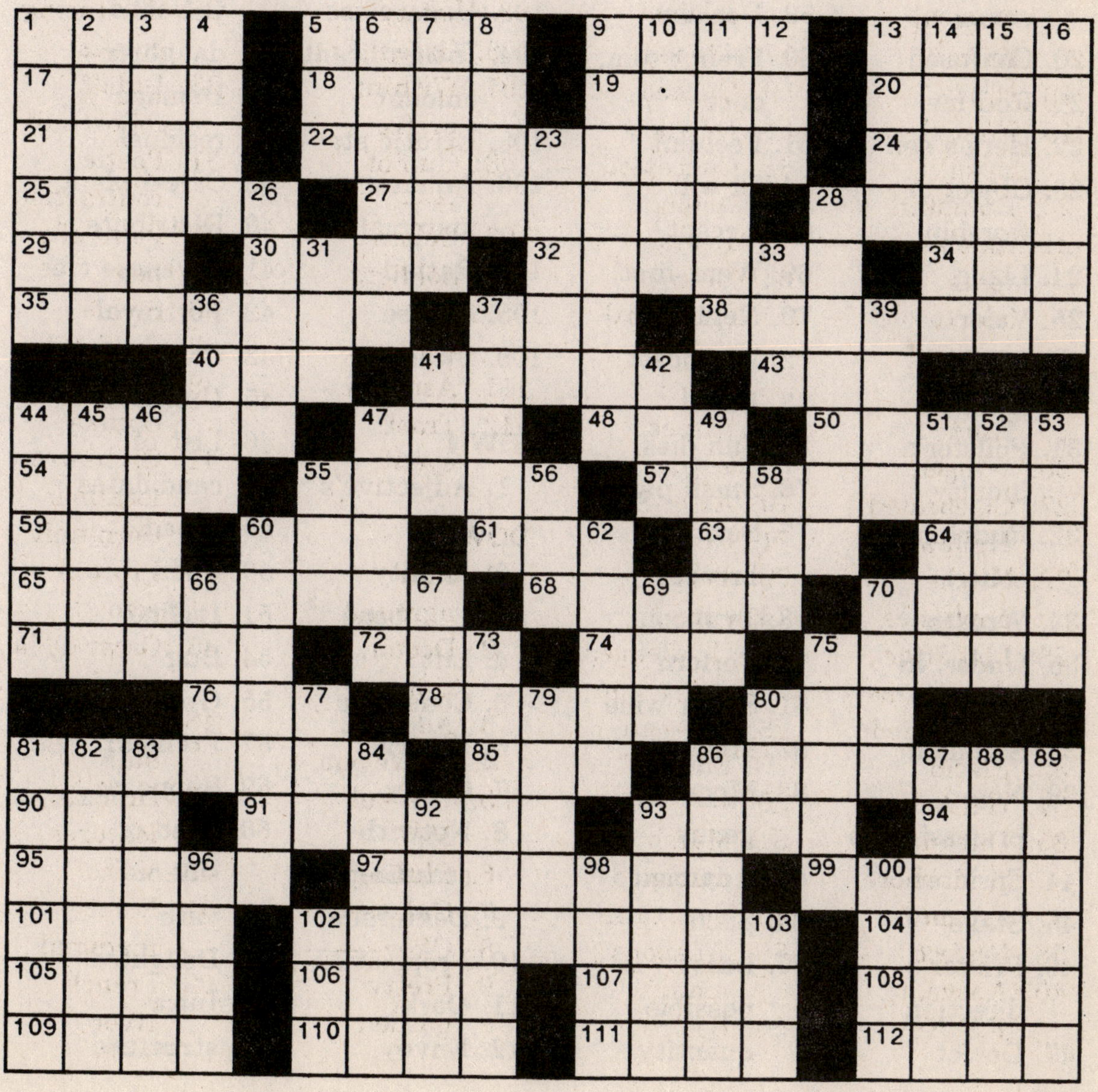

PUZZLE 387

ACROSS

1. Weathercock
5. Enthusiastic
9. Retired
13. Assay
17. Environmental sci.
18. Merchant's item
19. Sarcastic comment
20. Confused
21. Routine
22. Hera's son
23. Object of worship
24. Liang
25. Valor
27. Sidekick
29. Sea god
31. Pollster's inquiry
32. Rudolph's cohort
34. Woman
35. Under, in Milan
38. Summon
39. Non-professionals
44. Sprinted
45. Stake
46. Printer's direction
47. Detect
48. Particular
49. Attract
50. Piccolos' cousins
52. Frazier's competitor
53. Model
55. Shine
56. Forfeiter
58. Rd.
59. Declaim
60. French coin, once
61. Feel out
64. Ill will
65. Accept
69. Went first
70. Negligent
72. Downcast
73. Remit
74. Sun disk
76. Small piglet
77. Seth's brother
78. Typhoon
79. Forlorn
81. Sweet wine
82. Men
83. Mouse genus
84. Adamant
86. Zilch
87. Least possible quantity
91. "When I ___ a lad . . ."
92. Casters
96. Directly
97. Moreno of "West Side Story"
99. Electron's home
101. Acknowledge
102. Chinese wax
103. Univ. class
104. Insignificant amount
105. Erratic star
106. Aquatic mammal
107. Ratted
108. Course
109. Swarm

DOWN

1. Adjective's kin
2. Acidity
3. ___ bene
4. Lift
5. Conscious
6. Diverge
7. Choler
8. Notwithstanding
9. Dexterous
10. Proposition
11. Dark
12. Envoy
13. Squeals
14. Rebekah's son
15. Studied
16. Parable
26. Vanity
28. Split
30. Touch
32. Gross
33. Character
35. Station
36. Eugene O'Neill's daughter
37. Damage residual
38. Cereal plant
40. Distribute
41. Javanese tree
42. Portrayal
43. Commotion
45. Unmixed
46. List of candidates
49. Treadle
50. Pads
51. Incline
54. Bug
55. Ground grain
57. Pronoun
59. Supposes
60. Kind of silk or yarn
61. Delighted
62. Infrastructure

PUZZLE 387

63. Certain literary works
64. Dirty mark
65. Settled
66. October gem
67. Farewell, to Caesar
68. Glances at
71. Deletions
72. Stall
75. So-called
77. Pirate
78. Chivalrous
80. Scottish chimney
81. Coat type
82. Wire measurement
85. Sharp, nasal tone
86. Drifter
87. Plots
88. Strophanthus product
89. Lopez's theme song
90. Shiny mineral
92. Ecclesiastical court
93. Shout of a Bacchanal
94. Stray
95. Emulated Spitz
98. Great deal
100. Furthermore

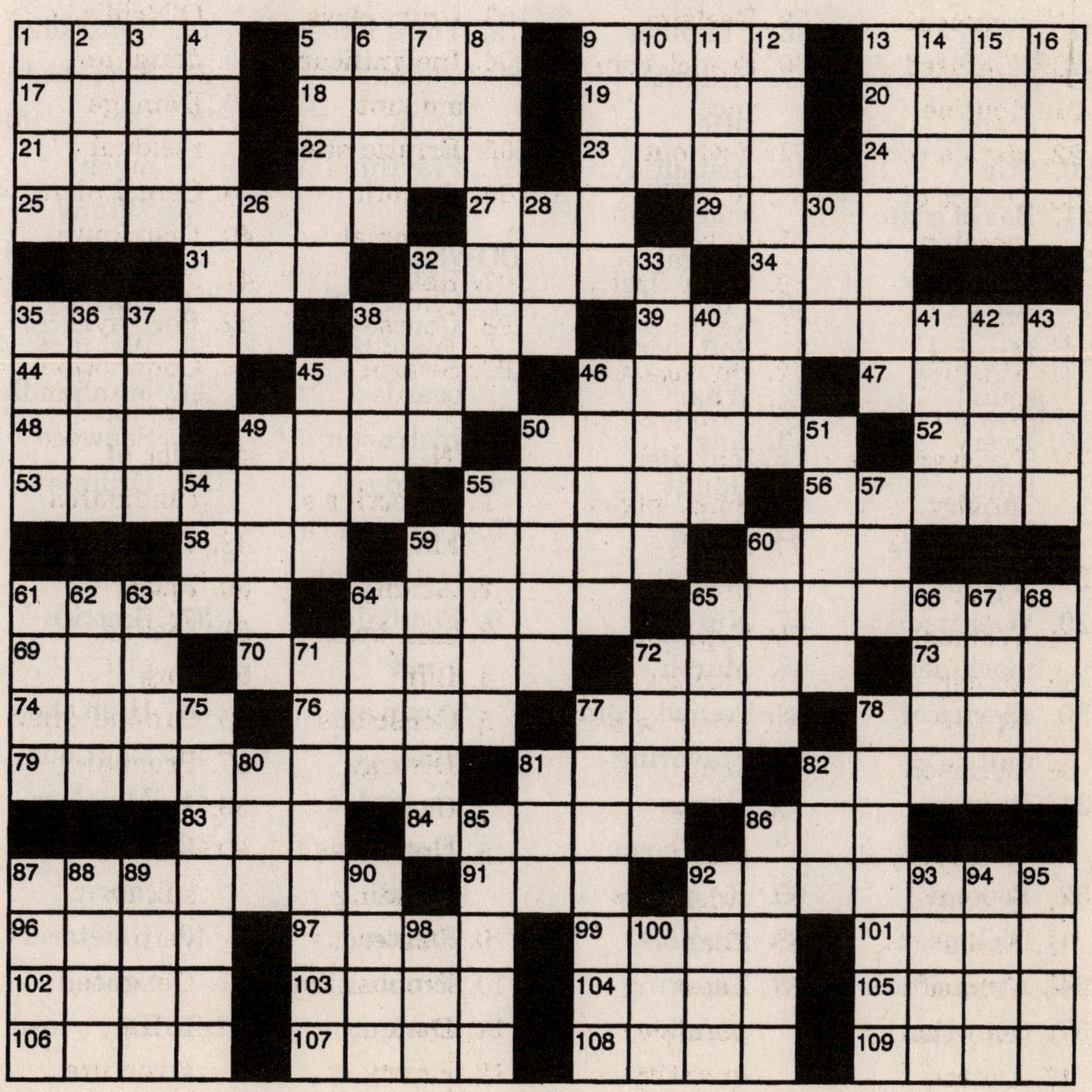

PUZZLE 388

ACROSS

1. Spiteful woman
4. Salty drops
9. Out of tune
12. Visage
13. Direction sign
14. Book page
16. —— Fe
17. Jerusalem: 3 wds.
20. Stir
21. Bar of soap
23. Feather scarf
24. Musical sound
25. Every thirty days
27. Quizzes
29. Operated machinery
30. Electrical unit
31. Persian king
32. Poetess Dickinson
34. Army officer
37. Cut of pork
38. Very dry, as champagne
39. Unsymmetrical
40. Caution
41. Noisiest
44. Sound of disgust
45. Endure
46. Chamber
47. Knight's title
48. British soldiers in Bengal
50. Price
51. Soft drink
52. Wharf
53. Any
54. Gaunt
55. Water mains
57. Nip
58. Marsh
59. French coin
60. Flavoring plants
62. Roof beams
66. Penpoints
68. Payable
69. Tapering seam
70. Baseball stick
71. Perry Mason's secretary: 2 wds.
74. Satire
76. Civil disturbance
77. Church path
78. Kitchen basin
79. Third letter
80. Cutting beam
81. Plaything

DOWN

1. Church law
2. Tread the boards
3. Instructor
4. Dowdy
5. Cleveland's waterfront
6. Football great Donovan
7. Self-appointed Texas judge: 2 wds.
8. Rustling sound
9. Antique
10. Remarkable deed
11. Local candidate: 2 wds.
12. Portuguese dance
15. Crucial exam
16. Yosemite ——
18. Suet
19. Contradict
22. Everybody
26. De —— (too much)
27. Skinny
28. Blood fluid
31. Classify
33. Wet dirt
34. Manhandle
35. Seaweed
36. Ordinary citizen: 3 wds.
37. Scottish girl
38. High shoe
40. Cautious
41. Misplace
42. Chinese fabric
43. Cafeteria utensil
45. Dog's lead

46. Capital of Italy
49. Billiards stick
50. Folding beds
51. Jargon
53. Place of enforced isolation
54. Radical
55. Remain undecided
56. Less cordial
57. Savage
58. Distant
61. Magazine execs
62. Grader
63. Black wood
64. Military grade
65. Pig's digs
67. Wild plum
69. Remove from print
72. Took food
73. Nineteenth letter
75. —— de Janeiro

PUZZLE 388

PUZZLE 389

ACROSS

1. Brown paper item
4. Shoo!
8. TV's predecessor
13. Retreats
17. Self
18. Buckeye State
19. Black wood
20. Theater sign
21. Bear up under
23. Goes without food
24. Spanish fruit
25. London apartment
26. "—— of Wax"
28. Broad chisel
30. Train tracks
32. Viking
33. Dishearten
34. Writer Ferber
35. Swell out
36. Basque's hat
37. "—— Day Afternoon"
38. Blouse type
39. Pep up
40. Sacred city
43. Slangy dice
44. Piglike animal
45. Nazimova
46. Table coverings
49. A, E, I, O, or U
50. Heavy blow
51. Does housework
52. All tied up
53. Overcast
54. Peruses
55. County celebrations
56. Swindler
57. With competence
58. Hitchcock villains
59. Confidence
60. Footlike organ
61. Ciphers
62. Crucifix
63. River in Scotland
66. Greek ship launcher
67. Parade sight
68. Cruel
69. Ushers in again
72. Muscular strength
73. Endures use
74. Bay windows
75. Inclined (to)
76. Lemon peel
77. Touched the starting line
78. Encore!
80. Pave the way for: 3 wds.
84. Brink
85. Most unpleasant
86. Thus
87. Atmosphere
88. Pod member
89. Makes wet
90. Sleuth Nancy
91. —— Turner

DOWN

1. Wager
2. Time gone by
3. Out on the links
4. Marsh birds
5. Small talk
6. River isle
7. Slight footings: 2 wds.
8. Turn down
9. Make humble
10. Medicinal portion
11. Bank statement abbr.
12. Mollusk fisher
13. Banish
14. Synonym of 13 Down
15. Mets and Yankees
16. Asterisks
22. "—— Cinders"
27. Roman revelry
29. Frank
30. Christmas color
31. "Much —— about Nothing"
32. Undraped statues
33. Lucifer
35. Ties tightly
36. Two-footed animal
38. Complains
39. Front yards
40. Jeer
41. Dodge
42. Woodland deity
43. Like a bad guy's eyes
44. French city
45. On high
46. Quarrel
47. West Point cadet
48. Spanish silver coins
49. Renders null
50. Group
52. Powerful industrialist
53. Bread border
55. Conflagrations
56. Reaction to a pun

PUZZLE 389

58. Wood-cutting machines: 2 wds.
59. Smoothed plaster
61. Ardent desire
62. Tribe
63. Not showing emotion
64. Spike of corn
65. Half ems
66. Took note
67. Facades
68. Restaurant list
69. Routines
70. Decompose
71. Flock of herons
72. Effervescent
73. Black —— spider
75. India rubber
76. Blow wildly
79. Sticky substance
81. Blunder
82. Aunt, to Pedro
83. Bread morsel

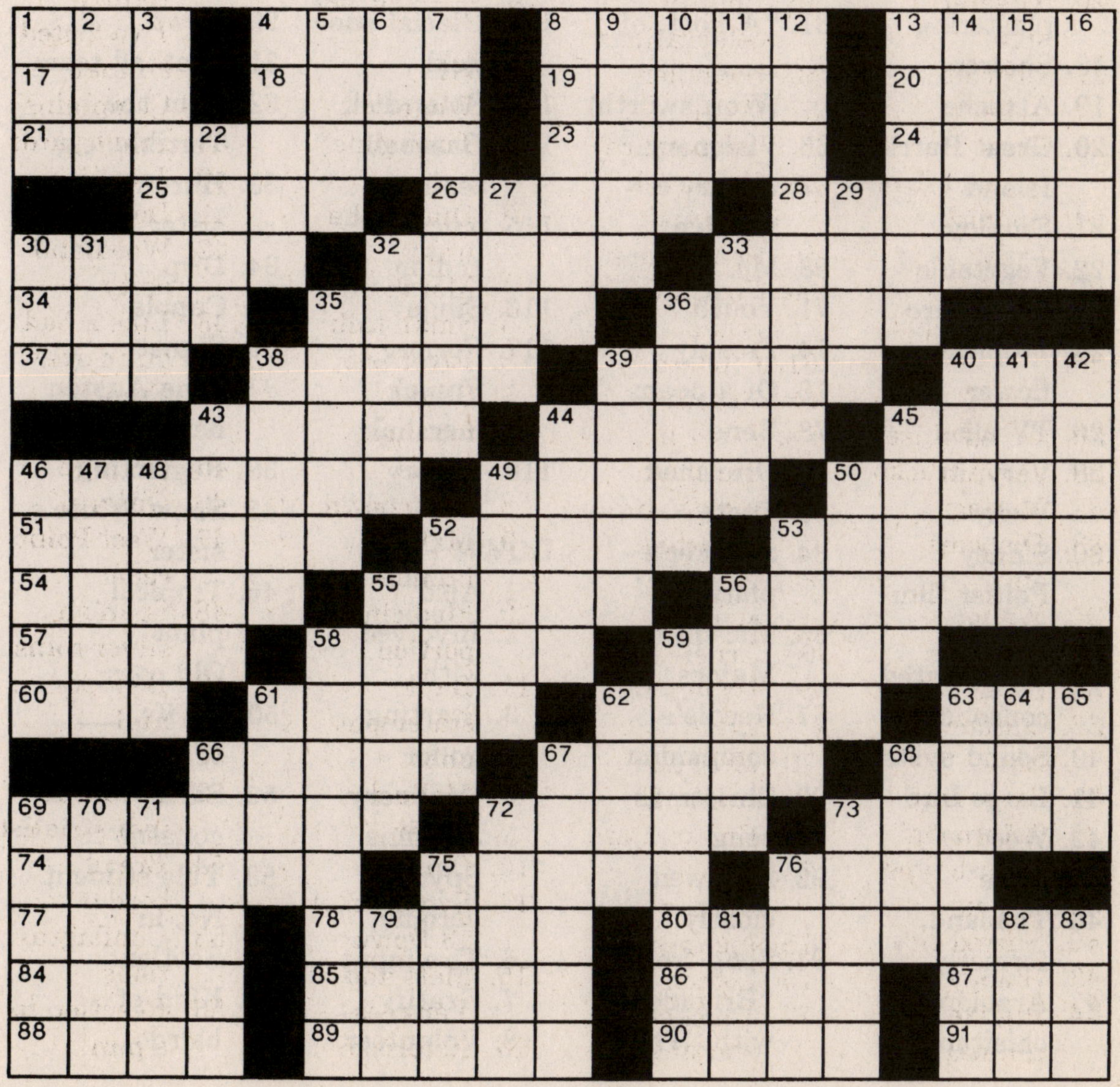

PUZZLE 390

ACROSS

1. A Jackson brother
5. General Arnold
8. Small dogs, for short
12. Lag behind
16. Unique person
17. Do some plastering
18. Shower
19. Attache
20. Great Barrier Island
21. Employ
22. Vegetable
23. Fan's hero
24. Tropical flower
26. TV alien
28. Very, in Vichy
30. Sidney Poitier film
36. Placid
39. Unaspirated consonants
40. Sound system
41. Large bird
42. Weed
44. Seize
46. Thailand, formerly
47. Arabian chieftain
49. New star
51. Tennis star Lacoste
54. ____ out (make do)
55. Memory's route
56. Rug-weaver's knot
59. Palmer's game
61. "A host, of ____" (Wordsworth)
66. Visionary
67. Canary's relative
68. Ms. Kett
71. Youth
74. Freshly
76. Of a poem
78. Bend
79. Drenched
81. Facts
84. Speaker's platform
86. Marvin or Majors
87. Needle's companion
90. Christmas song
92. Followed closely
94. Song from "Brigadoon," with "The"
97. Federal agcy.
98. ____ was saying
99. Ornamental shrub
102. Sunrise
105. Strong drink
107. Heraldic wreath
109. Lodging places
111. Jai ____
112. Glacial snow field
113. Solar disk
114. Baseball team
115. Yucatan Indian
116. Singe
117. Former French marshal
118. Theory

DOWN

1. Also
2. Involved with
3. Starting golfer
4. Visionary
5. Johanna Spyri's heroine
6. Tire input
7. Gratify
8. Volunteer
9. Furniture wood
10. Laughter
11. Traps
12. Shastas, e.g.
13. Disencumber
14. Commotion
15. Set
17. Pertaining to Santiago's country
25. Allude
27. Lengthy
29. Newt
31. Football team
32. Ivan the Terrible, e.g.
33. Huron's sister lake
34. Drip
35. Cupola
36. Signet
37. Jane Austen heroine
38. Regretting
43. Snow White's sister
45. Tropical plant
48. Old cars
50. No ifs, ____, or buts
52. Silent consent
53. Yale student
57. No, in Scotland
58. Kind of hairdo

PUZZLE 390

60. Went by jet
62. Grazing ground
63. Hideaway
64. Violin
65. Delay
69. Playhouse locale
70. Emulated Rich Little
71. Wood slat
72. Arthur ____ of tennis
73. Mrs. Copperfield
75. Texas city
77. Countryman
80. Porky Pig's love
82. Scarlet songbird
83. Part of B.A.
85. Casa's room
88. Exclamations
89. Condescends
91. Buckeye State inhabitant
93. Fighting ____ (Big Ten team)
95. Street show
96. Actor Jack ____
100. Camelot lady
101. "Green Gables" girl
102. Beaver's handiwork
103. Southern st.
104. Method
106. Eggs: Lat.
108. Itinerary: abbr.
110. East China, e.g.

PUZZLE 391

ACROSS

1. More protracted
6. Fish sauce
10. Mr. Martin
14. Lively
15. Roman statesman
16. Italian river
17. Baseball film
19. Arachnid
20. Decided
21. Sun. talk
22. Sharpener food
24. Singer Bandy
26. Figure mug
27. On deck
30. Baseball film
33. Guitar's kin
34. Tall tale
35. "Gimme a Break" gal
37. Besides
38. Loved to excess
39. Cap site
40. Oracle
41. "The African Queen" screenwriter
42. Designer Geoffrey ____
43. "The Pride of ____"
45. Riding horses
46. Units of work
47. Eur. nation
48. Body-hugging dress
51. ____ and away
53. Tango number
56. Dangle
57. Baseball film
61. Matty and Felipe
62. Where the Shannon flows
63. Make up
64. Doctor's amount
65. Split
66. San ____

DOWN

1. Scientific rms.
2. Malarial fever
3. Incline
4. Architect's addition
5. Hair color
6. Brazilian state
7. "Cowardly Lion"
8. Delphi vowel
9. Mixture
10. Baseball film
11. Singer Clapton
12. Hero or dote prefix
13. Yuletide tune
18. Like tag-sale items
23. Diminish
24. Baseball film
25. Spanish gold
26. A crowd?
27. Goat's-hair fabrics
28. Hay bundles
29. Start
30. Scolds
31. Actress Adoree
32. Mingle
34. Famous bear et al.
36. Pinky and Peggy
38. Daddy's girl
42. Heat meas.
44. Morsel
45. Gilbert of "Roseanne"
48. Roe producer
49. Salt: pref.
50. Adam's grandson
51. Maidenhair
52. Dill
53. Meadowlands offering
54. Decline
55. Bread spread
58. Hustle
59. Skye cap
60. Large lizard

PUZZLE 392

ACROSS

1. Bessie's home
5. Windstorm
9. Beauty parlor
14. Melville work
15. Caspian Sea feeder
16. Sierra ____
17. Lorre role
18. Go down
19. Synthetic fabric
20. Expanded
23. Liquid meas.
24. "____ Girls"
25. Like some beaches
27. Postponed
31. Farmer, at times
33. Bow's companion
34. Anon
35. "Had I ____ for a century . . ."
38. Problem
39. Easel
40. The Bard's wife
41. Melody
42. Paves
43. French school
44. Summoners
46. Interlocked
47. African desert
49. Grass genus
50. See 41 Across
51. Peace offering
58. Botch
60. Turkish liqueur
61. Matador's foe
62. Tear
63. Seed covering
64. Lulu
65. ____ Ababa
66. Of sound mind
67. Like some lawns

DOWN

1. Box-office flop
2. Cupid
3. Sacred Roman ____
4. Lunch time
5. Spewed
6. Sky ram
7. "One if by ____"
8. Nevada county
9. Scheduled
10. Atmosphere: pref.
11. New Jersey resort
12. Ryan or Tatum
13. "____ Bly"
21. Ball of yarn
22. Affect drastically
26. Nautical cries
27. Soviet news agency
28. Pisa's river
29. Highway feeder
30. Open arcade
31. Glides
32. Time periods
34. Lead
36. Type of poison
37. Lack
39. Bargain
43. Limerick man
45. Literary devices
46. Calder creation
47. Israeli
48. Felt sick
49. Illinois city
52. Cleopatra's maid
53. Unit of length: Sp.
54. Speck
55. Taboo
56. Kind of cut
57. Cornucopia
59. Egg: pref.

PUZZLE 393

ACROSS

1. Octagon word
5. Cooking verb
10. Clock face
14. Cavity
15. Whirling
16. Atop
17. Wide-mouthed vessel
18. Layers
19. Colorado Indians
20. Dixie drawl: 2 wds.
23. Conger
24. Above, to poets
25. Hiding places
29. Behave like sheep
32. Forefront
35. Concerning
36. Pretense
37. Sand hill
38. Fiji and Samoa, e.g.: 3 wds.
41. Dancer Miller et al.
42. Small pie
43. Watchful
44. Series
45. Movie dog
46. Stage whispers
47. "____ a Camera": 2 wds.
49. Letter addenda: abbr.
50. 1946 Disney film: 4 wds.
58. Seaweed
59. Path
60. Shelley or Keats
62. Blockage
63. Tapestry
64. Stare
65. Rosebud's rider
66. Hollers
67. Designate

DOWN

1. Haggard novel
2. Pulls
3. Bread spread
4. Land of the Incas
5. Washes
6. Spirit in "The Tempest"
7. Clairvoyant
8. Sea bird
9. "Born Free" lioness
10. "Irma La ____"
11. Mediated
12. Solar disk
13. Missing
21. Canines
22. Bashful
25. Houses: Sp.
26. "To a rag and ____": 2 wds.
27. Trusting in : 2 wds.
28. Shanties
29. Scarlett ____
30. Fisherman's need
31. 911 people: abbr.
33. Author Schwarz-Bart
34. Bird sites
36. Subway scarcity
37. Surrealist painter
39. Aves.
40. Lariat
45. I love: Lat.
46. Appraise
48. Marble
49. Flower part
50. Duffel bag
51. Earthen pot
52. Skirmish
53. Raced
54. Fling
55. Above
56. Roman robe
57. Tiller
61. Shirt type

PUZZLE 394

ACROSS

1. Flowery
5. Comedian Wilson
9. European capital
13. Global area
14. Work perk
15. Mixture
16. Gautier novel: 2 wds.
19. Stretch
20. Bay window
21. Odoriferous
23. Handbag
25. Engages
26. Depository
27. Alt. spelling
30. Lucre lover
31. Trade
32. High note: 2 wds.
33. Certain receivers
34. Body section
35. Tidbit
36. Andrea ____ Sarto
37. Sojourn
38. Principle
39. Sooner than
40. Impulse
41. New ____, Ct.
42. French river
44. Cafe chompers
45. "American Bandstand" host
47. Notice
48. Dickens novel: 3 wds.
54. Quarry of the carver's wife
55. Rome's port
56. Zola heroine
57. Court celebrity
58. Polanski film
59. Sprouted

DOWN

1. Varnish
2. Dos Passos trilogy
3. Small drink
4. Carolina cape
5. Whim
6. Steal
7. Leb.'s neighbor
8. As thick as ____ soup
9. Tusked animals
10. Holmes novel: 2 wds.
11. ____ and shine
12. December song
14. Moroccan coins
17. Rhone delta city
18. "Murphy Brown" role
21. Brawl bruise
22. George Eliot novel
23. Garden bloom
24. Bring to ruin
26. City in Vermont
28. E.T. and ALF
29. Lost in delight
30. Persian's pal
31. Comic pianist
34. Mountain pool
35. Dividing
37. Finnish port
38. Spud
41. Seaport in 7 Down
43. Napoleon's men
44. ____ Island
45. Cook book
46. Pitcher Tiant
47. Minnesota ____
49. Little one
50. Function
51. Attention
52. From Miami to Hartford
53. Small crow

PUZZLE 395

ACROSS
1. Bones
5. NATO and SEATO
10. So be it
14. Soared
15. Permit
16. Golf goal
17. New Year's figure: 2 wds.
19. Normandy town: 2 wds.
20. Water or wine
21. Bog fuel
23. Layer
24. "Metropolis" director
26. Surprised look
28. Encouraged
31. Athens's rival
34. "____ Alibi"
35. Stuffed
37. Upper atmosphere
38. Aphrodite's son
40. ____ eclipse
42. Ilk
43. Ceremonies
45. Diving feats
47. Wallet item
48. Saw
50. Fountain treats
52. Ohio Indians
54. Train-track runner
55. Flub
57. Type unit
59. "Lady and the ____"
62. "GWTW" home
64. Certain reporters: 2 wds.
67. Fiddler on the reef
68. Cape Cod town
69. Isaac's son
70. Detest
71. ____ Hall University
72. Humid

DOWN
1. Switch label
2. Reuben ingredient
3. Son of Adam
4. For a bit
5. Type of guidance
6. Jet's elevation: abbr.
7. Football infraction
8. Weighty books
9. Perspires
10. Sounds of surprise
11. Maternity
12. That girl, in Paris
13. Las Vegas light
18. Les ____-Unis
22. Duct ____
25. Outfit
27. Darn it!
28. Penthouse
29. Ronald Reagan film: 2 wds.
30. Jeans' material
32. Gulls
33. Comedian Johnson
34. Spice
36. Senegal's capital
39. Prophet
41. Aunt or uncle
44. Marina offering
46. Rouses
49. Jefferson and religious followers
51. Very happy
53. Put to music
55. Delineate
56. ____ avis
58. Border on
60. Flat-topped hill
61. Hyde Park sight
63. Humorist Burrows
65. Broadway hit sign: abbr.
66. Grab a bite

PUZZLE 396

ACROSS
1. Ear part
5. Athenian
10. Mr. Charles
13. Baal
14. Couple
15. Margarine
17. Space
18. Certain tanker
19. Alpha's follower
20. Refuge
21. Toothpaste holder
22. Panacea
24. New England state
26. TV sitcom
27. Circa
29. Conspiracy
30. Hobby
33. Holy book
34. Lawrence Taylor, for one
35. Mined matter
36. Roman poet
37. Baseball's Dean
38. Connect
39. Singer Shannon
40. Snit
41. Tub occupant
42. French season
43. Ms. Bombeck
44. Belt part
45. Singer Laine
46. Penniless
47. Astrologer's chart
50. Riot
51. Notable time
54. Excited
55. Eagle's weapon
57. October stone
58. Excuse
59. Mountain nymph
60. ___-mell
61. Be human
62. Prepared
63. Playing card

DOWN
1. Money in Venice, once
2. Redolence
3. Traveling library
4. Kind of tree
5. Proliferate
6. Clan
7. Story
8. Diamonds
9. Wedding, e.g.
10. Batman's partner
11. Author Haley
12. Sasquatch's cousin
16. Rowboat adjunct
21. Fork part
23. Latvian
25. "___ Lang Syne"
26. "Up ___ River"
27. Home
28. Rosie's fastener
29. Kind of pie
30. Accountant
31. Satellite of Uranus
32. Category
34. One of the "Gremlins"
37. Woody Allen, e.g.
38. Face card
40. Honduran seaport
41. Ocean marker
44. Spirit
45. Proud father's handout
46. Expansive
47. Shoot
48. Gawk
49. Activist
50. Tiny circus performer
52. Chest sound
53. Friend
56. 100 square meters
57. Choose

PUZZLE 397

ACROSS

1. Austen's Woodhouse
5. Rugs
9. British veggies
14. Prone one
15. Atop
16. In disguise: abbr.
17. Catching on: 4 wds.
20. Bird genus
21. El Dorado find
22. Feature of "pfennig": 2 wds.
25. Harems
30. Previous to
31. Sweet treats
33. Clock sound
34. ____ wait (ambush): 2 wds.
35. Scholar's lair
36. Gist: 3 wds.
41. Woodsman's activity
42. Dim
43. Bit
44. Prayer beads
46. Merry: Fr.
49. "The Genius" author
51. Spencer's co-star
53. Madre's sis
54. First name in fictional villains
55. Words of support: 5 wds.
62. Gourmand
63. Russian river
64. Bleaching vat
65. Type of shooting
66. Actress McClurg
67. Riley's life

DOWN

1. Go by
2. Above-ground
3. Interfere
4. Take for ____: 2 wds.
5. Coffee holder
6. Fitting
7. Haul
8. Siesta
9. Assign blame to: 2 wds.
10. Rump
11. Be a ham
12. Plant
13. Freud find
18. Yangtze city
19. Son of Zeus and Hera
23. Bound
24. Omega preceders
26. Perfume
27. Proper ____
28. Aussie rock band
29. "Say Anything . . ." actress
32. Ignores
34. Veranda
35. Don't leave!: 2 wds.
36. Uttered
37. Wife: Lat.
38. Bit
39. Listless
40. Parched
44. Bridle part
45. Delphi figure
46. ____ pig
47. Porthos's friend
48. Belong
50. Set in motion
52. In the red
55. Affirmative
56. Sturdy as an ____
57. Shoshonean
58. Carriage spring shape
59. British ref. work
60. Single: pref.
61. Scot's denial

PUZZLE 398

ACROSS

1. Zeno's specialty
8. Cane
13. Limited autonomy: 2 wds.
14. Shot
16. Youngman's specialty: hyph.
17. AL player
18. Fanatical
19. Postulate
21. Stannum
22. ____-and-span
23. Salisbury, for one
24. One trillionth: pref.
25. Lower-case poet's initials
26. Karpov's forte
27. "____ the Family": 2 wds.
28. "Gil ____"
29. Rickles' specialties
31. Lively dance
33. English homework
34. Plaintiff's award
36. Former ruler
37. Foreshadowings
38. Cautious
40. Charade
43. Shred
44. French soldier
45. Peak: pref.
46. Evian, for one
47. Imply: 2 wds.
48. Mohegan chief
49. American Rockies' high point
51. Eastern, for one: 2 wds.
53. Speak indirectly about something: 2 wds.
54. One of the Aleutians
55. Poor
56. Picks

DOWN

1. Pacific island
2. Protozoan
3. Dig find
4. Unproductive
5. Demand payment from
6. Certain esters
7. King of Persia
8. Haunter
9. Fixed period
10. MacGraw of movies
11. Naval group
12. Joy
13. Sense or opera
15. Partners of mortises
20. Romanian city
23. Condition
24. Luxurious
26. Dancing shoes
27. Test
28. Wishy-washy
30. Indian leader
31. Strategy: 2 wds.
32. Submissive
34. Part of Wessex
35. Glaswegian
36. Cracker
39. Missing part
40. Confront
41. Model T features
42. "...pussycat went ____"
44. Trifling
45. Commonwealth soldier
47. Alum
48. Ubangi feeder
50. Increase
52. ____ de mer

PUZZLE 399

ACROSS

1. Fume
6. Grimalkin
9. Suit fabric
14. Overhangs
15. "____ from the Heart"
16. Lend ____: 2 wds.
17. Ashes
18. Margosa
19. Peruvian ruminant
20. Hair strand, to Medusa
22. Hair ointments
24. Full of vim
26. Ship component
29. Helpful push
30. Nelson or Mary Baker
34. Beverages
35. Places for coins
36. Terrible
37. Wooden nail
38. Great amount
39. Wading bird
41. Ninnies
46. Old wound's leaving
47. Office article
48. Baseballer Hank ____
49. Actor Rip ____
50. Inside info
53. Certain colors
56. Sweet-smelling
60. South American timber tree
61. Boatman's item
63. Disposed
64. Secure
65. "Born in the ____"
66. Rich brown
67. Kills
68. ____ Aviv
69. Automotive lemon

DOWN

1. Matched groups
2. Horse
3. Finished
4. Certain zoo employees
5. German industrial city
6. Regulate
7. Tropical bird
8. Storm
9. Game dish
10. Intertwined
11. Interpret
12. Plucky
13. Notable periods
21. Bird beaks
23. Mel's family
25. Stickum
26. Agreeably flavored
27. New cadet
28. Protection
31. "Saturday Night Fever" music
32. Bleak
33. Pine
40. Incomplete
41. British hoosegow
42. Goes to a restaurant: 2 wds.
43. Ahead of
44. Sisterly
45. Geraint's wife
46. Played the lead
51. NYSE memberships
52. Shrubby undergrowth
53. Butter bits
54. Seed covering
55. Legendary account
57. Sorry!
58. Unicorn fish
59. Close tightly
62. "Peer Gynt" character

PUZZLE 400

ACROSS
1. Envelope abbr.
5. Unconstrained
9. Rebuff
13. Hillside, in Dundee
14. Buzz
15. Cato's robe
16. Points
17. Kilns
18. Shortly
19. Anderson/Weill tune: 2 wds.
22. Dele
23. Den
24. The sun
27. Writer Buntline
30. ____ culpa
31. ____ Beta Kappa
32. Astronaut Shepard
36. Incas' land
38. "Sunshine of Your Love" group
40. Crazy: 5 wds.
43. Unsuitable
44. Poet Khayyam
45. Approval
46. Dunderhead
47. Ocean: abbr.
49. Alkaline substance
51. Pose
52. River nymph
54. Plant of forgetfulness
59. U.S. financier: 2 wds.
63. Recedes
65. Gunwale pin
66. Soft cheese
67. Story
68. Madagascan tree-dweller
69. Miss Kett
70. Spotted
71. Belgian river
72. Film spool

DOWN
1. Demean
2. Judge
3. Florida city
4. Aeries
5. Seize
6. Scoundrel
7. Kind of sports
8. Smith of the blues
9. Bandleader Kenton
10. Colorado mountain: 2 wds.
11. Past
12. Kitchen utensil
14. Comic DeLuise
20. Although, poetically
21. Goosefoot
25. Scarlett or John
26. English sailor
28. Antipollution group: abbr.
29. Wrecks
32. Improperly
33. Veranda, in Hilo
34. Equipped to conform
35. Short sleep
37. Aries
39. Greek letter
41. Actor Arnold
42. "____ Freedom"
48. Tensely
50. Pipe joint
53. Mouth: suf.
55. Three-handed card game
56. Rich cake
57. Bring together
58. Filch
60. Secondhand
61. Partially obscure
62. Always, to poets
63. Summer, in Lyon
64. Leaf or window

PUZZLE 401

ACROSS
1. People of Cardiff
6. Buss
10. Tuber
14. Let up
15. Territory
16. Submissive
17. Cattle breed
18. Competed
19. Troubadour's song
20. Therefore
21. Impudent talk
22. Abbey man
23. ____ it (hurry): 2 wds.
25. Marks of behavior
27. Trudge
29. Henry or Lew
32. Sesame plant
35. Leak
37. Transferred legally
38. Father of Seth
40. Type of light
42. Excite
43. Naysaying
45. Brother of Seth
47. Foul place
48. Supplier to equestrians
50. Clipper clink
52. Shone brightly
54. Wind about
58. Revelations of Allah
60. Trough filler
62. "... ____ ready to pardon": 2 wds.
63. Actor Richard
64. Grass bunch
65. Stradivarius's rival
66. Lacerate
67. Porch
68. French impressionist
69. Profits
70. Shuck
71. Overconfident

DOWN
1. Night vigils
2. Chicago critic
3. Not petite
4. Sharpens
5. Ahem!
6. South Seas beverage
7. ____ coffee
8. Playground contraption
9. Lugubrious
10. Brings up short
11. Hudson site
12. Shield knob
13. Treasured
21. Reef rover
22. Heap
24. Of the past
26. Tormented
28. Actor Gerard
30. $0.01
31. Vortex
32. Small boys
33. Notion
34. Government donation: 2 wds.
36. ____ Zadora
39. Part of England
41. Decline
44. Actor Bates
46. ____ Yutang
49. Disprove
51. Allure
53. English novelist
55. Town in Guam
56. Pens
57. Archie's dingbat
58. Letterspace
59. Arch type
61. And the other people: 2 wds.
64. Cooking abbr.
65. Diplomat: abbr.

PUZZLE 402

ACROSS

1. Pike
5. Watery color
9. Sad songs
14. ____-and-shut case
15. Revolve
16. Jitterbug
17. Midas's love
18. Chore
19. Include: 2 wds.
20. Prompt: 2 wds.
22. Writer Waugh
24. French season
25. Permit to travel
27. Large deer
29. Purplish red
32. Courage
36. "____ Town"
37. Blunt
40. Andrea ____
41. Pindarics
43. Oven-cook
45. Moisturizes
46. Cambodian money
48. Marked
50. Occur
51. Musical composition
53. Made into law
55. Blemishes
57. Pro ____
58. ____ ideal
61. Racing distance
63. Deep red
67. Adage
69. Against
71. Moslem lord
72. ____ France: 2 wds.
73. Horn sound
74. FDR's dog
75. Choir member
76. Catch sight of
77. Comic Philips et al.

DOWN

1. Trademark
2. Onto
3. Irishman
4. Leafy veggie
5. Verifier
6. Sine ____ non
7. ____ Major
8. Leg part
9. Polished
10. Cover
11. Wavy, in heraldry
12. Redact
13. "Auld Lang ____"
21. Penny press
23. Freddy Kreuger's street
26. Hebrew high priest
28. Store
29. Heathlands
30. Sound control
31. Kermit's color
33. Halloween goody
34. Soda measure, abroad
35. Facilitated
38. ____ Paolo
39. Fragrant compound
42. Wallop
44. Perseverance
47. Speech defect
49. Fruit
52. Onassis
54. Wine unit
56. Agenda
58. Send out
59. Wind
60. Yoke pullers
62. Eve's grandson
64. Mosque priest
65. Missile site
66. Time periods
68. Two words in June
70. Acme

PUZZLE 403

ACROSS

1. Screen
5. Aroma
9. Stashed away
12. Zone
13. Got up
14. Mine yield
15. Sightseers
17. West of films
18. Composition
19. Visit
21. Get closer
24. Took a chair
25. Baking ingredient
28. Hint
30. Vatican leader
33. ". . . have you ____ wool?"
34. "____ on a Grecian Urn"
35. Clash of arms
36. Hibernates
38. Was introduced to
39. Feed the kitty
40. Support
42. ____ between the lines
44. Wet
47. Free
51. Inventor Whitney
52. Play practice
55. ____ off steam
56. Boast
57. Additions
58. Cube or tray
59. Timeless toy
60. Indulge

DOWN

1. Counterpart
2. Miscalculates
3. Oceans
4. Fine cigar
5. Wise bird
6. Forest female
7. Gumbo ingredient
8. Takes a nap
9. Place of origin
10. Persia, today
11. Boy scout's accomplishment
16. Hurricane center
20. Dance or water
22. Tiny particle
23. Passenger
25. Blue
26. Half of two
27. Stump remover
29. Rose or Seeger
31. TV host Sajak
32. Before, in verse
37. Drink daintily
39. Worshiped
41. Bowler hat
43. Pie ____ mode
44. Pastrami shop
45. Actor Guinness
46. Famous fiddler
48. Norway's capital
49. With a grain of ____
50. Alternative
53. Horse food
54. Self

PUZZLE 404

ACROSS

1. Pep
4. Finn's craft
8. Thaw
12. Cider girl
13. Once more
14. In charge of
15. Mesh fabric
16. Still
17. In order
18. Crates
20. Barely warm
22. Compete
24. Pearl gatherers
27. "The grass is always ____ . . ."
31. Magic lamp dweller
32. Youngster
33. Hunting dog, for short
35. Camp bed
36. Keen
39. Thinga-majigs
42. Iron-on pictures
44. "You ____ There"
45. Assumed name
47. Force
51. Price
53. Flower holder
55. Poem
56. Unfenced
57. Easily bruised items
58. Barbie's guy
59. Prove
60. Take an apartment
61. To the bitter ____

DOWN

1. ____ oxide
2. Brainstorm
3. Butter servings
4. Cereal fruit
5. Plus
6. Thick wool
7. Suit fabric
8. Reason
9. Proof
10. Guided
11. Have a go at
19. Actress Arden
21. ____ out (overeat)
23. Snakelike fish
25. Uprising
26. Puts
27. Happy
28. Compete
29. Teaches
30. Tatter
34. Meadow sound
37. Skill
38. Actor Wallach
40. Most arid
41. Treasure
43. Pack rat
46. Stuffing herb
48. Jab
49. First garden
50. Advance, as money
51. Spoil
52. Mimic
54. Cain, to Adam

PUZZLE 405

ACROSS

1. Sky color
5. Donations for the poor
9. ___ mitzvah
12. Flees
13. Travel by clipper
14. Fuss
15. Pupil site
16. Spent lavishly
18. Parking lot device
20. Andean nation
21. Aspects
23. Sprint
27. The old college ___
30. Lass's mate
31. Venetian road
32. Accumulated
34. Sovereigns
35. Vex
36. Typewriter key
37. Itty-bitty
38. Roused
39. Old-fashioned
41. Brunch, e.g.
43. Divans
47. Collar smudge
51. Crisp, filled tortilla
52. "___ to a Nightingale"
53. Mystery solver's aid
54. Repeat
55. Cooking vessel
56. Sacred song
57. Perceived

DOWN

1. Upper edge
2. Fishing decoy
3. Squadron
4. Dangerous curves
5. Ninny
6. Drank like a kitten
7. Murphy Brown's boss
8. Speak indistinctly
9. Purse
10. Hoosier humorist
11. Lightning attractor
17. Rustic
19. James Whitcomb ___
22. Pop
24. Again
25. Part of TLC
26. You're something ___!
27. Melt
28. Divorce city
29. Pull sharply
31. Certain solids
33. Works by Browning
34. Hamelin pest
36. Perfumed powder
39. Morning paper
40. Is overfond
42. Imprint firmly
44. "___ the Nation"
45. Dull pain
46. Shortly
47. Prune
48. Boise's state: abbr.
49. Fountain ___
50. Actor Olin

PUZZLE 406

ACROSS

1. Light on radar screen
5. Writing instrument
8. Move through the air
11. Helper
12. Grow old
13. Ohio Indian
14. Finely sharpened
15. Line of seats
16. Intend
17. Makes into a statute
19. Reduces gradually
21. Charged particle
22. Use a chair
23. Expensive steak
27. Legendary stories
31. Skilled person
32. Young swine
34. Court
35. Splitting device
38. Roped
41. Affirmative vote
43. Was introduced to
44. Held responsible
47. Shelflike beds
51. Freedom from difficulty
52. Congeal
54. Diva's forte
55. Snow runners
56. Sooner than, poetically
57. Caution
58. "____ and Sympathy"
59. Down in the dumps
60. Moved quickly

DOWN

1. Use an oven
2. Property claim
3. Concept
4. Lead-filled writing tool
5. White edible root
6. Freudian term
7. Salamanders
8. Without charge
9. Fibber
10. Craves
13. Containing nothing
18. Furthermore
20. Goal
23. Maxim
24. Solid water
25. Blushing color
26. Naught
28. Duet number
29. Soil-breaking tool
30. Turf
33. Played for money
36. Amusements
37. Potato bud
39. View
40. Drinking tubes
42. Borders
44. Most suitable
45. Huron, e.g.
46. India's continent
48. Golf hazard
49. Put on the payroll
50. Seashore material
53. Baseball stat

PUZZLE 407

ACROSS

1. John Wayne's nickname
5. Brush's counterpart
9. Vigor
12. Grandma Moses
13. Smell
14. Writer Levin
15. Limit food intake
16. Placed ahead
18. Takes the wheel
20. Prepare for publication
21. Deep grooves
23. Kind of egret or owl
26. Unobserved
28. Buffalo's lake
29. Gorilla
30. Pulls
33. Hotel
34. Misplaced
36. Public squares
38. Come in
40. Fodder tower
41. Starring role
43. Shops
47. Slicker
50. Dinner, e.g.
51. Ornamental vase
52. Brink
53. Or ____!
54. Plead
55. Shortly
56. ____-in-the-wool

DOWN

1. "My Two ____"
2. Segment
3. Joint
4. Restaurant patrons
5. Glider
6. Eccentric
7. Change position
8. Small nails
9. Actress Principal
10. Fury
11. Crazed
17. On cloud ____
19. Regretted
22. Ginger cookies
24. Triumphs
25. Hankering
26. Atop
27. Snuggling
29. Pub drink
31. Sparkle
32. Pepper's partner
35. High-schooler
37. Went rapidly
39. Marathons
42. Extinct bird
44. Depend
45. Alleviate
46. Winter toy
47. Massage
48. "Chances ____"
49. Time past

PUZZLE 408

ACROSS

1. Nuisance
5. Secret agent
8. Enrage
11. Tropical plant
12. Buckeye State
13. Vote against
14. Broad
15. Stink
16. Ascot
17. Crazy
19. Rely
21. Certain facial hair
25. "To ___ With Love"
26. Owned
27. Mideast nation
29. Strategy
32. Sooner, to Keats
33. Himalayan country
35. Flying saucer, for short
36. Look after
38. Extreme
39. Father
40. Index
42. Bureau parts
44. Profited
47. Citrus cooler
48. Curve
49. Tidy
51. Dawdles
55. Baltic or Black
56. Gentle
57. Queue
58. Sidekick
59. Foxy
60. Soot

DOWN

1. Fido's foot
2. Clockmaker Terry
3. Dirt
4. Swarms
5. That girl
6. ___ Piper
7. Teams of oxen
8. Pause
9. "Purple ___" (Prince film)
10. Looked at
12. Directed
18. Similar
20. Domino spot
21. Sharpen
22. Rabbit
23. ___ twin
24. Fast
28. Tell
30. Way off
31. Signals assent
34. Star
37. Aykroyd or Rather
41. Aptitudes
43. Water sources
44. Pant
45. Neighborhood
46. Bargain
50. Author Tan
52. Goal
53. Wildebeest
54. Harden

PUZZLE 409

ACROSS

1. Serpent
4. 4047 square meters
8. Flying pros
12. Gaming cube
13. Victim
14. PBS science series
15. Sudden onrush
17. Singer Campbell
18. As well
19. Flash of light
20. Short stories with messages
23. "Roses ____ Red"
24. Adjoin
25. Perform surgery
29. Off one's feed
30. Visorless cap
32. Young boy
33. Alleviate
35. Fuse metal
36. Maiden name word
37. Just
39. Turns aside
42. Inferno
43. Healing plant
44. Malicious pyromaniac
48. Confound
49. Begonia's beginning
50. Billiard stick
51. Verse maker
52. Classroom response
53. Vote type

DOWN

1. Classified items
2. Pose for a portrait
3. Green vegetable
4. Winesap, e.g.
5. Salad green
6. Decorate again
7. Aesthetic sense
8. Fisherman
9. Soft drink
10. Ceaselessly
11. Rational
16. Beer ingredient
19. Worry
20. Evenhanded
21. Ready, willing, and ____
22. Matador's foe
23. Tailless primate
25. Unrefined metal
26. Helm position
27. Lanky
28. Whirlpool
30. Honey producers
31. Actress Plumb
34. Dimple
35. Little bird
37. Penny pincher
38. Wear away
39. Stinging insect
40. Female voice
41. Licentious man
42. Gratis
44. Burnt wood
45. Frosty
46. Litigate
47. Oolong or pekoe

PUZZLE 410

ACROSS
1. Those people
5. Defeat
9. Use a shovel
12. Roof overhang
13. Not working
14. Period in history
15. Territory
16. New Jersey athletes
17. ____ Bernardino
18. Mirthful
20. Emptiness
22. Trunk cover
24. Recognize
25. Baby enclosure
29. Stage production
33. Lend an ____
34. Arrest
36. Carry with effort
37. Inquired
40. Parcel
43. Experiment site, briefly
45. Managed
46. Genteel
50. Brother's daughter
54. High card
55. Attired
57. Overcast
58. "____ Done Him Wrong"
59. Actress Raines
60. Wilderness walk
61. Very warm
62. ____-in-the-wool
63. Golf course mounds

DOWN
1. Sports group
2. Jack rabbit
3. Continuously
4. Annual publication
5. Storage container
6. Eve's home
7. Choir members
8. Tried
9. Lucy's love
10. Persia, today
11. Band
19. Bark sharply
21. That woman
23. Cozy room
25. Soup legume
26. ____ Palmas
27. Little Rock's state: abbr.
28. Afternoon rest
30. Pie ____ mode
31. Coffee cup
32. Ripen
35. Pub counter
38. Colonist Yale
39. Waltzed
41. Garbage receptacle
42. Chivalrous one
44. Stomach
46. Reckless
47. Resound
48. Yard units
49. Cartoon chipmunk
51. Toledo's lake
52. Birthday treat
53. "For Your ____ Only"
56. Mom's mate

PUZZLE 411

ACROSS
1. Balmy
5. Edge
8. Poet Angelou
12. Stink
13. ____ nutshell
14. Roasting chamber
15. Certain pasta
17. Greasy
18. Intimidate
19. Tennis player Ivan ____
21. Used a stool
23. Maiden
26. MacGraw of "Love Story"
27. Keats poem
28. October sign
32. Graven image
34. Arid
36. Small duck
37. Narrow paths
39. My stars!
41. Gone by
42. Earnest plea
44. Formerly named
45. Artificial waterway
47. Weaken
49. Exclusive
50. Comic strip caveman
55. Mischief-makers
56. Billiards stick
57. Swing singer Morse
58. Remainder
59. Quiche ingredient
60. Money or pearl

DOWN
1. Dad's mate
2. Ms. Lupino
3. Site
4. Deadlock
5. "Flying Down to ____"
6. Tavern
7. Sends, as a letter
8. Like some nights
9. Zealous
10. Shout
11. ____ day now
16. Modernize
20. Slippery as an ____
21. Jib, e.g.
22. Actor Alan ____
24. Total
25. Unite
29. Tall, lanky person
30. Fad
31. Sunburn soother
33. Most slender
35. Opposite of nay
38. Belgian resort
40. Different
43. "A ____ in the Sun"
45. Arrive
46. Swiss mountains
48. Pro votes
49. ____ Walter Scott
51. Cart
52. Journey part
53. Barcelona cheer
54. Shoulder enhancer

PUZZLE 412

ACROSS

1. Grand Coulee, e.g.
4. Black bird
8. Lure
12. Put to good ____
13. "Superman" reporter
14. Pilaf ingredient
15. Added spices
17. Last word in prayer
18. Eagle's claw
19. Make a dress
21. Tidings
24. Vigilant
28. Swindle
31. Edges
33. Blemish
34. Excitement
35. Spirit
36. Outrage
37. And not
38. Writing fluids
39. Three-way joint
40. Beaten path
42. Halt
45. Cunning
47. Spaghetti or fettuccini
51. Cry lustily
54. Monarchs
57. Fencer's weapon
58. Midday
59. Vain man
60. Fishing boat items
61. Female pigs
62. Commercials

DOWN

1. Fine powder
2. Totally confused
3. Repast
4. Replica
5. Rushed
6. Half a pair
7. Espouses
8. Barroom fight
9. Purpose
10. Cool cube
11. Sawbuck
16. Beau or Jeff, to Lloyd
20. Let up on
22. Small songbird
23. Descends gradually
25. Send forth
26. Hamburger order
27. Tall woody plant
28. "____ Smile Without You"
29. Fragrance
30. Ibsen woman
32. Fog
35. Fish feature
41. Cays
43. Unseals
44. Golf term
46. Desires
48. Couch
49. Walked on
50. Dangerous snakes
51. "Growing Pains" role
52. Gorilla
53. Soaked
55. Cow's sound
56. Explosive noise

PUZZLE 413

ACROSS

1. Scoop
4. Morse ____
8. Authentic
12. Nest egg letters
13. Ice pellets
14. Buffalo's lake
15. Save
17. Green gem
18. Join
19. Repeat
21. Sample
23. Suit maker
27. Hold title to
30. Gab
32. View
33. Competed
35. Crew
37. Corrodes
38. Fall flower
40. Fuel
42. Cook's vessel
43. "The Piano ____"
45. Pod vegetable
47. Baal
49. Obscure
53. Fragrance
56. Arrange systematically
58. Walk through water
59. Eternally
60. Sunbathe
61. Stared at
62. Copenhagen native
63. Bashful

DOWN

1. Chop
2. Press
3. Huff and puff
4. Red fruit
5. Rower's need
6. Seedy nightclub
7. Choose
8. Gladden
9. Baseball stat
10. Help
11. Singer Brenda ____
16. Congealed
20. Owns
22. Colorful tuber
24. Pounce
25. Aware of
26. Take a break
27. Elliptical
28. Savvy
29. Court dividers
31. Nail holder
34. Wanted
36. Forty winks
39. Angler's need
41. Safe
44. Famous
46. "____ in the Family"
48. Fluid rock
50. Horse food
51. Provo's state
52. Refuse
53. Be in the red
54. Doris or Dennis
55. "____ on a Grecian Urn"
57. Actor Kingsley

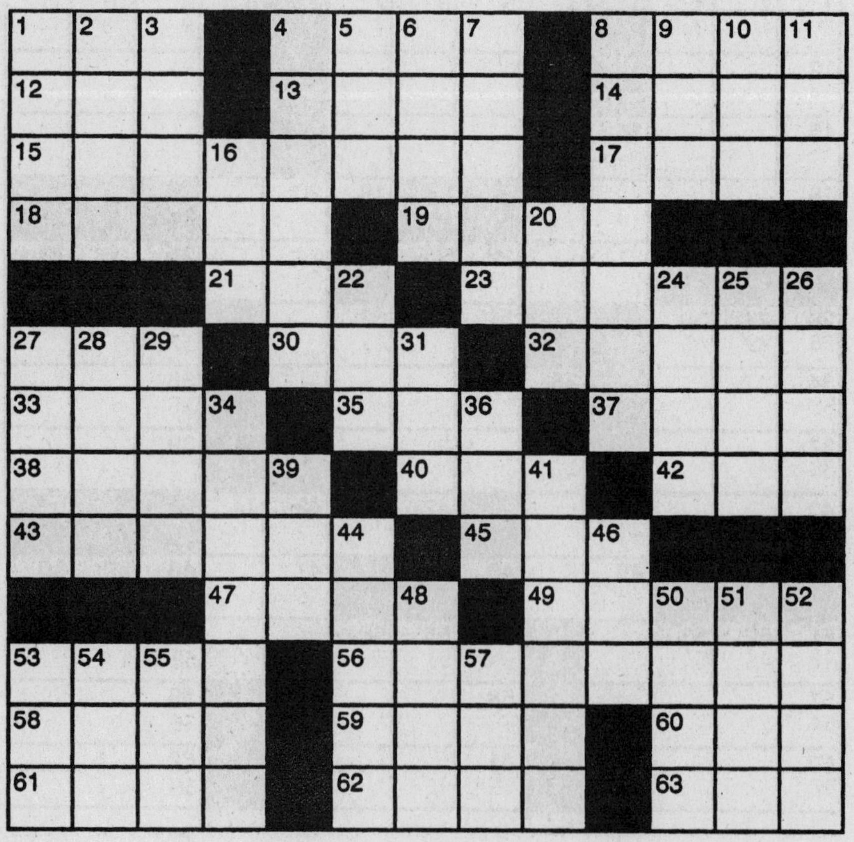

PUZZLE 414

ACROSS
1. Existed
4. Pillow cover
8. Cushions
12. Hops beverage
13. Bistro
14. Mine entrance
15. Beau or Jeff, to Lloyd
16. Study of stars
18. Flower part
20. Night before
21. Perfect
24. Dodge
28. "____ Softly to Me"
30. Listen to
32. Doze
33. King Kong, for one
34. Ship's crane
35. Singer Ho
36. Ballpoint or felt-tip
37. In the sack
38. Norm's wife, on "Cheers"
39. Record
41. Speed detector
43. Golly
45. Relative by marriage
48. Bachman-Turner ____
53. Anger
54. Blaze
55. Fail to include
56. Maiden name indicator
57. Three in a yard
58. Mineral springs
59. Ramble

DOWN
1. Stinging insect
2. Lily species
3. Opinion
4. Climb
5. Possesses
6. Fore's counterpart
7. Nothing more than
8. Wall section
9. Commotion
10. Faint
11. Piggery
17. Not concealed
19. Citrus beverage
22. Melville's captain
23. Crowbar
25. Subordinate
26. Gateway
27. Author Ferber
28. Sleeveless coat
29. Ready for business
31. Verdi character
34. Took a chance
38. Morrison of song
40. Heron
42. Food regimens
44. Cupid
46. Expanse
47. Garden invader
48. Not on
49. Contend
50. Before, in poetry
51. Little demon
52. By way of

PUZZLE 415

ACROSS

1. Recreational area
5. Sail support
9. Howl
12. Destroy
13. Aroma
14. Mine find
15. Formerly
16. Brown syrup
18. Precipitous
20. Lassos
21. Tempts
23. Facial features
26. Conflict
29. Pop
30. Skirt feature
31. Power
33. Yeltsin's country
34. Bait
35. Forbid
36. Attempt
37. Dog-paddled
38. Likewise
40. Master
42. Perplex
46. Denver's state
49. Genuine
50. Tavern fare
51. Hymn ending
52. Caviar
53. Sunburn shade
54. Nude
55. Take it easy

DOWN

1. Paid athletes
2. Female relative
3. Pilaf ingredient
4. Bow down
5. "Mr. ____"
6. Worshiped
7. Arias
8. Snare
9. Most domineering
10. "We ____ the World"
11. Of course!
17. Vends
19. Chubby
22. Sunbeam
24. Au ____ (nanny)
25. Stick around
26. Marries
27. Again
28. Remembered
30. Kicks
32. Juliet's love
33. Tattle
35. Notebook
38. Play
39. Weasellike swimmer
41. Sheik
43. Persuade
44. Coffee cups
45. Annoyance
46. Sedan
47. Flamenco cheer
48. Washington bill

PUZZLE 416

ACROSS

1. Belfry inhabitant
4. Golly
8. Marble slice
12. Hollywood's Gardner
13. Actress Moreno
14. Caesar's garb
15. Jumped the track
17. Ready for business
18. Was aware of
19. Lock of hair
20. Rip
23. Postpone
25. Let
27. Wipe gently
28. Select
31. Brief snooze
33. Widespread affliction
35. Lennon's wife
36. Vat
38. Deserves
39. "Full ____ Jacket"
41. Remainder
42. More senior
45. Actor Mostel
47. Tree's anchor
48. Rhythmic beats
52. Fit
53. Fury
54. Fearful reverence
55. Lascivious look
56. Baseball's Hershiser
57. Stroke

DOWN

1. Flawed
2. Madison or Park: abbr.
3. Roofing material
4. Wide smile
5. Lubricated
6. Simmered
7. Possessed
8. Anecdote
9. Easy gait
10. Ripens
11. Forbids
16. Ohio city
19. Dining surface
20. Mexican dish
21. Verve
22. Choir voice
24. Lick, like a dog
26. Irrigate
28. Mean monster
29. Plays on words
30. Try out
32. Place
34. Slugger Henry ____
37. Eastern market
39. Gauge
40. Sill
42. Type of exam
43. Ear part
44. Mete
46. Film spool
48. ____-Magnon
49. Beret, e.g.
50. Ram's mate
51. Matched group

PUZZLE 417

ACROSS

1. Register
4. Folding beds
8. Sprinted
12. Shock
13. Table spread
14. Protagonist
15. Insisted
17. Bridle part
18. Caesar's date
19. Longs for
20. Din
23. Costa del ____, Spain
24. Sunbeams
25. Expression of regret
29. Tennis term
30. Foot lever
32. Constrictor
33. Meaning
35. Drench
36. Tango's need
37. Vinegar vessels
39. World carrier
42. Abel's brother
43. Trench ____
44. Haughty
48. Eternal city
49. Competition
50. Fawn's mom
51. Supplemented
52. Caresses
53. Have

DOWN

1. Youth
2. Be in the red
3. Sapphire, e.g.
4. Apartment
5. More mature
6. Casual shirts
7. Turf
8. Piercing
9. Hammer part
10. Pennsylvania port
11. Knotts and Rickles
16. Points
19. Billiards
20. Stuff
21. Frilly trim
22. Yes votes
23. Baden-Baden, e.g.
25. Summer refresher
26. Woodwind
27. Ruminant
28. Gabs
30. Furry feet
31. Conceit
34. Uttered
35. Warbled
37. Insertion mark
38. Public disorders
39. Farm unit
40. Stole
41. Ornate fabric
42. Northern Indian
44. Current measure, for short
45. Fuss
46. Immediately
47. Hamilton bill

PUZZLE 418

ACROSS

1. Not cooked
4. Territory
8. Quick
12. Manipulate
13. Floral necklaces
14. Irritate
15. Cinemas
17. Notion
18. Strong wind
19. Poppy and sesame
20. Lid
23. Pleasure
24. Poems
25. Food fish
29. Buck's mate
30. Paces
32. Honey maker
33. Missions
35. Shoe part
36. Gloomy
37. Hex
38. Poet Robert ____
41. Sycamore, e.g.
43. Solitary
44. Large stones
48. "____ the Rainbow"
49. Jelly ____ Morton
50. Nautical response
51. Annoyance
52. Brewery products
53. Suit to a ____

DOWN

1. Furrow
2. ____ Wednesday
3. Diminutive
4. Church table
5. Film spool
6. Irish republic
7. Donkey
8. Pal
9. Military assistant
10. Toboggan
11. Oriental beverages
16. Matures
19. Lather
20. Morse ____
21. Aroma
22. Swerve
23. Plump
25. Towel word
26. Woodwind
27. Prison unit
28. Ship's centerboard
30. Tiny fly
31. Attach
34. Affirm
35. Raced
37. Retails
38. Fiasco
39. Drift
40. Smallest bills
41. Instrument
42. Reign
44. Bikini part
45. Have lunch
46. Deli bread
47. Understand

PUZZLE 419

ACROSS

1. Butter portion
4. Canine comment
7. Transmit
11. Sherbet
12. Fish bait
14. Beseech
15. Tot's game
17. Weak, as an excuse
18. Before
19. Made fun of
21. Tacked on
24. Portable beds
25. Skinny
26. Grove
30. Nosh
31. Wet snow
33. Director Spike ____
34. Saltine, e.g.
36. Actor Alda
37. Suggestion
38. Land of the Pharaohs
39. Runways
42. Hatchet
43. Crude metals
44. Signed up
49. Go on horseback
50. Perches
51. Author Levin
52. Wrench or hammer
53. Kettle
54. Snoop

DOWN

1. Small seed
2. Expert
3. Football stand
4. Prize
5. Judge's garb
6. To and ____
7. Daryl Hannah film
8. Epochs
9. Title
10. Changed colors
13. Engines
16. Sharp
20. Engrave
21. Actor Guinness
22. Cherished
23. Information
24. Woo
27. Comrade
28. Harvest
29. Fender bender mark
31. Hop, ____, and a jump
32. Contact ____
35. Sculptor's device
36. Grows older
38. Have being
39. Type
40. Threesome
41. Update
42. Choir voice
45. Bite
46. Point
47. Go astray
48. Doris or Dennis

PUZZLE 420

ACROSS

1. Notable time
4. Young cow
8. Surpasses
12. Replacement, for short
13. Opera solo
14. Wicked
15. Headstrong
17. California wine valley
18. Clamor
19. Capital of Oregon
20. Not fastened
22. Writing implement
23. Wander
24. Meteorologist's concern
28. Rifle or pistol
29. Leaks
31. Summer drink
32. Name
34. Very dry
35. Water barrier
36. Rides the air
38. Appraiser
41. Swap
42. Lamb's pseudonym
43. Gifts
46. Plummeted
47. Ceremony
48. Moray or conger
49. Notices
50. Actor Sharif
51. "One ____ at a Time"

DOWN

1. Dangerous curve
2. Boring routine
3. Plentiful
4. Log structure
5. Got up
6. Italian money, once
7. Ventilating device
8. Resident
9. Egg-shaped
10. Smoking device
11. Bang
16. Flourish
19. Oceans
20. Egg on
21. Part of speech
22. Energy
24. Tiny
25. Congealed
26. Singer Adams
27. Cincinnati nine
29. Celebrity
30. Nightmare street of film
33. High standards
34. Assistant
36. Actress Garbo
37. Surgical light beam
38. Umps
39. Toward shelter
40. Floor covering
41. Slim
43. In favor of
44. Oolong or pekoe
45. Crafty

PUZZLE 421

ACROSS

1. Insect
4. Zone
8. Quote
12. Dollar
13. Christmas
14. Chess piece
15. Moral wrong
16. Hairstyling aids
17. Poker bet
18. "____ Magnolias"
20. Group
22. Morning moisture
24. Bread ingredient
28. Smooth wood
31. Oriental staple
34. Untruth
35. Follow orders
36. Have being
37. Carbonated beverage
38. Pub drink
39. Unlock
40. Abound
41. Piano part
43. Couple
45. Image of worship
48. Kitchen garment
52. Supporting limbs
55. Accustomed
57. Actor Vigoda
58. Elliptical
59. Fencing blade
60. Cut the grass
61. Used to be
62. Doe
63. Domestic animal

DOWN

1. Supervisor
2. Part of a whole
3. Actor Hackman
4. Viewpoint
5. Fish eggs
6. Wiggly swimmers
7. Too
8. Wooden container
9. Charged particle
10. Small child
11. Squeak by
19. Whirlpool
21. Type of whiskey
23. Shawl
25. Succulent plant
26. "West ____ Story"
27. Lakers, e.g.
28. Sudsy substance
29. Qualified
30. Deficiency
32. Anger
33. Penny
37. Traffic sign
39. Ancient
42. Theater lane
44. Seltzer, e.g.
46. Was indebted to
47. Gait
49. Incline
50. Woodwind instrument
51. Salamander
52. Not high
53. Night before a holiday
54. Elongated fish
56. Born as

PUZZLE 422

ACROSS

1. Transparently thin
6. In front
11. Greeting
12. Films
14. Fragrance
15. Green gem
17. Officer
18. Monarch
20. Author Tolstoy
21. Understood
23. Title of respect
24. Sports competition
25. Neighborhood
27. Audacity
28. Rated
31. Flipped, as a coin
32. Resided
33. Moistens
34. Poetic works
35. Male heir
36. Three feet
40. Actor Vereen
41. Highlanders
43. Mr. Gehrig
44. Exploded
46. Sedates
48. Peaceful
49. Take on as one's own
50. Planted
51. Full of information

DOWN

1. Hut
2. Long-legged bird
3. Wed on the run
4. Shade tree
5. Bellow
6. Aviator Earhart
7. "Iliad" poet
8. Always
9. Melody
10. Merchants
13. Garment part
16. Was overly fond
19. Secondhand
22. Walks in water
24. Untidy
26. Ruby
27. Believe it or ___
28. Orb
29. Passengers
30. Streets
31. Camper's shelter
33. Covered with trees
35. Landscape
37. Let
38. Frolics
39. Powdery
41. Goulash
42. Read hastily
45. Expert
47. Fruit drink

PUZZLE 423

ACROSS

1. Society page word
4. Sends forth
9. Top pilots
13. Rows
15. Indian princess
16. Poi ingredient
17. Greer Garson film
19. Despot
20. Whole
21. Arbitrate
23. Sample
26. Sphere
27. Insane
30. Fights
32. Bridge expert Culbertson
33. Muzzles
35. Exclamation of triumph
37. North Pole worker
38. Deputy: abbr.
40. Thanksgiving dessert
41. Zilch
42. Red or Black
43. Painting surface
45. Auditor: abbr.
46. Agave fiber
48. Batter's place
52. Decay
53. Evade
54. Merchant vessel
58. Car shelter
62. Turkish regiment
63. Bing Crosby film
66. Comedian Foxx
67. Uncanny
68. Wash
69. Ottoman governors
70. Large antelope
71. Affirmative answer

DOWN

1. Alaska city
2. Deserve
3. Formerly, of old
4. Author Hemingway
5. ____ tai
6. Bill: abbr.
7. Swarm
8. Dry
9. Apparel
10. Humphrey Bogart film
11. Quod ____ demonstrandum
12. Tender
14. Strike hard
18. Persia, today
22. Drench
24. Camping shelters
25. Old Tokyo
27. Frances and Ruby
28. Model Macpherson et al.
29. Audrey Hepburn film
30. "Agnus ____"
31. Transports
34. Thread holder
36. Winglike expansions
38. Playing marble
39. Thicken
44. Haggard novel
47. Cubes, e.g.
49. Grimaced
50. Mild cheese
51. Green mineral
54. Dress
55. Sheltered
56. Double curve
57. Carol
59. Out
60. Donated
61. Peepers
64. Tax shelter: abbr.
65. Diarist Anais ____

PUZZLE 424

ACROSS

1. "Married to the ____"
4. Forest measure
8. Prayer ending
12. Reverence
13. Twofold
14. Mountain hollow
15. Dawn moisture
16. Encourage
17. Works by Keats
18. Lazy
20. Mother or father
22. Apportion
24. Lower face part
25. Ocean movement
26. Close loudly
27. Lemon drink
30. Singletons
31. Sunbather's goal
32. Surrounded by
33. ____ capita
34. Sand
35. Highway division
36. Baseball feature
37. Consumed
38. Occur
41. Foundation
42. Emerald ____
43. Equipment
45. ____ and downs
48. Tilt
49. Corrupt
50. Knock smartly
51. Country
52. Depend
53. Cunning

DOWN

1. Furious
2. Be in debt
3. Perplex
4. Mature
5. Heal
6. Dustcloth
7. Dumbo, e.g.
8. Squirrel's treat
9. Created
10. Equal
11. Birdhouse structure
19. Accom- plishes
21. Intention
22. On the apex
23. Draw the ____
24. Assertion
26. Outsider
27. Novices
28. Enjoy a banquet
29. Genesis garden
32. Woeful word
34. ____ whiz!
36. Pay out
37. Ahead of time
38. Road incline
39. Confused
40. Strategy
41. Suspect's release money
44. Christmas ____
46. Buddy
47. Secret agent

PUZZLE 425

ACROSS

1. Wine valley
5. Meeting plan
11. Camel's-hair coat
14. Actor Bates
15. Chestnut
16. ____ Yutang
17. Limited thinking
20. Of South American mountains
21. Quenches
22. Memorize
23. Sharp point
26. With an ____
27. Western plant
30. Hoopla
33. Ryan and Dunne
34. "____ on Down the Road"
38. Stubborn
40. Gleam
42. Oppositionist
43. Twitted
45. Country hotel
46. Leased
49. Military cap
52. Unhappy
53. Got up
57. Downy ducks
59. Smoothed
60. Obsesses
64. ____ Aviv
65. Poetess Wylie
66. Official deeds
67. Opposite of NNW
68. Voiced
69. Bodies of water

DOWN

1. Twangy
2. Straighten
3. Bearlike animal
4. Maddens
5. Hymn finish
6. Hood's weapon
7. Be wrong
8. Blue Eagle inits.
9. Medics
10. Tarsi
11. Similar
12. IQ name
13. "____ to bed"
18. Hawaiian porches
19. Commotion
23. Wavers
24. ____ Saud
25. Compelled
28. Actress Garbo
29. Theater seater
30. Eureka!
31. ____ Cupid
32. Table scrap
35. Friend: Fr.
36. Japanese coin
37. Sea eagle
39. Shirt front
41. High hopes
44. ____ loss
47. Steeds
48. Plays
49. Irish clans
50. Employs
51. Ms. Astaire
54. In abeyance
55. Actress Berger
56. Norse myths
58. Alone
59. Saucy
61. Writer Anais ____
62. Stop ____ dime
63. ____ compos mentis

PUZZLE 426

ACROSS

1. Easy task
5. Blue or news
10. Obstruct
14. Pueblo Indian
15. Seed anew
16. Italian river
17. Auditory
18. 10th-century emperor
19. Durocher and Gorcey
20. Afternoon break in Kent
22. Rascality
24. Baseball official
25. Falsehood
26. Saw-toothed
30. Patio
34. Revoke
35. Martin and Jones
37. Milit. rank
38. Ascots
39. Hoes
40. Hotness
41. Under the weather
42. Bandleader Shaw
43. Parsonage
44. Snuggles
46. Miser
48. Arab garment
49. Awesome, dude
50. Male felines
54. Kitchen item
58. Rumlike drink: var.
59. Marble man
61. Actor Lincoln
62. Racetrack fence
63. Rajah's wife
64. Author Uris
65. French pronoun
66. Dazzles
67. Kind of devil

DOWN

1. Kaput
2. Memo
3. Samoan port
4. Paintings
5. Punctual
6. Network
7. Devotee: suff.
8. Cranny's partner
9. Kind of camera
10. Serving tray
11. Banyan, e.g.
12. ____ about
13. Carnation
21. Muslim priest
23. Affectations
26. Rich cloth
27. Roman magistrate
28. Lively dances
29. Makes revisions
30. Rumors
31. Representative
32. Discontinue
33. Enroll
36. Clockmaker Terry
39. Tab payers
40. Camera type
42. Duchess of ____
43. Farrow et al.
45. Gridiron ploy
47. Groups of three
50. Weed
51. Of the mouth
52. Post
53. Wood strip
54. Ich ____, motto of Prince of Wales
55. ____-bargain
56. Cupid
57. Not any
60. Wildebeeste

PUZZLE 427

ACROSS
1. Lab fluid
5. Make small talk
9. Scottish hillsides
14. Colt's mama
15. Routine
16. Weird
17. Prayer ending
18. Black, to a poet
19. Russian kings
20. Dispatched
21. ____ a plea
22. Fence crossings
23. Horse-drawn winter vehicles
25. Walk through mire
26. Actress Lyon
27. Justice
31. Bed boards
34. Country
35. Red on a traffic light
36. Lend an ____
37. Stored up
40. Paddle
41. Bargain-event term
43. Competes
44. Pocket linen
46. Breaks, as a mirror
48. Snoopy or Sandy
49. Scores, in baseball
50. Laments
54. Essences
57. Feel poorly
58. "Pumping ____"
59. Wading bird
60. Poker stake
61. California wine region
62. Traffic sign
63. Resist temptation
64. Gait
65. German steel city
66. Otherwise
67. Hardy heroine

DOWN
1. Accumulate
2. Dromedary
3. Goodnight girl
4. Plaque-fighting man
5. Nativity scene
6. Tramps
7. Spin like ____
8. Little Indians count
9. Gambler
10. Gives up a job
11. Asian lake
12. Republic of Ireland
13. Meeting: abbr.
22. Playground chute
24. Pour forth
25. Singer Tommy ____
27. Bus fees
28. British school
29. Drench
30. Agile
31. The seven ____
32. Flog
33. Leontyne's song
34. Lions' resting places
38. Oasts
39. Arabian boat
42. Flaky
45. Opposing
47. Soup dish
48. Remove from print
50. Tastes
51. Angry
52. Slow gallops
53. Breaks
54. Highest point
55. Very, to Pierre
56. Sea dogs
57. Blue dye
60. Cooling drink

PUZZLE 428

ACROSS

1. Defeat
5. Courtier in "Hamlet"
10. Jones or Martin
14. Cupid
15. Office worker
16. Motionless
17. Current
18. Barbarian of film
19. Author unknown: abbr.
20. Criterion
22. Staid
24. Essence
25. Tender
26. Airy
29. Harm
34. Retard
36. Minstrel's instrument
37. By birth
38. Drones
39. German poet
41. Principal
42. Single
43. Shipshape
44. Prevents
46. Remedied
49. Not as good
50. Aspiration
51. Writer Waugh
53. Riviera wear
56. Playfully
60. Norse god
61. Actress Ekberg
63. Neighbor-hood
64. Gambling city
65. Forty-____
66. Unpleasantly moist
67. Complains
68. Coasters
69. Discontinues

DOWN

1. Louisville sluggers
2. Issue
3. Cracker or fountain
4. Ditches
5. Acting award
6. Laid away
7. Tear apart
8. Actress Claire
9. Associated
10. Crown
11. Writer Ferber
12. Thanks ____
13. Bird of Hawaii
21. Morse elements
23. New York canal
25. Overwhelm
26. Work
27. Goddess of peace
28. Avarice
30. Choice group
31. Enroll
32. Approaches
33. Succinct
35. Troupers
40. Lessen
41. Military prison
43. Sign gas
45. Maas that baa
47. African mammals
48. Sped
52. Truth changers
53. "____ Free"
54. Thought
55. Kong of the jungle
56. Penalty
57. OPEC member
58. Furnish
59. Wild oxen
62. Nothing

PUZZLE 429

ACROSS

1. Moiety
5. Sharpen, as a razor
10. Oodles
14. Russian mountain
15. Bouquet
16. Great Lake
17. Very small
18. Infant at a pool
19. Domesticated
20. Morose
21. Flower plot
22. Snuggled
24. Black suit
27. Take legal action
28. Confronted
30. Beet color
32. Printing machine
36. Juice fruit
38. Immediately
40. Use scissors
41. Policeman
42. Maddened
45. Turn right, Dobbin!
46. Employed
48. Polka ____
49. Pattern
51. Family car
53. Snyder or Brown
55. Languished
56. Acquired
58. ____ control
60. Playbill
64. Ignited
65. Double curve
68. Affection
69. Turning point
71. Tuneful threesome
72. Declare positively
73. Omit in pronunciation
74. Man of valor
75. Cravings
76. Make laugh
77. Paradise

DOWN

1. Shanties
2. Opera solo
3. Improved a lawn
4. Go on a jet
5. Cut wood
6. Stockbroker
7. Actor Steiger
8. Foretoken
9. Peels
10. Alphabet symbols
11. Verbal
12. "As ____ Goes By"
13. Kernel
21. Insignia
23. Have an evening meal
25. Writing tool
26. Ted Kennedy, for one
28. Adjust a camera
29. Came forth
31. Terrier, for one
33. Contrived artfully
34. Prolonged attack
35. Lay out money
37. Finish
39. Marry
43. Decay
44. Railway station
47. Sharp weapons
50. Perch
52. And not
54. Tune
57. Records
59. Small insects
60. "____ It Again, Sam"
61. Wander
62. Baking chamber
63. Grinding machine
66. Father
67. Directly
70. By way of
71. Article

PUZZLE 430

ACROSS
1. Bear's hideout
5. Gaucho's rope
10. Spill the beans
14. Summit
15. Bitter-____ (diehard)
16. Russian river
17. Assay
18. Sour
19. Shake-speare's river
20. Flightless bird
22. Truant
24. Syn.'s opposite
25. Youngster
26. Masked mammal
30. Cause ____
34. Touch
35. Strictness
37. Small amount
38. Wager
39. ____ out (renege)
40. "Where the Boys ____"
41. Helm position
43. Pumps
45. Legal claim
46. Wood-eating insect
48. ____ highway
50. Put to work
51. Prattle
52. Church dignitary
56. Came in
60. Distinctive air
61. La ____ (opera house)
63. Acclaim
64. Debt voucher
65. Window type
66. Very: Fr.
67. Willow or walnut
68. Artists' subjects
69. Tug

DOWN
1. Roman patriot
2. Copies
3. Waistcoat
4. Pull out
5. Atomic device
6. Move slowly
7. Summer quaff
8. Semester
9. Judge
10. Dynamited
11. Son of Jacob
12. Soon
13. Big ____ theory
21. Sea goddess
23. Mr. Hurok
26. Moroccan city
27. White poplar
28. Prettier
29. Recess
30. Managed
31. Interweave
32. Street show
33. Correct, as texts
36. Sticky stuff
42. Imitate
43. Texan's hat
44. Traffic lights, e.g.
45. Freedom
47. "Rose ____ rose . . ."
49. Large tub
52. Treaty
53. German district
54. Eastern canal
55. Beige color
56. General Robert ____
57. ____ avis
58. Tied
59. Rolltop
62. Live or first

PUZZLE 431

ACROSS

1. To and ____
4. Shock
9. Grand Coulee, e.g.
12. My mistake!
14. Possessor
15. Auction
16. Lost
17. "____ Barbara"
18. Robert ____
19. Deserve
21. Christmas figure
23. Witch town
25. Resound
26. Poems
28. Chore
32. Eternally
35. Page
38. Like a beaver
39. Male sheep
40. List
42. Sooner than, poetically
43. Korean, for one
45. Distance measure
46. Boast
47. Make a home
49. ____ duck
51. Camper's need
53. Highway divisions
56. Splashes
61. Office copies
63. Newsman Sevareid
64. Departs
66. Bad
67. Peril
68. Proportions
69. Descartes
70. Ruler: abbr.
71. Breaks suddenly
72. Normal: abbr.

DOWN

1. Froth
2. "The Subject Was ____"
3. Verdi work
4. Distress call
5. "____ the night before . . ."
6. Singer Moffo
7. Bind again
8. Medium's state
9. Surrealist artist
10. Actor Guinness
11. Unassuming
13. Tar
15. Married woman: Sp.
20. Actor Bessell
22. Crowd number
24. Dissolve
27. Appear
29. Curing chemical
30. Roman despot
31. Sketched
32. Epochs
33. Urn
34. Give out
36. Friend, to Francois
37. Complete
40. Estuary
41. Ardor
44. Charge
46. Core
48. Puts in a ledger
50. Pas' partners
52. Man from Austin
54. Roof parts
55. Limit unduly
56. Withered
57. Prudish
58. Speech impediment
59. Actress Hayworth
60. Pace
62. Toboggan
65. Induction initials

PUZZLE 432

ACROSS
1. Mineral springs
5. Literary collection
8. Neighbor of Cambodia
12. Agreement
13. Singer Falana
15. South American mountains
17. Tolstoy's Karenina
18. "____ Old Cowhand"
19. Tour of duty
20. ____ -do-well
21. Grandmas, to some
23. Winds up
24. Now and ____
26. Jewels
28. Mixes
30. Opera song
31. Poisonous snake
34. Goatees' locales
35. Tarkenton et al.
36. Education gp.
37. Put up, as a picture
38. Thin mud
39. Horse gait
40. Assoc.
41. Actress Martha et al.
42. Musical groups
43. Tiny
44. Waiters' rewards
45. Bombard
46. Actor Lugosi
47. Originate
48. Western alliance: abbr.
51. Maliciousness
53. Tattle
57. Actress Dunne
59. Eternally
60. Solitary
61. Grows wan
62. Speak wildly
63. Long periods
64. ____ Trueheart
65. Modern: pref.
66. Locale

DOWN
1. Bridge
2. Window glass
3. Complexion woe
4. Commencing
5. Straightens
6. "____ is an island"
7. Actor Alda
8. ____ Vegas
9. Pot fillers
10. Norse god
11. Transport
14. Word scrambles
16. Rds.
22. French river
25. Time units: abbr.
27. Pas' spouses
28. Portion
29. Faint coloration
30. Zodiac ram
31. "____ in Paris"
32. Barroom perch
33. Butter portions
34. Food, informally
35. Adhesive trap
38. Goes to sea
39. Shakes
41. Map line: abbr.
42. Definite article
45. Sound equipment
46. Make no ____ about it
47. Comic Martin
48. Small bite
49. I smell ____!
50. Prefix with vision or phone
52. Tennis's Lendl
54. Circle
55. ____ Domini
56. Top
58. Curvy letter

PUZZLE 433

ACROSS

1. Hullabaloo
5. Quick
9. Speechify
10. Queues
12. Foolishness
13. Stadiums
15. Writing tablet
16. Apportion
18. Moves stealthily
20. Pub drinks
22. Camper's shelter
23. Kingly
24. Skin openings
26. Profound
28. Sandwich shop
29. Respond
31. Uppish one
33. NYC summer hours
34. Lose one's footing
36. Ooze
38. "My Mother the ___"
41. Golf cry
43. Taunted
47. Filled with wonder
49. Sports group
51. Inane
52. Fray, as threads
54. Loyal
56. Ore-deposit vein
57. Hemingway's forte
58. Come in
60. Marry
61. XI
63. More hackneyed
65. Fashion
66. Downy duck
67. Ball holders
68. Actress Donna ___

DOWN

1. Part of TGIF: abbr.
2. Mt. Etna's yield
3. Inclined
4. Rang
5. Knocks down
6. Atmosphere
7. Derisive look
8. Took care of
9. Commands
11. Drooped
12. Claw
14. Closes tightly
15. Mama's mate
17. Change for a five
19. Skirt feature
21. Bastes
25. Ego
27. Bard
30. Mob scene
32. Busy insects
35. Feigns
37. Bucket
38. Find fault
39. Cognizant
40. Uprising
42. Merit
44. More snaillike
45. Senior
46. Colored
48. Gobi, for one
50. Grumble
53. Embankment
55. Uncanny
59. Go on horseback
62. Chemical suffix
64. Rocker Nugent

PUZZLE 434

ACROSS

1. Rope fiber
5. Tear
10. Begone!
14. Mideast bigwig
15. String along
16. ____ and hearty
17. Run for Coe
18. Enthusiastic
19. "Pumping ____"
20. Corks
22. Washed lightly
24. Lends a hand
25. Diamond source
26. Rejects
29. Rear entrance
33. Melodies
34. Rawboned
35. Fib
36. Like the Sahara
37. Spares
38. Scrabble piece
39. Go on pension: abbr.
40. Salad utensils
41. Did a half gainer
42. Memento
44. Furnishes food
45. Scottish girl
46. Harbor
47. Go
50. Railroad employee
54. "Once ____ a time . . ."
55. Boo-boo
57. Gown
58. Simple
59. Turnpikes
60. Singer Fitzgerald
61. Pollinators
62. Feel intuitively
63. "The ____ Hunter"

DOWN

1. Corny actors
2. Radiate
3. Venus de ____
4. Boned up
5. Spirited horses
6. Listens
7. From ____ to riches
8. Opposite of WNW
9. Oil-well towers
10. Polished
11. Hatchbacks, e.g.
12. Medicinal plant
13. Baby-sit
21. Bowlers' targets
23. Black
25. Hefty tresses
26. ____ raving mad
27. Processor's output
28. Join
29. River boat
30. Kalamata, for one
31. Tank ship
32. Orchestra section
34. Golf course
37. Pop-up appliances
38. Snickered
40. Autocratic ruler
41. "Wait Until ____"
43. Carpenters' tools
44. Unrefined
46. Urges
47. Stupid
48. Fencing sword
49. Skin opening
50. Wheat husk
51. Tunneler
52. Competent
53. Close
56. Caviar

PUZZLE 435

ACROSS

1. Role for Dustin Hoffman
5. Yokemates
9. Heroic tale
13. Gush
17. Healing shrub
18. New Delhi princess
19. Zing
20. Gulch
21. Revolving server
23. Self-control
25. Get melodramatic
26. Advantage
28. Cheer
29. Arctic abundance
30. Montana tribe
31. Encircle
32. Like
35. Blacktop
36. She, in Toledo
37. Health spot
40. Cookie-jar filler
43. Kojak's candy
45. And so on: abbr.
46. Connect
47. Not hers
48. Guideline
49. In a chair
51. Sister's superior
54. Geologic samples
55. Came out on top
57. Galley blade
58. Sweater material
60. First appearance
63. Worn down
66. Victorian fashion
70. Wotan
71. Badge metal
72. Cay
74. ___ and cry
75. '70s singer
78. Bird's game
81. Pulver, for one: abbr.
82. Border lake
83. Schulz character
84. They give a hoot
85. Author Hunter
86. Seed coverings
87. Spring mo.
89. Talisman
92. "Swan Lake" costume
93. Astonish
97. Kansas crop
99. Earth mover
101. ___ spumante
102. Lurch
103. Great Barrier Island
104. Fairy-godmother's stick
105. Peasant
106. Craves
107. Breaking story
108. Mexican miss: abbr.

DOWN

1. Angel's hat
2. Norwegian king
3. Exude
4. Pocket item
5. Cease-fire
6. Side of Manhattan
7. Santa ___
8. Roman Athena
9. Thick fabric
10. Away from the wind
11. Motorist's buy
12. Busy place
13. Turf
14. Poker holding
15. Actress O'Brien
16. Among
22. Pouch
24. Rustic
27. Mysterious
30. Large showy flower
31. Lustrous
32. Precambrian and Paleozoic
33. Windy-day toy
34. Andes empire
35. Greek letter
36. Site of ancient Olympic games
37. Horse goad
38. Vault or bean
39. Gibraltar denizens
41. Bail out
42. Galloped
44. Does a pressing chore
47. ___ and now
50. Harass
52. Contribution
53. Like Leroy Brown
54. Dressing jar
56. Confine
59. Up to snuff
60. St. Paul's feature

61. Adam's orchard
62. Dressmaker's cut
64. Plentiful
65. Phonograph records
67. Soften
68. Soothe
69. Slippery customers
73. Limit height?
76. Flat
77. Speech-making
78. Dry
79. Ornithologist painter
80. Takes a loan
85. Small
86. Opposite of knits
87. African mountain range

PUZZLE 435

88. Travel on foot
89. Immediate inits.
90. Clio, Euterpe, or Thalia, e.g.
91. "Do ____ others . . ."
92. Prom attendee
93. Disposed of
94. Russian despot
95. Fasting period
96. Norse earth goddess
98. Like Willie Winkie
100. Colorado tribe

PUZZLE 436

ACROSS

1. Oriental sashes
5. Children's game
8. Macaws
12. Gouda's kin
16. Askew
17. Drink flavoring
18. Nests
19. Mother of Castor and Pollux
20. Columnist Barrett
21. Endorse
22. Leer
23. Pickle flavoring
24. Stiff
26. Have a repast
28. Abadan native
30. Palavers
34. Make esteemed
37. Speak
38. Fall blooms
40. Needlefish
41. Printer's instruction
43. "To ___ and a bone . . ." (Kipling)
45. Clip
46. Bridge support
48. Winter downpour
50. Aperture
53. Abundance
54. Any
55. Herd
58. Greek deity
60. Prattles
66. Look
67. Touches
68. Landed
70. Certain trains
73. Author Ludwig
75. Arrest
77. Dancer Moreno
78. "Cape ___"
80. Comedian Imogene ___
83. Blame
85. Dachshund's doc
86. Saloon
89. "The ___ Purple"
91. Just as much
93. Run off at the mouth
96. Under, poetically
97. Occupied the sofa
98. Supplied with oxygen
102. Actress Merrill
104. Hearty's mate
106. Similar
108. Actor Andrews
109. Spoken
110. Z ___ zebra
111. Mr. Chamberlain
112. Emerald Isle
113. Cheers
114. Magazine magnate
115. Early hours: abbr.
116. Motored

DOWN

1. Blades
2. Blemish
3. Island off Scotland
4. Thinly scattered
5. "___ Rose"
6. ___ mode
7. Merriest
8. One more
9. Equip
10. Impromptu
11. Mexico's ___ Madre
12. Fork-tailed hawks
13. Inhabitants
14. Cool drink
15. Picture frame
17. Associates
25. Lindbergh, for short
27. ___ girl!
29. Roman bronze
31. Instructors
32. Time spans
33. American lake
34. Support
35. Influential person
36. "Six Degrees of Separation" is one
39. Belgian city
42. Peculiar to a particular place
44. Funnyman Jackie ___
47. Confederate soldiers
49. Philanderer
51. Sun or moon
52. Craggy rock

PUZZLE 436

56. Life, in Lille
57. Supplements
59. Fly high
61. Honeyed insect?
62. Lunar vehicle
63. The bull: Sp.
64. Tapenade ingredient
65. See 12 Down
69. Wields a shuttle
70. Salamander
71. Rachel's sister
72. Georgia city
74. Moonstruck
76. Piquant
79. Discloses
81. Aquiescence
82. Seaweed
84. Rancid
87. Ireland's Lough ____
88. Son of King David
90. Canadian capital
92. Conductor
94. Sacred city of Lamaism
95. Brads
99. Hawaiian root
100. Camelot lady
101. Scandinavian
102. Click beetle
103. Author Wolfert
105. Fleur-de-____
107. Model Alexis

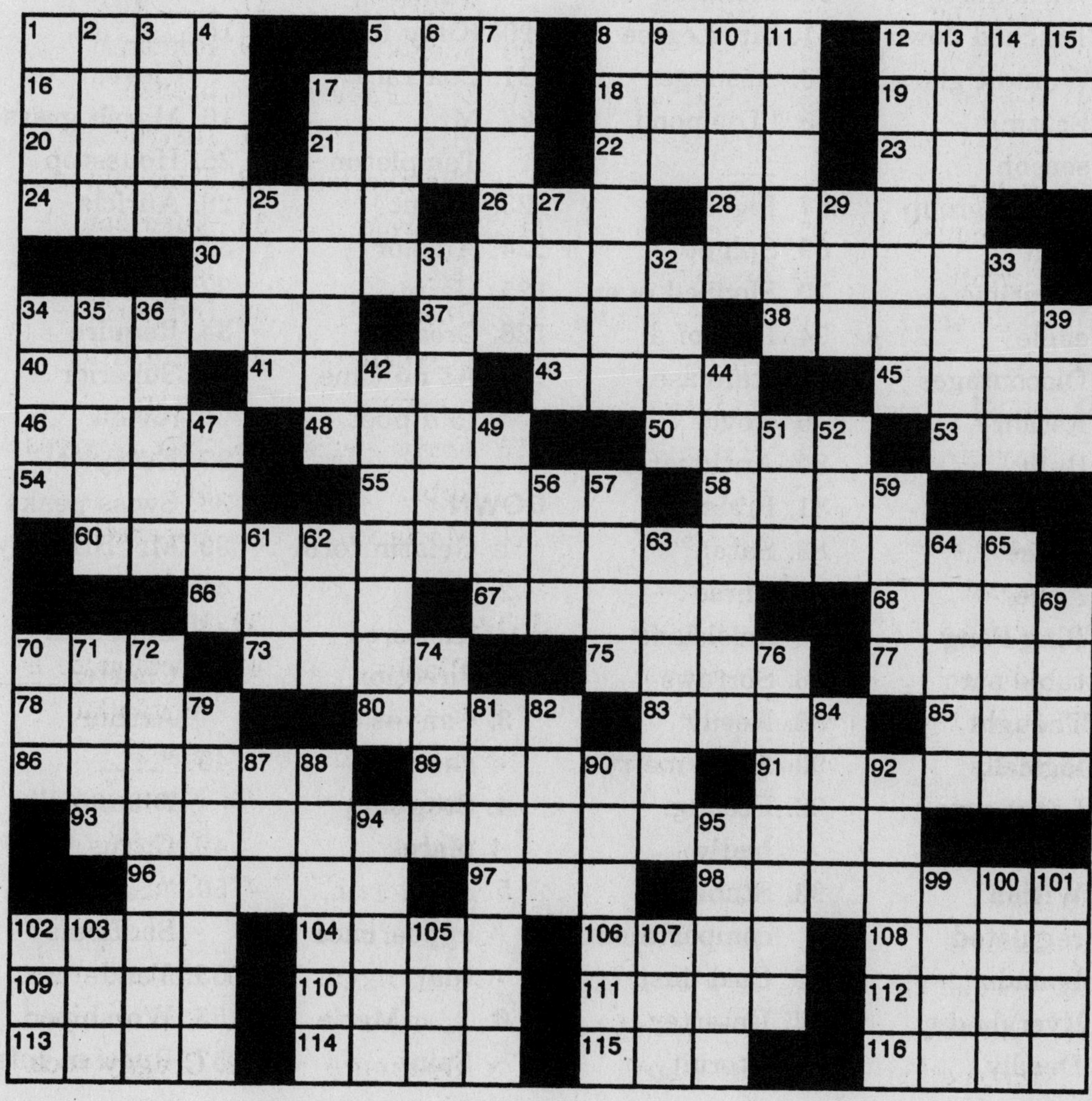

PUZZLE 437

ACROSS

1. Calculating subject
5. Special favorites
9. Corny actors
13. Hollywood luminary
17. Buttery substance
18. Wickedness
19. Touched down
20. Window glass
21. Fasting season
22. Ethnic group
23. Wan
24. Maritime eagle
25. Discourages
27. Retain
29. Built
31. Weaver's frame
33. Ache
35. Ping-Pong table part
36. Thought logically
40. Large coral head
42. Within regulated bounds
46. Everybody
47. Deadly
49. Large quantity
51. Part in a play
52. Celebrities: abbr.
54. Smooth
56. Food regimen
58. Remind constantly
59. Mollified
61. Mr. Legree
63. Assuages
65. "Diamond ____"
67. Pigeons
69. Spigot
70. Slopped over
74. Part of a staircase
76. Roves
80. Antiquated
81. Praise
83. Satan
85. Three musicians
86. Sorrows
88. Needy
90. Make merry
92. Feeling badly
93. Stable compartment
95. Coal dust
97. Deserter
99. Eternity
101. Chamber
103. Eat at eight
104. Published
108. Antlered deer
110. Attained
114. Split
115. Seasoning
117. Mild expletive
119. Greater amount
120. Kitty food
121. Coatrack
122. Mr. Templeton
123. Orient
124. Anchor
125. Germ
126. Created
127. At no time, to a poet

DOWN

1. Gelatin form
2. In a sheltered direction
3. Canvas shelter
4. Stopping places
5. ____-appearance tour
6. ____ Marie Saint
7. Woodland pest
8. Slumber
9. More content
10. Heart of Dixie: abbr.
11. "Walk a ____ in My Shoes"
12. Back of a ship
13. Ghost
14. Piquant
15. ____ of Cleves
16. Marsh grass
26. Housetop
28. Auricle
30. Long fish
32. Distributes
34. Require
36. Superior review
37. Essayist
38. Swiss peaks
39. Mr. Brinkley
41. Flunk
43. Departed
44. Chester ____ Arthur
45. "____ Diamond"
48. Citrus fruit
50. "____ Me in St. Louis"
53. Vend
55. Worshiped
57. Russian ruler

60. Pickle spice
62. Fresher
64. Catch sight of
66. Jump
68. Cut in two
70. Female hogs
71. Parcel
72. Cogitation
73. Couples
75. Resided
77. Sung solo
78. Gentle
79. Only
82. Solid gate
84. Mercy
87. Slim
89. Perched
91. ____ the Hyena
94. Homesite
96. Small child
98. Resident of Berlin

PUZZLE 437

100. Bird nurseries
102. "Call Me ____"
104. English baby carriage
105. Divorce capital
106. Division preposition
107. Defy
109. Festive
111. Organ of smell
112. Cleveland's waterfront
113. Precious
116. Pinky ____
118. Mr. Skelton

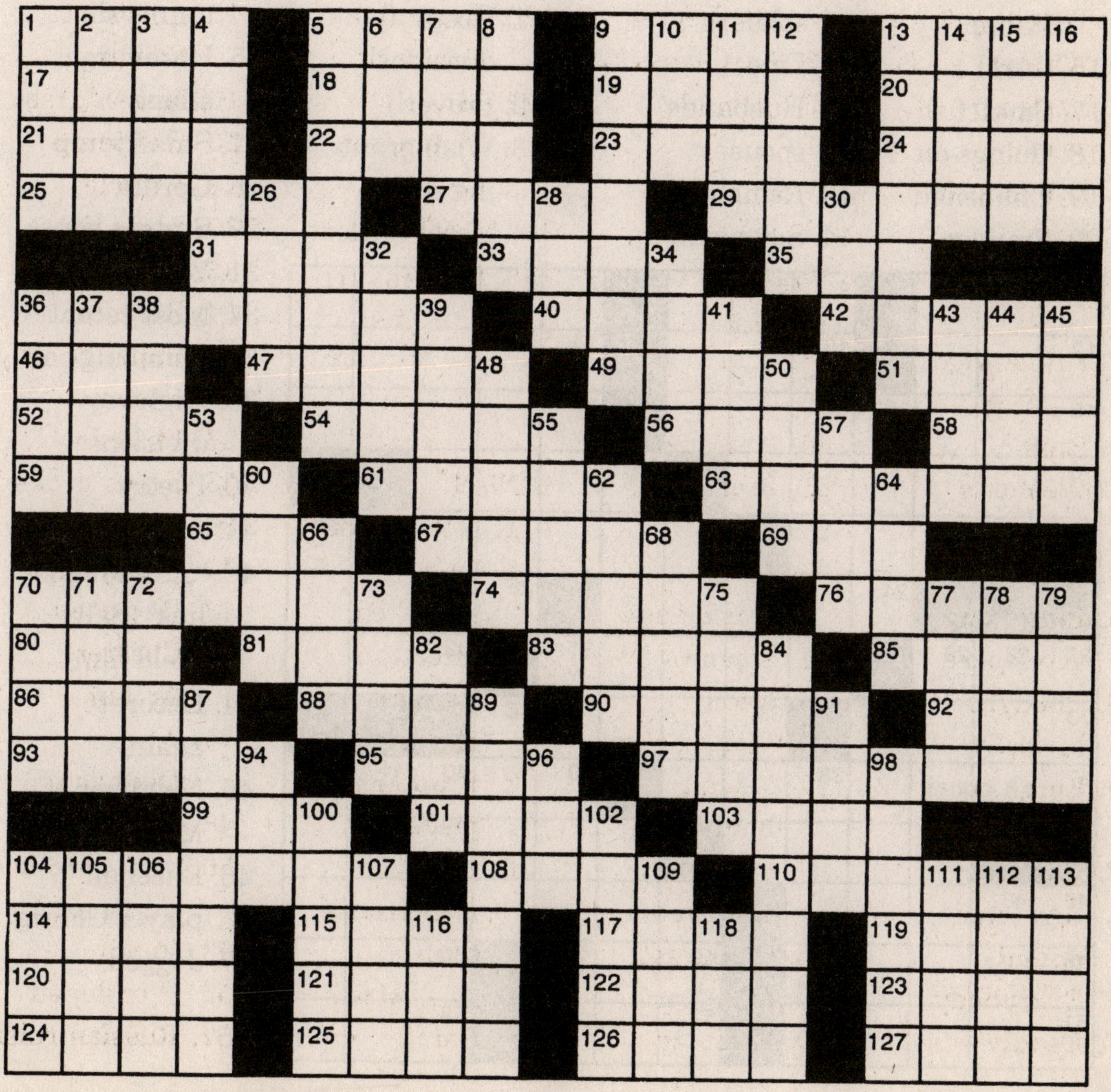

PUZZLE 438

ACROSS

1. Move back and forth
4. Chum
7. "Aida" or "Carmen"
12. Hatchet
13. Skating rink surface
14. Ancient Italian
15. Curl
17. Small fish
18. Goings-on
19. Challenge
20. Smudge
21. ____ spring (spa)
24. Rubs dry
26. Extinct flightless bird
27. Bad actor
30. Month before April
32. Steal from
33. Milky gem
35. Company of soldiers
37. Fine
39. Husbands' spouses
43. Remain
44. Say again
45. Foreigner
47. Opposite
48. Unconfined
49. Fruit drink
50. Observe
51. Mother's sisters
52. Neither's partner
53. Building addition

DOWN

1. Hospital divisions
2. Proverb
3. Wish-granting spirit
4. Early settler
5. Expert pilots
6. Permit
7. Keyboard instrument
8. Rained hard
9. Monarch
10. Knock
11. Whatever
16. Chew
19. Nightclub
21. Cheerful
22. Fuss
23. Certain tennis shot
25. Hamburger shape
27. Small jump
28. Gorilla
29. Stately house
31. Yet
34. Most recent
36. Plumbing part
38. Highway divisions
40. Poetry
41. Artist's stand
42. "____ Magnolias" (Sally Field film)
44. Decorate again
45. Neighbor of Miss.
46. Baseball player Gehrig
47. Jogged

PUZZLE 439

ACROSS

1. Table seasoning
5. Catch
8. Deep tracks
12. Pub orders
13. Neighbor of Wash.
14. Once more
15. Trail
16. Wooden nail
17. Leaning Tower site
18. Unruly kid
20. Like sandpaper
22. Into error
25. Comfort
26. Ill will
27. Self
28. Gloomy
31. Cooking items
32. Watch
33. Decorate again
34. Hog's home
35. Night bird
36. Howdy
37. Expected
38. Responsibilities
39. Earlier
42. Bungle
43. Minerals
44. Beige
46. Very bad
50. Cleo's river
51. Actor Wallach
52. Spacious
53. Butterfly catchers
54. Edge
55. ____ for granted

DOWN

1. Tree fluid
2. Pie ____ mode
3. Permit
4. Teens' wardrobe items
5. Frosty
6. Picnic drink
7. Suitcases
8. Fast
9. Platoon
10. Experiment
11. Rock back and forth
19. Actress West
21. River, in Madrid
22. Snakes
23. Small quarrel
24. Little
27. Snakelike fish
28. Supermarket department
29. Lazy
30. Pasture sounds
32. More sugary
33. Hideaway
35. Belonging to us
36. "Ben ____"
37. Medicinal amounts
38. Durable material
39. German city
40. Buffalo's lake
41. Sensed
45. Famous boxer
47. By means of
48. Bother
49. Soap-making ingredient

PUZZLE 440

ACROSS

1. Smidgen
4. Summon
8. Stinging insect
12. Selfish kind of trip
13. Sign
14. Huron's neighbor
15. Forest
17. Table supports
18. Take five
19. Boise's state
20. Arrived
23. Winter toys
25. Full steam ____!
27. House wing
28. Gorilla
31. Previous
33. Pasture
35. Hurricane center
36. Olive center
38. Sir Francis ____
39. ____-pocus
41. Singing brothers
42. Anticipate
45. Fishhook part
47. Guitar part
48. Clergyman
52. Appoint
53. Single units
54. Prospector's find
55. Made do
56. Monster
57. Lily leaf

DOWN

1. Morning moisture
2. In the past
3. Halloween greeting
4. Column
5. Gather
6. Tender
7. Tip
8. Fuses
9. Zone
10. Yearn
11. Mexican coin
16. Imagine
19. Lingered
20. Small restaurant
21. Sailor's hello
22. Slight
24. "A Nightmare on ____ Street"
26. Train station
28. Hoss's brother
29. Elbow
30. Woolly creatures
32. Guitarist Ocasek (The Cars)
34. Saudis, e.g.
37. Floating down the river
39. Walked
40. More sensible
42. Designer Klein
43. Not strong
44. High point
46. ____ and shine!
48. Cow sound
49. Spinning toy
50. Age
51. Traffic-light color

PUZZLE 441

ACROSS

1. "Betsy's Wedding" star
5. Building annex
8. Rim
12. Gasoline, for one
13. Sticky stuff
14. Gentle
15. Desert dweller
16. Complained
18. Just said no
20. Path between buildings
21. Mire
22. Tint
23. Idaho's capital
26. Most peaceful
30. Help
31. Pig
32. Neither's partner
33. Magic-lamp owner
36. Mommy's partner
38. Liquor in a daiquiri
39. Goal
40. Glossy fabric
43. Headache cure
47. Sayings
49. Challenge
50. Farmland measure
51. Grand ____ Opry
52. Hits the slopes
53. Now and ____ (sometimes)
54. Moisten
55. Examination

DOWN

1. In the distance
2. Tempt
3. Unable to hear
4. Scrapbooks
5. Urged
6. British nobleman
7. Baseball player Gehrig
8. Symbol
9. Pickling herb
10. Happiness
11. Small whirlpool
17. Heavy hammer
19. Take to court
22. Witch
23. Sheep's call
24. Liquid for frying
25. Actress Lupino
26. Pro's opposite
27. Finish
28. Grass
29. Attempt
31. That man
34. Compelled
35. Desert or beach hill
36. Short swim
37. Surrounded by
39. Thing of value
40. Argument
41. Curved doorway
42. Ripped
43. Capable
44. Leaf-gathering tool
45. Colored part of the eye
46. Bird's home
48. Tough ____ to hoe

PUZZLE 442

ACROSS
1. Not hard
5. Tresses
9. Auction offer
12. Locale
13. Woodwind
14. "Bells ____ Ringing"
15. Athletic group
16. Tennis star Sampras
17. Testing ground
18. Scarlet
20. Highest
22. More impersonal
25. Notice
26. Malt liquor
27. ____ or never
29. Do the two-step
33. Eyesore
35. Immerse
37. Gentle creature
38. Mails
40. ____ and tonic
42. Actress MacGraw
43. Popular street name
45. Pond resident
47. Breakfast food
51. Beach color
52. Pedro's river
53. Legendary
55. Hand out cards
58. "Much ____ About Nothing"
59. Defense
60. Land amid water
61. Allow
62. Shipped
63. Capital of Norway

DOWN
1. Posed
2. Raw metal
3. Brave
4. Domesticated
5. Move like a rabbit
6. Aid in a wrongdoing
7. Little bits
8. Staggered
9. Cotton unit
10. Levin and Gershwin
11. Liability
19. Library
21. Guide
22. ____ David
23. Biscuit topper
24. Lightning ____
28. Toupee
30. Tidiness
31. Prisoner's room
32. New York canal
34. Goblet feature
36. Cherry center
39. Slumbers
41. Fanatic
44. Syrup source
46. Ham operator's item
47. Word-of-mouth
48. Nurse's ____
49. Horn's sound
50. Legal claim
54. Tabby
56. Totally
57. Zodiac lion

PUZZLE 443

ACROSS
1. Country singer McEntire
5. Now hear ____!
9. ____ Grande
12. Oklahoma city
13. Conceal
14. Tack on
15. Presidential "no"
16. Certain golf club
17. Scarlet
18. Not any
20. Frock, e.g.
22. Leering
25. Chamomile drink
26. Media
27. More distant
31. Mazel ____!
32. Very long time
33. Citrus beverage
34. Cheat
37. Actor/director Woody ____
39. Acorn tree
40. Adjust to surroundings
41. Bunch of bees
44. Head coverings
45. Paving material
46. Scheme
48. Slant
52. Lyric poem
53. Lake, in Scotland
54. Great Lake
55. Pod vegetable
56. Tibetan oxen
57. Require

DOWN
1. Race in neutral
2. Opposite of WSW
3. Piece
4. Handsome Greek god
5. Object
6. Employ
7. Wedding words
8. "Return to ____"
9. Uncommon
10. The ____ of March
11. Betting numbers
19. Light switch positions
21. Ship deserter
22. Chooses
23. Get bigger
24. Jeans mogul Strauss
25. Light brown
27. Enemy
28. Patriot Nathan ____
29. Garden of Paradise
30. Lease
32. Large deer
35. Neither's partner
36. Moistly
37. Singer Garfunkel
38. Heed
40. Solemn vows
41. Cease
42. Walk through water
43. Region
44. Pawn
47. Mauna ____
49. Rage
50. Fib
51. Newsman Koppel

PUZZLE 444

ACROSS

1. Winged
6. December song
11. Osculate
15. Suez ——
16. Blackberry drupelets
17. Tooth: prefix
18. Promise of prosperity, with "A": 4 wds.
21. Imprudent
22. Certain gridders
23. GIs' wall hangings
24. Have being
25. Assigned character
26. Catlike beasts
27. Like the monsoon
29. Makes replete
30. Hopes
33. Secret group
34. Evian, e.g.
37. Aussie beast
38. Lively dance
39. Deneb
40. Prosper: 4 wds.
44. Samovars
45. Nostrils
46. Diacritical mark
47. Unpub- lished bks.
48. Malarial chills
49. Austere
51. Small valleys
52. Quiet
53. Zeal
55. Mr. Musial
56. Leg
59. Verdi works
60. Ankara native
61. Hence
62. Prosper: 4 wds.
66. Outline
67. Orleans's river
68. Wedding walkway
69. Actor Jack or Tim
70. Castle ditches
71. Attack

DOWN

1. Capital of Ghana
2. Volcanic landslide
3. Liqueur flavoring
4. RPM meter
5. Moose's kin
6. Artillery pieces
7. Tartly
8. Laundry cycle
9. Unit
10. Actress Ullmann
11. John Maynard ——
12. Computer fodder
13. Halts
14. Poses
17. Nonsense
19. Spooky
20. Last tribute
26. Actor Sebastian
27. Brooks
28. Fine horse
29. Comedian Soupy
30. Ancient Ethiopian capital
31. Rides on thermals
32. Hurts
33. Is concerned
34. Avocet's kin
35. Ling Ling, for one
36. "As You Like It" forest

PUZZLE 444

38. Skirt panels
39. Eddy
41. The King's ——
42. Defect
43. And others: abbr.
48. Make bubbly
49. Deprives of nourishment
50. Comedian Lee
51. Guide
52. Artist Gilbert
53. Agnew
54. Ride a bicycle
55. Furrow
56. Crab or blue
57. Nimble
58. Impressionist Claude
59. Rel. type
61. N.Y. canal
63. Shade tree
64. Viscid stuff
65. Bill

PUZZLE 445

ACROSS

1. Sale term: 2 wds.
5. Chemical suffix
8. Owned
11. Hts.
15. Talk wildly
16. Prom bouquet
18. Manner of running
19. Best picture (1935): 4 wds.
22. Earth pigment
23. Showed a film again
24. Majestic
25. American Indian
26. Old-fashioned
28. Father
30. Vane dir.
31. Stack
33. Exchanged
36. Pods
38. Expert pilot
39. Met melodies
42. Ring
43. Avoid
46. Markets
48. Hill builder
49. Algonquin brave
50. New Zealand parrot
52. Falsify
53. Busybody
56. Madden
58. Datum
59. Later
61. Failure
62. Hopi and Yaqui
64. Remnants
66. Literary villain
67. Fairy queen
70. —— Jima
71. Pamphlet
74. Ms. Hagen
77. Flawless
79. Delicate
81. Lotus- ——
83. Best picture (1983): 3 wds.
86. Fencing blade
87. Account books
88. Carouser's cry
89. Comedian Freeberg
90. —— Moines
91. Wall and Fleet: abbr.
92. Sun. discourses

DOWN

1. Military equipment
2. Gravy
3. "—— the Night" (best picture, 1967): 4 wds.
4. Commotion
5. Frigid
6. Entrances
7. Sea eagles
8. Sound of merriment: hyph.
9. Schedule
10. Society gal
11. Chills and fever
12. Actress Jessica
13. Giant
14. Format
17. Expand
20. Asian country
21. Commands
27. Church recesses
29. Oklahoma city
32. Architectural addition
34. Smelled strongly
35. Perish
36. Health clubs
37. Hair coloring
38. Yield
40. Best picture (1950): 3 wds.
41. Sliver
44. Tragic

PUZZLE 445

45. Sebaceous cyst
47. Establishes
51. Garret
54. Mel____
55. Dangers
57. Wild horse
58. Pear-shaped fruit
60. Uncooked
63. Assessor
65. Columbian export
67. Insects
68. Dexterous
69. Kentucky town
72. Goes by car
73. Warn
75. Vocalist
76. Comedian Johnson et al.
78. Revival shout
80. Beatty film
82. Iowa town
84. Decrepit
85. Imbecile

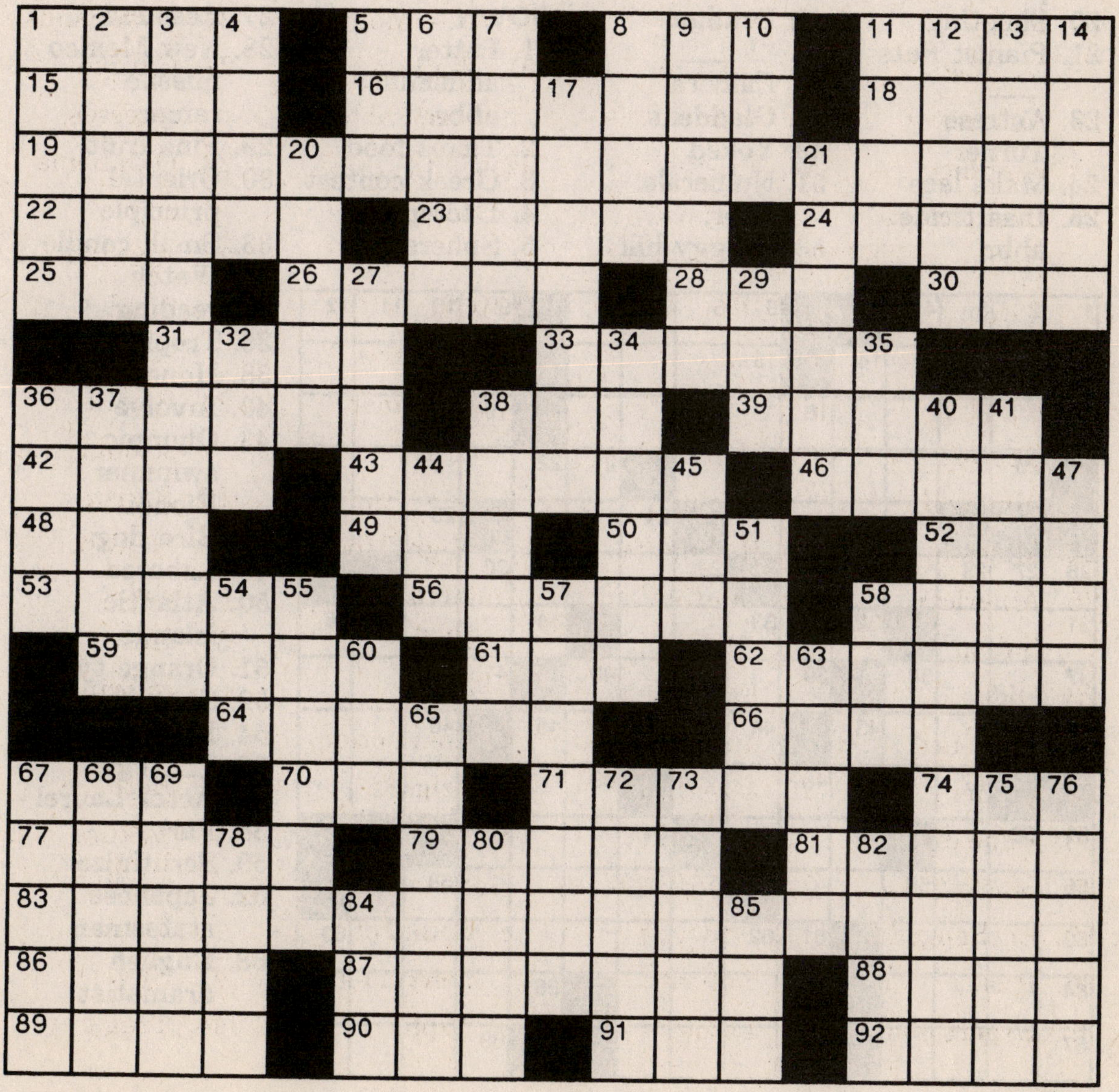

PUZZLE 446

ACROSS

1. Snow ____
5. Choir voice
9. Basic facts
13. Wiser
15. Speckled horse
16. Blessing
17. English monument
19. Continent: pref.
20. Shooting
21. Pianist Fats ____
23. Actress Turner
24. Make lace
25. Insecticide: abbr.
26. Least
29. Prairie wolf
31. Oh!: Ger.
32. Wyoming range
34. Stores
37. Wedge
39. "Inferno" poet
41. Of a lyric poem
42. Clan emblem
44. Drudges
46. "I ____ Camera"
47. Gladdens
49. Yoked
51. Numerals: abbr.
53. Craggy hill
54. Swiss coin
55. Come in!, Sicilian style
57. Beaux
60. Liana
61. Capital of Arkansas
64. Termini
65. Coup d'____
66. Pass on
67. For fear that
68. Fully cooked
69. ____ packing

DOWN

1. Letter addenda: abbr.
2. Takes food
3. Greek contest
4. Decrepit
5. Sphere
6. Protracted
7. Running game
8. Street sign
9. Second son
10. Colorado River barrier
11. Prepared apples
12. Short drink
14. Meal
18. Insinuated
22. Molecule
24. Lone Ranger's pal
26. In a snap
27. Resound
28. New Mexico missile range
29. Pine fruit
30. Oriental principle
33. Small candle
35. Watch reading
36. Tropical fish
38. Honey
40. Involve
43. Olympic swimmer Biondi
45. Bird dog
48. Labored
50. Atlantic islands
51. Orange type
52. Sheeplike
54. Montana city
56. ____ egg
57. Actor Laurel
58. Part
59. Scrutinize
62. Japanese statesman
63. English dramatist

PUZZLE 447

ACROSS
1. Additional
5. Talk
8. Aware of
12. Last word
13. ___ de Janeiro
14. Downpour
15. Jumble
16. Craft
17. Skillful
18. Pranks
20. Past, present, and future
22. Rift
23. Dawdle
24. Portrays
27. Builds
31. Make a mistake
32. Hard wood
33. Property
37. Trivial
40. Sooner than
41. Honest ___
42. Peddle
45. Rogue
49. Gain
50. Ignited
52. Tender
53. Words of understanding
54. Mine find
55. Candid
56. Require
57. Marry
58. Tidy

DOWN
1. Mother
2. Portent
3. Repose
4. Navy officer's rank
5. Understands
6. Ventilate
7. Vial
8. Valencia
9. Seizes
10. Roofing material
11. Singles
19. Tiger
21. Sound receiver
24. For each
25. Metric land measure
26. Gershwin brother
28. Narrow bed
29. Paving material
30. Heavens
34. Inclined
35. Three: pref.
36. Butter-colored
37. Left
38. Arab robe
39. Assignment
42. Check
43. Comfort
44. Arbor
46. Deal
47. Region
48. Period preceding Easter
51. Anger

PUZZLE 448

ACROSS
1. Small bite
4. Auction shout
7. Reporter's hope
12. Birds ___ feather
13. Ostrichlike bird
14. Framework
15. Bureaucracy
17. Command
18. Slight
19. Sleep noisily
21. Watchful
23. Religious woman
24. Star pilot
27. Martin's pal
29. Forehead
30. Life's work
33. Round shape
35. Came down
36. Actress Dunne
38. Sleeping place
39. "A Chorus Line" hit
40. Of birth
44. Heathen
46. Forest member
47. Assumed name
50. Stubborn loser
52. Dig
53. House extension
54. Swine
55. Bargain events
56. Ump's relative
57. View

DOWN
1. "___ Rae"
2. "___ a Song Coming On"
3. San Diego player
4. Actress Arthur
5. Little devils
6. Spanish chaperone
7. Disdain
8. Concern
9. Like Simon's couple
10. Raw metal
11. ___ annum
16. Harness ring
20. Part of a pound
22. Foot digit
24. Curve
25. Denver's st.
26. Sheep
28. Squeeze moisture from
29. Inhalation
30. Taxi
31. Ginger ___
32. Expel
34. Tavern
37. School book
39. Havens in deserts
41. Snares
42. Eagle's home
43. Shelf
44. Make an avenue
45. Cleo's river
47. Business getters
48. Grassy meadow
49. Not well
51. Santa's helper

PUZZLE 449

Diagramless crosswords are solved by using the clues and their numbers to fill in the answer words and the arrangement of black squares. Insert the number of each clue with the first letter of its answer, across and down. Fill in a black square at the end of each word. Every black square must have a corresponding black square on the opposite side of the diagram to form a diagonally symmetrical pattern.

ACROSS
1. Invite
4. Bat wood
7. Curtsy
10. Lawyer's charge
11. Honey insect

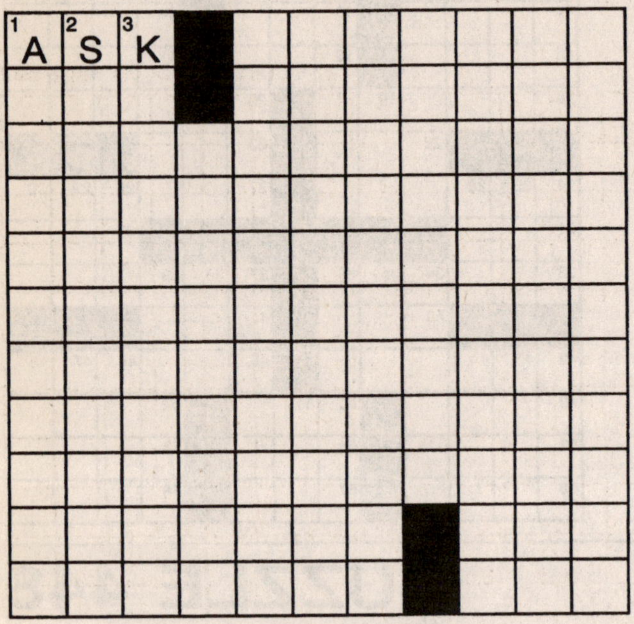

12. Stalk of corn
13. Snarled
15. Dehydrate
16. Book of accounts
18. Flat tableland
21. Eat away
24. Curved lines
25. Muddy the waters
26. Take a break
28. Electric units
29. Despot
32. Turned on a lamp
34. Assumed names
38. Building wing
39. Tree fluid
40. Affirmative vote
41. Ginger drink
42. Curvy letter
43. Archery wood

DOWN
1. Toward the back of a boat
2. Ocean
3. Barbie's boyfriend
4. Competent
5. Kernel
6. Shrub fence
7. Sleeping chamber
8. Paddle
9. Twisted
14. Smooth and shiny
17. Printing mistakes
18. Motorist's guide
19. Historical period
20. Sink deliberately
22. Scoop of ice cream
23. Overhead trains
27. Clean a blackboard
30. Woe is me!
31. Pinches
32. Meadow
33. Sick
35. Utter
36. Needle hole
37. Take stitches

PUZZLE 450

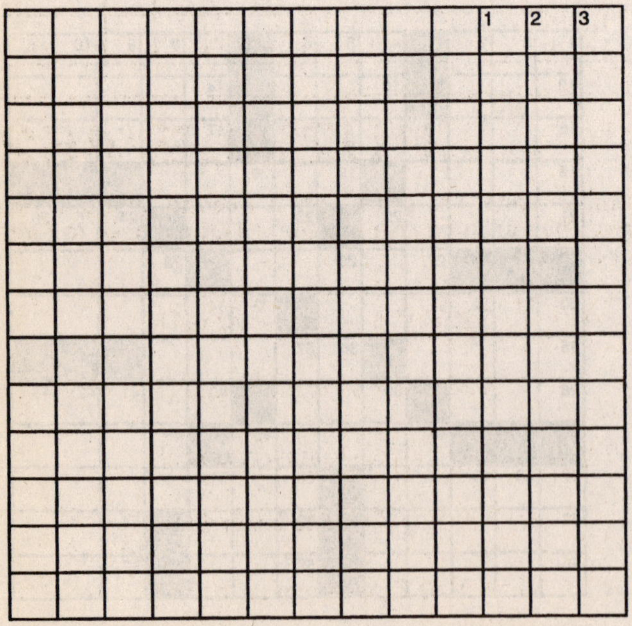

ACROSS
1. Household animal
4. Book leaf
5. Skirt edge
8. Oust dissidents
9. Mr. Clapton
11. Merchandise
12. Prohibited action
13. Sat for an artist
14. Transgression
15. Start a poker pot
16. Ipso ____
18. Withered
19. Uncooked
22. Thirst quencher
23. Opera solo
25. Clues
26. Grant temporary use
27. "Aida" composer
28. Years of life
29. Mine yields
30. Marry

DOWN
1. Removed rind
2. Omelet items
3. Golf peg
4. Thick soup
5. Biddy
6. God of love
7. Short skirt
8. Serenely rustic
10. Paper shower at a party
11. Habit
13. Harness racing horse
17. God of war
18. Beaches
20. Neighborhood
21. Bird's flapper
22. Installed electricity
24. Citrus drink
25. In this place
27. Solemn promise

PUZZLE 451

ACROSS

1. Health resort
4. Warning
6. Throng
7. Hoop attempt
9. Give off
12. Shy
13. Underground being of folklore
14. Tangle
16. Portly
17. ____ and letters
20. Winter precipitation
21. Forbid
22. Set afire
24. Radio operator
25. Enclosure
26. Native metal
27. Solidify
28. Sidestepped
30. Tart
31. Bonus
32. Prepare for publication
33. Buddy
34. Day's beginning
35. Made a winning chess move
37. Burrow
38. Vitality
39. Endowment
40. Climb
42. Flying toys
43. Headed

DOWN

1. Narrow opening
2. Golfer's goal
3. Eager
4. Nautical hail
5. Office note
7. Flat-bottomed boat
8. Fiery
10. Representation
11. Gull-like bird
13. Needlefish
14. Blackguard
15. Wanderer
16. Team's supporter
18. Striped cat
19. Strict
20. "____ Drives Me Crazy"
21. Flower area
22. Anger
23. Large deer
25. Part of a flower
26. Lamp fuel
29. A ____ a dozen
30. Tablet
31. Walden, for one
33. Writing tool
34. "A Few Good ____"
36. Assigned job
37. Membership fees
39. Ran away
41. Consumed

Starting box on page 562

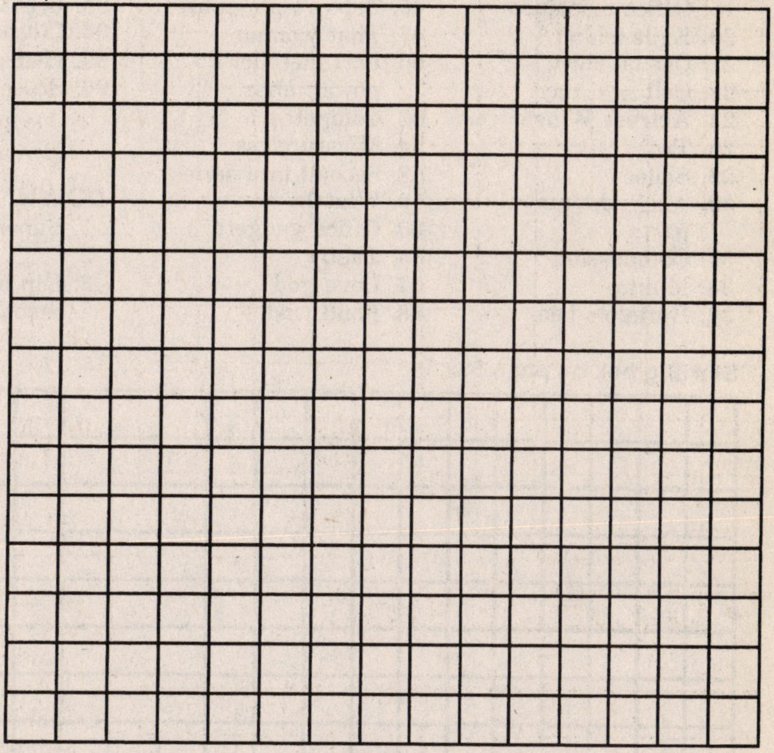

Codebreaker

PUZZLE 452

Each group of five letters is a word in a simple substitution code. The same code is used throughout. The clue next to each group gives you one of the real letters. The ten clues give you the ten letters used to form all the words. As a starter we'll tell you that K stands for D in all words.

1. H B W J K — one letter is D
2. K B M H V — one letter is R
3. H W C M B — one letter is L
4. M H B W Q — one letter is O
5. X B M Q K — one letter is G
6. J H H V B — one letter is U
7. V M X C V — one letter is E
8. B W J Q K — one letter is N
9. J H V Q K — one letter is P
10. H M Q K M — one letter is A

PUZZLE 453

• OFFICE SUPPLIES •

ACROSS

1. Take food
4. Lincoln's nickname
7. Conflicts
11. Easy task
13. Actress Ullmann
14. Theater sign
15. Office machines
20. Exile island
21. Casual shirt
22. Call ____ day
24. Actress Winger
26. Twit
29. Sailor
30. "____ the ramparts . . ."
31. Compassion
34. Manta
35. Buffalo's lake
37. Time ____ half
38. Norse explorer
39. Sault ____ Marie
40. Office equipment
43. Zola heroine
44. Republic of Ireland
45. Catches sight of
46. Topsy's playmate
47. That woman
50. Fortuneteller's power: abbr.
52. Compete
54. Moistureless
58. Second in a series
59. Whittle
60. Office gadgets
64. Tabby
67. Love god
68. Fond wish
71. Small case
72. Candlenut
73. Military grade
74. Expert
75. Dancer Miller
76. Lavender flower
78. Actress Berger
81. Mauna ____
82. Under the weather
83. Battery fluid
84. Office storage
91. Actress Foch
92. "Long ____ and Far Away"
93. Lightly colored
94. Close noisily
95. Heir
96. Sn

DOWN

1. Superlative suffix
2. "____ Wednesday"
3. Dip (into resources)
4. Ryan's co-star in "Love Story"
5. Morsel
6. Pre-holiday night
7. Tare, e.g.
8. Wheel rod
9. Office-machine supply
10. Gawked
12. Office fund
16. Minuscule
17. Brings up
18. Formal acts
19. Begin
23. Diva's solo
25. Sky altar
27. Made a lap
28. Potato bud
31. Office implements
32. Of wrath: Latin
33. Prong
36. Fencing weapon
37. Have being
41. "I Want to ____!" (Susan Hayward film)
42. Important times
48. Eternally
49. Actress Moreno
51. Office fastener
53. Life of Riley
55. ____ avis
56. Golf club
57. Office furniture
58. Buzzer
61. And others: abbr.
62. ____-the-mill
63. Mideast peninsula
64. ____ Tech
65. Friend: Fr.
66. Actress Shire
68. Is afflicted with
69. Waters of the world
70. Office implement
77. Linen vestment
79. Songstress Turner
80. Rich or West
85. ____ Palmas
86. Conceit
87. Against
88. Slave Turner
89. Inventor Whitney
90. Hamilton bill

Starting box on page 562

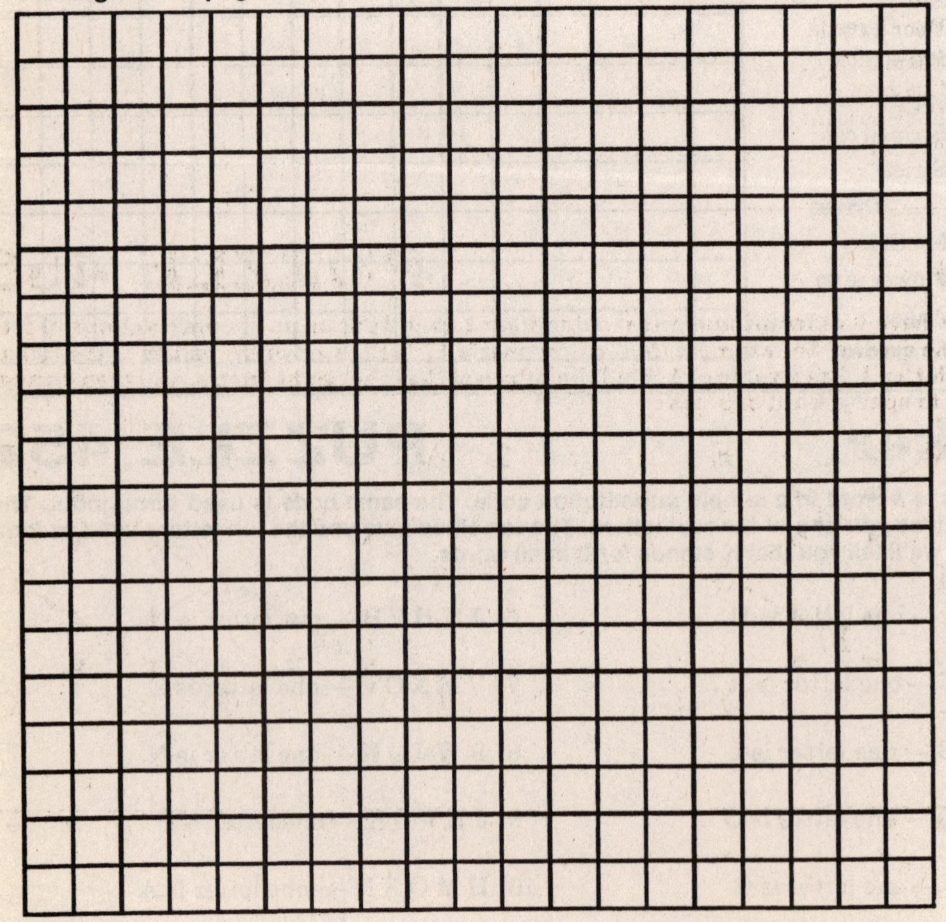

PUZZLE 454

ACROSS
1. For both sexes
5. Up to it
6. Flourished
10. Tranquility
12. Brushed leather
13. Distant
16. Serpent
18. Likeness
19. Cream of the crop
21. Have a longing
23. Energy
24. Roman robe
25. Medicine
26. Cut of pork
27. Requirement
29. Jack rabbit
30. Oxidation
34. Boulder
38. Single time
39. Talk wildly
41. Mortgage
42. In what way
45. Sag
47. Unaccompanied
48. Maxim
50. Explode
52. Clear profit
53. Sweetheart
54. Mortise fitting
56. Guitar neck ridge
57. Rational
58. Erupt

DOWN
1. Bottle top
2. Overweight
3. Verve
4. Rot
6. Chicle
7. Gather a harvest
8. Brim
9. Cry
11. Barely got by
12. Scorch
13. Retrieve
14. Hawaiian greeting
15. Hardship
17. Work for
20. Small candle
22. Regret
28. Oddly amusing
31. Labor group
32. Vista
33. Article of faith
35. Command
36. Auto
37. Door handle
40. Racetrack tipster
42. Fifty percent
43. Aroma
44. Flutter
46. Printing machine
47. Make amends
49. Obtain
51. Break suddenly
55. Modern

Starting box on page 562

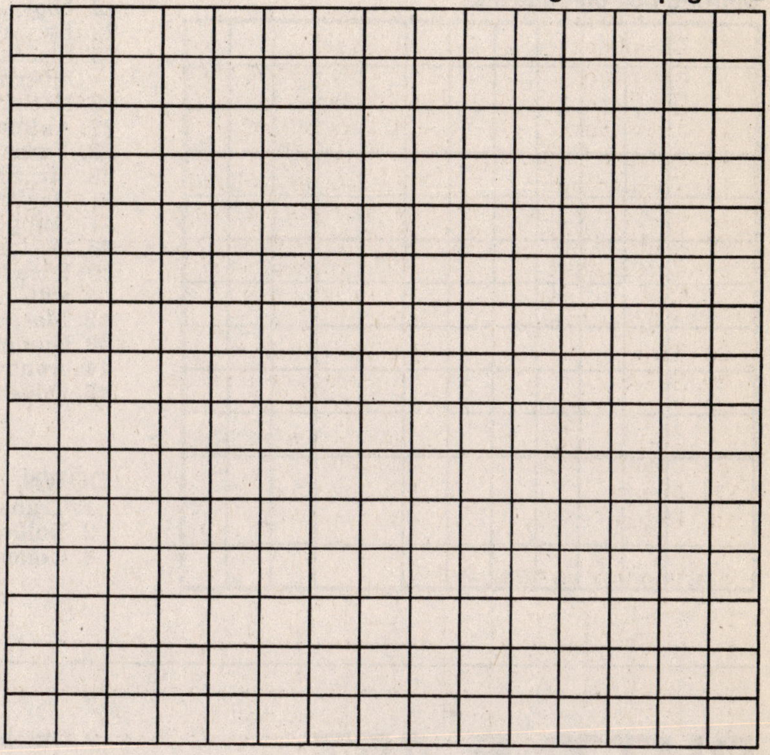

Foursomes

PUZZLE 455

In each puzzle the letters have a different numerical value from 1 to 9. Four sums of combinations of four letters are indicated by the arrows. For example, in the first puzzle 17 is the sum of the values of the letters I, S, C, and Y. The center letter, I, has a value of 1. Find the values of the other eight letters, and then arrange them in order from 1 to 9 to spell a word or phrase.

1.

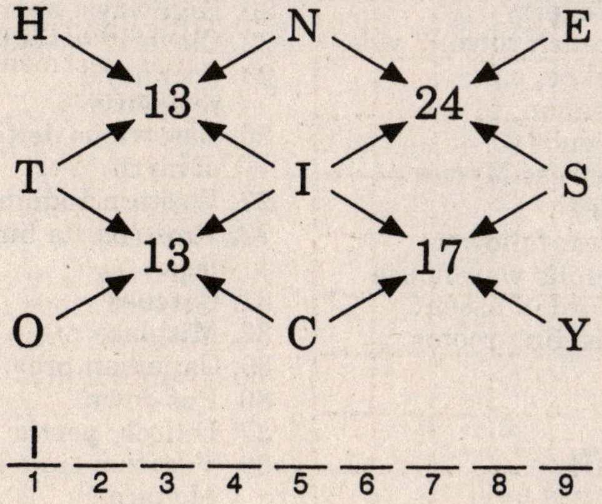

2.

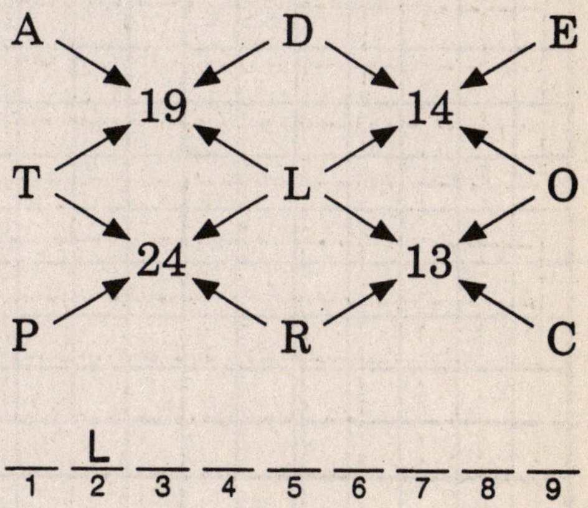

PUZZLE 456

ACROSS

1. TV show of controversy
5. Measuring strip

Starting box on page 562

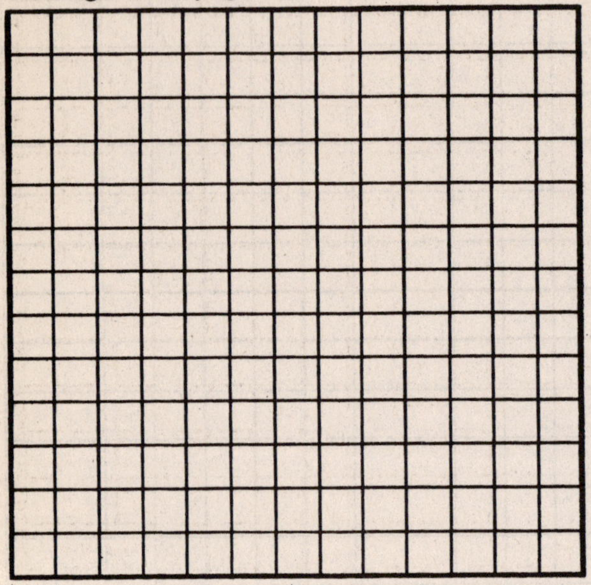

9. Perceived
11. —— energy (wave of the future?)
12. Tiny village: 2 wds.
14. Oz., lb., etc.
15. Cleopatra's river
16. Vane point
17. Not any
19. Look- —— (twin)
22. By way of
25. Places for hibernating
26. Not pre-recorded
27. Animal bag
28. Yarns
29. Mr. Shriner
31. Health resort
34. Competes
36. Doctor's charge
39. Race track bettors: 2 wds.
42. Margarines
43. Guides a car
44. Annoyance
45. Odds and ——

DOWN

1. Transmitted
2. Dollar bills
3. Cigarette residue
4. Unskilled laborer
5. Sandboxer
6. African lily
7. Cat's feet
8. Aerie denizen
9. Scatter seed
10. Martini, vodka collins, etc.
11. ". . . —— but not heard"
13. Wild plum
18. Wicked
19. Newspaper revenue
20. Meadow
21. Part of the foot
23. "—— Got Sixpence"
24. D.D.E.'s opponent
26. Tags
28. Journey
30. Nights before holidays
31. Window—— (look but not buy)
32. Point on an electric battery
33. Greek war god
35. Glut
36. Animal dinner
37. Miscalculates
38. Curved letter
40. Tippler
41. Longing

PUZZLE 457

ACROSS

1. Not unruly
5. Temporary bed
8. Attempted

Starting box on page 562

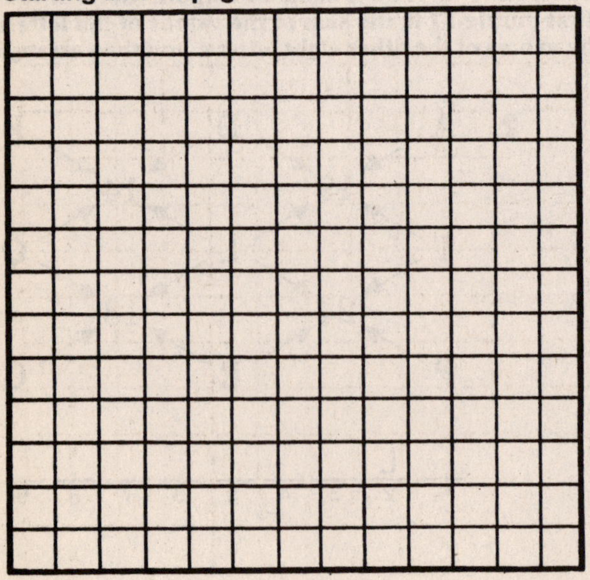

9. Oktoberfest offering
10. Feels sorrow
11. Blushing
12. —— of consent
13. W.W. II area
15. Ago
17. Hedy ——
21. Stuck to one's guns
23. Roll of a die
24. Printers' spaces
25. Used a ruler
29. Property
30. French town: 2 wds.
34. Pekoe, e.g.
35. Reagan, to his friends
36. Actress Myrna ——
38. Meal
41. Mar. follower
42. Public warehouse
43. Word of assent
44. Reading rooms

DOWN

1. Lines up
2. Ozone
3. "—— in White"
4. Detroit lemons
5. Billiard shots
6. Bullring cheer
7. Emcee Mack
8. Roman wear
10. Plan
14. Oriental porgy
16. Fork prongs
18. Suit to ——: 2 wds.
19. Tears apart
20. Highways: abbr.
22. Cleverly executed
23. Cockney's residence
26. Lascivious deities of myth
27. Western Indian
28. Arose on its hind legs
31. Catches
32. Misplace
33. Canadian prov.
36. Put down
37. Unlock: poetic
39. Vacation-time in Monaco
40. Disney's Peter

PUZZLE 458

ACROSS

1. Domesticated animal
4. Shade
6. Musical instrument
8. Impartial
9. Spoil
10. Restrain
11. Imitate
12. Ship's spar
13. Sphagnum
14. Twofer
15. Batter
16. Reckless
17. Window ledge
18. Sausage meat
19. Stop
20. Girl's name
21. Liberty ——
22. Last dinner course
24. Wake from sleep
25. Allow

DOWN

1. Teem
2. Graceful tree
3. Highest
4. Bed
5. Harvests
6. Acid
7. Attempt
8. Commotion
10. Ready money
11. Fuel
12. False face
13. Dissolve
14. Lady's sunshade
15. Bird beak
16. Wanderer
17. Great —— Lake
18. Cushion
19. At this point
21. Most suitable
23. Bring suit

Starting box on page 562

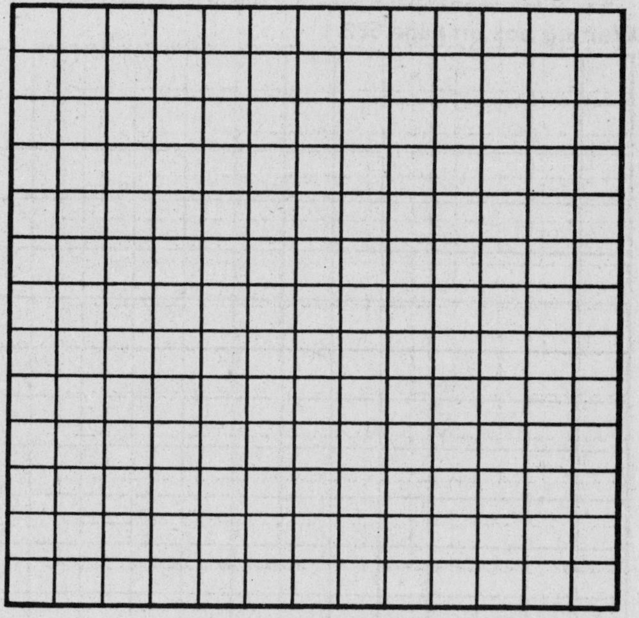

PUZZLE 459

ACROSS

1. Plug
4. Lariat
5. Harsh
7. Actress Turner
8. —— a course
10. Grain storer
11. Pack away
13. Friend in Paris
14. Mast
16. Departed
18. Stand up to
21. I'm all ——
24. Enemy
25. Precious metal
27. Evergreen trees
28. Honey maker
29. Hue
30. Explain
32. Pit
33. Pigpen

DOWN

1. —— Scotia
2. Gorilla
3. Microbes
4. Nevada city
5. Tearlike
6. Devours
7. Key —— pie
9. Kind of corn
10. Observed
12. Roll of money
15. Purify
17. ——, you're it
19. Garrison
20. Affirmative
22. Burglarize
23. Eskimo vehicle
26. Judges
27. Delicate
29. —— Tim
31. Suit

Starting box on page 562

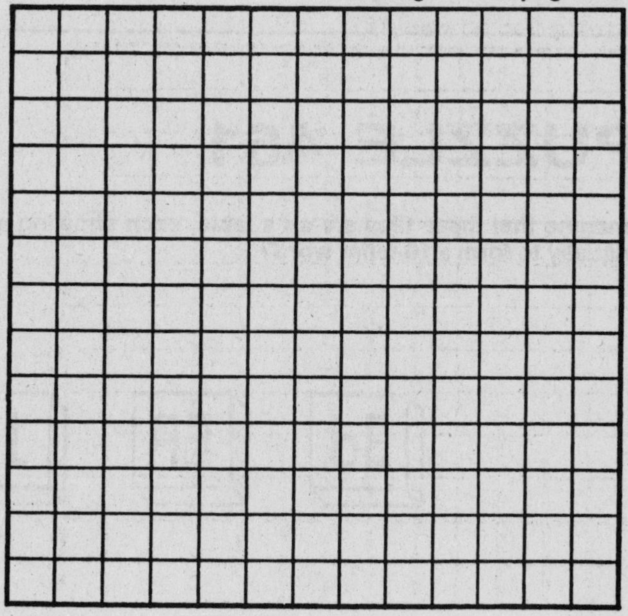

PUZZLE 460

ACROSS

1. Dawn to dusk
4. Pub brews
6. Water ___ (squirt gun)
8. Average
9. Craze
11. Physique
12. Blessing close
14. Dog-paddles
16. Social equal
18. Soothe
19. Beloved one
21. Fire residue
22. Hoover, for one
24. Verse writer
27. Ready
28. Extra
30. Ogre
31. Door feature
33. Fencing match
34. Hoopla
35. Lower-leg part
36. Soak up
38. Red-tag event
39. Engine fuel

DOWN

1. Donald Duck's love
2. Furthermore
3. To date
5. Love seat
6. Seedcases
7. Light fixture
8. A few
10. Property title
11. Chess piece
13. Formerly called
14. Mediterranean or Red
15. Stinging insect
17. Tire type
20. Knocks
23. Encountered
25. Large deer
26. Canned fish
27. Coral formation
29. Bubbly beverage
30. Tulip starter
32. Dylan and Hope
33. Challenges
35. Drink flavoring
37. Droop

Starting box on page 562

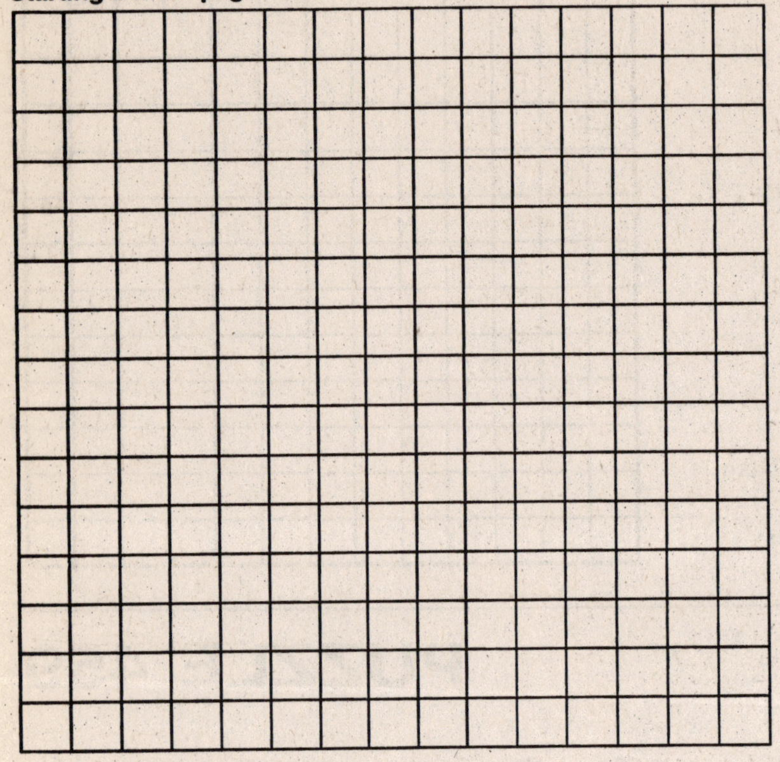

PUZZLE 461

TILES

Imagine that these tiles are on a table, each showing a 2-letter combination. Can you rearrange these tiles visually to form a 10-letter word?

PUZZLE 462

ACROSS

1. Package of bread
5. Military gp.
9. Actress Harlow
13. Rose's lover
14. Jacket section
15. Folk-singer Guthrie
16. Actress Lollobrigida
17. Think
18. Elbe tributary
19. Make the opposite of the expected occur
22. Thirst: Ital.
23. Recent: pref.
24. Brigham Young University site
26. Doubt
31. Arson, e.g.
32. British river
33. ____ the knot
34. Marilyn Monroe movie
38. Blackjack card
39. Futile
40. Enticed
41. Interfering ones
44. Rural structures
45. Make public
46. State founder
47. Be oblivious
53. Arizona Indian
54. "____ You Like to Take a Walk?"
55. Arrow
57. Poker stake
58. Sea birds
59. Hodgepodge
60. Writer Uris
61. ____ Sea
62. Hawaiian goose

DOWN

1. Tarry
2. Newspaper notice
3. Japanese aborigine
4. Terrible
5. Anatomical seam
6. Mayberry tot
7. Outdoor-wedding item
8. Detergent
9. Turnkey: var.
10. Celtic
11. Sudsy drinks
12. Negative word
14. Gambling game
20. "____ on Sunday"
21. Play the horses
24. Value
25. Shattered
26. '60s skirts
27. Golf club
28. Traffic no-no
29. Fathers
30. Watch over
31. Force
32. At a distance
35. Greatly intimidated
36. African antelope
37. Activated
42. Connecticut town
43. ____ Yutang
44. Turns
46. Heaped
47. Pitch
48. Until
49. Auger
50. Moon goddess
51. New England university
52. Miss Moran
53. Actor Linden
56. Water tester

PUZZLE 463

ACROSS

1. Author Wallace
4. Precious metal unit
9. Let it stand
13. Rara ____
15. Wind: pref.
16. Buckeye State
17. 13th president
20. Everywhere
21. Shut forcibly
22. ____ over on
23. Vast expanse
24. Puppy cry
25. Soul
29. Resort
32. Legend
35. Verbal
36. Predicament
37. Mr. Spade
39. Declination
41. High note
42. Twitch
43. Golf club
44. Ego
46. Moose
47. Print medium
49. Son ____ gun
51. Altar vow
53. Shore birds
57. Pudding flavor
61. Pensioner
62. Vice president
64. Captured, in poems
65. "____ Grows in Brooklyn"
66. There's ____ in them thar hills!
67. Terrier type
68. Cultivate
69. Nose: pref.

DOWN

1. Actor Fernando ____
2. Diabolically
3. 25th president
4. Actress Black
5. "____ del Sarto"
6. Ump's kin
7. Kingsley ____
8. Bridge fare
9. French river
10. 3rd president
11. Irish republic
12. ____ the line
14. Messy
18. Macao money
19. Old car
26. Name words
27. April addressee
28. Dutch river
30. Chum
31. Doctors' gp.
33. Libyan port
34. Mister: Ger.
37. Sault ____ Marie
38. Suffer
40. Enemy
45. Affectionate
48. Frolics
50. Ring of color
52. Actress Keaton
54. Dike
55. Native: suff.
56. Broadcasts
57. Tanks
58. Aleutian island
59. TV producer
60. Movie dog
63. Three: pref.

PUZZLE 464

ACROSS

1. Support
5. French river
10. Towel word
14. Beak membrane
15. Quebec city
16. Wild ox
17. Acrobatic feat
19. Unwilling, old style
20. Summer, abroad
21. Red planet
22. ____ tennis
24. Sink a putt
25. Cheongsam feature
26. Quench
28. Skeletal
32. Expiate
33. Relatives
34. Deep mud
35. New York college
36. Curt
37. Sioux tribesman
38. Type of cherry
39. Melody
40. Rotates
41. Sap
43. Quotes
44. One, in Bonn
45. British spa
46. North African fox
49. Emanation
50. ____ Tse-tung
53. District
54. How lovers walk
57. Expired
58. Oration
59. Toward shelter
60. Withered
61. Wines and ____
62. Emulates Dorcas

DOWN

1. Throb
2. Cadence
3. Sea eagle
4. Newscaster Koppel
5. Pierce
6. European industrial region, to Pierre
7. Shield
8. Nancy's mate
9. Aubergine
10. Precarious
11. Oklahoma town
12. Rock's companion
13. Store event
18. Indian's signal
23. Isle
24. Combat weapon
25. Small drum
26. Discoloration
27. Actor Greene
28. Solitary
29. Bishop's wear
30. Actor Jeremy ____
31. Average grades
32. French clergyman
33. Flume
36. Stopped the bleeding
40. Cronus, for one
42. Compete
43. Dentists' concern
45. Tennis great Don ____
46. Fancies
47. Cleveland's waterfront
48. ____ -do-well
49. Soon
50. "The ____ Animal"
51. Again
52. Lyric poems
55. Clay today
56. Possesses

PUZZLE 465

ACROSS

1. Put into symbols
6. Mythical galley
10. Sleuth Spade
13. Limber
14. Phony
15. Drooping
17. Pearl White's serial
20. Stage apparatus
21. Places for fleurs
22. Actor David ___
23. Miss Adams
24. Doctrine
25. Desires
28. Actor Robert ___
30. Superior
31. Column style
32. Johnny Reb's gp.
35. Ancient banquet's threat
39. ___ rule
40. Aquatic fliers
41. Caper
42. Those who oppose
43. Doubter
45. Cat genus
47. Weeded
48. Jacket features
49. Alpine heroine
51. One of the Stooges
54. How 17 Across ended
57. ___ fixe
58. About
59. Sea duck
60. Mme., in Madrid
61. Kind of poker
62. Pouring

DOWN

1. Kepis
2. Type of arch
3. Gossip
4. Actor Wallach
5. Mislead
6. Garbo's condition
7. Prevalent
8. Openings
9. ___ pro nobis
10. Briny
11. Vibrant
12. "Water Lilies" painter
16. Sty
18. Hindustani titles
19. World agcy.
23. "Be it ___ so . . ."
24. Prune
25. ___ Grande
26. Noisy quarrels
27. Wild ox
28. Styles
29. Munson et al.
31. Moroccan enclave
32. Shore digger's find
33. Napoli evening
34. Invites
36. Actress Darcel
37. Dinner scraps
38. Bumpkin
42. Hollyhock
43. Bustle
44. Young cow
45. Parries
46. Door sign
47. Backpacked
48. Cato's lucky number?
49. Suspicion
50. Off-white
51. South of France
52. Portent
53. Spooky: var.
55. Old Serbian capital
56. Ramona's aunt

PUZZLE 466

ACROSS

1. Golf scores
5. Healthy
9. Bring closer together
14. Newspaper notice, for short
15. Arabian Sea gulf
16. Juliet's love
17. Make over
18. Protective smoke producers
20. Lofty
22. Girls
23. Enthusiasm
24. Scratch
25. Abrades
28. Smoke ____
33. Tangelo variety
34. Skid
36. "Othello" villain
37. Bind, nautically
38. Napkin material
39. ____ monster
40. Celebration
41. Extras
42. Ancient
43. Moved up and down
45. Wire nails
46. Sleeping place
47. Wings
49. Seventh planet
53. Best
57. Smokey the Bear's concern
59. Tijuana treat
60. Fat
61. North African dress
62. Isaac's son
63. Chairs
64. Prolonged howls
65. Dispatched

DOWN

1. Leaf opening
2. First victim
3. Carnival attraction
4. Smoke conduits
5. ____ manana
6. Madison Avenue workers
7. Medieval tenant
8. Finish
9. Concoct
10. Expression of surprise
11. Andy's partner
12. Sampras of tennis
13. Pitch
19. Flour components
21. Jolson and Hirt
24. One who yields
25. Lace collars
26. Consent
27. Blackboard
28. Had a feast
29. Smokes
30. Northern woodland
31. Stared at
32. Streets
34. Most sluggish
35. Survived
44. Mistreats
45. Ovine sound
47. Attire
48. Sly looks
49. "Close Encounters of the Third Kind" ships
50. Dressing gown
51. Zone
52. Snug retreat
53. Egyptian city
54. Comfort
55. Scrutinize
56. Praise
58. Lie

PUZZLE 467

ACROSS

1. Deceive
5. Ashen
9. Headliner
13. Hair style
14. Accustom
16. Pakistani language
17. Performs
18. Exalt
20. Wind direction: abbr.
21. Burden
22. Crest
23. ____ operandi
25. British princess
26. Hedge shrub
28. Wooden pin
32. Whets
33. Dens
34. Genetic letters
35. Prayer ender
36. Coal sources
37. Arabian sultanate
38. ____ Francisco
39. Rope twists
40. Backbone
41. International under-standings
43. Metric units, in London
44. Age
45. Group for people with high IQ's
46. Book parts
48. Salvage
49. Bar bill
52. Distinction
54. Paddy product
55. Long ago
56. Panic
57. Sweet place?
58. "____ of Eden"
59. Individuals
60. Wallet items

DOWN

1. Pops
2. Alien sightings
3. Superior
4. Goddess of the dawn
5. Kind of butter
6. Scottish county
7. Carries with effort
8. Bungle
9. Abrupt
10. Math student's subject
11. Wood-worker's tool
12. Regret
15. Wage recipients
19. Baseball numbers
21. Pindar works
24. Baking chamber
25. First sign of the zodiac
26. Stage
27. Director Polanski
28. Armored vehicles
29. Esteem
30. Lacking sense
31. Country roads
33. Flax fabric
36. Method of cell division
37. Chooses
39. Assume a prayerful position
40. Mathe-matician's curve
42. Young bird of prey
43. Embank-ments
45. Large: pref.
46. Malay sailing boat
47. Pretensions
48. Problem
50. Zenith
51. Hive inhabitants
52. So long!
53. Master pilot
54. Greek letter

PUZZLE 468

ACROSS

1. Fly high
5. Triple ____
8. Abel's brother
12. Unemployed
13. California Indian
15. Movie dog
16. Adore
17. New Delhi's country
18. Military vehicle
19. London landmark
22. ____ Moines
23. Center of the solar system
24. French capital
27. Crosby, Stills & Nash, e.g.
29. Eternity
32. Cliff nest
33. Slender
34. Stuffing herb
35. Ship swallower?
38. Bathing suit tops
39. Bacchanalian cry
40. Certain runner
41. Serpentine letter
42. Unlock
43. Sleeveless garments
44. Title for John Gielgud
45. Umpire's call
46. Coterie
55. Dwarf buffalo
56. Sudden rainstorm
57. Origin
58. Luminary
59. Gluts
60. Misplace
61. Whetstone
62. Football's Dawson
63. Makes do

DOWN

1. Sediment
2. Aroma
3. Thomas ____ Edison
4. Atoll
5. Tunes
6. Icelandic literary work
7. Coconut fiber
8. Louisiana native
9. Cruising
10. Pliny's road
11. Back of the neck
13. Jazzman Davis
14. Fashion designer Oleg ____
20. Monet's farewell
21. Status ____
24. Noblemen
25. Rich tapestry
26. Margins
27. Wyoming range
28. Exceptional
29. Philadelphia athlete
30. Eyes
31. ____-do-well
32. Monastery head
33. Bathe
34. Cut quickly
36. Dishearten
37. Italian violinmaker
42. Texas tea
43. Mends
44. Petrify
45. Frequently
46. Money
47. Division word
48. Horse color
49. Iridescent gem
50. Fortune
51. Mystery author Gardner
52. Corner
53. Doctor's amount
54. Religious women: abbr.

PUZZLE 469

ACROSS

1. British letter
4. Information
9. Raced
13. "Trinity" author Leon ___
15. Ski resort
16. Charlatan
17. Largest portion
19. Taj Mahal locale
20. Eradicate
21. Fitting together, as boxes
23. Bread spreads
26. Twice five
27. Sustains
30. Egyptian president
32. Greek vowel
33. Indian shelter
35. Chum
37. Gratuity
38. Pedro's uncle
40. Buddhism or Catholicism: abbr.
41. Bullfight cheer
42. French island
43. ___ la vista
45. Barbie's boyfriend
46. "The Stu ___ Show"
48. Bank payment
52. Can material
53. Emulate Dick Button
54. Small ornament
58. Soils
62. Fury
63. Speak frankly
66. At any time
67. Bandleader Shaw
68. Connery of "The Russia House"
69. Spooky
70. Alan and Cheryl
71. Sault ___ Marie

DOWN

1. Bantu language
2. Ireland, in literature
3. Designer Christian ___
4. Quicker
5. Silvery-gray color
6. Auditor: abbr.
7. Gull's kin
8. Cut
9. Placed on a schedule
10. Unseen bargain
11. Attain
12. Haul
14. Pry
18. Song for one
22. Author Madame de ___
24. Kruger and Preminger
25. Opposite of NNW
27. Bristle: pref.
28. Useful
29. Blusterer
30. Observe
31. Stories
34. Trick
36. Loaned
38. Believe
39. Actor Buchanan
44. "___ the season . . ."
47. Claret producer
49. Flavors
50. "___, Brute"
51. Nurtures
54. Willow, e.g.
55. Rant
56. Latin abbreviation
57. Scarlett's home
59. Boone and Turner
60. Meticulous
61. Auld lang ___
64. Incorporated, in England: abbr.
65. Young goat

PUZZLE 470

ACROSS

1. On the ocean
5. Clothing junction
9. Walks heavily
14. Pennant
15. Diva Gluck
16. Large duck
17. Mountain lake
18. Conceited
19. "____ Gay"
20. Frequent fliers?
23. Withered
24. Charged particle
25. Nick and Nora's pet
27. Child's toy
30. Fight
34. Wish
36. Storage building
38. Chicken ____ king
39. Phileas Fogg, e.g.
42. Actress Lupino
43. Ping's partner
44. Typewriter types
45. Actress Susan and family
47. High-school student
49. Showy flower
50. Shoe tip
52. Fish-eating birds
54. "Around the ____ Days"
60. Kingly
61. Staffs
62. "Dies ____"
64. Sphere of action
65. Toward shelter
66. Tow
67. Obeys
68. Gives silent assent
69. Try to find

DOWN

1. At the stern
2. Dross
3. James ____ Jones
4. Unbeliever
5. Rescuer
6. In high spirits
7. Muslim nobleman
8. Hand: Sp.
9. Take care of
10. Bedding
11. Fragrance
12. Hardens
13. Spanish lady: abbr.
21. Endure
22. "____ the Toiler"
25. Stage whisper
26. Scatter
28. Kansas river
29. 54, to Caesar
31. Singer LaBelle
32. Century plants
33. Surfaces a road
34. Tasting like vinegar
35. Overacted
37. Looking at amorously
40. Opposite of SSW
41. Dirigibles
46. Maroon
48. Required
51. Earthenware jars
53. Ascends
54. "____ No Angels"
55. Curved molding
56. Mideastern country
57. ____ contendere
58. Factual
59. New Haven school
60. Cheerleader's shout
63. Wapiti

PUZZLE 471

ACROSS

1. Thumbtack
4. Prop for Chagall
9. Charlotte had one
12. October birthstone
14. Thwart
15. Inform
16. Be born with a silver spoon in one's mouth: 5 wds.
19. Indian, for one
20. Niche
21. Aggravated
22. Chill
24. Belief
25. Daydreams: 4 wds.
34. Palo ____
35. Units of farmland
36. Caper
37. Rita or Grande
38. Crude
39. Aunt, in Madrid
40. Hautboy
42. Peter, to a pumpkin
44. Symbol
45. "A ____ Dream": 2 wds.
48. College between Pittsburgh and Allentown: abbr.
49. Family member
50. Hawkins or Thompson
53. Haggard novel
56. Duke, dame, or lord
60. Not well: 3 wds.
63. Hit the ____
64. Sculled
65. Ages and ages
66. One
67. Fragrances
68. Amer. Indian

DOWN

1. Marco or water
2. Majestic
3. Bestowed
4. Slippery one
5. Ardent
6. Unharmed
7. First garden
8. Carrillo or Durocher
9. Unstressed
10. "... leave all ____ to the gods"
11. Became diffuse
13. Shed: hyph.
15. Designated
17. Indigo dye plant
18. Abe Vigoda role
23. Sweet veggie
24. ____ a boy!
25. Ricochet
26. Excuse
27. Got up
28. Vamoose
29. Piqued
30. More fresh
31. After gee
32. Oaf
33. Equines
41. Observed
42. Ostrichlike bird
43. Medical workers: abbr.
44. Light
46. Consumer
47. Whit
50. Koran chapter
51. By and by
52. 6/6/1944: hyph.
53. Herring
54. Star
55. Pitcher
57. "____ shalt not ..."
58. Pre-Easter time
59. Gaelic
61. Also
62. Sullivan and Begley

PUZZLE 472

ACROSS

1. Cabbage salad
5. Titles
10. Very fine rain
14. Scan (over)
15. Bar of metal
16. Opera melody
17. Cool liquids
18. Repent
19. Lab animals
20. Washington city
22. White weasels
24. Large-mouthed jars
26. Allow
27. Looked fixedly
30. Copycat
35. Chili con ____
36. Golf club
37. Erie or Placid
38. "We ____ the Champions"
39. Between tic and toe
41. Grow older
43. Break a Commandment
44. "____ Drink the Water"
46. Pork or beef
48. Evaluated
50. People with guns, at races
52. "Gunsmoke" star
53. Keen tonal sense
54. Heaps
56. Hunting expeditions
60. European thrush
64. Winter wear
65. Basketball player
67. Always
68. Feed the kitty
69. Press or secret
70. Steak style
71. Slender grass
72. Titles
73. Winter weather

DOWN

1. Resorts
2. Mine vein
3. Sector
4. Cowboy movie
5. Used the phone
6. Go in
7. Inflated ____
8. Completed
9. Thoroughly excellent
10. Kind of bliss
11. Persia, today
12. Scene
13. Soviet news agency
21. Chirp
23. Bumped into
25. Galahad's title
27. Oodles
28. Seer's deck
29. Sports center
31. Castle ditch
32. Sample
33. Dust-bowl refugees
34. Tears asunder
36. Froster
40. "The Ugly ____"
42. Goofed
45. Paid the tab
47. Cleo's snake
49. Replies
51. Roofing liquid
52. Informs
55. Goodnight girl
56. Aftereffect of trouble
57. Splendid: hyph.
58. Destiny
59. Long tale
61. The Terrible Tsar
62. Roman emperor
63. Waxed
66. Ruby or diamond

PUZZLE 473

ACROSS

1. Campfire refuse
6. Diddly-oop-bop
10. Actress Moore
14. Lois's pal
15. Major or Minor
16. Arabian noble
17. Country comic and novelist: 3 wds.
20. Type measures
21. Squirrel home
22. Stimulates
23. Fidget
24. Loot for the Knave of Hearts
25. Game fish
28. Sled
29. Bath
32. Tradename cookies
33. Barn adjunct
34. Comic Freberg
35. Horror author meets simian star
38. Type of line or step
39. Way-down
40. Water with a mouth
41. Assent
42. Don ____
43. No buts about it
44. Call's partner
45. Rhymer
46. Showy shrub
49. Amorous deity
50. Spelling contest
53. "God's Little Acre" star meets leading man: 3 wds.
56. Singles
57. Get paid
58. Sheds
59. Espouses
60. Search
61. Scratch out

DOWN

1. Zenith
2. ____ pickings
3. Artist Holbein
4. Marine raptor
5. Antsy
6. Great!
7. Algonquian language
8. Fit ____ fiddle: 2 wds.
9. Herb for a vinegar
10. Opening
11. Flightless birds
12. Farmer's wife's victims
13. Annoys
18. Hibernia
19. Old wives' tales
23. Inclined plane
24. Bell-shaped blossom
25. Unlike a rolling stone
26. Bandleader Shaw
27. Musical pipes
28. Compare
29. Pot spot
30. Switchboard
31. Huffy
33. Skulk
34. Go around
36. Makes lessons stick
37. Macabre
42. Hoot
43. By and by
44. Approve
45. Escapade
46. "All in ____": 2 wds.
47. District
48. Under covers
49. Bronte heroine
50. Actor Lugosi
51. Vittles
52. Otherwise
54. "The Facts of Life" star
55. Conjunction

PUZZLE 474

ACROSS

1. ____ breath
6. Shave sheep
11. Alums-to-be: abbr.
14. Fine fiddle
15. Nez ____ Indians
16. Carson
17. Vivacity: 2 wds.
19. Night before
20. Smooth and glossy
21. Chan portrayer
23. Saw eye to eye
26. Rule
27. Goddess of wisdom
28. Noah's landing
30. Disguise
31. Schedule
32. Palm leaf
35. Get up
36. Battle of the ____
37. Nabokov work
38. Choose
39. Concerns
40. Slammer
41. Type of nickel
43. Lead ore
44. Gomer Pyle, e.g.
46. Raids
47. Like a tower in Pisa
48. Stiller's spouse
50. Makeshift bed
51. Verdi opera: 3 wds.
57. "____ O'Clock Jump"
58. Social group
59. Eldritch
60. Saul's grandfather
61. Lugged
62. Old-fashioned

DOWN

1. Scrooge's statement
2. Parisian pal
3. Fox tail tip
4. Old English letter
5. Separative action
6. Emulated 007
7. Roll-call response
8. Estrada or Satie
9. Play part
10. Give back
11. Versatile opener: 2 wds.
12. Yellow or Orange
13. Firm
18. Kind of bargain
22. Caviar
23. Anchor position
24. Behind-the-scenes author: 2 wds.
25. M. Coty
26. Tower
27. Hair style
28. Director Woody ____
29. Riches' opposite
31. You bet!
33. Legal rights
34. Novelist Seton
36. Commanded
37. Actress Negri
39. Kind of lens
40. Marched
42. Upton Sinclair novel
43. Tennessee politician
44. Georgia city
45. Expiate
46. Simulated
48. Crow's-nest site
49. Ariosto's patron
52. Former Chinese leader
53. TV's Arthur
54. Museum exhibit
55. Golfer's concern
56. Took the fore

PUZZLE 475

ACROSS

1. After-bath sprinkle
5. Ledge
10. Cooking fat
14. Muffin topper
15. Hard resin
16. Neighborhood
17. Thailand, once
18. "Aida," for one
19. Shipshape
20. Military excavator
22. Brains
24. Pub brews
26. Important periods
27. Party game
31. Famed Hun
35. Poe's bird
36. Expiate
38. Dry, as wine
39. Folksinger Burl ____
40. Actor George ____
41. Bed support
42. Sea: Fr.
43. Lets up
44. Lawrence or Martin
45. Sets foot in
47. Banished
49. Land parcels
51. Went like sixty
52. Leech
56. "____ Mater"
60. Wotan
61. Seeps
63. Manufacture
64. Fix
65. Eric the Red, e.g.
66. Hibernia
67. Remnants
68. Gaiters
69. Divide

DOWN

1. Pitch
2. Inter ____
3. Frog or year
4. Likens
5. Earned points
6. Bound
7. Fencing sword
8. Gigantic
9. Disgraceful
10. Most recent
11. Scotto song
12. Mr. Foxx
13. Time periods
21. Dash
23. Detest
25. Roebuck's partner
27. Felony
28. Refuge
29. Prevent
30. Charger
32. Ait
33. GI's furlough
34. Performed
37. Attack
40. Bulwarks
41. Banner
43. God of love
44. Kind
46. African antelopes
48. Sheriffs' forces
50. Crouch
52. Fleshy fruit
53. Arabian gulf
54. Orange skin
55. Bible book
57. Exposed
58. Related
59. Take care of
62. Superlative suffix

PUZZLE 476

ACROSS

1. Tangy
5. Separated
10. ___ Hari
14. Persian poet
15. Street show
16. Religious painting
17. Leader
19. Bell town
20. Furtive
21. Fez feature
23. Observes
24. Anna's post
25. Depression
27. Santa Maria, for one
31. Drink noisily
32. Save up
34. Assam silkworm
35. "Penny ___"
36. Shindig
37. Soon
38. Coach Parseghian
39. Weeps
40. Rely upon
41. Relate
43. Outdated
44. "___ She Sweet?"
45. Irritate
46. Dash
49. Set off
53. Dash
54. Ruled out
56. Lease
57. Musical show
58. "___ Smile Be Your Umbrella"
59. Corrodes
60. Austrian geologist Eduard ___
61. Appear

DOWN

1. Goes beyond
2. He loves: Lat.
3. Marathon
4. Cherish
5. Mountain crests
6. Trails
7. Bohemian
8. Female ruff
9. Third in degree
10. Noxious atmosphere
11. Emotes
12. Ripped
13. Indigo plant
18. Snooze
22. Swiss river
24. Highlanders
25. Proclaim noisily
26. Of the moon
28. Most brilliant planet
29. Eaten away
30. Dryer fuzz
31. Strike sharply
32. Holy person
33. Quattro minus uno
36. Pressmen
37. Ammunition dumps
39. Son of Adam
40. Eagle's claw
42. Contaminates
43. Has compassion for
45. Uncle ___
46. Withered
47. Entreaty
48. Rave
49. Jackknife, e.g.
50. To ___
51. Head: Fr.
52. Dutch cheese
55. Romanian coin

PUZZLE 477

ACROSS

1. ____ la la
4. Creator
9. Employ
13. Apiece
15. Writer Rogers St. Johns
16. Germanic deity
17. Florentine river
18. Salmonoid fish
19. Penitence period
20. Race event
21. Magician's garb
22. Old saying
23. Excruciation
25. Liz
26. Lodestone
29. Bolivian city
31. Residence
32. Destruction
33. Standard quantity
37. Messy chap
38. Middle name
39. Make over
40. Proofreader's catch
41. Emulate Charlie Brown
42. Fissile rock
43. Saw feature
45. Propped
46. Golf club
49. Farther within
51. Frequently
52. Malayan vessel
53. Bagpiper, perhaps
57. Ananias
58. Drive
59. Different
60. "Vissi d'____" (Tosca's aria)
61. Unaided
62. Unique
63. Portland college
64. Studied hard
65. Put on

DOWN

1. Players
2. Undercooked
3. Skin problem
4. Group's talisman
5. Promo producer
6. Don't get upset: 4 wds.
7. French for 42 Down
8. Informant
9. Now, calm down: 3 wds.
10. Lifetime endeavor
11. Famed drummer
12. Computer key
14. Seeing red: 3 wds.
22. Rhine feeder
24. Gosh
25. Performer Tommy
26. Ship spar
27. With competence
28. Burgess boor
30. Religious procedure
32. Source
34. Approximate
35. Actor Eric
36. Kicked
38. Vamoose
42. Female
44. German one
45. Entangled
46. Tooth
47. Blazing
48. Condition
50. Nary a soul: 2 wds.
52. Early visitor to China
54. Clump
55. Scandinavian capital
56. "____ Beat"
58. Fairy queen

PUZZLE 478

ACROSS

1. Catch you later!
5. Wallop
9. Coalition
13. Proficient
15. Plumbing part
16. " . . . to love ____ other"
17. Laziness
18. ____ smasher
19. Acreage
20. High-strung
21. Place for thieves
22. Church instrument
23. Allege as fact
25. Set inward
26. Packing box
29. Summit
31. Vacates
32. Thrash
33. Grad
37. Hostile
39. Refuse
41. Spelling contests
42. Prior to
44. Keep
45. Shut forcefully
46. Nasal harrumph
47. Ponies
51. Support
53. Abscond
54. Wildebeest
55. Utters scratchily
60. Sagelike
61. Beloved
62. Be in store for
63. Uniform
64. Picnic pests
65. Gambling game
66. Others
67. Intersect
68. Bound

DOWN

1. Kind of iron or party
2. Useless
3. Long period of time
4. Selects
5. Card symbol
6. Not idiomatic
7. At the time of
8. Prized item
9. Vandyke
10. Enormous
11. Atlantic or Pacific
12. Mantra
14. Play place
22. Washington's bill
24. Watercraft
25. Dunk
26. Surrender
27. Good review
28. Birds
30. Rogue
31. Dr. Jekyll's haunt: abbr.
33. Highest male voice
34. Slanderer
35. Of a Christian group: abbr.
36. Gents
38. Epoch
40. Middle
43. Issue forth
45. Observe
47. Lumberjack
48. Green shade
49. Valentine's gift
50. Used up
52. Rupture
54. Actor Wilder
56. Army absconder
57. Fully satisfy
58. Pocket bread
59. Brake
61. Aswan, e.g.

PUZZLE 479

ACROSS

1. Tropical vine
6. Kilts' companions
10. "The Heat ____": 2 wds.
14. Misbehave: 2 wds.
15. Shoot forth
16. Italian painter
17. Boast: hyph.
19. N.C. college
20. Rich dessert
21. Nurse's specialty: abbr.
23. Brother
24. "____ On Down the Road"
27. Misplace
29. One who withstands
33. Mennonite
35. Prayer ending
36. ____ impasse: 2 wds.
38. Beyond: prefix
39. Unwilling to share
41. All by ____ (unaided)
44. Project Blue Book subject
45. Jumbo truck
47. Membrane
48. Belt
50. Noms de plume: 2 wds.
52. Peking nanny
53. Understood: 2 wds.
54. African antelope
56. Scoundrel
58. Young-Ameche film
63. Latvian seaport
65. Soi-disant: hyph.
68. Sore
69. Sandusky's lake
70. Clean
71. Apportion
72. Snick-or-____
73. Screams

DOWN

1. Final
2. Bakery employee
3. King of the Huns
4. ____ said!
5. "Wizard of Oz" missiles
6. Sympathy's companion
7. Friend: Fr.
8. Drizzle
9. Midler movie (1990)
10. Choler
11. Ego: hyph.
12. ____ about: 2 wds.
13. Hirschfeld daughter
18. Looping lariats
22. ____ il faut
25. Adam's son et al.
26. Age
28. Mexican nap
29. ____ Addar
30. Australian birds
31. Educated out of school: hyph.
32. Squeal
34. German city
37. Ancient Egyptian provinces
40. Author Asimov
42. 'Frisco eleven
43. Musical notes
46. Upon: prefix
49. Stages
51. Tidier
54. Weight measure
55. Riviera town
57. Actor Bruce ____
59. "____ Breckinridge"
60. "Good Earth" wife: hyph.
61. Aerie
62. Thirst quenchers
64. Mm-hmm
66. Prevaricate
67. Charge

PUZZLE 480

ACROSS

1. Wound crust
5. Chinese party
9. Slide a slope
14. Toodle-oo: hyph.
15. Sulawesi ox
16. Propose
17. Shy fellow
19. Vestige
20. Cool, man
21. Jet: abbr.
23. Leavings
24. Former Colt quarterback: 2 wds.
28. Filthy place
29. Arizonan Yuman tribe
33. Type of race
37. Numerical prefix
39. Pass a law
40. Former lightweight champ: 3 wds.
44. "____ Grows in Brooklyn": 2 wds.
45. Dawber or Shriver
46. "East of ____"
47. Edible mollusk
50. Utter
52. Come down hard: 3 wds.
58. Portico
61. Dr. J's org.
62. Raisin, once
63. Chicago busy spot
65. Boasters
68. Prenatal
69. Helen's ma
70. Don Diego marks
71. Seed covering
72. "My Favorite ____"
73. First Christian Scientist

DOWN

1. Smart
2. Crete's capital
3. Perfume
4. "A Midsummer Night's Dream" actor
5. Hebrew letter
6. Single
7. Scandinavian
8. Fitzgerald character
9. Camp bed
10. "...touch the honey ____": 2 wds.
11. From a distance
12. Faction
13. Three: Sp.
18. Amazed cries
22. ____ T: 2 wds.
25. Sarge's dog
26. Ship compass
27. Baking chamber
30. Receipt stamp
31. Facial bumps
32. Don't rub ____: 2 wds
33. Arab garments
34. Milit. org.
35. Unit of syllabic length
36. Suspect: 3 wds.
38. Rascal
41. ____ Horizonte, Brazil
42. Spar
43. Canton nurse
48. Have
49. Rocky
51. Safecracker
53. Street show
54. Solder
55. Paddled
56. Chose
57. Untidy
58. Squishy
59. "Of ____ I Sing"
60. Sow wild ____
64. Guido's high note: 2 wds.
66. Novel by Nabokov
67. Needlefish

PUZZLE 481

ACROSS

1. Charlie Brown's cry
5. Varnish ingredient
10. Irani ruler, once
14. Lode access
15. Cleverly escape
16. Ice cream holder
17. Actor Jamie ____
18. Confused fight
19. Mystic's character
20. Sedition
22. Naval officer
24. ____ King Cole
25. Baby's seat, sometimes
26. Jack Webb's show
30. Iceberg or Romaine
34. Stormed about
35. Got up
37. Sister
38. Assert
39. Army bigwigs
40. Great trumpeter
41. For each
42. Pat or Daniel
43. Cafe patron
44. Beg
46. Theft
48. Ogee shape
49. Appetizer in Oahu
50. Eating room
54. Dismissed: 2 wds.
58. Golden calf
59. Gone on a jet
61. Russian range
62. African lily
63. Common
64. ____ mater
65. Advance money
66. Seculars
67. Onionlike veggie

DOWN

1. Tom Sawyer's craft
2. Hebrew month
3. Exhaust
4. Truth, compared to fiction
5. Far
6. Like six or eight
7. "My Gal ____"
8. Thought
9. Unnecessary
10. Handwriting
11. Sixty minutes
12. "____ Karenina"
13. Foot part
21. Pearl seed
23. Spouse
26. Curtain
27. Poe's bird
28. Prevent
29. Seer's deck
30. Born ____
31. Become one
32. Doctor, for one
33. Diary notation
36. Did a marathon
39. Like a braggart
40. Customary
42. Ultimate
43. Black, to poets
45. Staggered
47. Aboveboard
50. Telephone part
51. Unemployed
52. Lunchtime, for some
53. Famous lioness
54. Smack
55. Shield border
56. Irene Cara film
57. Anti-aircraft fire
60. Parisian aye

PUZZLE 482

ACROSS

1. Hit sharply
5. Stop
9. Kitty
12. String
13. Diva's big moment
14. Bullfight cry
15. Before: pref.
16. Cake froster
17. YMCA members
18. Harass
20. Dance movement
22. Ring of light
24. Wetland
27. Lancelot's title
30. Bench or stool
32. A Great Lake
33. Lyric poem
34. Paper
36. Opposite of WSW
37. Be in front
39. Not front or back
40. Dover's st.
41. Artist's stand
43. Shadowbox
45. Had bills
47. Speaker
51. Cargo unit
53. Author Sheehy
55. Delivered
56. "Where the Boys ___"
57. Lily's relative
58. Sword
59. Blood color
60. Contact ___
61. Broadcast

DOWN

1. Smack
2. ___ and dine
3. Tiny tunnelers
4. Molars
5. Bald
6. Joan of ___
7. "sex, ___ and videotape"
8. Bakery items
9. Matched
10. Brewery product
11. Half a score
19. Comfort
21. Wool provider
23. Desert area
25. Quarry
26. Fruit skin
27. Fillet of ___
28. View
29. Speculated
31. Young frogs
35. Fifty-two weeks
38. Grass moisture
42. Lawful
44. Blows up
46. Valley
48. Masking ___
49. Cake baker
50. Organ pipe
51. Old sailor
52. Crude mineral
54. Charged atom

PUZZLE 483

ACROSS

1. Money for the poor
5. Pub beverages
9. Manage
13. Minor disagreement
17. Knock for a ____
18. Prime-time time
19. Jai ____
20. Mexican coin
21. Not worth ____
24. Over again
25. Hunting dogs
26. "We ____ the World"
27. Moral error
29. A Bobbsey twin
30. Anti's answer
31. Plays the lead
33. Neutral color
35. Riser
38. Benefit
39. Nice
43. Chore
44. Distrust
45. Legal attachment
46. Leg joint
47. Chicken ____ king
48. Brown quickly
49. Multi-movement composition
51. Fasten a shoelace
52. Early pioneer
54. Ducked away
55. General direction
57. First slice
58. Not together
59. Afternoon program
60. Greene of "Bonanza"
62. Weighing device
63. Write music
66. Hail!
67. Eraser's locale
69. Red planet
70. New Zealand parrot
71. Final letters
73. Modern gaslight
74. Display anger
75. Precious
76. Put at risk
78. Long fish
79. Cold spreaders
80. Butter look-alike
81. Funeral hymn
83. Bro's sibling
84. Girl
86. Coat sleeve
88. Future fish
89. The minimum
93. Singer Guthrie
95. Unsympathetic
98. Actual
99. Flair
100. Organization
101. Shredded
102. Poet
103. Fully cooked
104. Affirmative votes
105. "Graf ____"

DOWN

1. Woeful word
2. Bounding gait
3. Mew
4. Russian satellite
5. Grouchy
6. Untruths
7. Means justifier
8. Upper House member
9. Unexpected blow
10. Wapiti
11. Highlanders' negatives
12. Industrious
13. Health facility
14. Cheap card game
15. On a voyage
16. Small city
22. Equipment
23. Neighbor of Pakistan
28. Gun gp.
31. Take to the air
32. Piano
34. Pop the question
35. Train depots: abbr.
36. Story
37. Phony ____ bill
38. Panda or teddy
40. Be ahead
41. No, in Munich
42. ____ off
44. Detect
45. French river
48. Be in dreamland
49. Will
50. Tiny particles
53. Finger count
54. Madrid's country
56. Knock
58. Agreement
59. Kind
60. Goof off
61. Julia Child's prop

PUZZLE 483

62. Snick-and- ____
63. Soup containers
64. Row of stitches
65. Things to lend and bend
68. Swallowed greedily
69. Man
72. Actor Mineo
74. Style of furniture
75. Gobi and Sahara
77. Teachers' org.
78. Greek god of love
79. Kind of monster
82. Actress Dunne
83. Bangs a toe
84. Clothing
85. Surroundings
87. Venus de ____
89. Bluish green
90. At the pinnacle
91. Dried up
92. Family ____
94. No spring chicken
96. Moving truck
97. Torero's hurrah

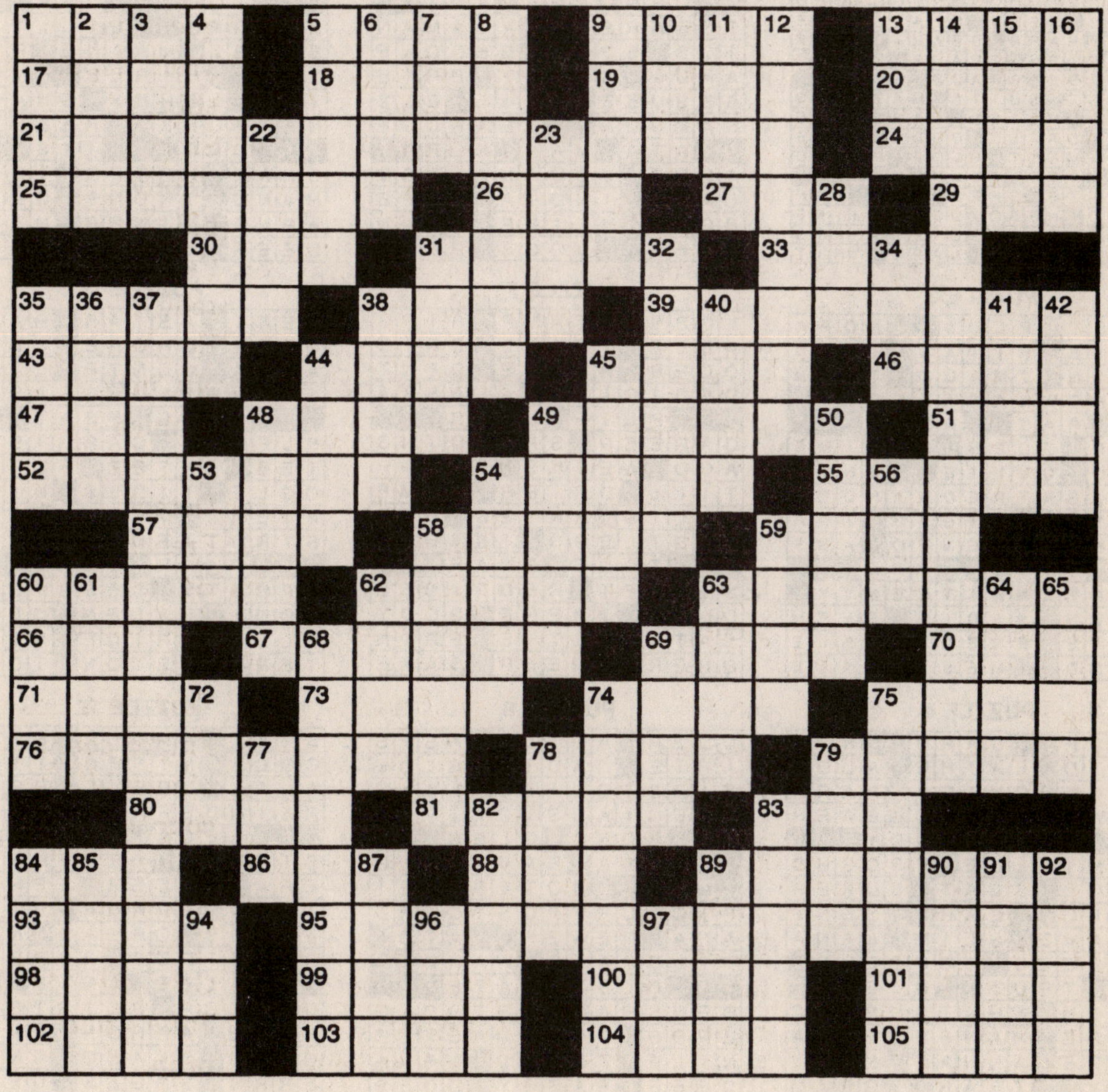

PUZZLE 1

FRA CADS PARI
ROLL CARAT OMEN
ASIA AGATE RANT
THENINETEENTHTO
END LOS
TEN TIAS RIVET
ERE REST DICE
NOWPASHURTHESON
ESTA MIRA OLD
TESTS POET RES
EAT SEL
THELORDWASREADY
HURL ARISE ALOE
ALIA CARPS DILL
ILES EWES TEL

PUZZLE 2

TATS ABED SLED BOSS
ARIA BARE HERE ABET
KEEPSAKES RANT LORE
EAR USE THEN REDEEM
ARE CREW WAGE
LAPSE MOON RECORDED
AIRS VERY HEATS ALE
DDE RARE SEARS TRIP
DESPISE TEARS TREAT
EASE BRADS WOOD
SENSE SUITS MATTERS
ALTO PLIES CARE VIE
SSE ORALS GODS HIDE
SEDIMENT SLOE PILED
MITT PEAK GEM
CREATE BRED SEA LAP
LONG NERO DETERMINE
ALOE DRAW EVES EATS
PEWS SAGS NAPE GRIT

PUZZLE 3

LAST PLUS NORA
ARTE RITAS INON
GAIN IMAGO TERN
BROWNASABERRY
RAT NERO
FIR TOES REGIME
ONO CURIE ENID
CAUGHTREDHANDED
ANTA STEAM INA
LEERED ENTO ASS
DYES CRO
GREENWITHENVY
LIEN SADIE SEEM
ALIE ERECT ERLE
BAND MESS TALL

PUZZLE 4

MESH SARD SPY
ALTO LATHE ALOE
SMEW ONTOP RARA
HOWDOYOUDO EWER
ORA ANDY
AMIBLUE EPOCHS
AWOL SLAT SURER
SILO ERR SENT
KNAVE SLIM LANA
AGREES YOUBEMY
TROT STE
PATH WHATSUPDOC
OBOE HANSE IONA
PURE ANNAL NOEL
STY TEAR GRAM

PUZZLE 5

URDU SARAH SERAC HESA
ROAR OMEGA URIEL EVER
SPLITLEVEL POPCONCERT
AYE RENE SLIDE TOASTY
END ONE HURT
PACKET STAVE FIRMEST
ERRED WHOSE KOREA HIM
PLAN BREAKDANCE GAGA
LES GUARD FOUR FAKER
ASH ANTE STOWS ALPERT
CLOTH SPOON PLIES
SPOILS START FAIR PBS
TOURS SLOT MARAT ERA
AURA WISECRACKS PAUL
RRS EPICS OATES PERIL
SEALANE SHEET GAIETY
RETE PTA OAR
ASPECT GRANI ERLE PPS
SCATTERRUG TUMBLEWEED
EACH READE EPPIE OKRA
AREA NOYES MISTY WEEK

PUZZLE 6

HEYS MOAT LBS
ANEW EFLAT EACH
IDLE AGILE MLII
GOLDILOCKS OTOS
OEN LEA ANI
TOWNRED ATAMAN
ICS EBEN REDONE
ARUM SNORT ERIE
REBUKE VEIL ELS
SAMSON TEAROSE
ATA MAI NOR
AGRA JOURNALISM
LAIR INDIA LOPE
POND MAINE ULAN
LES DOGS PEND

PUZZLE 7

LOSS STAMP RIPS
ABET TRIAL ERIE
DOER RIDGE GENT
DEDICATE ALASKA
PLIE USER
CAREEN SPENDING
AGO WEEKS SENOR
TILL DRIER DOME
ELLIS ANTES NEE
RESTLESS INTEND
TONE GNAR
STREET REDPINES
OMAR IRENE BODY
LATE RETIE ERIN
ONER EMEER SATE

PUZZLE 8

ODER AGILE ASPS
ARTE RADIX SLOE
FIRSTCLASS KALE
SPECIALS OLIVES
RONS GLEN
LISA RAVAGING
MOP NOTES REI
PICTUREPOSTCARD
ANA NEWER ATO
WILDCATS WARE
OLDS FATE
REDSEA PARTSONG
EROS POSTMASTER
NILE TRIAL ETNA
DEER SASSY DOES

PUZZLE 9

DAY GLOW VIDI
EROS AERO VENOM
SCUT MEAN ARADA
CHARLESLDODGSON
CEES ELIE
ALOSS FARES COO
LOUSE LALA EARP
TYPE HARAN MUNI
HALS AMON MACON
OLE AMIND ACUTE
ALAN TRIS
THEKINGOFHEARTS
RELIC OMAR TAIL
IRATE ENCE ECRU
MAME SITE EER

PUZZLE 10

ABES MAC SALK
DAVE OHARA ERIN
ALAN TULIP RENE
INA TREAT ISAW
TOO AAA
ASTORS LILLIAN
SHORE MAINE RTE
TIL GIRLS MAS
IRE LENNY SHALT
NETWORK REESES
ONO ITS
CHAN NOTED TED
HAND INONE OVEN
ARNE MINER NEMO
DEER OTE SNOW

PUZZLE 11

BEST ASTAR RAPT
ODOR CHORE ELIA
AIDA CONTE LAND
STANDING FEASTS
CODE PEAT
SLEEVE CARRIERS
TEE ENTER POPUP
OGLE TIDES NIPA
PIERS MEDAL CEN
STRUTTED LEASES
PARR SEAL
SPOTTY SESSIONS
LONI SALEM GLOW
OLEO TRINE HIRE
TERN SETON TOAD

PUZZLE 12

SPAT AMOLE STOP
COLA NINES TIME
ALAN TREAT REEL
REINDEER ETERNE
EELS VERA
STEREO REMEMBER
ERA SPEER EERIE
WORD ERASE RIDE
EPEES OREAD NED
REDBIRDS ROPERS
ALEE ANTE
UNSTOP BLISTERS
RETE AARON TRIP
GEAR SLANG ENTE
ERRS SAGES DEED

PUZZLE 13

ASH EDGE CHAP BAAL
PEEP ROOM ROLE AWRY
SARI ATOP EWER NEAR
ELDERS FIDDLEFADDLE
ANEW RIO ELI
AVILA IBEX LOCATES
LARA SPAS FASTS LAB
DIAMETER MAILS SUE
ANNOYED BURRO SCALE
DEW LUTES LAO
WAGES MIXED NATURES
HIM SILOS MATERIAL
ODE MADAM GONE AFRO
ANGELIC DEAN AGENT
USE CON YALE
OLDFASHIONED FLOATS
LOAF MICA RANI URSA
ELLA ARES ITER SLAG
SLEW NEST CEDE ORE

PUZZLE 14

HIP AMBER AFAR FILE
ALAS TOADY DANA EMEND
RIDE HORSELAUGH ABATE
PARABLES AGNES RISEN
DEFIED CEREAL FIBERS
OTT SHAGS CANE
ECHO ESTATE FLUNG HOP
WOOD WAR PLIES BOAR
ERR HORSESHOES TORTE
RESCUERS GLASS MARSHY
EASED BRASS PUREE
DIPPED PEEVE GALOSHES
IDLED HORSESENSE ARE
NEAR BAKES JOT PINT
GAY COMET THEMES ORES
TENS DEUCE TOO
ASCEND FERRET TODDLE
COAST CREES HURDLING
ELITE HORSEOPERA ELSE
SANER OTIS WRING STUN
REDS WHEY NORSE SEE

PUZZLE 15

PARK SPUR DEBT FANG
ERIE CASE OVER URAL
TINY ACES MELODRAMA
SAT ALE TRESTLE BED
IDLE TOAD LAP
CANAL HORN CHERRIES
ARTY BALE BUOY ORAL
LEI LEND CURLS LOSE
MANKIND CARVE HONED
NOD HOUSE FUN
BATON ROAST TANGLED
ABET PASTE CART AVA
SLAT AGES BALM KNIT
SELECTED BARK SIDLE
DOT COLD BATS
ERA SEVERAL PAW COW
PENETRATE ACID TAXI
IDOL NINE SANG OPEN
CONK SNAP TREE PEND

PUZZLE 16

SHAD RAFF MOW
CORA EVER ANI
ABUT SIRE GET
ROMANCANDLE
OUTS OLLA
CAM TEE POLAR
AGATES BANANA
SENOR DEN NAB
TRIP READ
FIRECRACKER
PRO ACID LORE
OIL MADE ELAN
POD SPED FAST

PUZZLE 17

BELT SCALP REDS
OLEO ERROR EDIE
TIER NOISE LIME
HART ASA PRATED
OPTS TAUT
RETIRE BARBELLS
AROSE TOMES EAT
DOTE PRAMS DATA
ADE DAISY MISER
RESTRICT DESERT
RANK CENT
SCRAWL RAT APED
ARID ELITE NOTE
POSE SEDER CLAN
SPED SEERS ELLS

PUZZLE 18

SPA JUDO FAST
LOU ASIA AREA
YES CENT LOWS
TROD HELMET
THROB READY
RUIN BRAIN
AMA PAUSE JOY
WORTH FADE
STAIN LINEN
POLLEN TAXI
EDIT AMEN TAP
EAVE PUNK OLE
DYED EDDY RAN

PUZZLE 19

YAP BRAG DABS
ECU LONE ELEE
SESSIONS GAEL
HUNT TARIFF
CHORD PURE
LOVE FERMENTS
ABE TONES ORA
PORTIONS ASIN
ALLY THEME
SHUNTS HOED
TANG CHARMING
EVIL AIMS VEE
METE PESO EEL

PUZZLE 20

STAR SETS BOG
TAXI EDEN EMU
ELLS NINETEEN
MEEKEST EARNS
IRE URN
MINER ASS TOP
OVER OWE FARE
BYE ALL TIGER
ATE EAR
APART PARENTS
LIMEADES MORE
ACE CUTE EPEE
SAN HOES NEED

PUZZLE 21

HOME ASP ALMS
IDEA ROE WOOL
DENS END AIDE
TAN DARNED
CAMERA LIE
ALERT PER NUN
MOAN HER CONE
PET FAN FRUIT
SUN GIANTS
ALMOND ANT
TOUR LAB EVIL
OGLE ELL RICE
PEER SEE SEED

PUZZLE 22

FLAT AFT TAMP
RODE ROE OLEO
OPERATES OPTS
MESSY STY HEY
EEL SOFA
HOT SAW NOBLE
AIRY POD REEK
GLEAM ERR TOE
AMEN YES
ASS TUB STAGS
BOUT BACTERIA
LURE BRA MILK
EPEE YEN SALE

PUZZLE 23

ABLE CAR THAN
LEAD LIE IOWA
EAVE ARDENTLY
CRANES SKY
SPOKE BOA
ASHES DISTANT
NEAR LON ALTO
TERRIER AXIOM
END RASPS
JAR UPBEAT
BEGINNER EASE
ARAB ERS ERIE
NAPE DEE SLAM

PUZZLE 24

PART GELD WASP ALAS
ALAR LEAR OBIE PILE
ROME AGREEMENT OMAN
REPAIR ASSET ISLAND
TREK DEN ETAL
KENYA NOEL PRISONER
ARE STERN LENOS ERA
NICE RED LATIN SWAT
ENEMIES ALBEE PASTE
SIRE FLOOR HELP
AISLE SATYR MANSARD
IRAE SPIED TON APAR
DAR STARR PANDA EVA
ANYWHERE TENT CAREW
RENE FOR EVIL
ABROAD SATIN EDWARD
BRAN HALLOWEEN ARIA
LANG AMES INRO YELL
EGGS LADE GERM SALE

PUZZLE 25

HARSH ASSET
PANAMA FEWER
BOUNCES AWARE
RUN EATER TIE
ARTS RED USES
KEEPS NEST
EDDIES NITWIT
LAID NEIGH
VEAL LAS RENO
ELM POLKA NOR
NOBEL LANTERN
OPERA ATTIRE
MERRY SEEMS

PUZZLE 26

NOW MESS THAW
ELI IGET RITA
WELLDONE ILAY
TOLLS IMPEL
OTTO ASSES
LADY IRKS ILL
ERODED NOODLE
NEW RENO READ
SANTA EBBS
TASTE ROSES
ATON ADMONISH
DOWD PLOW ATE
DENY SEWN MAD

PUZZLE 27

KITTY BOWL SCOT
ADORE ARIA EASE
RERUN CARDTABLE
LASS TOLEDO SON
LOTION SENT
SOW RIOTED
PRO NEWLY CURVE
LEAP LAYER REIN
UNTIL RESIN ELS
GOSSIP LET
ALEC METERS
SPA ABROAD NUNS
COMICBOOK STRAP
USED LAZE KHAKI
MESA EKES ISLET

PUZZLE 28

GALE OBESE IRKS
EDEN ALOHA MEAL
LIED SANER PALE
STROKES ANGERED
REST SIR
CEASE SUN NINES
ALIENS NEW LOVE
BUS ELITE BEA
IDLE WIT DESERT
NEEDS PER MELTS
WIG EVIL
SINATRA WATERED
ODOR ALIAS COLE
WEED STORE TILE
SALS PONDS SLAP

PUZZLE 29

SLOP SLOT ARC
LAVA LANE RIO
ICESKATES INN
PEN IVE TRADE
STE TEE
SEALS PADDLES
ARLO ARM DINO
PEEPERS WEEDS
EVE RAN
LEASE LOS PTA
ERR NEIGHBORS
TIE TAME SLAP
SEA STAR ALPS

PUZZLE 30

CLAM MACAW OWLS
LIDO AVENA SHOW
AMID POINT SIDE
WATERLILIES TEE
LIED RECENT
TOWELS FALLOW
EVADE KILO LABS
NET SWALLOW TRY
TREY ARMY IMEAN
RAPTLY ADOREE
TOWHEE ASOR
ARI TREADSWATER
SETS BRIDE VOTE
TACO ONDES INON
EDHS YEARS AGNI

PUZZLE 31

CHEFS AREO OGRE
LADLE REAL DEAD
OLEAN ESSE ETTE
PENNSTATE ASTER
NEE FLIMSY
BASE EMU MIASMA
APTLY ILIAD BUM
SRO ATT ENS ULA
TIN SEEDS TARTS
ELYRIA OIL EGIS
BECKON OAR
VERSA DARTMOUTH
ALOE TOTO ISSUE
SLOT CREA SOMME
TSKS USSR SLAPS

PUZZLE 32

CITES LOAF RAT
ARETE ELLA MILO
PILOT ADAR AVER
ESE TYPEWRITERS
PLEA INERT
SHARP ALECS
ETON SONORA COB
DANES LTS SCOPE
ORE OWLETS OMIT
AURAS AGAPE
PARSE LULU
FAXMACHINES TAB
RILE KATE SWEDE
AGED ELAN EERIE
YES DOLE TESTS

PUZZLE 33

SEES OMIT ASHES
LARA RANI STERE
AVON IRON TRAIN
WESTPOINT RELET
IONA HOE
ARAL NOLA PAS
OMEGAS ZIP RIA
COLORADOSPRINGS
ALI LON YEMENI
ETA AGES CPLS
BED ERAL
VALID ANNAPOLIS
ELIDE COAT RUDE
NOMEN ESTE ELLA
TENDS DYED DUET

PUZZLE 34

BACH COD BAS
EERIE LIRE PERT
RECAP ALEX ALIA
ASH CASSIUSCLAY
ITALS LAKES
DEBATE LETTS
ORAL SPARSE ZEN
WILES ANN SMILE
NED ESTEEM OMIT
ANTES AROMAS
PINTA CRETE
LEONARDSLYE RHO
ETTU TRUE LEMON
SEAL SARA ERASE
ERS BEN DENS

PUZZLE 35

IRED GLAND STOW
DEMO ROMEO PAPA
ODIC AGING AXED
LORENZODEMEDICI
NEE AWE
ORATE ACE ESSAY
MAR DIPOLAR EGO
ATE CAVIL TAD
HEN SECEDES UTE
ADAGE EYE LAPEL
ARC VAN
LEONARDODAVINCI
AXON EAVES MOOD
SIZE PLEBE ANNE
STET TENTS LEES

PUZZLE 36

FOAL ISLE SPEW
ECRU SPERM ERLE
THEVILLAGEGREEN
ESA DAIS LEAFED
LENT DOLCE
CREED DADA RAG
SLED EMIT ETO
CALAVERASCOUNTY
ORA IRAN NCAA
TAX ONCE SEDER
ALLEY MANO
ARTIES CARO ARI
PAINTTHETOWNRED
EVOE SUDEN EMIL
SEND BERG TYNE

PUZZLE 37

CLAD JALAP COLA
HAIR ORATE ALAR
UNDERCOVERAGENT
MASSEUSE GEODE
SANE BRED
ABOARD ALAN HAD
BERG CHORD ODA
UNDERTHEWEATHER
SEI ARIAN RULE
ETE POND BLAMED
KITE PAIN
CAINE MOLASSES
UNDERONESBREATH
PEEL LASSO PROA
SWAT ATSEA TANG

PUZZLE 38

CHAD EARPS ACTS
HERO SLURP SHIP
ERIC TAMER HIDE
FELTCHIPPER PAL
ORE SEAWALL
SPIRITED SNOW
EON BEVEL TRAPS
TOTS SELAH DYAK
APHID NOMAD ALI
ELIA NARRATES
ACCOSTS DEL
RAH CHIPPEDBEEF
BRIG ORION IDLE
OGPU MEESE OGLE
ROSY ENDED NEAT

PUZZLE 39

THIS SHOTS CADS
AERO HOSEA ARIA
FRANCISSCOTTKEY
TON AREA REST
AUKS PEER
BARNS BERN TOW
ABATES RANT OVA
COGS POISE SPIN
ODE TEND SALINE
NED RACE DICES
FAKE DRAM
DOOM FROM DAW
JOHNPHILIPSOUSA
ADIT ALIVE REIN
MOOS PETER BLAT

PUZZLE 40

BURP GRADE ROUT
ORAL RETIE EASY
DAVYJONESLOCKER
ELI OPEN LASSO
SKEW SHIP
DEFIED SLAV MAP
IVAN GAYLE EGO
JACKOFALLTRADES
ODE DALEY BENS
NED DRAM DEBATE
BEES NILE
OLLAS HATS EAR
GOODTIMECHARLIE
RANG LORRE ELMS
EDGE LASER BAST

PUZZLE 41

HIFI ABE AFAR
EDEN PAY LILY
PEAS IRE ANTE
ARISE LASSO
DOC IRK
SERENE DEACON
AWE OWE
MEDALS REVOLT
GAP AGE
CARGO BONET
BABE ROB IRIS
ISLE TRI CAPE
DEED SET ELSE

PUZZLE 42

LAS LEN
PRIDE COLE
LEMON ASIAN
GASP DAM STEW
ATE SIPS ERA
BETTE DEPENDS
ODD DOG
FLOWERS TOOTH
LOW NEAR LEE
YANK AGE ADAM
DENIM PAVES
RELY ADORE
SEE YEN

PUZZLE 43

RADAR BOB SSW
ADORE ARE TEA
GEESE READERS
ODOR DRAFT
HORN BEN ELSE
AWE DENIES
MEDLEY NOSILY
UNEVEN COO
HAFT DOT SEWN
OGRES TYPE
TRESTLE ADMEN
LET OER NAIVE
YES WAS ENDED

PUZZLE 44

BAR BETS ROD
ABE AREA HERO
GENERALS ADAM
STEER HANDLE
LEAK IKE
ATE LIE RENTS
LEND DIM REAL
LACED TIS DRY
LAY HATE
STOLES ELITE
LOSE AMERICAN
ONER GALE EMO
BED ARLO DES

PUZZLE 45

NONE ILL LOLL
EVIL RYE ARIA
TEND KEG RAMP
SNEEZE SALES
RODENT
HELLO BOY AGE
AWAY BOW WREN
YEW EON DATED
BAYOUS
SCRUB COHOST
LAIR HOE EPEE
IRON ERA RARE
PETS MEN SLED

PUZZLE 46

BAT EGO BIB
ALE GRAD SORE
COLORADO CREE
HELLO RAREST
DONS HE
SPA VAT ASHE
COLLEGECAMPUS
IDLE NAT YES
AW OPTS
PAWNEE EASED
ALEE BEANPOLE
STAR BEND DAN
TON SLY ANT

PUZZLE 47

RITE ADD ATOM
ODES RUE NOPE
MELT DEN KNEE
PALACE TALENT
TON AGE
ABSENT LOSERS
WOE GOO
LAWYER BARGED
ERE ORE
ALTARS NEARER
TIER INN MADE
OMEN GEE EYES
PENS NET DENT

PUZZLE 48

HAM ELM WASP
ERAS YEA ALTO
MISTREAT SPED
AHOY HUT
REST SENSE
WINK AIDE OLD
IRE MAE NAG
TAR FERN TOTE
SNORE AYES
OWL LALA
OBEY INDIRECT
TOGA FOR SARI
TOOL TRY PEP

PUZZLE 49

HUT RACE ABBE
ANY ELAN DRAW
TIP WISE MUSE
STOMACH LINES
ARE GATE
SCALD DEW TWO
HALE AIL STAR
EMU ARM SIEGE
MIST SAT
EDITS FEDERAL
DONE ARID ERA
GLUM GONE AIR
ELMS OMEN DAD

PUZZLE 50

GRIP ROAM DAD
AIDE UNDO EGO
SPEEDBOAT LOG
SALE METE
ENDS LEGAL
BOLD RED DALE
APE AVA TON
SAME GEM TEED
SLOTS NEAR
NAPS SEAL
ERA ICESKATES
SOD RARE TONE
SEE ETNA SPAT

PUZZLE 51

ETC WAVE PAWN MATA
GARB ABET ALAI OVAL
ARIA KATE NORM HOLE
DABBLE RESEMBLANCE
IONS NAY LEI
SCREW WEAR CHEERED
HOED PEAL BLESS DAD
AMA WHET PLANT EDO
WORSHIP NEARS MYNAS
OYL VERNE GOO
FLAPS FIORD BELUSHI
OAR CANNY PORT OUT
ENA JOKES PONE URGE
ALLUDES LIED ENTER
ADD PAC SLED
CONSOLATION ELUDED
ABUT IRAN IOTA LICE
BODE NENE CHIS YORE
SEED GAGS SOME RUM

PUZZLE 52

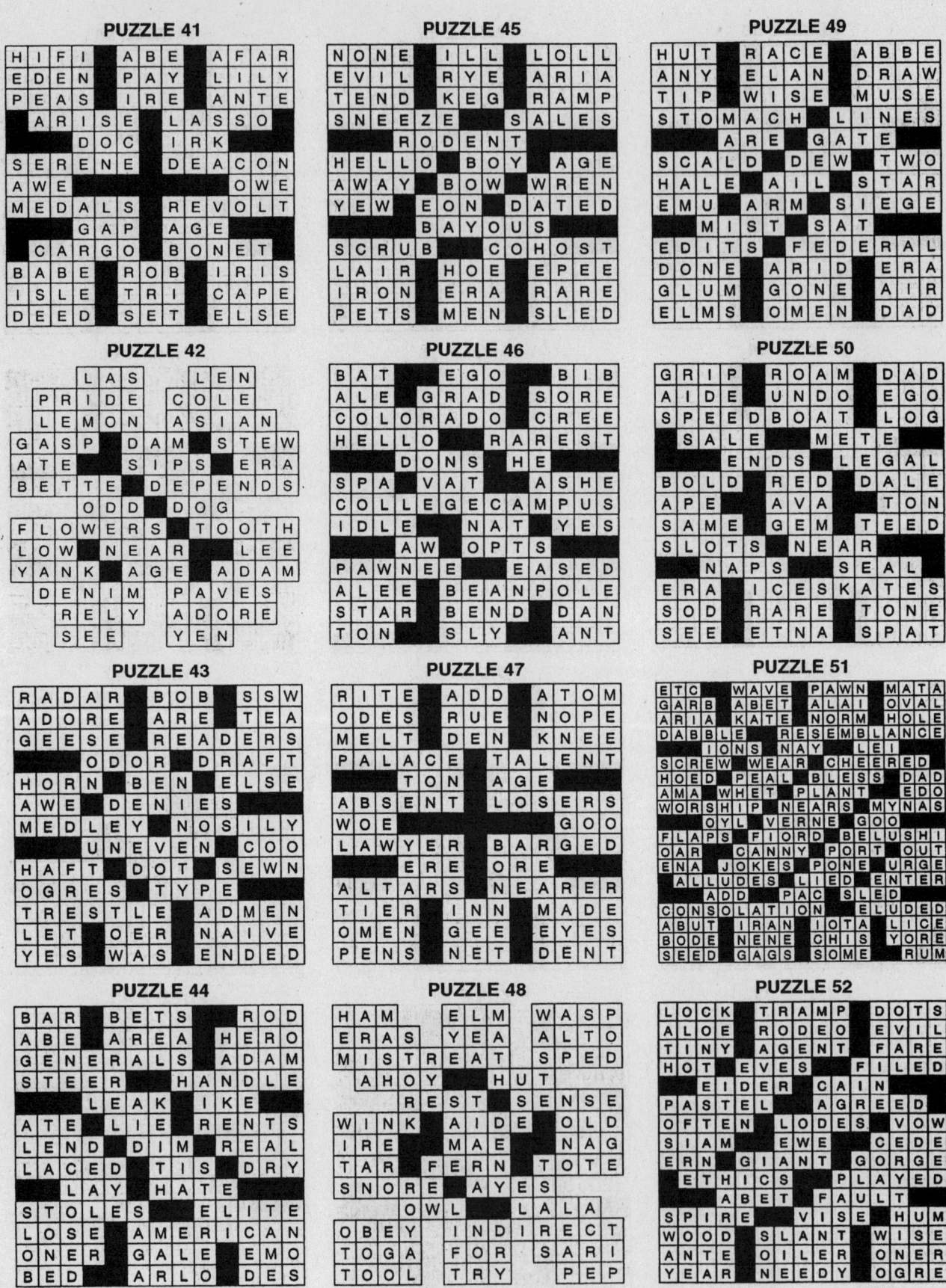

LOCK TRAMP DOTS
ALOE RODEO EVIL
TINY AGENT FARE
HOT EVES FILED
EIDER CAIN
PASTEL AGREED
OFTEN LODES VOW
SIAM EWE CEDE
ERN GIANT GORGE
ETHICS PLAYED
ABET FAULT
SPIRE VISE HUM
WOOD SLANT WISE
ANTE OILER ONER
YEAR NEEDY OGRE

PUZZLE 53

SPED RASH SMOTE
POLE OLIO HOPED
ARAL SILO ATALE
THEPINKPANTHER
TINE GEL
AMAIN STAR EARN
TAROTS ESE REE
LIONANDTHEMOUSE
ENS OUR DUBBED
SEER REAP FLATS
ALE ASTI
LADYORTHETIGER
ADIOS REAR AVOW
MARNE ARNI TINA
PRESS MESA ELAN

PUZZLE 54

RAGA WHALE MAIA
EARL IOWAN ATLI
ARAB DUETS SOIL
DEMETER EUROPA
RON CLEAN
SKETE FLY FREYA
LEDA LIE STYLES
ERG MARMOTS MAC
PREFER EAU LETO
TYROL TNT WORST
REARS SAO
SEMELE ALCMENE
ALDO TBONE IVAN
SUES ELITE NEMO
HERA RELIT GREW

PUZZLE 55

CHOLER BEACH
THERAGE ENDEAR
HOLDSONESTONGUE
ARLES DATES GEN
TIER WESER SAFE
INN PORED SERUM
SEESAWED KINDLY
ICED RUGS
WEDDED REDHEADS
IDOLS PILOT NEP
DINE DAVIS NYSE
ETA URGES WOMEN
NOTBREATHEAWORD
REAGAN ESCORTS
DYADS SPORES

PUZZLE 56

CASE AIRES AGED
OLLA SLOPE SOLO
RAES CLOSE SLIT
GREECE TOPSIDES
IMPOUND MAIZE
UTTER GLENDA
NEWT STILE SAIL
ORR ETO GNU
RIOS BRAVE DEEM
MENTHE SEATO
GOODS DRAPERS
FIDGETED TIPTOE
IOOI IRISH LUST
SNEE MURAL EDIT
TARS EMERY RENO

PUZZLE 57

SHUT BARB SWAY
EASE ESEL PARE
LASER ATTU ASEA
ALTERS OARS TAR
TEE ATTRIBUTE
ERMA RAIL PANDA
AMOEBA PROOF
TAKEUP SEPTET
ALERT ASTRAW
DISCI STOA NAGS
WENTALONG NRA
ERA GALA DEBTOR
LISP ETNA SANTA
INTO LETS SHOT
AGED SDAK OTTO

PUZZLE 58

FLAT REMOP LIME
LAME ERICA OLAS
AREA CLASSROOMS
PANCAKES TESTEE
HAOS NICE
ANDEAN DEMERITS
DOER SLOVEN TOE
IRISH UTE TSALA
TIS ASTERS CLAM
SEMESTER INIONS
STAS ANNE
FASTEN ASCENDED
ATTENDANCE CARE
STAR ENDOR ELIS
TUBS ENATE SEEK

PUZZLE 59

DISC PACER GOLF
ADAR ADORE IDOL
MERE SATAN AONE
PAINTTHETOWNRED
SEAS VET
MASHES BRAT MAP
ECLAT RAT ANA
THEWHITEFEATHER
REP DEE PEACE
EST CLAD SPANKS
VIE BALM
ONCEINABLUEMOON
POUR EGRET ABLE
ANTS SEINE TILL
LOSE SEEDS ETAL

PUZZLE 60

MANNA BARS CLAM SKATE
ICIER ARAP LUXE ANWAR
SETAE NAVE OREL HOAGY
STOPDEADINONESTRACKS
YON CANA DUES DARKE
HESA LESS TOGA NED
ASTONE PARE WOWS MILO
SHORTSTOPS GUNN PINUP
PAYS RIP DORY MINGLE
SRO PAIL HALS PANG
PULLSOUTALLTHESTOPS
OATS ORLY INTO RAT
DOMINO TIDY ALA BOLA
APART LILY PULLEDOVER
DELE AITS ZANY YOYOMA
ANA UPTO CART WIGS
MANET LENA SONG OTO
PULLSONESELFTOGETHER
ARTIE RITA LORD RIATA
KEENS ATOR ERAS ERROL
APSES LANE LADY LEANS

PUZZLE 61

WAFT HULK STOP
ODIE EPEE APARA
KILN IRAE LACER
STET DONNYBROOK
ASIA OAT
ELECT RANK ACME
GALLOP NEED RAS
RIVEROFNORETURN
ENE ESAU SERENE
TESS STLO DELES
EMU ITSA
STREAMLINE DARE
LOOMS ASKS LIEN
ONSET ILET EDEN
WEED REDS SALA

PUZZLE 62

BASES BASS ABA
RUPEE ALOE MOLE
ATOLL WANT BOLD
TOT ENLIGHTENED
LACES ARENA
PINTO SALT
RIGGS PRESUMER
ACHE RIATA NONE
POTLATCH STOOD
BEEN REINS
AGATE PANEL
LIGHTHOUSES IDS
TARE AGRA ARGON
ONER TEAL TAHOE
TEE HELM ENTRE

PUZZLE 63

LAS SPAT
FRONT TRIO
CLOUDED ROME
SHOAT PAVE
POUR VATS
URN MINCE
REDS SOD HAND
ELITE FOE
ROLE CARE
WEEP WORMS
JADE PIRATES
AGES NEVER
WONT TOY

PUZZLE 64

REDS ELIS OHARA
ALEE SOCK TONIC
DOES SLEIGHRIDE
APPT ELS LEASES
REFER STEER
RTES AME PADS
ATE BRUTE VENUE
THELIONINWINTER
LAZED SODAS ALE
EWES TEN STAR
FURZE ARCED
FACTOR ELL OTOE
ABOMINABLE MISE
REVEL WREN ACID
EDENS LAND SANS

PUZZLE 65

SNAP HART WASH LEGS
LAVA OLIO ARIA AMIE
EPIC REPRESENTATIVE
DESIGNS NAPS METES
FEE BASS SEAR
REMIT MADE EELS IMP
ALEC AUTO LEWIS NEE
TAD ALMS PARIS OGRE
ENIGMA SATIN SLEEK
CROSSONTHEGREEN
STAIR PROSE INSERT
MITT HAIRY CULT ROE
ERE PUREE CASE CAPE
WED REEL BORE HOLES
PASS EONS PER
ASSET ASST MARRIED
UNCLETOMSCABIN EDGE
NEAT IDEA COLE CLAN
TENS MANY TALL TEDS

PUZZLE 66

SPAT CHOP CHAR MALT
PURR HONE LOGE EDIE
EMMA IRIS APED RAMS
WASPS NOTED SHRIMPS
EKE NET EAT
BLAZING ROW LAW BED
RARE DAB NOMAD PISA
ICE MIA RAG MADAM
MEAT PANCAKE GIVEUP
REAL RIO PAGE
DESERT PERUSES DRAW
ALTAR SEA TAR ENE
SLAT BINGE PIG DANE
HAG PET EAR LILYPAD
TEA SAG NUN
DEPORTS STIRS GAVEL
ERIN LARK SAID MILE
LINE ETUI IDLE IVAN
LESS SEND NEON CANT

PUZZLE 67

SOAP LAIR CHEF SWAB
IDOL ACRE HIDE HONE
LONE STOP AMID ANNA
TREAD SNEER TEMPTED
SON SAD ROE
GREETED TED NAB WEB
ROAD WET NEWEL FILE
ASS POD LET RINSE
BEER ROTATED GARDEN
ALIT MAT SANE
NODDED PATENTS STAB
AHEAD BAG DUE HUE
PIER CIDER TAG PANT
SOD HAG DUB DECANTS
COT SAL MUG
DEMOTED BERET BEATS
ATOM RIPE RARE ALEE
MOLE EVEN EVER NONE
ENDS DENT DEER TESS

PUZZLE 68

FOAL CAPS DAMP DOSE
ABLE OGLE EWER EVER
ROOT NOUN FATE FANG
MEETINGS PER FELTS
ERE LAD BUN
CORRECT CUT SUNDERS
ADO TENEMENTS ERIE
SOLES AID DUO DICE
TREATS PAR TRY NED
RYES RUG KITS
LAB WEE BOB PAPERS
AVID ALA AYE PAPAL
METE FRIGHTENS EGO
PRESSES RES DARKEST
POD LEA DUE
RAPID EER INDENTED
ACES SEMI ARIL NILE
THEE AVON GONE ERIC
EELS GANG ONES LEAK

PUZZLE 69

BEAST HIDES MADAME
LEANER ANELE ALAMOS
DADDYWARBUCKS STRITCH
INDIA AIRE STOA HAE
EDIE FATTEN IONIC EPA
TAN PAGE TROTS HIRER
SUGARDADDY UNO FOAMED
PIER OEILS ILONA
OFFEND STARE CROSSCUT
HEART MOTHERGOOSE HRH
ARTY BIRL URNS ARIA
RAH SISTERKENNY SLEET
ELEVATES HOAGY STEELS
RARER MONTH ALAR
RAFTER MAD SOBSISTERS
ELISE SERAC ETCH VEE
BAG STELA HATTIE PANE
EMU ATTU INRE EIDER
CORRECT DADDYLONGLEGS
DEARIE EVERS TAGORE
ESTATE RESET TESTS

PUZZLE 70

SOBS MACE DETER
ALEE ORAL ARISE
NEEDLEANDTHREAD
KOREA SEAL SUE
RIFT ROIL
ADS REEK SAILOR
ROT SLANT SMILE
OWES TRIED ANIL
MEATS STARS EVA
ALLOTS SLOW REX
WEIR SPOT
ASK PLEA ROMEO
SCISSORSANDPINS
PATIO AIRY EMIL
STERN NAME REDO

PUZZLE 71

SALAD GNAT ARTS
ABODE RODE WIRE
SLOOP ERST ANEW
HEN ITEM HORDES
SCOT EVE
ESTATE LORE OAT
SPATS CAW RANGE
SALE ACE PIES
AROSE LED FRONT
YEN ARMS POINTS
ERA GIRL
PEDALS ARCS MAN
APES CAVE APACE
PINE AREA KARMA
ACTS LEST ENTER

PUZZLE 72

FARR SMEAR SALT
ERIE TARRY TRIO
TILT ARNIE RING
ALLIANCE BREAKS
RICH TRUE
SATIRE CREEPERS
EDEN TREAD VAL
TONG BREED PAPA
ORE VIEWS EDIT
NETWORKS SPEEDS
AIDS STOP
STANDS STEPSOUT
LAND ERNIE HIRE
ARTE YIELD OSSA
BEER EPEES WEAR

PUZZLE 73

USER GEO GOBS
SALON DRAY AREA
SKATE OATS RIAL
ENAMELS TENORS
TONES EMEND
TAMEST ERROR
ONO EASE TSARS
NET ARC ADE ROE
SWORD MADE IVE
EDGED ASIDES
SAFER OARED
STRIDE RESALES
PAIN EWER TIRED
ELSE TIRO SNIPE
DEES STS GETS

PUZZLE 74

LOCAL PANT PAWS SEE
AROMA ASIA ARIL PAN
DEBIT RING NATURIST
DECADE SIB MAKER
MAP RAGE TACIT RELY
AILS TOSSUP CARE
IDEAMAN PROF BALBOA
DEALER SIFTED CYRIL
AWAKEN AROSE ALE
CLAD CAN GOT STYX
HID ATLAS PURIST
AMASS ETUDES PARADE
REMOTE ELAN GETAWAY
DOLL LINDEN WERE
WEED FARES RODS DES
HELEN NUN BIDSUP
IRONICAL RAVE GALOP
SIP COTE ILES ARENA
TEE EWER ALLY RAKED

PUZZLE 75

HAW CAP SPA
EPIC SALAD SOOT
MESA ARENA ERNE
DEBATE TREATY
ARE CREAM
CENT WHY GEAR
ELLA SEE REDDEN
MOO STEAMER OLE
SUPPLY TAX DREW
DELE REP BEET
EELER PAN
REAPED GRAVEL
HORS AERIE EVIL
OPIE PEARY RENO
TEE MEL REB

PUZZLE 76

SLAT BOER DRS
RAGED ELSE BRAE
SNEER REEL RATA
DETAIL ANIMAL
EGRET TITAN
MORSE AGENT
AIM NEMO ELIAS
CLATTER ASSENTS
EERIE LODE COT
PALER DREAM
LAPSE BRAID
RUPEES ENDING
ICER SLIP ETONS
SIRS EIRE RELAY
EDS REAL DAWN

PUZZLE 77

LOWS ARARA ALMA
ALIA LADEN GEES
HENRYTHESEVENTH
RODEO SLIME DEE
FEND TIES
SAL DEAN ARMADA
IDO EASEL OBIS
EDWARDTHEEIGHTH
GEER ARADO OTE
ERRATA UPIN RON
NEBS TIER
AGO ALLOW AREAS
POPELEOTHENINTH
SEEN SPOOL ACTA
ESNE TEEMS SEAM

PUZZLE 78

SAND BANS AGAMA
TREE ELIA RUNES
REEL RING REIMS
INDIANAJONES
PAY CASA ASSESS
BRR MET RIN
NOTREDAME STORE
APIA SPANS ODER
SENDS SOUTHBEND
ARE COO RAY
LASHED PIES FLO
INDIANAPOLIS
EPODE TRAM RAMA
RAVER SINE ERIK
GLARY YSER SETA

PUZZLE 79

ALAMO LACES RACED
VITAL INERT ECOLE
ANODE MINOR FERAL
SEN AIM SANE ATE
TRES STAR WARBLE
HIP LOM YEA
KNEEL ASTOR EWES
NEEDLED ETAT LAHR
OAR SLEW AJAR SAY
TRIB APES AUSTERE
SEAT TRASH VASES
CAP ENE APT
ANKLES DARN EIRE
EVE EGIS TOY DIM
LIVEN THATS IRENE
ALERT EAGLE CEASE
MARES SHOES EELER

A critic is a man who knows the way but can't drive the car.

PUZZLE 80

IDLE RIDE LAMP
TAIL EDIT VALOR
EDAM LOAN IGLOO
MARSEILLAISE
WES CHRISM
TSKED STEN CEE
TAPIR JOEDUMARS
AMAS ADA URIS
MARSUPIAL GLUEY
ELK MELS GUESS
RESALE EEL
MARSHMALLOWS
ADIEU PAIR OBOE
BURNT ERLE BERN
EGAD DEED EYED

PUZZLE 81

PALL MAES MERE
ALEE TILER ELAS
CAESARSALADDAYS
ENS LAUDS RANEE
AIMS BAL
BLACKSEAMANSHIP
EERIE MURK ERA
ARID SLIDE BAER
DOS SLAG MARNE
STEAMIRONFISTED
LAP ALAS
FLOOR LOSES MEA
LIGHTHOUSEMAIDS
ALLA INSET SNIP
BYES DEER HITS

PUZZLE 82

TOM SCAM COLAS
ALEG POLE ABELE
LINO ALIT SENOR
COULDILEAVEYOU
IONA ADE
SAAR RAIL DAMP
PATTI TAUT DOE
ONEHANDONEHEART
KEN NOON RALES
EROS NOES OREL
TOE PENN
BEAUTIFULGIRLS
SLING RARA NEAT
TORCH AINT GENE
SWEET ELSE LAW

PUZZLE 83

SCAN STASH DYES
ERIE PELEE REAP
REDSNAPPER ELSA
FEATURES ADLER
DEE LINGO
TABLES MILDEWS
IDLES JELLY PIP
TAUS DUETS LARA
OPE BOLTS NODES
TRELLIS CAUSES
IRATE ARI
RABAT FLASHGUN
ORBS GREENHOUSE
SLOE YEARN WREN
EONS MITTY LURE

PUZZLE 84

THEONLYSUREWAYTOP
URUS OISE AMOS ALII
OILS NEED GUMS BLOC
YOKELS RANT BURBANK
H NATE NEAP ROY A
TELEVISE AGREED PAW
ICE ACTUP SAG SARI
WHAM KERRY MANDOLIN
YODEL ROYAL DOORMAN
E NOB SOMAS DOR E
NOSTRUM RENTS METER
OLEANDER NAILS LUNA
MEAL REB INEPT NOT
YON SPEARS TELECAST
N NOR DATA PIER H
ADDAXES HEAL TSETSE
GRUB SIAM LAMP DEAR
NERO ELSA IRAE INIA
IRBOTTONSIKCARTEC

The only sure way to pick a winner at the race track is not to bring any money with you.

PUZZLE 85

TABLE FUSE DOTS
AGAIN OVAL EDIE
MAYBELLENE CINE
ERSE IDA PLANED
RAPS SHAM
MAYANS MAYPOP
EXACT THINS BOA
WILE BRITT CENT
LOT IRATE DRACO
MAYDAY MAYHEM
AUKS ROYS
DIONNE GOA TOAD
YANK MAYONNAISE
AGEE ALMS ELLEN
NOSE NEST ESSAY

PUZZLE 86

AMOS MAFIA DAMP
BOTH APART ERIE
EDIE SPRAT CONE
DECATHLON VOWEL
FREE IMIN
ASE ASPS ASTRAL
SPRAY ITINERARY
TIER TEENY ODER
INCREASED PLATE
RETORT ROBE RES
GOAL LUSH
PLEAS IDENTICAL
EARN EVENT TARE
ERIC PEACE CREE
PANE IDLED HEAR

PUZZLE 87

HUBS DIP CATS TAB
ASTA ONA ALEE HUR
SOUTHCAROLINA ETA
EAT TALKS SMOG
RAW MOW TEE ROI
OLES RARER TODDLE
ASSES NOR ART DEW
DOTTED ASIDE SLOE
VOWELS RESALE
PAIN NOTRE SLEEPS
APR PIT END PEALE
DOGIES SHEEP TSAR
INN PEA LID TNT
TEND CEASE CUE
ELI NORTHDAKOTANS
ALA ERIE EVE OGRE
RAN WELD NED NEAR

PUZZLE 88

AVER SPAT ERAS
MATA HOUR AONE
INTHEMORNINGSOW
DEE MONET ULAN
LIVE ARE
ELATE IBIS OFF
AVON RIDE TEA
NOWASSOONASTHIS
EKE THAN RENT
WED OURS AVERT
ART GLEE
CAME SPAIN SAD
DAVIDDWELTINTHE
AVIS EASE ALAN
BEDS ANTS TOBY

PUZZLE 89

BOB LIED TASKS
ERE AALTO ALIEN
ILL SMOTE PIGGY
GOLDSOVEREIGN
ENSUITE DONATE
EST ALEC TAL
ITALIANLIRA OHM
SINS ATE PROA
LED JAPANESEYEN
EUR ADAR NOR
SPONGE STRIVEN
POUNDSTERLING
AROMA AMORE ODA
MOVER REVEL LEI
BOSNS NEED ADO

PUZZLE 90

ALEC JAIL YIP
SAGA ALDA ADO
SWORDPLAY RON
PEA MADLY
STREWN VATS
HEEDS DINETTE
OAF WEE IRA
EMERSON DICES
RIPE MONKEY
SHEBA OLD
TAN CIVILIZED
ARC ERAS COLA
BEE SENT TOLD

PUZZLE 91

AQUA BIDS TASTY
PUPS AREA IGLOO
RISK BOAR READY
IRE PENNAME WOO
LETTER NUDE
ERUPT DOLLAR
SHUN TRIP FLAME
OAT HOTEL NIL
DRAFT PLEA EDDY
ADHERE ELBOW
WARM OREGON
HOP PROVERB RUE
ADAGE RIND GATE
TOPAZ ASIA USED
ERASE LADY SPRY

PUZZLE 92

SPELL CREAM
STOGIES GROSSES
NARRATE RALEIGH
ENTER RAINY NAE
ADIT SPUNK MITE
DUC AMEND TENOR
PORTENT LATEN
HILT CASE
FRILL CONTROL
GRANT PONCE PET
LADE PRATE SEGO
ANI FLUTE SPRAY
STATION SATIATE
SITUATE TROTTED
CENTS EPEES

PUZZLE 93

CAPS REEL SILL
OBOE EAVES TRUE
MOLE PRIDE EARS
EVE ROLL THANKS
TESTERS ATOM
HAT ALLEYWAY
ALTER SLIER RUE
RAIN TWIGS RITA
AIL SHEEN MOTOR
BRETHREN CUP
ROUT BOLEROS
PLEATS PURE ART
ROAD TEARS URGE
OGRE SWINE SEAM
PENS ERST ERNS

PUZZLE 94

DEMI MAZES JABS
OMEN ALICE OGEE
PUTSINANUTSHELL
ASSURING SANDAL
ROAD FOGS
JAPANS FIVE LED
OPINE SAXE QUAY
NUTCRACKERSUITE
ARTE WOES CAGER
HES WAND SERINS
TAKE MONT
SPHERE BELIEVES
AHARDNUTTOCRACK
LETS ENURE ENCE
TWEE DOSED DEEP

PUZZLE 95

ORCA CAMPS HAT
LOIN ANISE RULE
LANSINGMICHIGAN
ARC ROLE ASSET
INANE RAVE
TENETS CEMENTED
ANNIE GREEN USE
IRAN BEADS ASSE
LOT SEAMS RICER
SLITHERS SEDANS
RATS STEEL
ALOOF MAAS OIL
DULUTHMINNESOTA
ABET OARED OSAR
REO PEERS BALD

PUZZLE 96

ABATE PLUCK CAT
BACON RUNON LIE
BRINGHOMETO ERA
ADD LISP CHASM
LIKE ELKIN
SPOUSE SMOOTHER
TENTH SHORN ORA
RATE SAUTE HURT
ACH GESTE BESET
PEERLESS GREEDY
HOARY ARIL
SPOON ADIT MAP
ARU CLOSETOHOME
GAS EERIE NEVER
EYE STEAM SPENT

PUZZLE 97

YEGG GRAY AYIN
OGLE BELA PELE
YOUNGSTOWN PSIS
OSTEO RENO RTES
SOLA ESTEE
STY NICER SHREW
HOER REP NEEDLE
ORLE ASIDE NAME
WALLIS CIV DYED
SHOES YSSEL SRS
WALDO PROM
DEBS AGAR LEERY
ABIE YUGOSLAVIA
CARR REVE TOCK
ENDS TREE YEAS

PUZZLE 98

VAMP CLAMP SCAT
ALOE LABEL HULA
RILL OPERA ABES
YELLOWSTONEPARK
MINE VENTS
MODEL BRAID
ABEL ADROIT LIP
YELLOWSUBMARINE
AYE NOOSES IOTA
WELSH IFNOT
TREAT HALF
YELLOWBRICKROAD
PEST ARENT ARNE
EDIE RANGE FAKE
DYER ENDED FLAP

PUZZLE 99

RANG CATER OATS
OVAL OPINE PLEA
DOME PESTS PANG
SWEATER REPORTS
MAD SATES
HAVEN HIP CEASE
AVID HEM BADGER
RED MEXICAN AIR
TREMOR LOG MINE
STOOD BAY WANED
METER PEN
STEELER DREAMED
HORN PATIO GIVE
EDIT ITEMS EDEN
DOCS DENSE SINS

PUZZLE 100

PAWN BASTE HASH
ALOE UNION EDNA
PANE NOTED LAIR
AND SYNE TEMPT
ELLA MOON
MAROON TERRACE
ALLOW DELAY HEN
GOAT PANEL BARE
INN SENSE PARIS
EDUCATE BULLET
TAKE ATEE
SPOON CURT SUM
CAPP APART ETNA
ALAI LARGE ROIL
BELA ENTER ANTE

PUZZLE 101

CAGES TERM FARO
ALIVE ARIA OMAN
FOREIGNLANGUAGE
EEL EKE TORTE
PENS CLAP
GEESE RELOAD
ERMAS SEES SLAT
LEER TAT TAME
KEEL SIRE DEMON
DRYRUN BARON
GANG SEWS
BEAST ETE PTA
MARTHASVINEYARD
ALIE NAIL RAREE
NESS SOLE EPEES

PUZZLE 102

SAFE ALANS TAMP
TRIM DANCE ALEE
ONES SHEAR NAST
AIL FORWARDNESS
TEDDERS ARI
GARB DETONATE
MORN CREEP NEE
SOAK FOILS SCAR
PAL SOLES RAHS
ANSWERED VINO
ATE DEMERIT
DRESSMAKERS ADA
RUNT OCEAN AGES
ALOE SHALE MEAT
BESS TESTS ISLE

PUZZLE 103

BARD SOLID HASP
AVER EVADE ERIE
LADY REGAL MELT
ASH FEN IDEALS
STEPIN PECAN
RARE ALAN TAP
MARIE ENATE HIE
ARIL SLATE MEDE
SIN SPACE DETER
SAG PINE PITH
PANDA AVERSE
ACROSS HUE ETA
LEAK TUNIS SEAS
ADZE ENURE ORLE
SEER RATED USED

PUZZLE 107

ASTI CARS AMIN
STEN OLIO STENO
TENGALLON TATAR
RESELL TAMALES
ORE LES TONER
BACKYARD MAB
LIFE TIO NEGATE
ANOAS NUT ERIES
GROTTO TOR ADES
SET INCHWORM
RENTA NAY DSM
BETTORS SENATE
GESTE PINTSIZED
ALTAR ELBE NEVE
MASS ROAR ASEA

PUZZLE 111

MIST CAFES MART
ASIA ORION OLIO
SLAM MARNE LANE
TEMPLE AWARDS
EAT FAKER
SCARY PAN ASTER
CAL PURSER EVE
ANA IRE WRY PEN
NOR CORNEA END
TEMPO TAR DIETS
ANNOY COD
COARSE OCEANS
ALMA WAGER ARIL
REED STALK LUNA
PONE YELLS SMEW

PUZZLE 104

SPY BRONC STREW
HOE REVUE PROVE
ALA AMEND LIBEL
HORIZON EVIDENT
RED ACE
MARINES STENCIL
OPUS LIFTS TOME
RAM ZOO LAG
EROS TEPID TOGA
STRIPED COLONEL
SEA LIT
CISTERN DESERTS
UNTIL ALOFT OUT
SCONE VENUE ONE
PAWED YIELD TAP

PUZZLE 108

SLED FLAW HEFT
LAVA LAIR ROSIE
AKIN OILY ARSON
BELABOR INSERT
ODDSANDENDS
FRACAS AVISO
RIGOR CLEO PISA
EDAM SHORN EVER
TERM TOOT CREAM
ACORN COASTS
OPENANDSHUT
CRADLE ASSAULT
TOTAL PORT PROA
EVENS ANTE IGOR
TORT DEER SENT

PUZZLE 112

RUBS SHRED PLOP
ETON TOILE RAGE
DANA ERNIE ANEW
SHOPPING SIDES
ENS BATS
COMETS BEQUEATH
ALINE RERUN RUE
FIND DELLA JINX
EVE TASTE NOSEE
SERPENTS CATERS
ASKS COP
START MOVEMENT
IOWA AZURE ERIE
TOLD LITER ANNA
ELSE APERS LEER

PUZZLE 105

MONTH RANI PERU
AMORE EDAM EGIS
TIROL BIGPARADE
STAMPOUT MULES
BELT NAPS
ACCORD BUGLERS
CYANS SORRY ATT
ANNE SOUSA DYER
DIN ACUTE PROVO
CYMBALS PRUNED
ELMS SHIM
SCALE SWIMMERS
MAJORETTE AERIE
OBAD LIED TRITE
GORY FAME ESSEN

PUZZLE 109

AMOR BABAR IRMA
VILE ATONE SEAL
ERAS THATS ATRI
REVERBERATE RIN
LIONS OBLONG
REPLAYS BRAE
ELIS REENTERS
ALE BRAYERS MAP
RETRIEVE CITE
ATTA RETILED
ROTTER LEARN
EVA RECONSIDERS
LIND AMVET EVAN
ANTE DIEGO RICO
YEAR SIREN SLEW

PUZZLE 113

LII AROMA POD
EDNA TUDOR BONE
NOTSTANDACHANCE
SLOPE EST ELDER
ENS LIB
STANDONESGROUND
EARS DOLCE ASEA
ACE TAR AWL
TINE VENUS OGEE
STANDARDBEARERS
GET EIN
EERIE SAP DAMES
STANDINGOVATION
TOTE ROUSE ERNE
ENE SWEET ESE

PUZZLE 106

ANDES OPAL SECS
CARNE VINE TROT
APART ENDS RARE
DEBATING SEESAW
GETS WEASELS
SPHERE TARTS
TEA SMART SEDAN
EARS SPEED SORE
PREEN EERIE LAW
NEARS EXALTS
POSTERS STAR
EMPIRE DESCRIBE
RAIN NOEL TIRES
THEE ABEL EVICT
HALL SIPS DESKS

PUZZLE 110

DEBT RABAT TRIM
ALOE AMORE EAVE
FIXE BOXCAMERAS
TAJ ABLY ROMANS
ARTIE DIRE
SACHET BREADBOX
TAKE SPOORS ONO
OREAD ELM SAXES
RAT EASIER ABRA
MUSICBOX EGRESS
DEUS PLIER
ASPENS ORAL RUM
THEATERBOX WINO
TALL RAISE REDO
AMES SPEED YSER

PUZZLE 114

OHARE POLA ETON
RANON ACES RARE
FLYOFFTHEHANDLE
FLA ARES CASED
SCAR ANON
STATEN FLYRIVER
TIMED ALIEN ORO
AROW FLYAT SLAM
FOR BOLES COTTA
FLYPAPER DAMSON
OSSE CAVE
OBOLI ARLO NEE
FLYINGSQUIRRELS
FEET NOUS TAROT
SURE UTAH STONE

PUZZLE 115

S	A	L	A	D		S	I	C		S	P	A
O	L	I	V	E		A	D	O		L	O	G
T	E	N	E	T		P	A	R	T	A	K	E
	S	E	R	E				R	O	B	E	D
			A	R	K		R	A	Y			
S	O	N	G		N	A	I	L		H	O	P
A	L	E	E		O	I	L		A	I	D	E
Y	E	W		A	C	R	E		S	T	E	W
			E	L	K		Y	E	T			
B	E	L	L	A				L	A	S	H	
A	M	A	S	S	E	D		M	I	N	O	R
D	I	G		K	E	Y		E	R	O	S	E
E	R	S		A	R	E		R	E	W	E	D

PUZZLE 119

K	E	Y		U	N	T	O		M	A	S	K
I	R	E		N	O	E	L		U	P	O	N
D	E	T	E	C	T	E	D		L	O	S	E
			A	L	E			A	L	L	O	W
S	P	I	T	E		L	A	S	S	O		
E	O	N	S		B	A	L	I		G	O	B
A	N	T		T	A	M	P	A		I	R	A
L	E	I		E	B	B	S		B	E	A	K
		M	I	L	E	S		A	I	S	L	E
P	E	A	R	L			A	S	K			
A	L	T	O		F	A	L	S	E	T	T	O
G	L	E	N		A	C	M	E		U	R	N
E	A	S	Y		N	E	S	T		B	Y	E

PUZZLE 123

C	O	A	T		D	A	M	P		D	I	N
A	N	T	E		I	D	E	A		Y	O	U
S	T	O	P		M	O	N	U	M	E	N	T
T	O	P	I	C		R	U	L	E			
			D	A	L	E	S		A	C	H	E
K	E	G		G	A	S		B	L	O	O	D
N	A	I	L	E	D		S	A	Y	I	N	G
E	S	S	A	Y		R	I	B		L	E	E
W	E	T	S		S	A	T	E	S			
			S	E	C	T		S	T	E	A	L
R	E	N	O	V	A	T	E		U	R	G	E
I	R	E		E	L	L	A		M	I	E	N
M	A	T		S	E	E	R		P	E	S	T

PUZZLE 116

L	E	F	T		M	A	R		H	O	B	O
O	K	R	A		A	L	A		A	D	A	M
R	E	A	R	V	I	E	W		R	O	B	E
E	D	I	T	E	D		B	A	R	R	E	N
		L	A	X		D	O	D	O			
A	M	E	N		R	E	N	O	W	N	E	D
L	A	S		T	I	L	E	S		E	R	A
I	N	T	R	E	P	I	D		V	A	R	Y
			O	R	E	S		M	A	T		
C	O	L	U	M	N		H	E	L	E	N	A
U	S	E	S		E	Y	E	L	I	N	E	R
F	L	E	E		S	E	A		S	E	E	M
F	O	R	D		S	A	D		E	D	D	Y

PUZZLE 120

B	A	R		S	W	A	M		C	H	A	R
O	R	E		H	A	R	E		Y	O	R	E
A	C	T		E	X	T	R	A	C	T	E	D
T	H	R	E	E		Y	E	L	L			
		E	S	P	Y			T	E	R	S	E
S	P	A	N		E	C	H	O		E	E	L
T	O	T	E		A	H	A		A	B	L	E
I	L	E		B	R	I	T		C	O	L	E
R	O	D	E	O			E	C	R	U		
			S	N	A	G		H	E	N	C	E
C	A	S	S	E	R	O	L	E		D	A	D
A	L	O	E		A	R	I	A		E	V	E
R	E	B	S		B	E	E	T		D	E	N

PUZZLE 124

G	A	P		S	T	A	G		E	D	I	T
E	R	R		T	A	L	E		M	O	R	E
T	I	E		E	X	T	R	A	C	T	E	D
S	A	F	A	R	I		M	O	E			
		E	R	N				R	E	C	U	R
P	E	R	K		B	A	I	T		O	R	E
A	R	R		S	A	U	N	A		V	I	E
A	L	E		I	R	K	S		D	E	S	K
R	E	D	I	D				F	O	R		
			N	E	B		R	A	N	G	E	R
C	R	O	S	S	R	O	A	D		I	R	A
A	I	D	E		E	L	S	E		R	I	P
P	O	E	T		W	E	E	D		L	E	T

PUZZLE 117

R	I	D	E		F	E	L	T		H	O	W
A	D	A	M		E	R	I	E		E	R	E
F	L	I	P		D	A	M	P	E	N	E	D
T	E	N	T	H			A	I	D			
		T	Y	I	N	G		D	I	S	C	O
O	B	I		D	A	L	E		T	H	A	W
S	E	E		E	P	O	C	H		A	G	E
L	A	S	H		S	A	R	I		R	E	D
O	T	T	E	R		T	U	L	I	P		
			E	A	T			T	R	E	S	S
G	R	I	D	I	R	O	N		A	N	N	A
O	A	R		S	O	D	A		T	E	A	K
O	N	E		E	D	D	Y		E	D	G	E

PUZZLE 121

J	O	B		S	P	E	D		S	H	A	D
A	W	E		C	A	G	E		W	I	F	E
R	E	C	H	A	R	G	E		A	L	A	N
		A	I	D	E		P	A	N	T	R	Y
S	I	L	K	S		G	E	L	S			
A	C	M	E		T	U	N	E		R	I	P
G	E	E		C	R	I	E	S		E	R	A
A	D	D		H	E	L	D		G	L	E	N
			H	E	A	T		H	O	I	S	T
M	O	T	I	F	S		L	I	E	S		
A	B	E	D		O	V	E	R	S	H	O	E
L	O	S	E		N	I	N	E		E	R	R
L	E	T	S		S	E	T	S		S	E	E

PUZZLE 125

S	P	A		S	L	A	Y		W	H	I	R
K	I	T		P	A	L	E		R	O	D	E
I	T	E	M	I	Z	E	S		O	M	E	N
			I	C	Y			K	N	E	A	D
A	L	L	E	Y		R	U	N	G	S		
B	E	A	N		D	E	S	I		T	O	T
L	E	T		T	I	B	E	T		E	K	E
E	R	E		A	C	E	S		W	A	R	E
		C	R	U	E	L		S	E	D	A	N
S	C	O	U	T			W	A	N			
A	R	M	S		C	H	I	L	D	I	S	H
P	O	E	T		A	U	R	A		R	I	O
S	P	R	Y		R	E	E	D		A	X	E

PUZZLE 118

C	L	A	Y		S	C	O	R	E		C	H	A	R
R	O	S	E		H	A	V	E	N		P	O	L	O
A	R	E	A		A	B	A	T	E		A	R	O	W
W	E	A	S	E	L		L	I	R	A		S	H	E
			T	A	L	E		E	G	G	H	E	A	D
B	I	G		S	O	T	S		Y	O	U			
A	G	O		E	T	H	A	N		G	E	T	U	P
N	O	R	M		S	E	V	E	R		S	A	L	E
G	R	E	A	T		L	O	P	E	S		I	N	A
			R	I	M		R	A	C	E		L	A	S
R	E	A	C	T	O	R		L	O	G	S			
U	R	N		I	R	O	N		R	O	U	S	E	S
M	A	I	N		A	W	A	R	D		D	U	L	L
O	S	L	O		S	A	T	I	E		A	R	I	A
R	E	E	D		S	N	O	O	D		N	E	A	T

PUZZLE 122

S	H	A	M		F	A	D		T	A	M	E
H	E	R	O		A	L	E		A	L	E	E
E	X	T	R	A	C	T	S		M	A	L	L
			T	I	E			T	A	N	S	
R	A	D	A	R			A	I	L			
I	C	E	R		S	E	G	M	E	N	T	
N	E	E		M	A	K	E	S		A	I	D
	D	R	E	A	M	E	D		R	I	D	E
			R	U	E			M	E	L	E	E
	R	E	A	L			H	E	N			
H	E	R	S		F	L	A	T	T	E	R	Y
A	N	N	E		O	I	L		E	L	I	A
D	O	E	R		G	E	T		D	A	M	P

PUZZLE 126

C	L	A	M		H	E	M		S	O	D	A
A	O	N	E		E	G	O		H	E	E	D
R	U	N	N	I	N	G	S	C	A	R	E	D
	D	E	A	R			T	A	R			
			C	A	R	T		T	E	N	O	R
	M	A	E		A	R	M	S		I	V	Y
O	A	R			T	E	A			L	E	E
A	T	E		S	E	A	M		D	E	N	
F	E	A	S	T		T	A	P	E			
			A	I	D			R	A	N	G	
R	U	N	T	R	U	E	T	O	F	O	R	M
I	S	E	E		P	A	R		E	M	I	T
D	E	E	D		E	R	A		N	E	T	S

PUZZLE 127

SORT NABOB EGOS
CROW IDAHO NOTE
ANTI CLIMB RATE
DEADBEAT SEASON
DESI SLAP
MALLET QUESTION
ALIEN GUIDE SHA
MOLD DIETS SLAM
AHA BURRS STERE
SACRISTY STATES
OATH TAUT
ASSISI SANDIEGO
COOL ELOPE OMAN
TILE SOREL NILE
SLID TOADY STAR

PUZZLE 128

APES MASS ALE
LINT ALIT LOW
ANTE PARADISE
STREW ERA
AROMA TRAMP
RAP EACH ELEE
IMP STRAW LET
DEER HERO IKE
ENDOW SPRIG
BOO ERASE
RESERVED ATIP
AYE SAME TOTE
NEW ELSE ERSE

PUZZLE 129

BARE LEI WHET
ALOE INN AURA
BADLANDS SNIP
ESS YESES GEE
PEN CAVE
HARASS TWIRLS
UPON SEAT
MEADOW WOODSY
SANE OUR
PIT EARLS ABE
ACID SOFTENED
RENO EVE REED
EDGE LED AWRY

PUZZLE 130

LIST GALA RUB
ARIA ONES ERE
MERCHANTS AGE
KIT ORDER
ADULTS FRO
NOSE BOTTLES
TOE OUR AWE
ERRANDS OVEN
ROD COWARD
BANKS RAN
LIE INTERESTS
ADE LEES REAL
BED YENS SEXY

PUZZLE 131

HITS CAD BRAY
AREA AGE ROLE
MEND ROB IDES
LAD TUB
FLAYS REFER
AID SIREN ERA
TEA NOR LOG
EGG INERT ODE
SEEKS OWNED
IMP MOO
OMIT LEA OPEN
RACE EAT DEMO
EYES ARE SNUG

PUZZLE 132

GEM BLEW SHOP
AWE RARE CURE
SENTINEL ELAN
ODD CANALS
BASE COME
BAGS DAME APT
ARE WOVEN CUE
RED HOED MERE
SIRS EASE
INFORM EAR
SOAR ARMRESTS
LORE TOIL HIP
EKES SETS YEA

PUZZLE 133

CLUE CAW RARE
EARL OBI EKED
DIGESTED MINE
ERECT LEBANON
TAP NOR
GLASGOW OKAYS
YAP DON LEE
MYTHS WARMEST
ELF TEE
PAPAYAS DROPS
ALIT TOBOGGAN
NOSE ERA ELLA
TEAR DEN DEEP

PUZZLE 134

STOW GRAPE CAR
LAMER LAGER AXE
OXIDE OZONE FIN
BIT FARE CHEST
JURY DOTE
DEMOTE PRO WARD
EVOKE QUIZ BOA
LATE CURVE ABUT
ADE HOSE PROSE
YELL ATE LOITER
AURA QUID
BLOWS HUGS JIB
RAP AERIE ELUDE
EKE GRAVE SATES
DEN EAGER MEAT

1-D, 2-P, 3-Q, 4-I, 5-O, 6-L, 7-M, 8-C, 9-G, 10-N, 11-U, 12-Z, 13-V, 14-E, 15-T, 16-J, 17-X, 18-W, 19-F, 20-K, 21-S, 22-B, 23-H, 24-R, 25-A, 26-Y.

PUZZLE 135

DATA SRS STEM
APER TWEET PETE
MILE RIVERBOATS
PALACES PAROLES
LAS FAN
MERIT DEFT ELD
SERUM ROI FLOE
CARIBBEANCRUISE
ADEN ANI ALTER
TED WREN TILER
CAR TEN
CATERED EASTERS
OCEANLINER OVAL
IRES SLAMS METE
NENE LES BRED

PUZZLE 136

HAM MACE GENT
ERIC RUNUP EDER
ETERNALTRIANGLE
LENIENCE DIRELY
MUCH WERE
BEWITH JAMS MIS
ASONE SOLI DADE
SQUARETHECIRCLE
KULL TONS RILED
SED REVS LOVERS
TORE WANE
SALOON SIDEWISE
EGYPTIANPYRAMID
TUNS TRIES YALE
SEXY YIPS SON

PUZZLE 137

SUED DEFER PLAN
ANTE ERODE ROME
WINS LARGE IDEA
STAPLE TENEMENT
IOTA RAVE
CLUSTERS CEDARS
RITES BESTS ROT
AMID POPES LOBO
MIL PERIL SIMON
STEWED ALIENATE
ENDS SNAG
GRIDDLES TREMOR
LORD EPODE RAGE
OBOE RADON INRE
BEND SLANT EYED

PUZZLE 138

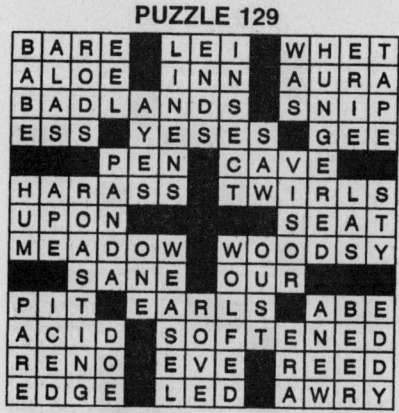

FLUFF MEDE BARK
RANEE ORAN AGUE
UNDERSTANDINGLY
ICE NOISE CARES
TERM AVE BELI
OTRA AIR EMS
PROTESTING OVAL
ROVED IST ARENA
ABEL COMICSTRIP
MER MAN SASH
STAB TON OGAM
SALES SECTS ALI
UNEXCEPTIONABLE
IDEA TARA ORLON
TIPS ORAL BEETS

PUZZLE 139

BRAT SET APES
EASE CAR LOVE
AREA ARE BREW
REASON ALIENS
END TON
MISDEAL TOAST
ORE LIP TOE
WEEDS TAFFETA
ROE PEA
DEFEND ENLIST
ARID GAR TOTE
RING EYE EWES
KNEE RED RAPT

PUZZLE 143

ASH RITA ADAM
RUE ATOM ROBE
TEA VENTUROUS
TEEM SORTS
TOWNS SLAW
AMAS STAG RTE
REV STONE ERA
ONE PORE SPOT
PIPE POETS
SOLAR SODA
PLACEMATS TIP
IGOT EPEE ERE
TASS NEWS DEW

PUZZLE 147

HIM AFRO FLEW
AWE GROW AIDE
MONTREAL CAGE
HEED FIRED
ISSUE TEA
RIMS PARALLEL
ADO BUYER ADE
NEGLIGEE AMEN
ITS ARENA
BRAGS COLA
OATH BAREBACK
RIOT EVER ROE
ELMS NEST FOG

PUZZLE 140

APES BON STEM
DOLL LEE HIRE
DELAWARE ARIA
STATES DIRECT
EAT ELIS
FLASKS DEFOGS
EER MIA
MAKEUP RELENT
ANKA EVE
CANTER LEARNS
ELSE STANDOUT
NEAR OAT ESTE
TESS NNE REST

PUZZLE 144

ALES STAR TAC
NEXT PALE ABE
TOTO EXPECTED
ENID SLATE
GONER CLEO
OLD ARIA SEMI
LEES ODD EXIT
DODO LEDA ACE
USER NAMES
LOOSE ANTI
EXPANDED ONCE
VEE DATA NEER
INN SWAM EDEN

PUZZLE 148

SWAP PEP SEAR
EARL OAR WANE
TREASURE ARTE
NUT TURNED
AGREE GERM
SOOT BING OFF
ELM BLADE VIE
ADE LENS BALE
DUST GALES
STARES MAT
EASY IRISHMEN
ERIE NET EAVE
STAR GOT DREW

PUZZLE 141

CAR LESS PEW
OLEO ASHE ROE
TENNESSEE END
STIR ADES
ONCE SLEDS
DARN ALF SNAP
IMA GAL TRA
AMID ETA ASKS
LONER EGAD
CLOT LOSS
MOO PINEAPPLE
ERA ERIE TOOL
GET DELL TEL

PUZZLE 145

MOM HELP ARID
APE ORAL RACE
KANGAROO OMEN
ELDER SWAM
ADD BACKS
CHAR ABLE LIE
HUTS TEA GATE
AGO EATS OWED
TEPEE SEA
GLEN ALONE
ONLY BEARSKIN
LEAP BITE AND
DEBT SLED YES

PUZZLE 149

RID SOFT SKIS
IRE PLEA TALL
CONSIDER ONLY
ENTIRE DOG
SIR SALAMI
BOAST SAN RED
ARMY WAG TOLL
NAB PAY WROTE
SLICED SEE
TAP PLATES
BAIL TELLTALE
AWOL ERIE USE
DENS ARTS TED

PUZZLE 142

OHIO RAFT
OPERA ELIOT
CABARET VERTIGO
CECIL SNOUT
MANE SPA ONES
ART TAR CEO
OVER AMADEUS METS
ERA IAN ARC ASH
WEIRD IRONY
TOP ODE
VENOM SODAS
ALI ROT ERG UMP
ADAM TOOTSIE NOAH
ROB MAP RIO
FREE STY ISLE
ELEGY LACES
SLEEPER JEZEBEL
MARGE ALONE
ROOF RIOT

PUZZLE 146

ARAB WEE RAMP
DODO ERA ELIA
STARWARS FELL
EAR IRISES
STARRY EON
EEL ASSENTS
MEL TRITE EAT
INSURED ARI
SOP COSTAR
POTATO ORE
ALOG STARTREK
RENE ERS TIRE
TOES SAT OPEN

PUZZLE 150

SET ABATE SOB
OAR COLAS HUE
WRESTLERS ONE
APED ERECT
EASED BONUSES
BROW BRACE
BEN PLATE MAD
CROSS HERO
SORROWS FARCE
CLAYS HEIR
RIG PANELLING
EVE EVERT LEE
WED RATES YET

PUZZLE 151

PUZZLE 152

PUZZLE 153

PUZZLE 154

1. Hard, Hark, Hack, Rack, Rock; 2. Sand, Band, Bald, Ball, Bill, Hill; 3. Mend, Mind, Mink, Sink, Sick, Sock; 4. More, Pore, Port, Pert, Pent, Rent.

PUZZLE 155

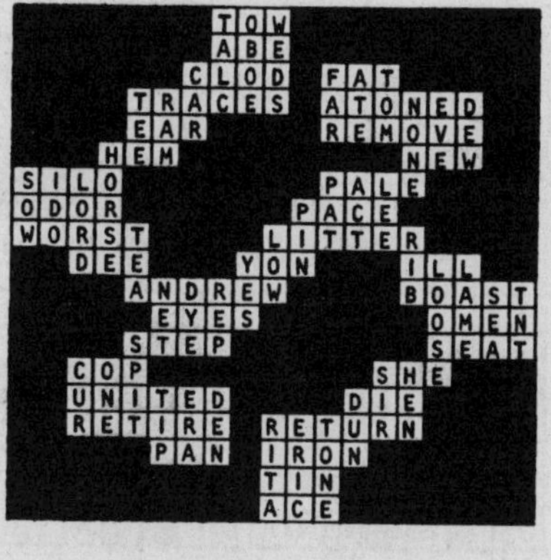

PUZZLE 156

PUZZLE 157

1. Sane, Panels, Personal; 2. Fuel, Ruffle, Fluffier; 3. Dart, Depart, Trampled; 4. Stir, Sister, Sinister; 5. Flat, Falter, Flattery; 6. Rent, Resent, Presents; 7. Oust, Stucco, Conducts.

PUZZLE 158

PUZZLE 159

Organic, Regular, Insight, Lozenge, Lengthy, Arrange. Bonus word: GORILLA.

PUZZLE 160

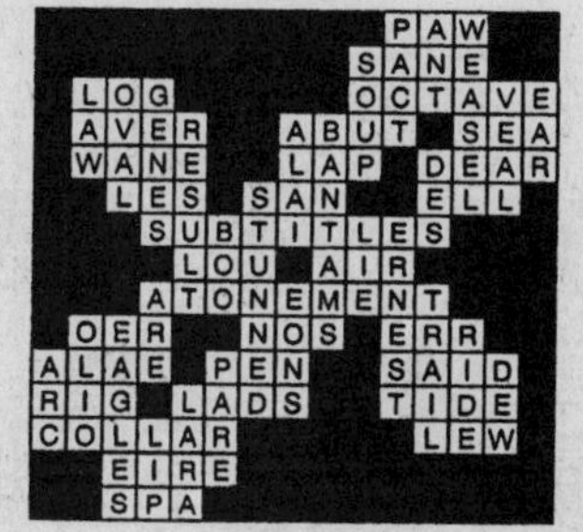

PUZZLE 161

1. Walk the dog, 2. Authorized, 3. Blacked out.

PUZZLE 162

PUZZLE 163

Clockwise: Yellow daffodils, purple crocuses, white tulips, pink hyacinths.

PUZZLE 164

PUZZLE 165

STEW MOTOR SLAB
PAPA ATONE PALE
EXIT STEED AREA
DICTATE ORDER
PERSPIRE
MATTER LANE PEG
ACHES DARK DIAL
CURE BONES UNTO
ATOM ODDS SATES
WEB CAGE COLORS
MATERNAL
TAKEN ANOTHER
ABED BALSA RODE
PLEA IDEAL OVEN
SELL TOOLS DENT

PUZZLE 166

MADE OARS LAB
IVAN ARGUE SANE
FORT LEASE EMIT
FIERCE REMODELS
DREARY ERA
ANTE DINNER
RAPT ETON OSAGE
IDA EDITION TON
CARED STEP ROSE
EMENDS CEDE
TIP ERASES
RETREATS ADORES
ERIE ROOST LORE
NINE EMOTE EDGE
ONE SETS DEER

PUZZLE 167

WED JET PER
MAXI UTE AVOW
HENCE SHE VITAL
ANTI STY ELUDE
MUSS PILOT NEE
EPIC FIEND
ZED ONE TEQUILA
AVAIL UTTER
PERCALE SEA YAM
EERIE IDLE
LAD PLAZA NEAT
AMEND DAM ILKS
MOVIE PUB AGGIE
KILN ELL AMIN
LET ATE RAN

PUZZLE 168

ASPEN INCA PEGS
QUOTE CAUL ALEC
UBOAT HIBERNATE
ASH TOOL EATON
POLAR ARACHNE
ERODES ANELE
COOED URSAMAJOR
RAH ALGER UNO
URSAMINOR ESSEX
CONAN PALTRY
ORACLES SATYR
TINED MARC IDE
TEDDYBEAR RIGOR
ETTE UGLI OPHIR
RIOS SOTS WATTS

PUZZLE 169

COBS TACIT CLIP
OVEN ORATE AURA
DATA WORSE DROP
ELAPSES ARENA
PRESTIGE
FLAMES CANE SEW
RAPID BARK CHAR
ABET HARDY RAGE
MEAT ALLY BAWLS
ELK ELSE TABLET
NOTATION
APRON MUSTARD
BOOM TRAPS AREA
COLA EASEL LIST
SLED ANKLE LATE

PUZZLE 170

APES FRAME RISK
LAMP LAGER ERIE
ELEE ARETE FIRE
EMULATED CHOSEN
LUTE STAR
CHASTE STSIMONS
HAD ORATE REVUE
ANAT YEARS DARE
ROMEO DREAD TSK
DISAGREE MELEES
TEES BOLA
SCARES COVERING
TUBA TIARA DOER
OBEY ELMER ETNA
PETS DEEDS RAES

PUZZLE 171

GAIT SEEP ABCS
INTRA TARE PLAT
SATON EVIL RANA
ORANGEPEKOE CON
IONA STACKED
BABE THE AROE
OWLS EELS LEASH
LOU ORATORY RIO
OLEAN DODO STLO
DISC NAB CHOP
SHAREOF JEER
TIN THEREDQUEEN
ELUL OMAR UPTON
ELBE RUCK ALONE
DYED TRES LENS

PUZZLE 172

F W C L C M T P
I A A O E E
T R S R W N R A
O S E T G
L O D D E E
E R S
S G P E A S T T
I U A X P E A
N R M L A E D P
E E M A
R P S S R N
O T L E E U
I U U E A N R T
N N N S T S I
A K D E S E E N

PUZZLE 173

AFT JAIL EMBER
SLIP UNDO NAIVE
PATE KELP CITED
ISLE EWE GONER
CHERUB SAD
STOW ITEMIZE
AMP EXHALE ODOR
REAP ICE DONS
ARIA AMENDS LET
BELLOWS TRIG
MAY UNISON
COVEY FAN AQUA
CORAL HUSK NUNS
AMBLE ERIE TACT
BESET PLAN BEY

PUZZLE 174

PROP ALAS POSES
ROPE DICE AMPLE
IDEA VEER LEASE
MEN SENSE ANTED
POSTERS NETS
WAS BANE GOT
RETIRE ODDS AVE
EDIT DOE FLEE
ADD POEM ABOARD
DYE OWLS TEA
FREE STELLAR
SMART GENES ARE
LABOR AMEN SNOB
ARENA TIED ACME
PETTY ERRS PEAL

PUZZLE 175

MIDAS MASH NIPS
ADULT ANOA OBOE
YELLOWJESSAMINE
SAL PROW LASER
APER SLID
HEAVEN THIN SAP
ERROR PHASE ANA
MOON ALERT SUED
ASS CLARK SONAR
NEE LANE SQUARE
LAST SAUL
STEAM TIRE BED
WILDPRAIRIEROSE
AMIE ABLE ZONAL
BEAN TEEN ENDUE

PUZZLE 176

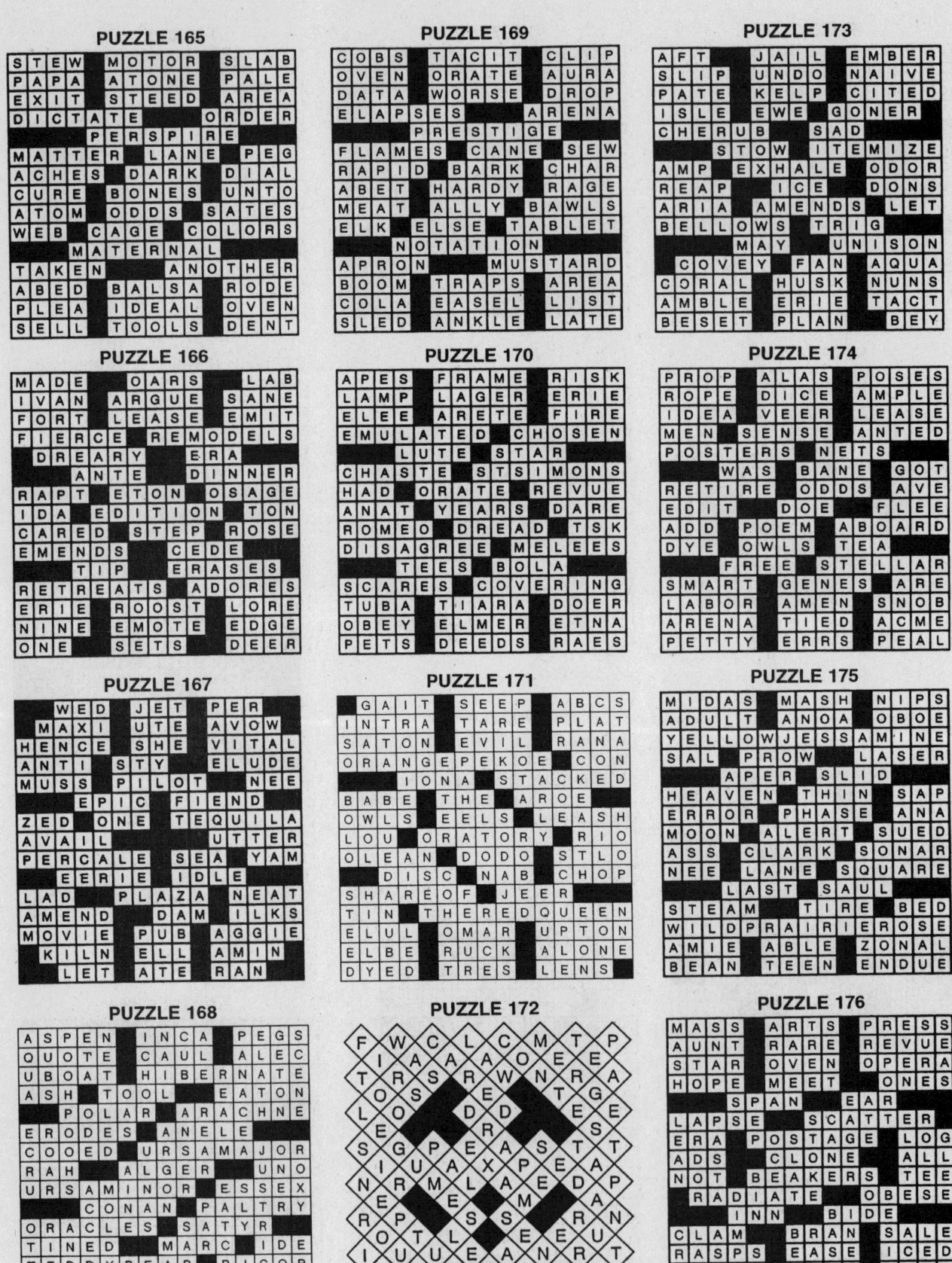

MASS ARTS PRESS
AUNT RARE REVUE
STAR OVEN OPERA
HOPE MEET ONES
SPAN EAR
LAPSE SCATTER
ERA POSTAGE LOG
ADS CLONE ALL
NOT BEAKERS TEE
RADIATE OBESE
INN BIDE
CLAM BRAN SALE
RASPS EASE ICED
ANKLE STEP DREG
BESET TEST EERY

PUZZLE 177

PAGED BOMB APSO
AGREE AMOR RATA
CHANT REDO GNAT
TAN ANDREWWYETH
TRIES SALLES
ROWENA SCENE
ETON POPART RIO
STOOD PUN SPENT
TOD ONEMAN AMOI
DRONE EOSINS
ANTRIM CAPON
MARYCASSATT GAP
UVEA DOUR ISTLE
LEAD ITER CHOSE
ESTS COTY SENOR

PUZZLE 178

CART CITE SHY
HOER ARENA STOA
ANDY RENDS TALL
NEW RENT SOIREE
HOUSE POURS
WINES PART AMP
HATES WAITS NEO
AVER ANN EDEN
LEA CADET PASSE
ERN AMES HASTE
DARED CORER
RUBBER ROME IDA
ERLE CRAVE SPAN
AGUE EATER PEST
DEE HERS ASHE

PUZZLE 179

SPIN BOONE SPRY
LADE OCTET HUES
OILS WHITEHORSE
TRESTLES EASER
OER CHALET
ERRAND BLURS
COAL GRANT DES
HORSETROUGHPEAK
ODE QUIDS RAVI
GULLY CRONES
SERIAL MAI
EILAT TERMINUS
CRAZYHORSE TITO
TETE ALONE CLEF
ONES METER HEST

PUZZLE 180

BETS AIRS DIKE
SALIC GOAT ARID
STONEHENGE TONG
RIP NISI PLUNGE
SKEWER CAPERS
ISEE SENATOR
SEWN SHIRT OPE
ETHER TAD OWNUP
ERE ARETE HESS
RETIREE SARI
STEAMS PUPPET
RETARD COIN ALE
ENOL STONEWALLS
MINI URNE ABEET
IDEA PIER YARN

PUZZLE 181

AGA PEAR ALMS
FALA SALLE BAIT
ALAS ASSET ANNA
RAISETHECURTAIN
AREA REE
TRAINS HONESTY
EAGLE BEVEL OER
EPOS BREAD RILE
SIR TRILL BELLS
DAIRIES ELDEST
DOG CREE
GIVETHESHOWAWAY
ASEA TREAD LONE
SLAT ELATE SODA
PELE NETS SYR

PUZZLE 182

PACK AGAS ROAD
ALLEY ROMP OBAN
STILE SOAR VERA
APPLEOFHISEYE
LEN NOD
LESTER SAKI SOS
ALOAD APPLECART
MOPE AGREE HIDE
APPLESEED MINER
REY APSE CENTRE
ARR AHS
APPLEPOLISHER
OLOR TAMP EERIE
SOLO TREE SANTE
OPEN YARN PEEN

PUZZLE 183

EDDA SABOT SCAN
FRET ADANO CARE
TECH VOICE UNIE
WILDERNESSROAD
EYRE TRESS
ALATE SORRY
SARI AVENUE ONA
THECOVEREDWAGON
ARA RETIRE MEET
CARON ABELE
STEAL SAAR
CUMBERLANDROAD
ANIL OILED SLAM
PELE YODEL IOTA
ARES SNARE ATEN

PUZZLE 184

ACTS BRIC LIED
MOAT ALAMO ASTO
PARA LUMPS UNTO
STARWARS TARTAR
FIST MARE
STAIN STARTLING
PARSON RIRE NON
INCH OPINE STOA
LGE TREE DETEST
LODESTARS DARES
LAHR ACER
CEDARS STARTREK
ARUT TULIP EIRE
MINE ANENT ROME
PEER REDS STAN

PUZZLE 185

BUST GAMUT AJAX
ASEA AGORA POUR
JERRYLEWIS TARA
ARAGE SASS NAY
EARL HEWER
SOFTSOAP LARIAT
AVA TOTAL MOVER
RENT FIRED SERE
ARNOS NITER RIA
HAYMOW SOMERSET
BELOW NOLA
MAR SOHO INANE
ONIT DONRICKLES
ONCE ESTER LOST
NEED NOOSE ETTE

PUZZLE 186

HASPS CAN SALT
INPUT SANE IVOR
STERE URNS DIRE
SIDELINE SMEARS
LENSES ESNE
ALLY SERPENT
POE PUT ANTENNA
ERASER COPIER
DESIRES AAR PAM
DUSTERS ASPS
ACES EATERS
SLOWER SIDECARS
COLA IBIS MELON
ANIL FEET UNTIE
NECK TAR STOLE

PUZZLE 187

PORCH BRAD GOSH
CLARA YORE ANKA
TAKES TAUT REIN
FEATHERBEDDING
TOE ACRE
BASE ABC TINSEL
ADA ARIEL NONNA
BEDANDBREAKFAST
ALAMO BENDS RUE
RETIRE SOL BEER
CAFE AGO
BREAKFASTINBED
LAMB OTHE ACTON
EVIL REOS WANNA
WIRE TROT STATE

PUZZLE 188

EMBED BUMS CHIN
SAUTE ASEA REBA
ARGOT TENTPOLES
USS RETRIAL LAT
PEARL ANATOMY
MIRACLE LITE
DRATTED SCONCES
CAY ARP
INSOFAR ALBANIA
ULNO SEASONS
PRORATA SALEP
AIL GOSSIPS EFT
CAMPSITES ARNIE
ETES NEAT MEESE
SACS ERNS SORTS

PUZZLE 189

GABES HABIT COAL
ALONE ERASE ARNIE
BADDAYATBLACKROCK
LIES ERIS BESSIE
ENS DATE HOSS ETS
LARS NAP
CHAN MODELS AHS
IRON CAT ROI BEA
SARAHPLAINANDTALL
ANN RIA COS ATEE
WEE STREET EDEN
KID PRES
MAP STEN KIEL COW
ARLENE TEED ALIA
JEANETTEMACDONALD
ANISE IRENE PAREE
ATES MANES STARS

PUZZLE 190

STARE AHEAD ACTED
LABOR EDIBLES MARCY
APATONTHEBACK ONION
NET SYNOD LEASABLE
TRET LAC STAIR SEES
EPOS STERNEST
LAPIN CHASE STAPLE
HELEN SHAFT ASIAN
OGLE SCARF ORAN NEV
TEE STATEOFMIND TRI
TNG LENS FOIST FATE
EDEMA SLATE FLIES
ASSIST TOILS TOOLS
SHOWOFFS LOBO
ADIT DANTE MAP DELL
SENATORS LOUIS ROE
SNAKE PICKANDCHOOSE
ESNES SLEEVES OLDER
TEENS SENAT PEERS

PUZZLE 191

LANAS CRAB CAME
AGENT HERE TALENT
TESTAMENTS STANCE
EST MOST TEAS TON
WILT OMAR PART
RAVINE SPAR POLES
ARENA KEEN TIM
CORE BEAR KEEPERS
ESS CONTAINER LIT
SEESAWS TOES HULA
ALL TOTE WIDER
STORM VERA CHEESE
HOPI PANS LAID
RIP POND GUNS LED
ELOPES OVERSTRIDE
DESERT NINE LUNGE
DENT SEES ENTER

PUZZLE 192

BITS LIT MAN STOP
EDIT ONE AGO TOME
SOLE STARTED ERIN
SLEET EMIT MEETS
POOR MENDED
HEM NAP REAL SOB
ORAL TROT WIT CUE
EASE SEVER SENATE
HAD TAPER DOT
TRIPOD LINER ATOP
HUN LEA DOSE HERO
EGG LENS PAW RED
PARTED OPEN
SPEAR CORN TESTS
WARN SPREADS WIRE
ALIT IRE TEA ELIA
TEES TOT EDD LOOM

PUZZLE 193

MAGNA ADAGE PLACATE
FABRIC REBEL REVERENT
ERRANT CRUEL EVANESCE
STOVES HIS ASSIST TON
TIGER LEVEE MUTT MERE
INA PURE SLIMY CADET
VET ALLY STATE LAY
ETERNAL SLASH FIREMAN
INN BLITHE AVERAGE
SABLE BRACE RAVED CIE
ALOE CRAVE FELON GOLD
BOO CHIDE CLEAR HONEY
ENTRAIN DRAINS GIN
RESERVE ROMES RINGLET
POE MISER COST IDA
EDSEL FEVER BOUT TUT
VEIL TINE AGENT ELECT
ATE CANARY RAT PLURAL
DESPOTIC ALATE AERATE
ESTIMATE LODES UNITED
TAPERED EXERT LADED

PUZZLE 194

HOSE SCARE GILDS SALT
EVIL ARSON ACORN TRUE
MERE LOPED REVUE RENT
PREVIOUS ODD EMACIATE
ATOP FRONT SKID
COTTEN PASTEUR STEINS
HAREM BARE RIOT ENDUE
USED SODA TOAD TELA
TIE SWORDS LISTEN ALL
ESSONITE AFOOT CELLOS
LEVY AKRON ELSE
MUDDLE OBEYS ALATIONS
ONE LLAMAS EGGERS NET
AFAR SLAT ONCE DIRE
TIRED PHIS DUET PROVE
STYLED ANCHORS LEANED
ESEL GRIND TERM
WINNIPEG ATE DISTANCE
ADIT AVAST GAITS TIER
DONE RELIC ANELE ILLS
SLED TEACH LADEN CETE

PUZZLE 195

SHARE WAFER CHORE
PAGAN EXILE HONOR
AGENT PERIL ARENA
GENT YARD
OPERA VIP SMEARS
SLUR PEEVISH CUE
PER GREET MARIE
YORE JOB REGIMENS
BOA ADE
PROBABLY POP SORT
ROUST EASED PIE
OPT BERATES METE
DESIRE NYE OVINE
RODS ALAN
BANAL PALER SUDAN
ELITE OLIVE EERIE
TALES TIDES STYLE

He who praises everybody praises nobody.

PUZZLE 196

HOLSTER THEFT
ATATIME QUAVER
SEDALIA SUBLIME
BEL CASTLES
LAS DEODAR
INCH PANTS FED
EIRE BEN ERMINE
STAMPINGGROUNDS
URGING LOS CLUE
PAS SHOER HERR
ORDEAL YET
HANGOUT BAT
ABOLISH ROUSING
REGALE ARRANGE
PLODS STARDOM

PUZZLE 197

A	G	E		S	L	O	E		E	S	N	E
L	E	T		T	O	R	N		A	H	E	M
I	T	E	R	A	T	E	S		G	U	A	M
			A	L	S	O		U	L	T	R	A
	R	A	N	K			O	R	E			
W	E	N	T		S	I	N	I	S	T	E	R
A	S	K		M	I	R	E	S		A	W	E
S	T	A	T	U	T	E	S		D	O	E	S
			O	L	E			B	U	S	S	
M	A	T	T	E		I	R	I	S			
A	C	R	E		A	D	A	P	T	E	R	S
S	H	E	M		M	E	M	O		S	E	E
T	E	E	S		P	A	I	D		S	O	W

PUZZLE 198

S	E	A	L		T	I	G	E	R			N	E	T
O	L	I	O		A	R	E	T	E		L	I	D	O
B	A	R	N	U	M	A	N	D	B	A	I	L	E	Y
S	S	E		R	E	T	E			P	E	E	N	S
			F	A	R	E			S	O	N			
C	A	B	A	L	S			N	E	L	S	O	N	
A	R	A	N				P	E	E	L		T	E	T
R	I	N	G	L	I	N	G	B	R	O	T	H	E	R
T	A	D		I	D	E	A				R	E	D	E
	S	A	L	T	E	D			C	O	U	R	S	E
			A	C	E			A	A	R	E			
T	O	U	C	H			A	R	N	E		A	S	E
S	E	N	D	I	N	T	H	E	C	L	O	W	N	S
A	N	T	E		I	R	E	N	A		R	E	I	N
R	O	O			L	E	M	A	N		O	S	T	E

PUZZLE 199

S	E	R	F			W	A	S	H		G	L	E	E
O	V	A	L		P	I	N	T	O		Y	O	L	K
M	E	M	O	R	A	N	D	U	M		R	O	S	E
E	N	S	U	I	N	G		B	E	L	A	T	E	D
			R	O	E				S	I	T			
T	A	C	I	T		C	U	B		L	E	A	D	S
A	M	O	S		S	O	N	A	T	A		T	O	E
M	I	C	H	A	E	L	C	R	I	C	H	T	O	N
E	G	O		S	T	O	L	E	N		E	A	R	S
R	O	A	S	T		R	E	D		V	E	R	S	E
			H	E	Y				C	O	D			
C	A	M	E	R	A	S		P	O	L	L	U	T	E
A	R	I	A		C	H	R	I	S	T	E	N	E	D
L	E	N	T		H	O	I	S	T		S	T	A	G
M	A	T	H		T	O	G	A			S	O	L	E

PUZZLE 200

E	A	C	H		S	C	O	L	D		A	B	L	E
S	H	O	E		O	A	K	I	E		B	R	A	M
P	A	A	R		C	R	A	N	E		R	U	N	E
	B	L	A	C	K	E	Y	E	D	S	U	S	A	N
			L	A	S	T				A	P	H	I	D
G	I	D	D	Y			A	R	E	N	T			
U	S	E	R		A	S	S	E	N	T		S	H	H
L	I	L	Y	O	F	T	H	E	V	A	L	L	E	Y
P	S	I		F	R	E	E	L	Y		E	A	R	P
			S	T	O	P	S			N	O	V	A	E
A	G	G	I	E				G	A	I	T			
Q	U	E	E	N	A	N	N	E	S	L	A	C	E	
A	R	E	S		L	O	A	N	S		R	O	A	D
B	U	S	T		M	A	M	I	E		D	I	V	A
A	S	E	A		S	H	E	E	T		S	L	E	D

PUZZLE 201

	M	I	C	E		S	I	R		L	E	G
T	O	D	A	Y		O	N	E		O	P	E
A	D	O	R	E		B	A	R	G	A	I	N
D	E	L	E				N	U	A	N	C	E
			S	O	F	T	E	N	S			
W	H	I	S	P	E	R				P	E	T
A	I	L		T	W	I	S	T		O	V	A
G	E	L				B	O	U	L	D	E	R
			R	E	V	E	N	G	E			
R	E	V	I	V	E				D	A	S	H
I	M	A	G	I	N	E		A	G	I	L	E
F	I	R		C	U	R		S	E	D	A	N
T	R	Y		T	E	N		P	R	E	Y	

PUZZLE 202

N	O	D	S		R	O	A	M		S	M	A	C	K
O	R	A	L		E	R	M	A		P	A	R	E	E
A	L	T	O		A	N	O	A		A	S	I	D	E
H	O	A	G	Y	C	A	R	M	I	C	H	A	E	L
				O	T	T		D	E	E				
A	D	I	E	U		E	T	U	I		D	A	R	E
L	E	V	A	N	T		O	R	O			M	A	L
G	E	O	R	G	I	A	O	N	M	Y	M	I	N	D
E	R	R			N	A	T		S	O	I	R	E	E
R	E	Y	S		G	A	S	H		U	N	S	E	R
			I	S	L			O	U	R				
T	W	O	S	L	E	E	P	Y	P	E	O	P	L	E
M	A	L	T	A		R	O	D	S		V	A	I	N
A	D	E	E	M		A	L	E	E		A	L	A	I
N	E	A	R	S		L	E	N	T		L	O	R	D

PUZZLE 203

C	A	T	O		A	W	N			A	S	E	A	
A	L	U	M		T	H	O	R		L	O	D	G	E
M	I	T	E		L	I	V	E		E	L	G	A	R
P	A	U	L	C	E	Z	A	N	N	E		A	P	O
			E	R	A		S	E	E		O	R	E	S
A	B	A	T	E	S				W	A	N	D		
R	O	N		S	T	E	E	L		N	E	E	D	S
C	A	D	E	T		M	O	O		A	R	G	O	T
S	T	Y	L	E		U	N	B	A	G		A	R	E
		W	A	D	E				P	R	I	S	M	S
C	L	A	N		E	G	O		P	A	R			
O	E	R		C	L	A	U	D	E	M	O	N	E	T
O	T	H	E	R		S	T	A	N		N	O	M	E
S	T	O	V	E		P	E	N	D		E	R	I	E
	S	L	A	W			R	E	S		D	A	R	N

PUZZLE 204

A	B	E	T		S	I	F	T			S	A	L	T
T	O	L	E		A	R	I	E	S		A	R	I	A
L	O	O	N		F	A	T	A	L		H	I	N	T
A	S	P		P	E	T	S		E	V	A	D	E	S
S	T	E	R	I	L	E		D	E	E	R			
			A	N	Y		R	E	V	E	A	L	E	D
D	R	A	F	T		T	O	P	E	R		O	R	E
R	E	N	T		C	H	A	O	S		M	U	S	E
O	A	T		F	O	I	S	T		H	A	T	E	D
P	R	E	C	I	N	C	T		J	O	T			
			R	A	C	K		F	E	D	E	R	A	L
A	S	T	U	T	E		A	I	R	S		E	R	A
G	O	R	E		R	A	V	E	S		E	G	G	S
U	N	I	T		T	W	I	N	E		T	A	U	T
E	G	O	S			E	D	D	Y		A	L	E	S

After all is said and done, there's a rerun.

PUZZLE 205

```
PET■PLANK■RAM
OLE■ROSIN■EGO
PINEAPPLE■MEL
■■■DYE■■AVAST
CITES■ADDER■■
HORN■SHOETREE
EWE■SPEED■IRA
FAMILIAR■HEIR
■■BLOND■LADEN
YOLKS■■CAR■■■
OBI■HONEYMOON
WON■EVADE■IDA
LEG■SABER■LET
```

PUZZLE 206

```
ORE■EMIR■NEWS
WAX■DONE■OVAL
LEA■URNS■MINE
■■MACE■PEALED
AGILE■ROAD■■■
DANE■VENT■BET
OLES■ASS■REDO
SAD■ERIE■OLEO
■■■COIN■SAINT
BANANA■SURE■■
AGED■NAPE■VIA
LUTE■TROD■ERN
LEST■SITE■SEA
```

PUZZLE 207

```
ALUM■SPEAR■AFAR
DOTE■ALATE■RILE
ARAL■RACES■IRON
REHOBOTH■TOSSED
■■■DONE■COMET■■
SAWING■HARASSES
ALIEN■LAGER■TAU
ILLS■MATES■PATE
GEM■LOPES■TOTED
ANIMATED■SERENE
■■NICOL■BALK■■■
SIGNER■DOVERAFB
KATE■INANE■IDEA
IGOR■SEWER■NULL
TONS■TENDS■DELI
```

PUZZLE 208

```
SIT■MILD■RANG
ADO■ERIE■ANON
PAL■SETS■VISA
■■EGAD■OMELET
PARE■■PLAN■■■
IRAN■PLAY■ASP
SITE■HAT■PITA
ADE■PACE■ERAL
■■■PINE■■ACRE
REGRET■PURR■■
AXLE■AMOS■AWE
VIES■SOLE■FOR
ETES■MELD■TEN
```

PUZZLE 209

```
SHOP■GABOR■STAY
EARL■ARETE■NONO
ALAE■FRAIL■ATTU
MONA■FANCYFREE■
■■■SLEY■■■ALMS■
CALAIS■BIRDS■■■
AMEND■ERNE■■DON
FANTASTICVOYAGE
ETO■■ETNA■LOIRE
■■■SETAE■DOUSED
■AMEN■■■PERT■■■
■FANDANGOS■HERO
ITSA■NOISE■FEAR
NEST■NEVER■URGE
CREE■ALERT■LYES
```

PUZZLE 210

```
LOB■ADE■■ABLATE
ABANDON■STEALER
BIGBEND■MOLDING
■■■ANNA■ANOS■■■
BED■■ANDREW■SPA
ALES■■GET■■SUIT
REFORMER■USABLE
■VICTORIAFALLS■
BANKED■DROWSING
UTES■■BEG■■AMES
NED■TARSUS■■ERA
■■■ERNE■ATTA■■■
PRORATE■BAHRAIN
REPLIED■LIAISON
EXTEND■■ENT■SUE
```

PUZZLE 211

```
GORE■ABLE■AGAPE
IDOL■IRON■CALLA
VOTE■LEGALITIES
ERECTED■MAD■TAT
■■■TED■MEDIC■■■
ARISE■COL■CAFES
MAN■■DOLLS■MATT
EDAM■INDIA■ECHO
NINE■ICING■■EEL
DIETS■ENG■CADRE
■■■EYING■MAR■■■
ADD■NOT■BEDEVIL
WEAPONRIES■NASA
EARED■IDEA■ALLY
DREGS■COPS■SEES
```

PUZZLE 212

```
COMB■STOVE■PREP
AREA■PAPER■LONI
SCAN■IRANI■AMAN
HAND■CALICOCAT■
■■■ALES■■■NENE■
TURNED■AFROS■■■
ARENA■STLO■■CEE
CATANDTHECANARY
OLE■■ROOD■VERNE
■■■SOUPS■SOILED
■AHAB■■■RING■■■
■ROBINHOOD■HAHA
DOVE■AURAL■BRAD
OMER■SENSE■OLLA
EARS■TRETS■ROOM
```

PUZZLE 213

```
MOPUP■TRIM■PRAM
IVANS■AURA■RATE
FARSIGHTED■IDOL
FLAT■EOS■DECANT
■■■AARE■REVERES
RABBLE■MINERS■■
AGILE■■ODES■CAB
SANE■ROVED■RONA
PRO■MUNI■■DEPOT
■■COULEE■WIDENS
BLUSTER■DANS■■■
RELIES■PEG■TUBS
AVAR■TELESCOPIC
TERI■HEAR■ENOLA
SESS■ERNE■TENET
```

PUZZLE 214

```
■WASP■VAST■■FAN
PARKA■IDIOT■OWE
ASSET■GONER■RAW
STOP■AIRS■INERT
TENTACLE■ABUSES
■■■IDEA■■WENT■■
BRACE■NAMES■ASP
OAFS■ACRID■BLUR
APT■KNEEL■ALLEY
■■EDIT■■LOGO■■■
STRESS■DIRECTOR
LAWNS■LONE■KITE
ALA■ERASE■BATHE
TOR■DIVER■IDLED
END■■MASS■BEER■
```

A teenager never takes no for a final answer.

PUZZLE 215

```
GERM■SALON■ELBA
AREA■AFIRE■FORM
MINH■TALES■FLEA
SCOOTER■STEALTH
■■■GAS■■■SAC■■■
RABAT■LOG■SEAMS
EDEN■ROTATE■RAH
FORYOUREYESONLY
ERG■PEERED■KITE
RESET■NOR■CLEAR
■■■LEA■■■TOA■■■
SHUDDER■GOPHERS
LAKE■SODOM■OLIO
AMES■OPINE■MIFF
TEST■PETES■ASEA
```

PUZZLE 216

```
JABS■RED■■ORB
ALOE■OVAL■RAE
ZEAL■DEDICATE
ZESTIER■VALET
■■■ZOO■PEP■■■
ALIEN■YES■BRA
DEAR■KEG■QUIP
SIN■TEN■BUDGE
■■■HAY■TEA■■■
BORAX■FIERCER
ALUMINUM■RARE
LED■SOME■EGGS
DOE■■WED■LEST
```

PUZZLE 217

ALP SPA SLOT
HAITI WATT NAPA
APERS ATLE OMAN
ELEPHANTWALK
OVID STE
STRIKEUPTHEBAND
AWE ERNE DECOY
RIGA ARI ERLE
ANODE CRUS OAR
SENDINTHECLOWNS
REO LIMN
ILOVEAPARADE
RAVE RILE EGGER
ICES SCAN RAISE
SENT SIT NED

PUZZLE 218

MILK WASP MARK
IDEA ARTIE ISEE
SLAY FRIENDSHIP
TED BEAR RESENT
EVERY DALY
TROD MAGI PTA
PASTE POLES ERR
ACHE CULLS SNIT
POI TARDY DIMES
ASP OPRY ERAS
ANTS PREEN
PRESTO WOOD SKI
AUTHORSHIP AHAB
RENE SHONE LINE
ADAR EATS APEX

PUZZLE 219

COMA RAFT PAL
UPON MINEO RACE
LIND AFTERHOURS
PET OIL ABLE
GABLE PASO
SCORE LETTER
TAMMY DEARE AES
ABE PIANO SRA
NOR DANTE SITAR
TYRONE ILONA
OVER MANOF
DANE ERS ETC
MAINSTREET IDOL
ARMY AUNTS TELA
YES BEDS ANDY

PUZZLE 220

STAT LARA SNAP
NINA EVERT LOMA
OMNIAVINCITAMOR
WEALS DESTINES
OPT AND
PADRES NONSENSE
ALI NADAR ROOM
CIVISROMANUSSUM
EVES LENIN ESA
REROTTED LEASES
TOR ESP
MOORINGS COEDS
VOXPOPULIVOXDEI
ALEE STENO ONER
LENS SEEN NAPE

PUZZLE 221

ADO HAT BED
LENS WIPED SORE
ANEW IRENE TONE
STRANGE SNEAKER
TUG OWL
TRESTLE STEEPLE
OIL SETTLER RED
OVA HOE IVE
LET STEREOS DEN
STEAMER PAMPERS
RUN TEE
STAGGER REWARDS
LULU TAPER COOL
OBOE SIRES HONE
WEE NOD FED

PUZZLE 222

DEPOSE SASH ESTEEM
LINEMEN TABOO STELLAR
ENTRANT AMORT PERSONA
EER NOR LIVEWIRE ENID
CRAW REMOTE ARIL GAI
HOPED AONE STATE PACA
LENTO STET SATAN
SHELLEY NATURE REMELT
WOMBAT LEMAN EAR
IVORY DAVIT MARGARET
METE HOMEDEFENSE ELAM
REDRIVER MORTE SLAKE
IVE SERRA STATEN
ESCAPE CRANKY PORTEND
SARGE RENT RADII
TREE SLAVE PIER POSIT
ICA OOZE HEREAT NODE
VETO OVERRATE DOG WEE
ANIMATE SAVIN ITALIAN
LEVERET ARETE SEVENTY
TEREDO LENE EMERGE

PUZZLE 223

STREW CABLES CASPER
ARENA AREOLE ALPINE
GOSSIPCOLUMN PLANTS
ENE FEAST AREA ERE
SAWS ROE TATER STET
PHIS NAMED TARES
PIQUES SOLES TIRE
ENURE TANKS SHRIEKS
SLOG SALES OHIO SEE
TOTE CHATTERER STEW
EVA GOOD URGED TAPE
RETINUE BRIAN WATER
ISAR TOKEN LAKERS
SMOLT FROES AIDE
PONE CRONY SST SAGA
ARM THOU OASES MES
TRALEE BLABBERMOUTH
HIRERS LILIES ENSUE
ESKARS EELERS WEEPS

PUZZLE 224

LAWS CAGED OSLO
ORAL AGILE CHOW
OILY REFLECTION
PAL BENT RANKS
SWEET CAIN
LATHER HOMETOWN
EGRET DAMES PRO
FREE ROBIN BEEN
TEE PANIC TENSE
SETPOINT BURSTS
RUDY TASTE
TRAIN PECK CAT
ROUNDSTEAK ERNE
ISNT HORSE METE
PETS YOKED STEM

PUZZLE 225

PAWS ACT FOREST
ANOA MAR EXETER
VIRTUOSO ATTUNE
ESSEN TULSA ITS
HEMS PATIO
FINAL ENSLAVES
SAP SOUSA HEMP
WRECKER TROUNCE
AGRO ANEAR TEE
NOSECONE MARIE
DEBIT ITAL
SAM RIATA OVATE
CREDIT INGRATES
OTIOSE NNE GOAT
TENNER GIN ERMA

PUZZLE 226

BARA WEDS EMILE PSAT
ULAN ARIA MODAL LUMEN
RAVISHING USERS AMANA
SMELLINGSALTS STATER
TON ANYA SALTLAKECITY
IVES PITY ELAN
ABODES CODE SALTSAWAY
LIVER TORE DAFOE VALE
ODES BART WORST BATON
PER DATA LANA MINCES
THESALTOFTHEEARTH
AMOUNT WETS MAID FAT
MANLY CRASS FIRN LIME
ICED SHUNS ROTS BARON
DESALTING MHOS WADERS
OENO MEET DARE
AGRAINOFSALT DIVE MEA
RIALTO WORTHONESSALT
AGILE SEETO OVERTURES
LOSER TRASS SERE RICE
TANS AGREE TROD FATA

PUZZLE 227

BALL BOISE CHOP
REAL INNER HOME
ARIA LOSER EMIT
NORMAL PARROTS
ASIA TIO
SHOSHONE ANKAS
PUB ENTRE GELT
ALEC ERN EPEE
OSHA DETER HER
TEEMS DELAWARE
YET RETE
ADRENAL MELTED
DEAN MERGE DOSE
AMIN PAEAN ETTA
MINE SNORT REEL

PUZZLE 228

ASIA FARM HOFFA
ROMP ALOU ELLIS
FLIPSIDES REINK
SINATRA EPA PEA
RAE FELLOW
DEFERRAL ADLIB
HULLO MIST ALLA
OBI FLIPTOP SAM
WIPE ASOU UPONA
ESSEX UNSTANCH
ATBEST WON
ABC BRA LIFENET
BOONE FLIPFLOPS
IDIOT EIRE ELEA
GENTS READ DOER

PUZZLE 229

COBB SEPAL REST
AGUE ATONE ERLE
RETE BUTTONWOOD
PET IRIS OASES
OATES SHOR
PANNED STANDBY
ELDER WHERE UPS
RIOT PARED ETRE
TAW SAKER CUTER
SNEERED LAROSA
LEAN BISON
TREAT TATA HAT
BUTTONHOLE COLE
ALOE EAGER HOAR
REND EGADS AKIN

PUZZLE 230

PLUS ACTOR TAGS
IOTA LLAMA AGRO
GOAL BONNY PAIL
THEMISSISSIPPI
MONEY CREED
JOB MOD RIA
ALOT BUNNYHOP
CLOUDFORMATIONS
KANGAROO NUTS
KOP AOK ROT
SOFIA ACRID
THEGRANDCANYON
RAIL GODOT LION
ARGO AMORE ALSO
DANO LENDS NYET

PUZZLE 231

ABA STAR PAAR
BOSC WORSE AIDA
ATTA OMITS CREW
STRAINAPOINT
ELAND ERNO NIB
DEY ESS GOOSE
YANKEEDOODLE
SHEA AISLE PEER
PULLUPSTAKES
ELMER NAT HOT
WAS DOTS NAIVE
TUGBOATANNIE
ICER RINGO EDEN
LODE ELDER WEDS
LOOK SLED ROY

PUZZLE 232

STOW BASER MELD
CORE ELOPE OLIO
ONCEINALIFETIME
TEA NONE DEMOS
ATIS AMATI
MARGOT ADAM NSF
ANENT NOEL SAAR
ONCEOVERLIGHTLY
RUES ARTE REEVE
IMP SIVA GADDER
TALLY SUBS
TIARA ETNA BIG
ONCEBITTENTWICE
TELA DOONE ITEM
SEES SENOR TEDS

PUZZLE 233

SCAD PILAF ABED
PERU ABOIL RAVI
ODIC USURY ARES
TEAK PET WABASH
PEEN THEY
CAVIAR BEER ELI
AGENT MINEO RAN
TOES BAGEL TACT
ERR BESOT BITER
RAY OAST PAGODA
CORE CODE
ARMAND OHM RIBS
DAUB OSTIA ECRU
ETNA WEIRD YEAR
NAIL NACRE EDDA

PUZZLE 234

AREA CORAL SOAP
PALM APACE ALLY
ESSE REWIN MEAL
SHARPEN DISPOSE
IRE EEL
DISCORD ENTERED
IDEA SADAT DAME
LID TAG DIN
LOGE RENEW HATS
STEMMED REMORSE
ION SAP
PLANETS ATTEMPT
LODE ALIVE FEAR
OVEN LACER UNDO
TEST STERN LUST

PUZZLE 235

RANT SEAMS CASH
ALOU PERIL OKIE
HERR ARENA CREW
CANADIANBACON
ELEE MYNA
WARDS CROIX
ALIT ATLONG ACT
COLOMBIANCOFFEE
SEE OBTUSE LADD
TRESS AIRES
ASIA STEM
ENGLISHMUFFIN
BRAE STAIN LOON
BIRR TOILE ATEE
BEES OARED MALE

PUZZLE 236

SLEPT ARIA AGHA
NOTER LONG GOAD
OUTRE LOCI ELLA
BRASSHAT TANDEM
UTAH PANDERS
BACALL RATTAN
EPODE FOVEA RAG
RIPE COWED CUBA
GAP BOXER GOLEM
ENAMEL GREEDY
ARROWED BOAR
BEHOLD IRONCLAD
HEED IOTA DIANA
OVAL AVEC MOTOR
REDE NAME ANENT

PUZZLE 237

ACTA CLAIR SPOT
POOR HANSE CLIO
SNAKEINTHEGRASS
END ACES RAYES
TSKS AMP
ESTATE ASH SOLE
LEAVEN DUO SOX
VII ROOMERS SIC
ENL UNI SUTURE
REOS TET ENAMEL
RTE ESNE
AMBIT ALEE TAT
RAINCATSANDDOGS
GIRT LOINS AREA
ODDS IRADE DYER

PUZZLE 238

TAPE SAP QUAD
MAXIM TEA USURP
EXILE ERR AERIE
WISER POKER APT
GAS ARTS
HAREM AZTEC
LANE OBIT OVAL
IRIS KORAN LATE
PESO YETI IDEA
SERGE CIDER
TOGA FEN
OFT GORGE JEWEL
FLING RAW ERODE
FINAL OLE CIVET
TYPE WAR TEEN

PUZZLE 239

CRAFT ARID RUDE
TULLE DOSE ITER
SEDAN ETAS FILS
SATO POKERFLAT
BROT RILEY
DEPOSE ANTAE
ARIA RESIST SPA
MISTS STD AFTON
ENA ESTEEM LALA
TRUER ARARAT
SPOIL ABET
SALTFLATS AFAR
PLAT IDOS COROT
ALTE EDGE TOGAE
REAR SASS STONE

PUZZLE 240

ABLE CALEB AMEN
LEAR ALAMO LALO
ALDA SCRUB IMAM
NAYS TAD BOVINE
BUREN TYPEE
FAIRER BASE EGO
ERRED MACON IRA
SODS CALIX ISIS
TAJ FIRST SCENT
SRO ASIA SPENDS
HALTS PEACH
SUNDAE ORA HOPE
URSA REGAL EWES
EDOM NOLTE SETS
DUNS SNEER TREE

PUZZLE 241

SPED ALL ATOP
OILY VIA RILE
ALEE ENTITLES
PEP ERECT TOT
HART HEN
STALE MEMENTO
PANT SAD WAIT
ATTEMPT BESET
ROE CART
AGA PALER IMP
MASTERED HEAR
PLEA EVE ISLE
SEAM DID STEP

PUZZLE 245

ACRE MART
ASP LAIR ALAI WAS
THEFARMER INTHEDELL
TONE ELM OLIO
APSE ADEPT ELSE
HORSESHOE
LOT ORT YAK CEE
EAR SSE REV HOG
STABLE SAWING
COO LAC
POTATO TURKEY
ADO SUM ARE ELA
PER CIA IDO NIP
HARVESTED
BACH MIRES TAME
ALOE NAT ORAL
BARNDANCE SPILTMILK
END ILEO OLEO DES
PLOW PLOT

PUZZLE 249

WAG COVE JADE
ALI RAIL AHOY
STREAKED CAGE
HOLLY DECK
MOB RADIOS
RED NAB PARKA
ICED TAG WARN
CREAM RAG NAG
HURRAH LAB
NEIL GABBY
GOBI KANGAROO
OVEN EVIL ERR
TANG DALE WEE

PUZZLE 242

ART RAP ERR
WEE SALAD NEE
AVA OHARE DES
RISES ENLIST
EVER ODD EVES
ERASER TIES
ERODE
PART VENEER
SOLE SEW ASEA
PLEDGE UTTER
EAR OVENS ELL
ANT BEGIN EEE
RDS ROB MDS

PUZZLE 246

GAME DEPT SET
OMEN IDEA ALE
NEAT VIRGINIA
ENTREAT GAD
URN TENTHS
HORSE BID RAY
EMIT GAP RAIN
WIG SAT MAPLE
STILTS CAT
DIE BANTAMS
ANIMATED ALOE
COT MATE NILE
TRY SPAT STEM

PUZZLE 250

EROS SHE TALK
GAVE TAW ERIN
OPEN OVERRIDE
STRANGE ERASE
STAY ONE
SLEET FAT TIP
EYES WAR CAVE
EER GAR TOKEN
SOY PINE
PASTA RESTORE
OVERLOOK EVIL
NINA ADO SETS
EDDY TEE TREE

PUZZLE 243

TAR AVID FIT
ODES SORE ADE
POPE STALLION
ELLIE TOLLS
SCALES TAN
PAL OTTO GRIP
AGES AIL SERE
REDO NEED SOW
BET ROBINS
SAWED MATES
CLARINET ATOM
ASK TIRE RENO
TOE SPED DEW

PUZZLE 247

PAW WAR SPA
ALIT ALE GOOD
TOTO ILL ROLE
GHOST IRATE
LEE EON
SENSED DETOUR
AVA ATE
LATHES WASTES
ONE OLE
PANDA NICER
ERNE SAD TROT
WAND ODE SILO
EYE NOR ELM

PUZZLE 251

T B L F P B G R
O O I U O A U
B W A B R S S N
E N E T I
R C D R M C
E O O E A B A
E D M P F L R N
O E T E O
R N L R T W
A A A U A
P P C B G P R B
A T O H R O
N I U A A A O B
O N R S N S A
N D T E T T T R

PUZZLE 244

MAC ACE CASH
SOLO LON AREA
OLDMILLSTREAM
STAINED RESTS
CAN EER
ELIA IDA BAT
MILLSBROTHERS
UTE HIE ETTE
BEN ERR
STILL CRIMPED
CECILBDEMILLE
ALES REC TOLE
TEDS OFT SPA

PUZZLE 248

SWAB CELL TAG
LACE ALEE ERE
IDEA NAVIGATE
MESSY PESO
TEASE REST
AWE APE AGREE
REPORT BLEARS
AREAS ROE SET
BEES GEARS
EARN TAMES
BOBSLEDS GORE
ADE SEEP ARIA
NET OKRA SENT

PUZZLE 252

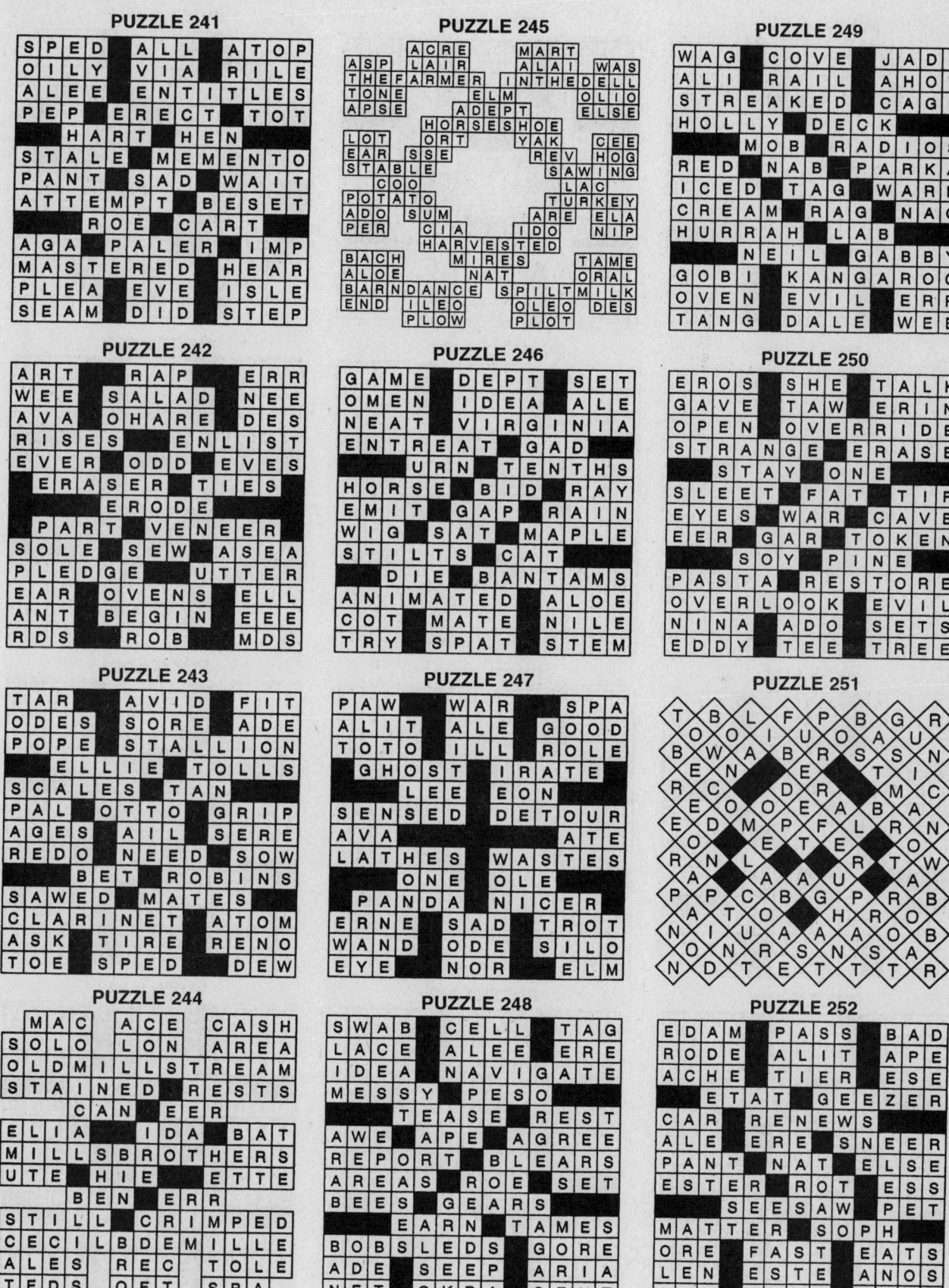

EDAM PASS BAD
RODE ALIT APE
ACHE TIER ESE
ETAT GEEZER
CAR RENEWS
ALE ERE SNEER
PANT NAT ELSE
ESTER ROT ESS
SEESAW PET
MATTER SOPH
ORE FAST EATS
LEN ESTE ANOS
EST REED STET

PUZZLE 253

LAB APED SEAM
ICE TRAY ANNE
ARE TORE VOTE
RETAINS WORST
IRE FARM
SPADE FIR OUR
PACE HAT FUSE
ART HUT POSED
ITEM PER
LOVER BLEMISH
IVAN SOAR DOE
NETS ANTE OLE
TREE DEED LED

PUZZLE 257

SHOT HIP SHOP
HIRE ARE PANE
EDEN NEE AMEN
SAD LAD
CHEW REBEL
ERA EGRET APE
YES AIR DEN
EAT EDGES GET
SMELL AGES
AMP GNU
HERD ILL LOPS
OVAL LEA FARE
PATE LED STOW

PUZZLE 261

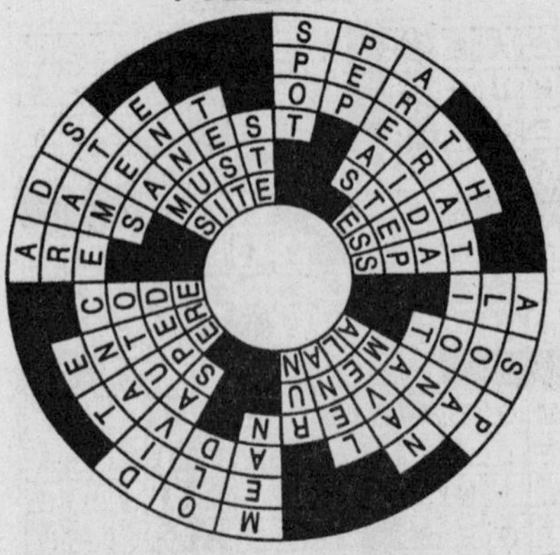

PUZZLE 254

POLE PET JAB
IDOL ROE HERO
PORE ONE ALTO
ERECT STARLET
TEA HIS
CLOSEST RHODE
AIL PAL YES
PEDAL NEEDLES
CAD EGO
ACROBAT GLEAM
BOOR NOW LACE
LOAN CUE ASEA
ELM ERE REST

PUZZLE 258

YIPS WAIT AMI
EDIT ECRU LID
SAGA ENERVATE
RIDE NESTS
STEERS BEE
PANDA HERRING
ALI JIG COO
REDUCED WROTE
SOD DRONES
ASPEN BAYS
GOODWILL TALL
ORE ALOE EPEE
GEM YEWS REST

PUZZLE 262

LOAN AHOY FOE
ABLE CASE INN
MOPS ENLARGED
PESTS DOSE
LEO TASTE
CALENDAR PLAY
HUE TOTAL OLE
URGE REVIEWED
MASTS EAR
CURT RACED
MUSHROOM SODA
AFT ELSE EVER
TOY REST RENT

PUZZLE 255

HAIL ARID SPA
OBOE LODE AID
TENT OBSERVED
TUNE PEERS
AROUSE LED
SINCE SIN PEN
POLE NUT HOLE
STY SON POSSE
PAD DENTED
BASIC CARE
INTERIOR SHOE
ATE ERIE TOIL
SEW DANS YELL

PUZZLE 259

TOP ACTS CREW
ALE NAIL HIVE
PET TREE EDIT
IRIS EASELS
ATTIC SPIT
LAID SWIM TAB
PRO EPEES ACE
SON DEER SPIN
DENT SHEDS
ALMOND KEYS
BEEP IDEA TEN
LANE NOEL RYE
EDDY GELS YET

PUZZLE 263

DINT ROD BAND
ODOR ARE OLEO
RENO GEM ROAN
MASON ORDERS
EPIC NEE
MAN PRO DRAMA
ALSO YAP SLAY
TEEMS RAW ADE
ION LAIR
BATTLE ROMPS
ABET VAN TILE
GLEE EGO ASEA
SEND ROW STAR

PUZZLE 256

CONE AOK STEP
APEX LIE PAGE
MARC ELEVATOR
ELDER PAR
PATH TEASE
PESTERED SILO
ARE ALI DUN
LINT PLATTERS
MEDAL OLEO
MAP EMEND
STEAMERS ALOE
ORAL LOP TAPE
BARE TEA ONER

PUZZLE 260

SUN TOTS HILL
ERE AVON ERIE
ANATHEMA RANT
THOR CRONES
ANNIE SKIN
VIES DAIS TEE
INS SWINE HAL
DES WING PATS
PANT MANSE
STRAND WALK
POOR LOOKSFOR
ALIT ERNE UTA
RELY DOTS LOW

Until Eve arrived, it was a man's world.

PUZZLE 264

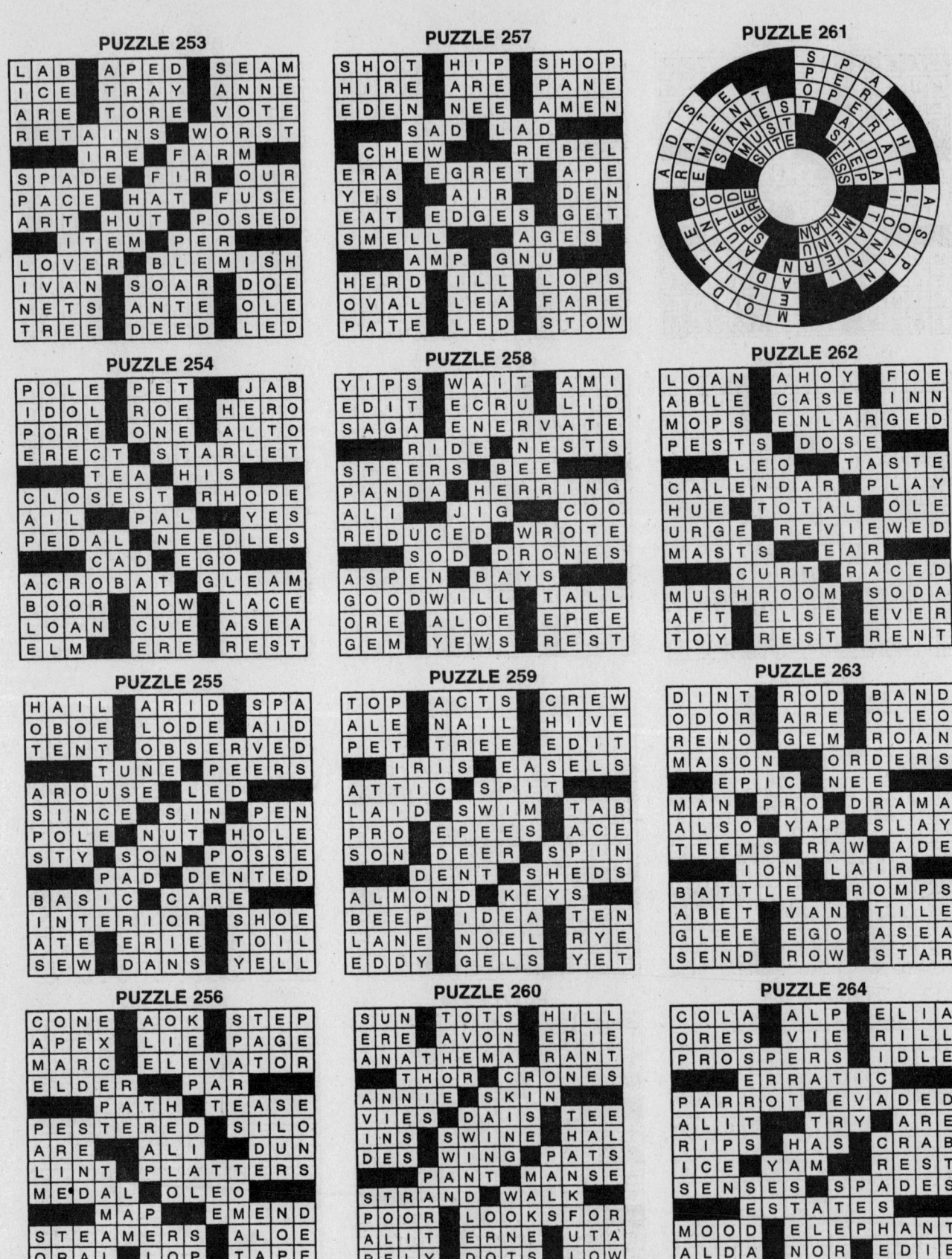

COLA ALP ELIA
ORES VIE RILL
PROSPERS IDLE
ERRATIC
PARROT EVADED
ALIT TRY ARE
RIPS HAS CRAB
ICE YAM REST
SENSES SPADES
ESTATES
MOOD ELEPHANT
ALDA NOR EDIE
TEEN SEN DALE

PUZZLE 265

CAB BAKE WRAP
HUE EMIR EAVE
ERA GENE AREA
WARNING CLERK
AND SAT
GARB BASHFUL
EGO PIECE ORE
MEETING MEND
HEN COO
MOLAR GARBAGE
ELAN LAND BID
LINK ALOE EVE
TOES BEER TEN

PUZZLE 266

AGE MORAN FLA
CORA AHOLE GRIT
ENID NADER LANE
SENATOR SANDS
ONA HAS
MAIN SALEMSLOT
MARTIN LEAS IVE
ALDA ODDER IVES
RTE SLUE TALENT
SANANTONE ROSS
MOE DRU
BELOW GENERAL
EVER ROMAN LARA
LINE AWARE MILT
ALS GLESS DOE

PUZZLE 267

PALM APPAL STAB
ALOE MARRY AARE
SOUSAPHONE OMEN
SUSAN BEST BAT
TUNAS ETO
CLARINETS CRUSE
RICE ITE SHERPA
ASCENT ESPIES
GLOVES SIT ANNE
SERER CASTANETS
DSO AUTOS
PSI SONS OFFER
AHOY PIANOFORTE
NONE ANGER REOS
TEST LEEDS DENT

PUZZLE 268

LEM RAT DATE
ARIA ELSA DARES
DALMATIAN ECLAT
AMER RESTHOME
ORO LEES
TDS ILE ETCHES
OUTSELLS STUPE
PERT FIR NOLA
TUBAS REPADDED
STEREO SOP ESE
RIAL PIA
GARNERED ESPY
USUAL GREYHOUND
STIRS SATE SLAY
HAND WAD ETE

PUZZLE 269

GABOR AGED MARC
ALAMO MOPE ALOE
FAKES OBIS LOUD
FRUITJUICE TOGA
EAR REEFER
AFFIRM FATED
ALECS NEVERMORE
HERE DATED IGOR
SANDPIPER BLEAR
COLES BAKERS
OCTOPI OER
SERF GINGERBEER
CLEF EVIL AORTA
ALEE NENE GLINT
RODE TSAR EDNAS

PUZZLE 270

ALAS BOSS HAME
CALM CARTE IRAN
THEUGLYDUCKLING
ARE ROIS TULES
SAWN SIDES
DUCKINGSTOOL
OLEAN IONS MAP
RANT REELS SAME
ANT RESP AKRON
SITTINGDUCKS
AEGIS ERMA
ANTIC SLOE ANA
ONESDUCKSINAROW
WONT LAYON RITE
ENTO EDEN CLAD

PUZZLE 271

VALET ASPENS PARTS
IMAGE SPROUTS ORIEL
PINON KEYSTONESTATE
END THEE SCANT TOE
ROOD ADDED KID RANT
FONT EVES LOBO
SLOE RASPS REAPER
TIMERS STOPS TRIBE
PAN DAYS IRANI ENOS
ORCS INTENTION DENT
STOW NORMA NORA TIS
ELLAS DUETS DESERT
DENIES TEILS TREE
NEAL ROUT CANE
CARS MEL NEARS ESAU
ADO MONET READ TOT
MOUNTAINSTATE APART
ERGON STAINED BETTE
LEEDS OREADS SPEAR

PUZZLE 272

SCAR CAMP BABA DAIS
PATE OVAL ABEL ALSO
AGOG NAPE TENT MILL
REPAST SALT DEBATED
LEER TEES RUG
DEMEANED DREW DENSE
AVE STREW YEAR DEAD
MINT SUGAR PROP AGE
ELDER NAVAL MOISTEN
SOB SEVER MEN
RATTLER REGAL ROGER
ACE LEAP LATER WIDE
TRAM TILL LEVEL LIE
SERUM LOAF SELECTED
MIG TRIP RENO
TUMBLES GEAR ATONED
ORAL NOSE RAPS PILE
OGLE TAPS TREE ELSA
LETS SPAT SEWS REEL

PUZZLE 273

ODDS COMAS TIFF
SERA ABATE EDER
APOD SENTA EERY
GOWESTYOUNGMAN
ERS TEE ASTAR
STYLE DAVID INA
ONO EIN ANDI
THECOVEREDWAGON
WELK ALI ORR
ORE FLIER EELER
SEPAL OSS EVE
THEOREGONTRAIL
DIAD ERATO EDNA
ACNE OILER SECT
SSTS SNARE TREE

PUZZLE 274

CASH STEM BABAR
ASTA ARTE AWARE
BEAN MISO NEROS
SANDSOFIWOJIMA
ITAL ZOG
SAFER EMMA HART
TERROR AIRS DOR
ARA BIGJAKE AGE
RIM ECHO STATUE
TEED HIRT TWEED
ROE ITEA
THEGREENBERETS
POISE ALGA DRIP
MORSE TIER ELLA
SLEYS SASS DEER

PUZZLE 275

CAPP ACTA DEFT
AMIR BLUNT IRAE
WATERCOLOR SADA
STYLI TIDEWATER
AVE PESOS
SHOWAND OTHER
LES ORBS LEONE
ONTHEWATERFRONT
SCION MULE PUA
HEARD FIVESIX
TOTEM DIX
FIREWATER ETAPE
IRON INHOTWATER
FIBS LATCH NELL
ESTE SAKE TETE

PUZZLE 276

CHIC ORAL STERN
RASH PELE ARNIE
AUTO AMIN NADER
BLOWSHOTANDCOLD
CAST OSE
DAHL ESTH RAPT
TAROT COO MAO
BLOWYOUROWNHORN
ALS FRA EERIE
RYES TIME ARES
ERE FARE
BLOWINGOFFSTEAM
LIVEN AMAT IDLE
OMERS RACE CITE
TENSE BRER STAT

PUZZLE 277

	M	A	P		C	O	D		E	D	G	E
D	E	L	I		A	V	E		L	E	A	D
O	R	A	L		R	E	S	E	M	B	L	E
T	E	N	O	R		R	I	G		T	E	N
			T	O	N		G	O	O			
C	O	O		T	O	W	N		F	A	L	L
A	U	N	T		V	I	A		F	L	E	A
B	R	E	W		I	N	T	O		P	A	W
			O	P	T		E	R	A			
S	P	A		A	I	L		B	I	N	G	E
C	O	M	P	L	A	I	N		S	E	A	R
A	L	E	E		T	O	O		L	A	I	R
R	E	N	T		E	N	D		E	R	N	

PUZZLE 278

S	W	A	T	S		M	A	R		S	P	A
P	I	L	O	T		I	C	E		W	A	X
A	L	A	M	O		R	E	S	P	I	R	E
T	E	N		O	R	E		U	R	G	E	D
			A	G	E		S	L	Y			
I	M	P	L	E	M	E	N	T		T	I	P
L	O	O	T		A	V	E		A	O	N	E
L	O	P		T	R	E	A	T	M	E	N	T
			A	R	K		K	E	Y			
B	A	S	T	E		D	Y	E		S	U	B
E	X	P	E	N	S	E		T	W	I	N	E
A	L	E		C	U	E		E	E	R	I	E
N	E	W		H	E	R		R	E	S	T	S

PUZZLE 279

T	A	M		A	R	I	A		S	O	R	T
A	L	I		W	A	R	S		P	L	E	A
R	E	S	H	A	P	E	S		R	E	A	D
		T	A	R	S		I	D	I	O	M	S
P	L	A	T	E		A	G	O	G			
R	A	K	E		L	I	N	E	S	M	A	N
O	N	E		B	A	S	E	S		A	B	E
M	E	N	D	A	B	L	E		D	I	E	T
			O	B	O	E		P	E	L	T	S
T	E	L	L	E	R		A	R	E	A		
A	R	A	L		E	N	C	U	M	B	E	R
M	I	C	A		R	E	E	D		L	A	Y
P	E	E	R		S	E	R	E		E	R	E

PUZZLE 280

L	A	D	D		H	A	T	S		S	H	E
A	L	A	I		O	M	I	T		H	E	M
B	I	D	S		T	I	N	E		E	L	I
S	T	A	C	K	E	D		A	D	A	P	T
			O	I	L		A	L	I			
R	E	R	U	N		M	I	S	S	I	O	N
O	V	E	R		W	A	R		C	O	N	E
D	E	B	A	T	E	D		B	O	N	E	D
			G	A	B		R	E	V			
C	A	P	E	R		C	A	T	E	R	E	R
I	C	E		G	O	O	D		R	O	D	E
T	E	N		E	L	L	A		E	V	E	N
E	S	S		T	E	A	R		D	E	N	T

PUZZLE 281

P	E	T	E		P	R	O		A	R	A	B
A	R	E	A		L	O	W		L	O	N	E
T	I	E	S		A	B	E		M	A	T	E
S	E	N	T	R	Y			G	A	M	E	S
			E	A	S	I	L	Y				
S	T	E	R	N		C	A	P		P	A	W
L	O	A	N		F	I	B		C	A	G	E
Y	E	T		S	A	N		O	I	L	E	D
				E	D	G	I	N	G			
S	C	U	B	A			D	E	A	C	O	N
L	O	S	E		S	E	E		R	O	D	E
I	D	E	A		P	E	A		E	N	D	S
D	E	S	K		A	L	L		T	E	S	T

PUZZLE 282

H	U	G	E		A	C	I	D		A	C	E
O	R	A	L		N	A	V	Y		V	O	W
O	G	L	E		T	R	E	E		O	D	E
P	E	A	C	H	E	S		R	A	C	E	S
			T	A	N		S	P	A			
H	A	G		S	N	A	P		E	D	G	E
E	G	O		P	A	R	E	S		O	A	R
W	E	B	S		S	C	A	N		S	S	E
			B	E	T		S	O	B			
M	O	L	A	R		L	A	W	L	E	S	S
A	B	E		A	M	E	N		A	L	O	E
N	O	R		M	O	A	T		M	A	L	T
Y	E	S		S	O	N	S		E	N	D	S

PUZZLE 283

C	O	P		E	P	I	C		F	E	A	T
A	R	E		N	E	R	O		A	N	T	E
S	E	A	F	A	R	E	R		I	D	E	A
E	S	K	I	M	O		R	A	N			
			B	E	N		O	B	T	A	I	N
H	O	T	E	L		A	D	E		W	O	O
O	V	E	R		I	C	E		R	O	W	S
M	E	N		A	N	T		D	E	L	A	Y
E	N	T	E	R	S		P	E	N			
			S	K	I		O	P	E	N	E	D
A	L	A	S		D	E	L	A	W	A	R	E
G	A	L	A		E	V	E	R		B	I	N
O	B	E	Y		R	E	S	T		S	E	T

PUZZLE 284

A	C	T	S		A	R	K	S		P	O	L
P	H	E	W		V	E	E	P		A	C	E
I	O	T	A		O	P	E	R	E	T	T	A
S	C	E	N	I	C		P	E	G			
			S	R	A	S		E	R	R	O	R
H	O	E		E	D	E	N		E	A	S	E
A	B	L	E		O	W	E		T	I	L	E
M	O	A	N		S	E	A	T		N	O	D
S	E	N	D	S		D	R	O	P			
			E	W	E		N	E	E	D	E	D
H	E	A	D	A	C	H	E		D	I	R	E
A	R	M		I	R	I	S		A	K	I	N
G	A	P		N	U	T	S		L	E	N	S

PUZZLE 285

S	E	E	S		P	E	T		S	C	A	R
P	E	A	T		E	R	A		T	A	L	E
A	L	T	O		E	N	D	O	R	S	E	D
			L	O	V	E		R	I	T	E	S
S	E	R	E	N	E		T	A	P			
E	R	A	S	E		R	E	L	E	A	S	E
A	I	M			H	O	D			P	I	T
R	E	P	L	I	E	D		C	R	E	D	O
			A	C	E		W	O	O	D	E	N
G	N	O	M	E		R	I	N	G			
R	E	V	E	R	S	E	D		E	D	G	E
I	R	A	N		O	D	E		R	E	A	L
D	O	L	T		N	O	N		S	E	L	L

PUZZLE 286

O	L	D		B	E	A	D		T	Y	P	E
M	O	O		I	D	L	E		H	E	I	R
I	N	N		S	I	L	T		E	W	E	R
T	E	A	P	O	T		E	L	M			
		T	O	N		S	C	I	E	N	C	E
A	R	I	D		D	A	T	E		A	R	K
C	O	O		S	E	V	E	N		T	O	E
R	A	N		A	P	E	D		T	I	P	S
E	N	S	U	R	E	D		B	O	O		
			P	I	N		B	L	O	N	D	E
S	A	N	E		D	A	L	E		A	I	D
O	M	E	N		E	G	O	S		L	E	G
S	P	E	D		D	E	B	T		S	T	Y

PUZZLE 287

H	A	T		C	A	S	T		P	O	D	S
E	V	A		A	N	T	E		E	V	I	L
R	E	P	O	R	T	E	R		R	E	N	E
	R	E	A	L		E	N	D	U	R	E	D
			R	O	A	R		A	S			
A	L	P		S	C	I		D	E	C	O	Y
S	E	A	M		E	N	D		D	A	R	E
K	O	R	E	A		G	O	T		T	E	N
			A	L		W	E	R	E			
F	U	R	N	I	S	H		I	L	E	D	
E	R	I	E		L	E	A	P	F	R	O	G
E	G	G	S		A	E	R	O		A	V	A
T	E	S	T		P	L	E	D		S	E	T

PUZZLE 288

H	O	T		A	L	S	O		W	E	P	T
A	D	O		N	E	O	N		A	R	A	B
L	O	T		C	A	L	E	N	D	A	R	S
F	R	E	S	H			S	E	E			
			P	O	L	L		E	R	R	O	R
C	A	N	A	R	I	E	S		S	O	R	E
A	C	E		S	E	A	L	S		B	E	D
F	R	A	Y		S	P	O	T	L	E	S	S
E	E	R	I	E		S	W	A	Y			
			E	L	L			R	E	A	R	S
S	T	A	L	K	I	E	S	T		C	A	T
A	R	I	D		M	E	A	L		I	C	E
G	Y	M	S		E	L	L	E		D	E	W

PUZZLE 289

ACER ATHOS ETNA
RODE BRIDESMAID
AVID LANDLOCKED
BET VOID FLEECE
EROSION GREENER
STREAM MOULD
QUILL FOLLY NOM
URAL HORDE DESI
EEL HADES LOFTS
SOTOL DEPART
ADAPTER SEVERAL
MEDIAL TINY ICE
AFICIONADO DOIT
SOMERSAULT OUZO
SEED THREE ISEE

PUZZLE 293

LAME IPSO SCAB
ENOL SUAVE ALLA
VEALCUTLET BUSS
EATER OKRA OBOE
ERS ELF SPOTS
BEEFSTEW TEA
RESOLE PASSKEYS
OCHO BAY NARK
CROSSBAR STAKES
SUR PORKCHOP
THANE AYN STE
CARA EBAN OATER
OBIT RACKOFLAMB
ROBE SCREW TIPI
MUSS KERN OREL

PUZZLE 297

LAG WADES RAGE
ONE DEVINE EVEN
TEN ORANGE VEND
SWERVE UMPIRES
RUE PULSES
FROG PUFF RENDS
LOS COMO ASSURE
OBI ALA DUO TOE
POTATO BURN ROD
STYLE LANA PIPS
TRAINS OUT
ATTESTS EMPIRE
DEAR OTTAWA OAR
DALE NEARER URN
SLED ENTER SEE

PUZZLE 290

DASH BASAL SCOW
UPTO ELENA RAKE
CARPETBAGS IRIS
TRIERS ESS PET
STARR SCROOGE
OLIO DONNA
MACAROON CARTON
IRAS ANITA GENA
CARSON CARTERET
ELMER ARTE
ESCUELA NOOSE
CAL ANT CORSET
AMIN CARVINGSET
ROTE AGAIN AIDE
EKED PENCE NESS

PUZZLE 294

LOADS MALL IRS
ANGER AREA ANET
PERFORMASERVICE
STET EBBS HETER
EWE STAS DERIDE
DODGERS LEA AES
LEO PAC STD
PERFORMANCE
SON IVY DEA
SES ERA RESTERS
TATTLE PANT NUT
ABEAM ERIC ANSA
PERFORMONESDUTY
LENT SITE EDILE
ESS TROD EASED

PUZZLE 298

NARC GAIT USES
OMAR ONER ATOLL
SOLITAIRE SOUSA
EYEBALL ENDPLAY
BRIE III
SPADE BACCARAT
STOGY SANK HIE
POKE SLITS NORA
EME MAZE CANER
CARDGAME CAPED
EER FARO
CANASTA IDOLIZE
ORALS SINGLETON
CAMEO CREE ONNA
OBER HERR NOES

PUZZLE 291

PATH BALER RAPT
ASHE ALATE EVOE
THEWORLDOFSPORT
EYE GRAY ELITE
PREY FACADES
REFUEL MARRY
ISIS BELIE WIT
ASTHEWORLDTURNS
LES SILLS SARA
SCREE DEEPER
STATUES HIND
EARED AONE LAB
THEWORLDSASTAGE
HOTE EIDER OMEN
SEED MESAS MEDE

PUZZLE 295

LAW SCAT PEA BOA
ALIT AMOLE SELMA JINX
MALA BILLYTHEKID ELEE
BILLFOLD WINO OPAL
ILOVE BIN RANI
SEABEE GMEN BRENNAN
ELMO AIR ROE TIRED
BUSY BOONE SHIER EDNA
ADO WILLIAMHOLDEN SEN
ENSILE IONS FIT
ARLO PLATE SOSO
LEO BEAM CRUMBS
ELS SWEETWILLIAMS ITS
RAHS STEIN YEARS CLAP
RIOTS AFT RON ALTO
CEREALS DENS BARBET
BEAR BUS CAIRO
IANA AARE WILLIAMS
BALK BUFFALOBILL ERAT
ALLY SMART OASIS DDAY
GAS PRO HAHA STE

PUZZLE 299

AHAS TACT ISIS
BARNS HIHO ANDA
ARTOO ANON MULL
FLIBBERTIGIBBET
TEC ESS RUTS
QUIRK KLEE SYM
GULP ARNO MATEY
RIAS REEFS IRAN
ANTES CATT MESA
USE ABED OSSET
ARAP VIA TIA
SENDINTHECLOWNS
PLEA TIER ERIES
AMAN EVAN MASSE
TOTO REDE LEST

PUZZLE 292

ABBA SAVES SCAM
NEAL AWARE ILLY
NATL MANNA MOAT
THEHORSESMOUTH
ROAD ANDES
SAGE ADALE
NOLI SENATE POE
THECATSWHISKERS
HOC BASALT ISNT
WAGER ONTO
ETHIC TREE
CHICKENHEARTED
LINK TIERS IMAS
ANTE CLASP CITE
TEST HERES STEW

PUZZLE 296

TRAP STEP AJAR
AIDE TAHOE ROLE
LAMP ATONE RHEA
ELI SKIM PLANED
ROWENA ASP
GALAS SHAM HIM
ALLAN JUNE ICE
GAFF FLEET FLOE
ERA FIEF TAINT
DER LEAF CARPS
RUE ELATES
PHASES RANA OAF
LOGE PASTE FUSE
AMUR ALOHA ASHE
NETS TINE DAYS

PUZZLE 300

MEIN TRIBES RIM
OTTO HODIAK OHO
CHARCOALBRIQUET
HEL ARNEL UTAH
ALOFT REPLIERS
OARS SUEZ
OMOO AAA DOZERS
CAPTAINMIDNIGHT
TIEPIN ALL COOK
EROS LEIA
TRIDENTS SLUMP
RAMA ATSEA NEO
INBLACKANDWHITE
PIE DIETED ETAS
END DORSEY RELY

PUZZLE 301

PUZZLE 302

Language has created the word loneliness to express the pain of being alone, and the word solitude to express the glory of being alone.

PUZZLE 303

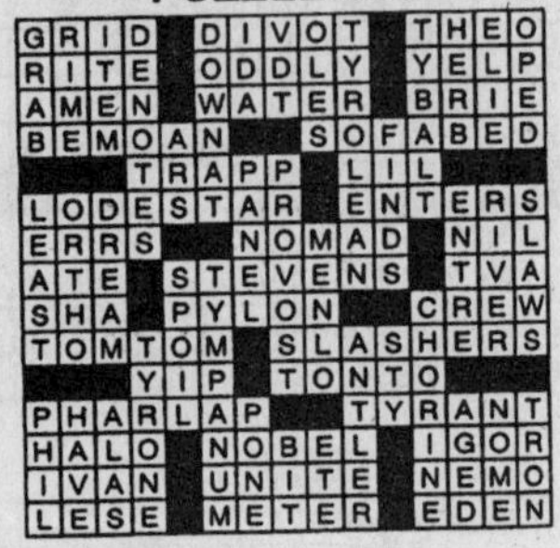

PUZZLE 304

Tune, Arch, Punt, Ache, Runt, Heap, Curt, Pane, Hurt, Cape, Turn, Chap.

PUZZLE 305

PUZZLE 306

1. Scheme, Upheld, Others; 2. Pirate, Garage, Sprain; 3. Mildew, Folder, Seldom; 4. Priced, Cliche, Icicle.

BONUS WORD: Heraldic

PUZZLE 307

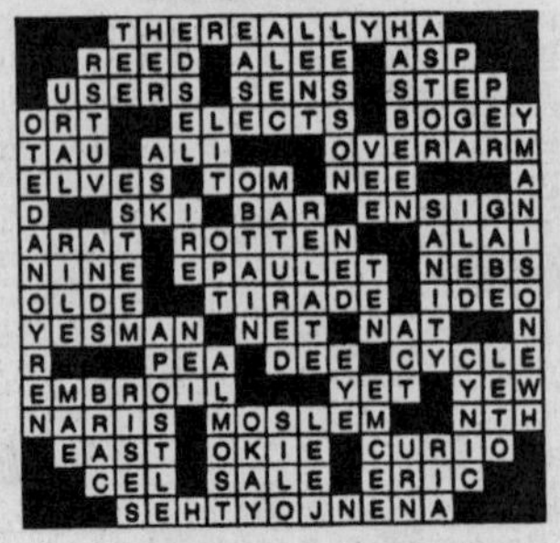

PUZZLE 308

PUZZLE 309

PUZZLE 310

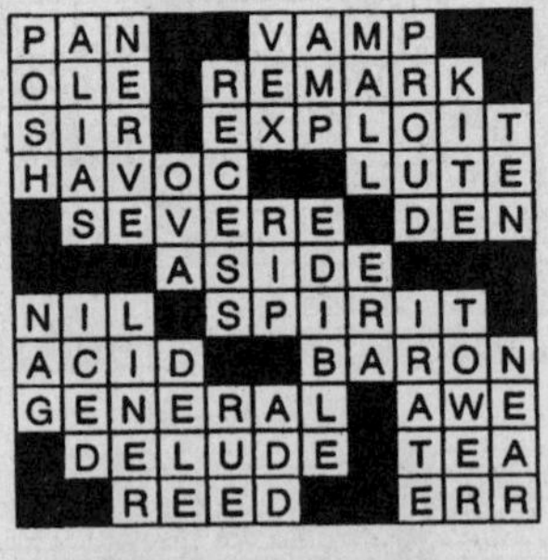

PUZZLE 311

PUZZLE 312

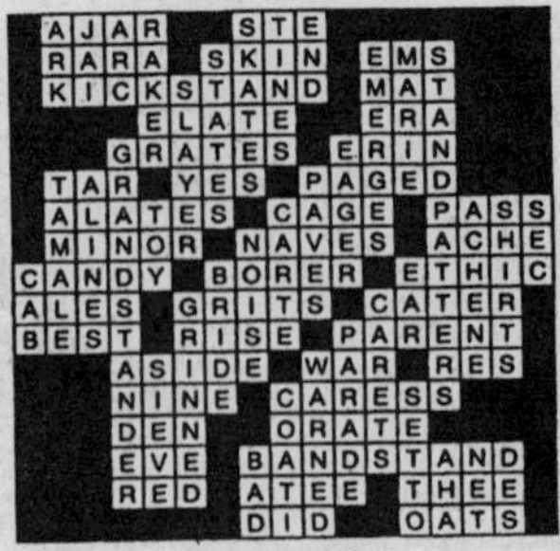

PUZZLE 313

1. Wood, 2. Fire, 3. Duck.

PUZZLE 314

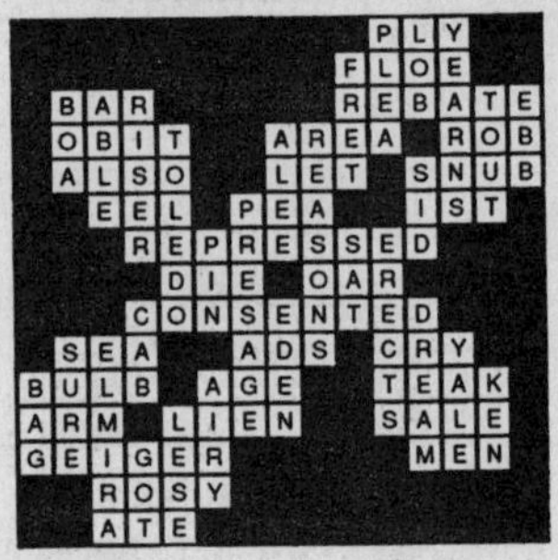

PUZZLE 315

Hatchet, Anchovy, Pitcher, Teacher, Ecology, Racquet.
Bonus word: CHAPTER.

PUZZLE 316

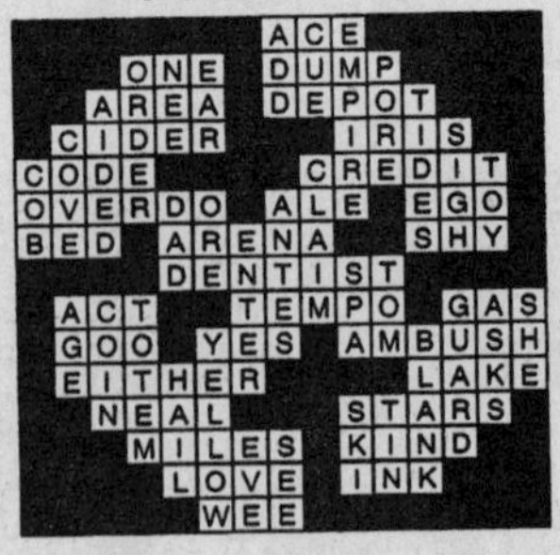

PUZZLE 317

A-7, B-4, C-2, D-3, E-5, F-8, G-1, H-6, I-9.

PUZZLE 318

SAIL
PETE LAPSE
SARIS AMPLE
MERITS MOLES
ARTEL RIVET
DER ELAPSE TUNAS
ANIL ORION OMAR
MADE SALAD TOR
EDGE TRAP PER
SEEKS AFOUL SWARM
HOT PLAT OLEA
DAB GENIE OMAN
LOGE ORANT SALA
BAGGY PARSED MIG
PADDY AMAZE
HILDA SKATER
ALLEY PATES
LEERS ARAR
LSTS

PUZZLE 319

1. Hand, Land, Lend, Lead.
2. Deal, Dell, Dill, Pill, Pile.
3. Bids, Bins, Bans, Bank, Rank.
4. Card, Care, Pare, Park, Pack, Peck, Deck.

PUZZLE 320

ASPIC
SPARE SALT
NOVELS OLEO
EKE LARGE AFTER
RED DEER STORE
PRAISES
HEM DEN
NIL VET
CAP TEA
WHISPER
STEAL ALSO ASS
PRESS PLEAD VIA
AIDE RECENT
TOSS BORGE
TOTED

PUZZLE 321

Theme, About, Noble, Psalm, Flask, Ovine, Gnarl, Clasp, Marsh, Upset.

PUZZLE 322

GALA
IMAM
BAYOU
TURN HUT
SLIP FIB ANO
HALO AURA ALTO
AHAB SCREEN SILO
MAT RAIL RAPIDS
SEND ROLE
CHAD FRET
NOEL PLOT
HERALD SLOW PAT
BEAD YELLOW HARI
FLAT SEED ACME
OUR IDE SILK
BET PLAN
YODEL
NIPA
GETS

PUZZLE 323

ARNO HERB HOHUM
MEAL AREA ALONE
AMOS BINS TITAN
SOMELIKEITHOT
SPINET ENO ADD
VAT SLIMMER
ATHLETES UNEASE
SHOAL DOS TALKS
WETTED DIRENESS
AMPERES REG
NEO EMS LENSES
THEDICEAREHOT
FLAIR LADY EASE
OATES ERNE DRIP
EPODE DEAD YENS

PUZZLE 324

SAL SAHIB ABUT
ROSA ARENA TUBA
EPIC NINES TREK
CHARADE EMIGRE
OPAL ABEL
BASEL GALAHAD
ERRS SCALE ELA
GAMESPEOPLEPLAY
AVA TINGE IONS
DESCEND CENTS
RAGS SOLO
ENCAMP CRICKET
CORD OFTEN HIDE
ORAL NOONE LEND
NAME GREER EVA

PUZZLE 325

KE RNEL BAR D
ENTE RALITORE
LAT ERABOV E
YAL E VAP OR
WRE CK POEM
IG UA NAPI ER
TEN TOAT LI E
TR Y ALO NE
TO NA BLERROD
APHI DBE DATE
G O NEE DE N
A C TSARTE
SLEETWA D E D

PUZZLE 326

JAM ULNA SABRE
ASIA TEAM ALIAS
BEER MANE HILTS
SANCHOPANZA LIE
HOST ARAGON
EJECT IMPALA
STORK SLIP ENOS
ETH SIMILAR NAP
WAND GEAL AMORY
WILLED EDENS
ADAGIO EMIR
MAT MOROCCOMOLE
UNSUB OBOE AXEL
STONE PELE NEAL
TENOR EYES NRA

PUZZLE 327

ASTA DAMS SGTS
ROAD ELIAS ARIL
ELKS SINAI SATE
ADE REVERE SNOW
STORES SLIT
SAFEST STEEPLE
TROTS DISAGREES
EER ORT RNS
ENGROSSES MAMIE
PAROLEE CABINS
AMEN SPARES
CANA IDEATE SAL
ASTI ORATE PIPE
LIEN RATER ROSE
LADE TORS ONER

PUZZLE 328

CLOVER MATER TIER
RAVINE OLIVE IDLE
AMENDS LATIN PEEP
MANE IFE OLD SAVE
SACK TEN
CAFE TRUED PARENT
ARIA LYE OBI
PORT GEE NOSEDIVE
USE SOB WIT MEN
TESTTUBE SET WANT
EAR LAP AGAR
REGARD FLATS RELY
EVA PROA
POLL PIP KEN SMEW
ELLA AVAIL DANUBE
AVON DANCE AVALON
LEND SNEER LEGEND

PUZZLE 329

WADED SMASH SEALS
ALONE PASTA HABIT
GIVES USHER ATONE
EVE MRS WEST VET
REST ETAL MOTHER
OUT GAS BEE
BONUS TEPID RATE
OPERATE STOW POND
NEW FANS SUED ASI
DREW ROOT BEARSUP
ALAS ROOST TOTES
YET TOO DEW
PASTED LOBE SLAT
WED TEAR NAB AVE
IRATE RAVEL ELDER
TIGER ERASE SEERS
SLEDS DENTS TASTE

PUZZLE 330

LAST BLAB SHES NEED
ASHE RARA COLT ERLE
MEAN ORAL ASIA VISE
BADNEWSBEARS MEEKER
INN FRY AMOR
PANSY ALUM DESCEND
ARA ANGEL PAIR RAYE
LESS ART ARNO YSER
MAHALIA AMASS EWES
VAL ARENA FLO
CLEW DRINK DOLLARS
POET REED CEO FLAW
AMAH PASS SHALE ONA
NOSEGAY OPEN DREAM
TESS SIR PIE
JOLIET MYLITTLEPONY
AGOG UPON NORA OBIE
RENE RANG GRIN RONA
SEER ELKE SOME TEAR

PUZZLE 331

WHO LOS
TEAMS HELP
DALMATIAN GREATDANE
ELS RANGE AIMS NEW
ECHO KNOT SOUP VISE
CANE POET
NORA OWL
TORSO ARISE
BOG MAN ALONE
SKI IRISHSETTER BTU
CLAUS ORE LES
THEME BOONE
PEA UPON
SOAR STUD
BAIT TRAP BELT SHAW
ANN REBA ARIAS OWE
RETRIEVER GREYHOUND
EAVE SUNNY
RYE NED

PUZZLE 332

ASH UTAH BRAG
JOE PITY ROLE
ADMITTED ABLE
RASCAL RAW
IKE ABLAZE
SHINE ONE WED
WING FAT MARE
ART ARK RAYON
PEOPLE LEG
APE AMIDST
SNAG DEDICATE
PACE OVEN TAR
AGES MEND ARM

PUZZLE 333

ACE MAR BAY
LOT DANA MARE
MOTORCYCLISTS
STENO EASES
OVER DEB
TAR ERAS RAGE
IVES MIL SLAW
MASC ANEW LYE
TRA SWAM
MAUDE ROOST
OUTBOARDMOTOR
ALES SEAS TOE
RED TEN ONE

PUZZLE 334

BUS TAMP BATH
ASP AVER ACHE
HEADLINE GEAR
OLD PRESTO
IRONY NAIL
NEWS FERN SAD
CEE PIPED OBI
ADD ALAS VALE
FULL BERET
EXHALE TEE
DRAM TOOLSHED
GALE EVIL OAR
EYED DALE PRY

PUZZLE 335

FUN SIS RIM
VINE TOW EASE
IRIS RUE AILS
METTLE ANGLES
LEE ROE
THREATS TREAT
HUE SAC EVE
ENDOW POWERED
AID LOS
TRUSTY LETTER
HARE ELI AURA
EGGS RID TRIM
NEE SEE ENC

PUZZLE 336

ALDA GEE AMES
SOIL RAN VICE
INVADERS ASHE
AGE RELIC TOP
PUN GERE
ASSUME NEARBY
COUP DEER
TOPICS SPADES
ELBA PER
MAR SMILE EPA
AMMO STARTREK
MEAN OTT OMNI
ANNE NOS MANN

PUZZLE 337

OAT STEEP CBS
FIR TANGO RAT
FLAMINGOS ASI
PAR TASTE
HOPIS PEACHES
ABEL BARGE
LID BRINE PEG
TRANS ALOE
REPEATS CRANE
OWING LET
SEN GRADUATES
IRE EERIE EVA
ESS DEEDS RED

PUZZLE 338

SPAN SOT IRED RIMS
TAPE TRIM VASE ERIE
EASE ALEE ATTENDANT
PREDETERMINE POINT
IVE BOA BELA
SEE OPEN CASTLED
APES ODOR ETTE ROT
CENTERED ANNE PINK
END TAR TSETSE ONTO
BET LINES TOE
ARTE ERODED SHA DOE
NOON ONER SHATTERS
TOR ESSE SOON ALOE
TEACHER PUNT ELL
ROES UAR ARE
STILL INTERCHANGER
CEASELESS SERE TALE
PARE ERLE TEEM ELLA
AMEN DEER LES DEEM

PUZZLE 339

BASS TEARS SPAN
ECHO RAVEN HOLE
ARID ASIDE ROUT
DEMANDED ALARMS
EEL SKIN
SPREAD SLEEKEST
ALERT SWORN MAR
LANE SHOPS BONE
ANT FAIRS DATES
DESERTED CIDERS
FEUD DOE
PREFER MEATBALL
LOGO DUETS ASIA
ODOR ASSET REED
TEST YEARS EASE

PUZZLE 340

ROMP SLOPE SLAM
AVER YODEL HERO
GATE SCOWL RAMP
ELEVATOR RINSE
ICE CLAM
REDEEM GRAPPLED
AVOWS FOUNT AXE
TOT JADED SPA
EKE TAROT STEER
RESTRICT POORLY
HOLE LOW
FAMED TEENAGER
OLEO OPERA RACE
REAR FEARS DIRE
DENY FALSE STUD

PUZZLE 341

BOSS SHARP REDS
OLLA TUTOR ELIA
WEED ENNUI VIES
SOWDRAGONSTEETH
LAM DOIN
BASENESS NEGATE
EWE TRACT DEMON
LADD PAR ROTA
TRAIT SMELL NAT
SENSED SEAEAGLE
PERO WAR
SOWONESWILDOATS
ALES ASIDE UVEA
NILE MILES SONS
GOLD SEEMS ENDS

PUZZLE 342

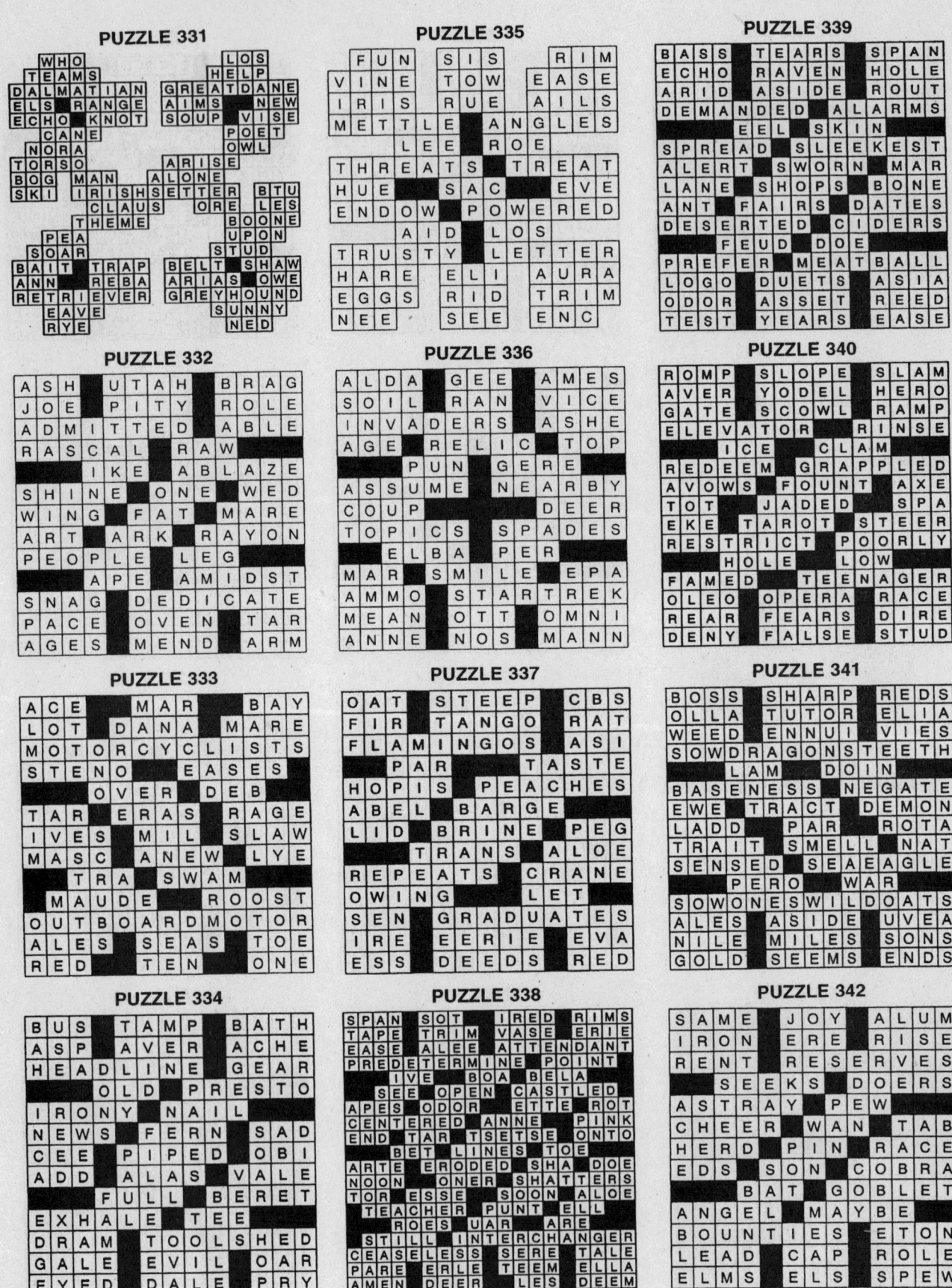

SAME JOY ALUM
IRON ERE RISE
RENT RESERVES
SEEKS DOERS
ASTRAY PEW
CHEER WAN TAB
HERD PIN RACE
EDS SON COBRA
BAT GOBLET
ANGEL MAYBE
BOUNTIES ETON
LEAD CAP ROLE
ELMS ELS SPEW

PUZZLE 343

ART WAF
KOALA ALIBI
ICIER LOSES
DRINKLIKEAFISH HERS
ROD ALE IRAN
ABLE STATE NONE
PEEL ASSET EDGE
EDDA SPY ASP SEER
NATE CROSS
NEE OIL
AFTER LEDA
SARI LSD ADD MARE
ELIS AWASH PLAN
DISH DAVES SORT
ACES GEL OER
NEST OTHERFISHTOFRY
OPINE REARM
RENTS ENSUE
YAK HEN

PUZZLE 344

EGG OFF ERAS
ARAB WOO VILE
RETAILER EMIT
WELL TON
ELMS ASKED
SAGS ALIT IRE
ALA DEN TIN
PAL MEET BEET
SNARE POLE
OWE ELBA
SHAD RESTLESS
PANE RAH SAIL
ALTO STY RAY

PUZZLE 345

DINA REP TAMP
ABEL AGE ERIE
REAL VOW AINT
EXPOSE TRADE
WINTER
ALLEN RAY SPA
FEED BIT REAR
TAG PET HEART
REELED
STORY ESCAPE
HIVE ERA ALAN
AMEN LOS POND
DENT LEE SEES

PUZZLE 346

LIFE EBBS ODE
ODOR LALA BOA
TORO FRONTIER
SLEDS OWES
FELONS AFRO
ERR OWS ERROL
LOOSEN RESOLE
BUNTS HER NEO
ETTE RESIST
ELIA EIDER
AFFRONTS NOTE
CAR OGEE GOAT
TRY TORN ERLE

PUZZLE 347

SCOT BARER
LEHAR ARMORED
UNITE FOOTAGE
ROC YARNS SAN
ERAS COT PELT
SAGEST EEL
SOLO REAP
MOP BRAVOS
GOYA UPI TALL
INA FRANK RIA
SILLIER EDICT
TOTALED RICES
NAMES NEED

PUZZLE 348

MAC APSE ASIA
ORE SEAT RING
OER HAWTHORNE
NAVIES AIM
ANN TAHOE
RANK EPIC ERA
ART LEACH MAR
VIE ALLY BILL
EASED DIN
LEO SINGLE
STEINBECK WAD
PORT OTOE AVA
YORE EATS YAM

PUZZLE 349

TACK APT CHEW
RULE SEASHORE
IRAN HASTIEST
PAWNS SKIN
EAR RASPS
POOLROOM ELI
LAW IDIOT MAN
EKE ELBOWING
ASSAY SPA
BOWL SIDLE
VALOROUS TEAL
ELEVENTH ELMS
TIDE TEE RIPE

PUZZLE 350

ALE SPA BAG
DENT LANE USO
SIDEBURNS RIN
NAG TENSE
EMBERS GELS
POUT PARADES
ORR EEL ORE
SENATOR TWIT
IRON TWINES
BASIN ARE
ASH EDDBYRNES
RTE SOIL SIRE
TAD GEE LAW

PUZZLE 351

GOLD ISLE TAM
LAIR MEAN OLE
ETNA MANDOLIN
ESKIMO DOME
NABS WARES
TRUSTIER RAGE
EAT ELDER TON
STEM EAGEREST
TENOR NILE
SOAR MYSELF
COINCIDE TSAR
OWL EDEN EASE
YES RENT DUST

PUZZLE 352

COAT RIP ANTE
OUCH IDA LOOK
TREE FOLKLORE
BALL NINES
POLITE PIG
ADAGE GETAWAY
COMB BAG TILE
TREATED ROSIN
DOG CARETS
STEWS POMP
COLOSSAL EARL
ABEL ACT ARIA
REEF YES REDD

PUZZLE 353

MESS SOW SHE
AMEN TIE STOW
TUNE ALE EASE
ESTEEM DANGER
ZAP SIS
ANGERED LEARN
DOE DIG BEE
SWEET PRECEDE
MOD AWL
BARBER NEATER
ALOE APT WAVE
NEAR FEE EPEE
GEM TAD DESK

PUZZLE 354

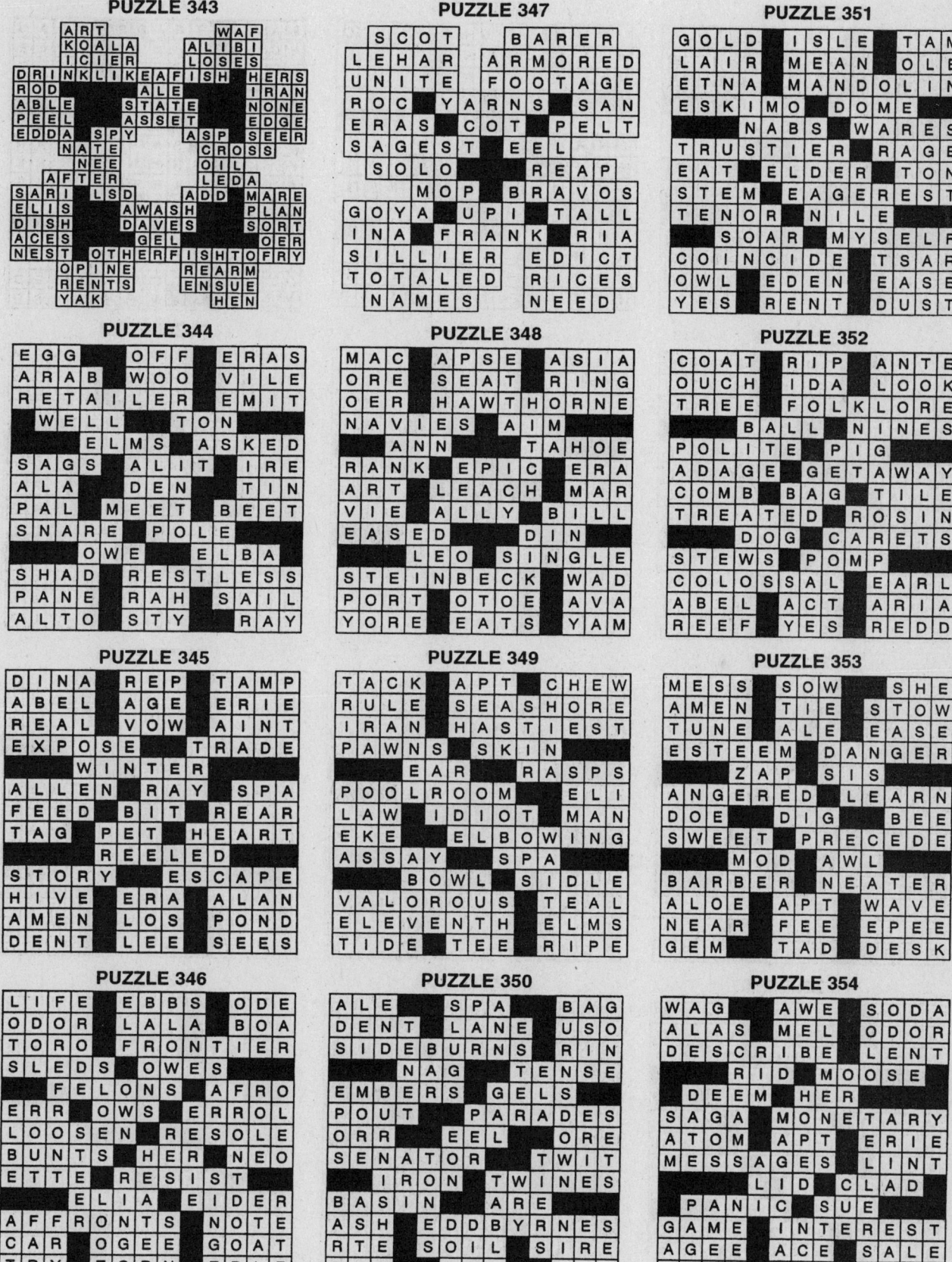

WAG AWE SODA
ALAS MEL ODOR
DESCRIBE LENT
RID MOOSE
DEEM HER
SAGA MONETARY
ATOM APT ERIE
MESSAGES LINT
LID CLAD
PANIC SUE
GAME INTEREST
AGEE ACE SALE
BEND NOT RYE

PUZZLE 355

S	T	U	N		A	D	D	S		F	O	E
H	I	R	E		D	A	R	E		R	A	W
E	D	G	E		S	L	O	W	P	O	K	E
D	E	E	D	S		E	V	E	R			
			L	I	T		E	D	I	B	L	E
R	I	P	E	N	E	D			M	O	O	D
A	R	E		G	A	I	L	Y		O	N	E
T	A	R	P			M	A	I	L	M	E	N
E	N	T	E	R	S		S	P	A			
			S	A	N	D		S	C	R	A	P
F	A	S	T	F	O	O	D		I	O	W	A
E	G	O		T	U	N	A		E	L	L	S
W	E	D		S	T	E	M		R	E	S	T

PUZZLE 356

H	A	U	L		O	P	T		H	O	B	O
A	L	S	O		V	I	A		O	W	E	D
I	D	E	A		E	N	R	O	L	L	E	D
L	A	D	D	E	R		P	A	L			
			E	A	T	S		F	O	R	C	E
D	E	W	D	R	O	P	S		W	O	O	D
E	R	A		P	O	E	T	S		P	I	G
A	I	D	E		K	E	R	O	S	E	N	E
L	E	E	R	S		D	A	L	E			
			R	I	B		Y	E	A	R	N	S
M	A	C	A	R	O	N	I		T	O	O	L
U	P	O	N		R	A	N		E	L	S	E
M	E	N	D		E	G	G		D	E	E	D

PUZZLE 357

B	O	L	T		R	A	M		T	I	R	E
A	W	A	Y		A	R	E		E	D	E	N
N	E	B	R	A	S	K	A		L	E	A	D
			A	S	H		S	A	L	A	D	S
O	P	E	N	S		F	U	S	E			
N	E	X	T		D	A	R	K	R	O	O	M
E	R	A		S	I	T	E	S		S	P	A
S	U	M	M	O	N	E	D		S	L	A	T
			A	W	E	S		W	H	O	L	E
A	R	T	I	S	T		L	I	E			
L	O	A	D		T	E	E	N	A	G	E	R
D	A	L	E		E	L	F		R	A	V	E
A	M	E	N		S	I	T		S	P	E	D

PUZZLE 358

J	A	W		M	E	S	S		W	I	P	E
I	D	A		O	R	A	L		O	V	E	N
M	O	S	Q	U	I	T	O		M	E	N	D
			U	S	E		W	E	E			
M	O	V	I	E		S	P	O	N	S	O	R
A	L	I	T		G	O	O	N		A	P	E
N	I	X		P	A	R	K	S		L	E	G
E	V	E		A	L	E	E		T	A	R	A
S	E	N	A	T	O	R		P	E	D	A	L
			A	S	S		P	A	L			
S	O	A	R		H	E	I	R	L	O	O	M
I	N	T	O		E	R	N	E		A	D	E
P	E	E	N		S	E	E	D		T	E	N

PUZZLE 359

J	A	M		S	P	U	N		S	I	L	O
A	L	I		N	E	R	O		A	R	I	D
W	E	S	T	E	R	N	S		H	I	V	E
		S	E	A	M			B	A	S	E	S
C	R	O	A	K			O	A	R			
H	O	U	R		R	A	D	I	A	T	O	R
E	A	R		C	A	R	O	L		E	V	E
F	R	I	L	L	I	E	R		F	E	E	L
			O	I	L			N	A	N	N	Y
G	R	O	U	P			I	O	W	A		
L	E	N	D		S	T	R	O	N	G	E	R
A	N	T	E		P	E	A	S		E	R	E
D	O	O	R		A	N	N	E		D	A	D

PUZZLE 360

H	U	L	A		P	A	D		W	I	L	L
O	P	A	L		A	D	E		A	R	E	A
G	O	N	G		V	O	W		V	A	S	T
S	N	E	E	Z	E			S	E	N	S	E
			B	I	S	H	O	P				
S	H	A	R	P		A	L	A		D	A	D
T	U	N	A		A	I	D		C	O	L	A
Y	E	N		O	W	L		E	A	T	E	N
				D	E	S	E	R	T			
D	I	V	E	D			B	R	E	W	E	D
I	D	E	A		R	I	B		R	A	V	E
C	O	T	S		O	R	E		E	D	E	N
E	L	S	E		W	E	D		R	E	N	T

PUZZLE 361

D	I	V	E		T	E	A		P	E	G	S
O	D	E	S		H	A	S		E	X	I	T
D	E	S	S	E	R	T	S		A	C	R	E
O	A	T		R	O	S	E	S		E	L	M
			B	I	B		R	I	C	E		
T	A	B	L	E	S		T	R	U	D	G	E
I	D	L	E						P	E	E	L
M	O	U	N	D	S		A	B	I	D	E	S
		E	D	E	N		F	A	D			
H	U	B		W	O	R	R	Y		M	A	E
A	S	I	A		R	O	A	S	T	I	N	G
T	E	R	M		E	L	I		O	N	T	O
E	D	D	Y		R	E	D		T	E	E	S

PUZZLE 362

A	C	R	E		T	A	B		W	O	R	D
L	O	A	M		O	D	E		E	V	E	R
D	O	N	E		K	E	G		L	A	N	E
A	S	T	R	A	Y			A	L	L	O	W
			S	C	O	L	D	S				
P	I	L	O	T		I	R	K		P	I	P
E	D	E	N		I	C	Y		H	A	R	E
N	A	G		A	R	K		P	O	W	E	R
				C	A	S	H	E	W			
S	O	L	V	E			O	P	E	R	A	S
O	B	O	E		D	E	N		V	A	S	E
R	E	S	T		A	G	E		E	R	I	E
E	Y	E	S		N	O	D		R	E	A	D

PUZZLE 363

H	O	E		B	A	A			P	A	T	S
I	N	N		A	L	P	S		A	L	S	O
D	E	D	I	C	A	T	E		S	E	A	T
			C	O	N		A	L	T	E	R	S
	W	R	E	N		A	S	I	A			
C	O	E	D		A	L	O	E		O	W	N
A	R	E		T	R	E	N	D		D	I	E
B	E	D		E	R	R	S		V	E	N	T
			F	E	E	T		C	A	S	E	
B	L	O	O	M	S		T	A	N			
E	A	R	L		T	A	R	G	E	T	E	D
A	C	E	D		S	L	U	E		A	W	E
M	E	S	S			L	E	D		P	E	W

PUZZLE 364

R	O	O	T		S	P	A		G	A	L	A
A	R	C	H		K	E	G		I	R	O	N
P	E	C	U	L	I	A	R		B	E	N	T
		A	D	E		T	E	A	B	A	G	S
M	A	S	S	E	S		E	G	O			
A	L	I		R	A	G		E	N	D	O	W
I	D	O	L		P	O	E		S	U	R	E
D	A	N	E	S		O	A	F		M	A	R
			G	A	B		R	A	M	B	L	E
E	N	R	A	G	E	D		T	A	B		
C	O	O	L		R	E	F	E	R	E	E	S
H	U	L	L		E	L	I		G	L	E	E
O	N	L	Y		T	I	N		E	L	L	A

PUZZLE 365

A	R	E	A		P	A	L	M		A	B	E
N	E	X	T		E	R	I	E		D	A	Y
N	E	A	T		P	I	N	A	F	O	R	E
A	D	M	I	T		S	E	L	L			
			C	U	B	E			E	V	E	S
V	A	N		B	A	N		D	E	A	L	T
E	L	O	P	E	D		B	O	T	T	L	E
I	D	O	L	S		R	A	Y		S	A	P
L	A	K	E			U	G	L	Y			
			A	S	P	S		E	A	R	T	H
K	I	N	D	N	E	S	S		W	E	R	E
E	R	A		A	S	I	A		N	A	I	L
G	A	B		G	O	A	T		S	L	O	P

PUZZLE 366

D	O	M	E		R	A	W		N	I	C	E
E	V	I	L		A	C	E		I	D	O	L
S	E	R	F		T	R	A	P	P	E	R	S
I	R	A		S	H	E	L	L		A	D	E
		C	L	U	E		T	E	A			
H	O	L	I	E	R		H	A	N	D	L	E
E	W	E	S						G	A	I	N
N	E	S	T	L	E		O	B	E	Y	E	D
			S	O	D		M	I	L	D		
C	A	B		A	I	M	E	D		R	O	E
O	R	I	E	N	T	A	L		S	E	N	D
D	E	A	R		E	Y	E		P	A	C	E
E	A	S	E		D	O	T		A	M	E	N

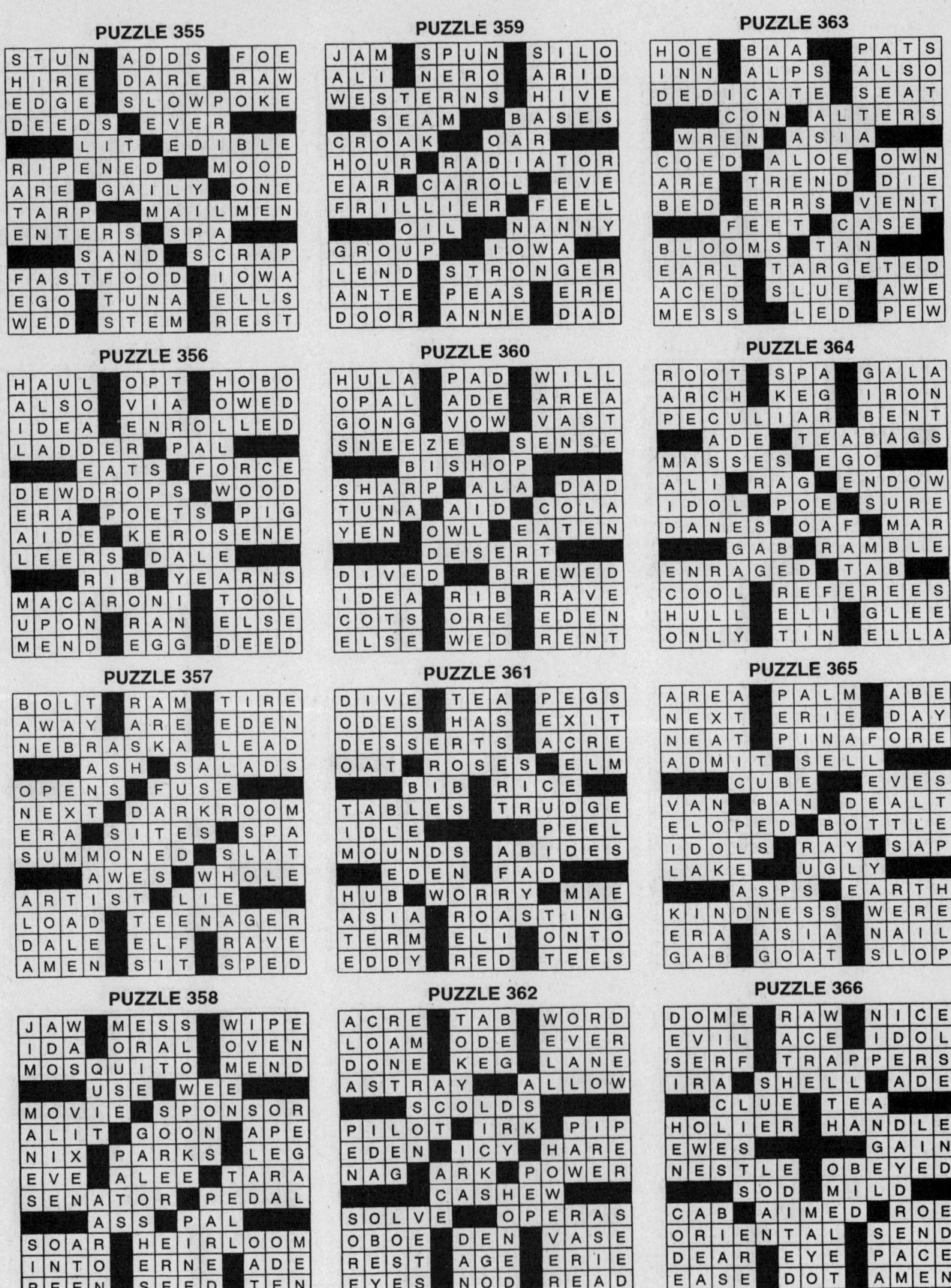

PUZZLE 367

WAD SPADE
SODA WADERS
HOLDS ECONOMY
OFF HIDES DUE
PASS RED BIDS
TWIN HINGE
COPIES BARGES
APART HOST
GETS PAN HALT
ERR MINDS FEE
DAIRIES CHINA
SCARCE OURS
KNEEL TEE

PUZZLE 371

CUR ABLE APED
USE NEAR DAVE
TAG TAME OPEN
ISSUE RANT
CASE SNARE
OUTER TIE APT
ARENAS RABBLE
TAR FAT DONOR
ATTIC DOWN
LORD LATER
AHEM ALSO MOP
MINI GETS ADE
BOOT ORES LET

PUZZLE 375

S F J C P W J N
O A U A A A O
G D R L T R V B
E A E A E
D T R P D R
E A E
S D D N G F S S
U U I E E I I
E E C N W S N R
L E T E
S A S S C R
L T A A I O
L A I P M T B D
I N O E E I E
L T T N S N N X

PUZZLE 368

PAPA FILE NAB
AGOG ORAL AMA
LEER REPORTER
ERE SPOONS
SCREAM EEL
HOE GAP DECAL
OVAL NAG SALE
PEDAL TAB SEA
MAT RESTED
DELETE MEN
EVIDENCE ABED
LEO SOON PITA
INN TROT STAY

PUZZLE 372

ERA BRAG MARE
LID IOWA ICED
FOOTBALL SHED
ELM LATELY
SHONE COLE
LAST SUPERIOR
OIL BORES DUO
PRODUCED JETS
ACID LEASE
ALASKA SIR
PUSH BLANKETS
ERIE LAKE GOO
DEAR EDEN OWN

PUZZLE 376

LOSE BAT ODD
AVOW LIE EPEE
MARE IRE LAME
ALERTS TAILOR
SAT HIT
HOW RED MELON
OWE ROD ADO
PLEAD GAY WED
BOW MAD
DEMOTE AMENDS
ARID EGG NEAT
WINE DOE TOTE
NED SOD SNAP

PUZZLE 369

SKY CRIB BALD
PIE AURA ALOE
ATTORNEY NAPE
GAGS WANED
CHARTS TAN
LAME PARADES
ARE SWARM ADE
PENGUIN SIGN
ANT ERASED
BLINK CLAN
REND BRACELET
ANTE RATE ORE
DOOR AWED WAD

PUZZLE 373

PUP BEG FAIL
ERA COAL AHOY
ANYPLACE LANE
SASHAYS
SLANT MEETS
OPALS SET RUE
FARM DAD TAIL
FIG DUD SHINS
NEWER STUNG
AWAITED
OAFS BROWSING
WRAP LIPS DUE
LENS ESS ATE

PUZZLE 377

WIRY NAP GRIN
AREA IDA LODE
GOAL PORTABLE
ENDED KISSED
IDEALS
OFT MAD TEAMS
NEAR BIB SLAP
EDGED TAB ANY
FROSTY
THREAD EAGER
YEARBOOK WIDE
PAGE RUE EVEN
ELSE STY DENT

PUZZLE 370

EGG FIR GUM
LOOP ADO ALSO
SEAL RAT DUES
ESTEEM TAMEST
AVE ELI
BATTED NITWIT
OLE ERA
ALASKA LITTER
WEB ACE
CABINS RELIED
OILS EWE LODE
ODES NOD STEW
PEW TWO ANY

PUZZLE 374

POD IRIS BOLA
ALE DICE RUES
WEE ABET ATOP
NORTH SHY
IOWA ASSES
CORN ECRU ODE
ARE FERAL AGE
LAD ADES EKED
FLOUR SHOW
RED VESTS
BULB OGRE OIL
ASIA NOON OLE
TEEN SOWS TED

PUZZLE 378

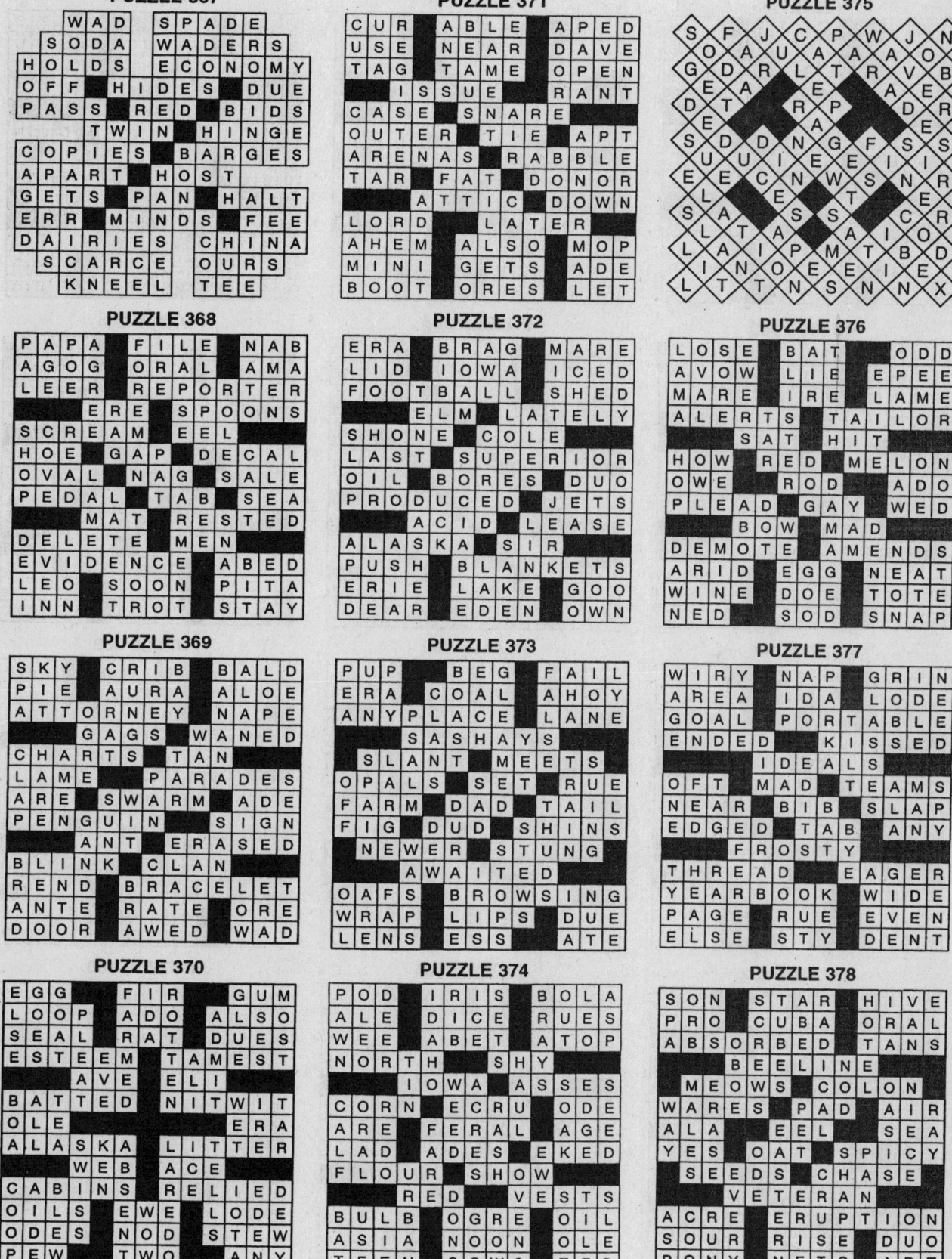

SON STAR HIVE
PRO CUBA ORAL
ABSORBED TANS
BEELINE
MEOWS COLON
WARES PAD AIR
ALA EEL SEA
YES OAT SPICY
SEEDS CHASE
VETERAN
ACRE ERUPTION
SOUR RISE DUO
PONY NETS ART

PUZZLE 379

LOW TEE MUM
ASH URN ONE
SLY BLED SWIM
TOSSES TONTO
PLAYPEN
HABIT ERA BAT
EDIT RAY RENO
ROB AIR PENNY
SIGNALS
SOLID BUTLER
LIAR RIBS ELI
ELK ODE ASP
DYE DAY FEE

PUZZLE 380

LAW BATH SPA
IRIS AREA TAP
PANE DIAL ADE
BEAD ALTARS
MOP SEW
BERSERK REPLY
AGE OIL AYE
RODEO TAMALES
ARE DIM
METALS LAMB
CAD TOES ZEAL
ODE OPAL EASE
PEN RELY TEE

PUZZLE 381

PAD TAP SPA
USE AIRS BEAD
RIB BLOT ONCE
RATTLE ACUTE
RED BAT
DENY ALL LED
AGO TOTEM AWE
MOD ACE OPEN
ALE ASH
VILLA CEMENT
ZOOS NOTE MOO
ALTO SLED INN
PEA EDS TEE

PUZZLE 382

MOTE BERT SHOE BIDE
EMIR ADOS PAPA UKES
SANG HIMALAYAS SEEP
ARSON SARI LENT
UPON SIP LILACS
CHAGRIN STOOD BELLE
REFUSE SCENTED SPED
ARTIE BEANS BAA HAG
WOES FOALS POUR ARE
REWROTE CORNCOB
ELS HATS PLEAT VEEP
RAH YUL SLOTH BETTE
AGAR DEFEATS TUNICS
SEVEN GIRTH BORSCHT
ERECTS NET BONG
RHEA ECRU SABER
OAHU UNDERLINE SORE
ALAI SKID INCA KILN
REST SAGS PEER SLED

PUZZLE 383

CRAB ANET STAT STOP
LOCO NENE TORE ARGO
OUTOFDATE OMEN LARD
GESTE LEPERS DRONES
HAM REAM LEANS
BRASSERIES DIRT LOP
OAT TWIN THIEF TAPE
AVOW LATE ANNOTATES
TEPID TONITE ORIENT
MAMA DOT STOW
STAPLE JUNEAU TAMER
COLLECTOR RUGS NAPA
OGLE HIKES GAIN GEM
WOO VANE COURTESIES
RAINY MARS EWE
BONSAI PIRATE ELATH
AROW COAX LITTLEJOE
NANA ABLE ENNA CARE
GLEN LIED SEAT TROD

PUZZLE 384

ERA LAMP GLAND GRAM
TAR OLEO LALIA RIME
CHESTERWNIMITZ ELBA
THUS DINES ZEALOT
COHOS VENTS ILLS
ROAD FARES PRESERVE
ALF MUSES SHIRE ION
BARTERED FLOSS ACTA
AUTOS PLATH ETHER
PINTER ALAMO CESARE
ASKED GLASS SURER
ISLE SLACK PLEIADES
LEI SCONE BLARE RAE
SINATRAS POETS POSE
BOAT TEXAS NODED
BEDLAM AIDES BORG
ERIE BARBARAWALTERS
ELMS LINEN NAST RAT
TEST EXERT TREE SPY

PUZZLE 385

EVES COLA GRIP DRAY
SECT AMOR HADA RIPE
PERI BEND ONER OPEN
PULLINGUPSTAKES
TIN HOST LESSER
LAZED POUT STAR PRO
AMID BARS SHIN BARA
RIO SAWN STRAD ONOR
KENNEL HIRER SIRS
CONESTOGAWAGONS
ETAT TAMMY RASHER
LINE COMMA CHAR DAY
SOYS HOPE MOAB ROSE
AGO EELS GENT CENTS
SANITY KALI SAG
THESANTAFETRAIL
LAIC NONO NERO LOON
ARCH NAST GRIN ENNA
PREY ERAS ESNE DEEP

PUZZLE 386

SHOO ALAD PLAY ALLS
TERM LOCO AONE LOUT
RANI LOOKERSON DUNE
ALATE TREATED RANGE
NET SEEN SERENE GEL
DRESSED HER SINLESS
OER PADRE BEE
PROWS FIT EAT GOOSE
LENS BATCH REPENTED
ANI BAN HID NED TIE
STONEAGE SETON PENN
MANIC SOD FOR DARES
PAR NEVER TEL
COWSLIP SER ARMORER
ERE MOROSE AGIO ENE
LILTS OVERAGE NESTS
LODE OVERSPEND DIRE
ALEE VERT ENDO ADEN
REDS ANTS STAR MEET

PUZZLE 387

VANE AVID ABED TEST
ECOL WARE GIBE ASEA
ROTE ARES IDOL TAEL
BRAVERY PAL NEPTUNE
AGE VIXEN GAL
SOTTO CITE AMATEURS
TORE POLE STET SPOT
ONE LURE FLUTES ALI
PATTERN GLARE LOSER
AVE ORATE SOU
GROPE SPITE APPROVE
LED REMISS BLUE PAY
ATEN RUNT CAIN GALE
DESOLATE PORT MALES
MUS STERN NIL
MINIMUM WAS ROLLERS
ANON RITA ATOM AVOW
PELA ECON IOTA NOVA
SEAL SANG ROAD TEEM

PUZZLE 388

CAT TEARS OFF
FACE ARROW LEAF
SANTA CITYOFDAVID
ADO CAKE BOA TONE
MONTHLY TESTS RAN
REL SHAH EMILY
MAJOR LOIN BRUT
ALOP WARN LOUDEST
UGH LAST ROOM SIR
LANCERS COST COLA
QUAY SOME LANKY
PIPES BITE FEN
ECU HERBS RAFTERS
NIBS DUE DART BAT
DELLASTREET IRONY
RIOT AISLE SINK
CEE LASER TOY

PUZZLE 389

BAG SCAT RADIO DENS
EGO OHIO EBONY EXIT
TOLERATE FASTS PINA
FLAT HOUSE TOOLER
RAILS NORSE DEPRESS
EDNA BULGE BERET
DOG MIDDY LIVEN FES
BONES TAPIR ALLA
SPREADS VOWEL CLOUT
CLEANS BOUND CLOUDY
READS FAIRS GRAFTER
ABLY BIRDS TRUST
PES ZEROS CROSS DEE
HELEN FLOAT MEAN
RESEATS BRAWN WEARS
ORIELS PRONE RIND
TOED AGAIN LEADUPTO
EDGE WORST ERGO AIR
SEED SOAKS DREW NAT

PUZZLE 390

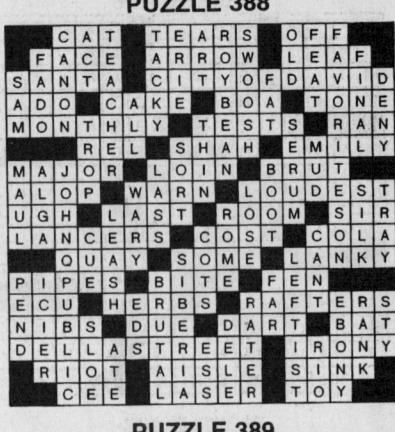

TITO HAP POMS DRAG
ONER CEIL RAIN AIDE
OTEA HIRE OKRA IDOL
ORCHID ALF TRES
LILIESOFTHEFIELD
SERENE LENES STEREO
EMU TARE GRAB SIAM
AMIR NOVA RENE EKE
LANE SENNA GOLF
GOLDENDAFFODILS
SEER SERIN ETTA
LAD ANEW ODIC WARP
ASOP DATA DAIS LEE
THREAD CAROL TAILED
HEATHERONTHEHILL
USIA ASI AZALEA
DAWN GROG ORLE INNS
ALAI NEVE ATEN NINE
MAYA SEAR NEY IDEA

PUZZLE 391

LATER ALEC DEAN
AGILE CATO ARNO
BULLDURHAM MITE
SET SER PENCIL
MOE TOBY
ABOARD RHUBARB
BANJO YARN NELL
ALSO DOTED KNEE
SEER AGEE BEENE
STLOUIS STEEDS
ERGS AUS
SHEATH FAR TWO
HANG THENATURAL
ALOU EIRE ATONE
DOSE RENT MATEO

PUZZLE 392

BARN GALE SALON
OMOO URAL LEONE
MOTO SINK ARNEL
BRANCHEDOUT GAL
LES PEBBLY
TABLED SEEDER
ARROW SOON LAIN
SNAG STAND ANNE
SONG TARS LYCEE
CITERS MESHED
SAHARA POA
AIR OLIVEBRANCH
BLOOP RAKI TORO
REAVE ARIL ONER
ADDIS SANE MOWN

PUZZLE 393

STOP BASTE DIAL
HOLE AREEL ONTO
EWER TIERS UTES
SOUTHERNACCENT
EEL OER
CACHES OBEY VAN
ABOUT SHAM DENE
SOUTHSEAISLANDS
ANNS TART ALERT
SET ASTA ASIDES
IAM PSS
SONGOFTHESOUTH
ALGA ROUTE POET
CLOT ARRAS OGLE
KANE YELLS NAME

PUZZLE 394

LUSH FLIP BERN
ASIA RAISE OLIO
CAPTAINFRACASSE
TRACT ORIEL
SMELLY PURSE
HIRES BANK VAR
MIDAS BANDY ELA
ENDS TORSO SNIP
DEL TARRY TENET
ERE URGE HAVEN
MARNE EATERS
CLARK FLIER
OURMUTUALFRIEND
MICE OSTIA NANA
ASHE TESS GREW

PUZZLE 395

OSSA PACTS AMEN
FLEW ALLOW HOLE
FATHERTIME STLO
WHITE PEAT HEN
LANG STARE
ABETTED SPARTA
HER SATED ETHER
EROS LUNAR SORT
RITES PIKES ONE
BEHELD MALTEDS
ERIES RAIL
ERR PICA TRAMP
TARA SOBSISTERS
CRAB TRURO ESAU
HATE SETON DAMP

PUZZLE 396

LOBE ATTIC RAY
IDOL BRACE OLEO
ROOM OILER BETA
ARK TUBE ELIXIR
MAINE AMEN
AROUND PLOT BAG
BIBLE GIANT ORE
OVID DIZZY JOIN
DEL TIZZY BAKER
ETE ERMA BUCKLE
CLEO BROKE
ZODIAC FRAY ERA
AGOG TALON OPAL
PLEA OREAD PELL
ERR READY TREY

PUZZLE 397

EMMA MATS PEASE
LIER UPON INCOG
ADDINGTWOANDTWO
PADDA ORO
SILENTP ZENANAS
ERE KISSES TOCK
LIEIN STUDY
SUMANDSUBSTANCE
AXING BLEAR
IOTA ROSARY GAI
DREISER HEPBURN
TIA URIAH
YOUCANCOUNTONME
EATER LENA KEIR
SKEET EDIE EASE

PUZZLE 398

PARADOX STAFF
HOMERULE PELLET
ONELINER ORIOLE
RABID AXIOM TIN
SPIC STEAK PICO
EEC CHESS ALLIN
BLAS INSULTS
GALOP ESSAY
DAMAGES SHAH
OMENS CHARY ACT
REND POILU ACRO
SPA GETAT UNCAS
ELBERT TIMEZONE
TALKAT UNALASKA
NEEDY SELECTS

PUZZLE 399

SMOKE CAT SERGE
EAVES ONE ANEAR
TREES NIM LLAMA
SERPENT POMADES
ENERGETIC
SPAR BOOST EDDY
ALES SLOTS DIRE
PEG SEA
IBIS GEESE SCAR
DESK AARON TORN
ESOTERICA
PASTELS ODOROUS
ARACA OAR PRONE
TIGHT USA SEPIA
SLAYS TEL EDSEL

PUZZLE 400

ATTN GLIB SLAP
BRAE DRONE TOGA
AIMS OASTS ANON
SEPTEMBERSONG
ERASE LAIR SOL
NED MEA PHI
ALAN PERU CREAM
MADASAMARCHHARE
INAPT OMAR OKAY
SAP ATL LYE
SIT NAIS LOTUS
AUGUSTBELMONT
EBBS THOLE BRIE
TALE LEMUR ETTA
EYED YSER REEL

PUZZLE 401

WELSH KISS SPUD
ABATE AREA TAME
KERRY VIED ALBA
ERGO SASS PRIOR
STEPON HABITS
SLOG WALLACE
TIL DRIP DEEDED
ADAM KLIEG SEND
DENIAL ABEL STY
SADDLER BRIG
GLARED ENLACE
KORAN FEED AGOD
EGAN TUFT AMATI
REND STOA MONET
NETS PEEL BRASH

PUZZLE 402

LUCE AQUA BLUES
OPEN TURN LINDY
GOLD TASK ADDIN
ONTIME ALEC ETE
VISA ELKS
MAGENTA METTLE
OUR TERSE DORIA
ODES ROAST WETS
RIELS NOTED ARE
SONATA ENACTED
MARS RATA
EGO MILE CERISE
MAXIM ANTI AMIR
ILEDE TOOT FALA
TENOR ESPY EMOS

PUZZLE 403

MESH ODOR HID
AREA WOKE ORE
TRAVELERS MAE
ESSAY ATTEND
NEAR SAT
SODA TIP POPE
ANY ODE WAR
DENS MET ANTE
AID READ
DAMPEN LOOSE
ELI REHEARSAL
LET BRAG ELLS
ICE YOYO DOTE

PUZZLE 404

ZIP RAFT MELT
IDA ANEW OVER
NET IDLE TIDY
CASES TEPID
VIE DIVERS
GREENER GENIE
LAD LAB COT
ACUTE GADGETS
DECALS ARE
ALIAS IMPEL
RATE VASE ODE
OPEN EGOS KEN
TEST RENT END

PUZZLE 405

BLUE ALMS BAR
RUNS SAIL ADO
IRIS SPLURGED
METER PERU
SIDES RACE
TRY LAD CANAL
HEAPED RULERS
ANNOY TAB WEE
WOKE DATED
MEAL SOFAS
LIPSTICK TACO
ODE CLUE ECHO
PAN HYMN SEEN

PUZZLE 406

BLIP PEN FLY
AIDE AGE ERIE
KEEN ROW MEAN
ENACTS TAPERS
ION SIT
SIRLOIN MYTHS
ACE PIG WOO
WEDGE LASSOED
AYE MET
BLAMED BERTHS
EASE GEL ARIA
SKIS ERE WARN
TEA SAD SPED

PUZZLE 407

DUKE COMB VIM
ANNA ODOR IRA
DIET ADVANCED
STEERS EDIT
RUTS SNOWY
UNSEEN ERIE
APE DRAGS INN
LOST PLAZAS
ENTER SILO
LEAD STORES
RAINCOAT MEAL
URN EDGE ELSE
BEG SOON DYED

PUZZLE 408

PEST SPY IRE
ALOE OHIO NAY
WIDE REEK TIE
MAD DEPEND
WHISKER SIR
HAD IRAN PLAN
ERE NEPAL UFO
TEND DIRE DAD
TAB DRAWERS
GAINED ADE
ARC NEAT LAGS
SEA TAME LINE
PAL SLY SMUT

PUZZLE 409

ASP ACRE ACES
DIE PREY NOVA
STAMPEDE GLEN
ALSO FLARE
FABLES ARE
ABUT OPERATE
ILL BERET LAD
RELIEVE WELD
NEE MERELY
WARDS FIRE
ALOE ARSONIST
STUN SEED CUE
POET HERE YEA

PUZZLE 410

THEY BEAT DIG
EAVE IDLE ERA
AREA NETS SAN
MERRY NOTHING
LID SEE
PLAYPEN DRAMA
EAR NAB LUG
ASKED PACKAGE
LAB RAN
REFINED NIECE
ACE CLAD GRAY
SHE ELLA HIKE
HOT DYED TEES

PUZZLE 411

MILD RIM MAYA
ODOR INA OVEN
MACARONI OILY
AWE LENDL
SAT DAMSEL
ALI ODE LIBRA
IDOL DRY TEAL
LANES GEE AGO
APPEAL NEE
CANAL SAP
SOLE ALLEYOOP
IMPS CUE ELLA
REST EGG SEED

PUZZLE 412

DAM CROW BAIT
USE LANE RICE
SEASONED AMEN
TALON SEW
NEWS ALERT
CON RIMS MAR
ADO GENIE IRE
NOR INKS TEE
TRAIL STOP
SLY PASTA
BAWL EMPERORS
EPEE NOON FOP
NETS SOWS ADS

PUZZLE 413

DIP CODE REAL
IRA HAIL ERIE
CONSERVE JADE
ENTER ECHO
TRY TAILOR
OWN YAK SCENE
VIED MEN EATS
ASTER GAS POT
LESSON PEA
IDOL CLOUD
ODOR TABULATE
WADE EVER TAN
EYED DANE SHY

PUZZLE 414

WAS SHAM PADS
ALE CAFE ADIT
SON ASTRONOMY
PETAL EVE
IDEAL ELUDE
COME HEAR NOD
APE DAVIT DON
PEN ABED VERA
ENTER RADAR
GEE INLAW
OVERDRIVE IRE
FIRE OMIT NEE
FEET SPAS GAD

PUZZLE 415

PARK MAST BAY
RUIN ODOR ORE
ONCE MOLASSES
STEEP ROPES
LURES LIPS
WAR DAD PLEAT
ENERGY RUSSIA
DECOY BAN TRY
SWAM DITTO
LEARN STUMP
COLORADO TRUE
ALE AMEN EGGS
RED BARE REST

PUZZLE 416

BAT GOSH SLAB
AVA RITA TOGA
DERAILED OPEN
KNEW TRESS
TEAR DELAY
ALLOW DAB OPT
CATNAP PLAGUE
ONO TUB EARNS
METAL REST
OLDER ZERO
ROOT CADENCES
ABLE RAGE AWE
LEER OREL PET

PUZZLE 417

LOG COTS SPED
AWE OLEO HERO
DEMANDED REIN
IDES PINES
CLAMOR SOL
RAYS APOLOGY
ACE PEDAL BOA
MESSAGE SOAK
TWO CRUETS
ATLAS CAIN
COAT ARROGANT
ROME MEET DOE
EKED PETS OWN

PUZZLE 418

RAW AREA FAST
USE LEIS RILE
THEATERS IDEA
GALE SEEDS
COVER FUN
ODES HADDOCK
DOE GAITS BEE
ERRANDS SOLE
SAD SPELL
FROST TREE
LONE BOULDERS
OVER ROLL AYE
PEST ALES TEE

PUZZLE 419

PAT ARF SEND
ICE WORM PRAY
PEEKABOO LAME
ERE TEASED
ADDED COTS
LEAN ORCHARD
EAT SLUSH LEE
CRACKER ALAN
HINT EGYPT
STRIPS AXE
ORES ENLISTED
RIDE SITS IRA
TOOL POT PRY

PUZZLE 420

ERA CALF TOPS
SUB ARIA EVIL
STUBBORN NAPA
NOISE SALEM
UNDONE PEN
ROAM WEATHER
GUN SEEPS ADE
ENTITLE ARID
DAM GLIDES
RATER TRADE
ELIA PRESENTS
FELL RITE EEL
SEES OMAR DAY

PUZZLE 421

BUG AREA CITE
ONE NOEL ROOK
SIN GELS ANTE
STEEL SORT
DEW YEAST
SAND RICE LIE
OBEY ARE SODA
ALE OPEN TEEM
PEDAL TWO
IDOL APRON
LEGS WONT ABE
OVAL EPEE MOW
WERE DEER PET

PUZZLE 422

SHEER AHEAD
HELLO MOVIES
AROMA EMERALD
COP RULER LEO
KNEW SIR MEET
AREA NERVE
GRADED TOSSED
LIVED WETS
ODES SON YARD
BEN SCOTS LOU
ERUPTED CALMS
SERENE ADOPT
SOWED NEWSY

PUZZLE 423

NEE EMITS ACES
OARS RANEE TARO
MRSMINIVER TSAR
ENTIRE MEDIATE
TASTE ORB
DEMENTED DUELS
ELY NOSES AHA
ELF AGT PIE NIL
SEA GESSO CPA
SISAL HOMEBASE
ROT ELUDE
GALLEON GARAGE
ALAI GOINGMYWAY
REDD EERIE LAVE
BEYS ELAND YES

PUZZLE 424

MOB ACRE AMEN
AWE DUAL CAVE
DEW URGE ODES
IDLE PARENT
ALLOT CHIN
TIDE SLAM ADE
ONES TAN AMID
PER GRIT LANE
SEAM EATEN
HAPPEN BASE
ISLE GEAR UPS
LEAN EVIL RAP
LAND RELY SLY

PUZZLE 425

NAPA AGENDA ABA
ALAN MARRON LIN
SINGLETRACKMIND
ANDEAN SLAKES
LEARN TIP EYETO
SAGEBRUSH
ADO IRENES EASE
HARDSET SHIMMER
ANTI TEASED INN
CHARTERED
SHAKO SAD AROSE
EIDERS PLANED
PREYSONONESMIND
TEL ELINOR ACTA
SSE SONANT SEAS

PUZZLE 426

SNAP PRINT STOP
HOPI RESOW ARNO
OTIC OTTOI LEOS
TEATIME KNAVERY
UMP LIE
SERRATE TERRACE
ADEEM DEANS GEN
TIES TILLS HEAT
ILL ARTIE MANSE
NESTLES STINTER
ABA RAD
TOMCATS DISHPAN
ARAK ELGIN ELMO
RAIL RANEE LEON
ELLE STUNS DARE

PUZZLE 427

ACID CHAT BRAES
MARE ROTE EERIE
AMEN EBON TSARS
SENT COP STILES
SLEIGHS SLOG
SUE FAIRNESS
SLATS LAND STOP
EAR HOARDED OAR
ASIS VIES HANKY
SHATTERS DOG
RUNS BEWAILS
ATTARS AIL IRON
CRANE ANTE NAPA
MERGE DIET STEP
ESSEN ELSE TESS

PUZZLE 428

BEST OSRIC DEAN
AMOR STENO IDLE
TIDE CONAN ANON
STANDARD SEDATE
CORE SORE
LIGHT DETRIMENT
ARREST LUTE NEE
BEES HEINE STAR
ONE NEAT DETERS
REDRESSED WORSE
HOPE ALEC
BIKINI FRISKILY
ODIN ANITA AREA
RENO NINER DANK
NAGS SLEDS ENDS

PUZZLE 429

HALF STROP LOTS
URAL AROMA ERIE
TINY WADER TAME
SAD BED NESTLED
SPADES SUE
FACED RED PRESS
ORANGE NOW SNIP
COP ENRAGED GEE
USED DOT DESIGN
SEDAN TOM PINED
GOT REMOTE
PROGRAM LIT ESS
LOVE PIVOT TRIO
AVER ELIDE HERO
YENS SLAYS EDEN

PUZZLE 430

CAVE RIATA BLAB
APEX ENDER LENA
TEST ACERB AVON
OSTRICH MISSING
ANT TOT
RACCOON CELEBRE
ABUT RIGOR DRAM
BET COP ARE
ALEE SHOES LIEN
TERMITE DIVIDED
USE GAB
PRELATE ENTERED
AURA SCALA RAVE
CHIT ORIEL TRES
TREE NUDES YANK

PUZZLE 431

FRO START DAM
OOPS OWNER SALE
ASEA SANTA ELEE
MERIT SAINTNICK
SALEM ECHO
ODES ERRAND
EVER LEAF EAGER
RAM ITEMIZE ERE
ASIAN MILE CROW
SETTLE LAME
TENT LANES
SPLATTERS STATS
ERIC EXITS EVIL
RISK RATES RENE
EMP SNAPS STD

PUZZLE 432

SPAS ANA LAOS
PACT LOLA ANDES
ANNA IMAN STINT
NEER NANAS ENDS
THEN GEMS
STIRS ARIA ASP
CHINS FRANS PTA
HANG SLIME TROT
ORG RAYES TRIOS
WEE TIPS SHELL
BELA STEM
NATO SPITE BLAB
IRENE EVER LONE
PALES RAVE EONS
TESS NEO SPOT

PUZZLE 433

FLAP FAST
ORATE LINES
TRIVIA ARENAS
PAD ALLOT EDGES
ALES TENT REGAL
PORES DEEP DELI
ANSWER SNOB DST
SLIP SEEP
CAR FORE TEASED
AWED TEAM SILLY
RAVEL TRUE LODE
PROSE ENTER WED
ELEVEN TRITER
TREND EIDER
TEES REED

PUZZLE 434

HEMP SHRED SCAT
AMIR TEASE HALE
MILE EAGER IRON
STOPPERS RINSED
AIDS MINE
SPURNS BACKDOOR
TUNES LANKY LIE
ARID TIRES TILE
RET TONGS DIVED
KEEPSAKE CATERS
LASS PORT
DEPART BRAKEMAN
UPON ERROR ROBE
MERE ROADS ELLA
BEES SENSE DEER

PUZZLE 435

```
HOOK TEAM SAGA SPEW
ALOE RANI ELAN WADI
LAZYSUSAN RESTRAINT
OVERACT EDGE HURRAH
ICE CREE GIRD
AKIN PAVE ELLA SPA
GINGERSNAP LOLLIPOP
ETC JOIN HIS RULE
SEATED ABBESS CORES
ACED OAR YARN
DEBUT ERODED BUSTLE
ODIN TIN ISLE HUE
MEATLOAF BASKETBALL
ENS ERIE LUCY OWLS
EVAN PODS APR
AMULET TUTU STARTLE
SUNFLOWER BULLDOZER
ASTI REEL OTEA WAND
PEON YENS NEWS SRTA
```

PUZZLE 436

```
OBIS TAG ARAS EDAM
ALOP COLA NIDI LEDA
RONA OKAY OGLE ANET
STARCHY EAT IRANI
SHOOTSTHEBREEZE
ENDEAR UTTER ASTERS
GAR STET ARAG SNIP
IBAR SNOW SLOT SEA
SOME DROVE EROS
BABBLESLIKEABROOK
SEEM FEELS ALIT
ELS EMIL STOP RITA
FEAR COCA ONUS VET
TAVERN COLOR NOLESS
HAVEALONGTONGUE
NEATH SAT AERATED
DINA HALE AKIN DANA
ORAL ASIN WILT ERIN
RAHS NAST AMS RODE
```

PUZZLE 437

```
MATH PETS HAMS STAR
OLEO EVIL ALIT PANE
LENT RACE PALE ERNE
DETERS KEEP ERECTED
LOOM PAIN NET
REASONED REEF LEGAL
ALL FATAL REAM ROLE
VIPS LEVEL DIET NAG
EASED SIMON LESSENS
LIL DOVES TAP
SPILLED NEWEL ROAMS
OLD LAUD DEVIL TRIO
WOES POOR REVEL ILL
STALL SOOT RENEGADE
EON ROOM DINE
PRINTED STAG EARNED
REND SALT DARN MORE
ANTE TREE ALEC ASIA
MOOR SEED MADE NEER
```

PUZZLE 438

```
WAG PAL OPERA
AXE ICE ROMAN
RINGLET GUPPY
DOINGS DARE
SMEAR MINERAL
WIPES DODO
HAM MARCH ROB
OPAL TROOP
PENALTY WIVES
STAY REPEAT
ALIEN REVERSE
LOOSE ADE SEE
AUNTS NOR ELL
```

PUZZLE 439

```
SALT NAB RUTS
ALES IDA ANEW
PATH PEG PISA
IMP GRITTY
ASTRAY AID
SPITE EGO DIM
PANS SEE REDO
STY OWL HELLO
DUE DUTIES
BEFORE ERR
ORES TAN EVIL
NILE ELI AIRY
NETS RIM TAKE
```

PUZZLE 440

```
DAB PAGE WASP
EGO OMEN ERIE
WOODLAND LEGS
REST IDAHO
CAME SLEDS
AHEAD ELL APE
FORMER MEADOW
EYE PIT DRAKE
HOCUS AMES
AWAIT BARB
NECK MINISTER
NAME ONES ORE
EKED OGRE PAD
```

PUZZLE 441

```
ALDA ELL EDGE
FUEL GOO MILD
ARAB GRUMBLED
REFUSED ALLEY
MUD HUE
BOISE CALMEST
AID HOG NOR
ALADDIN DADDY
RUM AIM
SATIN ASPIRIN
PROVERBS DARE
ACRE OLE SKIS
THEN WET TEST
```

PUZZLE 442

```
SOFT HAIR BID
AREA OBOE ARE
TEAM PETE LAB
RED TALLEST
COLDER SEE
ALE NOW DANCE
MESS DIP DEER
POSTS GIN ALI
ELM TURTLE
OATMEAL TAN
RIO EPIC DEAL
ADO PLEA ISLE
LET SENT OSLO
```

PUZZLE 443

```
REBA THIS RIO
ENID HIDE ADD
VETO IRON RED
NONE DRESS
OGLING TEA
PRESS FARTHER
TOV EON ADE
SWINDLE ALLEN
OAK ORIENT
SWARM HATS
TAR PLOT TILT
ODE LOCH ERIE
PEA YAKS NEED
```

PUZZLE 444

```
ALATE CAROL KISS
CANAL ACINI DENTI
CHICKENINEVERYPOT
RASH ENDS PINUPS
ARE ROLE CIVETS
RAINY SATES
ASPIRES CABAL SPA
KOALA GALOP STAR
SAILBEFORETHEWIND
URNS NARES TILDE
MSS AGUES SPARTAN
DELLS STILL
SPIRIT STAN GAM
OPERAS TURK ERGO
RIDETHEGRAVYTRAIN
TRACE LOIRE AISLE
HOLT MOATS BESET
```

PUZZLE 445

```
ASIS IDE HAD ALTS
RANT CORSAGE GAIT
MUTINYONTHEBOUNTY
OCHRE RERAN REGAL
REE PASSE DAD ENE
HEAP TRADED
SHELLS ACE ARIAS
PEAL ESCHEW SELLS
ANT SAC KEA LIE
SNOOP DEMENT FACT
AFTER DUD TRIBES
TRACES IAGO
MAB IWO TRACT UTA
IDEAL FRAIL EATER
TERMSOFENDEARMENT
EPEE LEDGERS EVOE
STAN DES STS SERS
```

PUZZLE 446

```
PEAS ALTO ABCS
SAGER ROAN BOON
STONEHENGE EURO
SNIPING WALLER
LANA TAT DDT
FEWEST COYOTE
ACH TETON MARTS
SHIM DANTE ODIC
TOTEM PEONS AMA
ELATES TEAMED
NOS TOR BATZ
AVANTI SUITORS
VINE LITTLEROCK
ENDS ETAT RELAY
LEST DONE SEND
```

PUZZLE 447

MORE GAB ONTO
AMEN RIO RAIN
MESS ART ABLE
ANTICS TENSES
GAP LAG
PAINTS ERECTS
ERR OAK
REALTY PALTRY
ERE ABE
RETAIL RASCAL
EARN LIT SORE
ISEE ORE OPEN
NEED WED NEAT

PUZZLE 448

NIP BID SCOOP
OFA EMU CADRE
REDTAPE ORDER
MERE SNORE
ALERT NUN ACE
ROWAN BROW
CAREER CIRCLE
ALIT IRENE
BED ONE NATAL
PAGAN TREE
ALIAS DIEHARD
DELVE ELL PIG
SALES REF SEE

PUZZLE 449

ASK ASH BOW
FEE BEE EAR
TANGLED DRY
LEDGER
MESA ERODE
ARCS ROIL
PAUSE AMPS
TYRANT
LIT ALIASES
ELL SAP AYE
ALE ESS YEW

PUZZLE 450

PET
PAGE
HEM PURGE
ERIC WARES
NONO POSED
SIN ANTE
FACTO
SERE RAW
WATER ARIA
HINTS LEND
VERDI AGE
ORES
WED

PUZZLE 451

SPA
ALARM
HORDE
SHOT EMIT
COY GNOME
KNOT FAT ARTS
SNOW BAR IGNITE
HAM PEN ORE GEL
EVADED PIE PERK
EDIT PAL MORN
MATED DEN
ELAN FUND
SCALE
KITES
LED

PUZZLE 452

1. Proud, 2. Drape, 3. Polar, 4. Apron, 5. Grand, 6. Upper, 7. Eagle, 8. Round, 9. Upend, 10. Panda.

PUZZLE 453

EAT ABE WARS
SNAP LIV EXIT
TYPEWRITERS ELBA
TEE ITA DEBRA
TEASE TAR OER
PITY RAY ERIE ANDA
ERIC STE STAPLER
NANA EIRE
SEES EVA
HER ESP
VIE ARID
BETA PARE
ERASERS CAT EROS
HOPE ETUI AMA RANK
ACE ANN LILAC
SENTA LOA ILL
ACID FILECABINET
NINA AGO PALE
SLAM SON TIN

PUZZLE 454

COED
ABLE GREW
PEACE SUEDE
FAR SNAKE IMAGE
ELITE YEARN PEP
TOGA DRUG
CHOP NEED
HARE RUST
ROCK ONCE
RANT LIEN
HOW DROOP ALONE
ADAGE BURST NET
LOVER TENON
FRET SANE
SPEW

PUZZLE 455

1. Itchy nose, 2. Old carpet.

PUZZLE 456

SOAP TAPE
SENSED SOLAR
ONEHORSETOWN
WTS NILE ESE
NONE
ALIKE VIA
DENS LIVE
SAC TALES
HERB
SPA VIES FEE
HORSEPLAYERS
OLEOS STEERS
PEST ENDS

PUZZLE 457

TAME COT
TRIED ALE
MOURNS RED
AGE ETO
PAST LAMARR
INSISTED
ONE ENS
MEASURED
ESTATE STLO
TEA RON
LOY REPAST
APR ETAPE
YES DENS

PUZZLE 458

PET
COLOR
TRUMPET
FAIR MAR
CURB COPY
MAST MOSS
PASS BEAT
RASH SILL
PORK HALT
AVA BELL
DESSERT
ROUSE
LET

PUZZLE 459

NAG
ROPE
SEVERE
LANA MAP
SILO STOW
AMI SPAR
WENT DEFY
EARS FOE
GOLD FIRS
BEE TINT
DEFINE
MINE
STY

PUZZLE 460

DAY
ALES
PISTOL
SOSO FAD
BODY AMEN
SWIMS PEER
EASE DEAR
ASH DAM
POET RIPE
PLUS BEAST
KNOB DUEL
ADO CALF
ABSORB
SALE
GAS

PUZZLE 461

TYPEWRITER

PUZZLE 462

LOAF ROTC JEAN
ABIE LAPEL ARLO
GINA OPINE ISER
TURNTHETABLES
SETE NEO
PROVO MISTRUST
CRIME AIRE TIE
RIVEROFNORETURN
ACE VAIN LURED
MEDDLERS BARNS
AIR PENN
TURNABLINDEYE
HOPI WOULD DART
ANTE ERNES OLIO
LEON DEAD NENE

PUZZLE 466

PARS HALE COAPT
OBIT ADEN ROMEO
REDO SMUDGEPOTS
ELEVATED LASSES
ELAN CUT
RASPS DETECTOR
UGLI SLIDE IAGO
FRAP LINEN GILA
FETE OVERS AGED
SEESAWED BRADS
BED ALAE
URANUS GREATEST
FORESTFIRE TACO
OBESE IZAR ESAU
SEATS BAYS SENT

PUZZLE 470

ASEA SEAM SLOGS
FLAG ALMA EIDER
TARN VAIN ENOLA
GLOBETROTTERS
SERE ION
ASTA DOLL SPAT
ASPIRE SILO ALA
CIRCUMNAVIGATOR
IDA PONG ELITES
DEYS TEEN IRIS
TOE ERNS
WORLDINEIGHTY
REGAL RODS IRAE
ARENA ALEE PULL
HEEDS NODS SEEK

PUZZLE 463

LEW KARAT STET
AVIS ANEMO OHIO
MILLARDFILLMORE
ALLOVER SLAMMED
SLIPONE SEA
YAP ANIMA SPA
MYTH ORAL JAM
SAM REFUSAL ELA
TIC IRON SELF
ELK PRESS OFA
IDO PLOVERS
VANILLA RETIREE
ADLAIESTEVENSON
TAEN ATREE GOLD
SKYE RAISE NAS

PUZZLE 467

DUPE PALE STAR
AFRO ENURE URDU
DOES AGGRANDIZE
SSE ONUS RIDGE
MODUS ANNE
PRIVET TREENAIL
HONES LAIRS DNA
AMEN MINES OMAN
SAN KINKS SPINE
ENTENTES LITRES
AEON MENSA
PAGES SAVE TAB
BRILLIANCE RICE
YORE SCARE HOME
EAST EGOS ONES

PUZZLE 471

PEG EASEL WEB
OPAL EVADE TELL
LIVEALIFEOFEASE
OCEAN DEN IRKED
NIP ISM
CASTLESINTHEAIR
ALTO ACRES DIDO
RIO RAW TIA
OBOE EATER ICON
MIDSUMMERNIGHTS
PSU SON
SADIE SHE TITLE
UNDERTHEWEATHER
ROAD OARED EONS
ANY ODORS UTE

PUZZLE 464

ABET ISERE HERS
CERE MAGOG ANOA
HANDSPRING NILL
ETE MARS PADDLE
HOLE SLIT
SLAKE ANATOMIC
ATONE CLAN MIRE
BARD SHORT OTOE
BING TUNE TURNS
ENERVATE CITES
EINE BATH
FENNEC AURA MAO
AREA HANDINHAND
DIED ELOGE ALEE
SERE DINES SEWS

PUZZLE 468

SOAR SEC CAIN
IDLE MODOC ASTA
LOVE INDIA JEEP
TRAFALGARSQUARE
DES SUN
PARIS TRIO EON
AERIE LEAN SAGE
BERMUDATRIANGLE
BRAS EVOE MILER
ESS OPEN CAPES
SIR OUT
CIRCLEOFFRIENDS
ANOA SPATE ROOT
STAR SATES LOSE
HONE LEN EKES

PUZZLE 472

SLAW DEEDS MIST
PORE INGOT ARIA
ADES ATONE RATS
SEATTLE ERMINES
EWERS LET
STARED IMITATOR
CARNE IRON LAKE
ARE TAC AGE SIN
DONT MEAT RATED
STARTERS ARNESS
EAR PILES
SAFARIS REDWING
COAT CAGER EVER
ANTE AGENT RARE
REED NAMES SNOW

PUZZLE 465

CODED ARGO SAM
AGILE LIAR ALOP
PERILSOFPAULINE
SET URNES NIVEN
EDIE TENET
CRAVES MORSE
AONE IONIC CSA
SWORDOFDAMOCLES
ASA ERNES LARK
ANTIS THOMAS
FELIS HOED
VENTS HEIDI MOE
INTHENICKOFTIME
IDEE INRE EIDER
SRA STUD RAINY

PUZZLE 469

ZED FACTS SPED
URIS ASPEN LIAR
LIONSSHARE AGRA
UNROOT NESTING
OLEOS TEN
SUPPORTS SADAT
ETA TEPEE PAL
TIP TIO REL OLE
ILE HASTA KEN
ERWIN INTEREST
TIN SKATE
TRINKET STAINS
RAGE TALKTURKEY
EVER ARTIE SEAN
EERY LADDS STE

PUZZLE 473

ASHES SCAT DEMI
CLARK URSA EMIR
MINNIEPEARLBUCK
EMS TREE ROUSES
STIR TART
MARLIN LUGE SPA
OREOS SILO STAN
STEPHENKINGKONG
SIDE DEEP RIVER
YES JUAN SURELY
BECK POET
AZALEA EROS BEE
ROBERTRYANONEAL
ONES EARN MOLTS
WEDS SEEK ERASE

PUZZLE 474

BATED SHEAR SRS
AMATI PERCE KIT
HIGHSPIRITS EVE
SLEEK TOLER
AGREED GOVERN
ATHENA ARARAT
FRONT SLATE OLA
RISE BULGE PNIN
OPT CARES POKEY
WOODEN GALENA
MARINE FORAYS
ATILT MEARA
COT AMASKEDBALL
ONE CASTE EERIE
NER TOTED DATED

PUZZLE 475

TALC SHELF LARD
OLEO COPAL AREA
SIAM OPERA TIDY
SAPPER EGGHEADS
ALES ERAS
CHARADES ATTILA
RAVEN ATONE SEC
IVES BRENT SLAT
MER EASES STEVE
ENTERS DEPORTED
LOTS TORE
PARASITE STABAT
ODIN OOZES MAKE
MEND NORSE ERIN
ENDS SPATS REND

PUZZLE 476

TART APART MATA
OMAR RAREE ICON
PACESETTER ATRI
STEALTHY TASSEL
SEES SIAM
BLUES CARAVEL
SLURP STORE ERI
LANE PARTY ANON
ARA CRIES TRUST
PERTAIN PASSE
AINT RILE
SPRINT DETONATE
ELAN ELIMINATED
RENT REVUE LETA
EATS SUESS SEEM

PUZZLE 477

TRA MAKER HIRE
EACH ADELA ODIN
ARNO SMELT LENT
MEET CAPE ADAGE
AGONY TAYLOR
MAGNET ORURO
ABODE RUIN UNIT
SLOB FORTE REDO
TYPO LOSE SHALE
TEETH SHORED
MASHIE INNER
OFTEN PROA SCOT
LIAR MOTOR ELSE
ARTE ALONE SOLE
REED BONED DON

PUZZLE 478

CIAO SLUG BLOC
ADEPT PIPE EACH
SLOTH ATOM AREA
TENSE DEN ORGAN
AVER INDENT
CRATE ACME
LEAVES LAM ALUM
ADVERSE DECLINE
BEES ERE RETAIN
SLAM SNORT
HORSES ABET
ELOPE GNU RASPS
WISE DEAR AWAIT
EVEN ANTS LOTTO
REST MEET LEAP

PUZZLE 479

LIANA TAMS ISON
ACTUP EMIT RENI
SELFPRAISE ELON
TRIFLE TLC FRA
EASE LOSE
RESISTER AMISH
AMEN ATAN META
SELFISH ONESELF
UFOS SEMI TELA
STRAP PENNAMES
AMAH ISEE
GNU CAD RAMONA
RIGA SELFSTYLED
ACHY ERIE ERASE
METE SNEE RANTS

PUZZLE 480

SCAB TONG COAST
TATA ANOA OFFER
INTROVERT TRACE
NEATO SST ORTS
GARYHOGEBOOM
STY YAVAPAI
ARMS TRI ENACT
BOOMBOOMMANCINI
ATREE PAM EDEN
SCALLOP SAY
LOWERTHEBOOM
STOA NBA GRAPE
OHARE BRAGGARTS
FETAL LEDA ZEES
TESTA YEAR EDDY

PUZZLE 481

RATS RESIN SHAH
ADIT EVADE CONE
FARR MELEE RUNE
TREASON ADMIRAL
NAT LAP
DRAGNET LETTUCE
RAVED AROSE NUN
AVER BRASS HIRT
PER BOONE EATER
ENTREAT ROBBERY
ESS POI
DINETTE SENTOFF
IDOL FLOWN URAL
ALOE USUAL ALMA
LEND LAITY LEEK

PUZZLE 482

SWAT HALT CAT
LINE ARIA OLE
ANTE ICER MEN
PESTER STEP
HALO SWAMP
SIR SEAT ERIE
ODE ESSAY ENE
LEAD SIDE DEL
EASEL SPAR
OWED ORATOR
TON GAIL GAVE
ARE ALOE EPEE
RED LENS SEND

PUZZLE 483

ALMS ALES FEND SPAT
LOOP NINE ALAI PESO
APLUGGEDNICKEL ANEW
SETTERS ARE SIN NAN
NAY STARS GRAY
STAIR BOON PLEASANT
TASK FEAR LIEN KNEE
ALA SEAR SONATA TIE
SETTLER SHIED TREND
HEEL APART SOAP
LORNE SCALE COMPOSE
AVE PENCIL MARS KEA
ZEES NEON RANT DEAR
ENDANGER EELS GERMS
OLEO DIRGE SIS
GAL ARM ROE ATLEAST
ARLO GIVESNOQUARTER
REAL ELAN CLUB TORE
BARD DONE YEAS SPEE

DIAGRAMLESS STARTING BOXES

Puzzle 153 starts in box 1
Puzzle 155 starts in box 8
Puzzle 156 starts in box 6
Puzzle 158 starts in box 1
Puzzle 160 starts in box 11
Puzzle 162 starts in box 10
Puzzle 164 starts in box 1
Puzzle 312 starts in box 2
Puzzle 314 starts in box 11
Puzzle 316 starts in box 8
Puzzle 318 starts in box 16
Puzzle 320 starts in box 1
Puzzle 322 starts in box 6
Puzzle 451 starts in box 7
Puzzle 453 starts in box 1
Puzzle 454 starts in box 4
Puzzle 456 starts in box 2
Puzzle 457 starts in box 3
Puzzle 458 starts in box 9
Puzzle 459 starts in box 5
Puzzle 460 starts in box 6

GUIDANCE YOU CAN TRUST

The Independent Study Catalog
The guide to over *10,000* correspondence courses! This *classic* provides the most complete listing available to courses at more than 100 accredited colleges and universities nationwide.

ISBN 460-7, $16.95 pb/ $23.95 CAN, 6th ed., 1995

Virtual College
A quick guide to *all you need to know* to get the degree you want with computer, TV, video, audio, and other distance learning tools.

ISBN 629-4, $9.95 pb/ $13.95 CAN, 1996

Peterson's Four-Year Colleges 1998
This *best-selling* guide- delivers *in-depth profiles* of more than 2,000 colleges and universities. **Bonus CD-ROM** eases the search process.

ISBN 783-5, $24.95 pb/ $34.95 CAN, 28th ed.,1997

College Money Handbook 1998
The *most comprehensive*, *up-to-date* financial aid locator available. **Bonus CD-ROM** helps explore options and estimate costs.

ISBN 832-7, $26.95 pb/ $37.95 CAN, 15th ed.,1997

Peterson's Scholarships, Grants & Prizes 1998
This *comprehensive* guide directs students to $2.5 *billion* in private aid– 770,000 separate financial awards! **Bonus CD-ROM**.

ISBN 833-5, $24.95pb/ $34.95 CAN, 2nd ed., 1997

The 90-Minute Resume
Teaches how to showcase skills, customize a resume, and job search on-line. **Plus–resume-writing software.**

ISBN 633-2, $ 15.95 pb (with disk) /$22.95 CAN, 1996

The 90-Minute Interview Prep Book
Step-by-step instruc- tions–plus **bonus soft- ware**–demonstrate how to polish interview skills.

ISBN 634-0, $15.95 pb (with disk) /$22.95 CAN, 1996

The Job Hunter's Word Finder
Builds resume, inter- viewing, and networking power with *thousands* of synonyms

ISBN 600-6, $12.95 pb/$19.95 CAN, 1996

ISBN prefix: 1-56079-
Dept. B8750

1-800-338-3282

Peterson's
Princeton, New Jersey
www.petersons.com

At Fine Bookstores Near You

Or Call: **1-800-338-3282**
Outside Cont. U.S.: **609-243-9111**
Fax: 609-243-9150
www.petersons.com/bookstore

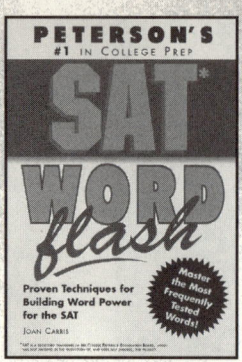